THE ROUTLEDGE HANDBOOK OF THE PHILOSOPHY AND PSYCHOLOGY OF LUCK

Luck permeates our lives, and this raises a number of pressing questions: What is luck? When we attribute luck to people, circumstances, or events, what are we attributing? Do we have any obligations to mitigate the harms done to people who are less fortunate? And to what extent is deserving praise or blame affected by good or bad luck? Although acquiring a true belief by an uneducated guess involves a kind of luck that precludes knowledge, does *all* luck undermine knowledge? The academic literature has seen growing, interdisciplinary interest in luck, and this volume brings together and explains the most important areas of this research. It consists of 39 newly commissioned chapters, written by an internationally acclaimed team of philosophers and psychologists, for a readership of students and researchers. Its coverage is divided into six sections:

   I: The History of Luck
  II: The Nature of Luck
 III: Moral Luck
 IV: Epistemic Luck
  V: The Psychology of Luck
 VI: Future Research.

The chapters cover a wide range of topics, from the problem of moral luck, to anti-luck epistemology, to the relationship between luck attributions and cognitive biases, to meta-questions regarding the nature of luck itself, to a range of other theoretical and empirical questions. By bringing this research together, the *Handbook* serves as both a touchstone for understanding the relevant issues and a first port of call for future research on luck.

Ian M. Church is Assistant Professor of Philosophy at Hillsdale College. He is the co-author (with Peter Samuelson) of *Intellectual Humility: An Introduction to the Philosophy & Science* (2017).

Robert J. Hartman is a Postdoctoral Research Fellow with the Lund-Gothenburg Responsibility Project at the University of Gothenburg, Sweden. He is the author of *In Defense of Moral Luck: Why Luck Often Affects Praiseworthiness and Blameworthiness* (2017).

ROUTLEDGE HANDBOOKS IN PHILOSOPHY

Routledge Handbooks in Philosophy are state-of-the-art surveys of emerging, newly refreshed, and important fields in philosophy, providing accessible yet thorough assessments of key problems, themes, thinkers, and recent developments in research.

All chapters for each volume are specially commissioned, and written by leading scholars in the field. Carefully edited and organized, *Routledge Handbooks in Philosophy* provide indispensable reference tools for students and researchers seeking a comprehensive overview of new and exciting topics in philosophy. They are also valuable teaching resources as accompaniments to textbooks, anthologies, and research-orientated publications.

Also available:

The Routledge Handbook of Consciousness
Edited by Rocco J. Gennaro

The Routledge Handbook of Philosophy and Science of Addiction
Edited by Hanna Pickard and Serge Ahmed

The Routledge Handbook of Moral Epistemology
Edited by Karen Jones, Mark Timmons, and Aaron Zimmerman

The Routledge Handbook of Love in Philosophy
Edited by Adrienne M. Martin

The Routledge Handbook of the Philosophy of Childhood and Children
Edited by Anca Gheaus, Gideon Calder, and Jurgen De Wispelaere

The Routledge Handbook of Applied Epistemology
Edited by David Coady and James Chase

For more information about this series, please visit: www.routledge.com/Routledge-Handbooks-in-Philosophy/book-series/RHP

THE ROUTLEDGE HANDBOOK OF THE PHILOSOPHY AND PSYCHOLOGY OF LUCK

Edited by Ian M. Church and Robert J. Hartman

NEW YORK AND LONDON

First published 2019
by Routledge
52 Vanderbilt Avenue, New York, NY 10017

and by Routledge
2 Park Square, Milton Park, Abingdon, Oxon, OX14 4RN

Routledge is an imprint of the Taylor & Francis Group, an informa business

© 2019 Taylor & Francis

The right of Ian M. Church and Robert J. Hartman to be identified as the authors of the editorial material, and of the authors for their individual chapters, has been asserted in accordance with sections 77 and 78 of the Copyright, Designs and Patents Act 1988.

All rights reserved. No part of this book may be reprinted or reproduced or utilized in any form or by any electronic, mechanical, or other means, now known or hereafter invented, including photocopying and recording, or in any information storage or retrieval system, without permission in writing from the publishers.

Trademark notice: Product or corporate names may be trademarks or registered trademarks, and are used only for identification and explanation without intent to infringe.

Library of Congress Cataloging-in-Publication Data
Names: Church, Ian M., author. | Hartman, Robert J., author.
Title: The Routledge handbook of the philosophy and psychology of luck /
edited by Ian M. Church, Robert J. Hartman.
Description: Abingdon, Oxon : Routledge, 2019. | Includes bibliographical references. |
Identifiers: LCCN 2018047506 (print) | LCCN 2018050928 (ebook) |
ISBN 9781351258760 (ebk) | ISBN 9780815366591 (hbk)
Subjects: LCSH: Fortune. | Chance. | Success.
Classification: LCC BD595 (ebook) |
LCC BD595 .R68 2019 (print) | DDC 123/.3–dc23
LC record available at https://lccn.loc.gov/2018047506

ISBN: 978-0-8153-6659-1 (hbk)
ISBN: 978-1-351-25876-0 (ebk)

Typeset in Bembo
by Newgen Publishing UK

Printed and bound in Great Britain by
TJ International Ltd, Padstow, Cornwall

For my wife, Corrie, who made me a lucky man indeed.

Ian

For my daughters, Eve and Leigh. I am lucky to have you two!

Robert

CONTENTS

Notes on Contributors	xi
Luck: An Introduction *Ian M. Church and Robert J. Hartman*	1

PART I
The History of Luck   **11**

1 Aristotle on Constitutive, Developmental, and Resultant Moral Luck *Nafsika Athanassoulis*	13
2 Aristotle on Luck, Happiness, and Solon's Dictum *Sarah Broadie*	25
3 The Stoics on Luck *René Brouwer*	34
4 Thomas Aquinas on Moral Luck *Jeffrey Hause*	45
5 Immanuel Kant on Moral Luck *Kate Moran*	57
6 Adam Smith on Moral Luck and the Invisible Hand *Craig Smith*	70
7 John Stuart Mill on Luck and Distributive Justice *Piers Norris Turner*	80

Contents

8 History of Luck in Epistemology   94
   Dani Rabinowitz

9 Thomas Nagel and Bernard Williams on Moral Luck   105
   Andrew Latus

PART II
The Nature of Luck   **113**

10 Modal Accounts of Luck   115
   Duncan Pritchard

11 The Lack of Control Account of Luck   125
   Wayne Riggs

12 The Probability Account of Luck   136
   Nicholas Rescher

13 The Mixed Account of Luck   148
   Rik Peels

14 Luck and Significance   160
   Nathan Ballantyne and Samuel Kampa

15 Luck as Risk   171
   Fernando Broncano-Berrocal

16 Luck and Norms   183
   Rachel McKinnon

PART III
Moral Luck   **193**

17 The Definition of "Luck" and the Problem of Moral Luck   195
   Daniel Statman

18 Kinds of Moral Luck   206
   Carolina Sartorio

19 Denying Moral Luck   216
   Michael J. Zimmerman

20 Accepting Moral Luck   227
   Robert J. Hartman

Contents

21 Luck and Libertarianism   239
    Laura W. Ekstrom

22 Luck and Compatibilism   248
    Mirja Pérez de Calleja

PART IV
Epistemic Luck   **259**

23 The Gettier Problem   261
    Ian M. Church

24 The Problem of Environmental Luck   273
    Benjamin Jarvis

25 Anti-Luck Epistemology   284
    Tim Black

26 The Luck/Knowledge Incompatibility Thesis   295
    Stephen Hetherington

27 Luck and Skepticism   305
    John Greco

28 Epistemic Luck and the Extended Mind   318
    J. Adam Carter

PART V
The Psychology of Luck   **331**

29 Cognitive Biases and Dispositions in Luck Attributions   333
    Steven D. Hales and Jennifer Adrienne Johnson

30 Luck and Risk   345
    Karl Halvor Teigen

31 Emotional Responses to Luck, Risk, and Uncertainty   356
    Sabine Roeser

32 The Illusion of Control   365
    Anastasia Ejova

33 Positive Psychology and Luck Experiences   377
    Matthew D. Smith and Piers Worth

PART VI
Future Research   **389**

34 Luck in Science   391
    J.D. Trout

35 The Philosophy of Luck and Experimental Philosophy   401
    Joe Milburn and Edouard Machery

36 Legal Luck   414
    Ori J. Herstein

37 Feminist Approaches to Moral Luck   426
    Carolyn McLeod and Jody Tomchishen

38 The New Problem of Religious Luck   436
    Guy Axtell

39 Theology and Luck   451
    Jordan Wessling

Index   464

NOTES ON CONTRIBUTORS

Nafsika Athanassoulis is an independent scholar who has previously held posts at Keele University and the University of Leeds. Her research focuses on Aristotle, virtue ethics, moral psychology, and moral education. Her works include the authored books *Virtue Ethics* (Bloomsbury, 2013) and *Morality, Moral Luck and Responsibility* (Palgrave Macmillan, 2010), the edited collection *Philosophical Reflections on Medical Ethics* (Palgrave Macmillan, 2010), the co-edited collection *The Moral Life* (Palgrave Macmillan, 2008) as well as numerous articles.

Guy Axtell is Professor of Philosophy at Radford University, Virginia, USA. He has published widely in epistemology, philosophy of science, and philosophy and psychology of religion. His recent books are *Objectivity* (Polity Press, 2016), and *Problems of Religious Luck* (Lexington Books, 2018).

Nathan Ballantyne is an Associate Professor of Philosophy at Fordham University. He has published articles on epistemology in venues such as *Australasian Journal of Philosophy*, *Mind*, *Philosophy and Phenomenological Research*, *Philosophical Quarterly*, and *Philosophers' Imprint*, and has a book titled *Knowing Our Limits* forthcoming with Oxford University Press.

Tim Black is Chair and Professor of Philosophy at California State University, Northridge (USA). He is the co-editor, with Kelly Becker, of *The Sensitivity Principle in Epistemology* (Cambridge University Press, 2012).

Sarah Broadie is in the Philosophy Department at the University of St Andrews, having previously taught at Princeton, Rutgers, Yale, University of Texas at Austin, and Edinburgh University. She has mainly published on Aristotle's physics and ethics, and Plato's *Timaeus*. She is a Fellow of the British Academy, the Royal Society of Edinburgh, the American Academy of Arts and Sciences, and the Academia Europaea.

Fernando Broncano-Berrocal is a Marie Skłodowska-Curie Fellow at the University of Copenhagen. His research interests mainly lie in epistemology. His work on luck, epistemic luck, modal accounts of knowledge, virtue epistemology, and perceptual justification has been published in *Philosophical Studies*, *Synthese*, and *Proceedings of the Aristotelian Society*, among other journals.

Notes on Contributors

René Brouwer teaches philosophy and law at the University of Utrecht (the Netherlands). He has published on a variety of subjects in the philosophy and history of law as well as in ancient philosophy, see especially *The Stoic Sage* (Cambridge University Press, 2014). He currently works on ancient conceptions of justice and on the interaction between law and philosophy in the late Roman Republic.

J. Adam Carter is a Lecturer in Philosophy at the University of Glasgow, working mainly in epistemology. His work has appeared in (among other places) *Noûs*, *Philosophy and Phenomenological Research*, *Analysis*, *Philosophical Studies*, and the *Australasian Journal of Philosophy*. Carter's first monograph, *Metaepistemology and Relativism*, was published in 2016 with Palgrave Macmillan.

Anastasia Ejova is a postdoctoral researcher at the Department of Psychology at Macquarie University in Sydney, Australia. Her doctoral research focused on issues with defining and measuring the illusion of control in experiments and psychological surveys.

Laura W. Ekstrom is the Frances S. Haserot Professor of Philosophy at The College of William & Mary (U.S.). She is currently working on a book entitled *God, Suffering, and the Value of Free Will*.

John Greco holds the Leonard and Elizabeth Eslick Chair in Philosophy at Saint Louis University. His publications include *Achieving Knowledge: A Virtue-theoretic Account of Epistemic Normativity* (Cambridge, 2010) and *The Transmission of Knowledge* (Cambridge, forthcoming).

Steven D. Hales is Professor and Chair of Philosophy at Bloomsburg University of Pennsylvania. His books include *Relativism and the Foundations of Philosophy* (MIT Press, 2006) and *This is Philosophy* (John Wiley & Sons, 2013). He is completing a book entitled *The Myth of Luck*.

Jeffrey Hause is Professor of Philosophy and Michael W. Barry Professor at Creighton University. He is editor of *Aquinas's Summa Theologiae: A Critical Guide* (Cambridge, 2018) and co-editor of the Hackett Aquinas Series.

Ori J. Herstein is an Associate Professor (Senior Lecturer) at the Hebrew University of Jerusalem and at King's College London. He works primarily in legal and moral philosophy.

Stephen Hetherington is Professor of Philosophy at the University of New South Wales (in Sydney, Australia). His publications include *Epistemology's Paradox* (Rowman & Littlefield, 1992), *Good Knowledge, Bad Knowledge* (Oxford University Press, 2001), *How to Know* (John Wiley & Sons, 2011), and *Knowledge and the Gettier Problem* (Cambridge University Press, 2016).

Benjamin Jarvis has worked on a number of topics in epistemology and the philosophy of mind, including mental content, the a priori, knowledge, and epistemic luck. He is a co-author of *The Rules of Thought* (Oxford University Press, 2013) and has published in professional journals such as *Noûs*, the *Australasian Journal of Philosophy*, and *Pacific Philosophy Quarterly*. He currently works for a Fortune 500 company on projects involving causal inference and advanced analytics.

Jennifer Adrienne Johnson is an Associate Professor of Psychology at Bloomsburg University of Pennsylvania. She has recent publications in *Teaching of Psychology*, *Philosophical Psychology*, and the *Journal of College Orientation and Transition*.

Samuel Kampa is a Ph.D. candidate in Philosophy at Fordham University, where he is writing a dissertation on the epistemology of doxastic and quasi-doxastic attitudes. His work has appeared in *Australasian Journal of Philosophy* and *Episteme*.

Notes on Contributors

Andrew Latus is an Assistant Professor of Psychiatry at Memorial University of Newfoundland in St. John's, Newfoundland and Labrador, Canada. He works clinically as a psychiatrist and teaches medical ethics and psychiatry in Memorial's medical school.

Edouard Machery is Distinguished Professor in the Department of History and Philosophy of Science at the University of Pittsburgh and the Director of the Center for Philosophy of Science at the University of Pittsburgh. He is the author of *Doing without Concepts* (Oxford University Press, 2009) and of *Philosophy Within its Proper Bounds* (Oxford University Press, 2017).

Rachel McKinnon is an Assistant Professor in the Department of Philosophy at the College of Charleston. She works on a wide variety of topics, including the nature of luck, norms of assertion, epistemic injustice, weakness of will, transformative experiences, trans issues, feminist philosophy, and propaganda and hate speech. Recently, she has begun work on trans athletes' rights, and is herself an elite internationally competitive cyclist.

Carolyn McLeod is Professor of Philosophy and of Women's Studies and Feminist Research at Western University, Canada. She is an editor of *Family-Making: Contemporary Ethical Challenges* (Oxford University Press, 2014) and the author of the forthcoming *The Power of Conscientious Objectors* (Oxford University Press).

Joe Milburn is a Visiting Professor at the University of Navarra in Pamplona, Spain. His research centers on epistemology and philosophy of religion. He is co-editing (with Casey Doyle and Duncan Pritchard) *New Issues in Epistemological Disjunctivism* (Routledge, forthcoming).

Kate Moran is Associate Professor of Philosophy at Brandeis University. Her research focuses on Kant's moral and political philosophy. She is the author of *Community and Progress in Kant's Moral Philosophy* (Catholic University of America Press, 2012) and the editor of *Kant on Freedom and Spontaneity* (Cambridge University Press, 2018). Her recent essays have appeared in the *Canadian Journal of Philosophy* and *Archiv for Geschichte Der Philosophie*.

Rik Peels is an Assistant Professor in the Philosophy Department of the Vrije Universiteit Amsterdam (the Netherlands). He recently published *Responsible Belief: A Theory in Ethics and Epistemology* (Oxford University Press, 2017) and the edited volume *Perspectives on Ignorance from Moral and Social Philosophy* (Routledge, 2017).

Mirja Pérez de Calleja is a Ph.D. candidate in philosophy at Florida State University. She specializes in philosophy of action and metaphysics, with a focus on free will. Her current research, in the intersection of philosophy of action and philosophy of education, concerns the conditions for autonomy, and in particular the reasons why an indoctrinatory education fails to meet these conditions.

Duncan Pritchard is Chancellor's Professor of Philosophy at the University of California, Irvine, and Professor of Philosophy at the University of Edinburgh. His monographs include *Epistemic Luck* (Oxford University Press, 2005), *The Nature and Value of Knowledge* (co-authored, Oxford University Press, 2010), *Epistemological Disjunctivism* (Oxford University Press, 2012), and *Epistemic Angst: Radical Skepticism and the Groundlessness of Our Believing* (Princeton University Press, 2015).

Dani Rabinowitz is a trainee solicitor at Clifford Chance LLP. He is co-editor with John Hawthorne and Matthew Benton of *Knowledge, Belief, and God: New Insights in Religious Epistemology* (Oxford University Press, 2018).

Notes on Contributors

Nicholas Rescher is Distinguished University Professor of Philosophy at the University of Pittsburgh. The author of more than a hundred books ranging over the whole of philosophy, and a specialist in the philosophy of Leibniz, he is the recipient of eight honorary degrees from universities on three continents and has been awarded the Helmholtz Medal of the German Academy of Sciences (Berlin Brandenburg.)

Wayne Riggs is a Professor and Chair of the Philosophy Department at the University of Oklahoma. His primary areas of interest are epistemology (especially virtue epistemology, understanding, epistemic luck, and social epistemology), philosophy of education, and philosophy of emotion.

Sabine Roeser is a Professor in the Ethics and Philosophy of Technology Section of TU Delft, the Netherlands. Her research focuses on moral emotions, intuitions, risk, and art. Her most recent monograph is *Risk, Technology, and Moral Emotions* (Routledge, 2018).

Carolina Sartorio is Associate Professor of Philosophy at the University of Arizona. She is the author of *Causation and Free Will* (Oxford University Press, 2016), and of articles at the intersection of metaphysics, agency, and moral theory.

Craig Smith is the Adam Smith Senior Lecturer in the Scottish Enlightenment at the University of Glasgow. A graduate of Glasgow and Edinburgh Universities, he researches the moral and political philosophy of the Scottish Enlightenment. He is the author of *Adam Smith's Political Philosophy: The Invisible Hand and Spontaneous Order* (Routledge, 2006), and one of the editors of the *Oxford Handbook of Adam Smith* (Oxford University Press, 2013).

Matthew D. Smith, Ph.D., is a Senior Lecturer in Psychology at Buckinghamshire New University, UK, where he is the co-course leader for the MSc Applied Positive Psychology (MAPP) program. He has also taught at Liverpool John Moores University, Liverpool Hope University, and Oxford Brookes University, all in the UK.

Daniel Statman is Head of the Philosophy Department at the University of Haifa. He is the editor of *Moral Luck* (SUNY Press, 1993) and, more recently, co-author of *War by Agreement* (forthcoming) and of *State and Religion in Israel* (forthcoming).

Karl Halvor Teigen is Professor Emeritus in Psychology at the University of Oslo, Norway, and adjunct Scientist at Simula Research Laboratory, Lysaker, Norway. His main research interests are in judgment and decision making, social cognition, and the history of psychology.

Jody Tomchishen is a Ph.D. candidate in the Department of Philosophy and a resident member of the Rotman Institute of Philosophy: Engaging Science at the University of Western Ontario, Canada. His Ph.D. research centers on the relationship between moral psychology and the law.

J.D. Trout is the John and Mae Calamos Professor of Philosophy at Illinois Institute of Technology. Most recently, he is the author of *Wondrous Truths: The Improbable Triumph of Modern Science* (Oxford University Press, 2016), and *All Talked Out: Naturalism and the Future of Philosophy* (Oxford University Press, 2018).

Piers Norris Turner is an Associate Professor of Philosophy at Ohio State University, USA, and has published in journals including *Ethics*, *Journal of the History of Philosophy*, and *Utilitas*. He has co-edited (with Gerald Gaus) *Public Reason in Political Philosophy* (Routledge, 2018).

Notes on Contributors

Jordan Wessling is a Postdoctoral Research Fellow in the Analytic Theology for Theological Formation Project at Fuller Theological Seminary, USA. His articles have appeared in journals such as the *International Journal of Systematic Theology*, *Theology and Science*, and the *International Journal of Philosophy of Religion*, and he has recently completed a book manuscript on God's love for humans.

Piers Worth, Ph.D., is a Reader in Psychology at Buckinghamshire New University, UK. He is a Chartered Psychologist and accredited psychotherapist. Piers is co-course leader of the University's MSc Applied Positive Psychology (MAPP) program. He is a co-author of the book *Second Wave Positive Psychology: Embracing the Dark Side of Life* (Routledge, 2015).

Michael J. Zimmerman is Professor of Philosophy at the University of North Carolina at Greensboro. He is the author of several books and articles on fundamental issues in ethics and the theory of value. His two most recent books are *The Immorality of Punishment* (Broadview, 2011) and *Ignorance and Moral Obligation* (Oxford University Press, 2014).

LUCK

An Introduction

Ian M. Church and Robert J. Hartman

Luck permeates our lives. Perhaps you were lucky to be born into a country experiencing relative political stability, whereas others were born into countries experiencing horrible civil wars. Many of us are lucky to enjoy the benefits of modern medicine and technology, as opposed to a medieval theory of humours. Precious few people are lucky to have won the lottery. In a very real sense, everyone reading this book is lucky to live in an age and time when information is so widely available and accessible, and to live in societies with enough resources that we can specialize enough so as to make things like academia possible. All current life-forms on earth are lucky that our planet was not formed slightly closer or slightly further away from the sun.

These observations raise interesting questions. Perhaps preeminently, what *is* luck? When we attribute luck to people, circumstances, or events, what are we attributing? Are events lucky primarily because they are not within our control? Or does luck have something to do with probabilities or relevant modal space? And what is the relationship between luck-related notions such as risk, fortune, uncertainty, ignorance, and accidentality? To what extent is deserving praise or blame affected by good or bad luck? Do we have any political obligations to people who are less fortunate to mitigate their relative bad luck? Although acquiring a true belief by an uneducated guess involves a kind of luck that precludes knowledge, does all luck undermine knowledge? And how accurate are our luck attributions anyway? Do we simply misattribute luck to things we do not understand? What can psychology and cognitive science tell us about our perceptions of luck?

While many of these questions have ancient pedigrees, the academic literature on issues surrounding epistemic luck, moral luck, and the science of luck have enjoyed a flurry of academic interest in the past few decades across several disciplines. One of the central aims of this *Handbook* is to bring together this interdisciplinary body of research into a single volume and to provide a basic and accessible overview of some of the central debates and issues that have developed in the philosophical and scientific literature in recent years. The *Handbook* is broken down into six parts: (i) the history of luck and its importance, (ii) the nature of luck, (iii) moral luck, (iv) epistemic luck, (v) the psychology and cognitive science of luck, and (vi) areas of future research. We will now, in very broad strokes, consider some of the central themes and issues to be explored in each part, and provide brief summaries of the chapters themselves.

1

Part I: The History of Luck

There has been a broad range of interest in luck throughout the history of philosophy. Aristotle, the Stoics, Thomas Aquinas, Immanuel Kant, Adam Smith, John Stuart Mill, Edmund Gettier, Bernard Williams, and Thomas Nagel, for example, have made some of the most important contributions to our understanding of luck, and to the place it should have in metaphysics, ethics, epistemology, and political philosophy. Paying attention to this history is not only valuable for its own sake, but can help to inform and challenge various features of contemporary debates. Here are some key questions to be considered in this part:

1. How do important historical figures think about luck? In what ways have views of luck changed over time?
2. How does luck fit within the broader philosophical projects of these important historical figures?
3. In what ways have historical contributions shaped contemporary debates about the metaphysics of luck, luck and flourishing, luck and moral virtue, luck and moral responsibility, luck and distributive justice, and luck and knowledge? Do some of those historical influences on contemporary debates rest on mistaken interpretations of the historical figure in question? Does this history contain resources to help us clarify or even solve contemporary problems?

Nafsika Athanassoulis (Chapter 1) begins her discussion by explicating Aristotle's view of lucky events as irregular, incidental, indeterminable, and unstable occurrences with good or bad effects. Subsequently, she explicates Aristotle's view of the good life and the kinds of people who have access to it with respect to that general account of luck and modern categories of resultant, developmental, and constitutive luck.

Sarah Broadie (Chapter 2) explicates Aristotle's subtle and rich view on the relationship between luck and happiness against the backdrop of other ancient views. Aristotle rejects the view that wisdom and moral virtue are sufficient for happiness, and accepts the view that various non-moral external goods are necessary to be happy, which makes happiness subject to luck in certain respects. Broadie discusses Aristotle's position in detail in relation to Solon's dictum: "Do not say 'happy' of the living, but only once the end is reached."

René Brouwer (Chapter 3) considers the role of luck in Stoic thought. In particular, he examines what luck is, how humans can know what luck is, and how humans should behave toward luck from the perspectives of three groups of Stoic philosophers: Early Stoics (Zeno, Chrysippus), Roman Stoics (Panaetius, Posidonius), and Imperial Stoics (Seneca, Epictetus, Marcus Aurelius).

Jeffrey Hause (Chapter 4) canvasses Thomas Aquinas's moral philosophy to determine whether Aquinas allows various kinds of luck to affect praiseworthiness and blameworthiness. Aquinas denies that the results of actions outside of the agent's control can affect her praiseworthiness or blameworthiness. Aquinas's view, however, is more complicated when it comes to circumstantial and constitutive luck; some kinds of each cannot affect a person's praiseworthiness or blameworthiness, but other kinds of each can do so.

Kate Moran (Chapter 5) explicates Immanuel Kant's complex views on luck, happiness, and moral responsibility. Although whether a particular person is happy can be subject to luck, moral virtue tends to bring about happiness over time at least at the level of the moral community. Furthermore, contrary to Kant's anti-luck reputation, his moral philosophy allows for certain kinds of luck in results, circumstance, and character to affect the agent's praiseworthiness and blameworthiness.

Craig Smith (Chapter 6) describes Adam Smith's view on luck and moral sentiments within his wider naturalistic descriptive project of explaining how the moral emotions that we have fit together. A. Smith observes an "irregular" sentiment in our attributions of responsibility: we believe that we merit praise and blame only in virtue of our intentions, and yet our praising and blaming responses are augmented and diminished by external actions and consequences. A. Smith considers where this irregularity comes from, what function it fulfills, and how it is connected to other features of moral experience.

Piers Norris Turner (Chapter 7) examines whether John Stuart Mill is a luck egalitarian—that is, whether Mill thinks that a just society must eliminate inequalities for which agents are not personally responsible. Turner argues that Mill does not think so. By examining Mill's principles of impartiality, sufficiency, and merit, Turner argues that Mill embraces relational egalitarianism, which is the idea that the just society must eliminate inequalities that undermine human dignity.

Dani Rabinowitz (Chapter 8) offers a narrative about the history of luck in epistemology. He describes the kind of luck identified in Edmund Gettier's counterexamples to the true justified belief account of knowledge, the way in which Duncan Pritchard sketches a modal account of luck to better understand the relationship between luck and knowledge, and the trend of building in various modal conditions to accounts of knowledge to avoid Gettier counterexamples.

Andrew Latus (Chapter 9) describes the way in which Bernard Williams and Thomas Nagel formulated the problem of moral luck, and how their papers spawned the contemporary moral luck debate. Williams and Nagel agree that our ordinary conception of morality is one that is immune to luck, but also agree that luck can make a moral difference. They, however, draw different conclusions. Williams revises our conception of morality, and Nagel accepts a paradox.

Part II: The Nature of Luck

The philosophical and psychological significance of luck has long been recognized; but only recently has there been focused attention to explore precisely what luck is. At least in the domain of philosophy, most credit Duncan Pritchard's (2005) *Epistemic Luck* as the catalyst for much of the current philosophical reflection on the nature of luck. There is, however, no consensus yet about what luck is; there are several competing accounts of luck in the literature. Here are some of the basic issues:

1. Are agents, propositions, events, or states of affairs the fundamental bearers of luck?
2. What is luck primarily? Is it mainly an improbable event? Is it chiefly an event over which a person lacks a certain kind of control? Is it principally an event that could easily have failed to occur? Is it predominantly an event that no one intends to occur or the occurrence of an event that we do not understand?
3. Does improbability, lack of control, modal fragility, accidentality, or ignorance stand alone as necessary and sufficient for luck? If one of those conditions does stand alone in that way, how do we explain why it is tempting to think about luck in other ways? If it does not stand alone, what are the other necessary conditions?
4. Must a lucky event be significant to some person or other? If so, must a lucky event affect her objective or subjective interests? And must she actually ascribe significance to that event? Or might it suffice that she would ascribe significance to it if she had all the relevant information or were rational?
5. What is the relationship between luck and related concepts such as accidentality, risk, fortune, chance, and uncertainty? Might focusing on one or another of these related notions help to sort out which account of luck is most plausible?

Duncan Pritchard (Chapter 10) sets out his modal account of luck, according to which an event is lucky if and only if it is modally fragile—that is, the actually occurring event fails to occur in a broad range of nearby possible worlds in which the relevant initial conditions are the same. Contrary to most accounts of luck and an earlier account of his own, he argues that a lucky event need not be significant to a particular agent. He also argues that the modal account provides a better account of luck than its rivals.

Wayne Riggs (Chapter 11) articulates the lack of control account of luck. On Riggs' view, an event is lucky for some person if and only if she does not skillfully and intentionally bring about the event, the event is good or bad in some respect for her, and she does not exploit the uncontrolled event for her own purposes. Subsequently, Riggs considers and responds to the objection that this account implies that too many uncontrolled events are lucky, such as the rising of the sun.

Nicholas Rescher (Chapter 12) further explicates his probabilistic account of luck. On his view, an event is lucky for some person if and only if it is improbable and significant for her. According to Rescher, there are various species of luck (finder's, gambler's, guesser's, and dumb luck), and this chapter makes the species of gambler's luck more precise by examining relationships between improbability and significance.

Rik Peels (Chapter 13) defends a mixed account of luck: a state of affairs is lucky for some person if and only if it is significant for the agent, the agent lacks intentional control over the event, and it could easily have failed to occur. He responds to three objections. First, the account is incomplete, because there is also a non-chancy species of luck. Second, the lack of intentional control condition is not a necessary condition of luck. Third, the modal condition is not a necessary condition of luck.

Nathan Ballantyne and Samuel Kampa (Chapter 14) examine the significance condition of luck by explicating and evaluating four specifications of the platitude that event E is lucky for subject S only if E is significant for S. The differences between these specifications turn on whether the agent must ascribe significance to the event, and whether it is the agent's subjective or objective interests that are impacted by the event. They also critically assess Pritchard's rejection of the platitude.

Fernando Broncano-Berrocal (Chapter 15) argues that luck and risk are parallel in various ways, and that two alleged differences between them are specious. Furthermore, he argues that paying careful attention to the relationship between luck and risk provides a reason to affirm the lack of control account of luck over the modal and probability accounts.

Rachel Mckinnon (Chapter 16) questions the common assumption that epistemic outcomes are either the product of an agent's skill or epistemic luck; instead, it is argued that all epistemic outcomes are a product of *both* skill and luck. On the basis of this lesson, Mckinnon suggests possible revisions to our understanding of the metaphysics of luck.

Part III: Moral Luck

The problem of moral luck arises from the intuitive moral principle that we are morally responsible only for what is within our control and the general fact that our character, actions, and consequences are shot through with luck. One way to frame the problem is that after we factor out all the luck from who we are, what we do, and what we bring about, it appears that there is nothing left us to be morally responsible for. An alternative way to frame the problem is that we have conflicting intuitions in concrete cases. Here are some examples: two drunk drivers manage their vehicles in the same way, and one but not the other kills a pedestrian; two trouble-makers would steal a bottle of Coca-Cola if given the opportunity, but only one gets an opportunity and does so. In these cases, the salient difference between the agents is a matter of luck, and so it is intuitive that the agents in each case pair deserve the same degree of blame. Nevertheless, in our everyday responsibility attributions, we also judge that the killer driver deserves more blame than the merely reckless driver, and that the thief deserves more blame than the mere would-be thief. So, our intuitions point us in contradictory directions. Although many in the history of philosophy were sensitive to the role of luck in our moral lives, it was not until the publication of papers by Thomas Nagel (1976, 1979) and Bernard Williams (1976, 1981) that they were sufficiently appreciated in our contemporary setting. Here are some of the relevant issues.

1. What account of luck best fits the role of "luck" in "moral luck"?

2. Is Nagel's basic taxonomy of resultant, circumstantial, constitutive, and causal moral luck exhaustive? Are some of these categories redundant? Should we be considering other forms of moral luck?

3. Does moral luck exist? That is, can factors outside of an agent's control affect the praise and blame that she deserves? Or, should all luck be factored out of desert of praise and blame? Can we factor out all luck without entirely eliminating moral praiseworthiness and blameworthiness for who we are, what we do, and what we bring about?

4. Would discovering the true nature of luck help to make progress in the moral luck debate? Or, should philosophers who are investigating this puzzle continue to use the lack of control conception of luck even if a different account of luck is correct or there is no adequate account of luck?

5. What is the relationship between luck and other moral properties such as moral obligation, moral virtue, or human flourishing?

6. What is the relationship between luck and free will? Do circumstantial and constitutive luck pose a skeptical threat to our self-conception as morally responsible agents even if free will and moral responsibility are compatible with causal determinism? If our actions are not causally determined, do they occur as a matter of luck? And if such actions do occur as a matter of luck, would their being lucky in this way undermine the "freedom" in "libertarian free actions"?

Daniel Statman (Chapter 17) argues that contrary to recent trends in the moral luck literature, ascertaining the true nature of luck will not help us to solve the problem of moral luck. In his view, a more promising route would be to develop a theory of praiseworthiness and blameworthiness that explains why luck can or cannot affect moral responsibility.

Carolina Sartorio (Chapter 18) explicates Nagel's fourfold taxonomy of moral luck. She focuses on neglected forms of each, such as resultant luck from omissions, the kind of circumstantial luck we observe in the situationist literature, and causal luck from non-deterministic causation. Subsequently, she considers new sources of moral luck that have to do with causation coming in degrees and with one agent's moral responsibility depending directly on what others do.

Michael J. Zimmerman (Chapter 19) examines whether luck can affect various moral properties such as moral obligation, leading a good or bad life, having a moral virtue or vice, and being morally responsible. He denies at least two kinds of moral luck. One cannot be morally obligated to do something that lies beyond her partial control, and one cannot be morally responsible for having done or brought about something that was not in her control.

Robert J. Hartman (Chapter 20) makes a case for accepting moral luck; in terms of the above examples, he argues that the killer driver deserves more blame than the merely reckless driver and that the thief deserves more blame than the mere would-be thief. His argument proceeds from the absurdity of blaming a person on account of what she has not actually done, an analogy from less to more contentious kinds of moral luck, and an explanation of the errant intuition that, for example, reckless drivers are equally blameworthy.

Laura W. Ekstrom (Chapter 21) considers whether pinning down the nature of luck might help to assess the luck objection to libertarianism. The objection is that the indeterminism involved in an agent's non-deterministically caused action makes whichever action occurs lucky in a way that undermines her freedom and moral responsibility with respect to it. She concludes in part that not all conditions of luck are fully pertinent to the core issue of freedom and moral responsibility and that objectors should put their luck objection in more appropriate terms.

Mirja Pérez de Calleja (Chapter 22) considers whether there can be luck or chance in a causally deterministic world. Subsequently, she examines two arguments about whether luck poses a skeptical problem for compatibilists—namely, for people who think that an action's being causally determined does not intrinsically rule out being free or morally responsible for that action. She also critically assesses replies to these arguments.

These six essays take up, even if very briefly, the question about what account of luck is relevant to solving the puzzles associated with moral luck and free will. One point of convergence between them is that lack of control is *the* important feature of luck, regardless of whether there are other necessary conditions on luck itself, to think about when engaging these puzzles. This convergence is not too surprising because the standard use of "luck" in the moral luck literature is the lack of control use of "luck" (see Hartman 2017: ch. 2).

Part IV: Epistemic Luck

It is a commonly accepted platitude that knowledge is incompatible with luck (e.g. lucky guesses generally do not seem to be good candidates for knowledge), but, arguably, not just *any* kind of luck rules out knowledge. If I just happen to be in the right place at the right time (i.e., as a matter of luck) to learn that I am going to be given a teaching award—perhaps simply overhearing the news as I walk past the Provost's office—that presumably does not preclude my *knowing* that I am going to be given the award. If I was very nearly blinded a moment earlier, that does not preclude my having visual knowledge now. So, what sorts of luck *are* incompatible with knowledge? The kinds of luck found in Gettier and Fake Barn cases are the obvious candidates; however, what distinguishes the luck in those cases from benign species of epistemic luck? Luck also seems to play a key role both in broad, historical skeptical challenges and in new, cutting edge epistemological research into the limits (and projected horizons) of human cognition. Over the past 50 years, a significant portion of the epistemological literature has been driven by luck. Some of the central issues include:

1. What account of luck best fits the role of "luck" in "epistemic luck"?
2. Is Pritchard's taxonomy of doxastic, evidential, content, capacity, veritic, and reflective epistemic luck exhaustive? Are some of these categories redundant? Should we be considering other forms of epistemic luck such as areatic doxastic luck?
3. What kinds of epistemic luck preclude knowledge? And is it possible to develop a theory of knowledge that viably avoids such luck? In other words, how might someone develop an adequately "anti-luck" epistemology?
4. Or perhaps the common assumption that knowledge is incompatible with luck (at least of a certain sort) is all wrong. Is knowledge really incompatible with luck in the way that so many epistemologists seem to assume?
5. The problematic kinds of epistemic luck have typically manifested themselves in particular cases or counterexamples. What is the anatomy of a Gettier counterexample, and why have they proven so incredibly difficult to avoid? And how is the environmental luck at work in the so-called "Fake Barn" style cases different, and what can they tell us about the nature of knowledge?
6. How does knowledge's apparent incompatibility with luck connect with much broader skeptical challenges with deep historical roots? And what does this reveal about the fundamental nature of knowledge?
7. What does our understanding of epistemic luck as incompatible with human knowledge reveal about our assumptions regarding cognition and the mind?

Undoubtedly, one of the central driving forces behind the contemporary epistemological literature on epistemic luck has been the Gettier Problem. Ian M. Church (Chapter 23) offers a diagnosis of the kind of luck at issue in the Gettier Problem, which elucidates why such counterexamples have been so resilient—that is, why the luck at issue in Gettier problems has proven to be so difficult to avoid. Church's grim conclusion is that no reductive analysis of knowledge can viably hope to avoid Gettier counterexamples.

Benjamin Jarvis (Chapter 24) considers the unique challenge posed by "environmental luck", the kind of luck at issue in "Fake Barn" style cases. In his chapter, Jarvis argues that the kinds of questions that many philosophers have focused on when it comes to environmental luck have been the wrong kinds of questions. Instead of asking whether environmental luck precludes knowledge, Jarvis asks whether environmental luck has any epistemic significance.

The problem of epistemic luck has, for many, been a problem of how best to understand and define knowledge so as to preclude the vicious species of luck. Tim Black (Chapter 25) considers some of the seminal "anti-luck" proposals that have been put forward in contemporary epistemology, including sensitivity theories, safety theories, and what he calls "internalistic anti-luck epistemology". Black concludes by considering a more radical "anti-luck" response that draws from the work of Søren Kierkegaard.

Stephen Hetherington (Chapter 26) takes a very different response to the purported problem of epistemic luck. Instead of trying to develop an "anti-luck" epistemology, Hetherington critically examines the guiding platitude in contemporary epistemology that knowledge is incompatible with certain kinds of epistemic luck. Hetherington concludes by suggesting that such a platitude might be fundamentally mistaken and that mere true belief might plausibly count as knowledge.

John Greco (Chapter 27) broadens the scope of the challenge posed by epistemic luck by highlighting the role luck has played in some seminal skeptical challenges in the Western philosophical tradition. Greco argues that such skeptical challenges are often driven by an overly "internalistic" understanding of the challenge posed by epistemic luck. Greco concludes by highlighting ways many contemporary epistemologists have rejected that internalistic understanding, opening up new and exciting ways to respond to longstanding skeptical challenges.

J. Adam Carter (Chapter 28) considers how our assumptions regarding cognition have shaped many of the seminal responses to epistemic luck. Carter argues that many responses to epistemic luck have assumed what he calls "cognitive internalism". He argues that if this assumption is replaced with a more "externalistic" conception of mind, a radically different view of luck and knowledge emerges.

Part V: The Psychology of Luck

Luck (and our perceptions of luck) can deeply affect our view of ourselves, others, and events. And as Pritchard and Matthew Smith (2004: 6) noted,

> Most of the work on luck in the recent psychological literature has taken place in terms of what is known as "attribution research", which is concerned with the way in which people construct causal explanations for why events happened, such as people's actions (e.g., why a person did what they did) or achievements (e.g., why a person succeeded or failed).

In fact, our luck ascriptions are deeply affected by our ability to emotionally regulate, our dominant attachment strategy, our ability to calculate risk, etc. This research into how and why people attribute luck to certain situations can inform or perhaps challenge purely theoretical conceptions of luck. But what is more, the psychological literature is also exploring how people experience and respond to luck; some researchers even explore ways we might help cultivate and promote healthy assessments and responses to lucky (or unlucky) events in life. Key issues to be considered in this part include the following:

1. What factors influence when and why we attribute luck to some situations and not others? From a psychological perspective, what tend to be the markers of a lucky event?
2. Are people consistent in their luck attributions? If they are inconsistent, what accounts for their variance?
3. How does assessment of lucky situations relate to assessment of risk?
4. What role do our emotions play when we evaluate and respond to luck and risk? Does better emotional regulation correspond to better luck assessments?

5. What factors influence how someone experiences luck? Is there any way to promote healthier responses to good or bad luck?

While we considered some purely theoretical accounts of luck in Part II of this *Handbook*, Steven D. Hales and Jennifer Adrienne Johnson (Chapter 29) argue that psychology and philosophy can work together to provide new insights into the nature of luck. In particular, Hales and Johnson argue that the literature on cognitive biases suggests that current theoretical accounts of luck are unable to viably distinguish good luck from bad luck.

Karl Halvor Teigen (Chapter 30) explores when and why people describe events as lucky (in everyday life and language) from a psychological perspective. According to Teigen's research, people are more likely to describe a situation as lucky if it involves risk—particularly in light of what people perceive to be close counterfactual situations. Teigen also explores how people make sense of lucky situations and what people are tempted to attribute to the particular results (e.g. divine action, chance, etc.).

Sabine Roeser (Chapter 31) explores what our emotional response to experiencing luck might tell us about how we evaluate luck. After all, an experience of luck is almost always accompanied by an emotion such as relief at narrowly avoiding an automobile accident or elation at winning the lottery. Roeser argues that these reactions appear to suggest that our assessment of luck is closely intertwined with risk and uncertainty.

The psychological literature seems to show that people routinely overestimate their ability to control random events—particularly when it comes to lotteries, roulette tables, etc. This is called the "illusion of control". Anastasia Ejova (Chapter 32) explores the psychological literature on the illusion of control and considers how such an illusion—especially in light of specific background beliefs—might affect our experience and understanding of luck.

And finally, Matthew D. Smith and Piers Worth (Chapter 33) look to how seminal ideas from the positive psychology literature might inform the psychological elements of how people conceive of and experience luck. By exploring links in this research between luck, on the one hand, and optimism and gratitude, on the other, Smith and Worth conclude that how we perceive and experience luck might be (at least partially) within our control.

Part VI: Future Research

While the academic research on luck has, thus far, centered primarily on questions concerning the nature of luck, moral luck, epistemic luck, and the psychology of luck, the literature continues to grow and develop. New, exciting questions are being considered, and even some old questions are being reconsidered from new or historically underrepresented perspectives. For example, both the nature of luck and luck attributions are deeply relevant to questions in theology and religion more generally. Sometimes luck is seen to be at odds with religious traditions that emphasize the sovereignty and providence of God; however, we might wonder if more careful reflection on the nature of luck reveals genuine conflict there. Additionally, issues concerning moral luck seem deeply connected to how we understand the legal system. The prevalence of epistemic luck might force us to reevaluate the history of science and the nature of scientific discovery. And we might think that variations in how people experience and perceive luck might force us to think carefully about the theoretical import of such experiences and perceptions. Here are some questions to be considered in this part:

1. To what extent does scientific progress rely on luck?
2. What does experimental philosophy have to teach us about attributions of epistemic luck?
3. How might a feminist understanding of moral luck reorient our practices?
4. Is there such a thing as legal luck? And what is the relationship between it and moral luck?

5. How does luck figure into religion and theology? What is the relationship between salvific luck, on the one hand, and moral and epistemic luck, on the other? Does the contingency of religious belief undermine rational religious belief? Can we understand luck as having a role in what is created, who experiences salvation, and whose prayers are answered?

J. D. Trout (Chapter 34) argues that contrary to the self-image of some conceptions of contemporary science, scientific progress is often affected by luck. Trout outlines various types of contingency common in scientific success including psychological idiosyncrasies of scientists, environmental features of civilizations, the timing of observing curious phenomena, convergence of political and scientific interests, attention paid to needs generated by cultural contingency, and contingency of our cognitive limitations.

Joe Milburn and Edouard Machery (Chapter 35) consider the relevance of experimental philosophy for anti-luck epistemology in part by surveying recent work. Current experimental philosophy supports the idea that defeasible true justified belief is not knowledge and that Gettier cases teach us something about knowledge, but they argue that more experimental philosophy needs to be done to determine whether there is an anti-luck condition on knowledge and how exactly such a condition should be understood.

Carolyn McLeod and Jody Tomchishen (Chapter 36) examine the complicated position feminists take on the relationship between luck and moral responsibility. There is a dominant trend in feminist philosophy that accepts that certain kinds of luck, such as the systematic luck involved in oppression, can affect moral responsibility. Nevertheless, other trends highlight limitations on luck affecting moral responsibility and duties.

Ori J. Herstein (Chapter 37) begins with the standard definition of legal luck as occurring when a person's legal status (rights, obligations, liabilities, or culpability) is affected by factors outside of her control. He explores general reasons to affirm and deny the existence of legal luck based on accepting and rejecting moral luck. He also canvasses particular reasons in favor of accepting legal luck in tort and criminal law, and offers clarifications for the standard definition of legal luck.

Guy Axtell (Chapter 38) surveys recent work on religious luck and explicates categories of religious luck in connection to categories from the moral and epistemic luck literatures. Subsequently, he offers the "New Problem of Religious Luck" from religious diversity for the claim that it is irrational to believe that one's own religion is uniquely true.

Jordan Wessling (Chapter 39) explores the way in which the doctrines of creation, salvation, and petitionary prayer involve luck. In particular, he considers the indeterminacy of autonomous creation that luckily leads to some possible life-forms and not others, whether a person's being a fit candidate for heaven or hell is lucky on various theological views, and whether there is luck involved in whether God answers petitionary prayers.

The Cover Artwork

The painting on the front cover is entitled, *Allegory of Fortune*, by Salvator Rosa. It portrays Fortuna, the Roman goddess of luck and fortune, pouring riches from her cornucopia upon undeserving beasts—representing how good fortune sometimes befalls the people who least deserve it or need it and how humans can perceive luck (and misfortune) in their lives.[1]

Note

1 The editors like the painting simply for its significance to the theme of this handbook. Andrew Beck at Routledge asked us also to mention the political context of the painting—namely, that Rosa used it to express his displeasure at being overlooked for papal patronage.

References

Hartman, R.J. (2017) *In Defense of Moral Luck: Why Luck Often Affects Praiseworthiness and Blameworthiness*, New York: Routledge.

Nagel, T. (1976) "Moral Luck," *Proceedings of the Aristotelian Society, Supplementary Volumes* 50, 137–151.

——, (ed.). (1979) "Moral Luck," in *Mortal Questions*, Cambridge: Cambridge University Press, pp. 24–38.

Pritchard, D. (2005) *Epistemic Luck*, Oxford: Oxford University Press.

Pritchard, D., & Smith, M. (2004) "The Psychology and Philosophy of Luck," *New Ideas in Psychology* 22, 1–28.

Williams, B. (1976) "Moral Luck," *Proceedings of the Aristotelian Society, Supplementary Volumes* 50, 115–135.

——. (ed.). (1981) "Moral Luck," in *Moral Luck: Philosophical Papers 1973–1980*, Cambridge: Cambridge University Press, pp. 20–39.

PART I

The History of Luck

1

ARISTOTLE ON CONSTITUTIVE, DEVELOPMENTAL, AND RESULTANT MORAL LUCK

Nafsika Athanassoulis

Discussing Aristotle's account of luck is challenging because he does not directly discuss luck in a way that is immediately comparable to modern debates; rather, the influence of luck permeates his theory. To make sense of Aristotle's diverse remarks on luck we will start with his definition of luck from the *Physics*. We will see how Aristotle defines luck as having five features: lucky occurrences are irregular, incidental, indeterminable, unstable, and their effects can be good or evil. Luck is then contrasted with both the purposefulness and the regularity we see in natural causes, and while it is understood as an intentional event, its results are incidental. In the next section we will consider how this definition of luck in the *Physics* relates to Aristotle's treatment of luck in his works on ethics and the good life, as well as how it compares with the modern understanding of moral luck in the debate introduced to philosophy by Bernard Williams and Thomas Nagel. To answer the question of how Aristotle conceives of the influence of luck on the moral life, we will consider what his theory has to say on the three types of moral luck discussed in modern literature, i.e. constitutive, developmental, and resultant moral luck. We will see how Aristotle grapples to reconcile the intuitively plausible claim that luck as well as wisdom can make one's life go well, with the equally plausible observation that if we want to praise and blame agents for their virtues and vices, the origin of these character traits cannot be luck. The conclusion of a complicated discussion is a distinction between good fortune, a rare state where naturally positive dispositions lead one effortlessly to virtue without the need for wisdom, and luck which retains all the features of the concept as developed in the *Physics*. We will then consider the constitutive luck which, given Aristotle's emphasis on the importance of education, practice, and the development of good habits, is the kind of luck that most affects Aristotelian theory. We will see how Aristotle embraces this kind of luck, accepting it as the features that make human lives vulnerable but, at the same time, precious. Finally, we will consider resultant luck and conclude that this kind of luck tends to be less influential for theories that focus on assessments of characters rather than outcomes.

Luck

For Aristotle luck[1] is a species of spontaneity,[2] as spontaneity is a wider phenomenon that encompasses cases of luck. Spontaneous events are events that have an external cause and that come to pass for the sake of something, but they do not come to pass for the sake of what actually results. Spontaneity applies to the actions of animals and inanimate objects, so we say, for example, the stool happened to fall upright spontaneously so that it can now be used as a seat, but it did not fall this way for the purpose of being used as a seat (note that it still fell for the sake of something, i.e. being a heavy object it fell downwards in accordance with its proper nature; landing on its feet, which makes it usable as a seat, was accidental). Lucky events are spontaneous occurrences that come about through the action of something capable of intention, so they fall under the realm of choice and make us fortunate or unfortunate, but they occur incidentally. Aristotle identifies five features of luck (Aristotle *Physics* Book II part 5):

1. Chance events are not regular. They do not happen, either always or for the most part, the same way.
2. Chance events are incidental, that is, they do not occur for the sake of something in the way that the housebuilding skill is, in virtue of itself, the cause of a house. So, for example, imagine that A is owed some money by B and A goes to the market to do his weekly shop where he happens to bump into B; we want to say that A recovered his debt by luck as his intention in going to the market was not to meet up with B. Wanting to shop explains A's being at the market and is the non-incidental cause of him being there; what explains A and B meeting is the incidental fact that they both attended the market at the same time. When we ask A how did you manage to meet B, the answer is "I happened to bump into him, just luck," so A's desire to shop and his trip to the market does not, in itself, explain the sequence of events that led to A getting his money back.
3. Chance events are indeterminable. Because chance events are incidental, there are an indeterminable number of them. So, A bumped into B because he wanted to go to the market, but he could have bumped into him because he wanted to meet someone else, or because he was following someone or avoiding someone, and so on. Having said that, Aristotle does point out that that does not mean that *any* two events can become connected through luck; some events are closer to others, e.g. warmth from the sun has a closer connection to health than getting one's hair cut.
4. Following on from that, we observe that luck is a thing contrary to rule, it is unstable and neither always true nor true for the most part. This makes luck unaccountable because it cannot be accounted for on a rational basis.
5. The effects of luck can be good or evil.

Aristotle then uses these insights about luck to set up a contrast with natural causes and develop a teleological argument about nature. At the heart of the Aristotelian account of teleology is the observation that every activity has a purpose. When Aristotle looks at the eye, he observes that it is constructed in order to see, and when he considers the activity of medicine, it is aimed at restoring health. The eye is *for* seeing, and medicine is *for* healing. One can use the eye to wink but that is not its characteristic function, for while eyes can be used for winking that is not what is essential about them. Similarly, medical skill can be used to torture but that is not what medicine is for, using medical skill to cause pain and extract information is a distortion of the function of medicine. This purposefulness is not something that is added later by our use of the eye or our application of medicine, nor is it something that is constructed by anthropocentric understandings of characteristics and activities. Rather this normativity is present in nature (Annas in Gardiner 2005: 13); what something is for is determined by its very nature. Luck is contrasted with both the purposefulness and the regularity we observe in natural causes (Johnson 2005: chs 3 and 4; Irwin 1990: ch. 5).

Both natural and lucky causes take place for the sake of something; they are the products of intention, but luck is incidental to the result. So, take the example of a sculptor who is working on a sculpture. His skill at sculpting is the cause of the sculpture but it is an internal cause, i.e. there exists a sculpture because he is a sculptor; there is a non-incidental link between his skill and its product. At the same time, there are an indefinite number of incidentals at work here as well, e.g. the sculptor is wearing a hat or not, has three brothers or not, etc. All these factors are incidental and external to the activity of sculpting as the sculptor sculpts in virtue of his skill in sculpting, not because he is wearing a hat or has three brothers. So to say "The man with the hat sculpted a sculpture" is true but accidental and does not tell us anything about the abilities of men with hats in general to sculpt sculptures. Natural causes are intrinsically related to their products, lucky ones are not; lucky ones just happen to come about. The function of sculpting explains why a sculpture was produced, in a way that is missing from the relationship between a lucky cause and its results.

Furthermore, if it is the function of activity A to produce result R we will see a lot of Rs coming about because of A. In nature we observe regularity, it is the function of eyes to see because natural things exist for the sake of something that is part of them, i.e. the eye exists for seeing. Equally, skills, arts, and activities exist for the sake of their products, sculpture for sculpting, and medicine for healing, so that where there are sculptors we expect to find sculptures and where there are doctors we expect to find healed patients. The opposite is true of lucky causes. Because luck is not intrinsically related to its results, there is no regularity to lucky occurrences; there are an infinite number of lucky causes for every single thing, because lucky causes are incidental.

In summary, Aristotle develops three concepts relevant to our purposes: spontaneous causes that are incidental and non-intentional, lucky causes which are incidental and intentional, and natural causes that are non-incidental and intentional. His discussion of luck serves two purposes, to account for luck as a cause and to contrast the features of lucky causes with natural causes thus setting the groundwork for the teleological argument that will underpin the definition of virtue.

The Link Between the *Physics* and the *Nicomachean Ethics*

So much for the definition of luck, a discussion of which takes place in the *Physics*, now we move on to what Aristotle has to say on the influence of luck on morality, a topic mainly developed in the *Nicomachean Ethics* and in part in the *Eudemian Ethics*. However, I have two concerns with framing our inquiry in this way, that is, as an approach that attributes two different and unrelated understandings of luck to Aristotle, i.e. the one developed in the *Physics*, and an incompatible one that underlies the discussions of luck and the good life in his works on morality. The first is the reasonable question, what is the relationship between the discussion of luck in the *Physics* and that in the *Nicomachean Ethics*? If we want to understand what Aristotle had to say about luck, we should attempt to understand all of it; it is not plausible that Aristotle intended for us to just set the *Physics* discussion to one side and move on.[3] The second concern, is that approaching the work of the *Nicomachean Ethics* and the *Eudemian Ethics* in isolation tempts us to impose modern conceptions of morality and luck on Aristotle, something that threatens to distort his theory. Let us consider this second point in detail first, and then we will return to the first concern.

The modern discussion of moral luck was ignited by and shaped in terms of the debate introduced by Williams (1993a) and Nagel (1993). Williams sets the scene from the beginning: the term "moral luck" is oxymoronic, because it encapsulates the tension between morality, responsibility, agency, and control on the one hand, and luck, lack of control, and the inappropriateness of ascribing responsibility, on the other. We feel the tension, as cases of moral luck are cases where admittedly there was lack of control on the part of the agent over a crucial aspect of the trait, action, or consequence but we still ascribe responsibility to him for it. The very definition of the phenomenon reveals a particular way of seeing things: an adversarial account between luck and morality, one that tempts us, along Kantian grounds, to reject moral luck altogether in favor of all powerful reason or at least to view cases of moral luck as extraordinary and as requiring special consideration. However, this is not Aristotle's view. For Aristotle, the moral life is steeped in luck. Williams himself seems to make this point in his postscript to the original paper on moral luck (Williams 1993b: 251). Williams suggests there were some misunderstandings in the way his original paper was read; moral luck poses a problem for a particular and well-entrenched conception of morality. However, if we think of ethics in the generalized sense, rather than morality as referring to a particular system of ideas, we do not have the same sense of conflict. That means that there are conceptions of the ethical that do not invite the problem of moral luck. Such wider conceptions of the ethical offer different insights into the distinctions between voluntary and involuntary which affect how we evaluate the influence of luck on human affairs. Rather than adversarial, luck becomes a benign part of the human experience. Furthermore, for Williams, a wider conception of the ethical challenges whether it is appropriate to see blame as a "divine, perfect, judgment" (Williams 1993a: 254). Williams urges us instead toward making more nuanced judgments suited to particulars, and toward accepting the importance of reactions other than blame, such as regret (Williams 1993b: 254–255). When approaching Aristotle, then, we should be careful not to import conceptions of morality that are alien to his thought, but rather to understand luck within a system of ethics that sees morality steeped in luck rather than opposed to it.

How is Aristotelian ethical theory steeped in luck? The answer comes from the *Physics* and will also answer our first concern over how the discussion in the *Physics* relates to Aristotle's treatise on ethics. In the *Physics*, Aristotle tells us that luck is only relevant where there is a possibility of benefit and, in general, of action (*praxis*) (Aristotle *Physics* 197b3). He links luck with action and luck is contrasted with spontaneity because spontaneity is only possible for inanimate objects and non-human animals, objects that cannot deliberate and make choices.[4] The very notion of deliberation and choice is linked to luck because of our human nature, and we cannot make sense of what kinds of people we should strive to become unless we see the commonalities between luck and thinking, namely that they both concern choice.[5] Not only that, but chance mimics causality; had the creditor known the debtor would be at the market, he would have gone there so as to meet him. "Luck comes about when the result that was *not* intended happens *as if* it had been intended" (Massie 2003: 23). This is why intention is so significant to luck and why it is defined separately from spontaneity; lucky events appear as if they were the objects of our intention, affecting us either positively or negatively, but they were not what was intended, as they are not done for the sake of the thing that results. For Aristotle, the concept of "luck" is linked to intentionality, choice, and deliberation, and can be properly understood only within this wider context.

Finally, then, the most important conclusion for our purposes is that our enquiry into choice, luck, and deliberation remains aporetic, that is, unresolved and questioning (Massie 2003: 16). We should not expect definitive and rigid answers from Aristotle as the subject matter does not permit them; "for it is a mark of the trained mind never to expect more precision in the treatment of any subject than the nature of that subject permits" (*NE* 1984b23–25). If the modern debate on moral luck forces us to take sides, either rejecting the very possibility of moral luck or surrendering to its influences, then Aristotle cannot be interpreted as taking part in the debate. Perhaps the most we can hope for from Aristotle is to shed some light on the question rather than arrive at confident answers, but that is not the fault of Aristotelian theory, this merely reflects the limits of the subject matter.

On the Different Types of Luck

If we are to learn something from the preceding discussion, then it is that luck exists and that it cannot be ignored but it makes us wonder at its place in nature.[6] Aristotle's remarks on luck are dotted around his works but there is no doubt that he considered the questions posed by luck to be important and central in ethics. To make sense of his diverse discussions, I will order them under the more modern distinctions of types of luck, namely constitutive, developmental and resultant luck.[7] In brief, *constitutive luck* affects who we are, the natural tendencies we are born with that may or may not assist us on the road to virtue. So, someone who is born naturally empathic may have an advantage when developing the virtue of kindness, whereas someone who is naturally irascible may have a weakness to overcome. *Developmental luck* refers to all the elements that go toward making us who we are, and which affect our moral development. These may include the ease or difficulty with which we develop good habits, the availability of appropriate role models for emulation, the conduct of our families and peers, the kinds of moral tests we are exposed to at different stages of development, the opportunity to learn from mistakes and failures, etc. Nagel's original discussion is slightly narrower and refers to the kinds of problems and situations one faces (Nagel 1993: 60), but I think the term "developmental" luck, with its broader connotations, captures more of the diverse factors which, along with the situations we come across, shape who we become.[8] *Resultant luck* affects the consequences of our actions. A callous driver shows utter disregard for the lives of others when he gets behind the wheel of his car while drunk, but if he does not encounter anyone else on his drive home, no one is hurt by his actions. What does Aristotle have to say about each kind of luck?

Constitutive Luck

The idea that who we fundamentally are affects who we become is crucial to any theory of development, but the thought that we have no control over our natural constitutive endowments, is disturbing. If we have no control over who we are, what chance do we have of shaping who we become? If constitutive luck does affect our characters then some of us are privileged and some of us are weakened in significant aspects of our moral development before we are even born. This suggestion is disturbing due to its unfairness, and it could lead us to despair about the very possibility of becoming virtuous before we have even begun on our journey.

Aristotle engages in a complicated discussion of the possibility of constitutive luck in Book VIII section 2 of the *Eudemian Ethics* where he tries to reconcile the intuitively plausible observation that luck as well as wisdom can cause one to lead a good life,[9] with the equally plausible claim that if we want to praise and blame agents for their virtue and vice, the origin of the character traits cannot be luck.

Aristotle starts by observing that even the foolish can sometimes luckily succeed in their endeavors, and that in some cases, such as navigation or strategy, there is an element of luck as well as skill involved. What is the source of such luck? It cannot be wisdom, because the wise can give reasons for their actions and the lucky succeed in spite of being unwise about the very matters about which they are fortunate. If you ask A how he recovered his debt, he cannot say because he searched out and found B in the market; he has to say that he was lucky to have done so. Luck also cannot be a gift of the gods because luck is random, and it is strange to think the gods would not bestow their favor on the wise. Nor can luck come from nature as nature is the cause of things that happen always or for the most part, and, as we noted above in the *Physics*, lucky events are the opposite. Does it then mean that there is no such thing as luck? This seems contrary to what we perceive so we cannot accept this conclusion.

To resolve this problem, Aristotle draws a distinction between what we will call from now on *good fortune* and *luck*.[10] Luck retains all the features of the concept we saw developed in the *Physics*, while good fortune accounts for the possibility of constitutive luck.[11] Those who have good fortunes do so because of their nature. Just as some musical people can sing without having to learn to sing but due to a natural talent, some of us lead virtuous lives due to inclinations and desires that naturally point toward the right actions without the need for deliberation and intellect. Such people are *naturally* virtuous as opposed to those who have *moral* virtue proper, where virtue proper requires the right reason and the right desire leading to the right action. The merely naturally virtuous will do the right thing even though they are foolish and irrational. They will be unable to account for their behavior or teach it to others, just as those who are merely naturally talented singers cannot teach singing. Such good fortune, whose origin is in the person's nature, saves the merely naturally virtuous person from his poor reasoning. Since the origin of the actions is in nature, this person will have continuous good fortune.

The lucky, on the other hand, succeed against their impulses. They have the wrong reason and the wrong desire but luck intervenes and brings about the right outcome. This maintains the characteristics of luck we saw developed previously, i.e. it is not regular, it is incidental and it is indeterminate. That means that the use of luck in the *Eudemian Ethics* is the same as that in the *Physics* but now this type of luck is restricted, in modern terms, to resultant luck, i.e. luck in how the effects of our actions turn out. Constitutive luck becomes the notion of the naturally caused, continuous good fortune, and good fortune is no longer luck as defined in the *Physics* as it is neither episodic, nor indeterminate, nor incidental.

Aristotle views good fortune, in this sense, as something people have from birth, in the same way they have blue or brown eyes. According to Aristotle's teleological account, nature continually reaches for its end, so the fact that some people are born naturally virtuous is not problematic; it is an expression of our nature acting unimpeded. It might be a rare phenomenon, and most of us who are not naturally fortunate have to work at bringing about the natural ends of humans *qua* humans through habituation, education, etc., but, for some of us, those ends come to fruition effortlessly due to having the right desires and impulses by our very nature. In this sense, deliberation and intellect are required where nature falls short of its own end and needs a helping hand.[12]

All this accounts for why some of us are virtuous without having wisdom and means that praising the naturally virtuous is unproblematic; they are both fortunate and praiseworthy as they are acting in ways natural to human beings. The link between morality and control is not so much abandoned but fades into the background. Control seems more important when corrective action is necessary, action on the part of the agent which brings him in line with the goals of nature. If such goals are already met, then moral praise is already appropriate and the requirement for control is not as relevant from the Aristotelian perspective. Here Aristotle breaks down the oxymoronic feature of moral luck, as good fortune is an expression of our very nature and there is no conflict between what we are due to fortune and what we should be due to nature.

Does a parallel argument work for natural vice? Much of what Aristotle has to say about virtue in terms of a cultivated, stable, and reliable purposive disposition is supposed to also be true for vice, but I think here we have a case where natural vice is not parallel to natural virtue. This is because natural virtue mirrors the goals of nature and therefore natural vice is an impossibility. Vice is only possible if one makes a deliberative choice in that direction, if one cultivates the wrong reason and the wrong desire to result in the wrong action. That would mean that constitutive fortune is possible but only with respect to natural virtue. Such a conclusion seems to me to be consistent with Aristotle's arguments but he does not make it, in fact, what he does say about how we are ruled by nature points to a bleaker picture. In the *Politics*, Aristotle tells us that while all humans are ruled by nature, different parts of the soul are present in different people differently. Thus, the slave has no deliberative faculty at all, the woman has the ability to deliberate but has no authority, while the child deliberates imperfectly (Aristotle *Politics* 1260a8–14). Further, Europeans are brave and spirited but lacking in intellect and art, Asians are intelligent and inventive but wanting in spirit and slavish, while only the Greeks are both high spirited and intelligent (Aristotle *Politics* 1327b19 ff.). These qualities are natural qualities that people have before any process of character development even begins.[13]

One might interpret Aristotle here as saying that we all participate in virtue, but not all in the same way; that in itself is unproblematic and could even be perceived as an advantage of his theory, as it allows for differing conceptions of the good life. In addition, we have also concluded that moral fortune is not objectionable in the constitutive case as it has been reduced to natural causes; this is a possible argument we can make in the case of good constitutive fortune. However, it seems to me that bringing these two conclusions together is problematic. The very reason why constitutive fortune is unproblematic is because nature aims toward the noble and the good. Since, however, the concept of nature expresses itself so differently in different people, we would have to accept that the life of a natural slave is a good life. Arguing that the naturally good life has many instantiations in one thing, asking us to accept that some of us are destined to be slaves, or destined to be women or Europeans where this is understood as being inherently less morally capable than Greek males, is problematic, even if we were to grant Aristotle that it is true due to our nature. It is not just that a different kind of good life is naturally available to those with good fortune, but rather that some versions of the good life available to the constitutionally gifted, i.e. the natural slaves or women, do not appear very good any more. While Aristotle does give an answer to the question of constitutive good and bad moral luck then, this answer is, at least in part, quite controversial.[14]

Aristotle then moves on in his discussion in the *Eudemian Ethics* to wonder what the source of reason is, the source of our ability to overcome natural deficiencies in the first place. In order to avoid an infinite regress, he argues that the starting point is God. I will not consider this argument further as it seems to move away from questions of constitutive luck to a discussion of antecedent luck. Antecedent luck is not widely discussed in the literature on moral luck and raises questions about determinism that are beyond the scope of this chapter, so we will move on to look at Aristotle on developmental luck.

Developmental Luck

Aristotle begins Book II of the *Nicomachean Ethics* by telling us that virtue is neither engendered in us by nature nor contrary to it.[15] Underlying this claim is the belief that the moral life is worth living if it can be secured by our efforts and cannot be entirely at the mercy of luck—the episodic, incidental kind of luck discussed above. The good life has to be within the capabilities of most people (Nussbaum 1986: 320), because it is an expression of natural excellence and, as such, the final and best end (Aristotle *NE* 1099b16 ff.). Aristotle specifically tells us that our understanding of the good life must be of a good that is widely shared among those who make an effort to study or practice it, so at least for most of us, who are not born naturally fortunate, the good life is within our possibilities.

Having the potential for something, though, is not the same as having the ability itself. Any moral theory that relies on the notion of character has to say something about the process of character development, and it is this process of developing the skills necessary for living the good life that is open to the influence of developmental luck. At its heart, Aristotelian theory is a theory about a gradual process of moral development, that eventually, and if all goes well, leads to established, reliable dispositions to act in accordance with reason, the characteristic function of human beings. Aristotle gives a complex and detailed account of this process of moral development with ties to moral psychology and education, but for our purposes, we can merely pick out its main elements. For a start, the student of virtue needs to develop the right habits. Virtue is not mindless habituation, but the first step on the road to virtue is to practice developing the right habits. The mind of the student of virtue must be prepared in advance to receive the seed of virtue, i.e. it must be habituated to take pleasure in the right things and feel dislike at the right things. If this appropriate habituation does not take place, it may be that the student will not be receptive to discussion and instruction in virtue later on (Aristotle *NE* 1179b23–27). A number of factors will influence the habits of the young, from their family, peers, and associations, to the law of the land which upholds and enforces the good (Aristotle *NE* 1179b31 ff.).

Central to this idea of habituation is the claim that we become virtuous by practicing the virtues (Aristotle *NE* 1103b6 ff.). This is a complex claim. For our purposes, it can be captured in the thought that the student of virtue begins by emulating an appropriate role model,[16] perceives the virtue in others, stands in awe of the virtue of others, and is motivated to aspire to the virtue of others. The first steps of this process involve copying virtue without fully understanding the details of the right reason but over time, with practice and the development of experience, the student of virtue comes to not only do the right action but understand why she does it. That is, she comes to understand how the complexities of the particulars of each situation generate the right reason, which, along with the cultivated right desire, lead to the right action. To make this move from the action to understanding, the student of virtue must learn to reason for herself, internalise the values involved and become an expert in judging the many aspects of each virtue that might be relevant to each situation.[17]

It is already evident that a very large number of factors crucial for this process of character development may be subject to luck; from the place of one's birth and upbringing, to the quality of one's parents and family, to the availability of suitable role models and friends, to the type of situations and moral tests one comes across, to the opportunities for learning from failure, etc. Whatever natural tendencies we may happen to be born with, a large number of factors, both positive and negative, have an influence on the process that goes toward developing our established and stable dispositions. As such, any theory that relies on character, and therefore has something to say about character development, is inherently vulnerable to luck.

Furthermore, luck affects not just the immediate period of character development but also the later opportunities for the expression of virtue and the living of the good life. The Aristotelian good life requires external goods, no one can act virtuously while starving; the exercise of virtue requires external goods such as wealth to be shared liberally with others; the living of the good life requires the support of virtuous friends.[18] This means that the vulnerability of the good life to luck extends to the whole of one's life, as external events and circumstances affect what situations we come across, what external goods are available to us, what happens to our friends, etc.

What should be our response to this influence of luck? Should we be concerned by the fickleness of it all, disturbed by the influence of random factors on something as important as moral development? The standard interpretation of the Aristotelian answer to the influence of luck comes from Nussbaum's highly influential work. Nussbaum argues that our very understanding of human excellence only makes sense as something of value *because* it is something vulnerable:

> [h]uman excellence is seen ... as something whose very nature is to be in need, a growing thing in the world that could not be made invulnerable and keep its own peculiar fineness. The contingencies that make praise problematic are also, in some as yet unclear way, constitutive of that which is there for praising.
>
> *Nussbaum 1986: 2*

Like a delicate plant, the student of virtue must find herself planted in fertile soil, nurtured by gentle rain, able to avoid sudden frosts and harsh winds.[19] The right circumstances will foster virtue, the wrong ones will tempt toward vice, but that is our nature as human beings, and much of what we value is based on this very human vulnerability. For Aristotle, this vulnerability brought about by luck is not inimical to morality, but rather goes to the heart of ethics (Nussbaum 1986: 264). William's oxymoron is not appropriate here as the tension dissolves; luck can have a profound influence on the good life, but the good life cannot be understood without the humanity that makes us vulnerable to luck. This is not a clash between morality and luck, but an interdependent relationship where what makes human lives valuable is the same thing that makes them vulnerable to luck; we cannot make sense of one without the other.

Yet at the same time the attainment of virtue, the end of the long period of character development, offers some protection against luck. The virtuous person possesses practical wisdom, a kind of applied expertise in making judgments about moral matters, which expresses itself in action, proceeding from settled and reliable dispositions. As such, the virtuous person will act kindly, for example, easily and effortlessly even when it is difficult to do so, or even when faced with what others perceive as tempting circumstances to do otherwise. The virtuous is insulated, by the reliability of his virtue, from the caprices of the world. Furthermore, like any good craftsman, the virtuous person makes the best of the materials at hand, so even when faced with bad tools in terms of the limited choices he may have, he makes the best of the situation. It is part of Aristotle's understanding of the nobility of virtue that one faces adversity in the right way. The virtuous man feels misfortune the same way we do, but his nature leads him to take the most honorable course available; like the good craftsman, the virtuous makes the best of the materials he has and faces the situation he finds himself in with dignity. Fundamentally this is because the good life is determined by our activities, which are the expression of our choices and therefore cannot be held hostage to good or bad luck.[20] It is virtue that determines *eudaimonia*, not luck (Aristotle *NE* 1100b4–10).

Aristotle's answer to the influence of luck on the good life, then, is complex. The developmental aspect of acquiring virtue is sensitive to many factors subject to luck. A lot has to go well in one's life before one can attain virtue, in terms of both the influences one is exposed to and the situations one comes across. The life of virtue requires activity, external goods, and good friends, but, at the same time, it also resists luck in that virtue is a purposive choice, it is the expression of the agent's practical wisdom in action.[21] Having said that, Aristotle inserts one last caveat: a life cannot be judged to be good until it has been lived to its end, as devastating misfortunes, the kind of comprehensive bad luck Priam suffered, might affect even the most prosperous of men (Aristotle *NE* 1100a5–9 and 1100a5–7). The *eudaimon* man, then, is "one who is active in accordance with complete virtue, and who is adequately furnished with external goods, and that not for some unspecified period but throughout a complete life" (Aristotle *NE* 1101a15–18).

Resultant Luck

Any normative theory that emphasizes the importance of having the right sort of character, of being the right kind of person, will be less vulnerable to luck affecting the consequences of one's actions. The virtuous person is virtuous because he perceives the right thing to do and feels the right way toward the right person and at the right time. This stable disposition toward the noble and the good will often result in action because the right choice often involves expressing one's state of being into doing, but the emphasis of the moral assessment of praise is on *who* you are, not on *what* you do.[22]

If the source of moral worth, then, is who one is, luck affecting the results of what one does is less problematic for character-based theories. If the good life is concerned with the kind of person you are, then all drunk drivers are equally culpable for being the kinds of people who recklessly disregard the welfare of others, and this holds true regardless of whether any one drunk driver is lucky to get home safely on a particular night or not.[23] Similarly, Aristotelians resist the pressure to evaluate whether a life has been well lived based on the consequences of one's choices; it is the choices themselves, and the reasonableness of the choices, that matter, not their incidental consequences. The virtuous person makes choices in light of the noble and the good, and while the fickle circumstances of the world can hijack the consequences of the virtuous action, they cannot hijack the essence of the character of virtue expressed in these actions. The reckless, vicious disregard for the welfare of others is expressed in the choice to drink when one knows one will drive and is not mitigated by the good luck displayed by pedestrians who happen to be indoors while one drunkenly veers one's car onto pavements. Equally, the virtuous concern with the welfare of others is displayed even in the failed effort to save another person from drowning; the praise is due for the genuine commitment to attempt the rescue, and is not negated by the, perhaps inevitable due to circumstances beyond one's control, lack of success.

This point is not merely a requirement for foreseeing the results of our actions, i.e. knowing that driving drunk endangers others, but is a more substantive point about knowing oneself and developing one's character in such a way that one's choices embody the right reason. Discussing Williams' famous Gauguin example, Kenny argues that our assessment of Gauguin should take place at the time he chooses to abandon his family to pursue his artistic career, rather than later on when we find out what kinds of painting he has produced. A painter who gives up on everyone in his life to pursue an artistic career when he has, at best, only a mediocre talent to develop, is not judged on his bad luck in producing mediocre paintings, but on his culpable lack of self-knowledge which led to the original deluded choice.[24] Other elements of Gauguin's choice can also contribute to our assessment of his character at the time the choice is made: for example, this is a person who is willing to abandon his wife to an extremely uncertain financial and social future to pursue his passion, this is a person who abandons his responsibilities to his children, this is a person who cannot reconcile artistic ambition and familial duties, etc. So, Gauguin's choice is not merely an assessment of the chances of artistic success but also a judgment that artistic success is more valuable than family commitments, a choice for which he can be held responsible at the time of the choosing and without needing to know how it pans out.

It is clear, then, that the good life resists the influence of resultant luck because virtue ethics is less concerned with *what* you do and more concerned with *how* you do it. The emphasis is on having the right dispositions and if their instantiation into action is occasionally perverted through bad luck this does not affect the moral assessment of the agent's character.

Conclusion

We started this chapter with Aristotle's definition of luck. Luck is a species of spontaneity that is brought about by something capable of intention and has five features: it is irregular, incidental, indeterminable, unaccountable, and may be either good or evil. This definition allows Aristotle to set up luck as a cause contrary to natural causes which are non-incidental and intentional. We then saw how Aristotle goes on to link luck and thinking because they both concern choice, luck also mimicking the kind of causality we observe in deliberate action. This understanding of luck makes it part of the human experience and we saw how Aristotelian theory is steeped in luck rather than setting luck against morality.

We then went on to consider the Aristotelian response to three kinds of luck discussed in modern debates: constitutive, developmental, and resultant luck. A complex discussion in the *Eudemian Ethics* concluded by drawing a distinction between good natural fortune which accounts for the possibility of constitutive luck, and luck that retains all the features of the concept as defined above. Developmental luck has the greatest influence on the Aristotelian good life as it can affect all the diverse factors that contribute to the long process of character development as well as the conditions for the expression of virtue in later life. Again, here the Aristotelian response to the possibility of luck is to accept the essential vulnerability of the human life but argue that much of what is valuable about the good life depends on this vulnerability. This is not an oxymoronic, contrasting, adversarial relationship between the demands of morality and the realities of luck; rather, it is a conception of morality as fully immersed in luck—a point to be embraced rather than resisted. Finally, we saw how, in the same way that character theories are more vulnerable to considerations of developmental luck because of their emphasis on a long period of character development, they are resistant to the possibility of resultant luck because of their emphasis on who one is as opposed to what one does.

Our final conclusion on Aristotle on luck and the good life can only be that the subject is complex and not easily captured in generalizations, reflecting the very complexity of the good life and its myriad interconnections with luck.[25]

Notes

1 The Ancient Greek term *tyche* is often also translated as "chance" but for ease of reference I will use "luck" throughout. Note that "*automaton*" can also sometimes be translated as "chance" but I have opted for "spontaneity" to avoid confusion.

2 The Aristotelian account of spontaneity and luck discussed in this section can be found in the *Physics*, Book II, parts 4–8.

3 Most authors interpret Aristotle as having a consistent understanding of luck as he moves from the *Physics* to works on morality. See for example K. Johnson (1997), Bodéüs (2000), and M.T. Johnson in Henry and Nielsen (2015). For an opposing interpretation see Woods (1982).

4 Aristotle, *Physics* 197b10, discussed in Shew (2008: 44).

5 Shew makes this wonderfully original argument in Shew (2008).

6 For more on this see Shew (2008: ch. 3).

7 These are introduced by Nagel, in Statman (1993).

8 For more on this see Athanassoulis (2005: ch. 3).

9 *EE* 1246b36–1247a1 is the passage that links good luck to *eupragia*. Kenny (1992: 57), doubts that *eupragia* should be understood as *eudaimonia* here, which would mean that luck cannot bring about true happiness, but I follow Johnson K. (1997: 94), who notes that Aristotle frequently substitutes *eupragia* for *eudaimonia* and Johnson M.R. (2015: 258), who concurs with this understanding, as otherwise the passage would not be setting up the problem of moral luck. If we do not interpret this passage as setting up the problem of moral luck the ensuing discussion and Aristotle's perplexity as to the role of luck do not make much sense.

10 Johnson, K. (1997), sees three distinctions here: those with bad reasoning who achieve success due to a desire which they may or may not have at other times, those with bad reasoning and bad desires who succeed due to external features of the world (resultant), and those who have continuous natural good fortune. It does not seem to me that there is sufficient evidence that Aristotle saw this as a triple distinction, so I follow Johnson, M.R. (2015), in distinguishing only between episodic luck and constant good fortune.

11 A similar distinction occurs in modern discussions, see for example, Hartman (2017: 28).

12 This argument on the natural sources of good fortune is developed in Johnson, M.R. (2015). Not everyone interprets these passages in this way, e.g. Leunissen (2013) paints a more moderate picture, interpreting such passages to show that there are natural attributes but they make moral development easier rather than predetermining it.

13 Some commentators interpret these passages as arguing for a strict division between races (Johnson, M.R. 2015), while others read Aristotle as saying that different races have these different characteristics for the most part (Leunissen 2012).

14 Admittedly this is a rather bleak point that Aristotle seems to be making here, however readers should not be put off his entire theory purely because of this. All it shows is that even Aristotle did not get everything right.

15 Aristotle, *NE* 1103a14ff. This is mainly a discussion of how virtue can be developed through habituation so therefore cannot be contrary to nature. However, Aristotle also explicitly says that virtue is not engendered in us by nature, a comment which does, on the face of it, seem to contradict the *Eudemian Ethics* discussion of constitutive, natural good fortune. Unfortunately, the scope of this chapter does not permit further discussion on how these points might be reconciled.

16 Aristotle discusses emulation in the *Rhetoric*; for this definition see 1399a35–1388b1. One of the few authors to discuss the Aristotelian concept of emulation is Kristjhansson (2007: 102–108).

17 For more on this move see Burnyeat (1980), Sherman (1989), and Vasiliou (1996).

18 On the need for external goods see Aristotle *NE* 1153b12ff., on liberality see *NE* Book IV, and on friendship see *NE* Book VIII.

19 The analogy comes from a poem by Pindar discussed by Nussbaum (1986: 1).

20 For all the above points see Aristotle *NE* 1100b23ff.

21 For more on how Aristotle both embraces and resists luck see Athanassoulis (2005: chs 3, 4 and 8).

22 Practically we make inferences from what people do as to what kind of person they are, but this is a different point.

23 For more on this see Athanassoulis (2005: ch. 3).

24 Kenny (1988: 110). A similar point is made by Andre (1983).

25 I am very grateful to Monte Johnson for kindly discussing ideas that inspired this chapter, and to Robert Hartman for extensive comments on earlier drafts of it.

References

Andre, J. (1983) "Nagel, Williams and Moral Luck," *Analysis* 43, 202–207.

Annas, J. (2005) "Virtue Ethics: What Kind of Naturalism?" in S. Gardiner (ed.) *Virtue Ethics Old and New*, New York: Cornell University Press.

Athanassoulis, N. (2005) *Morality, Moral Luck and Responsibility*, Basingstoke: Palgrave.

Aristotle *Eudemian Ethics*, H. Rackham (trans.) (1996) Cambridge, MA: Harvard University Press.

——. *Nicomachean Ethics*, J.A.K. Thomson (trans.) (1955) London: Penguin Books.

——. *Physics*, R. Waterfield (trans.) (1996) Oxford: Oxford University Press.

Bodéüs, R. (2000) *Aristotle and the Theology of the Living Immortals*, Albany: State University of New York Press.

Burnyeat, M.F. (1980) "Aristotle on Learning to Be Good," in A.O. Rorty (ed.) *Essays on Aristotle's Ethics*, Berkeley, CA: University of California Press, pp. 69–92.

Hartman, R.J. (2017) *In Defense of Moral Luck: Why Luck Often Affects Praiseworthiness and Blameworthiness*, New York: Routledge.

Irwin, T. (1990) *Aristotle's First Principles*, Oxford: Clarendon Press.

Johnson, K. (1997) "Luck and Good Fortune in the *Eudemian Ethics*," *Ancient Philosophy* 17, 85–102.

Johnson, M.R. (2005) *Aristotle on Teleology*, Oxford: Clarendon Press.

——. (2015) "Luck in Aristotle's *Physics* and *Ethics*," in D. Henry & K.M. Nielsen (eds.) *Bridging the Gap between Aristotle's Science and Ethics*, Cambridge: Cambridge University Press, pp. 254–275.

Kenny, A. (1988) "Aristotle on Moral Luck," in J. Dancy, J.M.E. Moravcsik, & C.C.W. Taylor (eds.) *Human Agency*, Stanford: Stanford University Press, pp. 105–119.

——. (1992) *Aristotle on the Perfect Life*, Oxford: Clarendon Press.

Kristjhansson, K. (2007) *Aristotle, Emotions and Education*, Aldershot: Ashgate.

Leunissen, M. (2012) "Aristotle on Natural Character and Its Implications for Moral Development," *Journal of the History of Philosophy* 50, 507–530.

——. (2013) "Becoming Good Starts with Nature," *Oxford Studies in Ancient Philosophy* 44, 99–127.
Massie, P. (2003) "The Irony of Chance," *International Philosophical Quarterly* 43, 15–28.
Nagel, T. (1993) "Moral Luck," in D. Statman (ed.) *Moral Luck*, Albany: State University of New York Press, pp. 57–72.
Nussbaum, M.C. (1986) *The Fragility of Goodness*, Cambridge: Cambridge University Press.
Sherman, N. (1989) *The Fabric of Character*, Oxford: Clarendon Press.
Shew, M.M. (2008) "The Phenomenon of Chance in Ancient Greek Thought," Dissertation submitted to the University of Oregon, https://scholarsbank.uoregon.edu/xmlui/bitstream/handle/1794/8545/Shew_Melissa_PhD_Summer2008.pdf?sequence=1
Statman, D. (1993) *Moral Luck*, Albany: State University of New York Press.
Vasiliou, I. (1996) "The Role of Good Upbringing in Aristotle's Ethics," *Philosophy and Phenomenological Research* 56, 771–797.
Williams, B. (1993a) "Moral Luck," in D. Statman (ed.) *Moral Luck*, Albany: State University of New York Press, pp. 35–56.
——. (1993b) "Postscript," in D. Statman (ed.) *Moral Luck*, Albany: State University of New York Press.
Woods, M. (1982) *Aristotle, Eudemian Ethics I, II and VIII*, Oxford: Oxford University Press.

2

ARISTOTLE ON LUCK, HAPPINESS, AND SOLON'S DICTUM

Sarah Broadie

Aristotle's thoughts on luck and happiness (*eudaimonia*) are not only seminal but subtle and rich. The question about luck and happiness was whether or to what extent human happiness depends on us, or is or could be under our control. In this ethical context[1] "what is by luck" simply indicates what, even by our best efforts, we cannot control, not merely in the sense of ensuring that it will or will not happen bur also in the sense of making it much more likely than not that it will or will not happen. What is by luck, therefore, is what is not our fault and what is not to our credit.[2]

It might be helpful to modern readers to start with a quick sketch of the role of *eudaimonia* in ancient Greek ethical theory.

Ancient thinkers disagreed on what happiness or *eudaimonia* is or consists in, but were united in holding it to be the highest or greatest good that humans might aspire to attain. (It will become clear as we go on that although "happiness" is probably the least awkward English translation, our modern use of this word can diverge significantly from the ancient understanding of *eudaimonia*.) In general it seems that the ancients did not anticipate John Stuart Mill in casting the highest good, whatever it might be, in the role of "foundation of morality" or "criterion of right and wrong" (*Utilitarianism*, the first paragraph). That is, they did not think of the highest good as that the pursuit of which makes right acts right. Nor did they think of conduciveness to the highest good as the mark or sign of rightness of acts. Instead, they tended to accept a commonsense pluralistic deontology of the morally right, in effect regarding the good, i.e. "What is good?," as a question whose solution stands in no very obvious or direct relation to the problem of determining which actions are right or wrong. (For if the rightness of an action is not assumed to depend, in general, on the goodness or expected goodness of its consequences, the question of what sorts of things would *be* good consequences is not generally germane to the question of which acts are right.)

For the ancients, as for us, the question "What is good?" hardly needs deep philosophical reflection to begin to answer. Obviously many goods and many kinds of goods are necessary or important for human beings, such as health, security, enough to eat, providing for one's dependants, peace, friends and family, freedom, a degree of honor or respect in the community, pleasure (which itself takes myriad forms), intellectual stimulation, knowledge, wisdom, virtues such as justice and moderation. Philosophical reflection raises its head when people, for whatever reason, begin to wonder about rankings among these goods, whether in terms of means versus ends or of some other principle of superiority/subordination. For example, once it is noticed that many people apparently pursue wealth, or power, just for its own sake, one can ask whether it makes sense to do so, or whether wealth and power are properly treated as means. And philosophical debate is definitely under way once people take the yet more systematizing step of claiming that this or that good is in fact the highest or greatest or best of all the many goods.

There are different ways of cashing out the claim that so and so (whatever it might be) is the highest or greatest or best of the goods. According to one ancient and axiologically austere perspective, for X to be the highest good is for X to be that from which the other so-called goods, including even non-instrumental goods such as honor, get their value. (Kant points toward this idea at the beginning of the *Groundwork of the Metaphysics of Morals*, when he speaks of the good will as the only unconditioned good, the implication being that other goods are only worth having on condition one has the good will.) If X is the highest good then unless the other goods co-exist harmoniously and supportively with X, whether in the life of individual or community, they lack positive value: they turn out to have been not worth the effort of obtaining or safeguarding, and they might even count as evils which it would be better to be without.[3] To the extent that X is absent from the life of a person or community, their life is, strictly speaking, devoid of value, however impressive their other possessions. It is not the case that, lacking X, they still have *some* good but less than the maximum.

This ancient perspective invites (although it does not logically necessitate) the identification of the highest good as *wisdom*: the wisdom to manage the other goods well: to live well from them and by means of them and to make good choices for how to get and use them. Wisdom, it is often held, includes or is even in some sense identical with standardly recognized virtues such as courage, justice, moderation, etc. In the absence of wisdom and the virtues, the presence of the other so-called goods adds no value to the agent's life and can even pave the way to disaster for her or him. If the point of seeking these objects is to have more *good* in one's life, vicious or foolish agents might just as well stop seeking—not that they are aware of their situation. If most of their existence (like most human existence in general) is a matter of going after those so-called goods as genuine *goods*, then most of their existence is a failure, whatever their own view of it and however comfortable they might be with themselves.

This is the perspective from which Aristotle says in his treatise on justice that although people pray for and pursue the non-moral goods (as we would call them)[4] their prayer and concern should instead be that these goods be goods *for them* (*Nicomachean Ethics* V, 1129b1–6). He is not saying that they should pray for the goods to be good for them in the way in which certain foods are good for us because they nourish the body. He is saying that people should pray and be concerned that they themselves become such that those commonly desired things should, in their hands, or in their orbit, be of genuine value—truly desirable—in the sense indicated above. (In this sense, nourishing food might *not* be "good for," i.e. not a genuine good as possessed by, some people; this would be the case with those who use their physical strength for evil deeds.)

There can be no doubt that for Aristotle it is moral virtue (which on his account entails practical wisdom) that we should seek and pray for as the good that "confers" value on the non-moral goods. He states this clearly near the end of the *Eudemian Ethics*:

> A good [i.e. virtuous] person is one for whom [i.e. in the hands of whom] the natural goods are good. For the goods that people fight over and that seem to be greatest—honour and wealth and bodily excellences and successes and powers—are good by nature but can be harmful because of people's dispositions. For neither a fool nor someone who is immoderate or unjust would get any benefit from operating with <those things>, any more than the sick person would from the healthy one's diet or the weak and maimed from the adornments of one who is well or who is unimpaired.
>
> *1249a26–34*[5]

So Aristotle definitely sees virtue and wisdom, or the lack of them, as what controls or determines the true value of the non-moral goods in an agent's life.

Aristotle on Luck and Happiness

At this point let us take stock. The overall topic of this chapter is luck in relation to *happiness* according to Aristotle, where "happiness" is simply a way of referring to the highest good (see *NE* I, 1095a14–20). But for some time now we have been discussing (1) the idea that what makes a certain good the highest good is its role as condition of value for the other goods. And we have seen how it is fairly natural to assume (2) that the condition of value for the other goods is nothing other than virtue and wisdom. We have also seen that Aristotle accepts this assumption. But (1) and (2) together entail that virtue and wisdom just *are* happiness. Yet virtue and wisdom need not be accompanied by much, at all, of the other goods. It is possible to be virtuous and wise—it is possible to be *actively* virtuous and wise—even if one is poor and sick. So is a person in that position *happy*? In other words, are virtue and wisdom by themselves a sufficient condition for happiness, the very highest good? This would be a paradoxical claim indeed. It implies that if the person in question became healthy and prosperous they would be no better off than before, since the highest and best good was theirs already. Is this outrageous position Aristotle's?[6]

The answer is no. We have been exploring just one ancient criterion for whether something is the highest good. But this criterion—conferring value on the non-moral goods—was not the only approach for identifying the highest good. In fact, Aristotle sets it aside in favor of a different criterion (or set of criteria), namely *completeness* and *desirability*. According to this emphasis, the true highest good, whatever it is, must not lack anything, and nothing else can be more desirable than it (see *Nicomachean Ethics* I, 1097a15–b21).[7] Aristotle does not give up (2) above, namely the tenet that the real value of the non-moral goods depends on their possessor's virtue and wisdom. But he rejects (1). For he recognizes that someone might live wisely and virtuously and yet be short of important natural goods, since a wise and virtuous life might happen also to be a life of pain or hardship or extremely limited opportunity. Aristotle, along with common sense, regards such shortages as *mattering*. Such an existence, however virtuous, is undesirable, unfulfilled, and incomplete by comparison with its better endowed counterpart. And so, along with common sense, Aristotle sees happiness as including a good measure of non-moral goods. He still regards virtue and wisdom as a non-negotiable element of happiness—even as its central element—but they are not by themselves a sufficient condition (see *NE* I, 1095b30–1096a2). The non-moral goods too have a necessary place in human *eudaimonia*.

This complex position has interesting implications for the relation of happiness to luck. Questions of whether, how, and to what extent happiness depends on luck generate questions of whether, how, and to what extent the two main components of Aristotelian happiness—moral goodness and the non-moral goods—respectively, depend on luck. If the answers come out different for the two types of component, this would help to explain why in the culture there were conflicting opinions on whether being happy is or is not a matter of being lucky: people on either side were focusing on just one of what Aristotle sees to be radically distinct aspects of happiness. The ability to explain and resolve the conflict would of course be an important point in favor of his view.

As we begin to enter the discussion of this in detail, it is worth noting that what has emerged as Aristotle's position has two rather surprising implications. In the first place, if the non-moral goods do not add genuine value to a life unless it is a life of active virtue and wisdom, then (arguably) their opposites such as poverty, ill-health, insecurity, loneliness, do not bring genuine bad or evil except to a life of active virtue and wisdom: but then it follows that a wicked or morally foolish person cannot, strictly speaking, be lucky or unlucky to lose or gain the non-moral so-called goods and evils. This is on the assumption that turns of luck, good and bad, do make one's life go genuinely better or worse. So when we wish each other good luck and hope for good luck in our own enterprises, we are, according to this austere philosophical vision, presupposing that we and those others are good people, ones for whom strokes of what are commonly held to be good luck and bad luck add genuine good or evil to life. If morally evil persons could clearly recognize the nature of their own moral condition, they would see that if they remain in this condition they have no reason to care whether so-called good luck and bad luck come their way. This is the first surprising implication.

The second one follows from the completeness criterion for happiness. "Complete" by itself is a highly indeterminate concept, and "complete life" is not much better. How complete is complete? For a life to be *eudaimōn* must it be so through and through from beginning to end of adulthood without any downturns? That might seem too demanding. On the other hand, *eudaimonia* is certainly not something that flickers in and out of a life in short and easily transient bursts. Perhaps the most rational position is that a life is *eudaimōn* only if it is *eudaimōn* for some very substantial part of itself, and, in particular, only if it remains so right up to the moment when it is rounded off by death. We feel a strong tug toward the sage Solon's dictum "Do not say 'happy' of the living, but only once the end (*telos*: the word also means 'completion') is reached" (*EE* I, 1219b6–8).[8] The force of the proverb is not merely due to a rather academic synthesis between (a) an abstract notion of *eudaimonia* as something essentially complete and (b) the verbal point that life is finished, hence in a certain sense complete, only at death. It is due to the fact that, however good a person's life might be while still ongoing, irreversible disaster can strike the part that is still to come. We have a sense that if a life takes this shape it is somehow a mistake to say retrospectively that the person *was eudaimōn* earlier. Hence we think that however good an ongoing life might be *now*, we should wait to see whether it continues good to the end before calling it *eudaimōn*. This is Aristotle's position in the *Eudemian Ethics*, and it seems not to rest on any assumption that disaster, if it does strike, was already being brewed from within the apparently good part of the person's life. If we assumed that, we could easily allow that the apparently good part was not really good, whether through a moral flaw in the agent or some hidden source of non-moral trouble on the side of the natural goods possessed. Thus we could easily allow that such a life had never in fact been *eudaimōn*. But Aristotle does not rest his Eudemian agreement with Solon on any such consideration. The point is that if misfortune wholly from the outside wrecks a life, then the good earlier part, although truly good while it lasted, does not count as *eudaimōn* or as instantiating *eudaimonia*. After all, the person could only, if at all, be said to have been *eudaimōn* during the good part because then they did not know that they would live to see their life in ruins—and there is something very uncongenial in the idea that the presence of *eudaimonia*, the pinnacle and glory of human life, should essentially depend on its supposed enjoyer's cognitive limitation. So perhaps it is right to predicate *eudaimōn* of a life or a person only if the life ends well.

But this generates the second surprising implication, namely that if we want to make the predication unconditionally, and if we want it to be more than a lucky or unlucky guess, we must withhold it until we can make it only retrospectively and in the past tense—when the life in question is over. Alternatively, we must frame it as the apodosis of a conditional: "*S* is *eudaimōn* now, but only if he or she ends well." Aristotle does not explicitly consider this second option, but it is clear that he would find it an uncomfortable straitjacket. For he and his culture have a definite place for the categorical predication where the referent is an individual.[9] In several places Aristotle discusses what seems to have been a recognized topic: the difference between the speech-acts of praise, encomium, and *eudaimonismos* or felicitation (*NE* I, 1101b10–27; *EE* II, 1219b8–16; cf. *Rhetoric* I, 1367b27–36). There is no hint that praise and encomium of individuals are only to be expressed in conditional sentences: such half-hearted statements would hardly be praise and encomium, and the same surely holds for felicitation. Moreover, categorical felicitations would typically have been addressed to the person concerned even if simultaneously to a wider audience as well. They cannot therefore typically be cast in a past tense reserved for use only when the person concerned no longer exists.

In the *Nicomachean Ethics* Aristotle distances himself from Solon's adage. He reflects on it and its implications at length, in Book I, 1100a1–1101b9. Here, too, he takes very seriously the completeness criterion of *eudaimonia*, but now he looks for ways to sidestep Solon's embargo. But first he disambiguates it. It might be taken to mean (a) that only the dead can properly be said to *be eudaimōn*, i.e. to be it now, *when* dead. But this is absurd and cannot be Solon's meaning, because, as Aristotle has emphasized, *eudaimonia* is not only essentially complete and lacking in nothing: it is also essentially *activity* (*NE* I, 1098a4–17; b30–1099a7; *EE* II, 1219a38–39; 1219b16–20)—not just possession of wisdom and virtue, but their active exercise. And the dead are not active. (They are not even potentially active.) So Solon must have meant (b) that in order to be on the safe side we must wait to predicate *eudaimōn* until the moment comes when we can only couch the accolade in the past tense. But Aristotle is not now satisfied with this restriction. He rejects it in a dense passage:

> So if we must look to the end and call someone blessed (*makarizomen*)[10] <only> *then*, not because he *is* happy (*eudaimōn*) but because he was so before, how is it not absurd to refrain from truly saying of him, *when* he is happy, what is the case—the reason <for refraining> being that one does not wish to felicitate (*eudaimonizein*) the living because of the changes <that can happen> and because one has assumed that happiness is something stable and not at all easily changed, whereas often the same persons undergo wheelings (*anakukleisthai*) of fortune?
>
> *NE I, 1100a32–b4*[11]

The argument seems to be: those who wait until *S* is dead before saying, in the past tense, that *S* was happy only speak truly because it *was independently the case* that "happy" applied to *S* during a significant part of *S*'s life continuing up to *S*'s death. (The retrospective felicitator does not, by his speech act, retrospectively make it the case that "*S* is happy" was true in the past.) Therefore when *S* was alive it would have been true to say "*S is* happy" during the relevant part of *S*'s life. Therefore if *S* is alive now and definitely exhibiting the truth-condition for "happy" (namely wise and virtuous activity with a decent measure of the natural goods), it is proper to say now that *S* is happy.[12]

This argument and its aftermath show that Aristotle assumes that the truth of applying "happy" to *S* during *S*'s lifetime does not depend on whether *S* continues happy to the grave. That is, he assumes that happiness is not such an all or nothing thing that logically I have it now only if I have it in the time leading up to when I die. In making this assumption he may be thought to beg the question against Solon's dictum. But notice that those who embrace the dictum need to do a better job of formulating their reason for doing so. They accept the dictum because of the well-known *wheelings* of fortune (*NE* I, 1100b4). These are not small variations but major ups and downs, heart-gripping to the spectator. But how are we to describe a spectacular downward wheeling—a catastrophe in which someone crashes from the heights to the depths—if we are not allowed to say that what he or she fell from was *happiness*? Obviously the person is not happy after the catastrophe, and if for an abstruse reason about the mere possibility of future disaster he or she did not count as happy before, what great change (cf. 1100a7) has taken place—from what to what?

Aristotle's rejection of Solon's adage seems to conflict with something he says at the start of the Nicomachean discussion:

> [T]here are many changes and all kinds of turns of fortune in the course of a life, and it can happen that one who enjoys the greatest prosperity is overtaken in old age by great disasters, as in the Trojan tales about Priam. Someone who encounters turns of fortune like that and who dies wretchedly (*athliōs*) is not called happy by anyone. Should we then refuse to call any other human being happy, but follow Solon's injunction to look to the end?
>
> *1100a5–9*

Certainly the notorious case of Priam, a good, noble, and extremely wealthy king who came to spectacular grief culminating in a terrible death, is a good place for launching the whole debate with Solon. If our analysis above is on the right track one might have expected Aristotle to wind up saying or implying that even Priam *was* happy up to the time of his downfall. But what he says here goes against that. He asks whether it follows from our reaction to the case of Priam that we should accept Solon's position for all *other* human beings. In short, he seems to take it for granted that Solon is right about Priam but possibly wrong about others. Is this coherent? Perhaps it is. What we react to in Priam's case is the whole well-known story with the dreadful end written in. Perhaps we cannot think of or refer to Priam without including Priam's terrible end in our conception of him. So perhaps we imagine that if we had met Priam in his days of prosperity, we, with our conception, would not have been able to say "Well, he's happy now, whatever the future holds" because we, now, are unable to think of him as heading toward an unknown future. It certainly seems in some way logically repugnant or inappropriate to think of him as happy now if built into our notion of the *him* in question is the story of the horrible end hanging over him. The Solonians take our reaction to Priam's case as a ground for withholding "happy" from living persons in general. But this is bad reasoning, since currently living persons are not legendary characters whose whole life stories we already know.

The discussion so far of Aristotle's Nicomachean reaction to Solon's adage has developed out of the very natural but vague assumption that happiness is something complete, which some participants in the debate interpreted so as to make it seem that no part of a life can count as happy unless the life ends (is completed) in happiness. However, Aristotle has an additional diagnosis of what makes this sort of view superficially attractive. His thought is that we are right to take happiness to be a stable condition (cf. 1100b2–3)—and from this we pass to the false conclusion that lost happiness could never have been real happiness.

For Aristotle the stability of *eudaimonia* is in contrast to the variability of luck. If, as some hold, *eudaimonia* were the same thing as good luck (*NE* I, 1099b7 ff.), or if changes in the former tracked changes in luck, then, since in the ordinary course of life luck in small ways goes to and fro between good and bad from day to day or hour to hour (at four o'clock I broke the heel of my shoe, but at five thirty I was just in time to get a seat on the commuter train), it would follow that the same person oscillates from moment to moment between *eudaimonia* and misery, changing like a chameleon. In fact, it is altogether wrong to think of *eudaimonia* and its opposite as tracking chance (1100b4–8). (It tells us something about the difference in meaning between *eudaimonia* and "happiness" as we often use it today that Aristotle can rely on his immediate readers to find it absurd that one might swing into and out of *eudaimonia* and its opposite as easily as one swings from annoyance at breaking the heel to relief at getting the seat.)

Aristotle now identifies the basis of the intuition that *eudaimonia* is stable. It is that *eudaimonia's* supreme determinant is activity of virtue. For the virtues, which are nothing but dispositions to be active in certain ways at any opportunity, are the most stable and longest lasting of human qualities (*NE* I, 1100b12–20; II, 1105a32–3).[13] Hence virtuous activity, the central and determining component of *eudaimonia*, is a steady, continuous, and spontaneous feature of the virtuous person's entire waking life regardless of possessions and circumstances.[14] Moreover, *eudaimonia* is flexible. Below a certain level of natural goods it is impossible, but active virtue ensures that agents adjust wisely to what they have got, making them more likely to maintain *eudaimonia*, not just virtue, under acceptable even if no longer grand conditions.

It is not easy to state precisely what it means to say that virtuous activity is the supreme determinant of *eudaimonia*. It is not by itself a sufficient condition since a certain abundance of the natural goods is needed too, and virtue or virtuous activity has, at best, limited control over that. Perhaps one can put the point by saying that *eudaimonia* is not a dance to the music of fortune, but a dance to the fortune-independent and fortune-transcending music of virtue, despite needing conditions that virtue alone cannot secure. Thus *eudaimonia* can be lost through serious misfortune, but the person who loses it never thereby becomes a wretch (*athlios*). For the true wretch stands at the other end of the moral universe from the *eudaimōn*. The wretch is one who does hateful and vile deeds, and it is not possible for anyone who really was once *eudaimōn* to fall as low as that. One may exchange good fortune for bad, but one cannot exchange virtue for moral ugliness (1100b28–1101a8).

In closing his Nicomachean discussion of luck and *eudaimonia* Aristotle seems to make a distinction between *eudaimonia* and blessedness (*makariotēs*).[15] He leads up to it by saying:

> So what is wrong with calling *eudaimōn* the person who is active in complete virtue, and who is adequately equipped with the external goods not for some random stretch of time but for a complete life?

> *1101a14–16*

From other passages beginning with the "What is wrong?" formula we know that nothing is wrong; this is a rhetorical question. We should also, I think, take it to be proposing a very abstract definition of *eudaimonia*, one that leaves open the interpretation of "complete life." However, the next sentence envisages an interlocutor who pushes for the "up until death" interpretation: "Or should we add that he also *will* live like this and will end his life on the same terms?" (16–17). Aristotle responds:

> Well, since the future is hidden to us, and if we posit that *eudaimonia* is a completion and complete in every way—given this, we shall call those living persons *blessed* (*makarioi*) who have, *and will have*, the things mentioned; but <we shall call them> blessed as human beings.[16]

> *19–21*

Here Aristotle says that *if* we want to interpret the completeness of *eudaimonia* so that it entails "up until death" (and he surely finds this understandable since it was his own view in the *Eudemian Ethics*) we should, by stipulation, substitute the term *makariotēs* to act as distinctive label of this logically far more demanding ethical profile.[17] This leaves us and him free to predicate *eudaimōn*, now, of people who are living now, and whose future is therefore unknown to us and could turn out drastically different from the good life they now enjoy.

As we have seen, the complex Nicomachean discussion partly rests on a contrast between the virtuous-activity component of *eudaimonia* and the variability of luck in respect of the natural goods. The point is not that the virtuous-activity component does not vary—of course it does in its specifics, in response to the agent's various commitments and relationships—but it does not, like the same person's luck, veer between being good and being bad. In addition, it is not a matter of luck that the virtuous agent, when active, is actively virtuous rather than actively vicious or actively mediocre. (For that to be possible it would have to be possible for the same agent to be both virtuous and vicious or mediocre, like an athlete skilled in both high jump and high dive, with its being a matter of luck which disposition gets triggered on a given occasion.) A passage of virtuous activity directed at making a difference in the world can be frustrated by bad luck; hence it depends for success on the lucky absence of bad luck. But the virtuous activity itself (the "trying"), as distinct from the intended result, wholly depends on the agent and so is invulnerable to luck. (Here we are on the brink of being able to argue that *if* being the good that confers value on the other goods—when they are present— were an adequate criterion for happiness, then identifying the value-conferrer with virtuous and wise activity means that human happiness would be wholly immune to luck.)

Nothing, however, in the foregoing discussion touches the question of luck in acquiring a virtuous disposition in the first place. At *NE* III, 1113b6–1114b25, Aristotle argues on a number of grounds that individuals are voluntary sources of their own ethical dispositions whether good or bad. One of his main concerns here is to oppose the asymmetrical view of Socrates and Plato that we are bad only involuntarily but good voluntarily. Another is to oppose the view that our ethical responses are wholly due to our genetically inherited nature, or to the play of external circumstance on this nature. In the end he comes out with the cautious assertion that "we ourselves are, in a way, co-causes of our own <moral> dispositions" (1114b2–23). The context shows that the other co-causal factor here is our genetically inherited nature.

But elsewhere Aristotle stresses the vital importance of good *upbringing* for developing a virtuous character (*NE* II, 1103b23–25; 1104b11–13; X, 1179b29–1180a4). One could put this by saying that even though an individual's virtue-building behavior must involve her or his voluntary input at every stage (good upbringing is a matter of getting the child to want or be willing to do the right things), good parents or guardians are absolutely necessary "co-causes" not only at the beginning but for a long time after that. But since it was in no way under my control whether I had good parents or guardians, wasn't it only by my past good luck that I became the virtuous person I now am, even if, as explained above, my present virtuous activity is an expression only of me and not at all dependent on present good luck? And in that case, if I also satisfy the other conditions for being *eudaimōn* isn't my *eudaimonia* today ultimately due to my luck as a baby?

Aristotle does not formulate this question (discussed today under the label of constitutive luck). A possible line of response for him would be to say that it is simply not a problem. The problem of allowing for the real possibility of human happiness while recognizing its vulnerability to luck comes from the thought that *eudaimonia* ought to be in some strong sense complete, together with the fact that a person's good luck can change. But, according to Aristotle, statements in the past tense are necessarily true or necessarily false because nothing can change their truth-value (*NE* VI, 1139b5–11). Even if it was by luck that I started life in a good home, this piece of luck is changeless now. Nothing can take it away from me, so on this score I am invulnerable. Aristotle might also consider that what we call "constitutive luck" is not luck at all. The thought would be that ascribing good or bad luck presupposes as its locus an agent with definite projects in the world to which the categories of success and failure apply, and with value-laden aspirations for a good life (The word *eutuchēs*, "fortunate," has connotations of success or hitting the mark.) But the so-called luck of starting life with good parents or good guardians is not something that happened to such an agent. It happened to what was only a potential agent, a creature that was completely indeterminate morally speaking. So it was not the case that the baby was lucky (or in the opposite circumstance unlucky), even though what happened to it was both a good thing and something over which it had absolutely no control. It would also be a mistake to think of the young products of good, bad, or "random" upbringing as lucky or unlucky results in relation to agents such as parents or supposed guardians or, in general, the older generation. This is because we and Aristotle think it the responsibility of older generations to bring up their children well.[18] This operation, then, and its products (although one can only speak very generally) is in the sphere of what human beings have some control over, so to that extent it is not in the sphere of luck.[19]

Notes

1 Aristotle also discusses luck, chance, and the fortuitous in the very different context of scientific explanation: see *Physics* II, chs. 4–8.
2 But the last paragraph of this chapter suggests a qualification of this point.
3 Cf. Plato, *Euthydemus* 280b–281d; *Meno* 87d–89a.
4 Aristotle sometimes calls them "the goods without qualification (or: in general)" (*haplōs*). This means that "goods" is a short-hand initial label picking out the things that everyone desires but leaving it open whether, for the life of a given individual or community, possession of them adds genuine, as opposed to apparent, value to that life. He also at times calls them "the natural goods," "the external goods," and "the goods of fortune."
5 Translation follows the Oxford Classical Text of Walzer and Mingay.
6 Somewhat later, this became the official position of the Stoics.
7 This is the highest good in something like the sense of Kant's *bonum consummatum*, whereas the unconditioned condition of the value of all other goods is Kant's *bonum supremum* (*Critique of Practical Reason* 2.2).
8 For the story surrounding Solon's dictum see Herodotus, *History* I, 30–33.
9 This is by contrast with a general class as in the Beatitudes "Blessed are the poor," or in Horace and Vergil "Beatus ille qui procul negotiis" ("Blessed the one who is far removed from burdens and cares" and "Felix qui potuit rerum cognoscere causas" ("Happy the one who has been able to learn the causes of things").
10 Here as in many places *makarios* and *eudaimōn* are synonyms, but at 1101a17–21 he seems to reserve *makarios* for the *eudaimōn* who continues so to the end. See below in the main text.
11 Translations from the *Nicomachean Ethics* mainly follow the Oxford Classical Text of Bywater.
12 This argument raises distinct questions of the predication's veridicality and its epistemic justification, but Aristotle does not treat them separately.
13 The vices too cannot just be laid aside or shaken off; see *NE* III, 1114a12–21 and VII, 1150b29–32 where vice is contrasted with acrasia as an incurable versus curable condition.
14 Virtues, like skills, are built up through practice of the relevant activity (*NE* II, 1103a17–b23; *EE* II, 1220a39–b5), and Aristotle might well think that even when attained they are reinforced—again like skills—through practice. Virtue is therefore strongly self-maintaining because it is not possible (as it is with skill) to possess it yet choose not to exercise it when one can.

Aristotle on Luck and Happiness

15 The interpretation is disputed and so is the text at 1101a17. I here follow Irwin in reading *epei dē* rather than *epeidē* (Irwin 1985).

16 I.e. our use of "blessed" does not imply that they are gods.

17 It is not clear whether we should assert on condition or make a conditional assertion, i.e. (1) say of someone dead that they were, when alive, *makarios*, but say it only on condition of our now knowing that their life was good up to the end, or (2) say of someone currently living well that they are now *makarios* provided they continue living well until death.

18 In fact, Aristotle takes it for granted as a piece of common sense that the task of political leaders is to make the citizens virtuous (*NE* I, 1099b30–32). The last chapter of the *NE* (X, 1079a33–1081b23) is a discussion of how best to effect moral education in society.

19 For completeness we should mention *Eudemian Ethics* VIII, ch. 2 (=VII, ch. 14) where Aristotle considers the question of what one might call "natural luck." Some agents seem to be lucky by nature in that they regularly succeed in achieving their ends despite being foolish and thoughtless. But is it right to call this "luck" or is it really something else? Aristotle's discussion is difficult, and seems to go to and fro on the question. See Kenny (1992: ch. 6) for some helpful elucidation. The topic of *EE* VIII.2 belongs to ethics considered as the general study of living well, since the naturally lucky are successful about the external goods, and having these is certainly part of living well. But it is clear that such agents are not candidates for *eudaimonia* since they lack wisdom and virtue.

References

Irwin, T.H. (1985) "Permanent Happiness: Aristotle and Solon," *Oxford Studies in Ancient Philosophy* 3, 89–124.
Kenny, A. (1992) *Aristotle on the Perfect Life*, Oxford: Oxford University Press.

3

THE STOICS ON LUCK

René Brouwer

Introduction

In this chapter, I discuss "luck" (*tuchē* in Greek, *fortuna* in Latin) as a central topic in Stoicism, from its early beginnings in the 3rd century BCE with Zeno of Citium (*c.* 334–*c.* 262), the founder of the school, to Marcus Aurelius (121–180), the last major self-proclaimed Stoic in antiquity. As we will see, the first Stoics took over the notion of luck from their Cynic teachers and developed it further in debate with Epicurus (341–271) and his followers as their main intellectual adversaries; later generations of Stoics remained faithful to the doctrine as it had been formulated by the first generations of Stoics.

The Stoic understanding of luck is best discussed from three points of view. The first point of view is ontological: does luck exist, and if so, what does luck refer to? The second point of view is epistemological: if luck exists, can human beings know it, and if so, how? The third point is ethical: how ought human beings behave toward luck? To put it upfront: for the Stoics luck does exist, not as blind chance, but rather as one of the ways of referring to the one, divine rational principle that pervades matter and thus forms the world. Due to their rational capacities human beings are, in theory, capable of understanding and aligning themselves with this principle. However, this understanding or aligning is seldom achieved, and so to imperfect rational beings this one rational principle appears as luck, either—from an epistemological point of view—in the sense of blind chance, or—from an ethical point of view—as good and bad luck.

The setup of the chapter is chronological. I will first discuss the early Stoic evidence on luck, starting with the Cynics' unconventional understanding of luck, which Zeno and his followers developed further. In the next section, I will shift to Rome, where in the 2nd and 1st centuries BCE Stoics such as Panaetius of Rhodes (*c.* 185–*c.* 110) and Posidonius of Apamea (*c.* 135–*c.* 50) introduced Stoicism to the Romans. These Stoics thus prepared the ground for the imperial Stoics, especially Seneca (1st century CE), Epictetus (*c.* 55–*c.* 135), and Marcus Aurelius (2nd century CE). Their writings have, in large part, survived: as we will see, Seneca is a particularly rich source for the Stoic understanding of luck.

The Early Stoics on Luck

The first Stoics were heavily influenced by the Cynics. Zeno of Citium, the founder of Stoicism, started his career as a pupil of Crates of Thebes (*c.* 365–*c.* 285), a follower of Diogenes of Sinope (*c.*

412/404–323), who was the first to call himself a Cynic, or "doggish" philosopher. According to the biographer and doxographer Diogenes Laertius (presumably 3rd century CE), whose *Lives of Eminent Philosophers* is one of our most important sources on Stoicism, Zeno's *Politeia*, the work that made Zeno famous, was written "on the dog's tail". This is Diogenes Laertius 7.2–3:

> Zeno went up into Athens and sat down in a bookseller's shop, being then a man of thirty. As he heard the bookseller reading from Book 2 of Xenophon's *Memorabilia*, he was so pleased that he inquired where men like Socrates were to be found. Crates [the Cynic] happened to pass by, so the bookseller pointed to him and said: "Follow that man." [...] For a certain time, then, he was instructed by Crates, and when at this time he had written his *Republic* some said in jest that he had written it on the dog's tail.

For the Cynics, the anticonventionalists par excellence, who propagated the simple life instead, that could be lived anywhere, or—as Diogenes coined it—as a "citizen of the world" (Greek: *kosmopolitēs*, see Diogenes Laertius 6.63, fr. 335 G.), luck was a major theme.[1] The Cynics questioned the conventional use of luck, which in the Hellenistic period, especially in the form of the worship of *Luck* as a god, had become a noteworthy phenomenon. The travel author Pausanias described a temple devoted to Luck in Thebes; from there the cult might well have spread rapidly over the Hellenistic world (Schneider 1967–1969: 830; Gasparro 1997: 81; Scheer 2005: 1093).

For Diogenes the Cynic, luck should not be worshipped, or simply passively accepted: instead, he regarded luck as a force that one needed to confront and overcome (Kindstrand 1976: 116, 207; Goulet-Cazé 2017: 429). In his excellent book on Diogenes, Étienne Helmer (2017: 100–101) characterizes Diogenes' "dealing with luck" ("*faire fortune*") as "to adapt oneself towards luck in taking as much as possible the initiative to act" ("*se réappropier la fortune en s'emparant autant possible de l'initiative de l'agir*"). In the ancient evidence, the point is usually conveyed in the forms of anecdotes, such as the one that survived in Stobaeus' 5th-century *Anthology*, at 4.44.71, p. 976.3–6 (fr. 351 G.): "When he fell prey again to some mishap, he would say, 'Thank you, Luck, for having confronted me in such a manly fashion!'; and on such occasions he would walk away humming a tune." In the words of Bion of Borysthenes (*c.* 325–*c.* 250), who—if not an outright Cynic himself—is at any rate to be associated with the Cynics (Kindstrand 1976: 58–67), the engagement consists in finding out the role in the world that luck has "assigned" to each of us, as the Cynic Teles of Megara (middle of the 3rd century BCE), *On Self-Sufficiency*, fr. 3 Hense 1909, via Stobaeus 3.1.98, pp. 37.8–38.6 (fr. 16A Kindstrand), reports:

> Just as a good actor must play to the best of his ability whatever role is assigned to him by the dramatist, so also must the good man play whatever role he is assigned by luck. "For like a poetess", says Bion, "she assigns now a leading role, now a secondary one, and sometimes the role of a king, and sometimes that of a beggar. So if you have a secondary role, do not aspire to a leading one; for otherwise you will be acting out of tune."
>
> *tr. Hard, modified*

If we have engaged ourselves, if we have found our role, if we know what is up to us, luck can no longer hit us. In an *Oration* ascribed to Dio of Prusa (*c.* 40–*c.* 115), at 64.18 (fr. 352 G.), this is how Diogenes is said to have become invulnerable against the strokes of luck, such that luck cannot affect him anymore. In English the wordplay with "luck" and "to hit," in Greek *tuchē* and *tuchein*, respectively, is unfortunately lost: "Diogenes the Cynic, in rustic manner (*agroikōs*) and downright uncivilised, used to declare loudly to Luck, claiming that, though luck shot many arrows with him as target, it could not hit him." Incidentally, in this anecdote, luck is connected with cosmopolitanism: the phrase "in rustic manner and downright uncivilised" may be taken as an allusion to Diogenes as a citizen of the world, distancing himself from conventional ways of living together but rather finding himself at home in the wider world. In Stobaeus, at 2.8.21, p. 157.7–9 (fr. 148 G.), a similar anecdote survived, again with the wordplay on *tuchē* and *tuchein*, to which a quote from Homer's *Iliad* 8.229 is added: "Diogenes said that he thought he could see luck storming out to attack him and exclaiming, using Homer's words: 'But that mad dog alone I cannot hit!'" (tr. Hard).

Just as the Stoics would do later, Diogenes stressed that his way of thinking allowed him to be prepared for luck, such that it could not attack him. See Diogenes Laertius 6.63 (fr. 360 G.): "When someone asked him what he had gained from philosophy, he said, 'This, if nothing else, that I am prepared for every form of luck'" (tr. Hard). Yet again, here a connection with cosmopolitanism is suggested: this anecdote on luck is immediately followed by the passage in which Diogenes declares himself to be a citizen of the world, already referred to above. In short: for the Cynics, luck is a force, with which active engagement should be sought, such that in the end it cannot affect us anymore. The outcome of this struggle would surely be living the simple life, being at home anywhere in the world.

Let us now move on to the Stoics.[2] According to a popular anecdote—it survived in several versions in the extant sources, conveniently collected in *SVF* 1.277, including Plutarch (*c.* 46–*c.* 120), *On Tranquility* 467d and *On Exile* 603d, Diogenes Laertius 7.5, and Seneca, *On Tranquility* 14.3 (for the Seneca passage see further below)—the philosophical career of Zeno of Citium, the founder of Stoicism, would even have started with luck. Here is the version in Plutarch (*c.* 46–120), *How to Profit by One's Enemies* 87a (*SVF* 1.277): "Zeno after having heard that his ship had been wrecked declared: 'You did well, Luck, that you have driven us to be dressed as a philosopher.'" Just as with regard to the Cynics, luck is here presented as a force that one needs to confront. Originally a merchant from Cyprus, who is confronted with a disaster, Zeno takes up the challenge that luck has brought to him: he decides to stay in Athens, becomes a pupil of the Cynic Crates of Thebes, and makes a career as a philosopher, founding an influential school of thought.

Fortunately, for a better understanding of the Stoic notion of luck, we do not have to rely on anecdotes alone. Despite the loss of almost all the writings of the early Stoics, there is just enough evidence about their doctrines to enable us to reconstruct their thoughts about luck. Just as for the Cynics, for the first Stoics luck was an important topic. Sphaerus of Borysthenes, one of Zeno's pupils, even wrote a whole book on it. Its title, *On Luck*, can be found in the catalogue of his books, which survived in Diogenes Laertius, at 7.177 (*SVF* 1.620).

In the accounts about the Stoic doctrine, we find that luck is used when the cause is unclear to a human being (or human understanding as other sources have it). These accounts include Simplicius (6th century CE), *Commentary on the Physics* 333.1–5, 7–10 (*SVF* 2.965), Alexander of Aphrodisias (fl. 200 CE), *Mantissa* 179.6–10, 14–18 (*SVF* 2.967), and his *On Fate* 174.1–5 (*SVF* 2.970). This is how the doctrine survived in the overview of the opinions of various philosophical schools written by Aëtius (around 150 CE; see further Mansfeld and Runia 1997: 121–125 and 2010: 173–180), who in his chapter on luck, after having set out the opinions of Plato, Aristotle, and Epicurus, offers us the Stoic doctrine (which he incidentally also attributes to the earlier "Presocratic" thinker Anaxagoras, *c.* 510–*c.* 428), at 1.29.7 Mau (*SVF* 2.966): "[Luck is] the cause unclear to human understanding." In a passage in his *Commentary on Aristotle's Physics*, which survived in the Arabic tradition only (fr. 1 Giannakis 1995–1996: 162, 171), Alexander of Aphrodisias adds the divine nature of the cause: "Alexander says: 'The Stoics say that luck is the divine cause which the mind does not grasp.'"

Before moving on to Aëtius' phrase "unclear to human understanding" or Alexander's "the mind does not grasp," let us first have a look at the Stoic theory of causation. The Stoics claimed that everything has a cause, with all causes and all things interconnected. For the interconnectedness of causes, they used the term "fate" (*heimarmene*; see further Sauvé-Meyer 2009), and for the interconnectedness of things, they used the term "sympathy" (*sumpatheia*; see further Brouwer 2015). They maintained that this interconnectedness would go back to a single immanent active principle. The Stoics gave this active principle different names, each name bringing out a particular aspect of the active principle (see Diogenes Laertius 7.135, *SVF* 1.102, LS 46B). In religious terms, they referred to it as God or Zeus (see Diogenes Laertius 7.88 (*SVF* 3.4, LS 63A), Stobaeus 1.31.12–14 (*SVF* 2.1062), Cornutus (1st century CE), *Greek theology*, ch. 11). In physical terms, they called it a special kind of fire (Stobaeus 1.213.15–21; *SVF* 1.120, LS 46D). In ethical terms, they also called it "law" (*nomos*), bringing out the power of the active principle as "king," "ruler," and "guide," as Chrysippus of Soli (*c.* 280–*c.* 206), the third head of the school, formulated it at the beginning of his *On Law*, in a passage which is quoted by the 3rd century CE lawyer Marcian, *Teaching Manual* bk. 1, and which survived in emperor Justinian's *Digest* 1.3.2, *SVF* 3.314, LS 67R (see also Cicero, *On the Republic* 3.33 (*SVF* 3.325, LS 67B), and further Brouwer 2011). They above all identified the principle with "reason" (*logos*), and the terms that connote with reason: with "intelligence" (*nous*), as the divine faculty of reason, and with "providence" (*pronoia*), as the plan according to which the active principle pervades everything. According to the Stoics, everything that happens is thus determined by divine reason (Aëtius 1.7.33, *SVF* 2.1027, LS 46A). As Plutarch, *On the Contradictions of the Stoics* 1045c (*SVF* 2.973), has it, Chrysippus thus claimed that the outcome of throwing a dice is also determined.

Already in antiquity the Stoics were criticised for their doctrine of reason as the active principle passive pervading matter and thus determining everything—above all by Epicurus and his followers.[3] According to Epicurus, *Letter to Menoeceus*, preserved in Diogenes Laertius at 9.133 (LS 20A), the Stoic doctrine of fate would involve an "inexorable necessity." Epicurus allowed for luck or blind chance as an independent force in this world, which in the soul he described as an "adventitious movement" (Plutarch, *On the Contradictions of the Stoics* 1045b (*SVF* 2.973); see further Long 1977). The Stoics, in turn, reciprocated and attacked Epicurus' account of luck as blind chance. According to Plutarch, *On the Contradictions of the Stoics*, at 1045c (*SVF* 2.973), Chrysippus criticized Epicurus for such an uncaused cause, because as he put it, "the uncaused cannot exist."

So much for the causes. Let us move on to the phrase "unclear to human understanding." In the Stoic account of the active principle of divine reason, human beings have a special position. As parts of the active principle, they successively occupy at least two steps on the scale of nature. At birth, just like any other animal, they develop a soul, understood as the principle of self-movement. In youth, however, unlike other animals, they move up a step, developing the faculty of reason, which allows them to get to an understanding of the course of the active principle or the order of things. However, whereas the faculty of reason develops naturally, they will have to bring this faculty of reason to perfection themselves. This faculty allows human beings to give an explanation of causes. A definition of explanation ascribed to Chrysippus can be found in Stobaeus, at 1.139.4–5 (*SVF* 2.336, LS 55A; cf. Mansfeld 2001): "An 'explanation' (*aitia*) is an 'account' (*logos*) of a 'cause' (*aition*), or an account on the cause as cause."

Now luck can be brought into play. It is the inferior person who, by virtue of his or her not yet perfect rationality comes to an incorrect understanding of the rational order of things, and who may either think that he or she is vulnerable to luck, or—already better—that he or she has not yet correct knowledge about the course of the active principle (Hankinson 1988: 153–157; Bobzien 1998: 175). From the point of view of the inferior person, luck can thus be used as a colloquial expression for that part of the divine rational force which guides all, but which is not yet properly understood.

For the inferior person, luck is thus a matter of subjective perception, and this is how other bits of evidence can now be understood. Alexander of Aphrodisias, *Mantissa* 179.7–8 (*SVF* 2.976) formulates the Stoic doctrine as follows: "Luck consists in people being in a certain state in relation to the causes." By "certain state" the state of ignorance must be meant. In his *Commentary on Virgil's Aeneid*, l. 8.334: "Almighty luck and unavoidable fate" (*SVF* 2.972), Servius states that this doctrine is Stoic, to which he adds that according to the Stoics, birth and death are assigned to us by fate, everything in between to luck. This must mean that for (imperfect) human beings only birth and death appear as certain, all other things in between as uncertain.

By contrast, the sage will be able to understand particular causes within the scheme of the whole. According to the Stoics, from the point of view of the perfectly rational person, luck in its conventional sense is thus but an illusion: any event ordinarily ascribed to luck can in the end be explained in terms of reason.

Thus far we have discussed luck from two points of view: from the ontological point of view luck refers to the divine force of nature, and from the epistemological point of view to the lack of understanding that goes with this usage. We can now move on the third, ethical point of view. According to the Stoics, happiness or the good life consists in living in accordance, that is having one's own nature in accordance with all-nature, having one's own disposition in accordance with the active principle. The Stoics claimed that, in principle, human beings should be able develop their rational faculty such that it becomes perfect. Out of the virtuous disposition of the perfectly rational being, correct accounts can be given all the time. For the good life only this perfect disposition matters: the only matter that is truly good is a virtuous disposition; that is, having one's rational disposition perfected, such that one lives in accordance with the course of the active principle of the world.

In their account of the good life, luck is discussed in another way, too. Luck is also used in the sense of personal lot, which can in Greek, next to *tuchē* also be rendered as *daimōn* (Gasparro 1997; Lawrence 2012: 502). In terms of personal luck: the good life or happiness in bringing one's personal *daimōn* in accordance with the divine cause that pervades the whole nature. The etymological connection between *eudaimonia* as the Greek term for the good life or happiness on the one hand, and *daimōn* on the other, will certainly not have escaped the Stoics. Again, the task that faces each human being is immense and not easy to bring to completion: each human being will have to find out who he or she is. In this search for self-knowledge, human beings may be helped by luck as an inner voice, which Socrates referred to as his *daimonion*, that is "little *daimōn*," which even in the imperfect condition sometimes presents itself as the voice that withholds. According to Plato (428/427–348/347), *Apology* 31d, Socrates at his trial formulated it thus: "It is a voice, and whenever it speaks it turns me away from something I am about to do, but it never encourages me to do anything."

With regard to good and bad luck, the implications of living in accordance with divine reason are that perfect human beings are both invulnerable against luck as well as in no need of it. "Invulnerable against luck" can already be traced back to Persaeus (*c.* 307–*c.* 246), Zeno's favourite pupil (Herzog-Hauser 1948: 1670; Busch 1961: 133). It survived in Themistius (317–390), *Oration* 32, at 358b Harduin (*SVF* 1.449): "The sage is not vulnerable against luck, not enslaved, not mixed, not suffering.""The sage is in no need of luck" survived in Proclus (412–485), *Commentary on the Timaeus* 1.197.28–9 Diehl (*SVF* 3.52): "The Stoics maintain that the sage is in no need of luck." The virtuous disposition is all that counts for happiness or the good life: it makes the sage invulnerable against bad luck, and in no need of good luck either. What for imperfect human beings appears as luck that gives or takes away, is thus for perfect human beings a matter that has been overcome.

However, achieving this virtuous disposition is extremely difficult: human beings let themselves "be led astray" (*diastrephestai*, as in Diogenes Laertius 7.89, *SVF* 3.228). With the exception perhaps of Socrates toward the end of his life (Brouwer 2014: 163–166), no human being has ever been able to achieve it. The early Stoics certainly included themselves among the imperfect or inferior persons (Brouwer 2014: 92–135). Almost all human beings, then, are vulnerable to the strokes of bad luck (or in a variation upon Persaeus' words "enslaved, mixed, and suffering") and might well think that they are in need of good luck.

The anecdote on Zeno's career change with which we started can now be easily understood in relation to the three points of view set out above. First, luck is presented ontologically as the divine force that pervades the universe: "Luck drives me." Second, from the epistemological point of view, the anecdote makes clear that its course is not known to human beings, who have not yet brought their rational nature to perfection, like Zeno himself: he is surely taken by surprise by this stroke of luck. From the ethical point of view, Zeno engages himself with luck: he abandons his career as a merchant and becomes a thinker of considerable importance.

The Roman Stoics on Luck

With regard to the "Roman" Stoics, a distinction can be made between those who experienced the rise of Rome to a world power on the one hand, and those who experienced it as an empire, under the auspices of a single ruler, on the other hand. Among the former, "Republican" Stoics, such as Panaetius and Posidonius need to be discussed, who contributed to the development of Rome as an intellectual center of the world, making it possible for others, like Polybius, to reflect on Rome's place in the world. Among the latter, "Imperial" Stoics, Seneca, Epictetus, and finally Marcus Aurelius will be discussed.

Just as for the early Greek Stoics, for the first Republican Stoics, who started working in Rome, our extant sources are yet again limited; the evidence on luck is therefore limited, too. For the Imperial Stoics, however, the situation is rather different: here complete treatises have been handed down to us.

Among the Republican Stoics, Panaetius was not the first Stoic to make his appearance in Rome. Other Stoics had prepared the grounds. In 168, Crates of Mallus (fl. 2nd century) came to Rome (since he broke his leg, he had to stay on for longer than he planned) and in 155, Diogenes of Babylon (c. 230–c. 150) had visited Rome as part of an Athenian embassy. However, Panaetius of Rhodes was surely the most important one, playing a significant role in the intellectual life in Rome in the second half of the 2nd century. In the learned literature, the phrase "Scipionic circle" is often used, where "Scipionic" refers to the elder statesman Publius Cornelius Scipio Aemilianus Africanus (born 185/4) and "circle" to the phrase "in our flock" (*in nostro grege*) in Cicero (106–43), *On Friendship*, at 69. This "circle" (if it was indeed that organized; cf. Ferrary 2014: 589–615, 734, with references) around Scipio and Panaetius also included the historian Polybius and the playwright Terence (first half 2nd century BCE).

Of the few bits and pieces of information that survived about, let alone from Panaetius, we know that he discussed the possibility of foretelling the course of the active principle in the world.[4] According to Cicero, *On Divination* 1.6 (fr. 137 Alesse), Panaetius was sceptical about the possibility of a science of divination, or of human beings being able to predict the course of divine reason. This is clearly in line with his more moderate interpretation of Stoicism, with less emphasis on the rigorous demands for perfection characteristic for the early Greek Stoics (see Cicero, *On Duties* 3.12 (fr. 75 Alesse), cf. *On Friendship* 18). Whereas Panaetius did discuss the active principle, unfortunately no evidence has survived that he did so in terms of luck, too.

With regard to Panaetius' pupil Posidonius, however, such evidence did survive.[5] In his historical and geographical writings, Posidonius used luck in the conventional sense of good luck. In a passage from his *History* (preserved by Athenaeus (fl. 200 CE), *Dinner-Table Talks*, at 212c, fr. 253.38 EK), Posidonius uses the expression "paradox of luck" in order to describe the unlikely fate of Athenion, who briefly became a tyrant in Athens in 88 BCE, the year Athens would be destroyed by Sulla. In his description of rich mines in Southern Spain, "every hill was material of coin" (preserved by the geographer Strabo (64/63 BCE–24 CE) 3.2.9, fr. 239.6 EK), Posidonius uses "bountiful luck." In his philosophical writings, however, Posidonius gives us the by now familiar Stoic account that we should not rely on good or bad luck but rather on reason. A quote has been preserved in Seneca, *Letter* 113.28 (fr. 105 EK):

> At this point, I want to tell you the view of our Stoic philosopher Posidonius: "You should never think that the weapons of luck will make you safe: fight with your own [i.e. reason]! Luck does not arm us against luck itself. Hence men who are equipped to resist the enemy are unarmed to resist luck."
>
> *tr. Long and Graver*

Earlier in his *Letters*, Seneca had already made a similar point, invoking Posidonius together with Chrysippus, at 104.21–22 (test. 81 EK):

Live with Chrysippus, Posidonius. […] There is only one haven for this stormy and turbulent life of ours: to rise above future events, to stand firm, ready to receive the blows of luck head-on, out in the open and unflinching.

tr. Long and Graver

More on luck is extant from the historian Polybius (*c.* 200–*c.* 120), who belonged to the "Scipionic circle" and thus must have been acquainted with Panaetius.[6] In his partly preserved *Histories*, luck plays an important role. As a historian, from hindsight, Polybius sets out to explain how it was possible that Rome had become a world power in some 50 years, from utter defeat by Hannibal at Cannae in 216 to the victory over the Macedonians at Pydna in 168, to be followed by the destruction of Carthage in 146. Most likely influenced by Stoic doctrine (Brouwer 2011; Krewet 2017), he does so with the help of luck as a universal power (Pédech 1964: 337–343). At any rate, he discusses luck under the ontological as well as the epistemological perspective that we already encountered when discussing the early Stoic understanding of luck. In the introductory pages of the *Histories*, Polybius explains that the Romans acted in accordance with luck as an overall active principle, even though its course might not have been clear to the Romans themselves. As a historian, Polybius considers it his task to reveal the operations of the Romans from this overall point of view, as he makes clear at 1.4.2: "The history should bring before its readers under one synoptical view the operations by which luck has accomplished its general purpose. Indeed it was this chiefly that invited and encouraged me to undertake my task." In the subsequent 40 books, Polybius then unravels the historical events from 264 to 146, from the beginning to the end of the war with Carthage; the synoptical point of view remains that of luck.

Among the Stoic authors in Imperial times, especially for Seneca, but also for Epictetus and Marcus Aurelius, luck is clearly a theme that they were interested in. In Seneca's—for the most part preserved—writings, luck occurs frequently.[7] In his philosophical works, it is mentioned 409 times (Hachmann 2000: 295). The frequency is already an indication that luck, especially the engagement with luck in the human condition of imperfection, is a central theme in Seneca's work. Like the early Stoics, Seneca discusses luck from three points of view: ontological, epistemological, and ethical.[8]

As for the question about the ontological status of luck, whether another name for the active principle or blind chance, Seneca formulates it in *Letter* 117.19 in the following manner:

Let us investigate the nature of the gods, or the nutriment of the stars and their various orbits, or whether human affairs develop in correspondence to their motions, or whether they are the origin of movement for terrestrial bodies and minds, or whether even so-called chance occurrences are bound by a fixed law and nothing ever happens spontaneously or outside the world's order.

tr. Graver and Long

The question is given a clear answer in e.g. *On Providence* 1.3: nothing happens without reason. According to Seneca, luck is in good early Stoic fashion one of the many names given to the active, divine principle, as he makes clear in *On Benefits* 5.8.3: "So now call him 'Nature', 'Fate' or 'Fortune': all are names of the same god using his power in different ways." Like Chrysippus, he argues against common people or "those who claim to possess wisdom," as he states in the Introduction to his *Natural Questions*, at 14–15, using a phrase that refers to Epicurus and his followers (Brouwer 2014: 169–170), who—as we have seen—maintain that the world order is accidental, and left to blind chance.

From the epistemological point of view, luck is used also by Seneca in order to refer to the active principle from the point of view of human beings that do not yet understand the course of the principle. For those who have been able to perfect their reason: they both understand as well as live according to it. See *On Providence* 5.4: "In the republic of this world: good men toil, they expend and are expended—and this willingly. They are not dragged away by luck: they follow it and match its pace."

Here we have already moved toward the ethical point of view of the good life, that is to say living according to luck as another name for divine reason. How, then, according to Seneca, should those who do not yet live the happy life, deal with apparent good, but above all bad luck? In the *Natural Questions* Praef. 1.15, Seneca discusses both. Since the rational, virtuous disposition is the only good, neither is good luck a good, nor bad luck a bad: "Raise your spirit above chance events; remembering your human status, so that if you are lucky, you know that will not last long, and if you are unlucky, you know you are not so if you do not think so" (tr. Hine) *On the Constancy of the Sage* 19.3–4 is an illuminating passage on how to deal with bad luck, such as injuries and insults. The sage has risen above such bad luck, above injuries and insults: he or she has won the battle and has become invulnerable to such things. For those who are striving for wisdom, they should simply expect that they must live with these things: "Everything that happens will be lighter, if they know to expect it." For the non-sage, luck is thus a force to be battled with, in the manner of Diogenes the Cynic or of "our" Zeno in the anecdote that also Seneca was happy to invoke in *On Tranquility* 14.3: "When a shipwreck was reported and he heard that all his possessions had sunk, our founder Zeno said: 'Luck is ordering me to strive for wisdom in a less encumbered manner.'"

The second Imperial Stoic that deserves mention here is Epictetus (*c.* 55–135). He was born as a slave, but nevertheless became an important teacher, first in Rome, then in exile in Nikopolis. His *Manual* has been preserved, his *Lectures* were written down by his pupil Arrian.[9] Even though luck does not figure as prominently in Epictetus' thought as it does in Seneca's work, Epictetus clearly follows Stoic orthodoxy here. The three aspects on luck come out nicely in a passage from Arrian's notes, which have been preserved by Stobaeus, at 4.44.65, pp. 974.14–975.2 (fr. 2.2 Schenkl): "He who is dissatisfied with what he has and what has been given to him by luck is a layman in the art of living" (tr. Hard). Luck is here presented as a power, whose course has to be understood and dealt with in order to be able to live the good life.

The last of the three Imperial Stoics is Marcus Aurelius, Roman emperor from 161–180.[10] Whereas his societal position could not have been more different from that of Epictetus, just like Epictetus, Marcus Aurelius remained faithful to the early Stoic doctrine, and also discussed luck from the by now familiar points of view.

In his *Notebooks* (or *Meditations*), he describes luck from the ontological point of view, like this, at 2.3.1: "The works of luck are not independent of nature or the spinning and weaving together of the threads governed by providence." From the epistemological point of view, the course of the active principle of divine reason remains unclear, as he states at 2.17.1: "In man's life his time is a mere instant, [...] his luck unpredictable, his fame unclear." In our actions, we should thus regard whatever happens to us as part of the workings of luck, at 3.11.4: "So in each case we must say: 'This has come from god; this is due to a conjuncture of fate, the mesh of destiny, or some similar coincidence of luck.'" As not yet perfect human beings, we thus best accept instances of good luck, such as the things that he got from his adoptive father, Emperor Antoninus Pius (see 1.16.16), and be prepared for bad luck, at 12.27.1: "Continually review in your mind those whom a particular anger took to extremes, those who reached the greatest heights of glory or disaster or enmity or any sort of luck."

Conclusion

Marcus Aurelius turned out to be the last self-proclaimed Stoic in antiquity. Since the beginning of the school, almost 500 years had passed. As we have seen, the different Stoics that we encountered in this long period were remarkably consistent in dealing with the doctrine of luck.

From the ontological point of view, the Stoics, from Zeno of Citium to Marcus Aurelius, dealt with luck as one of the names for divine reason pervading the world. From both the epistemological and ethical points of view, they used this particular name in order to refer to the fact that, whereas human beings by virtue of their rational faculty are acquainted with this active principle, they only very rarely are able to develop this rational faculty to perfection, such that they can not only understand its course but also live in accordance with it. Even so, whereas human beings should still strive to bring their own individual nature in accordance with the nature of the whole by becoming perfectly rational, and thus bring themselves in the virtuous condition of the sage, they otherwise should deal with or be prepared for the apparent bad or good luck that the active principle has in store, treating both types of luck with indifference.

The doctrine of luck is thus surely one of the central doctrines in Stoic thought, which—despite the disappearance of the school itself—has continued to fascinate, up until today.[11]

Notes

1 The evidence on Cynicism is collected in Giannantoni (1990; hereafter: G.). Hard (2012) is a useful translation of a selection of the evidence. For recent introductions on the Cynics see Desmond (2008), Goulet-Cazé (2017), and Helmer (2017).
2 The standard collection of the evidence is still von Arnim (1903–1905; hereafter: *SVF*). Selections thereof with translation are Long and Sedley (1987; with extensive commentary; hereafter: LS) and Inwood and Gerson (2008). Recent introductions to Stoicism include Inwood (2003), Sellars (2006), and Forschner (2018).
3 The standard collection of the evidence is Usener (1887). Long and Sedley (1987) offer a selection with translation and commentary. For an introduction to Epicureanism see Warren (2009).
4 Alesse (1997) is now the standard collection of fragments from and about Panaetius.
5 Edelstein and Kidd (1972–1999; hereafter EK) is the standard collection (with translation and extensive commentary) of what is left from and about Posidonius.
6 For the Greek text see Büttner-Wobst and Dindorf (1889–1905). For a recent translation see Waterfield (2010). About Polybius see Walbank (1972) and McGing (2010).
7 For the text of the *Letters* see Reynolds (1965), for the dialogues see Reynolds (1977), for the *Natural Questions* see Hine (1996). For recent translations see Asmis, Bartsch, and Nussbaum (2010–2017). About Seneca see Inwood (2005) and Wildberger (2006).
8 For the background of the Roman cult of *Fortuna*, comparable to the Hellenistic cult of *Tuchē*, see Asmis (2009: 117–118). Incidentally, she rather presents the engagement with luck as an innovation by Seneca.
9 For the Greek text see Schenkl (1916), for a recent translation see Hard (2014), about Epictetus see Bonhöffer (1890) and Long (2002).
10 For the Greek text of his writings see Dalfen (1987), for a recent translation see Hard (2011), for a recent introduction see van Ackeren (2012).
11 For the Stoic tradition see Colish (1990), Sellars (2016). On the depiction of Zeno and the shipwreck in Siena see Mönig (2008).

References

Ackeren, M. van (ed.) (2012) *A Companion to Marcus Aurelius*, Malden: Blackwell.
Alesse, F. (1997) *Panezio di Rodi. Testimonianze. Edizione, traduzione e commento*, Naples: Bibliopolis.
Arnim, H. von (1903–1905) *Stoicorum veterum fragmenta 1–3*, Leipzig: Teubner.
Asmis, E. (2009) "Seneca on Fortune and the Kingdom of God," in S. Bartsch & D. Wray (eds.) *Seneca and the Self*, Cambridge: Cambridge University Press, pp. 115–138.
Asmis, E., Bartsch, S., & Nussbaum, M. (eds.) (2010–2017) *The Complete Works of Lucius Annaeus Seneca*, Chicago: Chicago University Press.
Bobzien, S. (1998) *Determinism and Freedom in Stoic Philosophy*, Oxford: Oxford University Press.
Bonhöffer, E. (1890) *Epictet und die Stoa. Untersuchungen zur stoischen Philosophie*, Stuttgart: Enke.
Brouwer, R. (2011) "On Law and Equity: the Stoic View," *Zeitschrift der Savigny-Stiftung für Rechtsgeschichte. Romanistische Abteilung* 128, 17–38.
——. (2014) *The Stoic Sage: The Early Stoics on Wisdom, Sagehood and Socrates*, Cambridge: Cambridge University Press.

———. (2015) "Stoic Sympathy," in E. Schliesser (ed.) *Sympathy*, New York: Oxford University Press, pp. 15–35.

Busch, G. (1961) "Fortunae resistere in der Moral des Philosophen Seneca," *Antike und Abendland* 10, 131–154.

Büttner-Wobst, T., & Dindorf, L. (eds.) (1889–1905) *Polybios: Historiae*, Leipzig: Teubner.

Colish, M.L. (1990) *The Stoic Tradition from Antiquity to the Early Middle Ages* [1985], 2nd edn, Leiden: Brill.

Dalfen, J. (ed.) (1987) *Marci Aurelii Antonini ad se ipsum libri xii*, 2nd edn, Leipzig: Teubner.

Desmond, W. (2008) *Cynics*, Stocksfield: Acumen.

Edelstein, L., & Kidd, I. (1972–1999) *Posidonius: The Fragments*, Cambridge: Cambridge University Press.

EK = Edelstein, Kidd 1972–1999.

Ferrary, J.-L. (2014) *Philhellénisme et impérialisme* [1988], 2nd edn, Rome: École française de Rome.

Forschner, M. (2018) *Die Philosophie der Stoa*, Darmstadt: Wissenschaftliche Buchgesellschaft.

G. = Giannantoni 1990.

Gasparro, G.S. (1997) "Daimôn und tuchê in the Hellenistic Religious Experience," in P. Bilde et al. (eds.) *Conventional Values of the Hellenistic Greeks*, Aarhus: Aarhus University Press, pp. 67–109.

Giannakis, E. (1995–1996) "Fragments from Alexander's Lost Commentary on Aristotle's *Physics*," *Zeitschrift für Geschichte der arabisch-islamischen Wissenschaften* 10, 157–187.

Giannantoni, G. (1990) *Socratis et socraticorum reliquiae*, Naples: Bibliopolis.

Goulet-Cazé, M.-O. (2017) *Le cynisme, une philosophie antique*, Paris: Vrin.

Hachmann, E. (2000) "Der fortuna-Begriff in Senecas Epistulae morales," *Gymnasium* 107, 295–319.

Hankinson, R. (1988) *Cause and Explanation in Ancient Greek Thought*, Oxford: Oxford University Press.

Hard, R. (tr.) (2011) *Marcus Aurelius. Meditations*. Introduction and Notes by C. Gill, Oxford: Oxford University Press.

———. (2012) *Diogenes the Cynic. Sayings and Anecdotes with Other Popular Moralists*, Oxford: Oxford University Press.

———. (tr.) (2014) *Epictetus: Discourses, Fragments, Handbook*. Introduction and Notes by C. Gill, Oxford: Oxford University Press.

Helmer, É. (2017) *Diogène le Cynique*, Paris: Les belles lettres.

Hense, O. (ed.) (1909) *Teletis reliquiae* [1889], 2nd edn, Tübingen: Mohr.

Herzog-Hauser, G. (1948) "Tyche," in G. Wissowa, W. Kroll, & K. Mittelhaus (eds.) *Paulys Realencyclopädie der classischen Altertumswissenschaften* 7, Stuttgart: Metzler, cols. 1643–1689.

Hine, H.M. (ed.) (1996) *L. Annaei Senecae naturalium quaestionum*, Stuttgart: Teubner.

Inwood, B. (2003) *The Cambridge Companion to the Stoics*, Cambridge: Cambridge University Press.

———. (2005) *Reading Seneca: Stoic Philosophy at Rome*, Oxford: Oxford University Press.

Inwood, B., & Gerson, L.P. (2008) *The Stoics Reader*, Indianapolis: Hackett.

Kindstrand, J.F. (1976) *Bion of Borysthenes: A Collection of the Fragments with Introduction and Commentary*, Uppsala: Almqvist Wiksell.

Krewet, M. (2017) "Polybios' Geschichtsbild. Hellenistische Prinzipien seiner Darstellungen menschlichen Handelns," *Wiener Studien* 130, 89–125.

Lawrence, S. (2012) "Fate and Chance," in H.M. Roisman (ed.) *The Encyclopedia of Greek Tragedy* 1, Oxford: Wiley-Blackwell, pp. 502–506.

Long, A.A. (1977) "Chance and Natural Law in Epicureanism," *Phronesis* 22, 63–88.

———. (2002) *Epictetus: A Stoic and Socratic Mentor*, Oxford: Oxford University Press.

Long, A.A., & Sedley, D.N. (1987) *The Hellenistic Philosophers*, Cambridge: Cambridge University Press.

LS = Long and Sedley 1987.

Mansfeld, J. (2001) "Chrysippus' Definition of Cause in Arius Didymus," *Elenchos* 22, 99–109.

Mansfeld, J., & Runia, D. (1997) *Aëtiana 1: The Sources*, Leiden: Brill.

———. (2010) *Aëtiana 3: Studies*, Leiden: Brill.

McGing, B. (2010) *Polybius' Histories*, New York: Oxford University Press.

Mönig, K. (2008) "Zenons glücklicher Schiffbruch am Felsen der Weisheit. Eine stoische Allegorie im Dom zu Siena," in B. Neymeyer, J. Schmidt, & B. Zimmermann (eds.) *Stoizismus in der europäischen Literatur, Philosophie, Kunst und Politik*, Berlin: De Gruyter, pp. 487–500.

Pédech, P. (1964) *La méthode historique de Polybe*, Paris: Les belles lettres.

Reynolds, L.D. (ed.) (1965) *L. Annaei Senecae ad Lucilium epistulae morales*, Oxford: Clarendon.

———. (1977) *L. Annaei Senecae dialogorum libri duodecim*, Oxford: Clarendon.

Sauvé-Meyer, S. (2009) "Chain of Causes," in R. Salles (ed.) *God and Cosmos in Stoicism*, Oxford: Oxford University Press, pp. 71–89.

Scheer, T.S. (2005) "tyche," in H.H. Schmitt & E. Vogt (eds.) *Lexikon des Hellenismus*, Wiesbaden: Harrassowitz, p. 1093.

Schenkl, H. (ed.) (1916) *Epicteti dissertationes ab Arriano digestae. Editio maior*, Leipzig: Teubner.

Schneider, C. (1967–1969) *Kulturgeschichte des Hellenismus*, Munich: Beck.

Sellars, J. (2006) *Stoicism*, Chesham: Acumen.

———. (ed.) (2016) *The Routledge Handbook of the Stoic Tradition*, London: Routledge.
SVF = von Arnim 1903–1905.
Usener, H. (1887) *Epicurea*, Leipzig: Teubner.
Walbank, F.W. (1972) *Polybius*, Berkeley: University of California Press.
Warren, J. (ed.) (2009) *The Cambridge Companion to Epicureanism*, Cambridge: Cambridge University Press.
Waterfield, R. (tr.) (2010) *Polybius: The Histories.* With an introduction and notes by B. McGing, Oxford: Oxford University Press.
Wildberger, J. (2006) *Seneca und die Stoa: Der Platz des Menschen in der Welt*, Berlin: De Gruyter.

4

THOMAS AQUINAS ON MORAL LUCK

Jeffrey Hause

Introduction: Control and Responsibility[1]

In contemporary philosophy, the problem of moral luck is typically generated by reflection on paradoxes in our intuitions about the moral responsibility—typically the blameworthiness—of agents whose activity has been significantly affected by factors outside their control.[2] One drunk driver heads home without incident; another kills a pedestrian; a third passes out as she is headed to her car and does not drive at all. Are they equally blameworthy? Intuitions (we are told) might incline us in different directions. Perhaps the driver who kills the pedestrian is most blameworthy and the drunk who passes out least so. However, we might also think that there is no moral difference among the agents themselves. After all, the differences in these various cases stem from effects the agents themselves had no control over. Hence, contemporary theorists tell us, we face a paradox: We are inclined both to blame these agents to the same degree but also to blame them to different degrees. Other examples abound. An agent, taking all reasonable precautions, shoots what appears to be a deer but turns out to be a human. Is the shooter blameworthy for homicide? An agent born into a morally disordered society such as a gang family, expected to adopt this way of life, in fact does so. Is this agent less responsible than if she had opted for the gang life after a comfortable and privileged childhood in Beverly Hills?

Although contemporary treatments of moral luck draw chiefly on discussions from the past 50 years, the problems at issue had been recognized and addressed from Antiquity through the Middle Ages and into Modernity. One of the most sophisticated treatments can be found in the later writings of Thomas Aquinas (1225–1274), the preeminent ethical thinker of the Middle Ages. Aquinas does not treat the full variety of such cases under a single umbrella, as we do in speaking of moral luck. Nevertheless, he raises the same sorts of cases that contemporary theorists do, and in discussing them he asks whether an agent is blameworthy at all, or to a diminished degree, for events over which agents lack control or a certain measure of control. Hence, it is not anachronistic to think of Aquinas as a participant in the discussion of moral luck.[3]

However, Aquinas's approach to the problem of moral luck is somewhat different from that of contemporary thinkers. By contrast with writers such as Thomas Nagel and Bernard Williams, whose work in the 1970s generated an industry of writing about moral luck, Aquinas does not begin with paradoxes. In the *Summa theologiae*, his fullest and most mature treatment of the topic, he begins with the assertion that we are not responsible for anything that lies outside our control: "Now acts are

45

imputed to agents when they are in the agents' power in such a way that they have control over their own acts" (*ST* I–II 21.2c). And where our control is compromised but not eliminated, we are less responsible in proportion to the impairment of our control (*ST* I–II 73.6c). However, he recognizes that in some cases, moral luck does at least appear to be relevant to the evaluation of an agent's behavior. Aquinas's task in the *Summa*, then, is not to determine *whether* luck plays a role in these evaluations, but rather how to accommodate the intuition that luck does play a role into an account of responsibility that asserts that luck plays no such role.

Thomas Nagel (1979) has identified four varieties of moral luck: resultant moral luck, when factors outside one's control affect how one's deed or the consequences of one's deed turn out, thereby affecting one's praise- or blameworthiness; constitutive moral luck, when factors outside one's control affect one's dispositions or tendencies to conceptualize and behave in specific sorts of ways; circumstantial moral luck, when an agent finds herself living in conditions whose limitations, advantages, or pressures result in the agent acting in blameworthy or praiseworthy ways other circumstances would not have made possible or likely; and causal luck, when an agent is causally determined by factors outside her control to behave as she does. Aquinas addresses all four; I will not address causal luck, which requires separate (and lengthy) treatment and which commentators on Aquinas continue to disagree about.[4] For the other three cases, I will investigate key texts in Aquinas to establish that we are responsible only for those acts and events that we can exercise control over.[5]

Aquinas's Action Theory

Aquinas maintains that our actions originate and progress through the mutual activity of our intellect and will (*ST* I–II 8–17). Our intellect conceives of objects—Aquinas talks about objects variously as things or actions—in the light of one or more values that the agent sees as good or bad in various ways (say, as contributing to a meaningful life, as requiring painful self-sacrifice, as beautiful, or as shameful). Our will, which is our intellectual appetite, desires those objects that the intellect conceives as in some way good and suitable for the agent's own life. For instance, if our intellect presents the plan of becoming an architect as appealing, and if no other course of life seems as attractive to us in our particular position, then we might take up the plan to become an architect, which now serves as our intention. We might then deliberate about how to achieve that goal, determine that studying architecture at Chicago, MIT, or Cornell would each be appropriate, but in the end settle on starting at MIT next fall as the best option for our particular life. According to Aquinas, at each stage of this action, the intellect serves as a formal cause of a corresponding activity of will. In other words, the intellect presents an object that characterizes or informs the will's activity, and so each of the will's activities—its intention to study architecture, its consenting to study at Chicago, MIT, or Cornell, and its choice to study at MIT starting next fall—is the sort of activity it is because of the object presented by the intellect. The will is related to the intellect at each stage as matter to form because the will's activity is shaped by the intellect's object. After the agent chooses a course of action, the intellect and will put that choice into action. The intellect therefore commands that the plan be implemented, and the will moves our relevant capacities to execute the plan.

Aquinas calls the will's more generalized desire—in my example represented by the intention to become an architect—the will's *internal act* (*ST* I–II 19). The concrete plan as conceived by reason—in my example represented by the plan to study architecture, to do it at MIT, to begin studies in the fall—is called the *external act* (*ST* I–II 18). The external act includes not just the act's principal aim or "substance" (such as studying architecture), but also the act's circumstances, such as where, how, when, and why one studies it. The internal act and external act are not simply related as stages in a process; the internal act informs the external act, even when the goal of the external act is not by its nature directed to achieving the goal of the internal act. For instance, to live out her intention to express love for her neighbor, Liz might see fit to admonish Sue for her binge drinking, a pattern of behavior harmful to Sue. Although one person might admonish another with any number of intentions (to make herself seem superior, to put a stop to irritating and bothersome distractions, to fulfill a promise to the offender's parents), in this case Liz's intention to live a life of neighborly love is what moves her to admonish Sue, and so even her admonition becomes an act of love. Aquinas also calls one's deed, or the act that one finally executes, the external act (e.g. I-II 20.1 ad 1); and so we must distinguish the external act as conceived and the external act as performed. The external act as conceived by reason serves as the formal cause of the external act as executed by the will. Because of the network of formal causation linking all stages of this process from start to finish, Aquinas maintains that from the initial intention all the way to the execution, the agent performs just one unified human action that unfolds by stages. It is not a string of discrete acts, one just the efficient cause of the next, but a unified act comprising multiple stages.

Moral Luck and Frustrated Sinners in *On Evil*

A common question meant to elicit a philosopher's thought about the role of moral luck is this: If an agent is prevented by circumstances out of her control from executing an act that she intends to perform, does her failure change the moral value of what she does? For instance, suppose Connie plans to kill her sister, secures a weapon, loads it with bullets, aims it at her sister and pulls the trigger. However, the gun jams and she cannot accomplish her intention. Is she any less blameworthy than someone whose gun actually functioned well and successfully killed her target?

In the *Disputed Questions on Evil* and *Summa theologiae*, Aquinas raises just this sort of case to explore several questions about moral luck. I will begin by detailing what he writes in the earlier *Disputed Questions on Evil*, whose treatment is less clear than that in the *Summa* and in which Aquinas is willing to concede that moral luck might play a role in the evaluation of the acts of frustrated sinners. One such question arises from Aquinas's view that each time a person makes a sinful choice—even if it is a choice to perform the same sort of action one failed to accomplish earlier—that person incurs blameworthiness anew. In *On Evil* 2.8 ad 8, therefore, Aquinas explains that a person whose intention to perform a bad act is interrupted by circumstances outside her control and who later renews that intention is blameworthy twice over.[6] For instance, if Connie intends to kill her sister on Tuesday but is interrupted by an unexpected visitor, then renews her intention on Friday and carries out the plan, she is blameworthy for what she does on both Tuesday and Friday. By contrast, if the visitor had not arrived, she would have been blameworthy for just one event. However, nothing in this case implies that moral luck is relevant because the increase in blame is entirely in Connie's control. After all, between Tuesday and Friday she might have repented and not shot her sister.

Suppose a different sort of interruption had occurred, one that simply unnerved Connie, sufficient to prevent her from attempting the murder but not enough to keep her from persisting in (rather than dropping but later renewing) her plan. In that case, she makes a single choice to kill her sister, a choice she carries out several days afterwards. However, it is not clear that Connie is any less blameworthy in this case than she would be for two discrete choices. On Aquinas's view, *persistence* in a bad choice also makes that choice more blameworthy (*On Evil* 2.2 ad 8). Although he does not and probably cannot offer any precise measurement of blame here, we can see that he offers no reason to think that these impediments to Connie's action, by themselves, make any difference to the moral evaluation of her activity. Persistence is no better or worse than renewal of the choice, and in both cases it is always up to Connie to change her plans.

In *On Evil* 2.2 objection 9, Aquinas explicitly raises the question of whether an agent who is prevented from carrying out her bad choice is less blameworthy than one who succeeds in carrying it out. Aquinas writes:

Suppose there are two people with equivalent volitions to commit the same sin (say, fornication), and one has the opportunity and fulfills his will, and the other does not have the opportunity but would like to have it. It is clear that there is no difference between these two as regards anything that is in their power. But there is no issue of sin as regards what is not in a person's power. Therefore, one of these does not sin more than the other, and so it appears that sin consists in the act of will alone.

Aquinas responds:

No one gains merit or demerit because of his disposition [*pro habitu*], but because of his act. And so it happens that someone is so fragile that he would sin, should he face temptation, but if he does not face temptation, he does not sin. Nor does he gain demerit for this reason because, as Augustine says, God does not punish a person for what he would go on to do, but for what he does. Therefore, although having or not having the opportunity to sin is not in one's power, nevertheless using or not using the opportunity one has is in one's power. And on this basis he sins and his sin is increased.

In this response, Aquinas first establishes that an agent is not responsible for what he would do under counterfactual conditions, but only for what he actually does. In evidence, he explains that someone whose character is so weak that he would certainly sin if tempted is not blameworthy if he is lucky enough not to face circumstances that would ensnare him. The inveterate braggart commits no sin while sitting at home alone reading the newspaper, even though in the company of others he would eventually start to boast. Suppose, then, that our inveterate braggart begins to feel his habitual stirrings and wishes he did have the company of others so that he could boast. Aquinas's response to objection 9 might suggest that such a braggart does not sin unless he both has and seizes the opportunity to brag. This passage, it might seem, supports the view that Aquinas accepts the relevance of moral luck in the evaluation of agents, since the opportunity to brag is often a matter of luck.

What Aquinas writes elsewhere in *On Evil* should give us pause, however. For instance, at 15.2 sc2 and c, he explains that people do in fact commit sins, such as sins of lust, merely through their disordered passions. Hence, someone who would engage in a disordered sexual encounter but does not have the opportunity still sins. There are, then, two remaining interpretations of this ambiguous text. (1) Perhaps Aquinas means for us to think of seizing the opportunity to commit the sin as a deepening of that sin beyond the blameworthiness one incurs at the choice stage. In that case, we are more blameworthy if we act on an opportunity that might not be in our control to procure. If this is the correct interpretation, then Aquinas does admit the relevance of moral luck in this sort of case. (2) By treating the agent's choice to sin and the agent's seizing the opportunity to sin independently, Aquinas calls our attention to the fact that some agents do not carry through with their choices. If an agent seizes the opportunity, then the agent is more wholehearted in pursuing the action; but if the agent does not take advantage of the opportunity, then the agent is less fervent or more conflicted in pursuing the action. In this case, the sin does not itself become worse if we take advantage of the opportunity; rather, taking advantage of the opportunity is a sign that one is more committed to the sinful course of action. This line of interpretation faces a clear disadvantage over the first: It would require us to interpret "equivalent volitions" as meaning volitions for the same sort of objects rather than volitions of equal strength, which is the more natural interpretation. In this passage, therefore, Aquinas does appear to allow the relevance of moral luck.

Moral Luck and Frustrated Sinners in the *Summa Theologiae*

When we turn to the *Summa theologiae*, we not only find a more detailed and sophisticated account of moral luck, but we also find Aquinas rejecting the view he accepts in *On Evil*, namely, that moral luck plays a role in determining an agent's blameworthiness when circumstances out of her control prevent her from performing her chosen deed. In the First Part of the Second Part of the *Summa*, Aquinas offers a clear and more complete answer to the question he poses at *On Evil* 2.2 objection 9. Does the external act, when performed, add to the goodness or badness in one's volition alone? Aquinas explains that the external act

> is related to the volition as its terminus and end. And in this way it does add to the volition's goodness or badness, because every inclination or motion is completed in its reaching its end or attaining its terminus. Therefore, the volition is not complete unless it is of a sort that, given the opportunity, one would act. However, if that possibility is lacking, even though the volition is complete (so that one would act if one could), then the lack of completeness stemming from the exterior act is involuntary, absolutely speaking. However, just as what is involuntary does not merit punishment or reward in producing what is good or bad, neither does it take away anything of reward or punishment if a person involuntarily, absolutely speaking, falls short in accomplishing what is good or bad.
>
> *ST I-II 20.4c*

Here Aquinas finds a new solution to the problem that still accommodates the considerations he appeals to in the earlier *On Evil* passage, in particular the relevance of taking advantage of the opportunity to sin. If the volition to perform the act is complete—that is, if one is not indecisive, faltering in one's purpose, or otherwise hesitant to carry through with it—then this volition *includes* the desire to take advantage of the opportunity when it arises. If that opportunity lies entirely out of one's control, there is no moral difference between the agent who brings that volition to fruition and the agent who is frustrated in that goal. Where there is no difference in the quality of one's volition, there is likewise no difference in the praise- or blameworthiness of one's action, whether or not one achieves one's end. Whether one actually has the opportunity to sin, on Aquinas's later account, turns out to be irrelevant to one's blameworthiness, and so Aquinas eliminates the role he had earlier allowed for in these sorts of cases.

Aquinas does admit that agents who succeed in carrying out the external deed may find that the performance of this deed indirectly affects their praise- or blameworthiness because the execution of the deed can affect the quality of one's volition. Agents can be singlehearted in their volitions or, if they experience conflicting desires, can waver or act hesitantly. In addition, agents desire their objects with varying degrees of intensity. Because the will is a faculty of rational rather than sensory desire, intensity cannot be directly measured by its effects on our bodies, the way we can measure the intensity of anger or fear. Instead, we measure the intensity of a volition by its effects (how effectively it governs our behavior, how readily we fulfill it, how much we enjoy fulfilling it, and how powerfully it influences our lower appetites to conform to its desire). Aquinas explains that when agents carry out the external act, this execution itself can in fact affect our praise- or blameworthiness. That is because deeds that are pleasant or unpleasant naturally tend to increase or decrease the resolve or intensity of our volition. So, while the performance of the deed is, in itself, irrelevant to one's praise- or blameworthiness, that performance can itself influence the way we perceive and value the course of action we are engaged in and thereby indirectly affect one's praise- or blameworthiness.

Aquinas's strategy for accommodating intuitions about moral luck in these cases, then, is to move the locus of blameworthiness inward, to acts under our direct control, to characterize those acts as worse based not on their actually resulting in a bad external deed but on their tendency to produce such a deed. Is Thomas Aquinas, then, just Peter Abelard in Dominican clothing? Abelard (1079–1142) had famously argued that the sole criterion of sinfulness is the agent's consent or intention, that is, what the agent would carry out should the opportunity arise.[7] The deed is not itself a source of an act's moral badness, and so there is no moral difference between the agent who succeeds in carrying out her sinful intention and the one who is frustrated in her attempt (*Ethics* §29–30).

Likewise, Aquinas maintains that if an agent has a complete volition to perform a sinful act—that is, if the agent is ready to perform it when the opportunity arises—but is prevented from accomplishing her aim, that agent is no more or less blameworthy than the agent who succeeds. Despite this striking similarity, there is one important difference between Aquinas and Abelard. Abelard conceives of the deed as the efficient causal consequence resulting from the agent's consent. Aquinas conceives of the external act the agent executes as not just the efficient causal consequence of the activity of the agent's will but as an element in the complete act. The external act as conceived by reason is related to the external act as performed in the way that form is related to matter, and so they are unified parts of a greater whole. They are therefore united as one single act, not merely as multiple acts in which the internal cause the external.

One reason why this distinction matters is that, in Abelard's view, calling a deed a "sin" means only that the morally neutral deed is caused by a sinful act of consent (*Ethics* §106). Because the deed is not united to the act of consent, it is not part of the sin. On Aquinas's view, by contrast, the deed is a part of the complete sinful act. When an agent is blameworthy for her sin, therefore, that blame belongs to the entire sinful act, both those elements that take place in the agent's psyche and those the agent works in the world. However, as we have seen, the deed does not add any further blameworthiness to a complete volition to perform a sinful act. Therefore, in reading Aquinas's treatments of blameworthiness, demerit, and punishment, we must be careful to distinguish between what an agent is blameworthy for and how blameworthy the agent is. An agent might be blameworthy for more events if she succeeds in carrying out her will to sin, but she will not be any more blameworthy.[8]

Per Se and Per Accidens Consequences

The consequences of an agent's behavior are not limited to those that the agent intends to bring about. In addition to foreseen and intended consequences, there are unforeseen and unintended consequences. The *Summa theologiae* devotes two articles to these topics, the first in Aquinas's treatment of action theory (*ST* I-II 20.5) and the second in his treatment of sin and blameworthiness (*ST* I-II 73.8):

> A consequence is either foreseen or not. If it is foreseen, it is clear that it adds to [the act's] goodness or badness. After all, when someone who is aware that many bad things can follow from his activity does not for that reason forego engaging in it, it is clear that his will is more disordered.
>
> On the other hand, if the consequence is not foreseen, then we must draw a distinction. That is because, if the consequence follows from this sort of act per se and for the most part, then for this reason it adds to the act's goodness or badness; for it is clear that an act is better of its kind from the fact that more good things can result from it, and worse from the fact that more bad things naturally follow from it. However, if the consequence follows per accidens and rarely, then the consequence does not add to the act's goodness or badness, for we pass judgment on something not insofar as it is per accidens, but only insofar as it is per se.
>
> *I-II 20.5c*

> Harm can be related to sin in three ways.

> Sometimes the harm that stems from the sin is foreseen and intended, as when someone does something meaning to harm someone else, such as homicide or theft. And in that case the quantity of the harm directly increases the seriousness of the sin, because in that case the harm is a per se object of the sin.

Sometimes the harm is foreseen but not intended, as when someone rushing to commit fornication takes a short cut across a field knowingly causes harm to the young plants in the field, but without planning any harm. And in this case too the quantity of harm makes sin more serious, but it does so indirectly, that is, in that due to a volition highly inclined to sinning, it happens that someone does not avoid doing the harm to himself or another that he would not want, absolutely speaking.

But sometimes the harm is neither intended nor foreseen. And in that case, if it is related to the sin per accidens, it does not increase the sin directly; but due to a person's negligence in considering the harms that could result, the evils that occur outside her intention are imputed to her as regards her punishment, if she was doing something illicit. However, if the harm follows per se from the act of sin, even though it is not intended or foreseen, it directly aggravates the sin, because whatever follows per se on a sin belongs in a way to that species of sin. For instance, if someone publicly fornicates, there will follow scandal for many people; and although the sinner does not intend it, and perhaps does not foresee it, it nevertheless directly aggravates her sin.

ST I-II 73.8c

In these texts, Aquinas distinguishes between those effects that follow per se from one's sinful act and those that follow per accidens. According to Aquinas, A is a per se cause of B when, precisely in its capacity as A, it causes B. A builder might also be a grammarian, for instance, but it is in her capacity as builder that she is the per se cause of the house. It is that capacity of hers that *explains* the building of the house. It is still true to say that the grammarian builds the house, but her capacity as grammarian does not explain how the house comes to be. Therefore, the grammarian is the cause of the building per accidens and not per se. Likewise, in her construction work, the builder might in a single activity both build a house and block the neighbors' view of the mulberry trees. Her capacity to build houses makes it the case that when she uses that capacity, the result will always or for the most part be a house. This capacity *explains* why what results is a house. However, there is nothing about this capacity that makes blocking views of mulberry trees a usual result or that explains this result. This latter is therefore a per accidens result of the builder's activity.[9]

Aquinas treats effects that follow per se in much the same way as he treats the performed external act: Such an effect does increase the agent's blameworthiness, he writes, but not in any way that introduces moral luck into the evaluation of the act. It is not the actual occurrence of the bad effect that makes the act more blameworthy; rather, as I-II 20.5 makes clear, it is the act's tendency to produce the bad effect that makes the act worse of its kind.

Aquinas's treatment of bad consequences that follow per accidens is less perspicuous. At *ST* I-II 20.5 he simply asserts that per accidens effects do not make an act more blameworthy because "we pass judgment on something not insofar as it is per accidens, but only insofar as it is per se." Because we can predict and explain only the per se effects of our actions, those are the only ones that fall under our control and, therefore, the only ones that we are responsible for. However, the more thorough *ST* I-II 73.8, focused on the finer details of sin and responsibility, draws a distinction. If an agent is not engaged in any illicit activities and is not behaving negligently or recklessly, and yet some bad per accidens effect results from her activity, then she does not incur any blame. However, if some bad per accidens effect results from her negligence or illicit activity, Aquinas asserts that the resulting harm aggravates her sin: "Due to a person's negligence in considering the harms that could result, the evils that occur outside her intention are imputed to her as regards her punishment, if she was doing something illicit." Aquinas surely means this to be a disjunction: The unforeseen and unintended harms that result are relevant if the agent is either acting negligently or doing something illicit. Aquinas is nearly quoting from the *Decretales* (Gregory IX 1757), which treats these two conditions of illicit activity and negligence as individually sufficient for the agent to be responsible for the offense: "Accidental homicide is imputed to someone who was engaged in an illicit activity, or even a licit activity (on another interpretation) if he was not employing all the attentiveness that he should have" (*Homicidium casuale imputatur ei, qui dabat operam rei illicitae vel etiam licitae, secundum alium intellectum, si non adhibuit omnem diligentiam, quam debuit*, chap. 8 book v, title 12). Aquinas himself also treats them as individually sufficient conditions in his slightly later treatment of homicide at II–II 64.8.

As with sins in which the harm is either intended or foreseen, Aquinas asserts that in this case too the resulting harm increases the seriousness of the sin. However, in treating intended and foreseen harm, Aquinas explains that the seriousness of one's sin is in part a function of the *quantity* of harm the sin can produce. In treating unintended and unforeseen harm, he says nothing about this quantitative determinant of a sin's seriousness. If, as with the cases we have already treated, the seriousness of these sins is exclusively determined by how disordered the agent's will is, we can see why Aquinas does not mention the quantity of the resulting harm. If the harmful effect follows per accidens, its quantity cannot be predicted and therefore it cannot be a factor in determining just how disordered the agent's will is. But if the quantity of the resulting harm is not what affects the seriousness of the sin, then what does?

Although Aquinas offers no clear answer to this question, the one that best explains his claims here and accords well with the rest of his account is that we should measure the seriousness of these sins not by any single predictable or expected quantity of harm, but rather by the range, seriousness, and likelihood of various harms that could follow from one's negligence or illicit activity. It is not hard to see that different sorts of illicit activity risk greater or lesser harms of diverse sorts. Stealing apples from someone's tree might result in any number of consequences for the tree owner: disappointment at having no fresh apple pie for Aunt Liz's birthday, feelings of anger and distrust, an urge to make an extra expenditure on a security camera to make sure such a violation does not happen again—or perhaps the tree owner, like Augustine's neighborhood pear owner, might not care at all. Compare the sorts of harms that might ensue from a different sort of offense, such as breaking and entering: giving the homeowner a heart attack, inducing the homeowner to retrieve her firearms and shoot or be shot in turn, feelings of helplessness and anxiety requiring years of therapy. We can be sure the homeowner will not simply shrug off the invasion as one might shrug off the loss of one's apples, even if we do not know exactly how he will in fact react. This interpretation has the virtue of explaining how, even with effects that follow per accidens from one's activity, in which the quantity of harm is itself unpredictable, we can nevertheless see why certain sorts of negligence or illicit activities are worse than others. It would, after all, be implausible to think that every case of negligence is equally blameworthy.

Constituent and Circumstantial Moral Luck

Aquinas reflects not only on resultant moral luck, or luck at the downstream end of human actions, but also on the influence of factors outside our control at the upstream end. He treats what we now call "constituent moral luck" in multiple places when he notes that due to the differing constitutions of their bodies, human beings have various natural inclinations or appetitive tendencies to different sorts of emotions and behavior. According to one commonly accepted medieval medical view, someone in whom the cold and wet "humors" predominate, for instance, is mild and averse to anger; while someone with greater proportions of hot and dry humors will instead be prone to anger. Aquinas sometimes calls certain of these congenital traits, such as the tendencies to mildness and boldness, "natural virtues," since they often mimic the inclination of genuine virtues, such as courage or gentleness. They are, however, not genuine virtues but rather pre-reflective tendencies of the sensory appetites. The so-called natural virtue of boldness might look like courage in many circumstances, since our typical icon of a courageous person is someone who conquers fear and summons confidence in order to face dangers. However, the genuinely courageous person will not always act boldly and confidently because those feelings are not always warranted. A tendency to boldness, unlike genuine courage, might lead one into foolish risks or into the service of bad ends. Despite these concerns, we might think that natural virtues give an agent a distinct advantage by making it easier to train for the genuine virtues they resemble, and so they appear to afford their possessors a moral edge over others.[10]

However, Aquinas maintains that any such advantage is balanced out by corresponding disadvantages:

> A person can have a natural inclination to the activities associated with a *single* virtue. However, a person cannot have a natural inclination to the activities associated with *all* the virtues, because a natural disposition that inclines to one virtue, inclines to the contrary of another virtue (for instance, someone who is naturally disposed to courage, which consists in pursuing demanding things, is less well disposed to gentleness, which consists in checking the passions of the irascible appetite). That is why, as we see, animals that are naturally inclined to the act of some virtue are inclined to a vice contrary to a different virtue. For instance, the lion, which is naturally bold, is also naturally cruel.[11]

Aquinas here asserts that no natural disposition, or constellation of natural dispositions, makes the acquisition of virtue easier or harder, and therefore no one is at a moral advantage or disadvantage over anyone else in this regard. We might of course want to press Aquinas further on this reply, which seems entirely too quick and facile: Someone whose natural constitution includes a powerful inclination to boldness would not only have a disadvantage in becoming appropriately gentle, but would also face difficulties in developing genuine courage. After all, courage requires just the sort of thoughtfulness that a powerful inclination to boldness is likely to erode, and such a person, in the position of a soldier, could easily turn out to be unreliable and untrustworthy because of her tendency to evaluate how to act through the lens of boldness, to ignore the safety of her own comrades, and to take unnecessary risks. In addition, not all passions affect our rationality in the same way. Aquinas himself, following the tradition of ancient philosophy, holds that anger clouds our judgment more than other passions do (*ST* I-II 48.3c). Therefore, those born with irascible temperaments have a greater disadvantage than those born cool-headed and placid.

On the other hand, Aquinas admits freely that circumstantial moral luck plays an important role in the sorts of choices we make and the sort of people we become, even if in his view it does not control the moral outcome of our actions. Some people are born into less propitious circumstances than others, given poor moral education and training. They might be bombarded with moral challenges and have an underdeveloped capacity to reflect on how to approach those challenges. Others are more fortunate, raised to keep moral precepts in mind, corrected when they stray, and given models of virtue to emulate. Aquinas's moral writings are replete with examples. For instance, to make good decisions about complex practical matters, we must depend on the advice of others (*ST* I-II 14.3); and so we are at a moral advantage if we can rely on the counsel of those we trust. In our inexperience, we must also rely on the judgment of those who are more experienced and older (*ST* II-II 49.3); we are at a disadvantage if we have no trusted elders to consult. If we live in a community beset by public sinning, others' bad examples can induce us to sinning (*ST* II-II 43). By contrast, if we live in a community in which neighbors care for each other, we can expect moral advice and correction when we stand in need of it (*ST* II-II 33). Of course, no one is so lucky as to be born and raised into virtue without facing morally challenging situations. Even those with the most fortunate of upbringings must habituate themselves to virtue by the difficult work of performing virtuous actions, confronting challenges and bearing setbacks well, and coming to love what is fine and noble, even when it requires personal sacrifice. Nevertheless, some have a much greater edge in this effort than others, even though right action and virtuous character are, in principle, accessible to everyone.

Does Aquinas offer any consideration to mitigate the effect of moral luck here, as he does with constitutive moral luck? Abelard had built such a measure into his ethics. If (because of natural disposition or circumstances) one is more challenged to do what is fitting, then one gains greater merit for doing it (*Ethics* §5, §22). The initial difficulty is offset by the reward for success, a model used in athletic competitions such as gymnastics or ice skating. Aquinas's Aristotelian inheritance keeps him from adopting such a view: If one finds it difficult to pursue a good course of action because one has countervailing desires, that sort of challenge *detracts* from an act's value. If, however, one manages to forestall one's countervailing desires and keep them at bay by eliciting a particularly intense act of will for what is good, then that intensity adds to the value of one's act. But that is hardly an advantage to offset the initial inequity that besets people with unfortunate moral circumstances. That is instead a recognition of that disadvantage. Anyone without such a disadvantage can also benefit from this intensity of will, which does not require challenging circumstances.[12] We must admit that here we find not only that moral luck is at work in human life, but that the inequalities are widespread, some people severely morally hampered. Is there nothing to mitigate these effects of circumstantial luck?

Early in his career, admitting an uneven distribution of moral advantages and disadvantages, Aquinas nevertheless argues that whether we sin or not is in our control. In his *Commentary on the Sentences* he writes:

> Just as sin reduces but does not remove natural goods, a person cannot lose through sin what belongs to the nature of a natural power, even if it is weakened in him. Therefore since free election or the avoidance of good or bad belongs to the nature of free choice, it cannot be that the capability of avoiding sin is taken away from humans by sin, but only that it is lessened, so that that sin which a human had beforehand been able easily to avoid, he avoids afterwards with difficulty.
>
> In II Sent. 28.1.2c

Hence, although there is moral luck, each human—even someone who faces significant moral challenges—can overcome them and remain without sin. After all, each of us knows the basic precepts of morality and, by thoughtful attention, we can put them into action in each of our activities. By mid-career, Aquinas has abandoned this view: Although it was in the power of pre-lapsarian humans to refrain from sin, it is not in ours. His mature view is that we can avoid any sin singly—if we are watchful, singlemindedly dedicated to warding off temptation. This is sufficient control, he assumes, for moral responsibility. However, we cannot sustain this effort for long without sanctifying grace. A circumstance will eventually catch us by surprise as we let down our guard (*ST* I-II 109.8). Those in difficult moral circumstances, therefore, are particularly ripe for moral failure. But then, without God's grace, so are all the rest of us. Even the most fortunate of us are moving at a slower, reduced rate of moral failure.

Aquinas changes his early views out of concern that they are too Pelagian, not allowing God the governing role in determining human salvation. He nevertheless wants to retain something of the earlier view in that he holds we still have limited control: For each approaching sin, we have the power to avoid it, and this control is sufficient for our moral responsibility. If we did not have this power, then the sin could not have been attributed to us. It will be harder for us if circumstances press us, but unless we have developed vices, we can still defeat each oncoming temptation. Even this limited measure of control explains why Aquinas is willing to countenance the influence of circumstantial and constitutive moral luck, but not resultant moral luck. When we do eventually fail due in part to the pressure of circumstances, we see that this failure is something we could have overcome if we had been more focused, resolute, and loving. We can understand this failure as resulting from a flaw in ourselves, one we can strive to improve or even overcome (even if we will sometimes fail without divine help). What is more, even if we are more beset by serious temptations than others, if circumstances make it harder for us, we can still see our failure as our own capitulation to evil. At the downstream end, we see that we lack even the limited control we have at the upstream end: First, we could not have overcome at least some of these unlucky results by being more virtuous human beings, since even the virtuous see some of their actions go awry. And in cases in which several agents have the same sort of bad volition but that volition issues in further bad results in some but not other cases, those further bad consequences are not thereby further failures, further capitulations to evil.

There is, of course, a way in which agents can avoid all serious sin: through divine grace and the infused moral virtues that result from that grace. Aquinas distinguishes the acquired virtues we build through our own efforts from the infused virtues that are a divine gift in part by noting that if we use the infused virtues, we are guaranteed not to fail. They repair the defects of original sin sufficiently to allow us to stay on the path of righteousness.[13] Scholars disagree—vehemently and frequently—about how these virtues accomplish this goal, but at least this much is clear: These virtues do one thing the acquired virtues do not—they fix our wills on God so powerfully and with so much love that we would not want for anything to be separated from God and therefore we act with an attentiveness and persistence we could not muster without God. Of course, this way out of the problem of circumstantial moral luck just pushes the problem back one stage to yet another controversial question in Aquinas: Is grace on offer to everyone and in our control to accept, or is even receiving grace out of our control?[14,15]

Notes

1 I use the following abbreviations and conventions for Aquinas's works:

> *ST: Summa theologiae*
> I-II: First Part of the Second Part of the *Summa theologiae*
> II-II: Second Part of the Second Part of the *Summa theologiae*
> c = reply
> sc = on the other hand
> ad x = response to objection x
> Unless otherwise noted, all translations are my own.

2 The contemporary classical discussions are Nagel (1979) and Williams (1981). Hartman (2017) offers careful summaries and critical analyses of the treatment begun by Nagel and Williams as background to his own account.

3 Aquinas speaks of luck in praiseworthiness as well as in blameworthiness (e.g. I-II 20.5 ad 2). However, because his writing is meant in large part to clarify thinking about spiritual direction, he focuses on blame. After all, a common goal of spiritual direction, as one might find in the practice of confession, is to enable a person under direction to see how blameworthy she is, how far she has strayed from the right course of human life, and then to seek a return to that path.

4 See, e.g., Hoffmann and Michon (2017), Irwin (2007: 635, 678), Pasnau (2002: 200–233), MacDonald (1998).

5 On the nature of control in Aquinas, see Stump (2003: 277–306), Pasnau (2002), and MacDonald (1998).

6 "And so there is in him a twice evil will: one without, and one with an act" (*et sic est in eo duplex mala voluntas: una sine actu, et alia cum actu*).

7 Citations of the *Ethics* are to section numbers in Abelard (1995).

8 See Wilks (2014) for further comparisons of Abelard and Aquinas.

9 See *On the Principles of Nature* chapter 5.

10 On the natural virtues, see *ST* I-II 58.4 ad 3, 65.1c; see also *On the Cardinal Virtues* 2 in Aquinas (2010).

11 *Disputed Question on the Virtues in General* 8 ad 10, cited from the Hause and Murphy translation in Aquinas (2010).

12 Bowlin (1999: 202–212), rightly explains that serious moral challenges enable those raised in morally fortunate environments to reflect in such a way as to make their moral inheritance their own. To acquire the sort of virtue that makes us morally better agents, we must face serious challenges. This shows that there is a morally salutary aspect to certain occasions of temptation if we encounter them at the right time. It does not, however, mitigate the effect of circumstantial moral luck generally.

13 See *On the Virtues in General* 10 ad 14 in Aquinas (2010).

14 A topic the poet John Milton thought so Sisyphean he depicted the more erudite demons in *Paradise Lost* arguing endlessly and fruitlessly about this topic (Book II, 557–561).

15 I would like to thank the participants in the Rutgers *Pax et Bonum* Conference in honor of Marilyn McCord Adams for helpful comments.

Jeffrey Hause

References

Abelard, Peter (1995) *Ethics*, in P.V. Spade (ed. and trans.) *Ethical Writings*, Indianapolis: Hackett, pp. 1–58.

Aquinas, Thomas (1929) *Scriptum super libros Sententiarum* [*Commentary on the Sentences*] vols. 1 and 2, ed. P. Mandonnet, Paris: Lethielleux.

——. (1981) *Summa theologica* [*Summa theologiae*], trans. Fathers of the English Dominican Province [Fr. Laurence Shapcote], Westminster: Christian Classics.

——. (2003) *On Evil*, ed. Brian Davies, trans. Richard Regan, Oxford: Oxford University Press.

——. (2010) *Disputed Questions on Virtue*, trans. Jeffrey Hause & Claudia Eisen Murphy, Indianapolis: Hackett.

——. (2014) *On the Principles of Nature*, trans. E. Stump & S. Chanderbhan, in J. Hause & R. Pasnau (eds.), *Basic Works*, Indianapolis, Hackett, pp. 2–13.

Bowlin, John (1999) *Contingency and Fortune in Aquinas's Ethics*, Cambridge: Cambridge University Press.

Gregory IX (1757) *Decretales*, vol. 2, Coloniae Munatianae: J.R. Thurnisiorum.

Hartman, R.J. (2017) *In Defense of Moral Luck: Why Luck Often Affects Praiseworthiness and Blameworthiness*, New York: Routledge.

Hoffmann, T., & Michon, C. (2017) "Aquinas on Free Will and Intellectual Determinism," in *Philosophers' Imprint* 17, 1–36, Permalink: http://hdl.handle.net/2027/spo.3521354.0017.010.

Irwin, T. (2007) *The Development of Ethics: A Historical and Critical Study*, vol. 1: *From Socrates to the Reformation*, Oxford: Oxford University Press.

MacDonald, S. (1998) "Aquinas's Libertarian Account of Free Choice," in *Revue Internationale de Philosophie* 52, 309–328.

Nagel, T. (1979) "Moral Luck," in T. Nagel (ed.) *Mortal Questions*, Cambridge: Cambridge University Press, pp. 24–38.

Pasnau, R. (2002) *Thomas Aquinas on Human Nature: A Philosophical Study of* Summa Theologiae *Ia 75–89*, Cambridge: Cambridge University Press.

Stump, E. (2003) *Aquinas*, New York: Routledge.

Wilks, I. (2014) "Peter Abelard and St. Thomas Aquinas on Moral Intention," in J. Hause (ed.) *Debates in Medieval Philosophy*, New York: Routledge, pp. 85–96.

Williams, B. (1981) "Moral Luck," in B. Williams (ed.) *Moral Luck*, Cambridge: Cambridge University Press.

5

IMMANUEL KANT ON MORAL LUCK

Kate Moran

Introduction

This essay will focus on the role of luck in Immanuel Kant's moral philosophy. The first, shorter, part of the essay examines Kant's conception of happiness (*Glückseligkeit*), a conception that is fundamentally bound up with luck and circumstance. Of particular importance will be the observation that the moral law and an agent's autonomy stand as a kind of bulwark against the shifting winds of fortune. The second, longer, section of the essay considers Kant's stance on what philosophers now call questions of moral luck. Kant is sometimes charged with having an extreme, perhaps even naive, position on matters of moral luck—a position that insists that luck and circumstance should play no role in our moral judgments. This interpretation of Kant is understandable, but incomplete. Helpfully, Kant himself has a fair amount to say about these issues in lectures and published texts. Examining these statements and the contexts in which they appear yields an underappreciated Kantian stance on moral luck that helps to shed light on the contemporary debate and on Kant's moral philosophy itself.

Luck and Happiness

Though a complete discussion of Kant's conception of happiness and the role it plays in his moral philosophy is beyond the scope of this essay, it is important to note a few points in the context of our discussion of luck. Though happiness cannot serve as the ground or justification of moral action, on Kant's view, it is nevertheless crucial to his conception of moral life. Kant is not a Stoic. Happiness, coupled with and conditioned by virtue, is part of the complete good for embodied moral agents like ourselves. Happiness is good, insofar as it is consistent with morality, and a perfectly virtuous person who was not also happy would suffer a kind of privation.[1] Kant even suggests at some points that if we knew that happiness were impossible to achieve, we would be incapable of moral action.[2] But happiness is also bound up with and contingent upon luck. Of course, the German word for luck (*Glück*) is part of the word that Kant uses for happiness (*Glückseligkeit*), but the association between luck and happiness goes even further than this in Kant's theory.

To see that this is the case, we can turn to the second section of the *Groundwork of the Metaphysics of Morals*. That discussion is concerned, in large part, with the notion of an imperative, or the formula of a "representation of an objective principle in so far as it is necessitating for a will" (*GMS* 4:413). Famously, Kant distinguishes between hypothetical imperatives and categorical imperatives, where the former are imperatives that are set by the contingent ends that agents have, and the latter are set by ends that an agent must have, or, in Kant's terminology, by an "objectively necessary end" (*GMS* 4:414). Interestingly, however, Kant makes a further distinction between two types of hypothetical imperative. First, hypothetical imperatives can be so-called "imperatives of skill"—these are determined by the agent's "possible purpose(s)" (*ibid.*). Second, hypothetical imperatives can be "imperatives of prudence"—these are determined by an end that all agents necessarily and actually share, namely happiness. In the context of the second section of the *Groundwork*, it is noteworthy and perhaps even surprising that Kant would concede that happiness is an *actual, necessary* end for all rational agents. After all, Kant's argument in the text emphasizes repeatedly the need for the supreme principle of morality to be grounded in necessity, so in asserting that happiness is an end that all agents necessarily have, he might seem to be coming curiously close to the decidedly un-Kantian thesis that the basis of the moral principle might be found in the rational pursuit of happiness. Of course, this is not Kant's view, and it is easy to see why once we investigate his conception of happiness. Happiness, for Kant, consists in "a maximum of well-being, in my present and every future condition" (*GMS* 4:418). But "human beings can form no determinate and reliable concept of the sum of the satisfaction of all [inclinations] under the name of happiness" (*GMS* 4:399) because luck plays a large role in determining not just whether an agent will achieve such well-being, but what will contribute to her well-being in the first place. Kant offers a series of examples to prove the point: the person who attains wealth might also encounter "worry, envy, and intrigue"; the person who achieves wisdom might have the ills of the world revealed to him more clearly; and the person who wants a long life might find that this only brings him "long misery" (*GMS* 4:418).

Happiness is thus a necessary end for human beings, part of the complete good for sensible moral agents, but also fundamentally indeterminate, obscure, and mercurial. This suggests, if not a contradiction, at least an uncomfortable tension. How can something so important to the rational agent's moral life also be so contingent upon luck and fortune?

The answers to this puzzle help to fill in some important details about Kant's moral theory. First, Kant clearly endorses a version of the paradox of hedonism—direct pursuit of happiness is an almost certain path to misery, in no small part because of the indeterminacy of happiness described above. An excellent case study of this phenomenon is Kant's discussion of the miser (e.g. *TL* 6:432–434). The miser adopts an almost comical principle of savings precisely because he is so worried about being able to enjoy happiness in the future. All the while, however, he is consumed with jealous thoughts about his neighbors who spend their resources on goods that contribute to their happiness in the present (*V-Anth Parow* 25:250). Of course, if the miser were to spend his money like his neighbors, he would be consumed by fears about the future. The miser becomes unmoored. His only principle is the pursuit of happiness, and this can never provide a fixed foundation, either for morality or indeed for happiness itself.

There is thus a theme throughout Kant's moral philosophy that a moral will is the foil to the shifting winds of fortune. In lectures on ethics, Kant remarks that the moral agent must avoid "despondency," and instead recognize that he "possesses himself" and must "locate [his existence] in his own person, and not in things outside him."[3] In the same set of lectures, he puns on the similarity of the words "*sälig*" (fortunate) and "*selig*" (blessed, secure):

> [A] state whose comfort has its source merely in things of nature, or in good fortune, and of which I am not the author through my freedom, would not be called "blessed" (*selig*), and would have to be called "fortunate" (*sälig*), in that here the word "*Saal*" is at the bottom of it—as with every state of things—just as it has this meaning in the words *Schicksaal* (fortune) and *Trübsaal* (misfortune).

> *VMS-Vigilantius 27:644*

Of course, one should not adopt the principle of morality simply because one hopes it will contribute to one's happiness—this would be little more than a sophisticated iteration of the paradox of hedonism. But Kant is hopeful that happiness will *result from* moral action generally. This is perhaps nowhere so apparent as when he discusses the so-called highest good, the conjunction of virtue and happiness described at the outset of this section. Kant describes the relationship between virtue and happiness as causal—specifically, virtue *causes* happiness (*KpV* 5:112–113). (Compare this to Kant's conception of Stoic and Epicurean philosophers, whom Kant describes as simply equating virtue and happiness in distinct ways.) The nature of this causal relationship is hotly debated in Kant scholarship. In particular, there is no clear consensus about whether Kant thinks that agents will enjoy happiness in this life, or in an afterlife. But on at least one account the causal relationship between virtue and happiness is straightforward and this-worldly: virtuous agents who refrain from treating others merely as means to an end, and who adopt the happiness of others as their own will generally bring it about that others are more happy. The account is, of course, not impervious to luck. There is no guarantee that any particular agent will be as happy as virtue allows, but with respect to the moral community at least, virtue will tend to bring about happiness.[4]

Moral Luck

We turn now to the discussion of Kant's stance on moral luck. In his famous essay on the subject, Thomas Nagel repeatedly identifies Kant as a standard-bearer for the understandable but flawed view that matters of luck should never figure in to our moral assessment of an agent (Nagel 1979). On Nagel's view, Kant's theory captures the common sense intuition that we should instead be judged—and in turn judge others—only for what is in our control. Nagel acknowledges that this allegedly Kantian stance is difficult to leave behind. On the one hand, we regularly find ourselves making moral judgments that depend to some degree on luck and circumstance, as when we judge an agent for negligence that might just as easily have never come to light. But, Nagel observes, when we reflect upon these judgments, we cannot help but feel the theoretical pull of a view that says such judgments rest on a mistake. Nagel cites at least three reasons for this: first, that "people cannot be morally assessed for what is not their fault, or for what is due to factors outside of their control" (p. 25); second, that "something in the idea of agency is incompatible with the idea of actions being events, or people being things" (p. 37). Finally, he suspects a tendency to export judgments and attitudes about *ourselves*—guilt, shame, and pride, for example—into judgments and attitudes about *others*—for example, indignation, contempt, and admiration (*ibid.*). Nagel thus concedes that the Kantian stance retains a theoretical attraction. Nonetheless, "Kant's conclusion remains intuitively unacceptable. We may be persuaded that [judgments based in luck] are irrational, but they reappear involuntarily as soon as the argument is over. This is the pattern throughout the subject" (p. 33).

There is an obvious Kantian rejoinder to Nagel's observation, and this would be simply to insist that our practices of moral judgment are mistaken in many cases—that they are not phenomena that need to be accounted for by a theory, but simply errors in reasoning consistently. But such a reply would cut off philosophical discussion prematurely. In fact, Kant himself acknowledged many instances and examples of moral luck and did not take them to be ultimately devastating to his moral theory, or to his account of moral judgment. In what follows, I will argue that Kant's account of moral luck is capable of much more subtlety than is often acknowledged by examining each of the four subspecies of moral luck that Nagel identifies in his essay and considering the potential Kantian reply to each.

Constitutive Luck

Let us begin with what Nagel calls "constitutive luck"—this consists, he explains, of "the kind of person you are, where this is not just a question of what you deliberately do, but of your inclinations, capacities, and temperament" (1979: 28). We often make moral judgments involving the "inclinations, capacities, and temperament" of others (either directly or indirectly), even when these things are not ostensibly under the other person's control. Here, Nagel identifies clear Kantian resistance:

> Kant was particularly insistent on the moral irrelevance of qualities of temperament and personality that are not under the control of the will. Such qualities as sympathy or coldness might provide the background against which obedience to moral requirements is more or less difficult, but they could not be objects of moral assessment themselves, and might well interfere with confident assessment of its proper object—the determination of the will by the motive of duty.
>
> p. 32

Nagel points in particular to the first section of Kant's *Groundwork for the Metaphysics of Morals* for examples of Kant's resistance to constitutive luck's playing a role in our assessment of others. Two moments in that section stand out in particular in this regard. The first is Kant's opening assertion that the only thing good without qualification is a good will: "It is impossible to think of anything at all in the world, or indeed even beyond it, that could be taken to be good without limitation, except a good will" (*GMS* 4:393). Nagel appears to identify this assertion as an implicit statement about *all* forms of moral luck: the only appropriate object of moral judgment is an agent's will. To introduce any other consideration into one's judgment would be to lose sight of the locus of goodness in Kant's theory.

Kant's statement regarding the unique and unconditional goodness of the good will is certainly memorable, but it is important to keep in mind its argumentative context and aim. The passage adopts the structure of an argument that would have been familiar to readers versed in ancient philosophy— it identifies an ultimate good as an initial and general statement of the moral theory to be presented in the following pages. But, of course Kant only adopts the structure of the classical argument, since his is not a theory grounded in the pursuit of some good object, but rather in the form and content of willing. Kant, in other words, uses the structure of an argument familiar to teleological moral theories to introduce a non-teleological theory. Seen in this light, however, the "good will" passage is almost useless as a statement of Kant's views about moral judgment and moral luck. To see that this is the case, we can simply imagine that Kant had adopted a teleological view after all—perhaps identifying happiness as the ultimate good. Even a complete reversal on this score would tell us nothing about Kant's views regarding moral *judgment*. This is because questions regarding the foundation of a moral theory are largely separable from questions regarding practices of moral imputation on that theory. To be sure, Kant's assertion that only the good will is good without limitation suggests that *if* we were to make judgments about an agent's moral worth, we would have to do so on the basis of the content of her will. But nowhere in the "good will" passage does Kant suggest that moral agents ought to make it their business to engage in such judgment. Kant's emphasis on the agent's will can sometimes encourage an almost imperceptible slide from his account of the basis of morality to an account of judgment and imputation, but it is a slide nonetheless. And, as I will argue in what follows, Kant recommends a great deal of caution when it comes to judging others.

The first section of the *Groundwork* contains another passage that seems on its face to support Nagel's conclusion that Kantian judgment is resistant to constitutive luck and concerned only with the content of a person's will. This is Kant's discussion of moral motivation, in which he argues that only an action motivated by duty has moral worth (*GMS* 4:397–399). In that discussion, Kant considers four distinct action types—(1) actions contrary to duty; (2) actions in accord with duty where an agent has no immediate motivation to act (as when the shopkeeper charges a fair price so that he might preserve his business's reputation); (3) actions in accord with duty where an agent does have a direct inclination to act (as in the case of the person who finds joy in helping others); and (4) actions done from duty. In order to make the distinction between the third and fourth types of action explicit, Kant asks us to consider our common sense intuitions about the case of the friend of humanity, who was previously moved to beneficence by the joy it brought him, if that joy and compassion for others were to disappear as motivations.

> Suppose, then, that the mind of that friend of humanity were beclouded by his own grief, which extinguishes all compassion for the fate of others; that he still had the means to benefit others in need, but the need of others did not touch him because he is sufficiently occupied with his own; and that now, as inclination no longer stimulates him to it, he were yet to tear himself out of this deadly insensibility, and to do the action without any inclination, solely from duty; not until then does it have its genuine moral worth. Still further: if nature had as such placed little sympathy in the heart of this or that man; if (otherwise honest) he were by temperament cold and indifferent to the sufferings of others, perhaps because he himself is equipped with the peculiar gift of patience and enduring strength towards his own, and presupposes, or even requires, the same in every other; if nature had not actually formed such a man (who would truly not be its worst product) to be a friend of humanity, would he not still find within himself a source from which to give himself a far higher worth than that of a good-natured temperament may be? Certainly! It is just there that the worth of character commences, which is moral and beyond all comparison the highest, namely that he be beneficent, not from inclination, but from duty.
>
> *GMS 4:398–399*

Kant was almost immediately criticized for seeming to require that agents act *contrary* to inclination—even if that inclination is unselfish—if their actions are to have any moral worth.[5] Debate on this subject is extensive and far beyond the scope of this essay, but it is important to note that Kant almost certainly constructed the example above as he does because it would be otherwise impossible to know that the "friend of humanity" was, in fact, acting out of duty. For Kant, moral motivation is *fundamentally obscure*, and this applies just as much to our own motivation as it does to others' motivations. Of course, if I violate the moral law, I can know that I was not acting out of duty. But when my action accords with what duty requires, especially when I also have an immediate inclination to do what duty requires, it is impossible to know what my motivation is. From this observation, we can draw one important conclusion about Kant's views on moral luck and moral judgment—whatever his account of imputation and judgment turns out to be, it will not be one that asks agents to guess at others' motives, since knowing these is impossible. As we will see in what follows, Kant does suggest that agents pursue a kind of self-scrutiny about their *own* motivations, but he recommends this scrutiny in the service of moral improvement, not, in the first instance, as a way to ascribe blame or praise to oneself.[6]

It is also important to understand the role of the preceding argument in the first section of the *Groundwork*. Kant's aim in that part of the book is to arrive at a statement of the supreme principle of morality *via* an analysis of several common sense propositions about duty. The discussion above belongs to his explication of the first of these common sense propositions—that only an action done from the motive of duty has non-contingent moral worth. A similar claim appears in the Preface to the *Groundwork*:

> For in the case of what is to be morally good it is not enough that it conform with the moral law, but it must also be done for its sake; if not, that conformity is only very contingent and precarious, because the immoral ground will indeed now and then produce actions that conform with the law, but in many cases actions that are contrary to it.
>
> *GMS 4:390*

Kant's assertion presages his discussion of autonomy later in the text: only an action motivated by recognition of a law that the agent gives to herself will have non-contingent moral worth.

The point of the argument concerning the "friend of humanity" is thus to explicate a thesis about the non-contingency of moral motivation as part of a broader investigation into our common sense notions of duty. If we lose sight of the context and aim of the passage, it is easy to come to the mistaken conclusion that the passage is giving advice about how to go about making judgments about other agents' moral worth. But this is far from Kant's aim. The discussion in the passage above is about the moral worth of *action*, not of *agents*; it is a theoretical point about the type of motivation that would be required to guarantee morally worthy action, not a "how-to guide" about making judgments regarding others.

Luck in One's Circumstances

We can now proceed to discuss Kant's stance toward a second type of moral luck, so-called "luck in one's circumstances." The puzzle here, as Nagel observes, is that "the things we are called upon to do, the moral tests we face, are importantly determined by factors beyond our control" (1979: 33). Nagel concludes that one is, as a result,

> morally at the mercy of fate, and it may seem irrational upon reflection, but our ordinary moral attitudes would be unrecognizable without it. We judge people for what they actually do or fail to do, not just for what they would have done if circumstances had been different.
>
> *p. 34*

Kant himself is not oblivious to this type of concern. It is a common refrain in Kant's texts that what appears to be virtue is often just a matter of having escaped temptation to vice. For example, in an early set of lectures, he observes that,

> if, for example, an innocent country girl is free from all ordinary vices, that is because she has no opportunity for indulging in excess, and a husbandman who makes do with plain fare, and yet is content with it, is not content because he sees it as all the same to him, but because he does not lead a better life, and if he were given the opportunity of living better, he would also covet it.
>
> *Collins,* Lectures on Ethics, *XXVII 249, from Kant 1997*

We applaud the innocent country girl and the frugal husbandman, but notice simultaneously that this praise is bound up with the circumstances that the country girl and husbandman find themselves in. The country girl has no opportunity for vice, and the husbandman is apparently unaware of the better life he might otherwise covet. When Kant points to examples like these, he seems to be offering a word of caution. Crucially, however, his is not a word of caution about mistakenly ascribing virtue to *others*. Rather, Kant's warnings tend to be about ascribing virtue too hastily to *oneself*, as when he warns against arrogance and self-conceit in one's good conduct, which, he thinks is "strictly speaking, only in their good fortune in having so far escaped temptations to public vice" (*TL* 6:460).

When Kant does worry about mistakenly ascribing virtue to other agents, it is not because he is concerned that a particular agent is undeserving, but rather because of the negative effects that ascribing virtue to certain types of examples can have on our conception of duty generally. In this regard, Kant is particularly concerned with a kind of enthusiasm or fanaticism (*Schwärmerei*) that can emerge when agents focus excessively on examples of heroic conduct instead of the representation of duty. The worry is especially apparent in Kant's various discussions of moral education, for example in the *Critique of Practical Reason*:

> I do wish that educators would spare their pupils examples of so-called noble (super-meritorious) actions, with which our sentimental writings so abound, and would expose

them all only to duty and to the worth that a human being can and must give himself in his own eyes by consciousness of not having transgressed it; for whatever runs up into empty wishes and longings for inaccessible perfection produces mere heroes of romance who, while they pride themselves on their feeling for extravagant greatness, release themselves in return from the observance of common and everyday obligation, which then seems to them insignificant and petty.

KpV 5:155

When pupils are exposed to examples of heroic and noble action, there is a tendency to idealize or romanticize the characters in these stories. The student's focus is taken away from the representation of duty and instead directed toward the heroic and seemingly unattainable virtue depicted in the story. But of course, that seemingly unattainable virtue is a product not just of circumstance, but indeed a product of *fictional* circumstance.

This is not to say that Kant has no room for example in his moral philosophy—far from it. But Kant is very specific about the type of example that ought to be used in service of moral education. Of particular usefulness are hypothetical examples that require the reader or pupil to imagine herself in the position of the agent in question. The most famous of these is probably the "gallows example" from the *Critique of Practical Reason* (*KpV* 5:30). Kant's purpose in that example is to demonstrate to the reader that she implicitly recognizes a sphere of value beyond the merely prudential: the reader, like the character in the example, would not pursue the object of her *inclination* if it meant certain death. But she realizes that she could risk her life for an action required by the *moral law*. Aside from these sorts of interactive, hypothetical examples, Kant also appeals to historical example—Anne Boleyn is a particular favorite in this regard (*KpV* 5:155–156). Here, Kant's purpose is typically to show that a moral action that seems very difficult actually has been done, and is therefore possible.

Let us summarize these observations as they relate to the issue of circumstantial luck. First, Kant clearly recognizes that the judgments we make of ourselves and others are often at least in part the result of the circumstances that we and others find ourselves in. Notably, however, Kant's concern appears primarily to be with falsely ascribing merit to *ourselves*, rather than with falsely ascribing merit to others. This tendency toward unwarranted self-congratulation has the further effect of undermining the actual representation of duty in the agent. Similarly undermining is the tendency to ascribe supermeritorious virtue to examples of heroic conduct that derive their force from romanticized depictions of virtue. In this regard, it is far better to appeal to examples in which the agent can imagine how she might respond if she were lucky (or unlucky) enough to be faced with some particular circumstance.

Luck in How Things Turn Out

Perhaps the most well-known instance of moral luck is what Nagel describes as "luck in how things turn out." Our practices of judgment seem to have at least in part to do with consequences of actions that are often merely a matter of luck. So, for example, the penalty for attempted murder is typically less severe than the penalty for murder, despite the fact that the intent to kill is in both cases identical (29). And, of course, philosophers often return to the tragic example of a truck driver who strikes a child with his vehicle. Nagel notes that,

> If the driver was guilty of even a minor degree of negligence—failing to have his brakes checked recently for example—then if that negligence contributes to the death of the child, he will not merely feel terrible. He will blame himself for the death. And what makes this an example of moral luck is that he would have to blame himself only slightly for the negligence itself if no situation arose which required him to brake suddenly and violently

to avoid hitting a child. Yet the negligence is the same in both cases, and the driver has no control over whether a child will run into his path.

p. 29

Again, Kant acknowledges the tendency to base one's judgment at least in part on how things turn out. In the essay *On the Common Saying: That May Be Correct in Theory, But It Is of No Use in Practice*, Kant observes that our tendency to judge rebellions and revolutions is generally swayed by their outcomes. "It is hardly to be doubted," he explains,

> that if those uprisings by which Switzerland or the United Netherlands or even Great Britain won its constitution, now considered so fortunate, had failed, those who ready the history of them would see in the execution of their now celebrated authors nothing but the deserved punishment of great political criminals.

TP 8:301

Unlike murder, then, attempted revolution seems to lead to a harsher judgment than successful revolution (compare Nagel 1979: 30).

The problem of "luck in how things turn out" brings us to a discussion of Kantian judgment and imputation that this essay has so far avoided. While it is the case that Kant tends to recommend a principle of charity in the case of others, and a principle of rigorous scrutiny in one's own case, he nevertheless provides a rich account of imputation in both the legal and ethical spheres. Attending to the details of this account will help resolve many remaining puzzles about how Kant can accommodate the phenomenon of moral luck.

To begin, we must first make an important distinction between Kantian imputation in the legal sphere, or the sphere of right, and imputation in the sphere of ethics. As Kant understands it, matters of right have to do with external relations among agents, specifically the ways in which their actions might interfere with the freedom of others. Kant accordingly proposes the following "Universal Principle of Right"—"Any action is *right* if it can coexist with everyone's freedom in accordance with a universal law, or if on its maxim the freedom of choice of each can coexist with everyone's freedom in accordance with a universal law" (*RL* 6:230). Because right is concerned with the external relations of agents, it is unconcerned with their motivations or the maxims on which they act. Instead, right is concerned only with externally coercible actions. But coercion is only legitimate when it serves as a hindrance to a hindrance of freedom, since, in that instance coercion actually promotes freedom (*RL* 6:231).

It is in light of this last point about the legitimate use of coercion that a Kantian account of civil punishment can begin to emerge. Kant is sometimes held up as an example of a strict retributivist when it comes to punishment. However, depending on one's interpretation of retributivism, this would appear to run afoul of Kant's requirement that matters of justice (and therefore punishment) only concern themselves with actions, and not maxims or intentions. To see this point, consider Nagel's puzzle about the different punishments for murder and attempted murder. A retributivist account of punishment that recommended a lesser punishment for merely attempted murder would seem to have to make reference to something unknowable, namely the maxims and degree of guilt of each of the agents. The same could be said for a retributivist account that punished both crimes equally—in that case it would seem to be assuming the maxims of both agents are the same and should thus be punished identically. Notice, too, that the principle of equal punishment risks infringing on the innate right to freedom of the unsuccessful murderer, since he could plausibly argue that he is being punished for an infringement of another's freedom that never occurred.

Fortunately, Kant's account of punishment admits of more subtlety than this, and in so doing, it also helps to account for why our legal practices of holding people accountable depend to some degree on how things turn out. Let us see how this might be the case. In an influential paper, Sharon Byrd argues that Kant has a theory of punishment that is *deterrent in its threat of punishment*, but *retributivist in its execution of punishment* (Byrd 1989). The institution of punishment—in particular the threat of punishment—exists to serve as a deterrent to wrongdoing. So far, this is certainly consistent with the "hindrance principle" discussed above. However, once a person has been convicted of a crime, punishment is carried out simply because the person was convicted of committing a crime that carried with it a particular sentence. The sentencing of a person, in other words, is not a matter of deterrence, except in the indirect sense that people come to expect that people are generally punished according to what the law prescribes. And this is as it should be, since to sentence a person *merely* so that his case might serve as a deterrent to others would be to violate his innate right to freedom.

Now we can return to the puzzle of moral luck in how things turn out. The two-stage account of Kantian punishment helps to explain why a person would be punished more severely for negligence that led to the death of another person. Since an agent's motives cannot figure in to our assessment of an action from the perspective of right and punishment, all we have to go on is the agent's actions and, in particular, an assessment of whether and to what extent those actions have interfered with the innate right to freedom of others. Clearly, negligence that results in serious injury and death interferes more seriously with the freedom of others than negligence that fortunately does not. Of course, this is certainly not to say that mere negligence does not interfere with the freedom of others at all—at the very least, it endangers the security of others and creates unnecessary risk. From the perspective of the Universal Principle of Right, then, one would have every reason to discourage negligence *via* deterrence. Thus, it makes sense to institute and threaten punishment that accords with threat to the freedom of others that negligence signifies. Notice, too, that this means that we can punish a person for negligence without infringing on her own innate right to freedom, since we can punish her for an *action* (or a failure to act), and not just a *potential harm*. Far from having nothing to say on the matter of luck in how things turn out, the Kantian account of punishment gives a coherent account of why luck matters from a legal perspective, as well as an account of punishment that accommodates the phenomenon without infringing on the innate right to freedom of agents.[7]

Let us now turn to the sphere of morality, where Kant has a surprisingly detailed account of moral judgment and imputation that accounts for many of the types of moral luck listed above. When it comes to tracking praise and blame, we can consult what Kant says about ascribing "merit" to particular actions. Crucially, Kant makes an important distinction between "objective" and "subjective" merit. Objective merit simply corresponds to whether the action was owed or not. According to Kant, an agent earns merit (illustrated with the notation "+a") for the fulfillment of imperfect duty. An agent who violates perfect duty is culpable, or earns demerit (−a). But an agent who abides by perfect duty and does not perform imperfect duty earns neither merit nor demerit, unless, as Kant observes "the subject should make it his principle not to comply" with imperfect duty (*MS* 6:390). Notice that Kant's overview of objective merit makes no reference to the *motivations* of an agent. It merely asks whether an agent has violated perfect duty or performed imperfect ("meritorious") actions.

However, Kant's account of objective merit is only half of the account of Kantian judgment. Fascinatingly, he also carves out space for so-called subjective merit.[8]

> Subjectively, the degree to which an action can be imputed (*imputabilitas*) has to be assessed by the magnitude of the obstacles that had to be overcome. – The greater the natural obstacles (of sensibility) and the less the moral obstacle (of duty), so much the more merit is to be accounted for a good deed, as when, for example, at considerable self-sacrifice I rescue a complete stranger from great distress.
>
> On the other hand, the less the natural obstacles and the greater the obstacle from grounds of duty, so much the more is a transgression to be imputed (as culpable). – Hence the state of mind of the subject, whether he committed the deed in a state of agitation or with cool deliberation makes a difference in imputation, which has results.
>
> *6:228*

Unlike objective merit, subjective merit admits of degrees and accommodates facts about the agent's character and circumstance. An agent deserves more subjective merit if she has overcome greater "natural" obstacles in performing duty. Analogously, an agent who transgresses duty for the sake of some small inclination is subjectively more culpable. Of course, our inclinations and the "natural obstacles" that agents are subject to are almost entirely a matter of luck. Nevertheless, they figure centrally into the Kantian ascription of subjective merit and culpability.

Kant also mentions the "moral obstacle" in this passage, and there is understandable confusion about what he means (see Blöser 2015). One clue, perhaps, is Kant's comparison in the passage above between the state of "agitation" and the state of "cool deliberation" in an agent. Perhaps Kant means to argue that an agent deserves more subjective merit if her performance of duty was seemingly effortless, or of it did not involve a great struggle between morality and self-interest but rather a calm, reasoned recognition of what duty requires. Note that if this is Kant's suggestion, it is the opposite of what many take Kant to be saying about moral judgment in the "friend of humanity" example discussed above. Note, too, that whether a person encounters the "moral obstacle" as a struggle or not could also be a function of luck—for example, facts about her upbringing, moral education, or temperament. Far from denying the influence of luck and circumstance, Kant's account of subjective merit strives to accommodate these.

But what about the results of actions—whether these are intended or not? Here, Kant argues that whether the effects of an action are imputed to an agent depends on the type of action that it was. If the action was owed, then neither the good nor bad results of the action ought to be imputed to the agent. So if I am honest with a person and this brings about some good results, or if I pay back a debt and this brings about some bad results, neither of those results can be imputed to me. Things are different if I violate perfect duty—in that case, any bad results of the action can be imputed to me. Thus Kant's claim that the servant who lies about his master's whereabouts shares guilt for the crimes that his master is able to commit as a result (*TL* 6:431). If I perform an action that goes beyond what is owed as a matter of strict duty (that is, an imperfect duty), then the good results of that action can be imputed to me (*RLVI* 228). Finally, the results of accidents appear not to be imputable—for example, if "in a scuffle … someone pierces another with a dagger, but strikes an abscess, by the lancing of which the other regains his health" (*VMS-Vigil* 27:561).[9]

Again, however, it is essential to note that Kant's theoretical analyses of merit and imputation are still not tantamount to a *recommendation* that we engage in regular judgment of other agents. Where Kant discusses the practice of judging others in our day-to-day lives, he recommends a principle of charity—it is a "duty of virtue not to take malicious pleasure in exposing the faults of others … but rather to throw a veil of philanthropy over their faults, not merely by softening our judgments but also by keeping these judgments to ourselves" (*MS* 6:466). Even in cases of resentment, forgiveness, and gratitude, where blame and imputation would seem to play an important role, Kant's advice is measured. It is, Kant explains, a duty of virtue to avoid seeking revenge out of hatred—indeed, one should not even hope that God will exact revenge on one's behalf. And forgiveness appears justified, for Kant, not because a wrongdoer has undergone a moral change or asked for forgiveness, but because each of us "has enough guilt of his own to be greatly in need of pardon" (*MS* 6:460–461). Questions of imputation are perhaps most pressing for Kant when it comes to determining to whom we owe a debt of gratitude. Kant regards gratitude as an unpayable debt and sacred obligation. Even so, the degree of gratitude that we owe includes facts about *subjective merit*, which is, as we have seen, responsive to luck: "The intensity of gratitude, that is, the degree of obligation to this virtue, is to be assessed by how useful the favor was to the one put under obligation and how unselfishly it was bestowed on him" (*MS* 6:456).

Luck in Determination by Antecedent Circumstances

For Nagel, all of the above observations about moral luck seem to condense into a final observation: "The area of genuine agency, and therefore of legitimate moral judgment, seems to shrink under this scrutiny to an extensionless point. Everything seems to result from the combined influence of factors, antecedent and posterior to action, that are not within the agent's control" (1979: 35). The implications of such a claim for Kant, with his account of an autonomous will not determined by nature, would seem to be devastating. When we start to notice the myriad ways in which action is influenced by factors internal and external to the agent, the possibility of genuinely free agency, and thus judgment, seems to vanish.

But this is too quick. To be sure, Kant does insist on the possibility of a free, autonomous will, and the notion of an elective will (*Willkür*) that can choose to take the moral law as its guiding principle is central to Kant's view. But Kant's position about human freedom is not so unsubtle that it cannot admit of effects on one's character or virtue—for example, moral education—that might make it more or less easy to comply with what one recognizes as duty. How Kant's account of moral development is consistent with his account of freedom is, to be sure, a serious puzzle from the point of view of his metaphysics. But in the context of our discussion, it suffices simply to note that Kant recognized the real influence of antecedent circumstances and did not, as a result, revise his view about moral judgment. And as we saw in the above discussion of merit, Kantian *subjective* merit is clearly susceptible to all manner of influence by antecedent circumstance—one's inclinations, one's upbringing, the development of one's character, and one's material ability to help others, for example. Here we can draw an important conclusion: Kant's account of *freedom* does not necessarily imply an account of moral judgment that is completely blind to empirical circumstance. Far from painting himself into a corner when it comes to freedom and moral judgment, Kant again appears to have a sophisticated account of both that presages and accommodates many contemporary concerns regarding moral luck.

A Final Problem of Moral Luck

The preceding discussion has, I hope, shown that Kant's moral philosophy has the resources to offer a compelling response to concerns about moral luck. Indeed, Kant is far from oblivious to the philosophical challenge posed by the phenomenon. Evidence of this fact can be found in numerous passages in which Kant highlights a particular instance of moral luck that he takes to be particularly insidious and problematic. For example, in the discussion of benevolence in the *Doctrine of Virtue*, he remarks:

> Having the resources to practice such beneficence as depends on the goods of fortune is, for the most part, a result of certain human beings being favored through injustices of the government, which introduces an inequality of wealth that makes others need their beneficence. Under such circumstances, does a rich man's help to the needy, on which he so readily prides himself as something meritorious, really deserve to be called beneficence at all?
>
> *MS* 6:454

The phenomenon Kant describes here, sometimes referred to as "general injustice" acknowledges moral luck, but with a particularly Kantian twist.[10] Some people are in a position to be beneficent, and others are in need, because of circumstances brought about by "injustices of the government." But notice that Kant's concern with problem of "general injustice" is not about the judgments that we make of others. Rather, his concern is with our tendency to congratulate *ourselves* too readily for acts of beneficence. Kant thinks, in other words, that if we examined our circumstances and their histories carefully, we would be more cautious about ascribing unwarranted merit to ourselves. This underscores a point raised earlier—Kant is less concerned that we get our judgments of others "right," and more concerned that we apply careful self-scrutiny to our own case.

Conclusion

Let us briefly summarize the main claims in this essay. First, Kant has a conception of happiness according to which happiness is both essential to the moral lives of rational, yet sensible, agents yet fundamentally contingent upon luck. This conjunction of observations might seem to suggest a tension in Kant's thought, but it is relaxed to some extent when we observe that the moral law serves as a kind of bulwark against the whims of fortune. The single-minded pursuit of happiness will almost certainly lead to a kind of misery that only a grounding in moral principles can help to avoid. Further, Kant thinks that virtue tends to bring about happiness over time, at least at the level of the moral community.

With respect to the Kantian stance on moral luck, we can summarize several crucial points. First, one should not presume that Kant's explication of the supreme principle of morality, or his description of moral worth and acting from duty amounts to an account of moral judgment and imputation. These are distinct philosophical questions and Kant clearly treats them as separate in his texts and lectures. Second, motivation is fundamentally obscure on Kant's view. For any action that is in accord with what duty requires, we can never know for certain what the motivation for that action was. This applies in our own case and in the case of others. In part because motivation is obscure in this way, Kant does not think it should be the business of moral agents to try to guess at others' motivation in an effort to make a judgment about the worth of their actions. Insofar as their action accords with duty, they deserve praise and encouragement. In our own case, a practice of self-scrutiny with regard to our true motives is in order. But this is not so that we can make the "correct" judgments about ourselves, but rather so that we can avoid unwarranted self-congratulation and moral decay.

Third, where Kant does discuss judgment and imputation, the account is much more complex than one might initially expect. In this context, it is essential to keep in mind the distinction between right and ethics. In the sphere of right, we do not need to know people's motives or backgrounds in order to impute actions to them or punish them, and a "mixed" account of Kantian punishment, according to which punishment is a deterrent in its threat but retributive in its execution, explains why matters of luck should make a difference in punishment. In the sphere of ethics, Kant allows for both "objective" and "subjective" merit. Objective merit tracks the question of whether a person has violated duty, or performed a meritorious action. "Subjective" merit tracks other variables—for example, how difficult the action was for the agent, and how much of a moral struggle the agent experienced. Such variables are, of course, often subject to luck, but this appears not to be a concern for Kant. If anything, his distinction between objective and subjective merit is a prescient way of dealing with many of the problems of what we now call moral luck.

Fourth, while it is true that Kant clearly and forcefully rejects a determinist account of human action, his account of moral development does allow for the influences of education and upbringing, for example. More to the point, however, his account of subject merit *accommodates* the influence of antecedent circumstance. Finally, the type of moral luck that Kant seems most concerned with—the phenomenon of "general injustice"—has more to do with the judgments we make about our *own* merit, rather than judgments we make about others.

Notes

1 See especially *KpV* 5:110–111. References to Kant's works are by title initials (from the German original) and volume and page numbers from the "Akademie" editions of Kant's works (Kant: 1900–). Translations are from the following sources: *Groundwork of the Metaphysics of Morals* (*GMS*), (Kant 2011); *On the Common Saying: That May Be Correct in Theory But Is of No Use in Practice* (*TP*), *Critique of Practical Reason* (*KpV*), *Doctrine of Right* (*RL*) and *Doctrine of Virtue* (*TL*) (Kant 1996). Collins lectures on ethics (*VMS-Collins*) and Vigilantius lectures on ethics (*VMS-Vigilantius*) (Kant 1997).

2 *Mrongovius II Lecture*, 29:637. Here Kant argues that happiness provides only "confirmatory grounds" and not "motivating grounds" for morality. For a helpful overview of these topics, see Denis 2005 and Guyer 2002.

3 *VMS-Vigilantius* 26:606, author's amended translation.

4 The fact that there is no individual guarantee is, of course, a sticking point for some interpreters. For debate on this issue, Reath 1988 and a reply in Pasternack 2017.

5 For example, by Schiller, who jokes that one should start despising one's friends in order to behave dutifully toward them (Schiller 1987: 299–300).

6 See, for example, the "first command of all duties to oneself" in the *Doctrine of Virtue*: "know (scrutinize, fathom) yourself, not in terms of your natural perfection ... but rather in terms of your moral perfection in relation to your duty" (*TL* 6:441).

7 The case of attempted murder is more complicated, since attempted murder involves an intent to kill that negligence does not. Still, to punish attempted murder and murder identically would be to punish the attempted murderer for a hindrance of freedom that (fortunately) did not occur. But since we have reason to deter all attempts at murder (even unsuccessful ones), we can and should institute a separate punishment for attempts that are (fortunately) unsuccessful.

8 For excellent and detailed discussions of how degrees of imputation can be consistent with Kant's account of agency, see Blöser 2015 and Johnson 1996.

9 See also Hartman 2017: 113n–114n.

10 For a longer discussion of the phenomenon, Moran 2017.

References

Blöser, C. (2015) "Degrees of Responsibility in Kant's Practical Philosophy," *Kantian Review* 20, 183–209.

Byrd, B. (1989) "Kant's Theory of Punishment: Deterrence in its Threat, Retribution in its Execution," *Law and Philosophy* 8, 151–200.

Denis, L. (2005) "Autonomy and the Highest Good," *Kantian Review* 10, 33–59.

Guyer, P. (2002) "Ends of Reason and Ends of Nature: The Place of Teleology in Kant's Ethics," *Journal of Value Inquiry* 36, 161–186.

Hartman, R.J. (2017) *In Defense of Moral Luck*, New York: Routledge.

Johnson, R. (1996) "Kant's Conception of Merit," *Pacific Philosophical Quarterly* 77, 310.

Kant, I. (1900–) *Kants gesammelte Schriften*, ed. Königliche Deutsche Akademie der Wissenschaften, Berlin: De Gruyter.

———. (1996) *Practical Philosophy*, ed. and trans. M. Gregor, Cambridge: Cambridge University Press.

———. (1997) *Lectures on Ethics*, trans. Peter Heath, Cambridge: Cambridge University Press.

———. (2011) *Groundwork of the Metaphysics of Morals*, trans. J. Timmermann & M. Gregor, Cambridge: Cambridge University Press.

———. (manuscript) Mrongovius Lectures on Ethics, trans. J. Timmermann.

Moran, K. (2017) "Neither Justice nor Charity? Kant on General Injustice," *Canadian Journal of Philosophy* 47, 477–498.

Nagel, T. (1979) "Moral Luck," in *Mortal Questions*, Cambridge: Cambridge University Press, pp. 24–38.

Pasternack, L. (2017) "Restoring Kant's Conception of the Highest Good," *Journal of the History of Philosophy* 55, 435–468.

Reath, A. (1988) "Two Conceptions of the Highest Good in Kant," *Journal of the History of Philosophy* 26, 593–619.

Schiller, F. (1987) *Werke*, Munich: Hanser.

6

ADAM SMITH ON MORAL LUCK AND THE INVISIBLE HAND

Craig Smith

Such is the effect of the good or bad consequences of actions upon the sentiments both of the person who performs them, and of others; and thus, Fortune, which governs the world, has some influence where we should be least willing to allow her any, and directs in some measure the sentiments of mankind, with regard to the character and conduct both of themselves and others. That the world judges by the event, and not by the design, has been in all ages the complaint, and is the great discouragement of virtue

Smith 1976a: 104–105

The recent revival of interest in Adam Smith's moral philosophy has encouraged a series of papers on what Smith has to say about the pressing issues of contemporary moral and political philosophy. There has been a lively debate on Smith's conception of justice (Sen 2009; Verburg 2000; Witzum and Young 2006), liberty (Fleischacker 2003; Rasmussen 2008), and the virtues (Griswold 1999; Otteson 2002; Hanley 2009). One such set of discussions has arisen in connection to Smith's comments on the place of luck in moral judgment. Smith's discussion in Part II Section III of *The Theory of Moral Sentiments* (*TMS*), entitled "Of the Influence of Fortune upon the sentiments of Mankind, with regard to the Merit or Demerit of Actions," has been read as an episode in the history of philosophy which prefigures the concerns that arose in the classic articles by Williams (1981) and Nagel (1979).[1] Most of the contributions to this literature on Smith and luck seek to determine whether Smith in fact recognized something like the modern problem of moral luck, whether he saw it as a problem for moral philosophy, and the extent to which he offered a solution to the problem.[2] But for the purposes of this chapter I want to engage in a slightly different exercise. I want to place Smith's discussion of luck in the context of his wider system of thought and understand it as a product of his particular methodological approach to doing philosophy.

I will begin by making three initial observations that lay the ground for Smith's discussion of luck. The first of these is a comment on Smith's methodology in *TMS*. My reading of Smith is that he is primarily an analyst of the moral sentiments. This commits him to a number of basic positions. First, he is a naturalist about the moral emotions; second, he regards his project as the observational study of the operation of moral judgment; and third, he hopes to provide a systematic account of the actual lived experience of morality. Taken together these lead Smith to an approach that accepts that a successful account of moral experience will be one that succeeds in accommodating all of the elements that we observe are, in fact, part of that experience. Smith's account of the nature of philosophy in his *History of Astronomy*, underlines the fact that its main function is to provide a coherent account of observed experience in a fashion that calms the mind and settles emotional uncertainty (Smith 1980: 41–42, 45–46). For Smith philosophy works by joining together observed phenomena in a systematic fashion.

As a result, what we find in *TMS* is an attempt to discuss the major conceptual building blocks of moral life—the passions, reason, rules, utility, the virtues, justice, benevolence, self-interest, propriety, conscience, and so forth—as features that have to be understood and placed in their proper relation to each other. To this end, Smith's discussion of luck is embedded in a systematic account of how actual elements of moral judgment are related to each other.

The second observation arises from Smith's approach. He is writing in response to what he perceived as the failings of previous moral philosophy. In particular he is responding to Bernard Mandeville (1988). Smith's criticism of Mandeville's system is posited on the idea that he fails adequately to explain moral experience. The first sentence of Smith's book is a rebuke to Mandeville for failing to provide a satisfactory descriptive account of the place of benevolence in human life. Mandeville is an exemplar of a philosophical vice, the desire to provide an account of moral judgment that focusses on reducing it to one favored principle. In Mandeville's case this is self-interest; in the case of Smith's teacher Francis Hutcheson's system, developed in reaction to Mandeville, it is benevolence; in the case of Smith's friend David Hume it is utility. For Smith this is a fundamental error of method. Smith, as Hanley and Garrett (2015) argue, is better understood as a modern eclectic. He accepts the observed reality of different elements of moral experience and then attempts to build a system that places them in their proper relation. This is important for our present discussion as much of the animus behind the modern discussion of moral luck is drawn from the central place of the responsible will, by way of the so-called Control Principle, that has formed an important part of post-Kantian moral philosophy. As we will see below, the fact that Smith recognizes something like the Control Principle, which he calls the "equitable maxim" (Smith 1976a: 105), does not commit him to a position that views it as definitive of moral judgment. The reason for this is because it is simply one among many other aspects of moral experience that must be accounted for if the observational basis of Smith's account is to be successful.

Third, as I have argued elsewhere (Smith 2006), Adam Smith, like many of his fellow members of the Scottish Enlightenment, has a pervasive interest in unintended consequences. Smith's contribution to social theory, and in particular the oft-abused metaphor of the invisible hand, is shot through with explorations of social phenomena as the unintended outcomes of social interaction. The significance of this for our present discussion is that Smith develops a deep fascination with the implications of this for moral judgment. Mandeville's notoriety as an enemy of good morals stemmed chiefly from his satirical observation of the unintended social benefits of vice. But even if, as Smith believed, Mandeville was wrong to reduce all behavior to vice, the results of unintended consequences analysis decouple motivation and outcome in a way that appears to limit the usefulness of important moral concepts such as the Control Principle.

We can best see this if we look at some of Smith's classic statements of the approach in *TMS* and the *Wealth of Nations*:

> They [the rich] consume little more than the poor, and in spite of their natural selfishness and rapacity, though they mean only their own conveniency, though the sole end which they propose from the labours of all the thousands whom they employ, be the gratification of their own vain and insatiable desires, they divide with the poor the produce of all their improvements. They are led by an invisible hand to make nearly the same distribution of the necessaries of life, which would have been made, had the earth been divided into equal portions among all of its inhabitants, and thus without intending it, without knowing it, advance the interest of the society, and afford the multiplication of the species.
>
> *1976: 184–185*

> By preferring the support of domestick to that of foreign industry, he intends only his own security; and by directing that industry in such a manner as its produce may be of the greatest value, he intends only his own gain, and he is in this, as in many other cases, led by an invisible hand to promote an end which was no part of his intention. Nor is it always the worse for the society that it was no part of it. By pursuing his own interest he frequently promotes that of the society more effectually than when he really intends to promote it. I have never known much good done by those who affected to trade for the publick good.
>
> *1976b: 456*

In both of these passages the invisible hand is the mechanism by which a socially benign outcome is generated from the self-regarding actions of individuals. It is important to note what Smith is not claiming here. He is not claiming that all actions of economic self-interest will generate beneficial results, nor is he claiming that the results are ensured by the supernatural intervention of a Deity. Instead he provides an explanation of why, in cases like those stated, the intentions of the actors produce a meta-level order that can be assessed, by a favored normative criterion, as beneficial.

The problem that arises for moral philosophy is what to say about actions that might, by traditional accounts, have been criticized (selfishness) or applauded (trading for the public good) but which, in fact, issue in outcomes that by some important normative measure appear counter-intuitive. This, I will argue here, is the proper context in which to read Smith's interest in luck. Smith is interested in the relationship between different elements of our moral thinking, and in particular has to spend time discussing fortune, responsibility and judgments of merit precisely because he is aware that there is often a complete disconnection between the way philosophers talk about them and the way we actually think about them.

Smith on Luck

Smith's discussion of the influence of fortune on assessments of merit and demerit immediately follows a discussion of justice and beneficence where Smith criticizes Hume's account of justice grounded in utility and Hutcheson's account which grounds it in benevolence. Neither of their views satisfactorily accounts for the phenomenon, which Smith traces to sympathetic indignation and resentment. The chapter ends with a discussion of the "centinel" example (1976a: 90–91) where Smith addresses a situation where social utility dictates the punishment of a guard who falls asleep, but natural sentiments of justice do not reach the same conclusion. In such cases, Smith argues, it is difficult for us to act firmly as we feel the tension between these moral principles. We are torn, but ultimately we sacrifice justice to utility. But in so doing we find consolation in the belief that the person who suffers as a result will not be punished by "The justice of God" (Smith 1976a: 91) in heaven: justice, we believe, will be served in the long-run.[3] As we discussed above Smith is attempting to account for elements of moral experience, and, to the extent that this is a genuine and widespread experience, he needs to trace its origin in our sentiments and explain its relation to other elements of moral experience.

Before we begin we need to be clear what Smith believes is influenced by fortune: it is the sentiments. Our judgments of merit and demerit are sentimental, and we feel the impact of them on assessments of other people. My reason for stressing this is to point out that Smith frames his discussion in terms of a contrast between a generalized principle that we can only fairly be held responsible for intended actions and a lived reality where our judgments of others do not, in fact, work like this.[4] The point at issue is an irregularity, but we should not, from that, see Smith as worried by the fact that we do not honor the generalized abstract principle in everyday life—in practice we almost never do that in Smith's theory.

In Part II Section III Smith divides the object of praise or blame into three factors: intention, external action, and consequences. He then points out that neither of the latter two can be the foundation of merit, as the same external movement can issue in blameable and innocent actions—his example is a pull of a trigger that shoots a bird and one that shoots a man. The consequences also cannot be relied upon as they are too dependent on "fortune" (Smith 1976a: 93). This leads him to the view that reason dictates that only intended actions can be the subject of praise or blame.

At this point Smith introduces the impact on this of unintended consequences:

> Everybody allows, that how different soever the accidental, the unintended and unforeseen consequences of different actions, yet, if the intentions or affections from which they arose were, on the one hand, equally proper and equally beneficent, or, on the other, equally improper and equally malevolent, the merit or demerit of the actions is still the same, and the agent is equally the suitable object either of gratitude or of resentment.
>
> *Smith 1976a: 93*

But, as Smith points out, while this is accepted in the abstract as how we ought to approach the issue, we find that when we come to "particular cases" (Smith 1976a: 93) it is not the case and: "actual consequences" "almost always either enhance or diminish our sense" of merit or demerit (Smith 1976a: 93). This is an empirical observation for Smith and so his theory must account for it. In the rest of the section he sets out to explain it—by which he means identify what causes it, the extent of its influence, and its "purpose" (Smith 1976a: 93). The irregularity is "real" so the question is not whether it should be there—it is what it is—the question is rather where does it come from, what function does it fulfil, and how is it connected to other aspects of experience?

The Irregularity

The cause of this "irregularity" of the sentiments lies in the act of attributing responsibility. Drawing on the discussion of resentment in the previous chapter Smith argues that even in cases where intention is absent there is a "shadow" (Smith 1976a: 97) of merit or demerit. It is this shadow that accounts for the impact of fortune, and this becomes pertinent as "the consequences of actions are altogether under the empire of Fortune" (Smith 1976a: 97).

Smith's initial foray into the operation of the influence of fortune is to observe that its impact on judgment is to diminish the level of merit/demerit we accord to intended but unsuccessful actions, while equally increasing the merit/demerit of unintended actions that accidentally generate "extra-ordinary pleasure or pain" (Smith 1976a: 97).[5]

Moreover the "irregularity of sentiment"[6] is felt not only by those affected but also by those observing and even by the impartial spectator, Smith's internalized voice of conscience. We admire unsuccessful attempts to help others, but we admire them less than successful attempts. Similarly when it comes to blame we are capable of distinguishing between degrees of disapproval dependent on whether an action actually takes place. There is a real usefulness in this for Smith that becomes apparent in jurisprudence where the punishment for crimes committed is harsher than that for frustrated crimes even though the intention is the same.

This notion of apparently undeserved judgments of merit/demerit leads Smith into what is the heart of his discussion of luck—a discussion of the civil law notions of negligence and responsibility. His interest in this is based on the idea that legal thinking has long recognized that a person can be held responsible for the unintended outcome of his actions. Smith works his way through four notions of negligence and shows how the law treats each case.[7]

> When the negligence of one man has occasioned some unintended damage to another, we generally enter so far into the resentment of the sufferer, as to approve of his inflicting a punishment upon the offender much beyond what the offence would have appeared to deserve, had no such unlucky consequence followed from it.
>
> *Smith 1976a: 102*

Smith's example of a case of gross negligence, a man throwing a stone over a wall into the street, is designed to illustrate that the desire for retribution is in part driven by a desire to make others aware of their transgressions against other individuals. It is because such a person "wantonly exposes his neighbour to what no man in his senses would chuse to expose himself" (Smith 1976a: 102), that we resent him and hold him responsible to a degree that demands punishment. But there are lesser degrees of negligence. Carelessness leading to the injury of others raises our resentment, but not to the extent to warrant punishment. Instead such situations invite censure and the demand for compensation. The third type of negligence is "want of the most anxious timidity and circumspection" in considering all "possible consequences of our actions" (Smith 1976a: 104)—this is actually seen by Smith as blameable as it is debilitating for action. The fact that society assigns blame can lead to a neurotic fear of the slightest thing going awry, but excessive caution can go too far as people punish themselves and often avoid acting for fear of invoking criticism for negligence. Garrett (2005: 174–176) suggests that the Equitable Maxim with its focus on intention acts to prevent this sort of guilt becoming neurotic. A well-adjusted individual with a sense of proportion will be able to withstand this excessive fear of negligence and discern due diligence from over vigilance.

We see something similar with Smith's final sense of negligence. The "piacular" is a sense of shame from violation that Smith links to the ancient notions of impurity or the "fallacious sense of guilt" (Smith 1976a: 107) felt by the heroes of ancient tragedy. He wants to suggest that the piacular is not really a feeling of guilt, it applies in cases where there was no negligence, but where we nonetheless feel compelled to make some attempt to atone for the situation in which the sufferer finds themselves. This feeling is real in Smith's view and so must, again, be fitted into his account. He points out that it is involved in securing the same purpose as the other senses of responsibility: "by the wisdom of Nature, the happiness of every innocent man is, in the same manner, rendered holy, consecrated, and hedged round against the approach of every other man; not to be wantonly trod upon" (Smith 1976a: 107). The piacular appears to be something that weighs on the mind, and which must be borne with magnanimity.

Unlike Hankins who views the piacular as "remorse" (Hankins 2016:736) that prompts a desire to "apologise" (Hankins 2016: 711), or Flanders who views it as a version of Williams's "agent-regret" (Flanders 2006: 212), Eric Schliesser regards the piacular as a form of shame that forms a part of Smith's rejection of the selfish system of Mandeville (Schliesser 2017: 128). Piacular feelings motivate a desire to atone for an event for which we bear causal, but not intentional, responsibility. Schliesser points out that Smith links this to superstition and religious phenomena. What is particularly interesting about this is that the passage is expanded in the final edition of *TMS*. This is interesting when we consider that, as we noted above (Note 4), Smith removed a more explicitly orthodox religious passage on atonement at the end of the previous Section (II.II) of *TMS* in the same alterations. The passage on divine justice after the Centinel example was removed and replaced with a sentence noting that all religions have a notion of heaven and hell which corresponds to reward and punishment. The discussion of fortune and, in particular, the piacular refer to situations where we hold ourselves to account for things outside our control. Smith provides us with naturalized accounts of how these feelings arise and how they might be taken to extremes. The framing of these two sections, in effect, sets the scene for Smith's solution to the problem in the next Part where he discusses self-judgment and conscience.[8]

The "Purpose" of the Irregularity

Having demonstrated that the irregularity is real and has important implications for issues of responsibility, Smith now moves to his explanation of the purpose of the irregularity. "If the hurtfulness of the design, if the malevolence of the affection, were alone the causes which excited our resentment" then we would be resentful of anyone we suspected of ill intent.

> Sentiments, thoughts, intentions, would become the objects of punishment; and if the indignation of mankind run as high against them as against actions; if the baseness of the thought which had given birth to no action, seemed in the eyes of the world as much to call aloud for vengeance as the baseness of the action, every court of judicature would become a real inquisition.
>
> *Smith 1976a: 105*

Human jurisprudence limits itself to the actions that embody intent instead of seeking to punish the affections of the heart that we view as the actual source of disapproval. Judgment of sentiments is left to "the great Judge of hearts beyond the limits of every human jurisdiction" (Smith 1976a: 105). Smith dresses up this discussion by referring to God, Nature, Providence, and so forth. But we should be careful to realize what role is being played by God in the explanation here. Smith has shown us that the irregularity is real, he has described to us what effect it has, and he has shown how that effect can be beneficial. As with the two examples of the invisible hand that we discussed above, each of these explanations is fully naturalistic and so mention of providential design here does not invoke an active role for the Deity. The utility of the irregularity comes from the fact that it prompts us to moral action in order to realize the sentiments: "He must not be satisfied with indolent benevolence, nor fancy himself the friend of mankind, because in his heart he wishes well to the prosperity of the word" (Smith 1976a: 106). So, although we recognize on an abstract level that it is intent that matters, we are not in a position to be able to read intent in many cases of everyday judgment. This is why, for Smith, we have developed the ideas of degrees of negligence to which we apply differential legal, social, and internal sanctions. It is also why rewarding "latent virtue" is silly and punishing affections is "tyranny" (Smith 1976a: 106). Instead the irregularity teaches us a more general lesson. The lesson is that we ought to pay attention to our fellows and include their happiness in our calculations to the extent that we are capable, while avoiding the lack of proportion that can arise from the neurotic application of Smith's third form of negligence and the mania that can arise from the piacular. In many respects that is the project of Part III where Smith explains how the operation of the impartial spectator provides an internalized court which can judge our own behavior and confirm to us that we have acted with propriety even when actual spectators disapprove of us.

A Sense of Proportion

One of the running themes of *TMS* is the different ways in which humans are related to each other and interested in each other. The book starts with a clear attack on Mandeville's selfish system, but Smith's analysis does not depend on providing us with a single account of sociability. Instead there are a series of distinct elements of human sociability. The piacular, as Schliesser observes, is one of these, but it is also one that can be driven to excess. This is interesting because Smith's entire account is concerned with the smooth operation of the mind. His worries about "excessive" or "extreme" sympathy (Smith 1976a: 30, 140) lead him to favor a "moderated sensibility" to others (Smith 1976a: 143). We see a similar concern appear at several other key points in Smith's analysis, in particular it is one of the main themes in the discussion of conscience and duty. For example, when he discusses the famous Chinese earthquake (Smith 1976a: 136) example he is engaged in making more than one point. The main point is that our horrified reaction to the man who would prefer his finger to the lives of millions is evidence of the reality of the moral sentiments and their other-regarding nature. But he also provides us with a narrative of the individual thought process involved here. Smith's argument is that it is the voice of conscience that prevents our passive obsession with our own interests from becoming active. A well-adjusted person will not sacrifice the interests of others to achieve a trifle of his own, but he will also be able to express moral concern for the suffering of remote others without becoming debilitated by it. "Splenetic" philosophers (Smith 1976a: 127) or "whining" moralists (Smith 1976a: 139) who question how anyone can be happy while misery exists in the world are, in Smith's view, making a mistake. Their mistake is that their morality, however consistent, is not a morality for the imperfect and limited human being.

Here, too, Smith attributes this to nature and he discusses it in terms of, as Fonna Forman-Barzilai (2010) would have it, the circles of sympathy that embed individuals in a series of concentric sentimental relations that connect the appropriate degree of concern with the relevant level of proximity. It is a point he returns to in his discussion of justice and benevolence in Part VII. Perfect justice and universal benevolence are not within humanity's grasp. The "oeconomy of nature" (Smith 1976a: 77) directs us to the range of activity where we can make a meaningful difference to others.

We have already seen how Smith takes on the jurisprudential analysis of negligence to provide us with layers of warranted responsibility, and he does something very similar with the three senses of justice that he recognizes as existing in most languages: Commutative justice which underwrites jurisprudence, is justified by a high degree of resentment that warrants coercive punishment; distributive justice which is "proper beneficence" (Smith 1976a: 269); and a third platonic sense of justice which he associates with perfect propriety.[9] Each type of justice is carefully separated out, its individual thought process, mode of judgment, and scope of application analyzed, and then the whole connected together in a systematic fashion. But as our discussion so far has suggested, Smith also analyzes a fourth sense of justice that we might call heavenly justice.

The Invisible Hand

We can turn now to how all of this relates to the invisible hand. Thus far we have been discussing situations where an individual has in some sense brought about an outcome in relation to a concrete and contiguous other without intending that outcome. These interpersonal unintended consequences are real and Smith deploys a series of strategies to address them which he draws largely from the civil law tradition on justice, culpability, and blame attached to a sentimental moral psychology grounded in resentment and authorized by the impartial spectator. But the paradigm cases of the invisible hand do not provide so obvious a causal chain. In both of these cases we can see the beneficial social outcomes that arise from individual behavior, but, as Smith points out in the *Wealth of Nations'* discussion of the ordinary laborer's woollen coat (1976b: 22–23), thousands of intentional acts come together to produce a pattern that cannot meaningfully be understood as the responsibility of any one individual. In these particular examples the actions take place within the system of commutative justice and should, for reasons Smith explains, generate beneficial social outcomes. But these outcomes appear to come into conflict with our judgments of the intentional behavior of the actors involved.

As we have noted above, Smith is quite sanguine in accepting the reality of apparent contradictions between elements of our moral judgment. This, then, appears to be another such situation. The tricky question is whether the urge to judge an individual can lead us to believe that we can judge an entire causal chain. The idea that any one of us can be held responsible for the outcome of impersonal complex social interactions is difficult to pin down. We might hope that we can in some meaningful sense anthropomorphize the totality of agents involved and attribute responsibility to "society." But this would still involve a detachment of the judgment of the intention of the individuals who form that totality from the outcomes produced by that totality. To do so would be to attempt to extend judgment not only to unintentional actions that affect specific others, but to unintentionally generated outcomes affecting people unknown to us as well. Smith's discussion of fortune, negligence, and justice suggest he would be resistant to these arguments. This is mainly because he has other, more plausible, accounts of the moral sentiments of benevolence, humanity, generosity, and most importantly conscience, that are better able to account for the level of responsibility, to indicate the appropriate degree of concern, and to motivate morally correct action in situations like this.[10]

Even here, though, we are faced with situations where good or ill fortune might be experienced beyond the control of the individual and with no apparent other agent responsible. It is here that Smith's notion of heavenly justice comes into its own. Smith has explained to us where this desire comes from: the hope is that outcomes impacted by fortune will be corrected when we come before the ultimate judge. We want things to be different, but it is fortune that gets in the way. This leads us to seek to match outcomes to our preferred judgment of what they ought to be:

> [H]e is by no means able to render the fortune of either quite suitable to his own sentiments and wishes. The natural course of things cannot be entirely controlled by the impotent endeavours of man: the current is too rapid and too strong for him to stop it; and though the rules which direct it appear to have been established for the wisest and best purposes, they sometimes produce effects which shock all his natural sentiments.
>
> *Smith 1976a: 168*

A perfect match between our assessments of moral deservingness and outcomes is unattainable by human beings. But the belief that such a thing might be possible is part of our psychological coping mechanism. It is one of the ways in which our minds calm themselves and reconcile us to our fate. Or as Smith would have it:

> That there is a world to come, where exact justice will be done to every man, where every man will be ranked with those who, in the moral and intellectual qualities, are really his equals [is] so comfortable to the weakness, so flattering to the grandeur of human nature, that the virtuous man who has the misfortune to doubt of it, cannot possibly avoid wishing most earnestly and anxiously to believe it.
>
> *Smith 1976a: 132*

For Smith, the notion that humanity will ever be able to provide the perfect response to every incidence of fortune is for the next life. His theory accepts that elements of our moral experience will come into conflict, that we will have to live with the fact that fortune intervenes, or that centinels must be punished, and what Smith's theory provides us with is a naturalistic account of the emergence of various parts of our moral psychology that assist us in dealing with this fact. If fortune is ineliminable from human life, then what is left for the moral philosopher is the task of understanding how we come to cope with that fact about the human condition. In this sense the way to understand the place of luck in Smith's thought is to see that it slots into the discussion of the various degrees of responsibility, judgment, and justice that are governed by the approval of the impartial spectator in this life and the hope for heavenly justice in the next.

Notes

1 As both Russell (1999: 37) and Flanders (2006: 193) observe, Smith is only really concerned with consequential luck rather than any of the other modern formulations. See also the discussions in Timmermann (2002) and Garrett (2005).

2 As noted above, there is a developing critical discussion of this aspect of Smith's thought. It is worth framing our discussion of them with a reminder of the position that we have developed thus far. The point of Smith's discussion is an attempt to understand a real, observable, feature of moral experience. This is worth restating because both Chad Flanders and Paul Russell address at least part of their arguments to the weakness of Smith's "justification" (Flanders 2006: 193) or "rationalization" (Russell 1999: 46). They then offer alternative defences of Smith's view constructed from the basis of his approach. In Flanders' case the issue is epistemic— we cannot be certain of intentions, indeed intentions might not even exist in any meaningful sense, until we are about to act (2006: 202). This provides us with a useful limiting role for the irregularity. In the case of Keith Hankins (2016: 742) the utility argument provided by Smith fails, but the deeper point about the contribution that the irregular sentiments make to ease social life more than makes up for this.

   Paul Russell was the first to address the issue in a critical engagement that stressed the apparent weakness of Smith's naturalistic and utilitarian arguments. Put simply, he argues that Smith does not show that the passions are natural as he admits that they can be controlled by reflection or changed as society becomes civilized; while the utility argument fails as Smith does not consider that the disutility of the irregular sentiments might outweigh their utility, and that it is not clear that the irregular sentiments are required to generate interest in the good of others. As a result he thinks that Smith was not convinced by his own "rationalization" Russell (1999: 46). Perhaps the most obvious problem with these arguments is that they run against the position that Russell adopts in the second half of the paper where he comes to contrast Smith's discussion with the Kant-inspired discussion of Nagel (Hankins 2016: 743) and makes a similar point suggesting that the baleful influence of Kant has led to an unnecessary focus on the good Will that is simply absent from Smith's thinking. Here Russell argues that the Equitable Maxim of Smith is not the Control Principle of Nagel and that, as a result, Smith is freed from some of the intellectual baggage that Nagel brings along with him. Russell acknowledges that Smith sees no real problem in the existence of a divergence between our "reflective sense of justice" and our "moral feelings" (Russell 1999: 51, 53), because he does not envisage our moral feelings being fully subject to reason.

This is because, as Hankins clearly sees (Hankins 2016:741), Smith was suspicious of the idea of a single objective morality. The constant stream of Smith's argument is to suggest that if such a thing does exist then imperfect humans cannot have access to it. It is for God's justice. What we can have access to through observation, is a better idea of how we do, in fact, make moral judgments. For Hankins, the true utility of Smith's account is how the irregular sentiments contribute to making us social (Hankins 2016: 739). Flanders makes a similar point, but rests his argument on the epistemic issue (Flanders 2006: 201).

3 It is also interesting to note that in the final edition of *TMS* Smith removes a paragraph discussing the naturalistic origin of our desire to seek God's mercy.

4 What has come, in the secondary literature, to be known as the "equitable maxim" and the "irregularity of sentiments."

5 NB: this locution is used throughout the chapter, Smith says the discussion only applies to the "extraordinary."

6 For discussions of Smith on irregularity of sentiment see Griswold (1999: 240–243).

7 Smith's *Lectures on Jurisprudence* (1978) include a number of similar discussions.

8 This reading is supported by Flanders' (2006: 209) observation that the piacular seems to fall somewhere between justice and benevolence in its intensity and capacity to interest us in others. Taken too far it becomes an "irrational" guilt that is a psychological fact that we have to live with (Flanders 2006: 212). A point that Schliesser (2017: 129) also notes when he observes that the worst cases of the piacular can pose a threat to mental health—as indeed in the tragic figures of ancient drama they did.

9 For a discussion of this see Smith (2014).

10 Smith could perhaps turn to the notion of providence, but as we saw at the start, the references to providence in the Invisible Hand passages are not active—Smith explains why in each case the intentions transform into the outcomes without the need for providential intervention.

References

Flanders, C. (2006) "Adam Smith on Moral Luck," in L. Montes & E. Schliesser (eds.) *New Voices on Adam Smith*, New York: Routledge, pp. 193–218.

Fleischacker, S. (2003) *On Adam Smith's Wealth of Nations: A Philosophical Companion*, Princeton, NJ: Princeton University Press.

Forman-Barzilai, F. (2010) *Adam Smith and the Circles of Sympathy: Cosmopolitanism and Moral Theory*, Cambridge: Cambridge University Press.

Garrett, A. (2005) "Adam Smith on Moral Luck," in C. Fricke (ed.) *Adam Smith als Moralphilosoph*, Berlin: De Gruyter, pp. 160–177.

Griswold, C. (1999) *Adam Smith and the Virtues of Enlightenment*, Cambridge: Cambridge University Press.

Hankins, K. (2016) "Adam Smith's Intriguing Solution to the Problem of Moral Luck," *Ethics* 126, 711–746.

Hanley, R.P. (2009) *Adam Smith and the Character of Virtue*, Cambridge: Cambridge University Press.

Hanley, R.P., & Garrett, A. (2015) "Adam Smith," in J.A. Harris & A. Garret (eds.) *Scottish Philosophy in the Eighteenth Century: Morals, Politics, Art, and Religion*, Oxford: Oxford University Press, pp. 239–282.

Mandeville, B. (1988) *The Fable of the Bees*, ed. F.B. Kaye, Indianapolis: Liberty Classics.

Nagel, T. (1979) "Moral Luck," in *Mortal Questions*, Cambridge: Cambridge University Press.

Otteson, J. (2002) *Adam Smith's Marketplace of Life*, Cambridge: Cambridge University Press.

Rasmussen, D.C. (2008) *The Problems and Promise of Commercial Society: Adam Smith's Response to Rousseau*, University Park: Penn State Press.

Russell, P. (1999) "Smith on Moral Sentiment and Moral Luck," *History of Philosophy Quarterly* 16, 37–58.

Schliesser, Eric (2017) *Adam Smith: Systematic Philosopher and Public Thinker*, Oxford: Oxford University Press.

Sen, A. (2009) *The Idea of Justice*, London: Allen Lane.

Smith, A. (1976a) [1759] *The Theory of Moral Sentiments*, ed. D.D. Raphael & A.L. Macfie, Oxford: Oxford University Press.

——. (1976b) [1776] *An Inquiry into the Nature and Causes of the Wealth of Nations*, ed. R.H. Campbell, A.S. Skinner, & W.B. Todd, Oxford: Oxford University Press.

——. (1978) *Lectures on Jurisprudence*, ed. R.L. Meek, D.D. Raphael, & P.G. Stein, Oxford: Oxford University Press.

——. (1980) [1795] *Essays on Philosophical Subjects*, ed. W.P.D. Wightman, Oxford: Oxford University Press.

Smith, C. (2006) *Adam Smith's Political Philosophy: The Invisible Hand and Spontaneous Order*, London: Routledge.

——. (2014). "Smith, Justice and the Scope of the Political," in David F. Hardwick & Leslie March (eds.) *Propriety and Prosperity: New Studies on the Philosophy of Adam Smith*, London: Palgrave Macmillan, pp. 254–274.

Timmermann, J. (2002) "The Shadow of Fortune: Adam Smith on Moral Luck," in Verena Mayer & Sabine A. Döring (eds.) *Die Moralität der Gefühle*, Berlin de Gruyter, pp. 151–162.

Verburg, R. (2000) "Adam Smith's Growing Concern on the Issue of Distributive Justice," *The European Journal of the History of Economic Thought* 7, 23–44.

Williams, B. (1981) *Moral Luck*, Cambridge: Cambridge University Press.

Witzum, A., & Young, J.T. (2006) "The Neglected Agent: Justice, Power, and Distribution in Adam Smith," *History of Political Economy* 38, 437–471.

7

JOHN STUART MILL ON LUCK AND DISTRIBUTIVE JUSTICE

Piers Norris Turner

When and why are inequalities unjust? Luck egalitarians have argued that, as a matter of distributive justice, the focus should be on eliminating inequalities resulting from bad brute luck rather than those resulting from personal choice. G.A. Cohen, for instance, writes that his "animating conviction" with respect to distributive justice is that "an unequal distribution whose inequality cannot be vindicated by some choice or fault or desert on the part of (some of) the relevant affected agents is unfair, and therefore, *pro tanto*, unjust" (Cohen 2008: 7).[1] Luck egalitarianism makes personal responsibility the key factor affecting the justice or injustice of an unequal distribution of goods. It recognizes that in the course of pursuing our life plans, we may voluntarily choose to work more or less to earn certain goods, and we may benefit more or less from taking calculated risks. But it also emphasizes that a great many inequalities are traceable to factors beyond even our partial control, such as the wealth of one's parents or one's natural endowments, and that the influence of these factors on our opportunities and outcomes should be eliminated.

Luck egalitarianism has come under fire from relational egalitarians such as Elizabeth Anderson (1999, 2010) and Samuel Scheffler (2003, 2005) who argue that, by focusing on responsibility and luck, it loses sight of the core egalitarian justice concern. This core concern, as Anderson puts it, is to resist oppression and to establish a community of social equals (Anderson 1999: 288–289). Because luck egalitarianism, as a matter of distributive justice, allows in principle both extreme poverty and invasive or stigmatizing judgments of personal responsibility for those who have made bad choices, it threatens those individuals' ability to function as free and equal members of the moral community. The point is not just that ne'er-do-wells and criminals retain their basic moral rights. It is that honest, hardworking people who find themselves unable to provide for themselves (e.g., simply because their reasonable calculated risks did not work out) may then be *publicly scrutinized* for their failures before being provided aid. Relational egalitarians argue that whatever inequalities we allow, they must not undermine people's social dignity.[2]

My aim in this chapter is to place John Stuart Mill's distinctive utilitarian political philosophy in the context of this debate about luck, responsibility, and equality. Anderson has claimed that Mill should be counted as a relational egalitarian, because he accepts "the idea that a free society of equals is a society of mutually accountable individuals who regulate their claims on one another according to principles that express and sustain their social equality" (Anderson 2010: 3n; see also Morales 1996). But Daniel Markovits and others have thought that Mill endorses the intuition behind luck egalitarianism when he writes:

The proportioning of remuneration to work done, is really just, only in so far as the more or less of the work is a matter of choice: when it depends on natural difference of strength or capacity, this principle of remuneration is in itself an injustice: it is giving to those who have; assigning most to those who are already most favoured by nature.

Principles of Political Economy [PPE], CW II.210[3]

Either interpretation will challenge the set of admirers of Mill's *On Liberty* who tend to ignore his egalitarianism and eventual self-identification as a socialist (*Autobiography*, CW I.239).[4] But, taking his egalitarianism as well as *On Liberty* seriously, our question is whether the relational or luck-based view better captures Mill's core egalitarian commitment.

At first pass, it should not be surprising that Mill, as a utilitarian, might incorporate elements of both views. But it is also not very enlightening just to observe that Mill would endorse whatever egalitarian or inegalitarian arrangements maximize overall happiness. We must ask *how* Mill pursues the project of "moulding philosophical truths into practical shapes" through secondary principles appropriate to different states of society.[5] That is my focus in this chapter, and I hope it will reveal the extent to which his utilitarianism provides a helpful framework for synthesizing the competing claims of luck and relational egalitarianism.[6] I attempt to show that when Mill's distributive justice commitments are not decided by *direct* appeal to overall happiness—what he calls "expediency"— they are guided by three main public principles: an impartiality principle, a sufficiency principle, and a merit principle.[7] The question then becomes how luck and relational considerations figure into his articulation of these public principles. I will argue that Anderson is correct that relational egalitarianism is more fundamental than luck and responsibility in Mill's thought, but I also hope to show that any fleshed out picture of Mill's reform proposals must recognize his repeated condemnation of the role luck plays in determining the distribution of opportunities and outcomes.[8]

Elements of Luck Egalitarianism in Mill

Let us start by examining the many places where Mill points out the unjust effects of brute luck. Mill was a radical social reformer, and one of his main criticisms of existing social and political arrangements was the "injustice ... that some are born to riches and the vast majority to poverty" (*Autobiography*, CW I.239).[9] In making this claim, he does not simply argue that a more equal distribution of goods would better promote overall happiness.[10] Rather, he emphasizes the unfairness of the fact that "accidents of birth" rather than effort could so affect people's life prospects. His position is exemplified by the following lengthy passage from his *Chapters on Socialism*:

[T]here would be no ground for complaint against society if every one who was willing to undergo a fair share of this labour and abstinence could attain a fair share of the fruits. But is this the fact? Is it not the reverse of the fact? The reward, instead of being proportioned to the labour and abstinence of the individual, is almost in an inverse ratio to it: those who receive the least, labour and abstain the most. Even the idle, reckless, and ill-conducted poor, those who are said with most justice to have themselves to blame for their condition, often undergo much more and severer labour, not only than those who are born to pecuniary independence, but than almost any of the more highly remunerated of those who earn their subsistence; and even the inadequate self-control exercised by the industrious poor costs them more sacrifice and more effort than is almost ever required from the more favoured members of society. The very idea of distributive justice, or of any proportionality between success and merit, or between success and exertion, is in the present state of society so manifestly chimerical as to be relegated to the regions of romance. It is true that the lot of individuals is not wholly independent of their virtue and intelligence; these do really tell in their favour, but far less than many other things in which there is no merit at all. The most powerful of all the determining circumstances is birth. The great majority are what they were born to be. Some are born rich without work, others are born to a position in which they can become rich by work, the great majority are born to hard work and poverty throughout life, numbers to indigence. Next to birth the chief cause of success in life is accident and opportunity. When a person not born to riches succeeds in acquiring them, his own industry and dexterity have generally contributed to the result; but industry and dexterity would not have sufficed unless there had been also a concurrence of occasions and chances which falls to the lot of only a small number ... The connection between fortune and conduct is mainly this, that there is a degree of bad conduct, or rather of some kinds of bad conduct, which suffices to ruin any amount of good fortune; but the converse is not true: in the situation of most people no degree whatever of good conduct can be counted upon for raising them in the world, without the aid of fortunate accidents.

CW V.714–715[11]

Mill argues repeatedly that the great strength of socialism is its rejection, along luck egalitarian lines, of this state of affairs:

The distinction between rich and poor, so slightly connected as it is with merit and demerit, or even with exertion and want of exertion in the individual, is obviously unjust; such a feature could not be put into the rudest imaginings of a perfectly just state of society; the present capricious distribution of the means of life and enjoyment, could only be defended as an admitted imperfection, submitted to as an effect of causes in other respects beneficial ... Socialism, as long as it attacks the existing individualism, is easily triumphant; its weakness hitherto is in what it proposes to substitute.

"Newman's Political Economy," CW V.444

In these passages, Mill makes a pair of related points concerning brute luck and exertion: first, that birth and other "accidents" play the leading role in determining the distribution of goods in society and, second, that there is no "proportionality between success and merit," in part because the poor typically work harder than the rich. These circumstances, he believes, are "obviously unjust."

Questions remain. In particular, in focusing on exertion as an element of merit, does Mill believe that natural endowments are among the accidents that need to be corrected for? More generally, how do justice claims relate to the principle of utility in these cases, and so what is the nature and significance of the "complaint against society" generated by these inequalities?

The best way to approach Mill's commitments is to consider the immediate institutional reforms he proposes. I say "immediate" because there is a further question concerning the social and political arrangements Mill might have envisioned for some distant future state of society. As Helen McCabe (manuscript) has argued, any assessment of Mill's reform proposals must make clear which of them are intended as (a) practical reforms for the current or very near-term state of society, (b) the most desirable and sustainable institutions given steps that are discernible in the mid- to long-term, or (c) proposals concerning an in principle available, but unforeseeable, distant future.[12] To get a feel for Mill's commitments, then, consider four immediate reform proposals meant to undo inequalities due to brute luck: the elimination of primogeniture, heavy taxes on inheritance, guaranteed subsistence aid, and equal rights for women. Together, he thought, these would ameliorate many of the immediate injustices of inequality.[13] In considering them, we can glean certain mid-level principles organizing Mill's political thought.

Primogeniture. Throughout his career, Mill argues on luck egalitarian grounds that primogeniture, the practice of bequeathing one's property exclusively or primarily to the first-born child, is "radically wrong" ("Advice to Land Reformers," CW XXV.1231):

Unless a strong case of social utility can be made out for primogeniture, it stands sufficiently condemned by the general principles of justice; being a broad distinction in the treatment of one person and of another, grounded solely on an accident.

PPE, CW III.892

No strong case of social utility is available. Primogeniture certainly does not help the younger siblings, and there is no great social value to preserving large fortunes undivided in this way: "a person is more powerfully stimulated by the example of somebody who has earned a fortune, than by the mere sight of somebody who possesses one" (PPE, CW III.890). Even if it mattered to preserve these large fortunes, it would be better to reward "talent and education" rather than "being born heir" ("Primogeniture," CW XXVI.340). For Mill,

the more wholesome state of society is not that in which immense fortunes are possessed by a few and coveted by all, but that in which the greatest possible numbers possess and are contented with a moderate competency, which all may hope to acquire.

PPE, CW III.891, 755

Taxing inheritance. Mill also argues that although individuals may justifiably acquire great wealth in their lifetimes through their own effort, the inheritance received by their heirs should be taxed quite heavily. Besides general worries about "the tendency of inherited property to collect in large masses," he makes the luck egalitarian argument:

I see nothing objectionable in fixing a limit to what any one may acquire by the mere favour of others, without any exercise of his faculties, and in requiring that if he desires any further accession of fortune, he shall work for it.

PPE, CW II.224, 225; CW II. 226; CW III.811

What children may rightly claim from their parents is only "a fair chance of achieving by their own exertions a successful life" or a "fair chance of a desirable existence" (PPE, CW II.221, 222). Mill points out that a "fair chance" is all that was commonly understood to be owed to younger children or to children born out of wedlock. In cases when someone has not left a will, then, the state may rightfully withhold anything further than that for "the general purposes of the community" (PPE, CW II.223).

How much would he tax inheritance? In testimony before a parliamentary committee, he says:

[T]here is no injustice in taxing persons who have not acquired what they have by their own exertions, but have had it bestowed them in free gift; and there are no reasons of justice or policy against taxing enormously large inheritances more highly than smaller inheritances … I would do so to the utmost extent to which the means could be found for imposing it without its being frustrated.

"The Income and Property Tax," CW V.491[14]

Mill thus defends a tax on unearned income in luck egalitarian terms. And through this relatively simple mechanism of an inheritance tax, he hopes for a radical redistribution of wealth in society that would have far-reaching effects.

Subsistence Aid. Mill also came to argue that individuals are entitled to subsistence aid, regardless of their life choices: "The principle of securing, by a legal provision, the actual necessaries of life and health to all who cannot otherwise obtain them, we consider as now placed out of the reach of dispute by any unprejudiced person" ("The Poor Laws," CW XXIII.686; see also "French News [85]," CW XXIII.673, *Chapters on Socialism*, CW V.713–715). This runs counter to some luck egalitarian thinking that does not treat it as a matter of *justice* to rectify the situation of individuals whose poverty is the result of their own bad choices. But the present point is to note Mill's awareness that often mere chance leaves people in poverty—whether because one is born into poverty or placed there by some other misfortune—and that this demands a social remedy:

> [I]t may be regarded as irrevocably established, that the fate of no member of the community needs be abandoned to chance; that society can and therefore ought to insure every individual belonging to it against the extreme of want; that the condition even of those who are unable to find their own support, needs not be one of physical suffering, or the dread of it, but only of restricted indulgence, and enforced rigidity of discipline.
>
> *PPE, CW II.360; see Persky [2016: 204–205]*

For those capable of it, Mill thinks it reasonable to attach a work requirement to subsistence aid—"Aid guaranteed to those who cannot work, employment to those who can"—concluding that "the *droit au travail* is the most manifest of moral truths, the most imperative of political obligations" ("Vindication of the French Revolution of February 1848," CW XX.348, 349).[15] Subsistence aid is meant to provide an existence free of physical suffering and the stress of insecurity for all recipients. Though aid should not be so generous as to dissuade recipients from trying to find other work, Mill makes clear that the aid and work requirement must be consistent with respect for individuals' dignity: "In the workhouse, and the workhouse alone, can the bodily wants of the pauper be amply cared for, and yet pauperism be rendered not shameful (that is not the object), but undesirable" ("The Poor Laws," CW XXIII.688). While there is more to unpack about Mill's commitment to a right to subsistence, it is clear that part of his motivation is to undo the bad effects of brute luck: "These evils, then—great poverty, and that *poverty very little connected with desert*—are the first grand failure of the existing arrangements of society" (*Chapters on Socialism*, CW V.715; emphasis added).

Women's rights. Mill's life-long campaign for women's equal rights offers the most prominent example of his belief that it is an injustice to deny rights to any group on the basis of a mere "accident of birth." The "higher social functions" are closed to women, he observes, "by a fatality of birth which no exertions, and no change of circumstances, can overcome" (*The Subjection of Women*, CW XXI.275). He hopes instead that "before the lapse of another generation, the accident of sex, no more than the accident of skin, will be deemed a sufficient justification for depriving its possessor of the equal protection and just privileges of a citizen" (*Considerations on Representative Government*, CW XIX.481), so that "the aristocracies of colour, race, and sex" will be recognized as examples of "injustice and tyranny" (*Utilitarianism*, CW X.259). In their place, he proposes

> the habit of estimating human beings by … what they are, and by what they do: not by what they are born to, nor by the place in which accident or the law has classed them. Those who are fully penetrated with this spirit cannot help feeling rich and poor, women and men, to be equals before the State.
>
> *"Women's Suffrage [1]," CW XXIX.375; see also Harriet Taylor Mill,*
> *"Enfranchisement of Women," CW XXI.400–401*

On Mill's view, it is an injustice to allow a mere accident of birth, which is no moral reason at all, to justify a difference in treatment.

These proposals on primogeniture, inheritance taxes, subsistence aid, and women's rights, together with his effort to address overpopulation, constitute the core of Mill's immediate egalitarian reform program. We have seen that, in each case, his argument about justice turns significantly on claims about the influence of luck on people's opportunities and outcomes. But does Mill argue that *all* effects of brute luck should be eliminated? And *how* does he argue for the elimination of these effects?

The Impartiality Principle

To appreciate how Mill argues for the elimination of the effects of brute luck, I want to tease out three secondary principles—impartiality, sufficiency, and merit—that he believes should guide public discussion and reform. The most important of these, because it fundamentally shapes his account of what justice requires in any advanced state of society, is his principle of impartiality, or equal consideration. The question is: what does equal consideration require?

To begin, in *Utilitarianism*, Mill emphasizes that the principle of utility itself cannot be understood without appreciating its commitment to "perfect impartiality between persons," in which each person's happiness "is counted for exactly as much as another's" (CW X.257n, 257).[16] Now, as is often pointed out, this notion of impartiality is consistent with wildly inegalitarian social and political arrangements, if they promote general utility. Mill himself is clear that in early states of society even despotism is justified on utilitarian grounds—taking everyone's happiness into account impartially—in order to move from the terrible state of nature toward a spontaneously cooperative society (which he calls "civilization").

But in the same passage Mill emphasizes that the "highest standard of social and distributive justice" implied by utilitarian impartiality is that "society should treat all equally well who have deserved equally well of it" (CW X.257). As individuals develop and society progresses, equal justice claims will be asserted more and more, with fewer compromises for the sake of expediency ("Newman's Political Economy," CW V.445; *The Subjection of Women*, CW XXI.293–4; "Women's Suffrage [1]," CW XXIX.380). Overall happiness ultimately will require not just impartial consideration but "equality of treatment":

> The equal claim of everybody to happiness in the estimation of the moralist and the legislator, involves an equal claim to all the *means* of happiness, except in so far as the inevitable conditions of human life, and the general interest, in which that of every individual is included, set limits to the maxim … All persons are deemed to have a *right* to equality of treatment, except when some recognised social expediency requires the reverse. And hence all social inequalities which have ceased to be considered expedient, assume the character not of simple inexpediency, but of injustice.
>
> *Utilitarianism, CW X.257–258; first emphasis added*

Mill's principle of impartiality is the familiar justice principle of treating like cases alike unless there is some important reason to distinguish between them. The supporters of women's rights "are protesting against arbitrary preferences; against making favourites of some, and shutting the door against others. We are claiming equal chances, equal opportunities, equal means of self-protection for both halves of mankind" ("Women's Suffrage [1]," CW XXIX.374). And in *The Subjection of Women*, Mill emphasizes that the "presumption is in favour of … impartiality," thereby laying the burden of proof on those who would treat people differently: "the law should be no respecter of persons, but should treat all alike, save where dissimilarity of treatment is required by positive reasons, either of justice or of policy" (CW XXI.262; "The Admission of Women to the Electoral Franchise," CW XXVIII.152).[17] Those calling for equality against the "aristocracies of colour, race, and sex" need not prove their case; equality is the default.

Impartiality, understood to imply equal treatment, thus calls for the elimination of differences due to accidents of birth that lead to some enjoying greater opportunities or other goods. Although there are practical limits to this effort, Mill argues for a fair start—as equal as possible—for all (PPE, CW III.811).

The key thing at this point, however, is that the principle of impartiality is broader than the concern to eliminate inequalities due to bad brute luck. For example, it supplies Mill's core principle of taxation on earned income, the principle of equal sacrifice: "The just principle of taxation, I conceive to be, to impose as far as possible an equal sacrifice on all … each should be required to give up an equal share, not of their means, but of their enjoyments" ("The Income and Property Tax," CW V.472; also "Errors and Truths on a Property Tax," CW XXIII.550). As we have already seen, brute luck and personal responsibility play their part in Mill's overall views on taxation, but eliminating inequalities due to brute luck is just one aspect of Mill's more fundamental commitment to impartiality. And this more fundamental commitment, I will argue, is best understood in the context of Mill's relational egalitarianism.

The Sufficiency Principle

Mill's support for guaranteed subsistence aid regardless of life choices, with a work requirement for those capable of it, reveals a second public principle: sufficiency. He came to see the sufficiency principle as unassailable, and one of the chief building blocks of further social reform. While it is justified partly as a way to inoculate individuals against bad brute luck, it also goes beyond luck egalitarianism in its commitment to provide aid, as a matter of justice.[18] Mill emphasizes that poverty, not just undeserved poverty, is an evil that society must address (even if it is not society's fault that an individual has become poor):

> [I]f there be any who suffer physical privation or moral degradation, whose bodily necessities are either not satisfied or satisfied in a manner which only brutish creatures can be content with, this, though not necessarily the crime of society, is *pro tanto* a failure of the social arrangements.
>
> *Chapters on Socialism, CW V.713*[19]

Besides direct aid through workhouses, Mill's sufficiency principle also leads him to support a tax exemption for earned income up to the threshold required to provide the "necessaries of life":

> Our plan therefore would be, to relieve the smaller incomes from direct taxation entirely, up to the income which might be deemed fully sufficient to satisfy those physical wants of a human being which are independent of habit and convention: to keep off hunger and cold, and provide for old age, and for the ordinary chances of sickness, or other inability to work.
>
> *"Errors and Truths on a Property Tax," CW XXIII.553*

This passage also helps to characterize Mill's notion of a material subsistence consistent with human dignity, though he auditions a number of proposals concerning the acceptable place to draw that line ("The Income and Property Tax," CW V.474–476).[20]

The Merit Principle

In light of the principles of impartiality and sufficiency, the question becomes what *could* justify inequalities. The short answer is *merit*, but what does Mill have in mind?

Mill separates merit into three elements: exertion (effort, earnings), relevant talent (intelligence, skill), and virtue (roughly, public-spiritedness).[21] Let us start with talent. Mill generally attributes differences in talent to differences in opportunity (especially educational opportunities) and previous exertion, rather than to natural endowments.[22] He even argues that his own success is due to education and not to any natural intellectual superiority (*Autobiography*, CW I.33). But he admits there could be differences in talent even when two individuals have had equal chances and have exerted themselves equally in the same endeavor. Whether because of some difference in natural capacity or just because of the way their opportunities played out, one of them might be more efficient or creative. If so, could talent justify inequality of income or other goods? Mill's most famous discussion of whether to reward talent is decidedly ambivalent:

> In a co-operative industrial association, is it just or not that talent or skill should give a title to superior remuneration? On the negative side of the question it is argued, that whoever does the best he can, deserves equally well, and ought not in justice to be put in a position of inferiority for no fault of his own; that superior abilities have already advantages more than enough ... and that society is bound in justice rather to make compensation to the less favoured, for this unmerited inequality of advantages, than to aggravate it. On the contrary side it is contended, that society receives more from the more efficient labourer; that his services being more useful, society owes him a larger return for them ... that if he is only to receive as much as others, he can only be justly required to produce as much, and to give a smaller amount of time and exertion, proportioned to his superior efficiency. Who shall decide between these appeals to conflicting principles of justice? ... Social utility alone can decide the preference.
>
> *Utilitarianism, CW X.254–255*

I believe we can get some leverage on Mill's ambivalence by appealing again to the distinction between his immediate reform proposals and those meant for some distant state of society. For it seems that while he believes talent must be rewarded in any foreseeable state of society, he also imagines a future in which that would not be the case. Consider the following comment, only part of which we saw earlier:

> The proportioning of remuneration to work done, is really just, only in so far as the more or less of the work is a matter of choice: when it depends on natural difference of strength or capacity, this principle of remuneration is in itself an injustice: it is giving to those who have; assigning most to those who are already most favoured by nature. Considered, however, as a compromise with the selfish type of character formed by the present standard of morality, and fostered by the existing social institutions, it is highly expedient; and until education shall have been entirely regenerated, is far more likely to prove immediately successful, than an attempt at a higher ideal.
>
> *PPE, CW II.210*

The first sentence seems to express a "higher ideal" for a distant state of society, in which rewarding differences in talent (not reducible to differences in exertion) would be an injustice. The second sentence, by contrast, expresses the thought that rewarding differences in talent in the current state of society is "highly expedient," and is therefore justified (if not just).

Mill *hopes* for a future in which everyone, including the most talented, would be motivated by fellow-feeling and would see their own happiness as dependent on the flourishing of others in the community. In such a state, Mill imagines, the more talented would *themselves* reject receiving higher remuneration than others who have exerted themselves equally. He sees "great beauty" in Comte's idea that "we should regard working for the benefit of others as a good in itself ... we should desire it for its own sake, and not for the sake of remuneration" (*Auguste Comte on Positivism*, CW X.340). In *Utilitarianism*, he adds:

> [A]lready a person in whom the social feeling is at all developed, cannot bring himself to think of the rest of his fellow creatures as struggling rivals with him for the means of happiness, whom he must desire to see defeated in their object in order that he may succeed in his. The deeply-rooted conception which every individual even now has of himself as a social being, tends to make him feel it one of his natural wants that there should be harmony between his feelings and aims and those of his fellow creatures.
>
> *Utilitarianism, CW X.233*

In a society populated by such well-developed utilitarian individuals, the talented might not expect greater remuneration than their less-talented, but equally hard-working and conscientious, fellow community members.

With the rest of us, however, Mill recognizes that any reasonably foreseeable state of society is going to rely in part on selfish feelings to motivate productive behavior and set social expectations (*Autobiography*, CW I.241; *Auguste Comte and Positivism*, CW X.341). For instance, despite his support for socialist experiments, he thinks that society in the discernible future cannot do without a system of private property, but must shape property laws to the public's ends.[23] And where a system of private property exists, differences in talent will be rewarded:

> The inequalities of property which arise from unequal industry, frugality, perseverance, talents, and to a certain extent even opportunities, are inseparable from the principle of private property, and if we accept the principle, we must bear with these consequences of it.
>
> *PPE, CW II.225; but see "Centralisation," CW XIX.591*

Mill also accepts that when giving certain offices or responsibilities to the more talented is needed for everyone to receive an important benefit, then there is a positive reason for the difference in treatment as far as that goes.[24] For instance, he argues throughout his political works that competence should help determine who holds political offices, because promoting the general happiness requires skilled government.[25] But this is consistent with guarding against social and political inequalities that might result from rewarding talent, including by circumscribing income inequality, and taxing the earnings of the talented when they are passed on as unearned income to their heirs.[26] What we see in Mill's ambivalence about rewarding talent is precisely the sort of balancing act we expect from a utilitarian trying to fit his recommendations to a particular state of society while also imagining a society that differs in ways that could further promote overall happiness.

From the passages we have considered, however, it emerges that Mill principally identifies merit with "exertion": industry, work, or effort, as well as "abstinence" in the sense of accepting some immediate personal cost or inconvenience for some long-term or overall benefit. Abstinence, in this sense, requires that we make an effort, and I use the term "exertion" to include both positive effort and abstinence. Mill's core thought is that, as long as everyone has a "fair chance of a desirable existence"—and as long as one's exertion does not violate social morality or law (Mill does not mean to reward the industry of thieves)—then "the differences of fortune arising from people's own earnings could not justly give umbrage" (PPE, CW III.811; CW II.386). His basic merit principle might, therefore, be encapsulated by the claim that, given impartiality and sufficiency, there should be "proportionality ... between success and exertion" (*Chapters on Socialism*, CW V.714).[27]

The merit principle can also be illustrated by Mill's tax proposals. For example, after defending a flat tax on earned income above the sufficiency minimum, he allows an exemption for the portion of one's income that has been prudently saved for old age or for the upkeep of future children ("The Income and Property Tax," CW V.491). His overall system of taxation, we have found, neatly exemplifies the three principles of impartiality, sufficiency, and merit. Assuming that we are in a state of society in which everyone has a fair chance at a desirable existence, Mill proposes a sufficiency minimum exempted from tax altogether, a principle of equal sacrifice on earned income with an exemption for prudent or socially beneficial savings or investments, and a heavy tax on unearned inheritance income. Each public principle has its role to play, short of any direct appeal to utility or expediency.

Although Mill's three public principles include luck egalitarian elements, they also have a shape of their own. Ultimately, his egalitarianism follows from his understanding of what will promote overall utility. But is there more to say about how he arrives at the principles of impartiality, sufficiency, and merit?

Social Morality and Relational Egalitarianism

In this final section, I want to show that Mill's three principles should be understood primarily in relational terms, through his commitment to the progressive development of an egalitarian social morality. For society to exist at all, he argues, there must be a social morality—a widely shared set of normative expectations to ground practices of accountability.[28] As a moral and social campaigner, then, Mill sees his task as introducing *reforms* to current social morality (Turner 2017). But in order to revise social morality without undermining coordination and stability, he must offer principles that can guide a *public* process of moral and social reform. Among these are his principles of impartiality, sufficiency, and merit.

Impartiality is especially important because it reflects the very point of social morality: that we may rightfully hold each other accountable to a common standard set by shared expectations (letter to Ward, CW XV.650; Turner 2017, 382–383). In principle, a social morality may be inegalitarian. But insofar as some living under it are treated as second-class citizens they are denied social dignity and, inevitably, there will be tensions that threaten social stability and any goods dependent on fellow-feeling. Mill argues not only that inequality has powerful negative effects on the disadvantaged, but that it distorts the beliefs and character of the advantaged (*The Subjection of Women*, CW XXI.324; "French News [85]," CW XXIII.674).[29] This is why equal justice, as the core of social morality, is so important on Mill's utilitarian picture:

> [M]y argument is entirely one of expediency. But there are different orders of expediency; all expediencies are not exactly on the same level; there is an important branch of expediency called justice; and justice ... does require that we should not, capriciously and without cause, withhold from one what we give to another.
>
> *"The Admission of Women to the Electoral Franchise," CW XXVIII.152*

For starters, then, impartiality requires political equality:

> The feeling of obligation as it now exists, towards different individuals and different classes in the same community, is lamentably unequal. The comfort and suffering of one man, on the foreknowledge of which all rational sense of obligation towards him is based, counts in general estimation for something infinitely more than that of another man in a different rank or position. The great mass of our labouring population have no representatives in Parliament, and cannot be said to have any political station whatever; while the distribution of what may be called social dignity is more unequal in England than in any other civilized country of Europe.
>
> *"Taylor's Statesman," CW XIX.637, coauthored with George Grote*

Women's suffrage is needed to ensure that half of the population has "an equal hearing and fair play" ("Women's Suffrage [1]," CW XXIX.380). And, taking everyone into account, "[i]n any civilized condition, power ought never to be exempt from the necessity of appealing to the reason, and recommending itself by motives which justify it to the conscience and feelings, of the governed" ("Thoughts on Parliamentary Reform," CW XIX.324).

But even when there are equal political rights, Mill recognizes that economic forces can create social inequalities previously enforced by political means:

> No longer enslaved or made dependent by force of law, the great majority are so by force of poverty; they are still chained to a place, to an occupation, and to conformity with the will of an employer, and debarred by the accident of birth both from the enjoyments, and from the mental and moral advantages, which others inherit without exertion and independently

of desert. That this is an evil equal to almost any of those against which mankind have hitherto struggled, the poor are not wrong in believing. Is it a necessary evil? They are told so by those who do not feel it—by those who have gained the prizes in the lottery of life. But it was also said that slavery, that despotism, that all the privileges of oligarchy were necessary.

Chapters on Socialism, CW V.710; also PPE, CW II.383

Because significant inequalities exist, he argues, "[t]he working classes are entitled to claim that the whole field of social institutions should be re-examined" (*Chapters on Socialism*, CW V.711).[30] And the "proprietary class," for its part, must appreciate "the necessity of convincing the non-proprietary multitude, that the existing arrangement of property is a real good to them as well as to the rich" ("French News [85]," CW XXIII.674).

What is striking in these and other passages is Mill's effort to push society toward becoming a community of social and political equals, in which individuals address each other on terms of reciprocity. In *The Subjection of Women*, he writes:

[T]he true virtue of human beings is fitness to live together as equals; claiming nothing for themselves but what they as freely concede to every one else; regarding command of any kind as an exceptional necessity, and in all cases a temporary one; and preferring, whenever possible, the society of those with whom leading and following can be alternate and reciprocal.

CW XXI.294[31]

In this light, it seems that the main problem with uncorrected inequalities due to brute luck is that they are incompatible with social equality.[32] Impartiality, sufficiency, and merit are best understood either as public principles that can move us toward social equality and reciprocity, or as principles that would be sustained among a fully realized community of free and equal citizens.[33] Mill believes such a community will ultimately best promote overall happiness:

Already in modern life, and more and more as it progressively improves, command and obedience become exceptional facts in life, equal association its general rule … We have had the morality of submission, and the morality of chivalry and generosity; the time is now come for the morality of justice. Whenever, in former ages, any approach has been made to society in equality, Justice has asserted its claims as the foundation of virtue.

The Subjection of Women, CW XXI.293–294[34]

Notes

1 There are now many varieties of luck egalitarianism. Other canonical sources include Arneson (2000, 2011), Dworkin (2000), and Roemer (1993, 1996).

2 Luck egalitarians have responded to these and other charges—for instance, by arguing that distributive justice is not the only relevant consideration in many of the challenging cases—and so the debate about egalitarian justice continues. For an effort at reconciliation by a luck egalitarian, see Lippert-Rasmussen (2016). It bears mentioning that, at the practical level, both luck and relational egalitarianism require significant reforms to existing social and political arrangements.

3 See, e.g., Markovits (2008: 272) and Persky (2016: 214). Mill citations marked by "CW volume.page" refer to his *Collected Works*.

4 Mill saw, and numerous countries have now demonstrated, that social democracy is consistent with social, political, and economic liberty including freedom of speech, privacy rights, qualified property rights, and a regulated market economy.

5 Mill uses this phrase to describe the work of fellow public intellectuals, and himself, in a letter to Macvey Napier, CW XIII.483.

6 For another attempt to provide such a synthesis in Mill, see Persky (2016: Ch. 13). Persky's book makes a compelling overall case that Mill's political economy is more radical than is commonly appreciated. In doing

so, it argues that Mill's relational egalitarianism lays the groundwork for his luck egalitarianism, and sees "democratic equality as a transitional stage to luck egalitarianism" (Persky 2016: 215). By contrast, I argue that Mill's relational egalitarianism remains front and center in his thought, both shaping and limiting his commitment to luck egalitarianism.

7 These are not the only public principles Mill introduces (see Turner 2017), but they are the ones most relevant to questions of distributive justice.

8 Perhaps still the best single exposition of Mill's theory of equality can be found in Berger (1984: 159–204), but see McCabe (manuscript), Persky (2016), Claeys (2013), and Morales (1996).

9 At the time Mill wrote, the great majority of citizens in industrialized nations (and everywhere else) lived in poverty, and it is estimated that perhaps a quarter of UK citizens lived on less than the equivalent of $1/day (Ravallion 2016: 15).

10 Like Bentham, he accepts the egalitarian implications of diminishing marginal utility (see PPE, CW II.225–226). But his egalitarianism does not primarily rest on that point.

11 *Chapters on Socialism* was published posthumously, but this passage reiterates Mill's opinions from numerous other writings over the final decades of his life.

12 McCabe's article also provides a succinct and convincing account of Mill's socialist commitments. See also Claeys (2013: 145–146). For Mill's opposition to the *revolutionary* socialist movement in England, see *Chapters on Socialism*, CW V.749.

13 Mill recognized that these proposals would face resistance, but he proposed each of them as concrete, practical measures to be taken up in the near term.

14 Mill is then asked: "Consequently you would mulct the son for the virtues of the father?" He replies: "It is not mulcting him to prevent him from receiving what he has not exerted himself to earn," and concludes, "I would make taxation bear upon that which people acquire without exertion and talent, rather than upon that which they acquire by exertion and talent" ("The Income and Property Tax," CW V.493).

15 Here I set aside Mill's persistent worries about overpopulation, which complicate some of his comments. Mill argues that overpopulation threatens the well-being and future improvement of the poor and working classes, due to downward pressures on wages and the difficulty of supporting a rapidly growing population. In a luck egalitarian vein, he suggests that the opportunities people are born into would be more equal if parents were educated about and given birth control, and then voluntarily chose not to have more children than they can provide a fair chance. Yet, his answer to the problem of overpopulation is not to deny subsistence aid. Rather he first proposes to provide education about birth control and about parents' moral obligations to their children and, then, to place pecuniary restrictions on when couples may marry or to impose penalties on those who have children they cannot support (PPE, CW II.359, 368–372).

16 This does not mean we may not especially attend to those connected to us. For a brief summary of Mill's practical utilitarianism, see his letter to George Grote, CW XV.762.

17 In a manuscript unpublished in their lifetimes, Harriet Taylor Mill and J.S. Mill write that the public acceptance of this principle would be "nothing less than the beginning of the reign of justice, or the first dawn of it at least. It is the introduction of the principle that distinctions, and inequalities of rights, are not good things in themselves, and that none ought to exist for which there is not a special justification, grounded on the greatest good of the whole community, privileged and excluded taken together" ("Appendix B," CW XXI.380). Harriet Taylor Mill was herself an important voice for women's equality, and collaborated with Mill on some of his principal works.

18 Admittedly, Mill at one point proposes that the rule "they who do not work shall not eat, will be applied not to paupers only, but impartially to all" (*Autobiography*, CW I.239). But his point in that passage is to call for impartiality between rich and poor—because it is unfair that the idle rich enjoy great comforts when the idle poor suffer—not to undermine the right to subsistence.

19 All of this still leaves the case of a person who rejects subsistence aid, perhaps because of the work requirement. Mill seems to believe that while aid must be offered to people on reasonable terms, they must not be forced to accept it. One might yet suffer through one's own "voluntary fault," then, by an unwillingness to meet the work requirements (*Chapters on Socialism*, CW V.713).

20 The subsistence tax exemption, on Mill's view, also creates a graduated effect so that the rich are taxed more as a percentage of their income than the poor. With respect to *earned* income above the minimum threshold, Mill supports a flat tax. But this must be understood within his overall tax scheme including the minimum exemption and the heavy taxes on *unearned* income: "It seems to me that the just claims to graduation are sufficiently satisfied by taxing only the surplus above the minimum allowance to cover necessaries" ("The Income and Property Tax," CW V.497).

21 I focus only on differences in exertion and talent, but Mill does not mean to reward talent or exertion in the service of vice (*Chapters on Socialism*, CW V.714). In this account of merit, Mill broadly follows Bentham (*Considerations on Representative Government*, CW XIX.390, 392; Turner forthcoming).

22 He does not deny that some individuals have greater natural endowments, but in the main he emphasizes our common capacity for great improvement through education (*Autobiography*, CW I.109–110).

23 Mill writes: "The laws of property have never yet conformed to the principles on which the justification of private property rests. They have made property of things which never ought to be property, and absolute property where only a qualified property ought to exist. They have not held the balance fairly between human beings, but have heaped impediments upon some, to give advantage to others; they have purposely fostered inequalities, and prevented all from starting fair in the race" (PPE, CW II.207). In holding that "property is only a means to an end, not itself the end," Mill thus supports heavy inheritance taxes and other limits on property rights (PPE, CW II.223; also 226). For his qualified views on private property, see: PPE, CW II.214; *Autobiography* CW I.241; letter to John Jay, CW XIII.740–741; "French News [85]," CW XXIII.673–674; *Chapters on Socialism*, CW V.712–713; "Should Public Bodies Be Required to Sell Their Lands?" CW XXV.1232–1235; "The Right of Property in Land," CW XXV.1235–1243.

24 Anderson argues similarly that there is no reasonable interpersonal complaint against having the most talented surgeons perform surgery, and be rewarded for it, when everyone benefits thereby (2010: 11). Note that Anderson and Mill differ, at least in emphasis, insofar as Mill holds that those calling for equality need not prove an injury, but enjoy a presumption in their favor (Ibid.: 8).

25 For more on Mill's appeal to a principle of competence, see Turner (forthcoming, 2013). For an attempt to balance equality and competence, see "Thoughts on Parliamentary Reform," CW XIX.323–324.

26 See, e.g., his comment that "[t]he inequality of remuneration between the skilled and the unskilled is, without doubt, very much greater than is justifiable; but it is desirable that this should be corrected by raising the unskilled, not by lowering the skilled" (PPE CW II.388, 383–388).

27 Mill worries that exertion is not rewarded appropriately in the existing economic system: "The really exhausting and the really repulsive labours, instead of being better paid than others, are almost invariably paid the worst of all, because performed by those who have no choice" (PPE, CW II.383).

28 This paragraph summarizes the argument of Turner (2017). For more on the notion of social morality, see Gaus (2011, 2015).

29 This idea receives its most forceful expression in King (1963).

30 For an attempt to express a balance between the demands of equality and liberty, see Mill's letter to Arthur Helps, CW XVII.2002.

31 In his letter to Arthur Helps, he adds: "In my estimation the art of living with others consists first & chiefly in treating & being treated by them as equals" (CW XVII.2001). See also his letter to William George Ward, CW XV.650.

32 By contrast, the practice of rewarding exertion contributes ultimately to the benefit of the whole community, and its advantages are available to each of us.

33 Morales (1996) offers a valuable and detailed characterization of a well-constituted Millian society in relational egalitarian terms—such as these public principles might require.

34 I am grateful to Helen McCabe and Bob Hartman for comments that greatly improved this discussion.

References

Anderson, E. (1999) "What Is the Point of Equality?" *Ethics* 109(2), 287–337.

——. (2010) "The Fundamental Disagreement between Luck Egalitarians and Relational Egalitarians," *Canadian Journal of Philosophy* 40(supl.), 1–23.

Arneson, R. (2000) "Luck Egalitarianism and Prioritarianism," *Ethics* 110(2), 339–349.

——. (2011) "Luck Egalitarianism—A Primer," in C. Knight & Z. Stemplowska (eds.) *Responsibility and Distributive Justice*, Oxford: Oxford University Press, pp. 24–50.

Berger, F.R. (1984) *Happiness, Justice, & Freedom*, Berkeley: University of California Press.

Claeys, G. (2013) *Mill and Paternalism*, Cambridge: Cambridge University Press.

Cohen, G.A. (2008) *Rescuing Justice and Equality*, Cambridge, MA: Harvard University Press.

Dworkin, R. (2000) *Sovereign Virtue: The Theory and Practice of Equality*, Cambridge, MA: Harvard University Press.

Gaus, G. (2011) *The Order of Public Reason: A Theory of Freedom and Morality in a Diverse and Bounded World*, Cambridge, MA: Cambridge University Press.

——. (2015) "On Being Inside Social Morality and Seeing It," *Criminal Law and Philosophy* 9(1), 141–153.

King, Jr., M.L. (1963) "Letter from Birmingham Jail," originally published as "The Negro Is Your Brother," *The Atlantic Monthly* 212(2), 78–88.

Lippert-Rasmussen, K. (2016) *Luck Egalitarianism*, London: Bloomsbury Academic.

Markovits, D. (2008) "Luck Egalitarianism and Political Solidarity," *Theoretical Inquiries in Law* 9(1), 271–308.

McCabe, H. (manuscript) "Navigating by the North Star: The Role of the Ideal in J.S. Mill's Consideration of Social Reform."

Mill, J.S. (1963–91) *The Collected Works of John Stuart Mill*, edited by J. Robson, London and Toronto: Routledge and University of Toronto Press. Available digitally at the Online Library of Liberty: http://oll.libertyfund.org/titles/165. [CW]

Morales, Maria (1996) *Perfect Equality: John Stuart Mill on Well-Constituted Communities*, Lanham, MD: Rowman & Littlefield.

Persky, J. (2016) *The Political Economy of Progress: John Stuart Mill and Modern Radicalism*, New York: Oxford University Press.

Ravallion, M. (2016) *The Economics of Poverty: History, Measurement, and Policy*, New York: Oxford University Press.

Roemer, J.E. (1993) "A Pragmatic Theory of Responsibility for the Egalitarian Planner," *Philosophy and Public Affairs* 22(2), 146–166.

——. (1996) *Theories of Distributive Justice*, Cambridge, MA: Harvard University Press.

Scheffler, S. (2003) "What is Egalitarianism?" *Philosophy and Public Affairs* 31(1), 5–39.

——. (2005) "Choice, Circumstance, and the Value of Equality," *Politics, Philosophy & Economics* 4(1), 5–28.

Turner, P.N. (2013) "The Absolutism Problem in *On Liberty*," *Canadian Journal of Philosophy* 43(3), 322–340.

——. (2017) "Social Morality in Mill," in P. N. Turner & G. Gaus (eds.) *Public Reason in Political Philosophy: Classic Sources and Contemporary Commentaries*, New York: Routledge, pp. 375–400.

——. (forthcoming) "The Rise of Liberal Utilitarianism: Bentham and Mill," in J.A. Shand (ed.) *The Blackwell Companion to 19th Century Philosophy*, Malden, MA: Wiley-Blackwell.

8
HISTORY OF LUCK IN EPISTEMOLOGY

Dani Rabinowitz

Modern epistemology has labored under the light of two guiding intuitions. The first is the claim that knowledge is susceptible to a conceptual analysis involving true belief. In this sense "knowledge" is not conceptually basic. The holy grail of modern epistemology was thus a defensible analysis capturing the non-circular necessary and jointly sufficient conditions for knowledge. The amount of ink spilled in the pursuit of this goal has been staggering. It was not until Timothy Williamson (2000) upset the proverbial apple cart with his knowledge-first epistemology that the orthodoxy of this intuition came under pressure. In Williamson's framework, knowledge is conceptually basic and other epistemic concepts are examined with reference to it.

The second, and more relevant intuition in the context of this volume, is the claim that knowledge is incompatible with luck. Stated otherwise, one cannot be said to know a true proposition p when one is lucky that one's belief that p is true. The lucky guess is a simple expression of this guiding intuition. If I glance at a vase filled with a very large number of marbles and form the belief that "there are 102 marbles in the vase" without having counted them, then I do not know that "there are 102 marbles in the vase" since I am lucky that my belief is true. It was, after all, merely a lucky guess.

The lesson most garner from the lucky guess is that one's beliefs should be evidence-based. Epistemologists came to call this additional requirement for knowledge "justification." That I lacked evidence for believing that "there are 102 marbles in the vase" means that I do not know as much, despite my belief being true. Combining the two guiding intuitions, the notion of knowledge as justified true belief enjoyed a long period of popularity and came to be considered the traditional account of knowledge.[1] In Edmund Gettier's view, exemplars of this position included A.J. Ayer (1956: 34) and Roderick Chisholm (1957: 16). Gettier even went so far as to suggest that Plato should be included in this group, thereby deepening the account's theoretical roots and gravitas. As Gettier reads Plato's rejection of knowledge as mere true opinion (belief),[2] his objection rests on the inability of such an analysis to control for the undermining effect of luck, namely, true opinion must be grounded or supported by reason (justification) to effectively rule out a lucky guess as constituting an instance of knowledge.[3]

All this changed when Bertrand Russell (1948: 170) and, more famously, Gettier (1963) constructed counterexamples to such an analysis in which they showed that a justified true belief is insufficient for knowledge. The reason why the agents in the Gettier cases do not have knowledge is because luck still manages to infest the agent's true and justified belief in a way that is incompatible with knowledge.

Take the first Gettier case: Smith has excellent evidence that Jones will get the job and knows that Jones has ten coins in his pocket. Smith then believes the entailed proposition that "the man who will get the job has ten coins in his pocket." Jones does not get the job, however. Smith does. And Smith has ten coins in his pocket. Nevertheless, most intuitively deny that Smith knows that "the man who will get the job has ten coins in his pocket." That Smith got the job and just happened to have ten coins in his pocket is coincidental. Smith is lucky that his belief is true. Similarly, in Russell's case, even though an agent might be looking at a broken clock correctly reading the time (which it does twice a day) the agent fails to know the time since she is lucky that her justified belief is true.

Gettier marked a "crisis point" that unsettled the status quo. Many saw the solution to Gettier to lie in either a more robust justification condition or a fourth condition for knowledge.[4] One noteworthy attempt in the first camp denied that a true belief inferred from a false belief counts as justified (Harman 1973: 47). This effectively ruled out Smith's true belief as counting as knowledge in Gettier's first case since it was inferred from the false belief that Jones will get the job. One obvious problem with this modified justification condition is the narrow scope of its efficacy; that is, while it might account for the absence of knowledge in cases involving inferences from falsehoods, it nevertheless does not suffice for the exclusion of luck in most other cases. For example, this account of knowledge is incapable of accounting for the absence of knowledge in Russell's stopped-clock case, which involves no such inference.[5]

Others attempted to strengthen the justification requirement by insisting that the agent's justification be indefeasible by further factual evidence.[6] In their view, there should be no truth were it believed by S that would undermine or rebut the evidence S has for believing p.[7] This stronger justification requirement effectively rules out knowledge in Russell's case because there is a further truth, namely that the clock is broken, such that had the agent believed that further truth the agent's first belief would have been rebutted or undermined, thereby losing its original justification.

In criticism of the indefeasibility of justification, Jonathan Dancy (1985: 30) argued that the selection of which truths act as defeaters for the agent's evidence will be arbitrary. It is likely that in some cases had S believed a first truth S would no longer believe p. But had S then been apprised of a second truth, the defeat of p by the first truth could be overturned. The question is when to stop considering truths that could have an impact on the epistemic status of an agent's beliefs. Any termination point would be arbitrary. And if we insist that all truths be taken into account, then the scope of our knowledge would be greatly reduced.[8,9]

Realizing the shortcomings of tweaking the justification condition, several epistemologists sought a solution to the Gettier problem in a reliability condition on knowledge. The next section takes a closer look at the nature of luck itself to demonstrate why a reliability condition on knowledge became the accepted standard in the field. The chapter concludes with an overview of the manner in which safety theorists, Williamson in particular, have tackled the problem of epistemic luck.

Knowledge and Modality

A somewhat bizarre quirk of modern epistemologists is the lack of attention to the nature of luck itself. The maxim that "knowledge precludes luck" was accepted but with very little interest in the concept of luck itself. A modal condition on true belief equipped to exclude luck was deemed the most likely solution to the Gettier problem. But few bothered to analyze why that is the case. Duncan Pritchard (2005) was the notable exception to this trend. At a time when legal and moral philosophers were taking a lively interest in the nature of moral luck, Pritchard was able to draw on that material to develop a greater insight into the luck-quashing properties of a modal condition on knowledge.

First, Pritchard followed E.J. Coffman (2007: 158) in speaking of luck as "a relation whose domain contains individuals and whose range contains events (or obtaining states of affairs, or facts): luck obtains between an individual (of a certain kind) and an event."

Second, and more importantly, Pritchard was careful to distinguish two types of epistemic luck. The first, which he called "*benign* epistemic luck," is compatible with knowledge, whereas the second, "*malignant* epistemic luck," is not. Being cognizant of this distinction makes the job of isolating and accounting for the malignant forms of epistemic luck easier. Drawing on work by Peter Unger (1968), Pritchard identifies four categories of benign epistemic luck:

1. *Content Epistemic Luck* =$_{def.}$ it is lucky that the proposition is true.
   The example Unger provides to explicate this type of benign epistemic luck is that of an agent witnessing a car accident. That event occurred by accident and the content of the proposition is thus in a sense accidentally true. That the content of the proposition is only accidentally true does not impact upon the agent's ability to know that continently true proposition.
2. *Capacity Epistemic Luck* =$_{def.}$ it is lucky that the agent is capable of knowledge.
   Unger gives the case of an agent who, while looking at a turtle, narrowly misses getting hit by a rock in what would have been a fatal accident. That the agent is alive to see the turtle and thereby to know there is a turtle in the enclosure in no ways prevents him from having knowledge in this case.
3. *Evidential Epistemic Luck* =$_{def.}$ it is lucky that the agent acquires the evidence that she has in favor of her belief.
   Using a case from Unger (1968: 159), Pritchard describes a case in which a man walks past his employer's office only to overhear his employer say that he will be fired. That the man came by this information by mere accident does not prevent him from knowing that he will be fired.
4. *Doxastic Epistemic Luck* =$_{def.}$ it is lucky the agent believes the proposition.
   Consider a scientist who acquires evidence to support a hypothesis yet does not realize that the evidence does so. The scientist, at a later time, comes to realize the evidential relation owing to her mind being jolted into this realization by some random event, e.g. a scene from a movie jolts her mind into the realization. While the scientist was lucky to form the belief she did, this type of luck does not prevent her from knowing the hypothesis.

In opposition to these benign forms of luck, the malignant type of luck strikes a different cord with our epistemic intuitions. To understand the nature of this knowledge-denying form of luck, Pritchard took a closer look at the accounts of luck offered by others.[10] Unger (1968), William Harper (1996), and Carolyn Morillo (1984) define luck in terms of accident. Knowledge must therefore be justified true belief not acquired by accident. The problem with this explanation of luck, claims Pritchard, is that it does not capture the paradigm case of a lucky event—winning a lottery. That someone wins the lottery is lucky but is no accident. People purposely buy tickets in the expectation that they might thereby win. It would be incorrect to describe a lottery win in terms of accident. So cashing out luck in terms of accident is unsatisfactory.

Nicholas Rescher (1995) gives an analysis of luck in terms of probability. If *e* is a lucky event, the chance of *e* occurring is low. Rescher's analysis has intuitive pull. It neatly explains why it is lucky to win a lottery for the probability of doing so is very low. Pritchard finds this analysis unsatisfactory, however. The probability of a landslide occurring in a certain geographical location might be very low, but should it occur and no one be harmed or benefited in any way, we do not call that event lucky (Pritchard 2005: 126, 132–133). For an event to be lucky, it must be good or bad in reference to a person. Low probability alone will not do the trick in capturing what luck is.

The most popular manner of defining luck is in terms of lack of control (Nagel 1979; Greco 1995; Statman 1991; Zimmerman 1993). When *S* has no control over an event *e* occurring, then *S* is lucky with respect to *e*. The lottery win can be explained on this view since the requisite balls falling in the way they did was not something over which the lottery winner had control. But, as Andrew Latus (2000: 167) points out, the rising of the sun is an event over which no agent has control. Yet we do not consider ourselves lucky that the sun rose this morning. So luck cannot be understood as lack of control either.

Pritchard concludes that though luck does seem to be conceptually related to accident, chance, and absence of control, it cannot be fully captured by those concepts. Pritchard (2005: 128, 132) proceeds to offer the following modal account of luck:

(MAL) S is lucky in respect of an event e if and only if:

(L1) The event occurs in the actual world but does not occur in a wide class of the nearest possible worlds where the relevant initial conditions for that event are the same as in the actual world; and

(L2) The event is significant to the agent concerned (or would be significant, were the agent to be availed of the relevant facts).

Though Pritchard never says so expressly, I take it that he intends (L1) and (L2) to be both necessary and jointly sufficient conditions for an agent to be lucky with respect to an event e.[11] By "possible worlds" Pritchard means "possible worlds [as] understood, in the standard way, as ordered in terms of their similarity to the actual world (i.e., so that 'distant' possible worlds are very unlike the actual world, whilst 'nearby' possible worlds are very alike the actual world)" (p. 128).

Pritchard struggles to get very clear on the phrase "where the relevant initial conditions for that event are the same as in the actual world." If, e.g., the initial conditions specified include the precise manner in which the balls fall in the lottery machine, then it will turn out that the balls fall the same across all nearby possible worlds. Winning the lottery would not count as lucky if the initial conditions were thus specified on (L1). Instead Pritchard states that we do not set the initial conditions "in such a way that, individually or collectively, they determine the event in question" (p. 131). Pritchard does not offer more insight on the "non-determining" nature of the clause. He leaves it up to our intuitions to decide how the possible worlds are to be ordered. At this point in his work Pritchard is content to relax the accuracy of the clause.[12]

(L1) also captures why we consider an agent luckier with respect to some events more than others. If an event occurs in more nearby possible worlds than a second event, then we say that the agent is luckier with respect to the second than the first. Winning the lottery occurs in very few if any nearby worlds. As such it is deemed exceedingly lucky to win the lottery. But throwing a dice and getting the precise number to win a game is not as lucky since that event occurs in a good number of nearby worlds.

(L2) specifies that luck only obtains with reference to an agent: "this condition should suffice to capture the basic contours of the 'subjective' element of luck, and thus also captures the sense in which luck can be either good or bad" (Pritchard 2005: 132). Pritchard calls this the *significance thesis*. (L2) explains why it is inappropriate to talk of luck in the landslide case mentioned earlier, even though it does not occur in many nearby worlds and thus satisfies (L1), since that event does not bear any significance to an agent and thus fails (L2). However, were the landslide to destroy an agent's house, the landslide will be considered a stroke of bad luck for that agent. But if the landslide levels some terrain the agent wanted leveled, then the landslide is deemed to have been a matter of good luck for that agent. (L2) also captures the case of an agent who is lucky though unaware of it. Consider an agent who forgets that she bought a lottery ticket and her ticket is the winning ticket. Even though the agent is unaware of this, if she were apprised of her winnings she would deem herself lucky.[13]

With the modal character of luck thus exposed, Pritchard provides the conceptual link between malignant epistemic luck and the modal conditions on knowledge that became so popular after Gettier. The latter aim to control for malignant epistemic luck by stipulating modal conditions on knowledge that effectively quash the modal knowledge-denying properties of such luck. "Reliability," suitably defined, is a modal property, for it captures functioning across possible worlds.[14]

Modally-Inspired Epistemology

Despite a consensus building around reliability conditions on knowledge, the precise contours of such a condition have taken a variety of different forms.

Alvin Goldman (1976) proposed the idea that for S to know p, S must be able to discriminate between p and relevant alternatives to p. While it is not necessary that S be able to rule out every single possible alternative incompatible with p, those alternatives that are in some, yet hard to define, sense incompatible with p must be ruled out by S. For instance, if Henry is driving through a county with fake barns and Henry happens to look at the only real barn in the county and forms the belief that "there is a barn in the field," Henry does not know there is a barn in the field as Henry cannot discriminate between a real and fake barn.[15] Henry is thus lucky that his belief is true. Similarly in Russell's case, the agent does not count as knowing since the agent cannot discriminate between a working clock and a broken clock that is fortuitously reading the correct time. Goldman's account enjoyed limited popularity given the vagueness of his "relevant alternatives" condition.[16]

Others considered the notion of epistemic virtue to be the path toward an account of knowledge that adequately controls for epistemic luck. In their hands, a true belief produced by a virtuous cognitive faculty or process constitutes knowledge where, roughly, the notion of "virtue" is cashed out in terms of a cognitive faculty that is reliable by consequence of its exhibiting an intellectual or cognitive virtue (Sosa 1991: 277; Greco 2003: 111). Therefore, an instance of true belief by dint of luck does not count as an instance of knowledge, as the truth of the belief is not explained or accounted for by the deliverance of a virtuous process. One significant drawback of virtue epistemology is that it prima facie delivers the wrong result in Russell's case. In that case we have the agent employing a faculty or process that should count as a cognitive virtue. He is looking at a clock and forming a true belief about the time. All else considered, the employment of precisely the same perceptual faculty or process seems a prime candidate for knowledge; had the agent focused her attention on a nearby cup of tea, her belief that there's a cup of tea on the table would prima facie be an instance of knowledge.

The notion of virtue epistemology enjoyed significant popularity in the guise of the proper function epistemology promulgated by Alvin Plantinga (1993) who proposed, roughly, that a warranted true belief counts as knowledge where warrant is the property of being produced by a cognitive faculty functioning properly in an environment for which it is so designed to be reliable. In time Plantinga himself came to admit the shortcomings on his own account (2000: 156–161). In short, Plantinga realized that his account yields the wrong result in Russell's case, for in that case the agent's belief is, nevertheless, the product of a properly functioning process in the environment in which it was designed, etc. Plantinga attempted to revise his account to allow for this oversight but his tweak never gained any momentum in the epistemic community.[17]

The most noteworthy response to Gettier came from Fred Dretske (1971) and Robert Nozick (1981) who both proposed sensitivity accounts of knowledge where S knows p if S would not believe p in the nearest possible world in which p is false. Consider the case of a subject S looking at red widgets under a red light and coming to believe the proposition that the widgets are red. In the nearest possible world in which that proposition is false, e.g. a world where the widgets are white under red lights, S would falsely believe the widgets to be red. Therefore, S fails to know that the widgets are red in the actual world since S's belief is not sensitive to the truth of that proposition. The lack of sensitivity constitutes a lack of reliability and therefore does not adequately control for luck.

It soon became apparent that the sensitivity condition is fraught with problems. First, and quite obviously, the condition is blighted by any case in which the agent does not, for whatever mundane reason, believe the proposition in the nearest world in which the proposition is false. Gettier's first case demonstrates this weakness. Suppose, for example, that in the nearest world in which the believed proposition "the man who will get the job has ten coins in his pocket" is false the agent does not believe that proposition because he is distracted by a telephone call. In such a case the sensitivity condition renders the counter-intuitive result that in Gettier's case the agent counts as knowing that the man who will get the job has ten coins in his pocket.[18]

Second, and of more concern, is the inconsistency between the sensitivity condition for knowledge and the (single-premise) closure principle. One version of this principle states that if S knows p, competently deduces q, and thereby comes to believe q, while retaining knowledge of p throughout, then S knows q (Hawthorne 2004: 34). Closure is an intuitively appealing principle as it seems to be the means by which we expand our knowledge base. That said, if I know that I have a hand and deduce, and thereby come to believe, that I am not a brain in the vat, then I know that I am not a brain in the vat. The sensitivity theorist denies that one can know the entailed proposition since, *ex hypothesi*, in the nearest world in which that proposition is false one falsely believes that one is not a brain in the vat. Instead of denying knowledge of the quotidian proposition, the sensitivity theorist retains the intuition that we do not know the denial of radically skeptical hypotheses and ultimately sacrifices the closure principle in the process (Nozick 1981: 198 ff.), a price many felt too high to pay.

Third, the sensitivity condition cannot feature as a condition for knowledge of necessarily true propositions as there is no world in which such propositions are false since, by definition, necessarily true propositions are true in every possible world. The scope of the sensitivity condition is thus limited to knowledge of contingently true propositions. That the sensitivity condition cannot, for example, illuminate the nature of our mathematical or logical knowledge makes it less preferable, *ceteris paribus*, than a condition that can.

The latest attempt at a fourth condition can be found in the work of Duncan Pritchard, Ernest Sosa, and Timothy Williamson. Each formulates the safety condition differently, e.g. Sosa formulates the condition in the form of a counterfactual whereas Pritchard and Williamson do not. And unlike Sosa and Pritchard, Williamson is not engaged in the project of providing an analysis of "knowledge."[19] For sake of brevity, the discussion will center on Williamson's account since his work has been the most influential of the three. For Williamson, there must be no relevantly similar belief episode that results in false belief. The basic idea, then, is that S knows P only if S is safe from error; that is, there must be no risk or danger that S believes falsely in a similar case. Much work goes into identifying what counts as similar, but, at the core, similarity is for Williamson an intuitive judgment about the method of belief formation. We typically talk about methods or bases of belief in a coarse-grained way. Williamson, however, adopts a fine-grained, external individuation of bases. For example, Williamson (2009c: 307, 325 n.13) thinks that, other things being equal, seeing a dachshund and seeing a wolf count as different bases; believing that one is drinking pure, unadulterated water on the basis of drinking pure, unadulterated water from a glass is not the same basis as believing as much when drinking water from a glass that has been doctored with undetectable toxins by conniving agents; believing that one was shown x number of flashes after drinking regular orange juice does not count as the same basis as believing that one was shown x number of flashes after drinking a glass of orange juice with a tasteless mind-altering drug; and, finally, believing that S_1 is married by looking at S_1's wedding ring and believing that S_2 is married by looking at S_2's wedding ring count as different methods if S_1 reliably wears her ring and S_2 does not.

Williamson is inclined toward external, (super) fine-grained individuation of methods owing to his position vis-à-vis luminosity and skepticism.[20] Regarding the former, in some cases the circumstances of a case can change in very gradual ways that the agent fails to detect, such that the basis of belief is reliable at the start of the case while unreliable at the end of the case. Consider, for example, a case in which I see a pencil on a desk in front of me under favorable conditions. Assumedly I know that there is a pencil on the desk. I then begin to gradually walk backwards from the desk all the while keeping my eyes on the pencil until I reach a point at which it appears as a mere blur in the distance. At that point beliefs I form based on vision are no more than guesses. At each point in my growing distance from the desk my visual abilities start deteriorating slowly such that at some indiscernible point my eyesight no longer counts as reliable with respect to the pencil. Were bases of belief individuated in an internal, coarse-grained manner such that my looking at the pencil close-up and my looking at the pencil at a distance count as the same method, then I would fail to know that there is a pencil on the desk when close to the table since there is a close world in which I look at it from a distance and form a false belief that there is pen on the desk, which is intuitively the incorrect result. Consequently, minimal changes in the external environment result in a difference in the basis of belief formation.

The safety condition performs better when it comes to knowing the denial of skeptical hypotheses (and therefore maintains adherence to the closure principle) as well as accounting for knowledge of necessarily true propositions. As to the first issue, Williamson resists skepticism by exposing and undermining those claims that tempt us toward the idea that a brain in the vat and the agent in the good case have exactly the same evidence. According to Williamson (2000: 9) "one's total evidence is simply one's total knowledge." Since the agent in the good case has good evidence and the brain in the vat has bad evidence, this constitutes a sufficient dissimilarity between the cases. Therefore, the false belief in the bad case counts as irrelevant to true belief in the good case. Alternatively, Williamson can be read as saying that individuating methods externally and in a fine-grained manner leads to the conclusion that believing truly on the basis of good evidence is sufficiently dissimilar to believing falsely on the basis of bad evidence (ibid.: 169). The epistemic impoverishment of the brain in the vat is thus irrelevant.

As for the second issue, Williamson and Pritchard have no such problems with knowledge of necessary truths since both require global reliability. There are cases that demonstrate that the method used to believe a necessarily true proposition can be globally unreliable. For example, suppose I use a coin to decide whether to believe $42 \times 17 = 714$ or to believe $32 \div 0.67 = 40$, where I have no idea which is true without the use of a calculator. If the coin lands in such a way indicating that I should believe the first, which is necessarily true, then I am lucky to believe the necessary truth and not the necessary falsehood. I consequently do not know that $42 \times 17 = 714$ as I could just as easily have falsely believed the different proposition expressed by $32 \div 0.67 = 40$.

The safety condition is not without challenges of its own. In particular, safety theorists have a tough time with the relationship between probability and closeness. On the assumption that a proposition about a future state of affairs is either true or false, we take ourselves to know many things about the future; for example, that the Lakers game is next Tuesday, or that the elections will be held next month. This being the case, intuitively at least, Suzy knows that she will not be able to afford to buy a new house this year. On the other hand, we deny that Suzy knows that her lottery ticket will lose (even if the draw has already taken place and Suzy has not yet learnt of the draw result). This state of affairs, however, presents the following puzzle: assuming single-premise closure true, if Suzy knows that she will not be able to afford to buy a new house this year, and knows that this entails that her ticket is a loser, then Suzy should be in a position to know that her ticket will lose (by deduction). But it is commonly held that agents do not know that their lottery tickets will lose. (The aptness of this intuition is often demonstrated by the impropriety of flatly asserting that one knows that one's ticket will lose, or selling one's ticket for a penny before learning of the draw results.) The intuitive pull of single-premise closure is in tension with intuitions about what can be known about the future and about lottery tickets. Problems involving lotteries generalize (Hawthorne 2004: 3). For instance, we are willing to say that Peter knows that (P) he will be living in Sydney this coming year. Yet we are hesitant to say that Peter knows that (Q) he will not be one of those unfortunate few to be involved in a fatal car accident in the coming months. Assuming single-premise closure true, if we are willing to attribute to Peter knowledge of P, and Peter knows that P entails Q, we should then be willing to attribute Peter knowledge of Q.

One way of explaining why agents do not know that their lottery tickets will lose or that they will not die in unexpected accidents is that both events have a non-zero objective probability of occurring. That is, events with a non-zero probability of occurring can occur in close worlds. Naturally, then, one might think that the world in which one's lottery ticket wins or in which one dies from an unexpected motor accident is close and that therefore one's beliefs that one will lose the lottery or not die in an accident are unsafe. This line of thinking is devastating for safety, however, as it would effectively rule out knowledge of any propositions the content of which regards the future since, assuming indeterminism true, there is a non-zero probability that any proposition about the future will be false; that is, for any true proposition P about the future there will be a close world in which P is false and one believes P. If safety leads directly to skepticism about knowledge of the future this would be a good reason to give up safety.

One line of thought for a safety theorist to pursue in response to this problem is to support the following high-chance-close-world principle (HCCW): if there is a high objective chance at T_1 that the proposition P believed by S at T_1 will be false at T_2 given the state of the world at T_1 and the laws of nature, then S does not know P at T_1 as P is unsafe (even if P is true). The thinking behind this response is that if there is a high chance of some event occurring then that event could easily have occurred, which indicates that there is a natural connection between high chance and danger. For instance, if there is a high objective chance that the tornado will move in the direction of Kentucky, then it seems natural to say that Kentucky's inhabitants are in danger.

Hawthorne and Lasonen-Aarnio (2009) demonstrate that HCCW presents some rather unwelcome problems for the safety theorist. First, HCCW is in tension with knowledge by multi-premise closure. Suppose, by way of example, that at T_1 a subject S knows a range of chancy propositions P, $Q, R, \ldots$ about the future; that is, there is no close world in which any of those propositions are false. That said, while there might be a low probability for each proposition in that set that it will be false, for a sufficiently high number of propositions the probability at T_1 that the *conjunction* of $\{P, Q, R, \ldots\}$ will be true at T_2 will be very low. Accordingly, the probability of the negation of $\{P, Q, R, \ldots\}$ is very high at T_1. By the lights of HCCW there will then be a close world in which that conjunction is false. Therefore, while an agent might know each conjunct in a set of chancy propositions about the future, the safety theorist who is committed to HCCW must deny that the agent knows the conjunction of those propositions. HCCW is therefore incompatible with multi-premise closure.

HCCW also creates problems for single-premise closure. Consider Plumpton who is about to begin a significantly long series of deductions from a true premise P_1 toward a true conclusion P_N. Suppose that at every step there is a significantly low objective probability that Plumpton's deductive faculty will misfire, leading him toward a false belief. If the chain is sufficiently long then there will be a high enough probability that the belief at the end of Plumpton's deductive chain will be false, in which case, by HCCW, such a possibility counts as close. If closeness of worlds is cashed out in terms of HCCW, then Plumpton does not know P_N if he deduced it from P_{N-1}, which is effectively the denial of single-premise closure for whenever the chance that the next step will be false is high enough (for example, the step leading from P_{N-1} to P_N in Plumpton's case) the deduction from that previous step will be ruled out as unsafe. The same problem arises for knowing a proposition at the end of a very long testimony or memory chain when there is a non-zero objective probability that the process will go astray at any given link of the chain.

Moreover, HCCW also struggles to explain the inconsistency of why, in some cases, we *do* attribute knowledge to agents concerning events with substantially low probabilities of occurring, while in some cases we do *not*. For instance, we are happy to say, following Greco (2007) and Vogel (1999), that a veteran cop knows that his rookie partner will fail to disarm the mugger by shooting a bullet down the barrel of the mugger's gun, or that not all 60 golfers will score a hole-in-one on the par three hole, or that this monkey will not type out a copy of *War and Peace* if placed in front of a computer. Yet it is common to deny knowledge in the lottery case where the chances are substantially lower.[21]

Lessons Learnt

Gettier inspired a generation of epistemologists to devote their time toward the conceptual analysis of "knowledge." Thanks to the vagueness inherent in parts of our conceptual vocabulary and the peculiar nature of luck, this holy grail has remained unclaimed. We have learnt a tremendous amount along the way about our central epistemic terms and sharpened our intuitions as a result. Complex problems remain unresolved and there is much room for improvement. Perhaps the coming decades will vindicate a knowledge-first methodology. Perhaps they will show that project to be as ridden with problems as the Gettier project. At the very least it is going to be an interesting ride.

Notes

1 At least this is the picture of the status quo that Edmund Gettier presents at the outset of his seminal 1963 paper.
2 *Theatetus* 200d–201d.
3 From a historical perspective, it is interesting to note that Gettier makes no reference to epistemology in the medieval or early modern periods. One explanation for Gettier's silence might be the diverging role that certainty played in analyses of knowledge since Plato. Contemporary epistemology, on the whole, does not consider certainty to be a necessary condition for knowledge. However, from Aristotle through to Alfarabi, Maimonides, Descartes, and Hume, certainty was an essential element of knowledge, or at least the highest form thereof. Gettier might, therefore, have chosen to ignore all epistemology done under the umbrella of certainty. As far as I am aware there has been no discussion devoted to the transition from viewing knowledge as a species of certain belief to knowledge as justified true belief after Descartes and Hume. Nor have I seen a discussion by a contemporary epistemologist of why Aristotle was committed to the idea of knowledge being bound up with the notion of certainty while Plato (assumedly) did not. Both questions seem worthy of investigation. For helpful discussions on related issues, see Pasnau (2017).
4 Robert K. Shope (1983) produced an invaluable monograph detailing two decades worth of responses to Gettier. Rather than reproducing some of that material here, this chapter will focus on several notable responses to Gettier that continue to influence the current landscape in epistemology in one way or another. And unlike Shope, I will discuss material relating to the nature of luck itself.
5 The question of knowledge from an inference involving a false premise has enjoyed a resurgence of late. Many have taken up the challenge of defending, or at least offering alternative accounts of, Harman's position (Ball & Blome-Tillmann 2014; Coffman 2008; Feit & Cullison 2011; Fitelson 2010; Hiller 2013; Klein 2008; Rizzieri 2011). The opposite view is defended by Hawthorne and Rabinowitz (2018).
6 Klein (1971: 475), Ginet (1975: 80), Lehrer (1965), and Lehrer and Paxton (1969).
7 Views such as these have contributed to the robust interest displayed by epistemologists, especially those working in formal epistemology, in the topic of epistemic defeat. The explosion of work on peer and expert disagreement in recent years is one such example of epistemology driven by notions of defeasibility, especially as it interacts with the notion of evidence. Some have even gone so far as to defend positions according to which knowledge is compatible with defeat (Aarnio 2010).
8 A resolution to Dancy's problem might be found in non-standard contextualist or subject-sensitive invariantist semantics for "knows" where the relevant termination point for defeaters is determined from the viewpoint of the attributer. For more on such semantics for "knows," see Hawthorne (2004: 157 ff.).
9 The relevance of evidence beyond the agent's current grasp is currently a contentious matter as a number of scholars have begun to explore the epistemic repercussions of the realization that for many beliefs p, there is so much pertinent evidence beyond the agent's purview. See Goldberg (2016) for discussions on evidence that the agent does not have.
10 By luck I intend to include luck of both the good and bad kind.
11 Pritchard's commentators, e.g. Lackey (2006), work on the same assumption. Moreover, Pritchard tackles problems in the literature as if it were.
12 Pritchard is not alone when it comes to the problematic nature of the "initial condition." To avoid troubles arising from determinism, Williamson resorts to Lewis's "small miracle" to explain how close worlds diverge (Williamson in conversation).
13 In an interesting turn of events, Pritchard (2014) has come to drop his commitment to the significance thesis. See Chapter 14 by Ballantyne and Kampa in this volume for an excellent treatment thereof.
14 For more on the nature of reliability, see Goldman (1986: 81 ff.).
15 For a fascinating take on the multiple pitfalls facing various conditions on knowledge vis-à-vis fake barns, see Hawthorne and Gendler (2005).
16 In conversation Goldman has expressed his being open to solving this problem by adopting a form of non-standard contextualist or subject-sensitive invariantist semantics for "knows" where the relevant alternatives are determined by contextual factors or stakes relevant to the attributor.
17 Plantinga's work on warrant became the foundation for his very influential religious epistemology (Plantinga 2000). Briefly, a certain type of religious belief might count as warranted even if not based on any evidence (so-called "basic beliefs") where such a belief is the output of a properly functioning mental faculty designed

to produce such religious beliefs. Drawing on work from Aquinas and Calvin, Plantinga fleshed out the theological story needed to reach that conclusion. Similar epistemic considerations can also be found at the center of William Alston's religious epistemology (1991).

18 Thanks to John Hawthorne for pointing this out in conversation.
19 See Rabinowitz (2011) for a thorough elucidation of the safety condition for knowledge.
20 Following Williamson (2000: 95), a condition is luminous where for "every case α, if in α [condition] C obtains, then in α one is in a position to know that C obtains."
21 For replies to these problems, see Williamson (2009a: 327; 2009b: 27) and Pritchard (2008: 41; 2009: 29).

References

Aarnio, M. (2010) "Unreasonable Knowledge," *Philosophical Perspectives* 24(1), 1–21.
Alston, W. (1991) *Perceiving God: The Epistemology of Religious Experience*, Ithaca, NY: Cornell University Press.
Ayer, A. (1956) *The Problem of Knowledge*, Baltimore, MD: Penguin Books.
Ball, B., & Blome-Tillmann, M. (2014) "Counter Closure and Knowledge despite Falsehood," *Philosophical Quarterly* 64 (257), 552–568.
Chisholm, R. (1957) *Theory of Knowledge*, 2nd ed., New Jersey: Prentice Hall.
Coffman, E.J. (2007) "Thinking about Luck," *Synthese* 158(3), 385–398.
——. (2008) "Warrant without Truth?," *Synthese* 162 (2), 173–194.
Dancy, J. (1985) *Introduction to Contemporary Epistemology*, Oxford: Blackwell.
Dretske, F. (1971) "Conclusive Reasons," *Australasian Journal of Philosophy* 49, 1–22.
Feit, N., & Cullison, A. (2011) "When Does Falsehood Preclude Knowledge?" *Pacific Philosophical Quarterly* 92, 283–304.
Fitelson, B. (2010) "Strengthening the Case for Knowledge from False Belief," *Analysis* 70(4), 666–669.
Gettier, E. (1963) "Is Justified True Belief Knowledge?" *Analysis* 23, 121–123.
Ginet, C. (1975) *Knowledge, Perception, and Memory*, Dordrecht: Reidel.
Goldberg, S. (2016) "On the Epistemic Significance of Evidence You Should Have Had," *Episteme* 13(4), 449–470.
Goldman, A. (1976) "Discrimination and Perceptual Knowledge," *The Journal of Philosophy* 73, 771–791.
——. (1986) *Epistemology and Cognition*, Cambridge, MA: Harvard University Press.
Greco, J. (1995) "A Second Paradox Concerning Responsibility and Luck," *Metaphilosophy* 26, 81–96.
——. (2003) "Knowledge as Credit for True Belief," in M. DePaul & L. Zagzebski (eds.) *Intellectual Virtue: Perspectives from Ethics and Epistemology*, Oxford: Oxford University Press, pp. 111–134.
——. (2007) "The Nature of Ability and the Purpose of Knowledge," *Philosophical Issues* 17, 57–69.
Harman, G. (1973) *Thought*, Princeton, NJ: Princeton University Press.
Harper, W. (1996) "Knowledge and Luck," *Southern Journal of Philosophy* 32, 79–84.
Hawthorne, J. (2004) *Knowledge and Lotteries*, Oxford: Oxford University Press.
Hawthorne, J., & Gendler, T. (2005) "The Real Guide to Fake Barns," *Philosophical Studies* 124, 331–352.
Hawthorne, J., & Lasonen-Aarnio, M. (2009) "Knowledge and Objective Chance," in P. Greenough & D. Pritchard (eds.) *Williamson on Knowledge*, Oxford: Oxford University Press, pp. 92–108.
Hawthorne, J., & Rabinowitz, D. (2018) "Knowledge and False Belief," in C. De Almeida, R. Borges, & P. Klein (eds.) *Explaining Knowledge: New Essays on the Gettier Problem*, Oxford: Oxford University Press, pp. 325–344.
Hiller, A. (2013) "Knowledge Essentially Based upon False Belief," *Logos and Episteme* IV(1), 7–19.
Klein, P. (1971) "A Proposed Definition of Propositional Knowledge," *Journal of Philosophy* 68, 471–482.
——. (2008) "Useful False Beliefs," in Q. Smith (ed.) *Epistemology: New Essays* Oxford: Oxford University Press, pp. 25–63.
Lackey, J. (2006) "Pritchard's *Epistemic Luck*," *Philosophical Quarterly* 56, 284–289.
Latus, A. (2000) "Moral and Epistemic Luck," *Journal of Philosophical Research* 25, 149–172.
Lehrer, K. (1965) "Knowledge, Truth, and Evidence," *Analysis* 25, 168–175.
Lehrer, K., & Paxton, T. (1969) "Knowledge: Undefeated Justified True Belief," *Journal of Philosophy* 66, 225–237.
Morillo, C. (1984) "Epistemic Luck, Naturalistic Epistemology, and the Ecology of Knowledge," *Philosophical Studies* 46, 109–129.
Nagel, T. (1979) "Moral Luck," *Proceedings of the Aristotelian Society* 76, 136–150.
Nozick, R. (1981) *Philosophical Explanations*, Oxford: Oxford University Press.
Pasnau, R. (2017) *After Certainty: A History of our Epistemic Ideals and Illusions*, Oxford: Oxford University Press.
Plantinga, A. (1993) *Warrant and Proper Function*, Oxford: Oxford University Press.
——. (2000) *Warranted Christian Belief*, Oxford: Oxford University Press.
Pritchard, D. (2005) *Epistemic Luck*, Oxford: Oxford University Press.
——. (2008) "Knowledge, Luck, and Lotteries," in V. Hendricks & D. Pritchard (eds.) *New Waves in Epistemology*, London: Palgrave Macmillan, pp. 28–51.

——. (2009) *Knowledge*, London: Palgrave Macmillan.

——. (2014) "The Modal Account of Luck," *Metaphilosophy* 45(4–5), 594–619.

Rabinowitz, D. (2011) "The Safety Condition for Knowledge," *Internet Encyclopedia of Philosophy*: www.iep.utm.edu/safety-c/

Rescher, N. (1995) *Luck: The Brilliant Randomness of Everyday Life*, New York: Farrar, Strauss, and Giroux.

Rizzieri, A. (2011) "Evidence Does Not Equal Knowledge," *Philosophical Studies* 153, 235–242.

Russell, B. (1948) *Human Knowledge: Its Scope and its Limits*, London: Allen & Unwin.

Shope, R. (1983) *An Analysis of Knowing: A Decade of Research*, Princeton, NJ: Princeton University Press.

Sosa, E. (1991) *Knowledge in Perspective*, Cambridge: Cambridge University Press.

Statman, D. (1991) "Moral and Epistemic Luck," *Ratio* 4, 146–156.

Unger, P. (1968) *Ignorance: A Case for Skepticism*, Oxford: Oxford University Press.

Vogel, J. (1999) "The New Relative Alternative Theory," *Philosophical Perspectives* 13, 155–180.

Williamson, T. (2000) *Knowledge and its Limits*, Oxford: Oxford University Press.

——. (2009a) "Reply to John Hawthorne and Maria Lasonen-Aarnio," in P. Greenough & D. Pritchard (eds.) *Williamson on Knowledge*, Oxford: Oxford University Press, pp. 313–329.

——. (2009b) "Probability and Danger," The Amherst Lecture in Philosophy.

——. (2009c) "Reply to Goldman," in P. Greenough & D. Pritchard (eds.) *Williamson on Knowledge*, Oxford: Oxford University Press, pp. 305–312.

Zimmerman, M.J. (1993) "Luck and Moral Responsibility," in D. Statman (ed.) *Moral Luck*, New York: State University of New York Press, pp. 374–386.

9

THOMAS NAGEL AND BERNARD WILLIAMS ON MORAL LUCK

Andrew Latus

The modern philosophical luck industry began in 1976 with the publication of two seminal papers by Thomas Nagel and Bernard Williams, both entitled "Moral Luck." This was hardly the first time philosophers had taken an interest in the relationship between luck and morality, but 1976 marked the beginning of a still thriving philosophical industry.[1] A search of the Philosopher's Index helps make this clear. Searching for the word "luck" reveals six published papers in the decade from 1966 to 1975. After this, things picked up significantly. Between 1976 and 1985, 27 articles and reviews appeared. Over the following decade, there were 50 articles and reviews, most of which still directly referenced Nagel's and Williams's papers, although they began referring to one another. Over the next ten years, there were 219 articles and reviews, then 582 between 2006 and 2015. The scope of the literature also expanded beyond ethics. In 2016, papers were published concerning the relationship between luck and distributive justice, CEO pay, medical error, knowledge, talent in sports, and, of course, moral luck. Overall, the pattern in the literature is this. First, there was a fairly intense debate around the original issue, with objections and replies going back and forth. This was followed by a broadening of the debate as the elements of the original argument began to be applied in other areas. It is the classic picture of a modern academic industry.

But what is the debate about? Nagel's paper was officially a reply to Williams's, however, they are better thought of as operating in parallel. Both are about the role of luck in morality broadly construed, but their focus is very different. This has likely played a role in the subsequent flourishing of research into the philosophy of luck. A long-lasting franchise requires rich source material. From time to time, it is helpful to return to the origin story, which is what we will do here.

What is Moral Luck?

A case of moral luck occurs whenever luck makes a moral difference. The idea of a moral difference has been taken in a variety of directions including differences in how good or bad a person is and differences in the events for which a person is morally responsible. There is a *problem* of moral luck because, while many find it intuitively plausible that luck cannot make moral differences, the world provides many apparent examples of it doing exactly this. In the classic example at the center of many papers, two equally drunk drivers travel home equally recklessly along the same route. One swerves onto the sidewalk, killing a child. The other swerves on and off the sidewalk; but no child is present and no one is hurt. What do we do with the difference in moral indignation many of us feel toward

Williams on Moral Luck

these drivers when we reflect on the role luck played in the sequence of events? Has luck made a moral difference here?

This question of whether luck can make moral differences is at the heart of both Williams's and Nagel's papers. They both argue that it can, but draw very different conclusions from this.

Williams on Moral Luck

Williams's aim in "Moral Luck" is to discredit what he conceives of as a misguided but widespread conception of morality. He claims that the idea that morality is immune to luck is "basic to our ideas of morality" (Williams 1993a: 36). However, he sees these ideas as rooted in a tradition, emanating from Kant, that should be overthrown. He thinks the problem of moral luck is not solvable within this tradition, but goes away when one adopts a broader view of morality he refers to as "the ethical."

Williams begins by outlining the reason morality is thought of as being independent of luck. Luck permeates our lives. Some are born healthy; some are not. Some become wealthy by accident; others work hard, but remain poor. To those on the losing end, this might seem unfair, but we might also tell ourselves there is one type of value that is equally available to all of us, namely moral value. Morality thus provides us with a sort of comfort. In Williams's words, it offers "solace to a sense of the world's unfairness" (Williams 1993a: 36). However, Williams argues this will be cold comfort if morality is not particularly important. Thus, it is important not only that moral value is immune to luck, but also that it is the supreme sort of value. Moral value can give us solace only if it is both immune to luck and supreme.

It is against this picture of morality that Williams' argument must be understood. He presents us with a dilemma: either (a) moral value is free from luck but is not the supreme sort of value or (b) moral value is the supreme sort of value but is sometimes a matter of luck. In either case, we have to give up something important to the notion of moral value; hence, we should give up the notion of morality that leads us here.

Williams begins the drive toward this dilemma by focusing on *rational* justification rather than *moral* justification. It takes him a little while to make the reason for this shift of focus clear. For now, it is enough to note that moral and epistemic justification are closely related according to the Kantian approach to morality Williams ultimately wants us to reject. The key to his argument is the claim that rational justification is a matter of luck to some extent. He uses a thought experiment to make this point, presenting a story based loosely on the life of the painter Paul Gauguin. Williams's Gauguin feels some responsibility toward his family and is reasonably happy living with them, but nonetheless abandons them. He does so in an attempt to become a great painter. He goes to live on a South Sea Island, believing that living in a more primitive environment will allow him to develop his gifts as a painter more fully.

Williams asks how we can tell whether Gauguin's decision to do this is rationally justified. We might first ask what he means by "rational justification," but he never explicitly tells us. It appears, however, that he means some combination of epistemic justification with a certain set of practical interests. He is interested in the question of whether Gauguin was epistemically justified in thinking that acting as he did would increase his chance of becoming a great painter. Was it rational (given Gauguin's interests) for him to do as he did? Williams rightly observes that, at the outset of his project, it is impossible for Gauguin to know with certainty whether he will succeed. Even if he had good reason to think he had considerable artistic talent, he could not be sure what would come of that talent, nor whether the decision to leave his family would help or hinder the development of that talent. In the end, Williams says, "the only thing that will justify his choice will be success itself" (Williams 1993a: 38). Similarly, Williams claims the only thing that could show Gauguin to be rationally unjustified is failure. This is where luck enters into it. Since rational justification depends on success and success depends, to some extent anyway, on luck, it follows that rational justification depends, to some extent, on luck.[2]

What does this have to do with morality? Williams hopes to inflict damage on the notion of the moral by setting up a collision between rational justification and moral justification. Rational justification, Williams has suggested, is, at least partly, a matter of luck. But recall that moral justification, according to Williams, is not supposed to be a matter of luck at all if it is to provide us with the solace Williams identified. This leaves room for a clash between the two sorts of justification. The example of Gauguin is supposed to provide us with just such a case. Suppose that Gauguin's decision to leave his family is morally unjustified. Since luck has nothing to do with the moral value of this decision, we can say that Gauguin's decision is a morally bad one when he makes it and that it stays that way, regardless of how his project turns out. According to Williams, however, whether Gauguin's decision is rationally justified is not settled when he makes it. We have to see how the project turns out. Suppose that his Gauguin, like the real one, becomes a great artist. Once this is the case, Gauguin's decision is rationally justified though still morally unjustified. A problem now arises when we consider "where we place our gratitude" that Gauguin left his family and became a painter (Williams 1993b: 255). Suppose we are genuinely grateful that Gauguin did what he did and, as a result, became a great artist. We might say this shows that, on occasion, we have reason to be glad that the morally correct thing did not happen. But to say this is to call into question the point of morality, according to Williams. He maintains morality can offer us solace only if moral value possesses "some special, indeed supreme, kind of dignity or importance" (Williams 1993a: 36).

We are stuck between two supposedly unpalatable options:

Option 1: Moral justification and rational justification clash and rationality trumps morality. If so, so much the worse for morality. It loses its position as the supreme sort of value to a sort of value that is affected by luck and, in doing so, ceases to be a source of solace.

Option 2: Resolve the conflict by claiming that moral value and rationality do not clash here, because morality is itself subject to luck. This move will eliminate the threat that rationality poses to morality's supremacy, but this occurs at the expense of one of our core commitments about morality, namely its invulnerability to luck.

Either way, the notion of morality fails to escape intact, according to Williams. The problem of moral luck exposes a deep problem with our conception of morality and Williams recommends we would therefore do best to reject it.

Some Comments on Williams

At this point, it might seem that there are a couple of easy responses to Williams. For example, why must moral value be the supreme sort of value? Why can't it just be an important sort of value (and, according to what value are the various sorts of value to be ranked anyway)? Moreover, what is there to stop us from saying that our gratitude (if we have any) that Gauguin did what he did is just misguided and so that this is not really a case in which it is better that the rational thing rather than the moral thing happened? It might be that our gratitude is not a good indicator of whether Gauguin should have done as he did.

Developing this, one might focus on Williams's claim that a rational justification for a particular decision can only be given after the fact. This is what allows luck to enter into rational justification. If we do not accept this view of justification, Williams has given us no reason to think that either rational or moral justification is a matter of luck, and so we cease to have a reason to imagine a conflict between rationality and morality. This is a viable option on many accounts of justification. A common intuition about justification is that if we want to know whether Gauguin's decision to leave his family and become a painter was a rational one, what we need to consider is the information Gauguin had available to him when he made that decision. What did he have reason to believe would be the fate of his family? What indication did he have that he had the potential to become a great painter? Did he have good reason to think his family would hinder his quest after greatness? Did he have reason to believe a move to the South Seas would help him achieve his goal? And so on.

If the answer to the question about Gauguin's justification is to be found in the answers to the above questions, then justification is inherently forward looking and not backward looking. Luck has no toehold to enter into things.

Williams has an argument against this picture of justification. He appeals to the notion of "agent regret" (Williams 1993a: 43). Agent regret is a species of regret a person can feel only toward his or her own actions and their consequences. It involves a "taking on" of the responsibility for an action and the desire to make amends for it. Williams's example is of a lorry driver who "through no fault of his" runs over a small child (Williams 1993a: 43). He says that the driver should feel a sort of regret at the death of this child that no one else will feel. The driver, after all, caused the child's death. Furthermore, we expect agent regret to be felt even in cases in which we do not think the agent was at fault. If we are satisfied that the driver could have done nothing else to prevent the child's death, we will try to console him by telling him this. But, as Williams observes, we would think much less of the driver if he showed no regret at all, saying only "It's a terrible thing that has happened, but I did everything I could to avoid it." Williams suggests that a conception of rationality that does not involve retrospective justification has no room for agent regret and so is "an insane concept of rationality" (Williams 1993a: 44). He argues that if rationality is all a matter of what information we have when we make our decisions, then the lorry driver ought not to experience agent regret. He should simply remind himself that he did all he could and we have arrived at that "insane concept of rationality."

This, however, does not follow. The problem is that, in any plausible case of this sort, it will not be rational for the driver to believe that he could not have driven more safely. Drivers know all too well that they do not operate at the level of perfection. Indeed, what it is rational for the driver to do is to suspect there was something else he could have done which might have saved the life of the child. If he had just been a little more alert or driving a little closer to the center of the road … if he had been driving a little more slowly … if he had seen the child playing near the street … if his brakes had been checked more recently, and so on and so on. It will be rational for him to wonder whether he could have done more to avoid this tragedy and so rational for him to feel a special sort of regret at the death of the child (Rosebury 1995: 514–515). Agent regret exists because we can almost never be sure we did "everything we could." Thus, it provides us with no reason to believe there is a retrospective component to rational justification (and so no reason to conclude that luck plays the role in justification that Williams suggests).

None of this is to deny that the way things turn out might figure in the justifications people give for their past actions. It is just that, despite this, the way things turn out has nothing to do with whether or not those past actions really were justified. Sometimes the way things turn out might be all we have to go on, but this tells us nothing about the actual justification or lack thereof of our actions, not unless we confuse the state of an action being justified with the activity of justifying that action after the fact.

There are therefore some grounds for questioning Williams's argument. Indeed, despite being the article Nagel was commenting upon, Williams's argument seems generally to have been less convincing to philosophers than Nagel's. Williams has taken some of the blame for this, commenting in a postscript to his original article that "there are some misunderstandings [of his view] that I now think my formulations in *Moral Luck* may have encouraged" (Williams 1993b: 251). Williams's challenge to traditional conceptions of morality has been welcomed by some, but Nagel attempts to stay within that tradition, identifying a problem for morality but not a solution.

Nagel on Moral Luck

Nagel identifies the problem of moral luck as arising from a conflict between our practice and an intuition most of us share about morality. He states the intuition as follows: "Prior to reflection it is intuitively plausible that people cannot be morally assessed for what is not their fault, or for what is due to factors beyond their control" (Nagel 1993: 59).[3]

He then gives us a rough definition of the phenomenon of moral luck: "Where a significant aspect of what someone does depends on factors beyond his control, yet we continue to treat him in that respect as an object of moral judgment, it can be called moral luck" (Nagel 1993: 59).

Clearly cases of moral luck fly in the face of the above-stated intuition about morality. Yet, Nagel claims that, despite this intuition, we frequently make moral judgments about people based on factors that are not within their control. We might, as already noted, judge an unlucky drunk driver who kills a child more harshly than one who does not, even if the only significant difference between the two cases is that a child happened to be playing on the road at the wrong point on the unlucky driver's route home. This is the problem of moral luck for Nagel: the tension between the intuition that a person's true moral credit or discredit cannot be affected by luck and the possibility that luck nonetheless plays a role in determining this. Nagel suggests that the intuition is correct and lies at the heart of the notion of morality, but he also endorses the view that luck will inevitably influence a person's moral standing. This leads him to suspect there is a real paradox in the notion of morality.

At this point, it is worth noting that, if luck ever makes moral differences, there is more than one kind of difference it might make. Two sorts of difference are typically discussed in the literature on moral luck, although these are not always clearly distinguished. These two sorts of difference are represented by two different thoughts: (a) the thought that the unlucky driver is no worse a person than the lucky driver, and (b) the thought that since we cannot plausibly hold the lucky driver responsible for the death of a child (as no death occurred in his case), we cannot hold the unlucky driver morally responsible for that death. This second thought has to do with the assigning of moral responsibility for individual events, while the first involves an assessment of how much credit or discredit attaches directly to a person. We can use the term "moral worth" to capture both credit and discredit. So, we have two sorts of question to consider:

1. Can luck make a difference in a person's moral worth?
2. Can luck make a difference in what a person is morally responsible for?

Which of these questions is Nagel's? It is difficult to tell. Nagel does briefly refer to the problem of moral luck as a "fundamental problem about moral responsibility," but most of the time his worries are about blame, a notion with overtones of both sorts of moral difference (Nagel 1993: 58). About blame, he comments that "when we blame someone for his actions ... we are judging *him*, saying that he is bad, which is different from his being a bad thing" (Nagel 1993: 58). So, is he concerned that the driver will be blamed for the event of the child's death or that the unlucky driver himself will be rated morally worse than the lucky driver (that is, blamed more)? Nagel seems to entertain both possibilities, asking both whether the unlucky driver is to blame for more and whether he is a worse person than the lucky driver.[4] It might be the case that Nagel thinks the two questions are inseparable, that is, it might be that he thinks we cannot make sense of the idea of holding a person morally to blame for some event without this, at the same time, counting as a reason to lower that person's moral credit rating. (See Thomson (1993) for a discussion of this.)

Nothing Nagel says clearly reveals his position on this point. For now, it is enough simply to bear both sorts of moral difference in mind. The important point is that, in either case, there is something troubling about the idea that luck might make a moral difference. Yet, it seems we allow luck into our moral judgments all the time. We do think less of the unlucky driver. We do hold him responsible for the death of the child. On the face of it, this might not seem particularly troubling. We might admit that, on occasion, we judge people for things that happen as a result of luck, but simply claim that in any such case a mistake has been made. The mere fact that we *do* sometimes judge people for things that happen due to luck does not indicate that we *should* judge people for things that happen due to luck. The problem Nagel points out, however, is that when we consider the sorts of things that influence us, "[u]ltimately, nothing or almost nothing about what a person does seems to be under his control" (Nagel 1993: 59). That is, everything we do seems at some level to involve luck. Nagel makes a helpful comparison to the problem of epistemological skepticism. Just as the problem of skepticism emerges from the clash of our intuition that knowledge should be certain and non-accidental with the fact that few, if any, of our true beliefs are entirely certain or free from accident, so:

> The erosion of moral judgment emerges not as the absurd consequence of an over-simple theory, but as a natural consequence of the ordinary idea of moral assessment, when it is applied in view of a more complete and precise account of the facts.
>
> *Nagel 1993: 59*

This line of thought is made clearer through Nagel's discussion of several different types of luck.

Three Types of Moral Luck

Nagel identifies three distinct ways in which luck plays into our moral assessments:[5]

Resultant Luck: "luck in the way one's actions and projects turn out."
Circumstantial Luck: the luck involved in "the kind of problems and situations one faces"
Constitutive Luck: the luck involved in one's having the "inclinations, capacities and temperament" that one does (Nagel 1993: 60).[6]

These differing forms of luck operate at very different levels and make it possible for Nagel to formulate a powerful argument for the inescapability of moral luck.

Resultant Luck

Nagel gives us several examples of resultant luck. One is the case of the lucky and unlucky drunk drivers. Nagel also makes much of decisions, particularly political ones, made under uncertainty. He gives the example of someone who must decide whether to instigate a revolution against a brutal regime. She knows that the revolution will be bloody and that, if it fails, those involved will be slaughtered and the regime will become even more brutal. She also knows that if no revolution occurs, the regime will become no less brutal than it currently is. If she succeeds she will be a hero, if she fails she will bear "some responsibility" for the terrible consequences of that failure (Nagel 1993: 61–62). Thus, how the revolution turns out, something which might be almost entirely a matter of resultant luck, seems to have a great deal to do with the moral credit or blame she will receive. Again, Nagel means to suggest that luck will affect not just what praise or blame she actually receives, but also what praise or blame she deserves, regardless of how she is actually treated.

Circumstantial Luck

Just as luck might interfere in the course of our actions to produce results that have a profound influence on the way we are morally judged, so our luck in being in the right or wrong place at the right or wrong time can have a profound effect on the way we are morally assessed. Nagel's example is of a person who lives in Germany during the Second World War and "behaves badly" (Nagel 1993: 65). We are inclined to hold him or her responsible for what he or she did, but Nagel asks us to contrast this person with a German who moves to Argentina shortly before the War for business reasons. Suppose that the expatriate would have behaved just as badly as the German if he had remained in Germany. Are we willing to say the expatriate should be judged as harshly as the German? If not, circumstantial luck has made a moral difference.

Constitutive Luck

A natural reaction to worries about resultant and circumstantial luck is to suggest that what matters is not how a person's actions turn out or what circumstances they happen to encounter, but what is in that person's "heart" or character. As Nagel says, we "pare each act down to its morally essential core, an inner act of pure will assessed by motive and intention" (1993: 63). To do so, however, is to open oneself up to worries about constitutive moral luck. If we focus on a person's character, then what of the luck involved in determining what that person's character is? It might be that, in a given situation, Jane did not act with good intentions, but perhaps this was because Jane was unlucky enough to be born a bitter or spiteful person. Why then should her bad intentions figure in her blameworthiness? Nagel suggests they should not. He claims that we should not praise or condemn people for qualities that are not under the control of the will (and so not under their control). But as reasonable as this might sound, Nagel also claims we cannot refrain from making judgments about a person's moral status based upon just this sort of uncontrollable feature. If we did so refrain, it is not clear we would be able to make any judgments at all. In the end, people are assessed for what they are like, not for how they ended up that way.

The Problem Summarized

The notion of constitutive luck illustrates the difficulty of Nagel's version of the problem of moral luck. Our temptation is to avoid the other sorts of luck by focusing on what the person really is. In this way, we try to set aside worries about the luck that affects the way our actions turn out or the luck that places us in situations in which we make unfortunate decisions. We focus on the core of the person, on his or her character. But on reaching that core, we are disappointed to find that luck has been at work there too. The trouble is that there is nowhere further to retreat when we are at the level of character. If we retreat further, there is no person left to morally assess. Nagel concludes that "in a sense the problem has no solution" (1993: 68). The cost of not admitting the existence of moral luck is giving up the idea of agency. We seem driven to the conclusion that no one is blameworthy for anything. But the alternative is to preserve our notions of agency and responsibility by concluding that moral value is subject to luck.

Nagel and Williams thus agree that moral luck is real, but draw very different conclusions from this. For Williams, the idea of moral luck should lead us to an alternative form of morality. Nagel, who elsewhere says we should "trust problems over solutions," prefers to accept that the paradox is real (Nagel 1979: x–xi).

Conclusion

New ideas in philosophy might or might not exist, but it is certain that novel ways of expressing old ideas are impressive and animating to philosophers. The idea of moral luck provided a novel way of thinking about an old idea, namely the extent to which our lives are never entirely under our control. This is part of the idea's ongoing appeal. Philosophers also love an apparent paradox and the problem of moral luck provides that too. This is why many of the responses that followed consisted of attempts to dissolve the problem or show it did not really exist in the first place. This, in turn, contributed to the problem's longevity. Anytime your opponents start attempting to dissolve a problem that many other people find intuitively appealing, you are well positioned for the development of a philosophical industry. Finally, philosophers have an abiding love for vivid examples and thought experiments that lead us to uncomfortable conclusions. Nagel and Williams have several of these on offer, from Gauguin to pairs of drunken drivers to would-be Nazis.

The enduring nature of the literature on moral luck derives from the fact that Nagel's and Williams's papers hit upon all of the above points. Nagel and Williams challenge the idea that we can keep moral judgment as pristine and luck-free as we might naively expect and they do it vividly. Of course, it still might be that we can come to accept the presence of luck in morality. It could be that this will lead us to some alternative, better conception of the ethical, in keeping with Williams's intention. It might be that this will lead us simply to a clearer understanding of something that has been true about morality all along. Whichever of these or other options we select, collectively or individually, we will owe a debt to Williams and Nagel for helping to lead us there.

Notes

1 See Nussbaum (1986) for an extended discussion of ancient Greek opinions on the relationship between luck and morality and Feinberg (1962) for a more contemporary discussion of the topic.
2 There is a further wrinkle here that is not entirely necessary for understanding the overall argument. Williams distinguishes between *extrinsic* and *intrinsic* luck, claiming that only the operation of intrinsic luck is compatible with the result of a decision determining the rational justification of that decision. Roughly, intrinsic luck is luck that arises from the elements of the project or action under consideration, while extrinsic luck is luck arising from "outside" the project. If Gauguin fails because it turns out that living on a South Sea Island distracts him to such an extent that he becomes a worse painter, this will be a case of bad intrinsic luck and so he will be unjustified. On the other hand, if, at the start of his project, a freak accident causes him to sustain an injury that prevents him from painting again, he will be neither justified nor unjustified since his project is never really completed. His project will have failed due to extrinsic luck, so a verdict regarding rational justification will not be returned.
3 "Cannot" here refers to the way in which moral assessment should work if it is working properly.
4 Some have suggested that a failure to disambiguate these two ideas is part of what makes the problem of moral luck appear unsolvable (Greco 1995: 90–91; Hartman 2017: 124–127).
5 Nagel also identifies what has been called "causal luck" (Statman 1993: 11). This is "luck in how one is determined by antecedent circumstances." Like Nagel, I will mention this type of luck and then leave it aside. Nagel introduces this sort of luck simply to point out a connection between the problem of moral luck and the debate about free will and determinism. He wisely avoids the distraction of wading further into this rich debate.
6 Nagel does not give names to all these types of luck, but it is useful to have labels for them. "Constitutive luck" is a term he takes from Williams, although Williams intended the term to have a wider scope. "Circumstantial" luck is a term from Daniel Statman (1993: 11), while "resultant luck" comes from Michael Zimmerman (1993: 219).

References

Feinberg, J. (1962) "Problematic Responsibility in Law and Morals," *The Philosophical Review* 71, 340–351.
Greco, J. (1995) "A Second Paradox Concerning Responsibility and Luck," *Metaphilosophy* 26, 81–96.
Hartman, R.J. (2017) *In Defense of Moral Luck: Why Luck Often Affects Praiseworthiness and Blameworthiness*, New York: Routledge.
Nagel, T. (1993) "Moral Luck," in D. Statman (ed.) *Moral Luck*, Albany, NY: State University of New York Press, pp. 57–71.
———. (1979) *Mortal Questions*, Cambridge: Cambridge University Press.
Nussbaum, M. (1986) *The Fragility of Goodness: Luck and Ethics in Greek Tragedy and Philosophy*, New York: Cambridge University Press.
Rosebury, B. (1995) "Moral Responsibility and 'Moral Luck'," *The Philosophical Review* 104, 499–524.
Statman, D. (1993) "Introduction," in D. Statman (ed.) *Moral Luck*, Albany, NY: State University of New York Press, pp. 1–25.
Thomson, J.J. (1993) "Morality and Bad Luck," in D. Statman (ed.) *Moral Luck*, Albany, NY: State University of New York Press, pp. 195–213.
Williams, B. (1993a) "Moral Luck," in D. Statman (ed.) *Moral Luck*, Albany, NY: State University of New York Press, pp. 35–55.
Williams, B. (1993b) "Postscript," in D. Statman (ed.) *Moral Luck*, Albany, NY: State University of New York Press, pp. 251–258.
Zimmerman, M. (1993) "Luck and Moral Responsibility," in D. Statman (ed.) *Moral Luck*, Albany, NY: State University of New York Press, pp. 217–233.

PART II

The Nature of Luck

10

MODAL ACCOUNTS OF LUCK

Duncan Pritchard

The Modal Account of Luck in Outline

I was led to develop the modal account of luck in order to flesh-out an idea that I had (*c.* 2000) regarding a methodology in epistemology that I christened *anti-luck epistemology*. The thought was that there would be theoretical gains to be had by unpacking the widespread claim in epistemology that knowledge is incompatible with luck. While this thesis is routinely offered—relatedly, it is routinely cited as the reason why agents fail to have knowledge in particular cases, like Gettier cases—at the time there was no systematic attempt to spell out what this platitude amounted to. In particular, it seemed that there ought to be a straightforward three-stage process in play here. First, one offers an account of luck. Second, one explains the specific sense in which knowledge is incompatible with luck (knowledge can be compatible with some kinds of luck, after all, as in lucky discoveries). Finally, one brings the results from stages one and two together to offer an account of the anti-luck condition on knowledge. The result is a much more principled way of approaching the task of identifying this important necessary condition on knowledge than simply, as is usual, testing candidate conditions relative to particular cases. Relatedly, rather than trying to deal with particular cases that trade on the anti-luck platitude, such as Gettier-style cases, one is able to offer an account that can simultaneously deal with all cases of knowledge-undermining epistemic luck (e.g., lottery-style cases, cases of mere true belief through dumb luck, and so on).[1]

Almost immediately, however, I faced a very serious difficulty, which is that there was hardly any philosophical literature exploring the nature of luck. This is incredibly surprising given how analytical philosophers are apt to analyze just about everything. Moreover, luck is clearly a philosophically important notion, having a role to play in philosophical debates in a wide range of fields, from metaphysics (e.g., free will, causation), political philosophy (e.g., just deserts), ethics (e.g., moral luck), and epistemology (e.g., the Gettier problem). Aside from some interesting remarks about luck by some of the key figures in the moral luck debate, the closest anyone seemed to have come to anything resembling an analysis was within a book written by Nicholas Rescher (1995) intended for a non-philosophical audience.[2] So I was faced with the task of coming up with an account myself, pretty much *ex nihilo*.

The reason I mention this backstory is that I think it could well be significant. This is because it always seemed obvious to me that luck is primarily a modal notion, and hence would need to be understood in terms of possible worlds. I suspect that it is coming to this issue via epistemology that makes this so obvious, as modal epistemology had long since been an established feature of epistemological debate, and was employed, among other things, to deal with cases like the lottery case and Gettier-style scenarios that explicitly trade on the anti-luck platitude.

So, for example, why not think of luck along probabilistic rather than modal lines, such that lucky events are events that obtain even despite the odds being against them occurring? That would certainly capture some key cases of luck, such as being lucky not to be killed in a plane crash that killed nearly everyone else (your chances of survival were clearly very low). But anyone familiar with the epistemological literature, and in particular the lottery case, would immediately see the difficulty that such an approach would face.

One of the morals of the lottery case is that one cannot come to know that one's lottery ticket (for a lottery with very long odds) is a losing ticket simply by reflecting on the odds involved, even though one can come to know that it is a losing ticket by reading the result in a reliable newspaper. If knowledge were straightforwardly a function of one's epistemic support, probabilistically understood—i.e., such that the more the odds are in favor of your belief being true, the more likely one is to have knowledge—then this result would be puzzling. After all, the odds of the newspaper printing the wrong results, while very low, is not as astronomically low as one's ticket being a winner. But what lottery cases remind us is that probability is an imperfect guide to modal closeness. In particular, while low probability events will tend to be modally far-fetched, and high probability events will tend to be modally close, there can nonetheless be events that are both modally close and yet very low probability. Indeed, that is precisely what is happening in lotteries (and in fact is the reason, I would suggest, why people play lotteries, even though they would not normally "bet" on events with such long odds). After all, that one's ticket is a winner, while enjoying astronomically low odds, is nonetheless modally close—all that needs to happen is that a few coloured balls fall in a slightly different configuration. This is the reason why you cannot know that you have lost the lottery merely by reflecting on the odds involved, since that way of forming your belief could easily lead you astray (i.e., in the close possible world where you are a winner). Not so if you form your belief by reading the result in a reliable newspaper. While the odds are not so astronomically in your favor, this method of belief-formation will not easily lead you astray. In fact, in the close possible world in which you are a winner you will read different results and hence continue to have a true belief (albeit in a different proposition, as now you will truly believe that you have won the lottery).

With the foregoing in mind, it should be clear that a probabilistic account of luck will founder when it comes to dealing with low probability events that are nonetheless modally close. For example, if there is some feature of one's actual circumstances that means that there is a close possible world where you have been killed—your fate depends on the result of a lottery draw, say—then intuitively one is lucky to be alive, even though the odds of one being killed might well be very low (even astronomically low, as in lottery cases).[3] But of course the probabilistic account of luck would be obliged to claim that the exact opposite is true.[4]

We are now in a position to say what, at its core, the modal account of luck amounts to.

The Core Modal Account of Luck

An event that actually occurs is a lucky event to the extent that it fails to obtain in close possible worlds where the same relevant initial conditions for that event continue to occur. In particular, the closer the possible world where the event fails to obtain relative to the same initial conditions, the luckier the event.[5]

Let us unpack this claim, using an example as illustration. Suppose that one has narrowly avoided being shot by a sniper, with the bullet flying inches away from your head. You are clearly lucky to be alive. According to the modal account of luck, the reason for this is that there is a close possible world where you have been killed by a sniper's bullet. Moreover, notice that the modal account can neatly capture the idea that luck comes in degrees, such that some events are luckier than others. Imagine that in the actual world the bullet flies by not inches from your head, but feet. In that case, while we still might say that you are lucky to be alive, you are clearly less lucky than in the case where the bullet misses your head by inches. But that difference is reflected in the modal account of luck by the fact that such physical distance from hitting you in the actual world will entail that the closest possible world where you are hit by the bullet will be further out. This is just the point of the second clause in the core account above, to spell out how the modal account of luck can capture this "continuum" aspect of luck.

I think it is also clear that we need to keep the relevant initial conditions for the target event fixed if we want to capture the modal profile that we are after for lucky events. Again, that this is required will be a familiar point to those coming to this issue from epistemology, as modal conditions in epistemology also need to be "basis-relative," which amounts to the same thing in this setting.[6] Take the sniper case again. Perhaps in most close possible worlds you elected to go out in full body armour that day. In that case, there might be very few close possible worlds where you get shot and killed. But the possible worlds where you elect to wear full body armour do not seem to be relevant to an assessment of your luckiness to be alive in the actual world where you did not wear such protective armour. Similarly, perhaps in most close possible worlds our sniper has taken medication that makes him a dreadful shot (without the medication he is one of the best in the business). Again, while that might mean that there are few close possible worlds where you get shot and killed, the possible worlds where the sniper is drugged do not seem relevant to the assessment of your luckiness to be alive in an actual world where a highly skilled and unmedicated sniper shot at you. I think in most cases it is usually pretty clear what needs to be kept fixed, but that does not mean that there is a straightforward way of specifying, in advance, what kinds of things go into the initial conditions and what kinds of things do not.[7]

In any case, with the core modal account so described, one can see how it deals with a range of cases. Lottery wins are lucky events since one fails to win in relevant close possible worlds (e.g., worlds where one continues to buy a lottery ticket). Likewise, one's unskilled, but successful (i.e., one's hits the target), archery shot is lucky because in relevant close possible worlds one misses altogether. In contrast, when one's highly skilled counterpart hits the target this is not down to luck, but that is because in relevant close possible worlds—where, for example, the weather conditions are similar, she is not distracted or the shot interfered with, etc.—she continues to hit the target. And so on.

The Significance Condition

Before we consider some putative counterexamples for the modal account of luck, there is a further possible feature of the view that we need to outline. In my earlier presentations of the modal account of luck I incorporated a second condition, known as the *significance condition*.[8] The idea was to capture the thought that merely having the right kind of modal structure was not sufficient for an event to count as lucky; it also had to be an event that we either do, or should, find significant in some way. So, for example, there might be things occurring right now on distant planets, or at the microscopic level, that are absolutely of no significance for us, but which have the modal profile set out in the core modal account of luck. In that case, I argued, then they do not count as lucky.[9]

I now think that including the significance condition was a mistake. (This is especially unfortunate, as most contemporary theorists of luck have followed me in incorporating such a condition into their views). The issue comes down to what we are expecting from a theory of luck. Adding the significance condition certainly helps the account to match up with our ascriptions of luck, since we do not of course ascribe the property of luck to insignificant events, regardless of their modal profile. But I think that the fact that we do not ascribe the property of luck to insignificant events does not in itself suffice to show that insignificant events with the relevant modal profile are not lucky. After all, we do not tend to ascribe *any* properties to insignificant events, precisely because we are not interested in them. Nonetheless, such events surely do possess many properties. I think the same applies to insignificant events with the relevant modal profile. That is, I claim that once we understand the modal nature of luck, we realize that all events with this modal profile count as lucky, regardless of their significance. It is just that, since they are insignificant, we have no interest in these events (and rightly so).

One implication of dropping the significance condition is that it undermines an argument that Nathan Ballantyne (2011) has offered to the effect that incorporating the anti-luck condition into a theory of knowledge requires one to embrace pragmatic encroachment regarding knowledge. This is the idea that whether one counts as having knowledge can be significantly determined, at least in part, by purely pragmatic factors, such as the practical importance that one's belief be true. One can easily see how such an argument would proceed. What we find significant is inevitably determined in large part by pragmatic factors, and in particular by factors that are not relevant from a purely epistemic point of view, such as our practical interests, or even what kinds of things happen to have been made explicit to us. Accordingly, it seems to follow that what counts as a lucky event is, in part, determined by pragmatic factors. Hence, if there is to be an anti-luck condition within a theory of knowledge, then does it not follow that whether one counts as having knowledge is, in significant part anyway, determined by pragmatic rather than purely epistemic factors? If that is right, then one is obliged to endorse the pragmatic encroachment thesis regarding knowledge.

Now one might think that this conclusion is harmless. It is certainly true that a number of high-profile epistemologists have endorsed some version of the pragmatic encroachment thesis regarding knowledge.[10] Personally, however, I find pragmatic encroachment to be something to be resisted, though it would take us too far afield to evaluate the merits of the thesis here. In any case, even if Ballantyne is right that the significance condition inevitably introduces pragmatic factors into the nature of luck, I do not think it follows that anti-luck epistemology is committed to pragmatic encroachment about knowledge. For that to follow, one would need to in addition show that when the modal account of luck is incorporated within a theory of knowledge, as anti-luck epistemology advocates, it brings pragmatic factors specifically into the epistemic realm. But this further claim is far from obvious, and the reason for this is that the luck is targeted on the specific event of belief-formation. When epistemically evaluating beliefs, and in particular considering whether they satisfy the anti-luck condition, would we really think that pragmatic factors regarding the significance of the event of belief-formation would have any bearing? My instinct is that this is not the case. At the very least, I would need to hear more before being convinced on this score.

In any case, if one drops the significance condition from one's theory of luck, then this particular argument for why proponents of anti-luck epistemology should embrace pragmatic encouragement about knowledge does not go through anyway. Note that this is not to say that this is the only way in which a modal theory of luck could lead to a commitment to the pragmatic encroachment thesis regarding knowledge. One might argue, for example, that pragmatic factors are already in play in determining such things as modal closeness, in which case that would offer a different route toward the same conclusion.[11] But at the very least, we can say that the most straightforward way of committing anti-luck epistemology to pragmatic encroachment about knowledge is blocked, to the extent that those who wish to motivate this entailment still have a lot of work to do.[12]

The Modal Account of Luck and its Rivals

In response to the development of the modal account of luck, recent years have seen competing accounts of luck proposed. This is not the place to evaluate all of these competing accounts in detail, so what I propose to do instead is examine some of the most plausible contenders in this regard, including some putative counterexamples that have been proposed for the modal account of luck.

Consider first Rescher's (1995) theory of luck. In essence, Rescher claims that lucky events are events that the subject cannot rationally expect to occur.[13] For a wide range of cases, events that satisfy the modal account of luck will also satisfy Rescher's account, and vice versa. After all, a lucky event according to the modal account of luck is an event that could very easily have not occurred. One would thus expect it to be the kind of event that one could not rationally expect to occur. And it is at least often the case that events that one cannot rationally expect to occur, such as lottery wins, are also events that could very easily have not occurred. Crucially, however, these two accounts do come apart in terms of what they predict about particular cases, and where they do our judgments tend to go with the modal account.

For example, Rescher (1995: 35) gives the example of someone who receives a lot of money unexpectedly from a benefactor. Rescher argues that this constitutes good luck on the agent's part even if this bequest has been a long time in the planning. But I think we need to be careful here. Perhaps our agent might well be inclined to put this event down to luck, but it is not this judgment that should concern us (as it is almost certainly made while not being in possession of full information), but rather what we would say about the case once we are apprised of all the relevant facts. In particular, once it is clear that the bequest had been planned for a long time and hence was effectively guaranteed to occur, then the temptation to regard it as a lucky event subsides.[14]

A related kind of example that might be thought to present problems for the modal account of luck is offered by Jennifer Lackey (2008: §2):

> Sophie, knowing that she had very little time left to live, wanted to bury a chest filled with all of her earthly treasures on the island she inhabited. As she walked around trying to determine the best site for proper burial, her central criteria were, first, that a suitable location must be on the northwest corner of the island—where she had spent many of her fondest moments in life—and, second, that it had to be a spot where rose bushes could flourish—since these were her favorite flowers. As it happens, there was only one particular patch of land on the northwest corner of the island where the soil was rich enough for roses to thrive. Sophie, being excellent at detecting such soil, immediately located this patch of land and buried her treasure, along with seeds for future roses to bloom, in the one and only spot that fulfilled her two criteria.
>
> One month later, Vincent, a distant neighbor of Sophie's, was driving in the northwest corner of the island—which was also his most beloved place to visit—and was looking for a place to plant a rose bush in memory of his mother who had died ten years earlier—since these were her favorite flowers. Being excellent at detecting the proper soil for rose bushes to thrive, he immediately located the same patch of land that Sophie had found one month earlier. As he began digging a hole for the bush, he was astonished to discover a buried treasure in the ground.

Lackey describes Vincent's discovery of the buried treasure in this case as a "paradigmatic" instance of a lucky event, and yet this does not seem to accord with what the modal account of luck would say about the case. In particular, we are clearly meant to suppose that Vincent could not help but be successful in finding the treasure, and if that is right there will be no relevant close possible world where he is unsuccessful in this regard. As with Rescher's example of the bequest, however, I think we need to look a little more closely at the details of this case.

The example is rather ambiguous in certain respects, and once one notices this it ceases to be quite so obvious that Vincent is guaranteed to find the treasure. For example, how large is this "patch of land" that Sophie locates? The example only functions as Lackey wants it to if this patch is roughly the same size as the treasure, since it is only then that Vincent is guaranteed to find the treasure in this spot. Otherwise, he could have easily planted the rose bush on this patch of land and yet not found the treasure, and that would be consistent with the event being classed as lucky according to the modal account. Moreover, how deep was the treasure buried? Presumably a treasure chest would need to be buried fairly deep to prevent it from becoming exposed accidentally (e.g., from the effects of the weather), but if that is right then it is possible that one could plant a shrub on this ground without coming across the treasure (remember, after all, that our agent is not looking for treasure). Hence there is, again, no obvious inconsistency between this example and the modal account of luck. And so on.

We can remove these ambiguities by adding some additional details to the case. For example, we can stipulate that the areas on the island where one might bury treasure all come in distinct patches not much bigger than the treasure itself, and that the soil on these patches becomes too hard to turn very quickly, so that the treasure cannot be buried very deep. In this way, we can ensure that if anyone chose the patch of land in which the treasure was buried to dig (for whatever reason, including to plant a shrub), they would find the treasure. Now we further stipulate that there is only one patch of land on the island that is suitable for planting rose bushes, and that it is obvious that this is so to anyone who knows about these things.

With these details added, we now get the result that Lackey wanted, such that Vincent is guaranteed to find the treasure, but are we still inclined to judge that this discovery is lucky? In particular, remember that, just as with the case that Rescher offers, we need to set aside the fact that Vincent himself might well describe this discovery as lucky, since he is not availed of all the pertinent facts. The relevant judgment for us concerns someone who (like ourselves) knows everything salient to the case, and in particular knows that Vincent is guaranteed to find this treasure. I take it that once we make clear that Vincent is guaranteed to find the treasure, however, and so form our judgment about whether the event is lucky while being fully aware of this fact, then the temptation to characterize the event as lucky disappears. Sure, the discovery is *accidental*, since Vincent was not aiming to find the treasure, but it is not a matter of luck that he finds treasure in this spot, as he was bound to make this discovery in this case.[15]

Indeed, this case is, in many ways, akin to Rescher's example of the long-planned bequest. Although it is not an accident that the agent in Rescher's case receives the bequest (as it was planned that he should receive it), just like Lackey's case this pleasant turn of events can seem lucky at first glance simply in virtue of it being unexpected and surprising. But once one recognizes that the target event was bound to happen then, just like Vincent's discovery of the treasure, it no longer strikes one as lucky.[16]

This brings me to the relationship between luck and control. A recurring idea in the literature on luck, particularly moral luck, is that lucky events are events that the agent lacks control over.[17] Construed as a rough necessary condition on luck, the claim is quite plausible, but so construed it is also not in any obvious tension with the modal account of luck. For if an event is within one's control to bring about, and one does bring it about, then how could it not obtain in close possible worlds where the initial conditions for that event are the same (e.g., where one continues to try to bring it about)? (Indeed, it would be a very fishy sense of "control" if it did not generate this consequence). It is unsurprising then that events that are lucky on the modal account also tend to be outside of one's control. Hence there is no need for the proponent of the modal account to object to the idea that lucky events are events that are not in the agent's control (at least in some suitable sense of "control").[18]

The idea that lack of control is a sufficient condition for a lucky event is, however, highly dubious. To take a familiar example from the literature, the sun rose this morning, an event that none of us has any control over whatsoever, but that does not make it lucky that the sun rose—indeed, it was inevitable that it would rise.[19] It is thus incumbent upon proponents of the view that lack of control is sufficient for luck to propose a more nuanced rendering of this idea.

In recent work, Wayne Riggs (2009) has tried to resurrect the lack of control theory of luck.[20] Here is his statement of this view (where "E" stands for the target event):

E is lucky for S iff;
(a)   E is (too far) out of S's control, and
(b) S did not successfully exploit E for some purpose, and

(c)   E is significant to *S* (or would be significant, were *S* to be availed of the relevant facts).

Riggs 2009: 220

Notice that Riggs follows my earlier self in opting for a significance condition on lucky events. As I explained above, however, it now strikes me as a mistake to include such a subjective factor in one's account of luck. Relatedly, notice that Riggs is not defining lucky events per se (as I do), but rather the very different notion of events that are lucky *for a subject*. With the significance condition included in the account of luck this might well make sense, in that the relevant notion of significance will probably be an agent-relative one, and hence the resulting account of luck will be agent-relative too (different things can be significant to different people after all). But insofar as we reject the significance condition, then is there any reason to treat an account of luck as being relativized to agents in this way? I think not, though as we will see it might well be crucial to Riggs' account that he continues to conceive of luck in this fashion.

With the foregoing in mind, let us turn our attention to conditions (a) and (b) in Riggs' account of luck. Whereas (a) is relatively clear, (b) is more opaque. In particular, what does it mean to "exploit" an event for a purpose? We can get a handle on what Riggs has in mind in this regard by considering an example that he uses.[21]

Recall that we noted a moment ago that an obvious problem facing lack of control views concerns events such as the rising of the sun that are completely out of anyone's control but which are not classed as lucky. Riggs claims that our verdict in this regard is too quick. He asks us to imagine a case where two explorers—called Smith and Jones—are about to be executed by a local tribe, only for a total eclipse to come along and for this to lead to the tribesmen abandoning their plan to kill the explorers. Riggs now imagines that while one of the explorers—Smith—had no inkling that the eclipse was going to happen, the other explorer—Jones—knew full well that this event would occur. In particular, Jones was counting on the eclipse occurring as a means of avoiding possible execution by the natives.

Riggs concludes that while the event was not lucky for Jones, it was lucky for Smith. And note that this is even despite the fact that an eclipse is a nomically necessary event that is beyond anyone's control just as much as the sun's rising in the morning. In terms of the account of luck that Riggs offers, the difference between Smith and Jones relates to condition (b). For while, in line with (a), the event in question is equally completely beyond the control of either of them, it is only Smith who did not successfully exploit this event for his purposes (because he did not know it was going to occur).

That Riggs is here talking about an event that is lucky for one agent but not for another should give us pause for further reflection. For while it is undeniable that the event will seem lucky to Smith, since he was lacking crucial information about this event, we should not conclude from the mere fact that an event seems lucky to a certain individual who lacks relevant information that therefore it is lucky. Indeed, once we set aside the fact that Smith is lacking crucial information, there seems no obvious reason why we would regard the eclipse happening when it did as being lucky at all—after all, it was *bound* to happen when it did. The relevant judgment to follow in this regard is thus not Smith's but ours, which (since we are in full possession of the facts) would surely accord with Jones' judgment that this event was not lucky at all. Furthermore, notice that once we know the facts of the situation then it matters not one jot whether we failed to "successfully exploit" the event in question, since even when it is stipulated that condition (b) is met, we nevertheless do not regard the event as lucky.

In any case, this is all by-the-by since Riggs' account still fails to explain why paradigm cases of events that are outwith an agent's control do not thereby count as lucky. For example, what would Riggs say about the standard case of the sun rising in the morning? Doesn't this event satisfy the conditions on luck that Riggs lays down, and therefore count as lucky? Indeed, it is hard to see how adding the condition regarding the subject's failure to exploit this event for some purpose makes any difference to this perennial problem for the lack of control account of luck, given that it is *normally* the case that nomically necessary events such as this are not exploited in this way. It follows that the account of luck that Riggs is offering is untenable, at least unless one wishes to treat whole swathes of nomically necessary events as lucky. Even on a more nuanced reading, then, the lack of control account of luck is still implausible.

The alert reader will have noticed a common thread running through these responses to critiques of the modal account of luck. This is that we need to be alert to the details of the cases offered, and in particular to the point that what we are ultimately interested in is what our judgment of the case would be once we know all the salient facts. Once we fill in the relevant details, and draw our verdict in light of our possession of all the relevant facts, then the putative difficulties posed for the modal account of luck quickly disappear. Given the clear merits of the modal account of luck, and the problems facing rival views—and, for that matter, putative counterexamples to the modal account of luck—I think we can safely conclude that the modal account can reasonably lay claim to being the most credible theory of luck currently available.[22]

Notes

1 I develop anti-luck epistemology—including how it can be incorporated within a wider theory of knowledge that I call *anti-luck virtue epistemology*—in a number of places. See, for example, Pritchard (2004, 2005, 2007, 2008, 2009, 2012a, 2012b, 2015a, 2017a) and Pritchard, Millar, & Haddock (2010: chs. 1–4). See also the closely related account that I offer of *anti-risk epistemology*—and thus *anti-risk virtue epistemology*—in Pritchard (2015b, 2016, 2017b).

2 I discuss Rescher's (1995) account of luck below.

3 Incidentally, the empirical literature on luck ascriptions—and, relatedly, risk ascriptions, given the close conceptual connections between luck and risk—clearly bears this out. See, for example, the detailed work done on this topic by Teigen (1995, 1996, 1997, 1998a, 1998b, 2003). I discuss this empirical literature in more detail in Pritchard & Smith (2004). See also Pritchard (2014: §1).

4 Interestingly, the idea of offering a probabilistic account of luck has not been popular. This is especially odd given that the dominant account of risk in the literature—a notion that is very closely tied to luck—*is* cast along probabilistic lines, though I have argued in several places that it should be replaced by a modal account of risk. See, for example, Pritchard (2015b). For discussion of the probabilistic account of luck, see Rescher (2019).

5 This is essentially the account of luck that I originally offered in Pritchard (2004, 2005), and which I have elaborated upon in Pritchard (2014). As noted below in the next section, the original modal account of luck that I offered also had a second significance condition, but in more recent work I have dropped this condition.

6 See Dretske (1970, 1971) and Nozick (1981) for two early accounts of modal conditions on knowledge that incorporated basis-relativity.

7 One thing that is clear about our specification of initial conditions is that we absolutely do not want an account of them which entails that the event in question must occur, since in that case we would not be able to capture the idea that this event can be lucky (i.e., such that it could be an easy possibility that it does not occur).

8 See especially Pritchard (2005: ch. 5).

9 For further discussion of the significance condition, see Ballantyne & Kampa (2019).

10 See, for example, Fantl & McGrath (2002, 2009), Hawthorne (2004), and Stanley (2005).

11 I discuss the question of whether proponents of the modal theory of luck should be worried about some of the inherent difficulties associated with possible worlds in Pritchard (2014: §3).

12 For further discussion of the putative link between anti-luck epistemology, the significance condition, and pragmatic encroachment about knowledge, see Pritchard (2014: §2).

13 A similar proposal has recently been offered by Steglich-Peterson (2010).

14 Another point to make about this case is that it confuses luck with the related notion of fortune. It was always key to my defence of the modal account to differentiate luck from other notions in the vicinity, such as fortune, accident, chanciness, and so on, though this feature of the view is often overlooked. See, for example, Pritchard (2005: ch. 5, 2014). See also endnotes 15 and 16.

15 As I explain in Pritchard (2005, 2014), it is important to keep apart luck and accidents, as they are not the same thing. For example, if one plays the lottery and wins, that is lucky, but it is not an accident that one

won, as this was precisely what one was hoping to achieve by buying the lottery ticket. See also endnotes 14 and 16.

16 The similarities between this case and Rescher's example could explain why we might be tempted to characterize this example as one of good fortune. One point to keep in mind here is that Vincent is in this case finding a fortune (in treasure), and that this might well constitute background noise that impairs our judgment about the case. Would we describe a parallel case where the accidental discovery is not treasure but, say, a long-lost keepsake of sentimental rather than financial value as a case of good fortune? My instinct is that we would not, and I think this reflects the fact that good fortune tends to relate to long-term significant features of one's life. For further discussion of Lackey's critique of the modal account of luck, see Levy (2009, 2011: ch. 2). See also endnote 14 and 15.

17 The *locus classicus* when it comes to the debate about moral luck is the exchange between Nagel (1976) and Williams (1976). I offer my own response to this problem in Pritchard (2006; cf. Pritchard 2005: ch. 10). See also Driver (2012), who discusses the modal account of luck in the context of the problem of moral luck. For defences of (versions of) the lack of control account of luck, see Nagel (1976), Statman (1991), Zimmerman (1993), Greco (1995), Riggs (2007, 2009), and Coffman (2007, 2009). See also endnote 18.

18 That said, the idea that lack of control is even a necessary condition on luck has been criticized. See, especially, Lackey (2008). For discussion, see Coffman (2009) and Levy (2009, 2011: ch. 2). Note that Levy (2011: ch. 2) offers a hybrid account of luck that has both a modal and a lack of control element. Given that the modal account of luck offered here is consistent with the idea that lack of control is a necessary condition for a lucky event, it is thus not obviously inconsistent with Levy's proposal. Interestingly, Levy also thinks that there is a second kind of luck besides the type that we are discussing here which concerns lucky events. This is roughly equivalent to what Nagel (1976) had in mind when he wrote about "constitutive luck," which is luck in the traits and dispositions that one has. I must confess that I am skeptical that this is a genuine kind of luck, as I think the notion that Levy has in mind is probably best understood in terms of the distinct notion of fortune. On this point, see also endnote 14.

19 I believe Latus (2000: 167) was the first to offer this example. See also Pritchard (2005: ch. 5).

20 See also Riggs (2019).

21 The example is from Riggs (2009: §5).

22 Thanks to Ian Church for detailed comments on an earlier version of this chapter.

References

Ballantyne, N. (2011) "Anti-Luck Epistemology, Pragmatic Encroachment, and True Belief," *Canadian Journal of Philosophy* 41, 485–504.

Ballantyne, N., & Kampa, S. (2019) "Luck and Significance," in I.M. Church & R.J. Hartman (eds.) *The Routledge Handbook of the Philosophy and Psychology of Luck*, London: Routledge.

Coffman, E.J. (2007) "Thinking About Luck," *Synthese* 158, 385–398.

———. (2009) "Does Luck Exclude Control?" *Australasian Journal of Philosophy* 87, 499–504.

Dretske, F. (1970) "Epistemic Operators," *Journal of Philosophy* 67, 1007–1023.

———. (1971) "Conclusive Reasons," *Australasian Journal of Philosophy* 49, 1–22.

Driver, J. (2012) "Luck and Fortune in Moral Evaluation," in M. Blaauw (ed.) *Contrastivism in Philosophy*, London: Routledge, ch. 8.

Fantl, J., & McGrath, M. (2002) "Evidence, Pragmatics, and Justification," *Philosophical Review* 111(1), 67–94.

———. (2007) "On Pragmatic Encroachment in Epistemology," *Philosophy and Phenomenological Research* 75, 558–589.

———. (2009) *Knowledge in an Uncertain World*, Oxford: Oxford University Press.

Greco, J. (1995) "A Second Paradox Concerning Responsibility and Luck," *Metaphilosophy* 26, 81–96.

Hawthorne, J. (2004) *Knowledge and Lotteries*, Oxford: Clarendon Press.

Lackey, J. (2008) "What Luck Is Not," *Australasian Journal of Philosophy* 86, 255–267.

Latus, A. (2000) "Moral and Epistemic Luck," *Journal of Philosophical Research* 25, 149–172.

Levy, N. (2009) "What, and Where, Luck is: A Response to Jennifer Lackey," *Australasian Journal of Philosophy* 87, 489–497.

———. (2011) *Hard Luck: How Luck Undermines Free Will and Moral Responsibility*, Oxford: Oxford University Press.

Nagel, T. (1976). "Moral Luck," *Proceedings of the Aristotelian Society* 50 (suppl. vol.), 137–152.

Nozick, R. (1981) *Philosophical Explanations*, Oxford: Oxford University Press.

Pritchard, D.H. (2004) "Epistemic Luck," *Journal of Philosophical Research* 29, 193–222.

———. (2005) *Epistemic Luck*, Oxford: Oxford University Press.

———. (2006) "Moral and Epistemic Luck," *Metaphilosophy* 37, 1–25.

———. (2007) "Anti-Luck Epistemology," *Synthese* 158, 277–297.

——. (2008) "Sensitivity, Safety, and Anti-Luck Epistemology," in J. Greco (ed.) *Oxford Handbook of Scepticism*, Oxford: Oxford University Press, pp. 437–455.

——. (2009) "Safety-Based Epistemology: Whither Now?," *Journal of Philosophical Research* 34, 33–45.

——. (2012a) "Anti-Luck Virtue Epistemology," *Journal of Philosophy* 109, 247–279.

——. (2012b) "In Defence of Modest Anti-Luck Epistemology," in T. Black & K. Becker (eds.) *The Sensitivity Principle in Epistemology*, Cambridge, UK: Cambridge University Press, pp. 173–192.

——. (2014) "The Modal Account of Luck," *Metaphilosophy* 45, 594–619.

——. (2015a) "Anti-Luck Epistemology and the Gettier Problem," *Philosophical Studies* 172, 93–111.

——. (2015b) "Risk," *Metaphilosophy* 46, 436–461.

——. (2016) "Epistemic Risk," *Journal of Philosophy* 113, 550–571.

——. (2017a) "Knowledge, Luck and Virtue: Resolving the Gettier Problem," in C. Almeida, P. Klein, & R. Borges (eds.) *The Gettier Problem*, Oxford: Oxford University Press, pp. 57–73.

——. (2017b) "Anti-Risk Epistemology and Negative Epistemic Dependence," *Synthese*, doi: https://doi.org/10.1007/s11229-017-1586-6.

Pritchard, D.H., Millar, A., & Haddock, A. (2010) *The Nature and Value of Knowledge: Three Investigations*, Oxford: Oxford University Press.

Pritchard, D.H., & Smith, M. (2004) "The Psychology and Philosophy of Luck," *New Ideas in Psychology* 22, 1–28.

Rescher, N. (1995) *Luck: The Brilliant Randomness of Everyday Life*, New York: Farrar, Straus & Giroux.

——. (2019) "The Probability Account of Luck," in I.M. Church & R.J. Hartman (eds.) *The Routledge Handbook of the Philosophy and Psychology of Luck*, London: Routledge.

Riggs, W. (2007) "Why Epistemologists Are So Down on Their Luck," *Synthese* 158, 329–344.

——. (2009) "Luck, Knowledge, and Control," in A. Haddock, A. Millar, & D.H. Pritchard (eds.) *Epistemic Value*, Oxford: Oxford University Press, pp. 204–221.

——. (2019) "The Lack of Control Account of Luck," in I.M. Church & R.J. Hartman (eds.) *The Routledge Handbook of the Philosophy and Psychology of Luck*, London: Routledge.

Stanley, J. (2005) *Knowledge and Practical Interests*, Oxford: Oxford University Press.

Statman, D. (1991) "Moral and Epistemic Luck," *Ratio* 4, 146–156.

Steglich-Peterson, A. (2010) "Luck as an Epistemic Notion," *Synthese* 176, 361–377.

Teigen, K.H. (1995) "How Good Is Good Luck? The Role of Counterfactual Thinking in the Perception of Lucky and Unlucky Events," *European Journal of Social Psychology* 25, 281–302.

——. (1996) "Luck: The Art of a Near Miss," *Scandinavian Journal of Psychology* 37, 156–171.

——. (1997) "Luck, Envy, Gratitude: It Could Have Been Different," *Scandinavian Journal of Psychology* 38, 318–323.

——. (1998a) "Hazards Mean Luck: Counterfactual Thinking and Perceptions of Good and Bad Fortune in Reports of Dangerous Situations and Careless Behaviour," *Scandinavian Journal of Psychology* 39, 235–248.

——. (1998b) "When the Unreal is More Likely Than the Real: *Post Hoc* Probability Judgements and Counterfactual Closeness," *Thinking and Reasoning* 4, 147–177.

——. (2003) "When a Small Difference Makes a Large Difference: Counterfactual Thinking and Luck," in D. R. Mandel, D. Hilton, & P. Catellani (eds.) *The Psychology of Counterfactual Thinking*, London: Routledge, 129–146.

Williams, B. (1976) "Moral Luck," *Proceedings of the Aristotelian Society* 50 (*suppl. vol.*), 115–135.

Zimmerman, M. (1993) "Luck and Moral Responsibility," in D. Statman (ed.) *Moral Luck*, Albany, NY: State University of New York Press, pp. 217–234.

11

THE LACK OF CONTROL ACCOUNT OF LUCK

Wayne Riggs

In this chapter I will develop and defend a theory of luck often referred to as the "Lack of Control Account of Luck" or LCAL. The basic idea that motivates the view is simple: when something happens that you have no control over, its happening is a matter of pure luck with respect to you. The converse seems even more obvious: when something happens because you intentionally made it so, then its happening is no accident. Alas, as is all too common in philosophy, the obvious does not always hold up under critical analysis. And so the LCAL has to earn its keep the hard way, like any other philosophical view, by surviving rigorous articulation and objections.

The LCAL has been developed and portrayed in the philosophical literature as a "universal" theory of luck—that is, a theory meant to capture what we mean by "luck" in pretty much all circumstances. But what we mean, even in one circumstance, can be hard to determine. Paradigm cases of lucky events embody many features that could be (and have been) assumed central to what "luck" means. For instance, consider a fair lottery with 1,000,000 tickets. Only one ticket can be a winner, and mine is that ticket. Let us further suppose that I bought only the one ticket. This is clearly my lucky day! But what about that event makes it lucky? You might think that it is the fact that it was so unlikely beforehand. The odds were literally a million to one! Or, you might think it is lucky because if things had gone only the slightest bit differently, my ticket would not have won. Someone else's would have. Or, you might think, as the LCAL suggests, that it is because I had nothing at all to do with my ticket being picked as the winner. Each of these suggestions is embodied in a corresponding theory of luck.[1]

In later sections of the chapter, I will make the best case I can for LCAL as a universal theory of luck, but it is important to note that much of the motivation for such a view comes from LCAL's earlier success in two narrower domains: the moral luck literature and the theory of knowledge. Consequently, any defense of LCAL must begin by discussing the role of LCAL in those domains. I will touch briefly on the moral luck literature later, but I will begin with a detailed account of the origins of LCAL as a theory of epistemic luck. By "epistemic luck," I mean the kind of luck that undermines justification in one's beliefs, and hence undermines knowledge. It is helpful to see the origin of LCAL as a theory of epistemic luck in order to appreciate its considerable theoretical virtues, as well as its inherent limitations. Thus, I will summarize the argument for LCAL as a theory of epistemic luck in the first two sections. In later sections I will briefly discuss LCAL as an account of moral luck and examine the prospects of LCAL as a universal theory of luck.

125

Wayne Riggs

Gettier and the Internalism/Externalism Debate

In 1963, Edmund Gettier published a short paper titled "Is Justified True Belief Knowledge?" This paper had a monumental effect on the trajectory of work in epistemology until nearly the end of the century. The details of the "Gettier Era" in epistemology[2] are not relevant to the current topic, but some of its lasting effects are. I shall highlight two that are of interest here.

Gettier stipulated that (then) current attempts to analyze knowledge could generally be characterized by this formula (Gettier 1963: 121):

S knows that p iff

(i)   p is true,
(ii) S believes that p, and
(iii) S is justified in believing that p.

He even suggested in a footnote that this analysis of knowledge could be traced all the way back to Plato. This codification of the analysis of knowledge ultimately contributed to an intense focus on theories of justification, as justification was taken to be that which turns true belief into knowledge. This is the first effect.

But the point of Gettier's paper was to argue that this formula cannot be correct. He showed this by detailing two (hypothetical) cases in which someone has a justified true belief but seems not to have knowledge. Leaving aside much debate, disquisition, and detail, the key insight that was ultimately gleaned from Gettier's argument and his ingenious cases was that one could come to have a justified true belief in a way that was simply too "lucky" to count as knowledge.[3] Subsequent work in epistemology focused heavily on determining how to eliminate this pernicious element of luck. Many new theories of justification and knowledge were promulgated with ever more elaborate conditions designed to capture what is essential to knowledge while eliminating the pernicious element of luck. This is the second effect.

By the end of the Gettier era, epistemologists had become quite accustomed to talking about epistemic justification as that property which (all but) turned true belief into knowledge. And they increasingly saw justification as that which assured that one's true belief was not so by chance. Here are some characteristic quotes (these and more are cited in (Riggs 1998)).

> But true belief is not sufficient for knowledge, at least not in the strict sense of "know". If it is just accidental that you are right about p, then you do not know that p, even if you are correct in believing it … One traditional proposal for strengthening the requirements is to add a justification requirement.
>
> *Goldman 1986: 42*

> But knowledge is more than mere true belief. For your belief that it is raining could be true even if you didn't know that it is raining. Perhaps you have simply made a lucky guess. What, then, must be added to true belief to get knowledge? … The traditional or classic answer … is that knowledge is justified true belief.
>
> *Chisholm 1989: 90; emphasis original*

These are representative samples of the way in which Gettier-era epistemologists thought about epistemic justification. Textbooks, especially, were prone to explaining the need for a justification condition for knowledge by appeal to the possibility of "lucky guesses" and "accidentally true beliefs."

Yet despite wide agreement about the incompatibility of knowledge with luck, there were deeply entrenched disputes about the fundamental nature of the elusive property that was supposed to preclude lucky true belief from counting as knowledge—i.e., epistemic justification. The dispute most relevant to the development of LCAL is the internalism/externalism controversy. A vestige of this dispute rages on to some extent, but it was exceptionally lively in the last quarter of the 20th century. There are many ways of drawing the distinction between internalism and externalism, and these evolved over time. LCAL grew out of a version which pitted so-called "accessibility internalism," which emphasizes the importance of the believer's epistemic responsibility, and reliabilist externalism, which emphasizes the reliability of belief-forming processes at generating true beliefs.[4]

In (Riggs 1998), I argued that the solution to the internalist/externalist debate about the fundamental *nature* of epistemic justification was to be found in the widespread agreement about its apparent *function*—i.e., to preclude the possibility of lucky knowledge. My argument began by positing that externalist and internalist conceptions of epistemic justification do not actually articulate rival accounts of the same property, state, or phenomenon. In fact, I argue, each conception describes a legitimate and important epistemic property, each with its own distinct criteria of success. Hence, attempts to argue that one or the other is *the* correct account of justification are misguided and doomed to failure.

Epistemic Luck

This kind of "resolution by distinction" is a common strategy in philosophical rhetoric. When two camps have been arguing assiduously for some time without resolution, perhaps they are simply talking about different things. However, such a strategy raises two important questions in this case. First, what makes each of these kinds of justification distinctly necessary for knowing? Second, and relatedly, what explains why the need for this distinction was not apparent from the beginning?

The answers, I argued, are to be found in the consensus about knowledge and luck mentioned in the previous section. But though most epistemologists agreed that justification must preclude luck, internalists and externalists focused on different kinds of luck (or ways of being lucky). Externalists focused on ruling out true beliefs produced in ways that were very unlikely to yield a true belief, though they had done so in this instance. (Think lucky guesses, hunches, believing what one sees at a glance, etc.) Internalists focused on ruling out true beliefs whose bearers had been negligent in coming to hold the belief—bearers who had not done their due diligence to ensure that their belief was true. Sometimes this occurs through carelessness (e.g., hasty generalizations) and sometimes it is through culpably pernicious cognition (e.g., wishful thinking). In either sort of case, the idea is that when one comes to hold a belief in such a way, it is fundamentally accidental if it turns out to be true—one has not guided one's believing in such a way as to sufficiently safeguard an arrival at true belief.

Of course, paradigm "lucky beliefs" have both these characteristics—unreliable origins and irresponsible oversight. But ever more sophisticated and detailed counterexamples can (and did) pump one or the other of the intuitions behind each of these different ways of being lucky at the (apparent) expense of the other. Let us consider two of these.

On the one hand, we have Laurence BonJour's fanciful example of Norman, who possessed a reliable but unsuspected gift of clairvoyance. Through the operations of this power, Norman would regularly find himself with strong beliefs about the whereabouts of the U.S. president. Because he was unaware of his reliable clairvoyance, he had no explanation for these beliefs, nor any reasons to hold them. Now imagine that Norman has the true belief, by way of his clairvoyance, that the president is in New York City. Without any reasons for such a belief, Norman was irresponsible to believe the president was in New York, despite being in fact correct and reliable. To internalists like (then) BonJour, such a belief is only accidentally true with respect to the believer, hence it cannot count as being justified (BonJour 1985: 41 ff.).

On the other hand, consider Cho, a responsible but naive first-time visitor to Oklahoma. Being from a big city on the East Coast and relatively untraveled, Cho has no idea what to expect. On his flight there he meets Mary, an Oklahoma native returning home. Mary seems to be knowledgeable, friendly, and to genuinely want to help Cho. Among the things she tells him is that only cowboys are allowed to wear cowboy hats in Oklahoma. She is, of course, joking with him, but she says it in all apparent sincerity and Cho has every reason to believe her. As he steps out of the airport in Tulsa, he sees a man in a cowboy hat. Cho believes he is a cowboy, and he is right. Arguably, Cho is being responsible in employing the information given him by Mary, but identifying someone as a cowboy because they are wearing a cowboy hat is a very unreliable method of coming to hold true beliefs about cowboys.

The point of these two examples is that each kind of luck is independent of the other. Though they commonly occur together, one can construct examples like these where one is present but not the other. So the lesson to draw from the internalism/externalism debate is that all parties to the debate were mainly concerned to make sure lucky true beliefs never got counted as knowledge.[5]

All of this puts us finally in a position to answer the two questions posed earlier in this section to justify my "resolution by distinction" strategy. First, both internalism and externalism provide necessary conditions on knowledge because each wards off a distinct kind of epistemic luck. Falling prey to either kind undermines one's knowing. Avoiding both is required.

Second, until recently there were few extant analyses of luck. Most paradigm cases of lucky events are lucky in all regards, so the distinctions do not make themselves obvious. But when epistemologists started crafting counterexamples to defend accounts of justification that were addressed to one kind of lucky true belief but not another, the need for the distinction became more clear.

The step that takes us from epistemology to a general theory of luck is to wonder why epistemologists feel so strongly that knowledge is incompatible with luck in the first place. More crucially, why would they feel equally strongly about the presence of two different kinds of luck that are really quite different from one another? The answer brings us, finally, to LCAL. What the two kinds of luck have in common is that the presence of either one undermines the extent to which we had agency or authorship over some event or outcome. Another way of putting this is that, in order for some event to be considered something you did, both forms of luck must be precluded. For an event to be something you did, it must have been subject to your control.

The final chapter of the origin story for this version of LCAL is the observation that all this makes excellent sense if we understand knowledge to be an achievement that is attributable to the knower. This is one formulation of what has become known as the "Credit Theory of Knowledge." On such a view, what is central to cases of knowing is that you come to hold a true belief in such a way that your success in knowing is attributable to you as an agent (rather than as a mere physical object, for example.) The slogan for this view is that knowledge is creditworthy (or properly attributable) true belief.[6]

It turns out that this version of the credit theory of knowledge has a theory of epistemic luck at its heart. This total package offers many benefits, if correct. It resolves the internalism/externalism debate: both sorts of justification are required for your true belief to be attributable to you and thus count as knowledge. It makes accounting for knowledge a special case of accounting for the attribution of outcomes (more crudely, assigning credit) generally. It explains why Gettier cases arise and why they bother us so much. Gettier cases are, generally speaking, cases in which the agent is justified in all the usual senses yet we intuitively resist attributing knowledge to them. This makes perfect sense if we understand knowledge as an achievement that is generally undermined by various species of luck. What Gettier cases show us is that the two kinds of luck precluded by internalist and externalist accounts of justification do not quite exhaust the category of knowledge-undermining luck.

I conclude, then, my brief presentation and defense of the approach to the theories of knowledge and epistemic justification that gave rise to my original formulation of the LCAL as an account of epistemic luck. This is not the place to argue for any theory of knowledge, of course, but the point here is that a circumscribed version of LCAL emerges from this analysis of the epistemological literature and the theory of knowledge motivated by it. LCAL as an account of *epistemic* luck has a lot going for it.[7] As I will begin to discuss below, there are significant obstacles to LCAL as an account of luck more generally. But first, a brief foray into the topics of moral responsibility and moral luck.

Moral Luck and LCAL

As mentioned above, LCAL has a separate origin in the literature discussing the (alleged) phenomenon of "moral luck." This phenomenon arises allegedly in situations wherein we intuitively want to hold an agent responsible for some outcome of their actions, but where the outcome seems to have been (to some significant extent) beyond their control. Robert Hartman (2017: 23) expresses it succinctly:

> The *Standard View* of moral luck is that it occurs when factors beyond an agent's control partially determine her positive praiseworthiness or blameworthiness. The conception of luck implicit in the StandardView is the following lack of control conception: An event is lucky for a person insofar as it is partially determined by factors beyond her control. This definition of luck is universally accepted in the early moral luck literature, and many continue to accept it.

It is easy to see how a version of LCAL arises in response to the need to express the nature of moral luck. It is nearly just a restatement of the phenomenon itself. As Hartman notes, LCAL was once the universally accepted account of moral luck and is still considered the standard view. It says a lot for the significance of an LCAL conception of luck that it plays such a central role in not just a particular theory of knowledge, but also as the bedrock characterization of moral luck. This dual support for LCAL from both epistemology and ethics has been noted elsewhere as well.[8]

Moral responsibility is not my area of expertise, so I will simply cite the experts and move on. Still, it seems fair to say that at its core, LCAL is meant to account for the kinds of luck that are inversely related to our estimations of things such as responsibility, attribution, credit, and the like. Each of these notions is subtly distinct and would need to have its relationship to agency-undermining luck clarified, but the intuitive force behind LCAL is that agency in general is in tension with luck. This is the common guiding motivation behind LCAL as an account of both epistemic luck and moral luck.

LCAL Generalized

In its rough outline, LCAL is quite intuitive, though its fuller formulation inevitably becomes more complicated. If something occurs that you had no control over, that occurrence is a matter of luck with respect to you. And control is understood in terms of ability guided by intention. If either ability or intention is absent, then so is control.

Let me address a few preliminary points about discussions of luck before moving on. Notice it will not do to say that events uninfluenced by you are necessarily "lucky" for you. Unfortunately for philosophical analysis, the term "lucky" has connotations that a successful analysis needs to avoid. For instance, it is plausible to say that being struck by lightning is a matter of luck for someone (bad luck, to be sure), but we would not thereby call them "lucky." (Indeed, we would call them "unlucky," which *really* confuses the issue.) So we must generally abandon the terms "lucky" and "unlucky" for the more cumbersome expression "a matter of luck."[9]

Moreover, we have to relativize the notion to an individual. What is a matter of luck for one person might not be for another. If I plant explosives and competently and intentionally blow up a dam, the subsequent flooding is not a matter of luck with respect to me at all. But it constitutes (very bad) luck for those downstream.

Now let us turn to look more closely at LCAL. According to my view, there are really two distinct kinds of luck that clearly undermine agency and, hence, must be included in the account.[10] The first occurs when some event is simply not the product of one's abilities in any reasonable sense. Standard examples to pump this intuition are paradigm lucky events such as making wildly improbable shots in some sport or other. A novice who makes a hole in one on the tenth hole did not likely do so out of ability. They simply "lucked out." While in some technical sense, the novice scored the hole in one, in the more substantive and relevant sense, the success would be attributed much more to luck than to the novice golfer.

The other kind of luck is perhaps best called "inadvertence" or, more gruesomely, "accidentality." This refers to the occurrence of an event or outcome that is not at all intended by the agent. Consider Barbara, who is rather clumsy. Her friend insists that they go into a shop that is crammed full of delicate items, many of which are precariously balanced on their shelves. Being very careful, Barbara nonetheless stumbles on a bit of loose carpet and bumps into a shelf, causing several fragile items to fall to the floor and smash. Barbara is abashed and tells all in hearing that it was "just an accident." Although Barbara might be held in strict liability to pay for damages, the more relevant assessment here is that the smashing of the items is accidental. Barbara did not intend to smash the items—indeed she was trying very hard not to. It was simply bad luck (Riggs 2012: 290–292).

Having spelled this out roughly, a more formal representation of LCAL would look like this:

LCAL: E is a matter of luck for S iff E is (too far) out of S's control.

This formulation is accurate but not terribly detailed, so let us supplement it with this:

CONTROL: E is out of S's control to the extent that

(a) E is not the result of applying S's powers, abilities, or skills, or
(b) E is inadvertent with respect to S.[11]

The qualifier "too far" is necessary since control is a matter of degree. The extent to which my agency is responsible for bringing about some event is not absolute. I can be more or less in control of something. The threshold of control below which some event is a matter of luck for me is not something that can be designated with precision.

In what follows, we will be able to make do with the short version of LCAL, but it is important to keep the more detailed account of CONTROL in mind generally in thinking about these issues. I have already argued that LCAL is a plausible account of epistemic luck, moral luck, and of agency-undermining luck in general. The rest of this essay will be directed toward determining how far LCAL can be extended toward being a universal theory of luck.

Objections and Replies

Philosophers have raised a number of powerful objections to LCAL in recent years. The most troubling of these objections attack the claim that lack of control is *sufficient* for luck. I will consider and respond to a series of these objections. During the course of this consideration, LCAL will be modified as needed to accommodate the most cogent of them.

The most basic objection to the sufficiency of the two conditions for LCAL is that the overwhelming majority of events in the universe are due to neither my abilities nor my intentions. Hence, very nearly everything that has ever happened in the history of the universe is a matter of luck for me. This result is, to put it mildly, unintuitive. As I have suggested elsewhere (Riggs 2015: 182), it is possible to bite this bullet by offering an error theory of sorts. But I will not pursue that strategy here. I will assume that this implication of LCAL as it stands is unacceptable. So how should we modify it to handle the objection? I will offer two addendums to the current formulation to make some progress against this rather intimidating objection.

Significance

One way to winnow down the number of events that are a matter of luck for me in the universe is to limit them to those that have some sort of significance for me. This has become a common strategy in theories of luck. Neil Levy (2011), in describing Duncan Pritchard's early view, sums up the idea perspicuously:

Roughly, an event or state of affairs can count as lucky only if it is significant. It may be genuinely chancy how many hairs fall out of my head today ... Nevertheless, it would be strange to say that it is a matter of luck whether I have an odd or an even number of hairs on my head at 12 noon, because we generally reserve the appellation "lucky" for events or processes that *matter*.

Levy 2011: 13; emphasis in original

And Nathan Ballantyne says that

[e]veryone agrees that luck requires significance, but there is conflict over how to understand it. Significance is thought to make the difference between a merely unlikely event and a lucky one. An unlikely landslide that didn't affect anyone, for example, isn't lucky because it is significant for no one. All agree that for an event to be significant for someone, she must have *interests*. A lucky event somehow benefits the individual while an unlucky one brings detriment. The consensus just is, at bottom, that if an event is lucky for an individual, then it's somehow *good for* or *bad for* her.

Ballantyne 2012: 13

To respect this usage of the term "lucky," we could add a significance condition to LCAL. This means that to count as lucky, an event would need to be out of S's control *and* be a matter of significance to S. This would considerably narrow down the vast number of things that would count as lucky for any given individual, at least on a charitable understanding of "significance." Getting clear on just what significance amounts to is, itself, a contentious and complicated issue, and a full treatment of it is beyond the scope of the present work.[12] However, we need some idea of how to understand the scope of what counts as significant to assess how well the significance condition answers the objection it addresses.

Following Ballantyne's lead, E.J. Coffman formulates the condition this way: E is a matter of luck for S only if E is in some respect good (bad) for S. According to Coffman, this

seems the best way to understand the so-called significance condition on luck. Because an event can be good for you in one respect and bad for you in another, accounts of luck that utilize [this principle] correctly allow that an event can be both lucky *and* unlucky for you (cf. Ballantyne 2012: 331). For example, your lottery win may be good luck in that it enables you to retire early, but bad luck in that it makes you a salient target for extortion.

Coffman 2015: 479

The Coffman/Ballantyne formulation is admirably succinct, intuitively plausible, and determinate enough for current purposes. The version Ballantyne ultimately defends in the article quoted by Coffman is slightly more complicated, but the additional wrinkles are not relevant to the current discussion. Let us add it to our evolving analysis of LCAL:

E is a matter of luck for S iff

(a)   E is (too far) out of S's control, and
(b)   E is in some respect good (bad) for S.

Adding the significance condition helps LCAL considerably with the sufficiency objection. Plausibly, an awful lot of the events that are out of my control are of no significance to me. That is, they are neither good nor bad in any respect for me. At the very least, it seems to fend off the worry that vast numbers of events far distant from me in time and space are matters of luck for me. We are tightening a lasso with the goal of ultimately roping only things that are truly matters of luck. Requiring significance allows us to pull up a lot of the slack.

Exploitation

Although adding a significance condition narrows down the number of things that must be considered a matter of luck for me, it is clear that it does not do enough. There are still a lot of events that are in some respect good or bad for me, out of my control, yet not intuitively matters of luck for me. For instance, in a now much discussed paper, Andrew Latus (2003) points out that the rising of the sun each morning is out of anyone's control and deeply significant for all humans, but we do not consider it a matter of luck for anyone. Yet it seems LCAL must say that it is.

There seem to be two different problems that sunrise cases represent for LCAL. One is that things like the sunrise just do not seem like the sort of thing that *could be* a matter of luck, perhaps by virtue of their being a matter of natural law. Another is that such cases are numerous and leave LCAL still counting far too many things as matters of luck that seemingly are not. I will consider each of these two aspects of the problem in turn.

Is a sunrise the sort of thing that could ever be considered a matter of luck for someone? In two previous papers (Riggs 2009 and 2015) I have offered pairs of examples that I think show that it can. In one such pair, we consider two people in similar circumstances. Emelia and Francesca are each being pursued in the night by vampires (these are two separate incidents—the two women are not together). Emelia is harried and terrified. She has barely kept away from capture all night and is at the end of her resources. Just as she collapses in exhaustion in an open field near her home town, the sun rises and vaporizes the vampires, saving her life. This would seem to be a plausible case in which the sunrise is genuinely a matter of luck for Emilia (Riggs 2015).

Hopefully, this dispenses with the idea that sunrises simply cannot be a matter of luck for anyone. But the bigger problem is that sunrises happen every day, they are significant for everyone, and people are not generally in situations analogous to Emilia's. So we are still not tempted to say that every sunrise is a matter of luck for everyone.

My response to this aspect of the objection requires recounting the story of Francesca, the other case in the pair mentioned above. She, too, is being pursued by vampires, but she is neither harried nor terrified. She is confident and calculating. She leads the vampires on a merry chase all night, timing her run across the field to coincide with the dawn. When the morning's first rays vaporize her pursuers, she grins in satisfaction. This seems to be a case in which the sunrise is very much not a matter of luck for Francesca (Riggs 2015).

But notice that the way in which the sunrise is not a matter of luck for her seems very different from the way in which it is not a matter of luck for most of us most of the time. For us, the sunrise is significant in a diffuse, abstract sense. If it did not happen, we would all be dead. But for Francesca, the sunrise is significant in a very specific, immediate, and concrete way. Moreover, while Francesca did not control the rising of the sun, she did control the overall situation in which the sun's rising when it did played a crucial role in the outcome of the chase. She *exploited* the rising of the sun in the execution of her plan to kill the vampires. There seems to be a substantive sense in which the sunrise was not lucky for her because of how she incorporated it into her plans.

This provides another strategy for tightening our lasso still further. Events that we exploit in this fashion, even when they are out of our control and significant, are not lucky for us. We can modify our ever-changing formulation of LCAL to accommodate this insight.

E is a matter of luck for S iff

(a) E is (too far) out of S's control, and
(b) E is in some respect good (bad) for S, and
(c) E is not exploited by S.[13]

But we must ask again, how much does this help? Fanciful scenarios aside, most of us do not manipulate the rising of the sun to our advantage on any given day. It seems that LCAL is still saddled with an implausible implication that such things are matters of luck for us.

This might be the end of the road for LCAL. It might be only a special-purpose account of luck, useful for talking about agency but not an all-purpose notion that can always capture what we mean when we talk about luck. Hartman (2017) acknowledges this possibility from the perspective of defending LCAL as a theory of moral luck. But he argues that it is unreasonable to expect more than this.

> [T]he assumption that an adequate account of luck in moral luck must map onto all our ordinary uses of 'luck' is a false assumption, because the moral luck debate is about not luck per se but a tension in our ordinary thinking about moral responsibility.
>
> *Hartman 2017: 24*

In other words, LCAL could do the job asked of it for moral luck even if it does not fully generalize. The same is true for LCAL and its role in the credit theory of knowledge. It could even be that there is no single account of luck that can accommodate all the different intuitions we have about luck, accidents, chance, etc. If so, LCAL's situation is not so bad. At least, it is no worse off than any other theory in that regard.

Of course, there is always hope. I will end my defense of LCAL with one last proposal—one final tug at the lasso to see whether I can get hold of just the things that are truly lucky. This will be both speculative and sketchy, so consider it a gesture toward the future defense of LCAL as a universal theory of luck.

My last suggestion is to substantially expand the notion of exploitation. As I have described it, to exploit an event requires that one actively rely on it for the successful execution of some determinate plan. The examples I have given suggest that the agent must consciously realize that the event will happen and that it will contribute in the desired way. But what if exploitation need not be quite so intentional?

There is a sense in which each of us relies on the sun's rising every day. I make plans for the coming week that implicitly assume that I will be alive, that there will be daylight at the usual times, etc. I do not think about the role of the sunrise in the successful execution of those plans, but I would certainly plan differently were I to have some doubt about its happening as it usually does. All our plans, even the most mundane, implicitly assume that the background conditions of our lives will not vary enough to require accommodation. Though we do not control them exactly, we are not entirely unaware or taken by surprise when our assumptions turn out to be true. We can be wrong, of course, but in many of *those* cases it would be plausible to say that the variation that we do not expect *is* a matter of luck (often bad) for us. But in the vast majority of cases, this expanded notion of exploitation could help us classify the others as not being matters of luck.

Here are some examples to illustrate.

I make plans to meet a friend across town for lunch. I leave in plenty of time to drive there, given the usual traffic, even allowing a little extra time just in case. But along the way I encounter a stopped train at a railroad crossing. I cannot get out of my lane to turn around, so I am stuck for 40 minutes. I am subsequently late for lunch. Bad luck.

I agree to write a letter of recommendation for a student at the last minute. I have to write it from home, but a ferocious thunderstorm knocks out the power in my house, rendering my computer useless. Moreover, downed power lines make it impossible for me to travel. I do not get the letter written. Bad luck.

So let us say that all the things we implicitly and correctly assume will happen in order for our plans to be successful are also (implicitly) exploited, whether we consciously consider them or not. Then they will not count as matters of luck according to LCAL, allowing us to tighten our lasso considerably. The examples above suggest that when we incorrectly implicitly assume something will happen in order for our plans to be successful, at least much of the time those events *will* intuitively count as matters of luck.

Conclusion

LCAL is a strongly intuitive account of luck. It underwrites plausible and insightful views about moral luck and about knowledge, and there is some prospect for its extension to a fully universal account of luck. Much more would need to be said about how exploitation works. How exactly are we to tell when something we did not explicitly think about was nevertheless exploited in a way that renders it not a matter of luck according to LCAL? What do we say about cases in which we did not think about something but we should have? This will be challenging, to say the least. And over all of it hovers the question of whether there really is a universal theory of luck at all.

Notes

1 Illustrative examples of each are Rescher (1995), Pritchard (2005, 2015), and Riggs (2009, 2012), respectively.
2 We can somewhat arbitrarily stipulate that the Gettier era began to fade in 1983 with the publication of R.K. Shope's book, *The Analysis of Knowing: A Decade of Research*.
3 Here is a very simple case: Imagine believing (correctly) that the time is currently 2:05 by looking at your very reliable and expensive watch. You have a justified true belief. But now suppose that the watch stopped working exactly 24 hours ago. Intuitively, it seems that you cannot gain knowledge by looking at a malfunctioning watch at the one time of day it happens to report truly. That you had a true belief about the time was simply wildly lucky.
4 For a canonical (though slightly dated) account of the different varieties of internalist and externalist justification, see Alston (1986).
5 This is what Duncan Pritchard calls "the Luck Platitude" (Pritchard 2005: 3 ff.).
6 John Greco develops a very sophisticated version of a credit theory of knowledge from very different motivations, which also seems to speak in the theory's favor. See Greco (2010) for a full treatment of his view.
7 Intriguingly, Duncan Pritchard's well-known alternative account of luck in terms of modal safety also has its origins in his prior account of epistemic luck. See Pritchard (2005).
8 See Riggs (2009: 206 ff.), Levy (2011), and Hartman (2017).
9 Indeed, E.J. Coffman (2015) has argued persuasively that we need to modify our expression still further and treat "strokes of luck" as the fundamental "unit" of luck, so to speak. This seems a very promising strategy, though I cannot pursue it here.
10 I suggested in the last section that "Gettier luck" is distinct from each of the kinds of luck highlighted by the two theories of justification—internalism and externalism. And the presence of Gettier luck is generally agreed to undermine knowledge. It is to be hoped that a proper articulation of LCAL will capture the kind of luck involved in Gettier cases as well. But the cases are so complex and the literature so vast that addressing this question here would take us very far afield, especially because that issue is most relevant to the theory of knowledge rather than a universal theory of luck. So I will ignore the complication of Gettier luck in what follows.
11 This formulation is adapted from Riggs (2009: 218).
12 See Ballantyne (2012) for an extensive discussion of the issue.
13 Another intriguing possibility is that we build the exploitation condition into the control condition: E is out of S's control to the extent that (a) E is not the result of applying S's powers, abilities, or skills, or (b) E is inadvertent with respect to S, *or (c) E is not exploited by S*. I find this strategy appealing, since it keeps the bulk of the account still in terms of control. I also think exploitation is plausibly a kind of control, so this would be no mere ad hoc move to save the theory from counterexamples. Alas, there is no time to pursue this possibility here.

References

Alston, W. (1986) "Internalism and Externalism in Epistemology," *Philosophical Topics* 14, 179–221.
Ballantyne, Nathan (2012) "Luck and Interests," *Synthese* 185, 319–334.
BonJour, L. (1985) *The Structure of Empirical Knowledge*, Cambridge, MA: Harvard University Press.
Chisholm, R. (1989) *Theory of Knowledge*, Englewood Cliffs, NJ: Prentice Hall.
Coffman, E.J. (2015) "Strokes of Luck," in D. Pritchard & L. Whittington (eds.) *The Philosophy of Luck*, Oxford: Wiley-Blackwell, pp. 27–58.
Gettier, E. (1963) "Is Justified True Belief Knowledge?" *Analysis* 23, 121–123.
Goldman, A. (1986) *Epistemology and Cognition*, Cambridge, MA: Harvard University Press.

Greco, J. (2010) *Achieving Knowledge*, Cambridge: Cambridge University Press.

Hartman, R. (2017) *In Defense of Moral Luck*, New York: Routledge.

Latus, A. (2003) "Constitutive Luck," *Metaphilosophy* 34, 460–475.

Levy, N. (2011) *Hard Luck*, Oxford: Oxford University Press.

Pritchard, D. (2005) *Epistemic Luck*, Oxford: Oxford University Press.

———. (2015) "The Modal Account of Luck," in D. Pritchard & L. Whittington, (eds.) *The Philosophy of Luck*, Oxford: Wiley-Blackwell, pp. 143–167.

Rescher, N. (1995) *Luck: The Brilliant Randomness of Everyday Life*, New York: Farrar, Straus and Giroux.

Riggs, W. (1998) "What Are the 'Chances' of Being Justified?" *The Monist* 81(3), 452–472.

———. (2009) "Luck, Knowledge, and Control," in A. Haddock, A. Millar, & D. Pritchard (eds.) *Epistemic Value*, Oxford: Oxford University Press, pp. 204–221.

———. (2012) "Why Epistemologists Are So Down on Their Luck," in J. Greco & J. Turri (eds.) *Virtue Epistemology: Contemporary Readings*, Cambridge, MA: MIT Press, pp. 329–344.

———. (2015) "Luck, Knowledge, and 'Mere' Coincidence," in D. Pritchard & L. Whittington (eds.) *The Philosophy of Luck*, Oxford: Wiley-Blackwell, pp. 177–189.

12

THE PROBABILITY ACCOUNT OF LUCK

Nicholas Rescher

Our lives unfold in a setting where much that is of importance for our existence and well-being occurs in unpredictable circumstances. Pure chance alone all too frequently determines our fate and fortune. And then it is not fact-exploiting reason but probability-managing judgment that provides us with guidance in dealing with the world's affairs. And here luck is bound to enter in.

The concept of "luck" that functions in English usage in the stochastic sense of chance benefits is philosophically underdeveloped because neither the Latin *fortuna* nor the French *félicité* nor the German *Glück* comes close to capturing the conception at issue. In English, however, unlikelihood is of the essence and luck demands improbability. Take epistemic luck. If you discover the truth by investigation and inquiry, there is no luck about it, nothing is left to chance. But if you hit on the truth by sheer conjecture and guesswork, you are lucky—and lucky to an extent that depends on the likelihood of getting it right in this way. Or take moral luck. If you promised to meet Smith at 1pm tomorrow and—having totally forgotten this—just happen to run into him at that time, then despite your reprehensible proceeding you have at any rate not broken your promise, unlikely though this result might be. You are in this respect very lucky.

Luck is a matter of the positive (or negative) outcome for someone of a contingently chancy development that can yield positivities or negativities for this individual. One is lucky when, in a situation of uncertain outcome, one fares better than one has a right to expect, and is unlucky when one fares worse.[1] And this matter of an outcome-antecedent "right to expect" is inherently probabilistic in nature.

When an outcome is realized by predesign, by means of skill, by result-rigging, by cheating, or any such predeterministic ways of outcome-production, luck does not come into it. Only where there is chance, inadvertence, and absence of control is luck at issue. It requires the presence of chance—that default mode of "explanation" where all the standard versions of causal explanation fail to function and sheer accident is "the last man standing." Consider an illustration. X sets out to assassinate Y. He takes up his revolver, goes to encounter him, draws, aims, and pulls the trigger. Nothing happens. Did Y have a lucky escape? It all depends on the explanation, which could be any of the following: (1) X actually never loaded the revolver, (2) Z unbeknownst to X filed off the revolver's firing pin, (3) the cartridges in the large box from which X loaded the revolver were actually unsuitable for it, or (4) the few particular cartridges of this box that X happened to collect were defective. Here, only with (4) was pure chance at work, so this case alone rendered Y lucky, strictly speaking. In the other cases he was merely fortunate. To reemphasize: luck requires chance.[2]

Some theorists propose to construe luck in terms of an absence of agent control rather than chance.[3] However, this approach is very problematic. Good outcomes which are entirely beyond an agent's control might or might not be matters of luck. Thus winning the lottery could certainly be so, but falling heir to your parents' estate would not. (People might not control or even foresee what their parents leave to them in their will but receiving such a bequest is surely not a matter of luck.) Again, you do not control whether you are born male or female, but neither way are you lucky (or unlucky) about it. You fully control how you guess spelling "happenstance" in a spelling bee. But if you chance to be correct you are still quite lucky. When you stop at a traffic light you have no control over it. But when it turns to green and speeds you on your way at a particular juncture you neither controlled nor foresaw, there is nothing of luck about it. Altogether, it is more conducive to clarity to conceptualize luck in terms of chance rather than agent control or its lack.

So understood, someone is lucky (or unlucky) when they are the beneficiary (or maleficiary) of a fortuitous development. As such, luck can take very different forms, some standard versions being

- Finder's (good) luck: stumbling upon a treasure trove
- Gambler's (good or bad) luck: succeeding or failing in some sort of gamble
- Guesser's (good) luck: inadvertently hitting on the right answer (e.g. in a spelling bee)
- "Dumb" luck (good or bad): being in the right (or wrong) place at the right (or wrong) time: e.g. stumbling out of the way just as the bullet comes by, and similar "narrow escapes"

Each such mode of luck has characteristic features of its own, so that none is totally typical of the entire range. However, the present deliberations will focus on Gambler's luck, both because it is the most familiar form of the phenomenon and because it best admits of quantitative analysis.

The extent to which one is lucky has two distinct aspects. One pivots on probability alone: you are lucky to the extent to which you succeed "against the odds"—betting on the right horse out of dozens, say. This version might be called *odds-luck*. The other sort of luck—*yield-luck*, it might be called—pivots on how you fare in a chancy situation—on what luck has gained for you. When matters pivot on the toss of a coin, you are not going far against the odds, but if your life is at stake, a successful outcome means that you are being very lucky indeed.[4]

Odds-luck can be assessed at $1 - p$ where p is the probability of success. When this probability is small, luck is comparatively large (i.e., close to the maximum of 1); when the probability is great, luck barely comes into it (i.e., stands close to 0).

Yield-luck, accordingly, depends on the stake at issue, the difference can result for you as between success and failure, between "winning" and "losing." Here the crux is that the Δ is measured by the gap between a favorable and unfavorable outcome. In binary situations with a win-outcome (W) and a loss-outcome (L) this can be taken as the difference: $W - L$. Two questions are thus at issue with good luck, namely, (1) whether or not one succeeds and (2) the benefits consequent upon success. One can be very lucky in the former regard (in investing against the odds) and not particularly lucky in the latter (in deriving little if any benefit from this success). Odds-correlative luck and yield-correlative luck are related but still rather different issues. However, a combined or blended version of luck assessment will result if we simply multiply these two quantities:

$$\lambda = (1 - p) \bullet \Delta = (1 - p)(W - L)$$

However, yield-luck that is realized in obtaining the yield (Y) that is provided by a particular chancy outcome is reflected in the excess over (or the shortfall from) what is to be expected (E). This line of thought leads to the basic yield-luck measure:

$$\lambda = Y - E$$

Thus if you make a gain by what looks to be a fortuitous development of which you had no expectation at all—chancing upon a lost treasure, say, or inheriting something from a previously unknown relative—you are lucky to the tune of your entire gain. (Or if you sustain a wholly unforeseeable loss you are comparably unlucky.) However, in this formulation of the matter, the expectation will have to be assessed objectively. For with entirely unrealistic expectations $Y - E$ will be negative whereas the agent might, in actual fact, be very lucky. And since the expectation E that is at issue in a given uncertain-outcome situation is a fixed quantity, the amount of luck associated with a particular outcome is proportionate to its yield.

Since fortuitous outcomes are a matter of unfathomable haphazard, luck is not an agency to be employed or potency to be propitiated. Strictly speaking, even to use a noun here is problematic in its anthropomorphic connotations and reversion to the mythology of Lady Luck. It would be better to keep to the adjectival mode and say that various developments are lucky (or unlucky) for certain people. The expressions "by luck" or "by chance" describe how things happen and involve no descriptive claims regarding the causal or productive process that make for the happening: they answer the question *how* but not *why*?[5]

Luck thus flourishes in the gap between realization and expectation. One is lucky to the extent that achievement exceeds warranted expectations and unlucky to the extent that it falls short.[6] People who realize chancy positivities—length of life, say, or familial inheritance—to an extent that exceeds the average (which, after all, is the best they can reasonably expect) can be accounted as lucky in this regard.

Luck requires someone to be lucky (or unlucky): there is no luck without a beneficiary. This beneficiary can, to be sure, be both unidentified and hypothetical: "Someone who sailed on the *Titanic*, would have been very lucky to have escaped with their life." One is lucky in an uncertain-outcome situation to the extent that the actual outcome exceeds to one's antecedent expectation, and unlucky to the extent the matter is reversed: when the difference is positive, you have good luck; when negative you have bad luck. One person's good luck need not come at the cost of another's. Tom very much wants to inherit grandfather's watch; Tim his war medal. When the executor decided to award such personalia by a coin toss, both might well enjoy a lucky success.[7]

Suppose that you have entered into an arrangement where you are to toss a die and will get $2 for each resulting point. You throw the die, get a 4, thereby winning $8. How lucky are you? To resolve this requires knowing two quantities:

(1) Y: the actual yield consequent upon the after-the-fact outcome that has resulted. (In the present example $8.)

(2) E: the yield that was antecedently to be expected—the amount that the agent "has a right to expect." (In the present example $7.[8])

Your luck depends on the comparison of these two quantities, and is determined by the aforementioned *Basic Formula* for the assessment of luck: $\lambda = Y - E$. So in the present example you are lucky to the tune of $1. As a measure of the amount of luck at issue, λ can be viewed in a dual perspective. Retrospectively, after the fact, it indicates the amount of luck (good or ill) that was realized by the outcome at issue. Prospectively, in advance of the fact, it indicated the amount of luck (good or ill) that will be required to realize this outcome. In general, luck rules when yields are great and expectations low.

When the yield of an uncertain-outcome situation is measured with the expectation taken as a single unit, luck will correspondingly stand as per the simple linear relationship of Figure 12.1.

Usually when thinking about luck, we have in mind something like a lottery where a substantial gain has unexpectedly fallen into our lap. But the other side of the matter—the unexpectable avoidance of a great negativity also provides a vivid illustration. Luck dwells in the discrepancy between attainment and expectation. And the comparison at issue has three possible outcomes:

The Probability Account of Luck

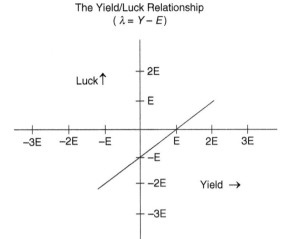

Figure 12.1 The yield/luck relationship
Note: E = the expectation (given that E is constant in a given unpredictable outcome situation, we have it that $\lambda \approx Y$).

$Y > E$. In this case the individual is lucky.
$Y < E$. In this case the individual is unlucky.
$Y = E$. In this case luck does not come into it.

The luck-definitive difference $Y - E$ thus determines both the direction and the magnitude of the luck at issue.

All this accords smoothly with our informal understanding of the issue. For example, with any sort of performance the augmented skill that results from training and practice will increase the expectation of better performance, so that the otherwise required amount of luck in achieving a favorable outcome will be diminished.

Even a high-probability outcome can be very lucky when a low-probability alternative that it averts is catastrophic. And even an outcome that is very negative can be quite lucky when its alternatives are substantially worse. Someone who survives an earthquake's collapse of his apartment building has every right to deem themselves very lucky to escape with a few scrapes and bruises.

To be sure, we sometimes prioritize probability over yield, speaking of "luck" simply to indicate personal inclinations. Thus, saying "When his house key fell from his pocket while he was crossing the field he was very lucky to find it again" seems plausible even though the item was of little value—no doubt because the key's subjective value to its owner is so great.

It is, however, important to heed the distinction between

- *what is to be expected*, i.e., what is objectively reasonable and appropriate to expect (and accordingly "what the agent has a right to expect")
and
- *what someone happens to expect*, i.e., what the individual subjectively expects.

And a parallel observation of course applies in respect to the evaluation of yields and the estimation of probabilities. One must accordingly distinguish between objective luck based on measurable quantities and subjective luck based on personal sentiments. All of the factors at issue with luck-yield evaluation, outcome probability, and result estimation can be assessed both on a personally subjective basis and with reference to measurably objective factors. Accordingly, there is both subjective and objective luck. However, the present deliberation will focus on the objective and measurable dimension. The subjective psychology of luck is an important but separate issue. The successful suitor doubly compliments his beloved in deeming himself as "the luckiest man alive." For, on the one hand, this suggests her being "a pearl of rare price." And, on the other, it suggests that she, being so desirable, was sought after by so many that his own chances were minute. Subjective luck inheres in the opinions of the agent. In accepting fool's gold as the real thing, he might think himself lucky. Or, again, if his friends rigged the lottery in his favor, so that chance is entirely absent. In neither case, however, do the objective facts confirm the subjective assessment of luck.

Letting λ^+ be the amount of luck for the best possible outcome (i.e., that providing for the maximum achievable yield Y^+, a given uncertain-outcome situation will have its particular max-luck outcome as per:

$$\lambda^+ = Y^+ - E$$

We may thus define *proportional luck*, namely $\lambda\star = \lambda/\lambda^+$, by the equation:

$$\lambda^\star = \frac{\lambda}{\lambda^+} = \frac{Y - E}{Y^+ - E}$$

This quantity affords a measure of the relative (rather than absolute) amount of luck at issue in a given outcome. Clearly when the actual yield is maximal ($Y = Y^+$) we will have $\lambda\star = 1$, and when the actual yield comes to the expectation ($Y = E$) then $\lambda\star = 0$.

An interesting situation thus arises in the theory of luck when an uncertain-outcome situation involves an alternative that is totally and absolutely unacceptable, one that effectively has an outcome of $-\infty$. Now as long as this outcome is a real possibility—and so has a non-zero probability—the expected value of the situation (calculated in the standard way) will itself be $-\infty$. (In effect, this means that situations with absolutely unacceptable outcomes should themselves be seen as unacceptable.) With respect to those alternative (non-catastrophic) outcomes we have it that the associated luck, assessed in the standard manner of the Luck Formula, $\lambda = Y - E$, will now be $+\infty$. The escape from absolute disaster, however achieved, has to be seen as a thing of boundless good luck.

A chancy, uncertain-outcome situation exists whenever events can issue in any one of several different outcomes. In such stochastic situations we will have various possible outcomes O_i with respective probabilities p_i and yields $<O_i>$. And as indicated, the amount of luck for an individual given the outcome O_i is measured by the difference between his yield given O_i, and the yield E that was antecedently to be expected, where this expectation can be measured by the probability-weighted sum of the various possibilities, which comes to:

$$E = \sum_k \left(p_k \bullet \langle O_k \rangle \right)$$

Accordingly an agent's luck for the outcome O_i will stand at:

$$\lambda\{O_i\} = \langle O_i \rangle - E = \langle O_i \rangle - \sum_k \left(p_k \bullet \langle O_k \rangle \right)$$

Thus in the preceding die-throw example your luck with every possible outcome will stand as follows: 1 produces luck to the tune of -5 because you get $+2$ but expected $+7$. And similarly, 2

The Probability Account of Luck

produces -3, 3 produces -1, 4 produces $+1$, 5 produces $+3$, 6 produces $+5$. Since the expected value is a fixture of the situation, the amount of luck at issue with various outcomes is aligned with the yield at issue. For the six outcomes at issue, the respective luck quotients $\lambda^{\star}$ are: $-$, $-$, $-$, $+$, $+$, and $+$, respectively. In the circumstances there is no scope for much of luck (good or ill).

These considerations convey some larger lessons. The main way to reduce the scope of luck is by increasing the expectation of a good outcome: the more you succeed in this the less scope there will be for the role of luck. When—and only when—success is assured can one say that "nothing has been left to luck." On the other hand, when the stake is large and the chance of achieving a successful outcome is very small, then its realization must be regarded as extremely lucky indeed. Thus, winning the lottery is the quintessential instance of good luck.

Here again, the distinction between objective (statistically measurable) probability and subjective (personally estimated) probability is crucially important for an understanding of luck. For, as noted, the magnitude of luck lies in the difference between yield (Y) and expectation (E) and expectation is measured via the probability of eventuations. Only when the probabilities at issue are objective will one be dealing with objective luck, which is something relatively unmanageable. But if the probabilities at issue are subjective, then this is something which, in the end, is a matter of the outlook of the individual. And the same goes for the assessment of outcomes. So, for present purposes, probabilities, outcomes, and expectations are to be construed in the objective mode, with personal (psychological) probabilities and other subjective evaluations reserved for the psychological treatment of luck-related issues.

Consider a binary win-or-lose gamble with the following yield of win and lose:

$$Y\{\text{win}\} = W$$
$$Y\{\text{lose}\} = L$$

So when the probabilities of win vs. lose stand at p and $1 - p$, respectively, the risk-runner will secure the following expectation:

$$E = p \bullet W + (1 - p) \bullet L$$

Accordingly the luck that arises with winning and losing, respectively, is:

$$\lambda\{\text{win}\} \quad W - E = W - p \bullet W - (1 - p) \bullet L$$
$$(1 - p) \bullet (W - L)$$

$$\lambda\{\text{lose}\} \quad L - E = L - p \bullet W - (1 - p) \bullet L$$
$$-p \bullet (W - L)$$

In such cases, we may define a participant's stake (Δ) as the difference between his win-yield (W) and his lose-yield (L) so that:

$$\Delta = Y\{\text{win}\} - Y\{\text{lose}\} = W - L$$

Accordingly, in the preceding situation of a binary win-or-lose gamble we arrive at the characteristic *Yield-Luck Equation* already encountered above:

$$\lambda\{\text{win}\} = (1 - p) \bullet \Delta = (1 - p) \bullet (W - L)$$

Thus in these binary situations, an individual's win-luck is to be measured as the product of the total stake and the loss-probability.[9] Accordingly, the larger the stake and the smaller the probability of winning, the greater is the luck attendant upon success. Observe that we now have $\lambda\{\text{lose}\} = -p \bullet \Delta$ so that the difference between win-luck and lose-luck, namely $\lambda\{\text{win}\} - \lambda\{\text{lose}\}$ exactly measures Δ, the stake at issue. The two modes of luck—win or lose—will thus be the same only when $\Delta = 0$. And the luck involved in winning will be 0 in just two cases, namely when the outcome is certain ($p = 1$), and when it makes no difference whether one wins or loses because $W = L$.

On this basis the amount of luck involved in a one-chance-in-ten win of \$110 [namely $(1 - .1) \bullet 110 = 99$] is much the same as the amount of luck in wining \$1000 in an unrealistically favorable nine-chances-in-ten lottery [namely $(1 - .9) \bullet 1000 = 100$]. As far as sheer luck goes, the greater yield at issue in the second case is offset by the far greater likelihood of its realization. While the yield is more substantial, the high probability of its attainment takes much of the luck out of it.

Consider a binary win-lose situation where the expectation is given by:

$$EXP = p(W - L) + L$$

There are, clearly, three ways to increase this quantity:

(1) by increasing the win-probability p
(2) by increasing the stake $\Delta = W - L$
(3) by decreasing loss-outcome L.

Recalling that the win-luck at issue is given by

$$\lambda\{\text{win}\} = W - E,$$

it transpires that as long as the win-yield W remains constant, any of those three ways of increasing the expectation will diminish the reliance on luck.

In view of the above-indicated relationships we also have it that in binary gambles:

$$\frac{\lambda\{\text{win}\}}{\lambda\{\text{lose}\}} = \frac{1-p}{-p}$$

Now with a fair (zero-expectation) binary gamble where $E = 0$, we have:

$$E = p \bullet W + (1 - p) \bullet L = 0$$

And this means that:

$$\frac{W}{L} = \frac{1-p}{-p}$$

Accordingly, in this special case we have it that for the parties at issue:

$$\frac{\lambda\{\text{win}\}}{\lambda\{\text{lose}\}} = \frac{W}{L}$$

The luck-ratio of the two outcomes amounts exactly to the yield ratio. And it deserves note that this relationship obtains independently of the value of p.

When would the two contesting parties in a binary gamble (X and Y) have equal luck upon winning? In view of the above formulas we have it:

$$\lambda \{X \text{ wins}\} = (1 - p) \bullet (<X> - <Y>)$$

with p as the probability of X winning. And on the same basis:

$$\lambda \{Y \text{ wins}\} = p \bullet (<Y> - <X>)$$

These quantities will be equal just in case

$$<X> - <Y> - p \bullet <X> + p \bullet <Y> = p \bullet <Y> - p \bullet <X>$$

And this means that:

$$<X> = <Y>$$

And so, on these binary gambles, equality of win-luck amounts to win-yield equality for the parties, and is entirely independent of win-probability.

Suppose that in a binary win-lose gamble you get +1 for a "win" and 0 for a "loss." Then your win-luck via the yield-luck equation $\lambda = Y - E$ is simply: $\lambda = 1 - p$. But your proportionate luck in winning will be $\lambda^\star = (Y - E)/(Y^\# - E) = 1$, the maximum. And your odds-luck will be $1 - p$. On the other hand, if you get +1 for a "win" and -1 for a "loss" then your win-luck doubles: $\lambda = 2(1 - p)$. However, your proportionate luck in winning stays at 1, and your success-luck remains a $1 - p$. So all that changes with regard to luck in the two cases is the amount that a win provides: the extent to which you are lucky in winning it remains the same.

But, as this example shows, the question "How lucky would you be in winning?" is decidedly equivocal. Luck is something that can be viewed from different angles.

There yet remains the problem of luck in the complex case of indefinite (or disjunctive) outcomes. In such multi-outcome situations we have a variety of outcomes O_i, each with a corresponding yield $<O_i>$ and a corresponding probability p_i. With luck measured by the difference between one's actual yield and one's expectation, the luck involved with the particular outcome O_i is:

$$\lambda\{O_i\} = <O_i> - EXP$$

where EXP is the expected value:

$$EXP = \sum_k \left(\langle O_k \rangle \bullet p_k \right)$$

So overall we have:

$$\lambda\{O_i\} = \langle O_i \rangle - \sum_k \left(\langle O_k \rangle \bullet p_k \right)$$

But one could also dualize the case into a two-outcome situation of O_i vs. not-O_i. On this basis one obtains

$$\lambda\{O_i\} = (1 - p_i) \bullet \Delta_i$$

where

$$\Delta_i = \langle O_i \rangle - \langle \text{not-}O_i \rangle$$

And so:

$$\lambda\{O_i\} = (1 - p_i) \bullet (<O_i> - <\text{not-}O_i>)$$

For these two measures of luck to agree we will need to have

$$\langle O_i \rangle - \sum_k (\langle O_k \rangle \bullet p_k) = (1-p_i) \bullet (\langle O_i \rangle - \langle \text{not-}O_i \rangle) =$$

$$\langle O_i \rangle - \langle \text{not-}O_i \rangle - p_i O_i + \langle \text{not-}O_i \rangle$$

This requires:

$$\sum_k \langle O_k \rangle \bullet p_k = \langle \text{not-}O_i \rangle + p_i \bullet O_i - p_i \langle \text{not-}O_i \rangle$$

or equivalently:

$$\sum_{k \neq 1} \langle O_k \rangle \bullet p_k = \langle \text{not-}O_i \rangle \bullet (1-p_i)$$

And this will only be the case when:

$$\langle \text{not-}O_i \rangle = \frac{1}{1 - p_i} \sum_{k \neq i} (\langle O_k \rangle \bullet p_k)$$

This construal for the yield of not-O_i means that those two measures for luck automatically yield identical results.

Thus returning to the die-toss example given above we have it that a toss-outcome of x has a yield of $2x$ with probability $\frac{1}{6}$. On this basis, the just-derived formula has it that

$$\langle \text{not-}4 \rangle = \frac{1}{1 - \frac{1}{6}} \bullet \left(\frac{1}{6} \bullet 2 + \frac{1}{6} \bullet 4 + \frac{1}{6} \bullet 6 + = \frac{6}{5} \bullet 10 + \frac{1}{6} \bullet 12 \right)$$

$$= \frac{6}{5} \bullet \frac{1}{6} (34) = \frac{34}{5}$$

And so by the indicated luck equation we have

$$\lambda \langle \text{not-}4 \rangle = \left(1 - \frac{5}{6} \right) \bullet (\langle \text{not-}4 \rangle - \langle 4 \rangle) = \frac{1}{6} \bullet \left(\frac{34}{5} - 8 \right) = \frac{1}{6} \bullet -\frac{6}{5} = -\frac{1}{5}$$

Not-4 is thus a result reflecting just a little bit of bad luck.

The Probability Account of Luck

The point is that any multiple-outcome situation can be partitioned into various binary win/lose reconstructions. And here the just illustrated mode of luck computation should yield results that are circumstantially appropriate.

In general, luck is governed by the basic formula $\lambda = Y - E$. Accordingly, someone who usually stands in the top third of a competition by beating some 70% of the field this time only makes the top half by having only 50% of the field below him, may be seen as having bad luck to the extent of $50 - 70 = -20$ percent. And if someone who usually beats 50 percent of the contestants this time beats 80 percent of them he should be deemed lucky to the tune of $80 - 50 = 30$ percent.

Can one control one's luck in reaching a certain favorable outcome O? The luck equation

$$\lambda = \Delta \bullet (1 - p) = (\langle O_1 \rangle - \langle \text{not-}O_1 \rangle) \bullet (1 - p)$$

conveys two important lessons here, namely that one can diminish the scope of luck in realizing an object in two ways:

- by increasing the probability of success
- by decreasing the penalty for failure.

Life being what it is, these parameters are, in general, change-resistant. A fortunate exception occurs in the medical arena where lifestyle changes and medical regimes can significantly reduce the probability for and the scale of misfortunes, thereby reducing the scope for sheer luck.

However, it is folly to think that good luck can be earned or deserved. Good luck might invite envy but it should never elicit admiration since its beneficiary got there by pure chance. Good luck is something to be happy about, but not really something to be grateful for. No larger potency in the scheme of things arranged for it to come your way; chance alone has been at work. So do not press your luck. Insofar as you can decrease reliance on luck you can diminish your exposure to risk, but do not count on luck itself to get you out of a tight spot.

An unusual sort of situation arises when one uncertain-outcome situation occurs as one component within the context of another. Consider, for example, the situation where one competitor must win the present match or lose the entire contest with it. And let it be that two alternative choices (A, B) are at his disposal, subject to the following condition.

Probability of Outcome:

Tactic	Win [+1]	Lose [–1]	Draw [0]
A	.2	.8	.0
B	.1	.1	.8

Here the comparison of expectations is clearly on the side of Alternative B. Yet despite the fact that alternative A is liable to produce a loss—and do this with far more likelihood than its alternative—it nevertheless represents the best option by affording the greatest chance for success in the larger context of procedure. The prospect of success that it affords to our contestant is very much a forlorn hope but, in the circumstances, our competitor had best chance it and entrust his fate to the uncertain security of good luck.

Some rather different questions revolve about the concept of luck. One is the *question of amount*: "How lucky would it be (or: was it) for X to realize the outcome O?" And it is this question that has mainly concerned us to this point. But there is also the *question of presence*: "Was it by luck that X realized the outcome O?" This (very different) question calls for reemphasizing that luck is, in fact, a default conception. For only if that outcome is not explainable in a chance-conflicting way—outcome "fixing," bribery, cheating—is it appropriate to ascribe it to luck.

Of course one of these alternative ways is that of skill. When someone succeeds in a chancy enterprise—be it a game or some more portentous venture—the question is often asked whether this happy result was due to skill or luck. This, of course, is something that can only be addressed on a statistical basis.

In comparing the role of luck and skill in accomplishing a certain aim we have to determine the proportion of cases in which the agent—or others at the same level of skill and competence—has achieved a comparable success in the enterprise at issue. But it is important to keep the two factors apart. For it is never by skill that you have good luck, which is, by nature, a matter of pure chance. And while *relying* on luck is something we might be able to control, *having* it is beyond our control in a chancy world in whose affairs haphazard almost invariably plays a role.

Notes

1 In ordinary discussion "luck" often means good luck, but not always. For while we might say that "it was just his luck" to be at the wrong place at the wrong time, we would not say that he was lucky to be there.
2 Yet one certainly should not identify luck and chance, because most chance developments in nature exert no effect on anyone for good or for ill. Only with matters of chance where someone's interests are at stake does luck come into play.
3 See, for example, Zimmerman (2002: 559).
4 It is this sort of thing that is at issue with what is called "epistemic luck." Thus if you correctly guess someone's (given) name you are lucky with regard to a range of several hundred, whereas if you guess their age you are lucky with respect to a range of a couple decades. Getting the former right requires a good deal greater luck.
5 There are three significantly different modes of chance: *physical chance* associated with the stochastic processes of nature, *unpredictability chance* arising when the information required for prediction is in principle unavailable, and *cognitive chance* in matters where the particular agent at issue is simply ignorant of relevant information. These different modes of chance give rise to varying determinations of likelihood—and correlatively of luck. But the principles of calculation with the resultant numbers remain the same.
6 The probabilities at issue in these expected-value assessments should, of course, be the prior probabilities obtaining in advance of the fact. The ex-post-facto probability that a head-yielding toss has yielded a tail is a here-irrelevant zero.
7 Subjective luck very much depends on how that agent values outcomes.
8 The expected yield is the sum of the products of the various outcome-yields and their respective realization-probabilities. In the present case this is $\frac{1}{6}(2) + \frac{1}{6}(4) + \frac{1}{6}(6) + \frac{1}{6}(8) + \frac{1}{6}(10) + \frac{1}{6}(12) + \frac{42}{6} = 7$.
9 This is the measure of luck specified in the Appendix of my 1995 Farrar-Strauss-Giroux book on *Luck*.

References

Rescher, N. (1995) *Luck: The Brilliant Randomness of Everyday Life*, New York: Farrar-Strauss-Giroux. (Re-issued by the University of Pittsburgh Press in 2005.)
Zimmerman, M.J. (2002) "Taking Luck Seriously," *The Journal of Philosophy* 99(11), 553–576.

Appendix 1

Measuring Luck

- General Formulas

    Odds-luck index: $1 - p^+$ (where p^+ is the (prior) probability of success/winning)
    Yield-Luck Measure: $\lambda = Y - E$ (λ for amount of luck)
    Max-luck: $\lambda^+ = Y^+ - E$ (Y^+ being the yield of the best possible outcome)
    Proportionate luck: $\lambda\star = \lambda/\lambda^+ = (Y - E)/(Y^+ - E)$

The Probability Account of Luck

- Binary Gambles

  Expectation: $E = p \cdot W + (1 - p) \cdot L$
  Stake: $\Delta = W - L$
  Win-Luck: $\lambda\{\text{win}\} = (1 - p) \cdot \Delta = (1 - p)(W - L)$

- Multi-Outcome Situations

  Expectations: $E = \sum \left(p_k \cdot \langle O_k \rangle \right)$ (Where p_k is the prior probability of outcome O_k)

  $\lambda\{O_i\} = {<}O_i{>} - E$

Notes

1 Y is the outcome-yield and E the expectation.
2 ${<}O_i{>}$ is the yield of outcome O_i.
3 With binary gambles, W is the win-yield and L the loss-yield.
4 p is the (prior) probability of the outcome at issue. With success-luck in binary gambles it will be the probability of winning.

13
THE MIXED ACCOUNT OF LUCK

Rik Peels

Introduction

On two earlier occasions, I have spelled out and defended what, henceforth, I call a *Mixed Account* of luck.[1] It is mixed because it combines the conditions of two main rival accounts of luck: the control condition and the modal condition. Moreover, it also has a significance condition (see Peels 2015: 77–79; 2017: 200–207). Since my account had to be sketchy on those earlier occasions, I am glad that the editors have invited me to spell out my view in more detail, contrast it with various other accounts, and defend it against objections.

Before I set out to do so, let me address a preliminary question: What is at stake? In other words, why does it matter how we think of the nature of luck? Of course, it might be of intrinsic epistemic value to get a better grasp on what it is for something to be lucky, but are there any further philosophical pay-offs? I think there are at least five of them:

1. What luck is matters for the well-known debate on moral luck, as Hales (2015), Peels (2015), and Pritchard (2005; 2006) rightly point out. The debate concerns whether people are morally blameworthy, praiseworthy, or otherwise responsible for things that are due to luck. Adherents of moral luck argue that we are, whereas others deny that we are. Whether or not there is such a thing as moral luck clearly depends on exactly what luck is.[2]
2. Others, such as Neil Levy (2011), have taken this issue a step further and have argued that there is no such thing as moral responsibility or that we should be skeptical about moral responsibility because too many things that make a difference to what we do and what we fail to do—the outcomes of our actions, the circumstances in which we find ourselves, the character traits that we have and fail to have—are due to luck. Whether this is true, indeed, partly depends on what luck is.
3. It is often said and argued that having knowledge excludes that the fact that one's belief is true is a matter of luck. An account of luck can shed light on exactly how one's beliefs should not be lucky in order for them to be instances of knowledge.[3]
4. What luck is also matters to one's theory of distributive justice. After all, one might think that it is merely a matter of luck that some people are talented, rich, healthy, gifted, and so on, whereas others are not. If so, then this might have radical implications for how we should organize our societies, given the relations one might think to hold between luck and fairness.[4]

The Mixed Account of Luck

5. Some—see Nagel (1979) and Mele (2006)—have suggested that if our actions are not determined, then they are merely a matter of luck and that this counts against the libertarian conception of free will. Again, whether this is convincing depends on what luck is.

Thus, I think that Jennifer Lackey is right that "[t]he concept of luck plays a crucial role in many philosophical discussions" (Lackey 2008: 255). I encourage the reader to explore these discussions with the Mixed Account and rival accounts of luck in mind. Here, I focus on defending the account. The chapter is structured as follows. First, I address the issue of what the analysandum should be. I argue that the primary analysandum is "the actualization of some state of affairs Σ being lucky for some person S." All other kinds of luck are in some way or other reducible to this phenomenon. After that, I briefly present the Mixed Account of luck and its main motivations. I lay out the three conditions of the Mixed view, roughly: (i) Σ is significant for S, (ii) S fails to exercise control over whether or not Σ obtains, and (iii) Σ could easily have failed to obtain. I contrast the view with its main rivals. Subsequently, I spell out in much more detail exactly what each of these three conditions amounts to. Finally, I discuss and reply to three objections to the Mixed Account and conclude that it survives unscathed.

What Sorts of Things Are Lucky?

When we try to analyze luck, what sort of a thing do we try to analyze? Well, clearly luck is not a material being, a number, a proposition, a person, or some such thing. Rather, it seems, luck is a *property*: things can be lucky. More specifically, things can be *lucky*, that is, have the property of being due to luck and being in some sense positive; things can be *unlucky*, that is, have the property of being due to luck and being in some sense negative; and things can be what we could call *non-lucky*, that is, they could not be due to luck.[5] If things are lucky or unlucky, they have the property of being due to luck or being the result of luck or crucially involving luck (the details between these various ways of phrasing it do not matter for our purposes).

If luck is a property, what sorts of things have that property, that is, what sorts of things are lucky or unlucky? It seems to me that in ordinary parlance, we say of four sorts of things that they are lucky or unlucky: persons, propositions, events, and states of affairs. What I mean by that is that you will find lots of examples on the internet, in newspapers, on blogs, and so on, of sentences along these lines and that there is nothing *grammatically incorrect* about them. They might be conceptually muddled, but I return to that issue after I have given examples of how we use the words "lucky" and "unlucky". As to *persons*, we say things like:

(a)   Andrea was unlucky not to pass the driving test on the first occasion.
(b)   Beatrice was lucky not to be hit by a lightning bolt.

With respect to *propositions* (or, at least, with respect to their truth value), we utter sentences like:

(c)   It was lucky that we got the tickets for Handel's *Messiah*.
(d)   It was lucky that the firefighters arrived quickly.

When it comes to *events*, it seems normal to say:

(e)   It has widely been thought that it was bad luck to change the name of a boat.
(f)   The police say the chance drug haul was good luck.

Finally, luck can also properly be attributed to *states of affairs* that are not events:

149

(g) His cancer was bad luck.
(h) Our house facing north is good luck.

In what follows, I focus on luck as a property of *states of affairs*. The reason is that this captures all other phenomena of luck. If some person is lucky, she is lucky that some state of affairs is (not) actualized. If a luck-sentence comes with a that-clause, the property of luck is also ascribed to the actualization of a state of affairs, such as our getting tickets for the concert in sentence (c) and the firefighters arriving quickly in (d). Finally, events are particular states of affairs, but it seems questionable that all particular states of affairs are events: is someone's having cancer an event, and is a house facing north an event? Thus, by focusing on luck as a property of states of affairs, we make sure we do not miss out on important phenomena that are a matter of luck.[6]

E.J. Coffman has argued that our focus should be on *strokes of luck* rather than luck as a property of states of affairs (the actualization of some state of affairs being lucky for someone), since the latter can be explained in terms of the former, but not vice versa. Here is how he defines the relation between the two:

> Event E is at t (un)lucky for subject S = df. (i) E is in some respect good (bad) for S and (ii) there's a stroke of good (bad) luck for S, E$\star$, such that *either* (a) E = E$\star$ *or* (b) E$\star$ is a primary (chief, main) contributor to E.
>
> *Coffman 2014: 36*

Thus, even though you living your life might counterfactually depend on your luckily narrowly escaping an accident as a toddler (a stroke of good luck), that does not imply that everything else that happens in your life is a matter of luck—which is indeed the result we want. Here is an example that he uses to illustrate this point:

> Our department meeting just happens to end early for once. As a result, I'm early to pick up my son Evan from school. Upon arriving, I spot him playing in the street. A car, whose distracted driver is texting on her cell phone, speeds toward Evan. But I'm in a position to push Evan out of the car's path, and I of course do so. Hugging Evan tightly moments later, I say: "I'm so lucky you're safe!"
>
> *Coffman 2014: 35*

He interprets this case as follows: it was a *stroke of good luck for me* (and for Evan) that I was in a position to save Evan, but it was *not* a stroke of good luck that I saved him, because that happened as the result of the exercise of my control. However, it is *lucky for me* (and for him)—rather than a stroke of luck—that Evan ended up safe. Coffman concludes that the notion of an event's being lucky is parasitic on something's being a stroke of luck (see Coffman 2014: 48).

I think we can do without appealing to the notion of "something's being a stroke of luck" (a phrase we use far less often than the word "lucky" anyway). It is lucky for me and for Evan that I am rightly positioned, because that meets all three criteria. It is *not* a matter of luck that I save Evan once I am so positioned, for in saving him I exercise control. Are Evan and I lucky that he ends up safe? Well, here I think we should hesitate to answer with a firm yes or no. After all, the fact that he is safe is partly explained by the lucky fact that I happened to be rightly positioned and by the non-lucky fact that I saved him. And I think that is exactly what we would do. We would say something like: "We're so lucky that Evan is safe. Or, I mean, of course, since I was there, I acted without thinking. Who wouldn't have saved his son in such a situation? But if the meeting had not ended early I wouldn't have been there. So, we've been extremely lucky that the meeting ended early." Appeal to the notion of a "stroke of luck" will not change our hesitation to call the state of affairs of Evan's being safe a lucky one.

So, I do not think that examples like these give us good reason to focus on strokes of luck rather than on states of affairs being lucky for someone. What these examples *do* make clear, though, is that there are certain boundary cases of luck. I am lucky that I was able to save Evan, it is not a matter of luck that I saved him, and it is not entirely clear whether or not it is a matter of luck that Evan is safe. One of the things that plays a role here is *temporal and causal proximity*: we hesitate to say that Evan's being safe is a matter of luck, because it is fairly close to, but does not straightforwardly follow from my being lucky that I was there to save him—what stands in between the two is *my actually saving Evan* and that, we saw, is not a matter of luck. In what follows, I put such boundary cases aside and leave discussion of them for another occasion.

The Mixed Account of Luck, and Its Rivals

Here is the Mixed Account of luck that I will defend in this chapter:

The Mixed Account of Luck

The actualization of some state of affairs Σ is lucky or unlucky for some person S at some time t if and only if (i) Σ is significant for S at t, (ii) the actualization of Σ is *not* the intended result of S's exercising control over the actualization of Σ at t, and (iii) Σ obtains in the actual world, but does not obtain in a wide class of nearby possible worlds.

I call it the "Mixed Account" because it combines two major accounts of luck that we find in the literature: the Control Account and the Modal Account (I return to these below). Something along the line of this Mixed Account has also been defended by E.J. Coffman (2007), Neil Levy (2011), and Wayne Riggs (2007).[7]

I call conditions (ii) and (iii), respectively, the *control* condition and the *modal* condition. The account also has a *significance* condition, condition (i), which further warrants the term "Mixed Account," as only some accounts in the literature include such a significance condition. I claim and will argue that each of these three conditions is necessary and that they are jointly sufficient for something's being lucky or unlucky for someone.

Now, there are two main rival accounts to the Mixed Account of luck: Control Accounts and Modal Accounts. But there are other accounts as well. There is, for instance, one in terms of accidentality. Here, I discuss three rival accounts and several combinations of the conditions they provide.

1. The *Control Account* is endorsed in some form or other by Nafsika Athanassoulis (2005: 20), Claudia Card (1990: 199), John Greco (1995: 83), Adrian Moore (1990: 301–305), and Michael Zimmerman (1993: 219, 231, 2002: 559, 2006: 585–590). It differs from my Mixed Account in that it leaves out a modal condition like (iii) and in that it states that what is necessary is that *S lacks control* over Σ; it does not say that *S fails to exercise control* over Σ. I reply that this will not do. As to the idea that we do not need a modal condition and that a lack of control condition will do, the differential rotation in the upper atmosphere of Jupiter is beyond my control, but clearly not lucky for me or anyone else. After all, the differential rotation in the upper atmosphere of Jupiter could not easily have been otherwise. We can, of course, add a significance condition like (i). So, what if something is of significance for me and beyond my control? Well, the differential rotation in the upper atmosphere of Jupiter is beyond my control, but of no significance; the law of gravity *is*, though. If the law of gravity did not hold, I would immediately cease to exist. Still, it seems false to say that I am *lucky* that the law of gravity holds. And the reason it seems we are not *lucky* that the law of gravity holds is that things could not easily have been otherwise.

As to the second part, which concerns the issue of control, E.J. Coffman provides a case which, I think, shows that what is relevant is not the *lack of* control but *not exercising* such control:

151

Without your having had any say in the matter, you find yourself holding a ticket in a lottery (...). There are two ways you can win: press a button that will make you the (illegitimate) winner, or let the lottery proceed fairly in hopes that your number will be the one selected. For you to win either way, you *must* keep your ticket. Although you're free to make yourself the winner, you refrain from intervening. Indeed, given your character, there was almost no chance you'd exploit the set-up to win illegitimately. Lo and behold, you win fair and square!

Coffman 2014: 46

It seems that in this case, I am *lucky* that I win, even though I *do* have intentional control over winning. I am lucky, because I in no way *exercise* that control; the actualization of Σ has nothing to do with my having control over Σ.

2. According to William Harper (1996: 276) and Carolyn Morillo (1984: 109, 125), an event is lucky just in case it is accidental or chancy. Let us, therefore, call this the *Chanciness Account* (even though I hesitate to call it an "account," as it is not developed in any detail by these philosophers). What do they have in mind? Unfortunately, they are not very specific on what this is supposed to amount to. Here are what seem to be the two main options:

a. Something is accidental just in case it is *metaphysically or logically contingent*. This, however, will clearly not do, as it implies, for instance, that all our actions are lucky, since they are all metaphysically and logically contingent. It is not a matter of luck, for instance, that I have read various papers on luck this morning. It was not a matter of luck, for I did so intentionally, in order to prepare certain material for this chapter.

b. Something is accidental just in case it is a matter of *chance*. The word "chance" is in fact used quite often by philosophers working on luck—e.g., Browne (1992: 345–346) and Harper (1996: 274). But what is it for an event to be due to chance? Well, they might mean that it is unlikely or improbable to occur. But mere improbability does not suffice for luck. If I see the exact same number of cars today that I saw yesterday, is that a lucky event? No, it is surely unlikely—unless one lives in, say, some remote area in Siberia and that number is 1 or even 0. It is unlikely in normal circumstances, but not lucky. What if we add condition (i), the significance condition? That will not provide a way out. If I hesitate to accept the job and it is likely that I will not, but I nonetheless—say, contrary to my overall character[8]—freely decide to do so, then the event of my accepting the job is unlikely and, its being a job, of significance. But that does not render the event lucky. I have chosen it myself; the consequences might be lucky or unlucky but my accepting the job was not.

3. A third and final account is the so-called *Modal Account*. On this account, defended by Duncan Pritchard, the actualization of some state of affairs is lucky just in case it could easily have failed to obtain in the sense that it obtains in the actual world, but fails to obtain in a significant number of nearby possible worlds. Slightly more precisely:

If an event is lucky, then it is an event that occurs in the actual world but which does not occur in a wide class of the nearest possible worlds where the relevant initial conditions for that event are the same as in the actual world.

Pritchard 2005: 128

Now, certain philosophers, such as Nicholas Rescher and Duncan Pritchard himself, add something like condition (i): the event should be of significance for the person in question (Pritchard 2014, 2005; Rescher 1993, 1995: 211–212).[9] Here is an example that, I think, can be used to illustrate how this is supposed to run. Imagine, for instance, that five different people intend to steal my car, but that all of them cannot make it, for very different reasons: one misses the train, another falls ill, the third one cannot find the car, the fourth person is attacked by a wild bison on his way to my car, and the fifth one instantly falls in love with a woman that he runs into and asks her out. In most nearby possible worlds, at least one person makes it and steals my car. And, surely, whether or not my car is stolen is of significance for me. I am lucky, then, that my car is not stolen, or, in other words, it is a matter of luck for me that my car is not stolen.

Unfortunately, combining condition (iii) with condition (i) will not do as an account of luck. We also need a control condition, for similar reasons as I mentioned in my discussion of the Accidentality Account with a significance clause. Here is an example that I have used in earlier writings to illustrate the point:

> Imagine that Sam is strongly inclined to ask Julia to marry him, so that it is highly probable that he does, that is, that he does so in most of the nearby possible worlds. Nevertheless, he decides not to propose to her. Would we say that his not proposing to her was a lucky event for him? I do not mean to ask whether his not marrying Julia or any of the other consequences of not proposing to Julia is a lucky event. Those may very well be. But it seems that Sam's not proposing to Julia itself is not a matter of luck. Improbability conjoined with significance might be necessary, but it is not sufficient for an event's being due to luck. We also need the absence of control as a separate condition.[10]
>
> *Peels 2015: 78, 2016*

The point generalizes: many of our actions are such that they are significant and we perform them in the actual world but *not* in a significant number of nearby possible worlds. But that does *not* make them lucky: they are *fully* under our control and we *exercise* that control. We not only need a significance condition and a modal condition, but a control condition as well, in order to construe a plausible account of luck.

The Three Conditions Considered in More Detail

Now that I have briefly mentioned the Mixed Account and sketched why it is to be preferred over the main rival accounts, let me spell out in more detail what each of the three conditions in the Mixed Account amounts to.

(i) *Significance condition.* This condition says that, in order for Σ to be lucky, whether or not Σ obtains should be significant for S. By this, I mean that it matters, that it is important, that it is of value for S, whether or not S is aware of that—which is why I now prefer the phrase "significant *for* S" to "significant *to* S." Things cannot be lucky or unlucky for S if they are in no way relevant for S. Thus, it is a matter of *chance* that I have the exact same number of atoms on my plate today as I had yesterday. But I am not *lucky* that this is so, as it makes no difference of value for me. If I were to win the lottery in case I have the exact same number of atoms on my plate as I did yesterday and that happens to be the case, then the actualization of this state of affairs *is* lucky for me.[11]

(ii) *Control condition.* Clearly, significance all by itself will not do. It is significant for me whether or not I accept the job offer, choose a particular medical treatment, propose to my loved one, or decide to have children (if one can have children). But these states of affairs are not matters of luck: I am in control of them and that is why they are actualized or not (unless special conditions hold). Exactly what sort of control is relevant here, though? I think two features of such control should be highlighted here:

(1) First, it is not so much *de re* but *de dicto* control that one should fail to exercise in order to be lucky. Imagine that number 123.456.789 will be the winning lottery ticket and that I can buy that ticket. Then I can exercise *de re* control over buying what is in fact the winning lottery ticket. If I did, I would still have been lucky to win the lottery and to buy the winning lottery ticket.

That is because, even though I intentionally bought *the ticket of which it is true that it is the winning ticket*, I did not intentionally buy *the winning ticket*—after all, I had no clue what the winning ticket would be.[12]

(2) What seems relevant here is the absence of both *direct* and *indirect* control. Some philosophers, such as Neil Levy (2011: 36), claim that luck requires the absence of *direct* control, but this scope is too narrow. Imagine that something is of significance for me and that I lack *direct* control over it, but that I *do* have indirect control over it. A well-known example from the literature on control is losing weight.[13] This is something we lack direct control over: we cannot simply choose to lose weight. Instead, we can choose to perform other actions, such as exercising, consuming a healthy diet, and so on, over a longer period of time. Unless special conditions hold, such as a severe illness, one will be successful in losing weight if one exercises such indirect control. If I intentionally exercise that indirect control and thereby lose more than 10 pounds, as I intended, then is my losing 10 pounds *lucky*? Clearly, it is not: it is something that I intentionally and reliably brought about. Hence, what luck requires is the failure to exercise direct control as well as indirect control.

(iii) *Modal condition.* This condition says that things could easily have been otherwise. This is important, for certain things that are significant for me and beyond my control, such as the law of gravity (I could not exist without it), are clearly *not* a matter of luck—they are physically necessary. It is not that clear, though, how we should spell out the phrase "Σ obtains, but could easily have failed to obtain." One way to do so—which I will accept for now—is that Σ obtains in the actual world, but not in a wide class of nearby possible worlds. Thus, I win the lottery, but in many nearby possible worlds I do not win.

In exactly *how many* nearby possible worlds should things be different from how they are in the actual world, in order for Σ to be lucky? I think Nicholas Rescher is right that that is *context-dependent* (see Rescher 1995). If I partake in Russian roulette with a six-chambered revolver and survive, it seems right to say that I have been lucky to survive, even if my chances of surviving were 5/6—so that I survive in most nearby possible worlds. Contrast this with a lottery case: imagine that I can win $10 with a lottery, that the lottery has only six tickets, and that I buy five of them, among which is the winning ticket, it seems I am *not* lucky that I win the lottery, even though in that case as well, the chances of the relevant state of affairs obtaining are 5/6. The reason is that there is much less at stake: there is an enormous axiological difference between merely not winning the lottery on the one hand and dying on the other. What this suggests is that the more that is at stake, the lower the number of possible worlds needs to be in order for the actualization of Σ to count as lucky (a similar point is made by Levy 2011: 36).

Before we move on, let me draw attention to the fact that this is a *radically objective* account. What I mean by that is that whether someone is lucky or unlucky depends on whether something *is* of significance for S (whether S thinks so or not), whether it *is* something over which S fails to exercise control, and on whether there *are* nearby possible worlds in which the event fails to obtain. It, thus, differs from subjective accounts, such as that of Andrew Latus (2000, 2003). Imagine that I take part in Russian roulette, but that, contrary to what I think, the revolver contains no bullets. I shoot and, of course, survive. The right thing to say seems that I *think* that I am lucky, but that I am not lucky to survive. After all, there was no chance I would die as a result of shooting.

Slightly more controversially, this suggests that if physical determinism is true and if there are, therefore, no nearby possible worlds, since things could not easily have been otherwise, then *there is no luck*. E.J. Coffman (2014: 30) believes this is misguided; after all, can we not be lucky in winning the lottery in an entirely determined world? I see no reason to accept that verdict: if the current total state of affairs in the world is determined by the conjunction of, say, the total state of affairs a million years ago and the laws of nature, then it could *not* easily have been the case that I would lose the lottery today. In that case it *would still seem as if* there is luck and luck-talk might be helpful in all sorts of ways. But there would be no luck: everything would happen as a matter of causal necessity. I was, therefore, not lucky to win the lottery, even though things might *seem* that way.

Three Objections and Replies

In this section, I discuss three main objections to the Mixed Account that can be found in the literature. I argue that they fail to convince.

1. A first objection is that the Mixed Account is not so much *mistaken*, but *incomplete* as an account of luck. Neil Levy has suggested that the Mixed Account gives us a good account of *chancy* luck, but that there is also such a thing as *non-chancy* luck (see Levy 2011: 36). Here, he thinks, for instance, of certain kinds of Gettier-scenarios and what Thomas Nagel calls "constitutive luck" (see Nagel 1979). Let me explain. As to the Gettier-scenarios, imagine that an alien space ship lands and the creatures that set foot on earth upon landing present you with a machine that is said to detect the chemical structure of any substance. You have good reason to believe them, but your belief is false: you are unaware that it is broken, so it will always tell you that the relevant substance is H_2O. Moreover, for some reason or other, the aliens, who are unaware that the machine is broken, make sure that it is highly likely that you select water (say, they love water, because they do not have it on their planet). Thus, you choose water and come to believe that its structure is H_2O. It seems that you are lucky that your belief is true and that you, therefore, do not *know* that the chemical structure of the substance is H_2O, even though in all nearby possible worlds your belief is true, because in all those worlds you select water (see Levy 2011: 25–29).

As to the second kind of non-chancy luck, what Levy has in mind is what Nagel and others in his wake refer to as "constitutive luck": "luck in the traits and dispositions that make one the kind of person one is; that is, in the traits and dispositions that constitute one" (Levy 2011: 29; see also Nagel 1979). Imagine Marie Josephine grows up in the right sort of family and educational circumstances, and thus has the virtue of open-mindedness. But, of course, things could have been otherwise; she might have grown up in different circumstances in which she did *not* develop this virtue, but the vice of narrow-mindedness, without any fault of her own. Psychological traits are, Levy rightly points out, not fixed by genes, so even if origin essentialism, such as that of Saul Kripke (1980), is true, there will still be constitutive luck. There is always plenty of room for cultural influence to make a difference to what virtues and vices we have. Clearly, whether or not one has a particular virtue or its correlated vice is something that is of significance. And in this case it is beyond one's control. However, one might also think that it seems Marie Josephine is *lucky* to have this virtue rather than this vice. But then there is luck that does not meet condition (iii), for the world in which Marie Josephine lacks this virtue is far away (e.g., worlds in which she has a different family); she has it in *all* nearby possible worlds.

Based on examples such as these, Levy suggests that with respect to non-chancy luck, we maintain the significance condition (i) and the control condition (ii), but add something similar to but crucially different from (iii). The alternative modal condition should be understood in terms of *the number of possible worlds* in which Σ fails to obtain rather than the *nearness* of those worlds.[14] Moreover, what is relevant is not so much the individual as beings relevantly similar to the individual:

> Rather than relativizing worlds to the individual, to understand attributions of constitutive luck we should understand the relevant worlds as those in which human beings like us exist: I am (non-chancy) constitutively lucky in those traits and dispositions that vary significantly in human experience.
>
> *Levy 2011: 33*

Thus, given the better nutrition available in the West, we should relativize luck when it comes to the IQ of, say, Canadians to the average IQ of people in the West: that is the relevant reference group. And if I survive an airplane accident but break both my legs, I am still lucky to survive, for the relevant reference group is that of airplane accidents and those are often fatal. The reference group can even be counter-factual, e.g., when it comes to the fact that this universe is fine-tuned for life: there is only one universe, but, it seems, there could have been all sorts of other universes and in the vast majority of them life is impossible (Levy 2011: 33–35).

Should we embrace the idea that there is chancy luck and non-chancy luck? I suggest that there is a better way to deal with the cases to which Levy draws our attention. For, as people such as E.J. Coffman (2007: 392) and Fernando Broncano-Berrocal (2015: 16–17) have pointed out, there is a concept rather close to luck that can easily be confused with it: fortune. *S* can be *lucky* that *Σ* is actualized; another, closely related, option is that *S* is *fortunate* that *Σ* is actualized. If *S* is fortunate that *Σ* is actualized, it is of significance for *S* and she fails to exercise control over it, and there is a substantial number of possible worlds in which *Σ* fails to be actualized, whether or not they are close. Marie Josephine is not *lucky* that she is open-minded; that is not a matter of luck, given her genes, family situation, and cultural circumstances, which could not easily have been otherwise. But we would surely say she is *fortunate* to have the virtue of open-mindedness (unless, of course, she has developed that virtue herself, in which case she *has* exercised control over it).[15]

How we should think of the other cases mentioned by Levy depends on the details, it seems to me. As to the alien case: I agree that in such a case I fail to know that the substance is H_2O. If the aliens could easily have picked another substance as their favorite substance, then there are nearby possible worlds in which the substance is *not* H_2O. If, for some reason or other, they could not have easily chosen another substance—let us say, they love water—it is a matter of *chance* or *coincidence* (not so much luck) that they choose water, and I am fortunate—a knowledge-undermining kind of fortune—to form a true belief on the issue. People in Canada with an IQ of 160 are fortunate to have such a high IQ. I am *lucky* to survive the airplane accident; in nearby possible worlds the plane makes a slightly different move or hits a different object and I die. And, unless some form of theism is true (on which God wanted there to be intelligent life), we are fortunate that out of the many universes that were possible, one is actualized in which life is possible, because all nearby possible worlds are worlds in which life is possible. This is not to deny that *at some point in the past* it might have been a matter of luck (luck for us) that a universe was actualized in which life is possible, because, *at that time*, there *were* many close possible worlds in which intelligent life was impossible.

2. A second objection, due to Jennifer Lackey (2008: 258), is that *Σ* can be lucky for *S* even if *S* *does* have control over the actualization of *Σ* and exercises that control. Thus, (ii) is not necessary. Here is the example she adduces in favor of this point.

> Ramona is a demolition worker, about to press a button that will blow up an abandoned warehouse, thereby completing a project that she and her co-workers have been working on for several weeks. Unbeknown to her, however, a mouse had chewed through the relevant wires in the construction office an hour earlier, severing the connection between the button and the explosives. But as Ramona is about to press the button, her coworker hangs his jacket on a nail in the precise location of the severed wires, which radically deviates from his usual routine of hanging his clothes in the office closet. As it happens, the hanger on which the jacket is hanging is made of metal, and it enables the electrical current to pass through the damaged wires just as Ramona presses the button and demolishes the warehouse.

Ramona's case, she says, is riddled with luck and even her blowing up the warehouse is due to luck, but she has full control over whether or not she blows up the warehouse. She says her blowing up the warehouse is due to luck, since if something had gone slightly differently—if her coworker had not hung his jacket in that specific location—she would not have blown up the warehouse. I think this is mistaken. There are all sorts of events in this case that are a matter of luck, such as a mouse chewing through the relevant wires (an unlucky event), her coworker hanging his jacket in that precise location (a lucky event), his deviating from his usual routine (a lucky event), and so on. However, *once these events have obtained* and the situation is as it is, Ramona is in full control and whether or not she blows up the warehouse is not a matter of luck. Not everything that is possible only because a lucky event took place is *itself* a matter of luck. After all, if that were the case, then virtually any event in the world would become a matter of luck—say, because the big bang was a matter of luck, or the emergence of life was a matter of luck.[16]

3. Third and finally, Jennifer Lackey also argues that the modal condition, condition (iii), is not necessary for luck. She illustrates this claim as follows:

> Sophie, knowing that she had very little time left to live, wanted to bury a chest filled with all of her earthly treasures on the island she inhabited. As she walked around trying to determine the best site for proper burial, her central criteria were, first, that a suitable location must be on the northwest corner of the island—where she had spent many of her fondest moments in life—and, second, that it had to be a spot where rose bushes could flourish—since these were her favourite flowers. As it happens, there was only one particular patch of land on the northwest corner of the island where the soil was rich enough for roses to thrive. Sophie, being excellent at detecting such soil, immediately located this patch of land and buried her treasure, along with seeds for future roses to bloom, in the one and only spot that fulfilled her two criteria. One month later, Vincent, a distant neighbor of Sophie's, was driving in the northwest corner of the island—which was also his most beloved place to visit—and was looking for a place to plant a rose bush in memory of his mother who had died ten years earlier—since these were her favourite flowers. Being excellent at detecting the proper soil for rose bushes to thrive, he immediately located the same patch of land that Sophie had found one month earlier. As he began digging a hole for the bush, he was astonished to discover a buried treasure in the ground.
>
> *Lackey 2008: 261*

Lackey suggests that Vincent was lucky to find the treasure, even though he finds it in all nearby possible worlds: after all, that was the only patch of land on the island where rose bushes can flourish. One might object with Neil Levy (2011: 20–22) to this case that finding the treasure might *seem* lucky to Vincent, but that it really is not. E.J. Coffman (2014: 32), however, responds to such a reply that we can simply stipulate that Vincent somehow, without sufficient evidence, *believed* that he would find a treasure there, so that it was not lucky *to* Vincent at all; still, Coffman suggests, finding the treasure is lucky *for* Vincent.

In reply, we should note that the case is riddled with luck. There happens to be only one patch of land on which roses can bloom, Vincent happens to like the same kinds of flowers as Sophie liked, and so on—all states of affairs that, as it turns out, are lucky for Vincent (whether or not Vincent knows about that). But, as I pointed out above, not everything that happens partly as a result of luck is itself a matter of luck. Now, let us turn to Vincent's finding the treasure: that state of affairs is significant for Vincent and it is beyond his intentional control. What about the modal condition; is it met? I think that depends on the details of the case. If he could easily have failed to find the treasure, say, because the patch is still fairly large, or because he decided not to plant a bush but write a poem or some such thing, then his finding the treasure is a matter of luck for him. If, however, he could not easily have failed to find the treasure—because the patch is really small, there was no serious alternative to planting a rose bush in memory of his mother, and so on—so that finding the treasure was pretty much unavoidable and happens in nearly all nearby possible worlds, he is not *lucky* to find the treasure, but just very *fortunate*. After all, the *chances* are very small: in the vast majority of possible worlds, he does not find the treasure, because the island has more patches of such land, his mother loves other kinds of flowers, he never even makes it to the island, and so on. Thus, again, the conceptual distinction between luck and fortune can explain why we should *not* use the word "luck" in such cases, but rather "chance," "coincidence," "improbability," or, given its significance and its being beyond Vincent's control, "fortunate" in this case.

Conclusion

I conclude that the Mixed Account of luck survives unscathed; it is victorious over the Control Account, the Chanciness Account, and the Modal Account. Any satisfying account of luck will have to include (i) a significance clause, (ii) a clause to the effect that one fails to exercise control, and (iii) a modal clause.[17]

Notes

1 It has also been call an "Augmentation View"—e.g., by Hartman (2017: 27)—since, as we shall see below, it augments a lack of control condition with a significance condition and a modal condition.
2 For various positions in this debate, see Statman (1993). Some, such as Hartman (2017: 23–31, 65–66), have argued that we do not need to grasp the nature of luck in order to solve the problem of moral luck, since the problem of moral luck really is a problem of lack of control, but this seems to be a minority position in the field (unfortunately, I cannot address it here; I do so in Peels (2019)).
3 For more on the non-lucky nature of knowledge, see Pritchard (2005); Zagzebski (1996).
4 Probably the best-known example of someone who has argued that distributive justice should rule out as much as possible things that are in some relevant sense due to luck, is John Rawls, especially in Rawls (1971).
5 Another possibility is, of course, that something is due to luck but neither positive nor negative. Since it is not relevant to the discussion in this chapter, I will not further explore it here.
6 In Peels (2015), I focus on *events*, but in Peels (2017), I broaden the focus of my analysis to *states of affairs*, so as to include beliefs (as beliefs can be lucky, or, at least, so I argue there).
7 Coffman's (2014: 44) account is also highly similar to it, but its analysandum is "an event's being a *stroke of luck* for *S*" rather than "the actualization of a state of affairs *being lucky* for *S*".
8 For various ways to construe "contrary to one's overall character" that maintain responsibility, see R.J. Hartman and B. Matheson (manuscript).
9 In a more recent publication, Pritchard (2014) drops the significance condition.
10 I now believe, though, in opposition to what I argued earlier, that what is relevant is not so much the *absence of* control, but the *failure to exercise* that control. I explain this in more detail below.
11 What if a friend of mine gives me a lottery ticket in which each ticket has a 1/1,000,000 chance of winning $1,000,000, and I happen to win, but I do not care at all about money or winning? In that case, it seems, it is a matter of chance or improbability that I win and *for many people, such an event would have been lucky*, but I am *not* lucky to win—winning is not lucky *for me*—since I do not care one bit whether or not I win.
12 It is a rather complicated matter exactly what *intentional* control requires. Does it require propositional knowledge or at least know-how, justified true belief, rational true belief? I leave this discussion for another occasion, since the conflict between the Mixed Account and rival accounts does not depend on this issue.
13 E.g. Alston (1989). I have spelled out the difference between direct and indirect control in more detail in Peels (2017: 61–87).
14 To be specific, he replaces (iii) with two other conditions: "(iii) events or states of affairs of that kind vary across the relevant reference group, and (iv) in a large enough proportion of cases that event or state of affairs fails to occur or be instantiated in the reference group in the way in which it occurred or was instantiated in the actual case" (Levy 2011: 36).
15 One might worry that distinguishing between luck and fortune does not help to solve problems having to do with luck, such as the problem of moral luck (since the problem seems equally to apply to moral fortune). I address this worry elsewhere, namely, in Peels (2019). Here, my aim is merely to cut the concepts at their joints.
16 In reply to Lackey, Levy (2011: 22) makes a point similar to the point I make here.
17 For their helpful comments on earlier versions of this paper, I would like to thank Valentin Arts, Wout Bisschop, Jeroen de Ridder, Geertjan Holtrop, Emanuel Rutten, Hans van Eyghen, René van Woudenberg, and especially Robert Hartman. This essay was made possible through the support of a grant from the Templeton World Charity Foundation. The opinions expressed in this essay are those of the author and do not necessarily reflect the views of the Templeton World Charity Foundation.

References

Alston, W.P. (1989) "The Deontological Conception of Epistemic Justification," in W.P. Alston, *Epistemic Justification: Essays in the Theory of Knowledge*, Ithaca: Cornell University Press, pp. 115–152.

Athanassoulis, N. (2005) *Morality, Moral Luck, and Responsibility: Fortune's Web*, New York: Palgrave Macmillan.

Broncano-Berrocal, Fernando. (2015) "Luck as Risk and the Lack of Control Account of Luck," in D. Pritchard & L.J. Whittington (eds.) *The Philosophy of Luck*, Oxford: Wiley-Blackwell, pp. 3–26.

Browne, B. (1992) "A Solution to the Problem of Moral Luck," *The Philosophical Quarterly* 42(168), 345–356.

Card, C. (1990) "Gender and Moral Luck," in Owen Flanagan & Amelie Rorty (eds.) *Identity, Character, and Morality*, Cambridge, MA: MIT Press, pp. 199–218.

Coffman, E.J. (2007) "Thinking about Luck," *Synthese* 158(3), 385–398.

——. (2014) "Strokes of Luck," in D. Pritchard & L.J. Whittington (eds.) *The Philosophy of Luck*, Oxford: Wiley-Blackwell, pp. 27–58.

Greco, J. (1995) "A Second Paradox Concerning Responsibility and Luck," *Metaphilosophy* 26(1–2), 81–96.

Hales, S. (2015) "A Problem for Moral Luck," *Philosophical Studies* 172(9), 2385–2403.

Harper, W. (1996) "Knowledge and Luck," *The Southern Journal of Philosophy* 34(3), 273–283.

Hartman, R.J. (2017) *In Defense of Moral Luck: Why Luck Often Affects Praiseworthiness and Blameworthiness*, New York: Routledge.

Hartman, R.J., & Matheson, B. "Moral Responsibility for Acting Out of Character," *unpublished manuscript*.

Kripke, S. (1980) *Naming and Necessity*, Cambridge, MA: Harvard University Press.

Lackey, J. (2008) "What Luck Is Not," *Australasian Journal of Philosophy* 86(2), 255–267.

Latus, A. (2000) "Moral and Epistemic Luck," *Journal of Philosophical Research* 25, 149–172.

——. (2003) "Constitutive Luck," *Metaphilosophy* 34(4), 460–475.

Levy, N. (2011) *Hard Luck: How Luck Undermines Free Will and Moral Responsibility*, Oxford: Oxford University Press.

Mele, A. (2006) *Free Will and Luck*, New York: Oxford University Press.

Moore, A.W. (1990) "A Kantian View of Moral Luck," *Philosophy* 65(253), 297–321.

Morillo, C.R. (1984) "Epistemic Luck, Naturalistic Epistemology and the Ecology of Knowledge or What the Frog Should Have Told Dretske," *Philosophical Studies* 46(1), 109–129.

Nagel, T. (1979) "Moral Luck," in *Mortal Questions*, New York: Cambridge University Press, pp. 24–38.

Peels, R. (2015) "A Modal Solution to the Problem of Moral Luck," *American Philosophical Quarterly* 52(1), 73–87.

——. (2016) Review of D. Pritchard and L.J. Whittington (eds.), *The Philosophy of Luck*, Oxford: Blackwell, 2014, *Notre Dame Philosophical Reviews*, September 23, http://ndpr.nd.edu/news/70033-the-philosophy-of-luck/.

——. (2017) *Responsible Belief: A Theory in Ethics and Epistemology*, New York: Oxford University Press.

——. (2019). "Is the Problem of Moral Luck a Problem of Lack of Control?," in A.C. Khoury (ed.) *Midwest Studies in Philosophy* 43: The Problem of Moral Luck, 2019.

Pritchard, D. (2005) *Epistemic Luck*, Oxford: Clarendon Press.

——. (2006) "Moral and Epistemic Luck," *Metaphilosophy* 37(1), 1–25.

——. (2014) "The Modal Account of Luck," in D. Pritchard & L.J. Whittington (eds.) *The Philosophy of Luck*, Oxford: Wiley-Blackwell, pp. 143–167.

Rawls, J. (1971) *A Theory of Justice*, Cambridge, MA: Harvard University Press.

Rescher, N. (1993) "Moral Luck," in D. Statman (ed.), *Moral Luck*, Albany: State University of New York Press, pp. 141–166.

——. (1995) *Luck: The Brilliant Randomness of Everyday Life*, Pittsburgh: University of Pittsburgh Press.

Riggs, W. (2007) "Why Epistemologists Are So Down on Their Luck," *Synthese* 158(3), 329–344.

Statman, D. (ed.) (1993) *Moral Luck*, Albany: State University of New York Press.

Zagzebski, L. (1996) *Virtues of the Mind*, Cambridge: Cambridge University Press.

Zimmerman, M.J. (1993) "Luck and Moral Responsibility," in D. Statman (ed.) *Moral Luck*, Albany: State University of New York Press, pp. 217–233.

——. (2002) "Taking Luck Seriously," *The Journal of Philosophy* 99(11), 553–576.

——. (2006) "Moral Luck: A Partial Map," *Canadian Journal of Philosophy* 36(4), 585–608.

14

LUCK AND SIGNIFICANCE

Nathan Ballantyne and Samuel Kampa

Philosophical debates about the nature of luck have for the most part endorsed the following condition:

> *Significance-generic:* event E is lucky for subject S only if E is significant for S.

The condition leaves open several questions about how events are significant. For an event to be significant for someone, must she consciously take an interest in it? Must she know the event's likelihood? Does she need to think of the event as being good or bad for her? Recent debates over significance take up these questions. Luck theorists have bracketed the correctness of Significance-generic in order to examine the kind of significance operative in that condition (see Rescher 1995: ch. 1; Pritchard 2005: ch. 5; Coffman 2007; Ballantyne 2012; and Whittington 2016).

In this chapter, we describe and evaluate four potential specifications of Significance-generic. We then consider the possibility that debates over significance are fundamentally misguided—a position defended by Duncan Pritchard (2014). In his early work on luck, Pritchard defended a significance condition for luck (2005: 132–133). More recently, he has changed his tune, insisting that "the very idea of adding a significance condition to the modal account of luck is wrongheaded" (2014: 604). If Pritchard is correct, Significance-generic is false and debates over the best account of significance are for naught. We examine Pritchard's challenge and ask whether it can be met.

Varieties of Significance

Why think that luck requires significance in the first place? We can begin to see why by considering a pair of scenarios. In the first, an active chocolate factory suffers an unlikely meltdown, causing chocolate production to cease immediately. In the second, an abandoned chocolate factory suffers an equally unlikely meltdown, but without impacting chocolate production. The former event is unlucky—dire, even. The latter event is neither lucky nor unlucky. What accounts for the difference? Facts about significance.

An unlikely meltdown that affects no one is not lucky. That is because it is significant for no one (cf. Pritchard 2005: 132). Nicholas Rescher notes that

Luck and Significance

[i]t is only because we have interests—because things can affect us for better or for worse—that luck enters in. A person is not ordinarily lucky to encounter pigeons in the park or to see a cloud floating overhead, since such things do not normally affect one's well-being.

1995: 32

Rescher observes that things would be different between you and the pigeons if you had bet $100 on their presence in the park, because money is something you care about.

Most discussions of luck focus on cases where an event is good or bad, in some sense, for someone. When you win the lottery, that is good luck for you. When you get hit by a falling meteorite, that is bad luck for you—and good luck for your nemesis. Philosophers have generalized from these sorts of observations to the claim that, in general, an event is lucky for someone only if it is good or bad for her.

As noted, debates over luck's significance tend to focus not on Significance-generic itself but on its proper specification. Theorists have tried to fill in the blanks by noting some typical features of lucky events. In many cases involving lucky events, subjects ascribe significance to those events. In other such cases, subjects' interests are impacted negatively or positively. Philosophers have thus defended accounts where what matters for significance is *ascriptions of significance* or *impacted interests*.

Two key questions divide competing accounts:

Q1: For an event to be significant for someone, must she ascribe significance to the event?

Q2: For an event to be significant for someone, must the event impact her subjective interests?

Philosophers who discuss significance disagree over the answers. In response to Q1, some say "yes" and others say "no." Call the former *constructivists* and the latter *realists*. Constructivists say that in order for an event to be significant for someone, she must take the event to be significant, either in the actual world or in a nearby possible world (Pritchard 2005: 132–133). According to constructivism, a meltdown at the chocolate factory is significant for Charlie only if Charlie *actually* ascribes significance to the event or *would* ascribe significance were he to know relevant facts about the incident (that it was highly unlikely to occur, that the meltdown rendered Charlie's Golden Ticket null and void, etc.). Realists, on the other hand, insist that whether an event is significant for someone does not depend on whether she ascribes significance to it (Coffman 2007: 386–388; Ballantyne 2012: 327). According to realism, a meltdown at the chocolate factory can be significant for Charlie even if Charlie does not ascribe significance to the event and would not ascribe significance to the event if he were privy to the relevant facts about the meltdown. Though realism might seem counterintuitive, there are strong arguments in its favor (see sections 4–5).

In response to Q2, some philosophers say "yes" and others say "no." Call the former *subjectivists* and the latter *objectivists*. According to subjectivism, an event is significant for someone only if she has a subjective interest in the event's obtaining, where a subjective interest is a personal desire or preference (Rescher 1995: 7–8; Pritchard 2005: 132; Coffman 2007: 386–388; Borges 2016: 467). For example, winning the Florida State Lottery is significant for Abraham Shakespeare only if he wants to win the lottery, in which case winning is good luck, or wants to lose the lottery, in which case winning is bad luck. Whether an event is significant for Shakespeare, and whether it is good or bad luck for him, is a matter of Shakespeare's subjective desires or preferences. Objectivism is the negation of subjectivism. We can distinguish between two types of objectivism: *weak objectivism* and *strong objectivism*. According to weak objectivism, an event is significant for someone if she has a subjective *or* objective interest in the event, where an objective interest "[depends] on particular natural and biological facts, which concern health or goal-directed activity" (Ballantyne 2012: 322–323). For weak objectivists, the question of whether winning the lottery is significant for Shakespeare is settled by

161

Table 14.1 Specifications of significance condition

	Subjectivism	Objectivism
Constructivist	E is lucky for S only if (CON) S actually or counterfactually ascribes significance to E and (SUBJ) E satisfies or frustrates a subjective interest of S. Pritchard (2005), Borges (2016), possibly Riggs (2007)	E is lucky for S only if (CON) S actually or counterfactually ascribes significance to E and (STRONG-OBJ) E satisfies or frustrates an objective interest of S. No known proponents
Realist	E is lucky for S only if (REAL) E is in fact significant for S, independently of whether S actually or counterfactually ascribes significance to E, and (SUBJ) E satisfies or frustrates a subjective interest of S. Coffman (2007), possibly Rescher (1995)	E is lucky for S only if (REAL) E is in fact significant for S, independently of whether S actually or counterfactually ascribes significance to E, and (OBJ) E satisfies or frustrates an interest of S. Ballantyne (2012), possibly Blancha (2015) and Whittington (2016)
Eliminativism	Whether E is lucky does not depend on whether E is significant for any agent S. Pritchard (2014), Milburn (2014)	

facts about his subjective interests (his preference for wealth and comfort) or his objective interests (his biological needs, his well-being) or both. Strong objectivism, on the other hand, says that an event is significant for someone *only if* she has an objective interest in the event. For strong objectivists, winning the lottery is significant for Shakespeare only if the event in some way satisfies his objective interests.[1] The authors of this chapter are of different minds about the best way to understand objectivism. For our purposes, we will use weak objectivism as the default view, with one exception. (See below for further discussion of strong objectivism, and see note 1.)

To recapitulate, debates over how best to specify Significance-generic turn on two ancillary debates. One concerns whether significance depends on ascriptions of significance; this is the debate between constructivists and realists. The other concerns which sorts of interests determine significance; this debate is between subjectivists and objectivists. Note that while constructivism is incompatible with realism and subjectivism is incompatible with objectivism, these views can be held in any other combination. Thus, one can be a constructivist subjectivist, a constructivist objectivist, a realist subjectivist, or a realist objectivist. In the literature on significance, three of the four combinations enjoy support (see Table 14.1). Though we do not know of any defenses of constructivist objectivism, we consider what might motivate someone to defend it. In the following sections, we critically examine each view.

Constructivist Subjectivism

In his initial account of luck, Duncan Pritchard (2005) identified two necessary conditions for an event's being lucky for someone: a modal condition and a significance condition. On the modal condition, an event is lucky only if it does not occur "in a wide class of the nearest possible worlds where the relevant initial conditions for that event are the same as the actual world" (2005: 128). Pritchard notes that for an event to be lucky, it is insufficient that the modal condition is satisfied. A chance landslide that affects no one might fail to occur in a wide class of nearby possible worlds, but it does not thereby count as lucky. An additional condition is needed: namely, a significance condition.

Pritchard proposes one such condition: "If an event is lucky, then it is an event that is significant to the agent concerned (or would be significant, were the agent to be availed of the relevant facts)" (2005: 132). Furthermore, Pritchard suggests that an event's being significant for someone depends not only on whether it frustrates or satisfies her subjective interests but also on "the significance that the agent *attaches* to the event in question" (2005: 133; emphasis added). Drawing these points together, Pritchard advocates the following thesis:

> *Constructivist subjectivism:* event E is lucky for subject S only if the following conditions hold: (CON) S actually or counterfactually ascribes significance to E and (SUBJ) E satisfies or frustrates a subjective interest of S.

Constructivist subjectivism reaches the correct verdict about the landslide case. Since a chance landslide that affects no one can have no impact on anyone's subjective interests, and since no one would ascribe significance to a landslide that affects no one, the landslide satisfies neither (CON) nor (SUBJ). Constructivist subjectivism also reaches the correct verdict in cases where someone fails to ascribe significance to an event simply out of ignorance. For example, if someone narrowly sidesteps a thunderbolt without noticing, she is clearly lucky to have escaped unscathed even if she did not in fact ascribe significance to the event (Pritchard 2005: 133). Indeed, (CON) is satisfied so long as the agent ascribes significance to the event in nearby possible worlds where she knows the event occurred. And, plausibly, this is true: had she known that she sidestepped the thunderbolt, she would have ascribed significance to the event. Finally, constructivist subjectivism reflects the received wisdom that, in general, people ascribe significance (or would ascribe significance) to events that are genuinely lucky.

Nonetheless, constructivist subjectivism has difficulty accommodating at least two types of cases. The first challenges (CON) while the second challenges (SUBJ):

> WOLF GIRL: A pack of wolves comes upon an abandoned one-year-old girl and take her into their care. One day, the child crawls from the wolves' den and accidentally crosses the path of a stampeding herd of bison. Just before the bison trample the child, a lone wolf who happens to be hunting in the area appears on the scene, redirecting the stampeding bison.[2]

> REX: Rex suffers from anorexia nervosa. He doesn't want to gain weight and so desires to forgo eating. By an unlikely accident, Rex's water faucet is connected to a tank filled with nutritional supplement. Rex drinks the water-like supplement and so maintains a healthy body weight, despite concerted efforts otherwise.
>
> *Ballantyne 2012: 322*

Plausibly, the baby girl and anorexic man are beneficiaries of good luck. But if constructivist subjectivism is true, neither WOLF GIRL nor REX is a case of good luck. Owing to her limited cognitive abilities, wolf girl is unable to ascribe significance to the bison incident in the actual world and in nearby possible worlds. WOLF GIRL thus fails to satisfy (CON). Rex is subjectively interested in losing weight, and so the accident that allows him to maintain a healthy body weight is *bad luck* on constructivist subjectivism. But plausibly, Rex enjoys good luck, not bad luck. So if REX satisfies (SUBJ), it is for the wrong reasons.

There are other cases that suggest constructivist subjectivism is false (see Ballantyne 2012 for discussion). Suffice it to say that cases such as WOLF GIRL and REX present a significant prima facie challenge to the view.

Constructivist Objectivism

To our knowledge, no philosopher has defended constructivist objectivism.[3] It is nonetheless a conceivable (and perhaps viable) view:

> *Constructivist objectivism:* event E is lucky for subject S only if (CON) S actually or counterfactually ascribes significance to E and (STRONG-OBJ) E satisfies or frustrates an objective interest of S.[4]

Someone who subscribes to the view will think that whether an event is lucky depends on whether the subject ascribes significance to it and whether it satisfies or frustrates an objective interest of hers. At first, this might seem curious. When a subject ascribes significance to an event, this presupposes that the event has some effect on her subjective interests. For if the event had no bearing on her subjective interests, why would she ascribe significance to it? Thus, it appears there is some tension between (CON) and (OBJ): if we affirm that luck requires ascribing significance to an event and that ascriptions of significance turn on subjective interests, we seemingly lack space for objective interests in our account.

It is, however, possible to motivate constructivist objectivism by collapsing the distinction between subjective and objective interests:

> *Interest Linkage:* if event E is objectively significant for subject S, then in the nearest possible worlds where S knows all the relevant facts about E, E satisfies or frustrates a subjective interest of S.

Interest Linkage might appeal to those who think akrasia is impossible. Suppose we think it is impossible for someone to simultaneously (i) know all of the relevant normative and non-normative facts about an event E, (ii) know that E is objectively more desirable for her than any other event, and yet (iii) not want E to occur (see Stroud 2014; cf. Milburn 2014: 582–583). We then have reason to accept Interest Linkage. For if (i) through (iii) are in fact incompatible, someone is objectively interested in E just in case she *would be* subjectively interested in E were she to know all the relevant facts about E. In other words, objectively interesting events are subjectively interesting under conditions of full transparency.

One worry about constructive objectivism begins with the observation that if an event is in a subject's objective interest, that is *independent* of the subject's standpoint. But since the effects of the event on the subject are an objective matter, it is not obvious what the subject's actual or counterfactual ascription of significance would add in addition to the event's objective effects on the subject. There is a kind of redundancy here. Suppose we assume that the event has some objective effect on a subject. If we also assume that the subject actually or counterfactually ascribes significance to the event, we should wonder what the subject's ascription adds to the event's significance that the event's objective effects did not already accomplish (see Ballantyne 2012: 330–331).

We will leave aside further discussion of constructive objectivism. For now, suffice it to say that a constructivist who denies the possibility of akrasia might have reason to accept constructivist objectivism. But such a constructivist should also explain what the subject's ascription of significance really adds to an event's significance over and above the event's objective effects.

Realist Subjectivism

Nicholas Rescher (1995) and E.J. Coffman (2007) defend realist subjectivism. Both concur with Pritchard that *subjective* interests are what count in determining significance. But unlike Pritchard, Rescher and Coffman deny that an event's significance for someone ultimately depends on whether she ascribes significance to it. We can state their view as follows:

> *Realist subjectivism:* event E is lucky for subject S only if (REAL) E is in fact significant for S, independently of whether S actually or counterfactually ascribes significance to E, and (SUBJ) E satisfies or frustrates a subjective interest of S.

Coffman's argument for (REAL) and against (CON) features cases where subjects are unable to ascribe significance to an event but nonetheless seem to experience good or bad luck:

> A toddler who crawls safely across several lanes of freeway traffic during rush hour without being noticed is lucky to have made it through the traffic uninjured. The LaGrange County (Indiana) horse that was fatally struck by lightning on May 11, 2004, suffered bad luck on the indicated occasion.
>
> *2007: 387*

This toddler is a beneficiary of good luck even though she is unable to ascribe significance to her perilous journey. The horse is a victim of bad luck even though he is unable to ascribe significance to the lightning strike. Constructivism conflicts with these apparent facts, for it says that an event is significant for someone only if she actually or counterfactually ascribes significance to it. But neither the toddler nor the horse actually or counterfactually ascribes significance to the respective incident. Coffman's cases thus put pressure on constructivism.

Although Rescher and Coffman deny (CON), they are not thereby committed to denying (SUBJ). That is because whether an individual has subjective interests does not depend on whether she is able to ascribe significance. It is commonplace to treat young children and animals as having subjective interests. A toddler wants to be safe even if she is unable to ascribe significance to fortunate events. A horse wants to live and continue consuming oats even if he is unable to ascribe significance to unfortunate events. This is just to say that subjective interests and ascriptions of significance can come apart.

While it is natural to think subjective interests can help to underwrite significance, realist subjectivism is not without challenges. Sometimes subjects appear to be lucky even though their subjective interests are not impacted:

> WILSON'S BRAIN: A group of rogue neuroscientists have Wilson's name and address, among thousands of others, in their database of "involuntary research subjects". For tonight's operation, they've randomly picked Wilson. The group kidnaps Wilson while he is sleeping at home and transports him unawares to their laboratory. Once in their care, the scientists extract Wilson's brain, plop it in a vat of nutrients, and use a computer to present him with experiences in concord with his earlier life. Poor Wilson can't discern any difference between his pre-surgery experiences and those stimulated in the laboratory. He doesn't suspect that his present experiences are unconnected with the real world.
>
> *Ballantyne 2012: 321; cf. Nozick 1974: 42–45*

We judge that Wilson suffers bad luck on account of the negative effects of the event. For one, his relationships and plans in the real world come to an end. For another, he loses his body. Notice how WILSON'S BRAIN challenges realist subjectivism in two ways. First, realist subjectivism presumes that the good or bad effects that make an event lucky must have some effect on a subject's interior, experienced life. But WILSON'S BRAIN shows this is false: the envatment event is unlucky for Wilson even though it "leaves no trace" on his interior life. Second, since Wilson's experiences in the laboratory are indistinguishable from his real-world experiences, WILSON'S BRAIN shows that unlucky events need not bring about pain and lucky events need not bring about pleasure (see Ballantyne 2012: 322).

Realist Objectivism

We have rehearsed some challenges for constructivism and subjectivism. These challenges help motivate an account of significance advanced by Ballantyne (2012) and perhaps David Blancha (2015: 88–115) and Lee John Whittington (2016):

Realist objectivism: event E is lucky for subject S only if (REAL) E is in fact significant for S, independently of whether S actually or counterfactually ascribes significance to E, and (OBJ) E satisfies or frustrates an interest of S.

(REAL) avoids the difficulties that WOLF GIRL and Coffman's cases pose for constructivism (see above). And (OBJ) avoids the trouble that WILSON'S BRAIN presents for subjectivism (see the previous section). Plausibly, Wilson is objectively interested in not being a brain in a vat, even if his envatment has no impact on his subjective interests. So (OBJ) but not (SUBJ) arrives at the correct verdict in WILSON'S BRAIN: namely, that Wilson is a victim of bad luck.

What allows (OBJ) to deliver the intuitively correct verdict is its appeal to natural and biological facts concerning health or goal-directed activity (Ballantyne 2012: 322–323), which Ballantyne identifies with objective interests. Becoming a brain in a vat is a stroke of bad luck for Wilson not because it affects his subjective interests but because it interferes with his proper biological functioning and frustrates his goal-directed activity. Objective interests are not a matter of subjective desires and preferences but of well-being and proper functioning.

According to (OBJ), anything that has interests can be lucky. Luck is not just for sentient beings, for every living thing engages in activities and processes that can be described teleologically, and any living thing that can be described teleologically has objective interests. Thus, a worker ant can be described as fulfilling her proper biological function if she successfully forages, defends her colony from rival critters, and so on. Moreover, we can think of success in foraging, defending one's colony, and so forth, as objective interests of the ant. The ant *has* these interests even if she cannot *take them on* as interests.

We suspect that not everyone will be on board with (OBJ). Here are a couple of cases that might spell trouble for the account:

SPACEWORMS: The space shuttle *Columbia* tragically burned up on reentry on 1 February 2003, strewing debris from east Texas to Louisiana and into southwestern Arkansas. Months later, five canisters containing hundreds of living *C. elegans* worms, which had been part of an experiment onboard the shuttle, were recovered from crash sites in Texas. The canisters housing the creatures exited the shuttle at a height of more than 30 km above the Earth, at velocities of 660–1,050 km/h. (A sixth canister was never recovered.) These tiny, pinhead-sized worms survived the extreme heat and velocity of reentry and the subsequent crash.[5]

LUNA THE REDWOOD: In the late 1990s, when an old-growth forest in northern California was threatened by logging, a young woman named Julia Butterfly Hill set out to protest. Ms. Hill conducted a "sit in": for 738 consecutive days, she lived on a small platform fastened to a giant redwood that she named Luna. The logging interests eventually backed down and Luna, along with a small area of nearby forest, was spared from the chainsaws. If Ms. Hill had chosen to dwell elsewhere in the forest (or had failed in her protest), it is unlikely that Luna or the adjacent trees would have been left standing.

If (OBJ) is correct, Luna and the space worms are lucky. In conversation, we have found that some philosophers resist the notion that trees and worms can be lucky. In our small, unscientific sampling of non-philosophers' opinions, we observed mixed verdicts on the question of whether worms and trees can be lucky.[6] While this is hardly a resounding "yes" in support of our view, mixed intuitions do not a refutation make.

In the end, we suspect that at least some disagreements about significance will bottom out in rather general questions concerning value and well-being. Since there are long-standing disputes about the nature of value as well as controversies concerning whether organisms such as worms and trees can have interests, we anticipate disputes over significance will continue.

We have, up to this point, explored four ways to specify Significance-generic. Each of these accounts faces challenges. But Pritchard insists that any account of significance is bound to fail. He thus rejects Significance-generic and with it the search for a significance condition. Let us now turn to Pritchard's provocative proposal.

Eliminating Significance

Recall Pritchard's suggestion that "the very idea of adding a significance condition to the modal account of luck is wrongheaded" (2014: 604; see Duncan Pritchard's chapter in this volume for more on the modal account). In earlier work, Pritchard defended constructivist subjectivism, according to which an event is lucky for someone only if she (actually or counterfactually) ascribes significance to the event and only if the event satisfies or frustrates a subjective interest of hers. In response to objections (see the second section of this chapter and Pritchard 2014: 603–606, especially note 20), Pritchard abandoned constructivist subjectivism. But instead of endorsing a rival account of significance, Pritchard rejected Significance-generic altogether. Pritchard now embraces what we will call *eliminativism* about significance conditions for luck. (Milburn 2014: 579–586 also defends eliminativism, but we focus on Pritchard's argument in what follows.)

How does Pritchard motivate eliminativism? First, he notes one positive upshot of eliminativism: luck theorists no longer need to address "various challenges" regarding specifications of Significance-generic. Writes Pritchard:

> Does it suffice to meet the significance condition that a subject (*any* subject?) merely regards the target event as significant (whether rightly or wrongly), or should we opt for a more objective treatment of significance whereby we focus on those events that the subject ought to find significant? Do we allow for subject-relative luck, such that an event can be lucky for subject A and yet not for subject B? Do we allow purely pragmatic factors—such as what kinds of things are being discussed in a given conversational context—to determine whether an event is significant? And so on.
>
> *2014: 603–604*

Pritchard seems to be developing the following idea. Theorists who try to specify Significance-generic have to answer difficult questions about the nature of significance and the extent to which facts about significance determine facts about luck. (Some of these questions have been explored in some detail in Ballantyne (2011, 2012, 2014) and Whittington (2015: ch. 4, 2016).) But by rejecting Significance-generic altogether, eliminativists short-circuit all of these prima facie problems. In other words, eliminativists have an easier path to success than non-eliminativists do. If luck theorists can be eliminativists without making undue sacrifices, they should accept the view. All things being equal, you are better off endorsing eliminativism than hitching your wagon to any particular significance condition for luck.

What else can be said in favor of eliminativism? Pritchard appears to think that significance conditions for luck lead to problematic consequences because they prevent theorists from understanding luck "as an objective phenomenon" (2014: 605). He considers a familiar example—that of a small avalanche on the South Pole. Pritchard observes that "no one will regard [the avalanche] as lucky since no one cares about it, and it makes no difference to anyone" (2014: 604). But Pritchard no longer sees why this fact precludes the avalanche from being a genuinely lucky event. He writes:

> We shouldn't expect an account of the metaphysics of lucky events to be responsive to such subjective factors as whether an event is the kind of thing that people care about enough to regard as lucky. That's just not part of the load that a metaphysical account of luck should be expected to carry.
>
> *ibid.*

The thrust of Pritchard's suggestion here might just be that there are lucky events, such as that small avalanche, to which no one (actually or counterfactually) ascribes significance. But if there are such lucky events—as defenders of realist subjectivism and realist objectivism will allow—then all constructivist accounts of significance are false. So one might think Pritchard is simply disputing constructivism. For a couple reasons, however, we doubt this is the best interpretation of his thinking. First, there are other viable accounts of significance left on the table, so this line of argument does not by itself vindicate eliminativism. Second, we doubt that many people will have a strong intuition that the small avalanche on the South Pole *is* lucky.

We think a more plausible reading of Pritchard's argument will acknowledge a more fundamental shift in Pritchard's thinking about luck. Pritchard now insists that the subject matter of a theory of luck is strictly "metaphysical." In theorizing about luck, he says, "our interest ought to be in luck as an objective feature of events" (2014: 604) and "our interest is ultimately … in luck as an objective phenomenon" (2014: 605). The upshot of such observations is that facts about our "subjective" judgments or feelings concerning luck are not the proper data for theories of luck.

Let us call *Pritchard's Truism* the claim that the fundamental facts about luck are "metaphysical" facts that do not depend on what subjects judge or feel. Add to Pritchard's Truism the further claim that on any viable significance condition, whether an event is lucky depends on what a subject judges or feels. It follows that Pritchard's Truism conflicts with significance conditions. We believe that argument plausibly captures Pritchard's reasoning.

But is Pritchard's Truism even true? For starters, it is not obvious to us (i) in what sense a robustly "metaphysical" account of luck rules out partial determination of luck facts by subjects' judgments or feelings, or (ii) what it means to say that luck is an "objective feature of events," or (iii) why we "ought" to be interested in luck as an objective feature of events. Moreover, it seems to us that philosophical interest in luck arises not from theoretical insight into the nature of risk or modal reality, but rather from everyday discourse about luck—that is to say, from our *folk conception* of luck. And here is a recurring theme in our pre-theoretical luck talk: we tend to ascribe luck only to significant events. So our folk conceptions of luck, far from being mere psycho-social phenomena, should guide theorizing about luck. Any attempt to intuit the nature of luck independently of our folk understanding simply grasps at air.

Let us leave this complaint aside and turn to Pritchard's minor premise: that significance is simply a matter of what subjects think or feel. Perhaps some accounts of significance satisfy Pritchard's minor premise; at any rate, constructivist subjectivism looks to be the main target. But realist objectivism clearly does not satisfy it. After all, according to realist objectivism, whether an event is significant need not depend on subjects ascribing significance to it or having a subjective interest in it. For realist objectivists, facts about significance can turn on mind-independent facts about what constitutes proper biological functioning for a subject, what contributes to a subject's well-being, what it means for a subject to be healthy, and so on. Realist objectivists can thus accommodate Pritchard's demand for an "objective" metaphysical account of luck that does not wholly depend on mere "subjective factors." At least one specification of Significance-generic—realist objectivism—is immune to Pritchard's criticism.[7]

Because Pritchard fails to show that all specifications of Significance-generic are implausible, his direct argument against Significance-generic is inadequate. Even so, Pritchard still might be right to suggest that the litany of prima facie difficulties for accounts of significance favor eliminativism. We agree with Pritchard that these difficulties require philosophical effort to overcome and that eliminativism neatly sidesteps them. The path of least resistance, eliminativism, wins out, all else being equal.

But are all things equal? We doubt it. Consider eliminativism's implications. If eliminativism is true, every chance event is a lucky event (given certain plausible assumptions about the nature of luck). An unlikely avalanche that affects no one is lucky. An unlikely quantum event that impacts no one's interests is lucky. Surely this strains credulity (cf. Borges 2016: 467). If eliminativism indeed suggests that chance events and lucky events are one and the same, eliminativism does not simply regiment or refine our conception of luck. It obliterates it.

Pritchard might be untroubled by this. He insists, after all, that "we are interested in our subjective judgements about luck only because of what they reveal about our folk concept of luck" and that our subjective judgments should be "evaluated relative to an objective standard for lucky events" (2014: 605). He appears willing to dispense with how we ordinarily think about luck. It is a bold move that raises important questions about the very enterprise of theorizing about luck. What should constrain our theories of luck? What do we have left to guide theorizing if we bracket out our folk conception of luck? Is the quest for an "objective standard," untainted by folk wisdom, simply quixotic?

Speaking for ourselves, we expect theorizing about luck to begin with our folk conception of it. It appears to be our primary source of insights or "data." What else could be our starting point? If we dispense with this data at the outset, we risk losing the motivations that spurred theorizing about luck in the first place. Eliminativism might reduce the philosophical burden, but the cost is intolerably high.

In sum, we do not think Pritchard provides sufficient reason to accept eliminativism. While each of the significance conditions currently on offer is controversial, we deny that the search for a plausible significance condition is misguided. In theorizing about luck, as in life in general, we are at our best not when we avoid pressing problems but when we meet them head-on.[8]

Notes

1 NB weakly favors weak objectivism; SK strongly favors strong objectivism. According to weak objectivism, an event is significant for someone just in case it satisfies or frustrates an objective *or* subjective interest of hers (Ballantyne 2012: 322–324; cf. Blancha 2005: 96–115). According to strong objectivism, an event is significant for someone just in case it satisfies or frustrates an objective interest of hers, full stop.

Here is why one might doubt strong objectivism. Say that I (SK) am playing video games instead of doing what I ought: grading my students' papers. Suddenly, my game console suffers an unlikely mechanical failure, forcing me to stop procrastinating and start grading. It might seem that weak objectivism neatly describes the situation. Weak objectivism implies that the mechanical failure is bad luck in one respect and good luck in another. It is bad luck insofar as I am subjectively interested in playing video games and good luck insofar as I am objectively interested in grading students' papers. And it is ultima facie good luck insofar as my objective interest outweighs my subjective interest. Weak subjectivism thus provides a tidy way to analyze cases of so-called mixed luck (cf. Ballantyne 2012: 331). Strong objectivism, on the other hand, seemingly cannot make sense of this phenomenon, since it says that what determines facts about significance are objective interests alone. Gaming neither conduces to health nor fulfills biological needs nor garners my partner's approval, so I appear to lack any objective interest in gaming. Strong objectivism thus has an implausible implication: the mechanical failure is in no way bad luck for me.

But strong objectivists have a line of defense. They can retort that I have an indirect objective interest in playing video games. If playing video games has any redeeming quality (a big "if," one might think), it is that it conduces to well-being in some way—by producing pleasure, reducing stress, and so on. Clearly, personal well-being is something I am objectively interested in. So given some plausible background assumptions, I have an indirect objective interest in playing video games. Of course, I also have an objective interest in grading students' papers, and this interest conflicts with my interest in gaming. But that is no problem. Interests can conflict. According to strong objectivism, the mechanical failure is bad luck insofar as it frustrates one objective interest but good luck insofar as it satisfies another. And the event is ultima facie good luck insofar as grading students' papers conduces to well-being better than playing video games. For the strong objectivist, this is a perfectly natural way to treat episodes of good luck. Moreover, it avoids comparing apples to oranges (i.e., subjective to objective interests) in determining facts about ultima facie luck, and it accommodates the plausible view that we are always objectively interested to some extent in satisfying our subjective interests.

2 Compare WOLF GIRL with NEWBORN in Ballantyne (2012: 324). A key difference between these cases is that in NEWBORN, but not in WOLF GIRL, there is an observer who can ascribe significance to the event.

3 But Ballantyne (2012: 330–331) and Milburn (2014: 582–583) discuss this sort of position.

4 The only interesting version of constructivist objectivism entails strong objectivism (STRONG-OBJ). We discuss strong objectivism in note 1.
5 For more on the story of the extraordinary worms, see Conley et al. (2005).
6 Empirical work on folk ascriptions of luck has not, to our knowledge, measured intuitions about the possibility of lucky non-sentient beings such as trees (though such a study is ripe for the picking). See Pritchard and Smith (2004: 6–15) for a survey of extant psychological work on luck ascriptions.
7 Does strong objectivism satisfy Pritchard's demand for an "objective" account of luck better than weak objectivism? Possibly, given that strong objectivism says that facts about significance *always* depend on mind-independent facts about well-being. For now, we leave the matter aside.
8 We are grateful to Ian Church and Joseph Vukov for helpful comments on an earlier version of this chapter.

References

Ballantyne, N. (2011) "Anti-Luck Epistemology, Pragmatic Encroachment, and True Belief," *Canadian Journal of Philosophy* 41(4), 485–503.
——. (2012) "Luck and Interests," *Synthese* 185, 319–334.
——. (2014) "Does Luck Have a Place in Epistemology?" *Synthese* 191(7), 1391–1407.
Blancha, D. (2015) *The Moral of Luck*, Ph.D. Dissertation, Columbia University, doi: 10.7916/D818360Q.
Borges, R. (2016) "Bad Luck for the Anti-luck Epistemologist," *Southern Journal of Philosophy* 54, 463–479.
Coffman, E.J. (2007) "Thinking about Luck," *Synthese* 158(3), 385–398.
Conley, C., et al. (2005) "*Caenorhabditis elegans* Survives Atmospheric Breakup of STS-107, Space Shuttle Columbia," *Astrobiology* 5, 690–705.
Milburn, J. (2014) "Subject-Involving Luck," *Metaphilosophy* 45, 578–593.
Nozick, R. (1974) *Anarchy, State, and Utopia*, New York: Basic Books.
Pritchard, D. (2005) *Epistemic Luck*, Oxford: Oxford University Press.
——. (2014) "The Modal Account of Luck," *Metaphilosophy* 45, 594–619.
——, & Smith, M. (2004) "The Psychology and Philosophy of Luck," *New Ideas in Psychology* 22, 1–28.
Rescher, N. (1995) *Luck: The Brilliant Randomness of Everyday Life*, New York: Farrar, Straus, and Giroux.
Riggs, W. (2007) "Why Epistemologists Are So Down on Their Luck," *Synthese* 158, 277–97.
Stroud, S. (2014) "Weakness of Will," *Stanford Encyclopedia of Philosophy*, <https://plato.stanford.edu/entries/weakness-will/>.
Whittington, L.J. (2015) *Metaphysics of Luck*, Ph.D. Dissertation, University of Edinburgh, <http://hdl.handle.net/1842/20409>.
——. (2016) "Luck, Knowledge and Value," *Synthese* 193, 1615–1633.

15

LUCK AS RISK

Fernando Broncano-Berrocal

July 4, 1943, 11:07 p.m. A Consolidated B-24 Liberator takes off from Gibraltar Airport. It carries Władysław Sikorski, the commander-in-chief of the Polish Army and the Prime Minister of the Polish government-in-exile. Sixteen seconds after takeoff the aircraft crashes into the sea. Sikorski dies along with ten other people. The pilot, Flight Lieutenant Eduard Prchal, survives.

Later investigations of this World War II event failed to pin down the specific cause of the accident, but it is believed that the elevator system of the aircraft was jammed. Prchal's efforts to move the stick of the steering mechanism were all in vain. He could not pull up and the plane lost height quickly. Inevitably, it ended in the waters of the Strait of Gibraltar.

Prchal's lucky survival and events alike suggest that there is a close connection between luck and risk. For a lot of risk is involved in taking off in an aircraft whose elevator system is jammed, and a lot of luck is involved if that risk is materialized, the aircraft crashes and yet one survives against all odds. Indeed, cases of this sort give prima facie reason to think that luck is a risk-involving phenomenon. In this chapter, I aim to explore this hypothesis.

Here is the plan. First, I will take a closer look at the luck-as-risk hypothesis in the light of the parallelisms between both phenomena and introduce three ways to spell it out: in probabilistic terms, in modal terms, and in terms of lack of control. In the next section, I will explain how luck can be naturally understood as a risk-involving phenomenon even if luck and risk are different—especially in view of the fact that risk concerns unwanted events, whereas luck can concern both wanted and unwanted events. Then, I will criticize the modal and the probabilistic models of the luck-as-risk hypothesis. I will argue, first, that they fail to account for the connection between risk and bad luck; second, that they also fail to account for the connection between risk and good luck. Finally, I will defend the lack of control view. In particular, I will argue that it can handle the objections to the probabilistic and modal views and that it can explain how degrees of luck and risk covary.

The Luck-as-Risk Hypothesis

Luck is a phenomenon that is attributed post hoc, i.e., to events that have occurred. Risk, by contrast, is attributed a priori (i.e., before the fact) and thus applies to potential events. In view of this, the luck-as-risk hypothesis cannot be simply that luck and risk are the same phenomenon, but that luck is risk-involving, in the sense that some kind of risk always precedes luck.

That there is some interesting connection between luck and risk is evident if we consider cases like Prchal's survival. But there are at least two further theoretical considerations that also lend support to this connection. The first is a distinction that applies to both luck and risk, which is often overlooked in ordinary parlance. The second is the fact that degrees of luck and risk covary. Let us start with the first.

Luck and risk come in two guises. Most of the time, we talk of luck as if it established a relationship between an agent and an event. For example, we say things such as "Prchal was lucky to survive the accident," "Sophie was lucky to hit the mark," or "James was lucky to guess the answer." In these cases, it is an agent who instantiates the relational property of being lucky with respect to the occurrence of an event. This is what we might call the *relational sense of luck*.[1] Sometimes, however, some luck attributions do not denote any relationship between an agent and an event: luck in those cases is predicated as a non-relational property of events. By way of illustration, we say things such as "That shot was by luck" or "It was a matter of luck that the wind suddenly rose and made the arrow hit the target." This is the *non-relational sense of luck*. Note that although the latter locutions can be (and are often) interpreted relationally (i.e., as implicitly being attributed to subjects), the distinction between the relational and non-relational senses of luck holds as long as the following does not necessarily hold: (1) an event E is a matter of luck if and only if (2) E is lucky for an agent S. Consider the following expression: "It is a matter of luck that the ball stays on the tip of the cone." We can plausibly imagine contexts in which this sentence is uttered as an instance of (1) but not of (2), i.e., contexts in which it is not implicitly attributed to an agent.

Exactly the same distinction applies to risk. An event may be risky in the sense that it is at risk of occurring. Let us call this the *non-relational sense of risk*—strictly speaking, it is the possible occurrence of an event that instantiates the property of being at risk of being materialized. But we also talk of risk as establishing a relationship between an agent and an event. For example, we say things such as "Jane is crazy to play Russian roulette, she is at serious risk of death" or "Max has left the king unprotected, he risks losing the chess game." Here the agents in question instantiate the relational property of being at risk with respect to the possible occurrence of an event (e.g., dying, losing). This is the *relational sense of risk*.[2]

The second parallelism between luck and risk is that *degrees of luck and risk covary*. Consider non-relational luck and risk. Playing Russian roulette with a six-shot revolver loaded with five bullets is riskier than playing with the same revolver but loaded with one bullet. In addition, surviving the former game is, unsurprisingly, luckier than surviving the latter. This lends support to the following thesis:

> *Non-Relational Risk–Luck Gradability Correspondence*: The more risk there is that an event E will occur, the luckier it is that E does not occur.[3]

Consider the previous example: the more risk there is that a Russian roulette player will die, the luckier it is that she survives.

The same point about gradability applies to relational luck and risk. A Russian roulette player pulling the trigger of a six-shot revolver that is loaded with five bullets is at more risk of dying than a player who shoots the same revolver with only one bullet in the chamber. Correspondingly, the former player is luckier than the latter if both survive. Again, this makes the following connecting thesis plausible:

> *Relational Risk–Luck Gradability Correspondence*: The more at risk an agent S is with respect to the possible occurrence of an event E, the luckier S is that E does not occur.

These two parallelisms (the relational/non-relational distinction and the gradability correspondence) suggest that luck relates to risk in an interesting way. However, this is not sufficient to secure the plausibility of the luck-as-risk hypothesis. What would really render the idea that luck is a risk-involving phenomenon plausible would be the fact that the same sort of conditions featured by accounts of luck can be also intuitively replicated as conditions on risk. If this were the case, we would have enough motivation to deem the luck-as-risk hypothesis something more than a mere working hypothesis. But before entering into details, two caveats are in order.

First, my focus will be on relational luck only. The reason is not just simplicity, but also the fact that the relational sense of luck is the most common one in ordinary parlance, i.e., more often we attribute luck to agents in connection to events (or to events in connection with agents) than to (the occurrence of) events simpliciter. Correspondingly, I will only focus on relational risk.

Second, the project of this chapter is to distinguish plausible ways to spell out the luck-as-risk hypothesis. I am not interested in judging whether the different available views on luck and risk that will serve to model luck as a risk-involving phenomenon are individually correct *qua* accounts of luck or risk.[4] In other words, I will be only concerned with investigating to which extent it is plausible to claim that, for a given condition (or set of conditions) C on luck, a significant event E is lucky for an agent S if and only if an analogous condition (or set of conditions) for risk C⋆ also holds for E and S. The methodological approach will be the following: the resulting luck-as-risk views will be deemed plausible if the relevant conditions they feature on luck (C) and risk (C⋆) go hand-in-hand, i.e., if there is no case in which C holds, but C⋆ does not, or the other way around—later, we will see that two prima facie plausible views actually fall prey to this sort of counterexample. Without further ado, let us start with the first way to model luck as a risk-involving phenomenon.

A natural way to understand the nature of luck is *in probabilistic terms*. Suppose that you win a lottery with long odds. Given the odds, the fact that you have won was very improbable. This suggests that a significant event is lucky for an agent if and only if it was improbable.[5] There are, of course, several ways to cash out this view depending on how the notion of probability is interpreted and on how many further constraints one includes in it. For example, the relevant probability of occurrence might be interpreted objectively, as a subjective expectation (a credence), might be conditionalized on one's evidence, on one's knowledge, on whether or not one is in a position to know that the event in question will occur, and so on. All these are valid ways to understand the nature of luck in probabilistic terms.[6]

The interesting point, however, is that the nature of risk can be also plausibly understood probabilistically. Suppose that you participate in a lottery in which you will die unless your ticket is the winner. There is a high risk of death and one explanation of this is that dying is very probable given the odds. So, in general, a plausible view of risk is that a significant event is risky for an agent if and only if its occurrence is probable.[7]

This automatically connects (probabilistically construed) luck with (probabilistically construed) risk. It seems that if an agent S is lucky that an event E occurs (e.g., surviving) it is because not-E (e.g., not surviving, i.e., dying) was risky for S in the first place, and this means that E was very likely. So luck would be risk-involving in precisely this sense. By way of illustration, imagine that you survive the aforementioned deadly lottery because your ticket is the winner. The reason why you are lucky to survive is that there was high probability (i.e., a high risk) that you would die. We can label this view *luck as probabilistic risk* or L-R$_{Prob}$ for short.

A quite popular alternative to the probabilistic model is to understand luck *in modal terms*. The idea is that a significant event is lucky for an agent if and only if the event is such that it effectively occurs but could easily have failed to occur. In possible worlds talk, this view can be formulated as follows: E is lucky for S if and only if E occurs in the actual world, and in most nearby possible worlds in which the initial conditions for E are the same as in the actual world, E does not occur. Consider a fair lottery. In most nearby possible worlds participants lose. That is why winners are lucky.[8]

Risk can be naturally explained in the same terms. Consider the deadly lottery again. Participants are at a serious risk of death. In modal terms, this can be put as follows: they risk dying because in most possible worlds where they hold a lottery ticket (i.e., in very similar circumstances to the actual ones) they would die.[9]

173

Once luck and risk are understood in modal terms, the two notions seem to go hand-in-hand. As in the case of L-R$_{Prob}$, the idea is to explain the fact that an agent S is lucky that a significant event E occurs (e.g., surviving) in terms of not-E (e.g., dying) being at risk for S before E's occurrence. In modal terms this would translate as the simple idea that S is lucky that E because E would fail to occur in most nearby possible worlds. Let us call this view *luck as modal risk* or L-R$_{Mod}$ for short.

The final intuitive way to understand luck is *in terms of lack of control*. Consider Prchal's lucky survival. A key factor is that he lacked control over the aircraft. In particular, what was beyond his control is the fact that he would survive the takeoff. In normal conditions where pilots can handle the steering mechanism of their aircrafts, surviving a takeoff is something they have control over and, moreover, something that it is not a matter of luck for them. This lends support to the following view: a significant event E is lucky for an agent S if and only if S lacks control over E (alternatively, just in case E is beyond S's control). There are, of course, several ways to interpret the relevant notion of control.[10] But it suffices for present purposes to understand it pre-theoretically (I will elaborate on the notion of control below).

The interesting point is that lack of control is also a plausible way to account for risk. Before crashing, Prchal was at a high risk of death. This is plausibly explained by the fact that he lacked control over the steering mechanism, because the elevation system of the aircraft was jammed. Generalizing, the view would be that a significant event E is risky for an agent S if and only if S lacks control over E (alternatively, just in case E is beyond S's control).

Once again we have a match between the notions of luck and risk. The hypothesis is that events are lucky for agents because they are preceded by risk. In terms of lack of control, this can be formulated as follows: a significant event E is lucky for an agent S insofar as E is beyond S's control. Let us call this the *luck as uncontrolled risk* view or L-R$_{Con}$ for short.

The fact that three intuitive ways to understand the nature of luck can be replicated without loss of plausibility as intuitive ways to understand risk and, moreover, the fact that the three *main* accounts of luck in the literature can be easily coupled with plausible corresponding accounts of risk, suggests that the luck-as-risk hypothesis is not a mere working hypothesis, but a very plausible way to think of luck. Later, I will evaluate which of the three distinguished views (L-R$_{Prob}$, L-R$_{Mod}$, and L-R$_{Con}$) is the most plausible candidate for modelling luck as a risk-involving phenomenon. But before that, we need to address two potential impediments to cashing out luck in terms of risk, namely two intuitive differences between the two phenomena that should be taken into account.

How Can Luck Be a Risk-involving Phenomenon if Luck and Risk Are Different?

The first difference, as Pritchard (2015) correctly points out, is that risk typically concerns unwanted events, but luck can concern both wanted and unwanted events. Winning a prize in a raffle, for example, is lucky but not risky, because it is something (typically) wanted. In addition, Pritchard thinks that a second difference has to do with the fact that we can meaningfully talk of very low levels of risk, but we cannot talk of low levels of luck in a meaningful way.

The question that naturally arises is whether these two differences are consistent with the hypothesis that luck is a risk-involving phenomenon. In what follows, I will argue that the former difference is compatible with the luck-as-risk hypothesis (so we can take it into account) and that the latter is controversial (so we do not need to take it into account). Let us start with the controversial one.

While it is true that we talk of low levels of risk meaningfully—e.g., think of any activity that we would regard as safe but not completely exempt from potential mishaps[11]—it seems wrong to deny that talk of low levels of luck is meaningful. Consider the following example:

Football Star
Leo Messi, one of the best football players in the world (if not the best), masterfully dribbles past ten players of the opposing team. He runs at great speed towards the goal. Several

defenders chase him. The goalie anxiously awaits wondering from what angle the shot will come, whether he should lunge left or right. Messi is determined to strike the ball to the lower-right corner of the goal. In a matter of milliseconds, he takes a look at the goalie's position, visualizes the trajectory of the shot and raises his left foot. When he is about to strike the ball, he trips over his right foot and makes a beautiful chip shot instead. The stumble goes unnoticed and the stadium celebrates what can be fairly considered the best goal in the history of football.

Since nobody in the history of professional football has dribbled past a whole team and scored, we would not consider Messi's play a mere matter of luck. Quite the opposite: we would deem it a very skillful and competent performance. But since the last part of the play (i.e., the shot) involves an unnoticed stumble, we cannot objectively say that it is completely exempt from luck either. The upshot is that cases of very competent performances like this are such that it seems appropriate to say that they involve low levels of luck, despite the great skill displayed. Moreover, correspondingly to such low levels of luck, these sorts of cases involve associated levels of risk. For example, the risk that Messi would trip over his own feet before effectively doing so was rather low (because he is unbelievably good at running fast while controlling the ball). Thus, in keeping with the luck-as-risk hypothesis, a low level of risk (of failing because of a stumble) precedes a corresponding low level of luck (of scoring because of a stumble). In sum, we should not be worried about Pritchard's claim that talk of low levels of risk is meaningful but talk of low levels of luck is not: not only are both meaningful, but they are also correspondingly related to each other.[12]

Let us turn to the second difference, namely the fact that risk concerns unwanted events whereas luck can concern both wanted and unwanted events. How does this difference bear on the idea that luck is a risk-involving phenomenon? Let us see this in more detail.

It is widely agreed that in order for an agent S to be lucky with respect to the occurrence of an event E (or for E to be lucky for S), E must be significant to S, in a subjective or in an objective way, i.e., E must somehow affect S's subjective or objective interests (e.g., one's desires, one's preferences, one's life, and so on).[13] The same can be plausibly said about risk. S is at risk with respect to the possible occurrence of E (or E is risky for S) only if E is significant to S in a subjective or in an objective sense.

By way of illustration, think of any insignificant event, such as a leaf that is about to fall from a tree that is 1,000 km away from you. Does this potential event pose any risk to you? Intuitively, it does not, and the reason is that none of your interests will be affected in any relevant manner. Exactly for the same reason it would not be lucky for you either (i.e., it would be neither good nor bad luck for you).

With these considerations in place, we can now explain in what sense risky events are negatively valenced by default: namely, in the sense that, if they materialize, the impact they have is always detrimental to our interests.[14] Bad luck is also detrimental to our interests (otherwise it would not be described as "bad"). This suggests an interesting connection between risk and bad luck:

Risk–Bad Luck Connection: An event E is bad luck for an agent S, only if E is risky for S and E occurs.

Suppose that you bet your life savings on one roulette spin. You are at risk of losing them insofar as this is something that would clearly have a negative impact on your interests. Suppose further that such a risk materializes and you lose. This is bad luck for you. So a risk precedes your bad luck.

The interesting question (as far as the luck-as-risk hypothesis is concerned) is: how can negatively valenced risk give rise to good luck? The answer is actually straightforward: since materialized risks give rise to bad luck, risks that do not materialize give rise to good luck. In other words:

Risk–Good Luck Connection: An event E is good luck for an agent S, only if not-E is risky for S and E occurs.

Consider the roulette example again. Suppose that you bet your life savings on one roulette spin. You are at risk of losing them (i.e., you are at risk of not winning) and, again, this is detrimental to your interests. Suppose, however, that such a risk does not materialize and you win. Winning is good luck for you. So a (negatively valanced) risk precedes your good luck.

This result is unsurprising. After all, our judgments about good and bad luck are typically made against a background of positive and negative expectations, i.e., with an eye on whether the relevant possible outcomes (or the absence thereof) will be beneficial or detrimental to our interests. The bottom line is that the crucial difference between luck and risk—namely, that risk only concerns unwanted events whereas luck concerns both wanted and unwanted events—is no impediment to interpreting luck as a risk-involving phenomenon. Quite the opposite: it follows naturally from how we ordinarily think about the impact of materialized and unmaterialized risks on our subjective and objective interests.

$L\text{-}R_{Prob}$, $L\text{-}R_{Mod}$, and $L\text{-}R_{Con}$ interpret these connections between risk and good/bad luck differently, insofar as they disagree on how to spell out the relevant notion of risk. In the next section, I will assess whether the probabilistic and modal interpretations can account for them. The upshot will be that they cannot.

Against the Modal and Probabilistic Interpretations

Let us start with $L\text{-}R_{Prob}$. On this view, risk is a matter of probable occurrence and luck is preceded by risk so understood. More precisely, the relevant notion of risk featured by $L\text{-}R_{Prob}$ is the following:

> *Probabilistic Risk*: An event E is risky for an agent S if and only if E's occurrence is probable and E would have a negative impact on S's subjective or objective interests.

With this notion of probabilistic risk in place, $L\text{-}R_{Prob}$ explains *Risk–Good Luck Connection* (the thesis that S has good luck that E occurs only if not-E was risky) as follows: if S has good luck that E occurs, then not-E was probable and would have a negative impact on S's interests. By way of illustration, suppose that you bet your life savings on one roulette spin and, luckily, you win. Your good luck can be explained by the fact that it was probable (i.e., probabilistically risky) that you would lose and by the fact that this would have a very negative impact on your financial and personal interests. But since this risk does not materialize, you are (positively) lucky.

However, while the connection between good luck and probabilistic risk seems pretty straightforward (I will cast doubt on this below, though), it is unclear how probabilistic risk relates to bad luck. Consider *Risk–Bad Luck Connection*, the thesis that S has bad luck that E occurs only if E was risky. This thesis, translated in probabilistic terms, would amount to the following: if S has bad luck that E occurs, then E was probable and would have a negative impact on S's interests. But this tweaked version of *Risk–Bad Luck Connection* is problematic. Consider the following two lotteries:

> *Two Lotteries*
>
> Lottery 1 is a standard fair lottery with long odds where only one participant wins (namely, the one whose ticket number is selected). Lottery 2 is a non-standard fair lottery with the same number of participants as Lottery 1, but in which the selected ticket number is the only loser, i.e., the participant in possession of it is the only person who does not receive a prize. In addition, suppose that losing is as negative for participants of Lottery 2 as it is for participants of Lottery 1.

In Lottery 1, the most probable event is that participants will lose (i.e., they are at probabilistic risk of losing). In Lottery 2, by contrast, the most probable event is that participants will win. $L\text{-}R_{Prob}$ and its version of *Risk–Bad Luck Connection* deliver a very counterintuitive verdict here. To see this, notice that since the probability of losing Lottery 2 is so low, such an event cannot be considered risky as per $L\text{-}R_{Prob}$ standards. But by assumption, losing Lottery 2 is at least as bad luck (if not more) as losing Lottery 1. After all, it is very bad luck that someone loses a lottery in which nearly everyone who participates will win—in comparison to losing a lottery in which nearly everyone will lose. Therefore, we have a case in which an improbable risk materializes and gives rise to bad luck. In other words, contrary to what $L\text{-}R_{Prob}$ professes, probabilistic risk does not track bad luck.

Le us turn now to $L\text{-}R_{Mod}$. This view understands risk in terms of easy possibility of occurrence, and luck as preceded by this kind of risk. Here is a more precise formulation of the relevant notion of modal risk:

> *Modal Risk*: An event E is risky for an agent S if and only if E would occur in most nearby possible worlds and E would have a negative impact on S's subjective or objective interests.

Let us see how $L\text{-}R_{Mod}$ explains the connection between modal risk and good luck. In brief, *Risk–Good Luck Connection* would be translated as the thesis that if an event E is good luck for an agent S, then E occurs in the actual world but would fail to occur in most nearby possible worlds, which would have a negative impact on S's interests.

This tweaked version of *Risk–Good Luck Connection* seems to capture the connection between risk and good luck (I will also cast doubt on this). By way of illustration, suppose that you bet your life savings on one roulette spin and, luckily, you win. In most nearby possible worlds (or in a sufficient proportion of them) you would lose. This would affect your interests negatively, but since this risk does not materialize in the actual world (because you win), you have good luck.

However, as in the case of $L\text{-}R_{Prob}$, it is dubious that $L\text{-}R_{Mod}$ can account for the connection between risk and bad luck. Consider *Two Lotteries* again. In Lottery 1, most participants would lose in most nearby possible worlds (i.e., they are at risk of losing). In Lottery 2, by contrast, most participants would win in most nearby possible worlds. This difference makes $L\text{-}R_{Mod}$ and its version of *Risk–Bad Luck Connection* get the wrong results. The modal risk of losing Lottery 2 is very low, almost nonexistent, given that what is easily possible is the fact that one wins. But by assumption, losing Lottery 2 is at least as bad luck (if not more) as losing Lottery 1—again, because nearly everyone who participates in Lottery 2 wins whereas nearly everyone who participates in Lottery 1 loses. Therefore, we have a case in which a remote possibility materializes giving rise to bad luck. This means that, contrary to the main tenet of $L\text{-}R_{Mod}$, modal risk does not track bad luck either.

The problems for $L\text{-}R_{Prob}$ and $L\text{-}R_{Mod}$ do not end with their inability to account for the connection between risk and bad luck. There is another problem in the offing. In a nutshell, significant events that arise from *coincidences* are paradigmatic instances of luck. But a coincidence might be such that its components are at no or little risk of failing to occur (i.e., they might be very probable or modally robust). This means that there are cases of luck that involve no modal or probabilistic risk. If this mismatch is not worrisome enough, these sorts of cases also serve to show that neither $L\text{-}R_{Prob}$ nor $L\text{-}R_{Mod}$ can explain the connection between risk and good luck. Let us look at all this in more detail.

A coincidence is an event that cannot be explained because there is no causal or nomological antecedent between its components.[15] Suppose that you are an ice cream lover. You crave an ice cream, so you head to your preferred local ice cream shop. Another person goes to the same shop. It is scorching hot and he/she wants an ice cream to cool him/her down. While waiting in line, you strike up a conversation with this other person. You like each other. You get to know each other. You fall in love. You live a long and happy life together.

There is a causal explanation for why you go to the ice cream shop: you are an ice cream lover and you fancy an ice cream. There is a causal explanation for why the other person goes to the ice cream shop: it is scorching hot and he/she wants an ice cream to cool him/her down. There is a causal explanation for why you fall in love: you like each other. However, there is no causal explanation for why you arrive at the ice cream shop simultaneously. This is an inexplicable coincidence.

Unsurprisingly, meeting your life companion is very good luck for you, not only because it is something tremendously positive, but also because it arises out of a coincidence.

One key feature of coincidences is the following: they are no less coincidental if their components are very probable or modally robust. In other words, the probabilistic or modal profile of their components is completely tangential to their being coincidences: all that matters is that such components have no common antecedent, i.e., that there is no causal explanation of why they eventually come together. By way of illustration, suppose that you are completely determined to buy an ice cream at the local ice cream shop so that the probability that you will go there is 1 or close to 1 (alternatively, there are no or few nearby possible worlds in which you would not go the ice cream shop). Suppose that the same applies to the other person. It is still a coincidence that you both meet in the line. That you meet is obviously very good luck for you and that you didn't would be certainly detrimental to your interests. However, note that, before getting to know each other, there was *no modal or probabilistic risk* that you did not meet. To make the point more vivid, consider this other example:[16]

Takeover

For the past three months, hundreds of corporations have been secretly trying to take over Sansa's firm, an event that would have very unwelcome consequences for her workers: they would be fired. Sansa knows how to stop these hostile takeovers. For any attempt, she just needs to file a legal complaint via an online submission system. However, unbeknown to Sansa, there is a problem with the document targeted against the takeover attempt of company number 978, the Cersei Group. An unusual interference in the data stream has modified the contents of the submitted file in such a way that the competent authority has received a document with so many arguments justifying the acquisition that it has decided to give green light. Everybody in the company is in panic. In particular, everyone fears that they will lose their jobs. However, when Cersei, the CEO of the Cersei Group, is about to seal the takeover effectively, the Stannis Group (its long-standing competitor) discloses a scandal that makes Cersei's company's shares drop 99%—no one at the Stannis Group, not even Stannis, the CEO, knows that Cersei was trying to take over Sansa's firm. As a consequence, the corporation goes bankrupt and the takeover does not succeed. In fact, it is the Stannis Group that takes over Cersei's company. The disclosure of the scandal was part of Stannis's meticulous and independent plan to bring down and take over the competition. As luck would have it, it was scheduled one year ago at coincidentally the same time Cersei was about to close the takeover.

L-R$_{Prob}$ and L-R$_{Mod}$ get the wrong results in *Takeover*, because they, respectively, entail that if an event E is good luck for an agent, not-E was probable/would be the case in most nearby possible worlds. In *Takeover*, Sansa's workers are lucky that the takeover does not succeed and that they can keep their jobs. This is good luck for them insofar as the fact that they are not fired arises out of an inexplicable coincidence, something that is obviously positive for their interests. More specifically, what is inexplicable is that the Stannis Group's careful plan to take over Cersei's company is executed at exactly the same time Cersei is about to seal the takeover of Sansa's firm—recall that the submitted legal document that would stop the takeover suddenly changes in a way that makes Cersei's takeover feasible.

However, given how determined to carry out his plan Stannis is, it is highly probable that Cersei's takeover will not succeed and that Sansa's workers can keep their jobs. Given such a determination, this event would also occur in most nearby possible worlds. In other words, there is no modal or probabilistic risk that Sansa's workers will be fired. Since the fact that Sansa's workers can keep their jobs is good luck for them and there is no modal or probabilistic risk involved, we cannot but conclude that modal and probabilistic risk do not track good luck.

Luck as Risk

The Lack of Control Interpretation: A Defense

We have seen that neither L-R$_{Prob}$ nor L-R$_{Mod}$ is an adequate way to model luck as a risk-involving phenomenon. A more promising candidate is L-R$_{Con}$. On this view, risk is a matter of lack of control and luck is understood as being preceded by this sort of risk, namely by an *uncontrolled risk*:

> *Uncontrolled Risk*: An event E is risky for an agent S if and only if E is beyond S's control and E would have a negative impact on S's subjective or objective interests.

Consider *Two Lotteries*. Recall that Lottery 1 is a standard lottery with long odds with only one winner, while Lottery 2 is a non-standard lottery with the same number of participants but with only one loser. The participants of both lotteries lack the same degree of control over the outcomes, i.e., the risk of losing is the same. Since the assumption was that losing would have the same negative impact on the interests of participants of Lotteries 1 and 2, and the risk (i.e., the degree of lack of control over the lottery outcomes) is the same in both, participants of Lotteries 1 and 2 are equally unlucky to lose. L-R$_{Con}$ accounts in this way for the connection between risk and bad luck.

But here is an interesting question for L-R$_{Con}$. If in a lottery with long odds all participants have the same degree of control over the outcomes (namely, none), why is it that we have the intuition that lottery losers are less unlucky than winners are lucky, i.e., why is it that the degree of "luckiness" of winning such a lottery is higher than of losing it? While the degree of lack of control over an outcome sets the baseline for how risky for a participant a possible lottery outcome is, the degree of significance that the outcome (or the absence thereof) has for the participant can dramatically increase its degree of luckiness. If you participate in a standard lottery like Lottery 1 where you know that nearly everyone will lose, you will not be very disappointed if you lose as well. Winning such a lottery, by contrast, would come with a much higher degree of significance. Consider now the opposite case, Lottery 2, where you expect that nearly everyone will win a prize. Here, it is losing that comes with a much higher degree of significance (namely, of disappointment), precisely because by buying a ticket for Lottery 2 you basically take for granted that you will get a prize.

These considerations give us a more accurate idea of how degrees of luck covary with degrees of risk. Recall *Relational Risk–Luck Gradability Correspondence*, the thesis that the more at risk an agent S is with respect to the possible occurrence of an event E, the luckier S is that E does not occur. Now that we know that degrees of luck and risk depend on degrees of significance, we can formulate two more specific theses:

> *Negative Significance–Luck Gradability Correspondence*: The more negative the occurrence of an event E for agent S is, the luckier S is that E does not occur.

> *Positive Significance–Luck Gradability Correspondence*: The more positive the occurrence of an event E for agent S is, the luckier S is that E occurs.

An analogous thesis can be formulated for degrees of control, on which degrees of luck depend:

> *Lack of Control–Luck Gradability Correspondence*: The more an event E is beyond an agent's (S) control, the luckier or unluckier S is with respect to E.

Notice that *Negative Significance–Luck Gradability Correspondence* and *Lack of Control–Luck Gradability Correspondence* together specify the sense in which risk (when understood in terms of lack of control) covaries with luck: namely, (1) the more negative the occurrence of E for S is and (2) the more E is beyond S's control, the luckier S is that E does not occur. L-R$_{Con}$ explains the connection between risk and luck in precisely these terms.

Consider Prchal's lucky survival. Obviously, (1) it would have been terribly negative for Prchal's interests to die in the accident. In addition, (2) this eventuality was also significantly beyond his control (the elevation system of the aircraft was jammed and there was nothing he could do about it). (1) and (2) explain both why dying in the accident was so risky for Prchal and why he was so lucky to survive—moreover, they explain why the degree of risk that Prchal died corresponds to the degree of good luck that he survived.

Finally, consider *Takeover*. As we have seen, the case is problematic for L-R$_{Prob}$ and L-R$_{Mod}$ because it shows that there can be luck without modal or probabilistic risk. Sansa's workers are lucky not to be fired (because it is coincidental that they are not), but before being so lucky, there was no modal or probabilistic risk that they would lose their jobs—given how determined Stannis was to take over the company that was trying to take over Sansa's firm (Cersei's), it was actually very probable that Sansa's workers would keep their jobs, and in no nearby possible worlds would they lose them. Intuitively, however, before Stannis's takeover was effective, Sansa's workers were at risk of losing their jobs. Otherwise how could it be explained that they panicked, fearing that they would be fired?

L-R$_{Con}$ can easily explain in what sense Sansa's workers were at risk of becoming jobless and why they are so lucky to keep their jobs in the company. In a nutshell, (1) this eventuality was negative for them and (2) was something beyond their control. In this way, L-R$_{Con}$ is able to explain the cases that are troublesome for its rivals, L-R$_{Prob}$ and L-R$_{Mod}$.

By way of conclusion—and in order to avoid common misunderstandings about lack of control views as well as hasty objections—we can say something more about the notion of control that is relevant here. The first thing to keep in mind is that there is no unique way to control an eventuality. Consider Sansa's typical way to stop hostile takeovers: filing a legal complaint. Her control arises out of the fact that her knowledge of the law is vast. In a way, she can competently bring an eventuality (namely, a possible takeover) to a desired state (namely, a frustrated takeover attempt). Now, the most common way to do this is by exerting some sort of *causal influence*. For example, Leo Messi has control over the ball in this sense when dribbling past a whole team by moving the ball and himself in certain desired ways. We can call this kind of control *effective control*.

But Sansa's or Messi's actions are not the only ways to exert control. Consider Sansa's workers. They clearly lack control in the effective sense: they are aware that the legal complaint filed by Sansa will not work, and there is nothing in their capacity as company workers that they can do to make it work. Interestingly enough, they have no inkling about Stannis's intervention. This leads to the following idea: had they known sufficiently about it, they would have been in a position to take proper action (e.g., they could have announced the scandal themselves, made sure that Stannis's takeover came to a good end, and so on).

This points to a second kind of control, which we can call *tracking control*. It is the kind of control that a sufficiently vigilant pilot has when flying on autopilot mode. The pilot neither exercises effective control (i.e., has no causal influence) over the aircraft, nor does she aim to bring the aircraft's flight to some desired state. However, we cannot say that the aircraft is beyond her control, because she is in a position to exert effective control if needed (e.g., in areas of turbulences).[17] In general, having tracking control is a matter of actively checking or monitoring whether something is in a certain desired state, in such a way that one is thereby in a position to exercise effective control over it if needed, or alternatively, to act in ways that would allow one to achieve goals related to the thing controlled (e.g., a pilot, knowing that there is no possible way to effectively control a broken down aircraft, can grab her parachute and jump; farmers, who have no effective control over the sun, can still competently count on there being enough sunshine in the next months so that they can sow their crops and make them grow).

The key point is that, depending on the practical context, one of the two forms of control will be the one needed to make oneself safe from risky eventualities. Sometimes, both are needed. What I hope to have shown in this chapter is that, no matter how probable, improbable, modally robust or fragile an eventuality is, if it materializes and it is bad luck for one, it is because it has a negative impact on one's interests, but also, and more importantly, because it is beyond one's control. If it is good luck

Notes

1　Some luck attributions are of the form "Event E is lucky for agent S" (e.g., "Surviving the accident was lucky for Prchal"). This suggests that luck in the relational sense can also be understood as a relational property of events with respect to agents. See Broncano-Berrocal (2016) and Milburn (2014) for further discussion on this distinction.

2　See Broncano-Berrocal (2016) for further discussion of this distinction.

3　For the sake of simplicity, here and in what follows I will omit time indexes.

4　See Broncano-Berrocal (2016) for a comprehensive review.

5　Here and in what follows, I will talk of *significant* events. The reason is that, when it is relational luck and risk we are talking about, an event does not count as lucky or risky for an agent unless it is significant to the agent. See below for discussion of the significance condition.

6　See Broncano-Berrocal (2016) for a review.

7　This view roughly corresponds to the notion of risk in science and contexts of decision-making. See Möller (2012) for discussion of the latter. See also Broncano-Berrocal (2015) and Pritchard (2015) for further discussion on probabilistic risk.

8　The modal account of luck has been most prominently defended by Pritchard (2005, 2014).

9　See Pritchard (2015) for this kind of account of risk.

10　See Broncano-Berrocal (2016) for a review of lack of control accounts of luck and Broncano-Berrocal (2015) for a defense of a specific version of this kind of view. See also "Luck as Lack of Control" by Wayne Riggs in this volume.

11　An example would be vaccines. Although they entail some risks (e.g., they might have some side effects), numerous randomized, placebo-controlled trials conclude that they are safe and effective in preventing potentially deadly diseases, so the benefits clearly outweigh the risks. In other words, the best available science considers vaccination a *low*-risk activity.

12　Pritchard's intuition that talk of low levels of luck is not meaningful is probably influenced by his own modal account of luck. In particular, he thinks that we can talk of low levels of risk when events are modally far off, but "once the non-obtaining of the target event becomes modally far off it no longer makes any sense to talk of luck" (Pritchard 2015: 446). In this way, for Pritchard, winning a lottery that (unbeknown to one) has been rigged in one's favor does not count as lucky. By contrast, lack-of-control theorists have different intuitions, because insofar as one lacks control over a significant event to some degree (e.g., the outcome of a lottery, kicking a ball without stumbling) one is correspondingly lucky to the same degree. This is, of course, compatible with there being low levels of luck. Other views in the literature also endorse the existence of low levels of luck. For instance McKinnon (2013: 510) defends a view according to which "we attribute credit proportional to the agent's skill, and the rest to luck." This obviously allows for cases where low levels of luck are involved. See Broncano-Berrocal (2016) for discussion.

13　This view is by Ballantyne (2012). Alternative (but more problematic) significance conditions on luck can be found in Coffman (2007) and Pritchard (2005: 132–133). See Broncano-Berrocal (2016) and Ballantyne (2012) for discussion. See also Ballantyne and Kampa's contribution to this volume on "Luck and Significance."

14　While the intuitive notion of risk seems inherently tied to unwanted outcomes, exposing oneself to some risks might lead to beneficial outcomes that otherwise could not be achieved. For instance, there is something intrinsically wrong about overprotective environments, namely they tend to prevent personal growth and development. By way of illustration, in order to develop abilities we often need to be exposed to stressors that push us beyond our limits (e.g., consider physical abilities). In addition, we also sometimes talk of investments as being risky (in that one might lose the amount invested), but insofar as they might produce high profits, they are typically considered "good" risks. In sum, our intuitions about risk seem to be parasitic on our intuitions about what the costs and the benefits of the possible outcomes are.

15　See Owens (1992) for this view.

16　The case is from Broncano-Berrocal (2018).

17　See Broncano-Berrocal (2015) for discussion of these two kinds of control.

References

Ballantyne, N. (2012) "Luck and Interests," *Synthese* 185, 319–334.

Broncano-Berrocal, F. (2015) "Luck as Risk and the Lack of Control Account of Luck," *Metaphilosophy* 46, 1–25.

——. (2016) "Luck," *Internet Encyclopedia of Philosophy*, <www.iep.utm.edu/luck/>.

——. (2018) "Purifying Impure Virtue Epistemology," *Philosophical Studies* 175, 385–410, doi: 10.1007/s11098-017-0873-x.

Coffman, E.J. (2007) "Thinking about Luck," *Synthese* 158, 385–398.

McKinnon, R. (2013) "Getting Luck Properly Under Control," *Metaphilosophy* 44, 496–511.

Milburn, Joe (2014) "Subject-Involving Luck," *Metaphilosophy* 45(4–5), 578–593.

Möller, N. (2012) "The Concepts of Risk and Safety," in S. Roeser, R. Hillerbrand, M. Peterson, & P. Sandin (eds.) *Handbook of Risk Theory*, the Netherlands: Springer, pp. 55–85.

Owens, D. (1992) *Causes and Coincidences*, Cambridge: Cambridge University Press.

Pritchard, D. (2005) *Epistemic Luck*, Oxford: Oxford University Press.

——. (2014) "The Modal Account of Luck," *Metaphilosophy* 45, 594–619.

——. (2015) "Risk," *Metaphilosophy* 46, 436–461.

16
LUCK AND NORMS

Rachel McKinnon

One might wonder why philosophers care about the metaphysics of luck. What, if anything, hangs on getting the nature of "luck" right? One reason to focus on the metaphysics of luck is that there seems to be the following platitude: we give agents less credit for obtaining outcomes through luck than we do for obtaining outcomes through skill. Relatedly, a recent focus in epistemology is to conceive of knowledge as true belief through the exercise of a cognitive skill. In that domain, there seems to be a related anti-luck platitude: knowledge of a proposition is incompatible with luck.[1] For example, one attractive account of Gettier cases in epistemology is that what explains why an agent fails to know is the presence of a kind of epistemic luck.[2] As Sosa (2011: 45) writes, Gettier cases are "competent and even true, but its correctness is due to luck and manifests no relevant competence of the performer's."

This chapter is concerned with the relationship between luck and the normative evaluation of performances. That is, how should we think about ascribing credit—or withholding credit—for performances that succeed due to luck? Since we are primarily concerned with evaluating *actions* and performances, this is typically discussed under the umbrella topic of "performance normativity." Some argue that the presence—or at least the presence of a certain kind—of luck undermines the creditworthiness of an agent's performance. On the contrary, I will argue that anti-luck epistemology has been too "anti-luck." Creditworthy—and praiseworthy—achievements often involve luck, and this does not detract from the credit- and praiseworthiness of the agent's performance. This mistake arises, I suspect, from a mistaken view of the metaphysics of luck: successful actions are not the result of *either* luck or skill. Rather, successful actions always involve *both* luck and skill.

There seems to be a very common unstated assumption that outcomes are either the result of skill or the result of luck. That is, we can attribute the attaining of an outcome to either skill or luck. I call this view *luck binarism*. Consider Sosa (2011: 63) discussing two theses of performance normativity: "Success is better than failure. Success through competence is better than success by luck." He further writes, "Reaching an objective must be distinguished, moreover, from attaining it, which requires that you reach it not just by luck" (2011: 64). Implicit here is the assumption that a successful action completely obtains its goal by luck or by competence. Moreover, it assumes that one can engage in a performance that attains its goal "just by luck." But I will argue that this is a false binary: all performances involve *both* luck and skill. No actions are entirely attributable to skill or to luck. Moreover, no actions—that involve the exercise of an ability—involve *no* skill or no luck.

In this chapter, I further develop my view of the metaphysics of luck—which I have called the Expected Outcomes View (EOV)—in McKinnon (2013, 2014) in order to advance our understanding of the relationship between luck and *achievement*. Very quickly, here is a recapitulation of my view of luck:

> I make the case that we can better understand the nature of luck by drawing an analogy with the expected value of wagers. A long series of wagers, each with a determinate expected value, itself has a determinate expected value. It's unlikely, however, that the outcome of the series will be the expected value. I argue that the difference between the actual results and the expected value is what we call luck. When we consider how actions, specifically when exercising a skill or ability, are similarly probabilistic, we can call the expected results of a series of actions "skill." Then, mutatis mutandis, the difference between the expected outcomes and the actual outcomes of a series of actions is what we call luck. Moreover, like a single wager viewed as part of a series of wagers, I propose that we view the outcome of an individual action as one element of a larger series of trials. Its status as creditable or lucky depends essentially on its place within that series. I subsequently argue that agents deserve credit for an outcome proportional only to their skill. Insofar as an agent's obtaining an outcome involves good luck, we should remove credit proportional to the good luck; similarly, insofar as an agent's obtaining an outcome involves bad luck, we should attribute credit proportional to the bad luck.
>
> *McKinnon 2013: 497*[3]

One upshot of my argument in this chapter will be a new treatment of Gettier cases such that some Gettier cases *are* knowledge. Some successful performances, where we attribute the success to the agent's skill, are compatible with the presence of some luck.[4]

Performance Normativity

One of the relatively recent innovations in epistemology is to conceive of knowledge not simply as a state—perhaps a mental state—but as the result of a *performance*. On Ernest Sosa's (2011) view, we evaluate knowledge just as we evaluate all performances, according to an AAA structure. Creditworthy performances are Accurate, Adroit, and Apt. A performance is *accurate* if it successfully attains its goal—an archer hits her target, a belief is true. A performance is *adroit* if it is skillfully performed. And a performance is *apt* if it is successful in attaining its goal by manifesting the agent's skill. That is, a performance is apt if it is accurate because it is adroit. The latter is important since we want to rule out cases where one skillfully performs an action, but the success comes about through luck. And since knowledge is understood in terms of performance normativity, I will speak interchangeably between a performance being successful and a belief being true (or perhaps even knowledge).

Here is a representative quote from Sosa (2011: 4):[5]

> The archer's shot is a good example. The shot aims to hit the target, and its success can be judged by whether it does so or not, by its accuracy. However accurate it may be, there is a further dimension of evaluation: namely, how skillful a shot is, how much skill it manifests, how adroit it is. A shot might hit the bull's-eye, however, and might even manifest great skill, while failing utterly, as a shot, on a further dimension. Consider a shot diverted by a gust of wind initially, so that it would miss the target altogether but for a second gust that puts it back on track to hit the bull's-eye. This shot is both accurate and adroit, yet is not accurate because adroit, so as to manifest the archer's skill and competence. It thus fails on a third dimension of evaluation, besides those of accuracy and adroitness: it fails to be apt.

For Sosa, actions that are successful but do not manifest the agent's skill are *defective*. Moreover, the archer's shot that hits its target through the double-wind is "deplorable" (2011: 45). These performances are inapt and fall "short simply because [their] success is in that way attributable to luck rather than fully enough to competence" (2011: 45).[6] Full credit goes to agents only for apt performances. There is an additional level of evaluation, though: meta-aptness. An archer can be skillful in taking her shot, but an archer can also be skillful in deciding *whether* to take a shot. And if a performance's aptness manifests an agent's meta-aptness, the performance is "fully apt." We reserve our highest praise for fully apt performances. However, for the sake of our discussion, we need only focus on aptness and apt performances.

The archer double-wind case nicely illustrates Linda Zagzebski's (1994) way of characterizing Gettier cases—in epistemology—as a result of double-luck. Here is a recipe for constructing Gettier cases: Start with a case of a justified false belief. The belief-forming process is generally reliable, but the belief happens to be false due to bad luck. Now add in a second, independent element of luck that makes the belief true. The second element of (good) luck thus cancels out the first element of (bad) luck. We have a justified true belief that, due to the presence of the luck, is not knowledge. In Sosa's archer case, the archer is skillful in taking her shot, and in normal conditions she will hit her target. She suffers some (bad) luck, with a gust of wind blowing her arrow off course. However, she benefits from some (good) luck, with a gust of wind canceling out the first gust of wind, blowing the arrow back on its original course. On this view, we should treat the archer hitting her bull's-eye just as we treat Gettier cases: she does not deserve full credit for her success, just as a Gettier belief is not knowledge.

The key behind this approach is that the success does not properly manifest the archer's skill. Much of the debate has thus been on what it means for an outcome to sufficiently "manifest" a skill. However, this is not yet to build in a metaphysics of luck. So far "luck" has been used as an unanalyzed primitive, where the assumption seems to be that it does not much matter how we think about luck, any concept of luck will do. However, I think that this is a mistake: the metaphysics of luck matters for how we conceive of performances and their creditworthiness.

Anti-Luck Performance Normativity

Saying something about how luck undermines credit for successful performances seems to say more about how we think about performances than the nature of luck. But the two seem to go tightly hand-in-hand. Gettier cases in epistemology are a common site for both debates, and sometimes at once. Duncan Pritchard's (2005, 2010, 2012, 2014) *modal account of luck* seeks to explain both what luck is, and why Gettier cases are fully explained by an adequate account of luck.

> L1: If an event is lucky, then it is an event that occurs in the actual world but which does not occur in a wide class of the nearest possible worlds where the relevant initial conditions for that event are the same as in the actual world.
> L2: If an event is lucky, then it is an event that is significant to the agent concerned (or would be significant, were the agent to be availed of the relevant facts).[7]

And while the anti-luck platitude holds that knowledge is incompatible with the presence of luck, Pritchard argues that it is not quite that simple: knowledge is incompatible with a particular species of luck, which he calls *veritic* luck.

Pritchard (2012) distinguishes between veritic and *evidential* luck. Consider the following two cases. There are ten coins under my desk, and I just guess that there are ten coins under my desk. I cannot see them. I have no idea whether there are any coins under my desk, but I guess and form the belief "There are ten coins under my desk." My belief happens to be true. *That* my belief is true is a matter of luck; specifically, it is veritically lucky. Veritic luck happens, in the epistemic case, when,

185

given our evidence, it is lucky that our belief is true. In a non-epistemic case, it is like an unskilled archer randomly shooting her arrow and it happening to hit its target.

Now suppose that there are the same ten coins under my desk and, rather than simply guessing, I happen to trip and fall. "Lucky" for me, I fall in a position to see that there are ten coins under my desk and I thereby form the belief "There are ten coins under my desk." There is nothing surprising about my forming a true belief here. However, that I was *in a position* to have the evidence for my true belief is a matter of luck. But given that I now have that evidence, that I form a true belief is not a matter of luck. Knowledge is consistent with evidential luck, but not veritic luck.

However, there are two varieties of veritic luck: *intervening* and *environmental* veritic luck.[8] On Pritchard's (2005, 2010) view, knowledge is incompatible only with intervening veritic luck. Here, the luck is just like the gust of wind in the archer case: although the archer exercises her skill (the performance is adroit), and she hits her target (the performance is accurate), the wind "intervenes" between her performance and the outcome, contributing to the causal chain. Her performance is still successful because two different gusts of wind intervene and happen to cancel each other out, but the result of hitting the bull's-eye is not entirely attributable to the agent's performance: the winds steal some credit. Pritchard writes that "luck of this sort is incompatible with achievements, since it entails that the success in question was not because of the exercise of the agent's abilities but rather down to luck" (2005: 28). Pritchard thus seems to take on board some version of luck binarism.

Environmental luck, on the other hand, is when an instance of intervening luck could have easily happened, but didn't. For example, an archer takes a shot and two gusts of wind are on their way to interfere with the flight—but in a way that cancels each other out. However, shortly before the winds reach the arrow, someone turns on a forcefield blocking all wind, and the winds have no effect. Luck is present: it was lucky that the forcefields were activated in time, but the forcefields did not "intervene" between the agent's performance and the result (of hitting the bull's-eye). And since the "luck" did not intervene in the agent's performance, their success is entirely attributable to their skill. However, can one both adopt the anti-luck platitude while allowing for the presence of some (kind of) luck in creditworthy performances? Ian Church (2013) suggests not.

Church has argued that if we think that Zagzebski's double-luck account of Gettier cases is right, and that the presence of this kind of luck undermines credit, then we are in trouble: for a given analysis of knowledge (or, as I would put it, performance normativity) we will always be able to construct Gettier cases. Or in Pritchard's terms, we will always be able to construct intervening veritic luck cases. The worry, then, is that we can never *fully* eliminate the problematic forms of luck from our performances: we can never fully satisfy the anti-luck platitude. The upshot of this is that we do not need increasingly sophisticated accounts of luck, such as Pritchard's modal account, for we can construct modally robust Gettier cases. Instead, Church argues, we should seek an account of knowledge that simply rules out the presence of luck entirely.

Here is the sort of modally robust Gettier case that Church uses. John Turri (2011) offers the following "Special Dog" case. Suppose that you come across a field in the countryside and you see a sheep-shaped object in the field. You form the corresponding belief, "There's a sheep in that field." But suppose that the sheep-shaped object you are looking at is not in fact a sheep; rather, it is a cleverly disguised dog. As it happens, though, there is a sheep nearby behind a tree. But you cannot see the real sheep. This is a classic Gettier case. But the dog is special: it loves the sheep so much that it follows it everywhere. So every time that you see the dog in that field, it is true that the sheep is in the field. So your true belief "There's a sheep in that field" is true in the actual world *and* most nearby possible worlds where the relevant initial conditions are the same as in the actual world. Your true belief is thus modally robust. However, the case is run-through with what seems like knowledge-undermining luck.

Church's argument is that once we admit that luck comes in degrees, then we can construct cases where only a tiny amount of knowledge-precluding luck is present. On Church's view, all we need is a tiny amount of knowledge-precluding luck to, well, preclude knowledge. He argues that this presents us with a dilemma: either we strengthen our analysis of knowledge to guarantee the truth of beliefs, or we have to admit that we can construct knowledge-like cases where luck is present. Church chooses the former: he fully adopts the anti-luck platitude and suggests that we need an analysis of knowledge where to know that *p* is to guarantee that one's belief that p is true.[9]

I disagree. The right response, I think, is to admit that fully creditworthy performances—and knowledge—admit *some* amount of luck. That is, we should deny the anti-luck platitude: it is hardly a platitude. The platitude gets the metaphysics of luck and performance normativity wrong. In what remains, I will apply my account of the metaphysics of luck—the Expected Outcomes View (EOV) of luck—to show how achievement is consistent with the presence of some luck, even some "veritic" luck. I will do so by connecting the EOV to an account of *achievement* as a kind of valuable success through skillful performance. One upshot of this is that some Gettier cases *are* knowledge.

Achievement, Skill, and Luck

There has been recent attention to the nature of achievement, much of which is attributable to Gwen Bradford (2013, 2015, 2016a, 2016b). She argues that achievements have the following features. They involve: a difficult process, the process causes the outcome, and the process is executed competently (2016a: 17). In short, she argues that "achievements are comprised by a process and a product, where the process is difficult, and competently causes the product" (2016a: 24). In effect, this seems quite similar to Sosa's view of apt (and perhaps fully apt) performances: a performance is apt if one skillfully brings about one's aim where the outcome manifests one's skill.

One important feature of achievement is *reliability*, which, like me, Bradford cashes out in terms of the ability to produce similar results in a sufficient number of nearby possible worlds. In McKinnon (2014) I offered a distinction between an *ability* and a *skill*.

> Subject S has ability A by performing action ϕ to produce outcome O in a range of contexts C iff were S to ϕ in C there would be a nonzero probability that S will O by ϕing in C. I have the ability, for example, to make a half-court basketball shot (by moving my body a particular way), even though it's extremely unlikely that I will succeed in making the shot. Contrast ability, then, with skill. I have both the ability and the skill, for example, to make a basketball shot from 1″ away from the basket by moving my body in a particular way. I have the ability but not the skill to make half-court basketball shots ….What it means to have a skill is that one ϕs with sufficient regularity and in the right way(s).
>
> *McKinnon 2014: 562*

Crucially, one can have a skill even if one will only have one opportunity to exercise it. What matters are not real-world results, but the counterfactual, modal features of one's skill. When our successes manifest our skills, we achieve them in a *non-accidental* way. Finally, for Bradford, the more competently caused an outcome, the better the achievement (2016a: 143).

For Bradford, though, the presence of luck seems to undermine achievement. She suggests adding an anti-Gettier condition to her account of knowledge as an achievement. But why? She appeals to the true claim that "it is widely held that knowledge requires a further, 'anti-Gettier' component" (2016a: 65). But part of my purpose here is to push back on that: some Gettier cases are consistent with achievement (namely, performance normativity) and thus, by extension, some Gettier cases are knowledge. Anti-luck (virtue) epistemology has become a little too "anti-luck," lately.

One interesting attempt to square anti-luck (virtue) epistemology with a performance normativity account of knowledge belongs to Lisa Miracchi (2015). She argues for a view she calls *direct virtue epistemology* (DVE). On traditional or "indirect" virtue epistemology accounts, one's epistemic (or perhaps cognitive—I take no stand on this distinction) skill in coming to know a proposition involves a skill aiming at obtaining true beliefs. Sosa's view of knowledge as apt belief is an instance of this.

However, Miracchi argues that our epistemic skills are not aiming at true belief; rather, they are aiming at *knowledge*. That is, our epistemic competences are not to form true beliefs, but to form knowledge. She argues that one only fully exercises one's competence to ϕ when one succeeds in obtaining one's goal of ϕing. She disagrees, then, with my claim that one can exercise one's skill but still fail to achieve its aim due to bad luck. She argues that such cases are instances of "degenerate" performances. That is, for Miracchi, there are two manifestations of competences: one of which is constitutively an achievement, and another of which is constitutively a failure. She places Gettier cases in the latter category, alongside justified false beliefs.

She suggests that her proposal can solve the Gettier problem. She writes,

> According to the present proposal, the exercises (constituted by the manifestation conditions) that are fundamental to competences to know are cases of knowledge, not anything that falls short of it. Thus there is no room for a success condition (e.g. true belief) distinct from the achievement condition (knowledge), and so no room for Gettier-style counterexamples.
>
> *2015: 47*

She offers the following as a definition of her *manifestation condition*.

> **Manifestation Conditions**: The manifestation conditions of C_K are whatever operations of subpersonal cognitive mechanisms and external conditions together (against a background of possession of C_K) constitute a particular case of knowing that p in the way characteristic of the competence (W_{CK}).
>
> *Miracchi 2015: 45*

For our purposes, the relevant sub-species of the manifestation condition for Miracchi's view is the following *proficiency condition*:

> **Proficiency Condition**: The proficiency condition of C_K requires that the objective probability of the manifestation conditions obtaining conditional on the basis of the competence being operative be sufficiently high. I.e., $Pr(M \mid O_B) \geq n$, for some sufficiently high $n \in (0, 1]$.
>
> *Miracchi 2015: 46*

However, her proposal falls victim to the same sort of Gettier cases that Church (2013) uses: for any "competence" view of knowledge that is not fully infallibilist, we can construct a pair of cases, holding an agent's proficiency constant, where one is "achievement" and the other is a Gettier case where the double-luck is present.

Here is the sort of set of cases I offer in McKinnon (2014) to illustrate this point. Gina is an expert archer. In a competition she takes a shot. Consider three ways to modify the case. In the original case, the arrow unsurprisingly hits its target: it is an achievement where her success manifests her archery skill. In the second case, Gina★ takes the same shot but a gust of wind blows the arrow off target, while a second gust of wind blows it back on target, and she succeeds in her aim. This is "intervening" luck on Pritchard's view. In the third case, Gina★★ takes the same shot, and the same two gusts of wind as in the Gina★ case are on their way to interfere with the arrow's path, but someone accidentally hits a button that closes shutters to the archery hall, blocking the wind, and her arrow unsurprisingly hits its target.

What will Miracchi's view say of these three cases? Gina is a straightforward case of achievement, and so Miracchi's view agrees. So far so good. But Gina★ seems straightforwardly to be a Gettier case, and Miracchi's view is that Gina★'s success in hitting the target does not sufficiently manifest her competence to count as an achievement. Instead, it is one of Miracchi's "degenerate competences" cases. Importantly, because the two winds cancel each other out, nothing has changed about the probability (even modally understood) of Gina★'s shot. Miracchi is forced to say that the presence of the double-wind means that the manifestation condition is not met, because succeeding with the presence of wind is not to succeed "in the way characteristic of the competence." Let us set that aside for the moment.

What about Gina★★? On Miracchi's view, Gina★★ might collapse into the original Gina case, and so count as a genuine instance of achievement (and thus not a Gettier case). But why? If Gettier cases can often be characterized by the presence of "double-luck," what about the triple-luck of Gina★★? The wind "intervenes" in the Gina★ case, but the archery hall window shutters "intervene" with the wind that would have intervened in the Gina★★ case. The proficiency conditions in all three cases are crucially the same. So how can we treat Gina★ differently from Gina★★ and Gina? Is it merely that the wind "touches" Gina★'s arrow, but not Gina's or Gina★★'s? I criticized this sort of view as the "don't touch my stuff" view of causation in McKinnon (2015).

But let us return to Gina★. Is it really the case that when the double-wind "intervenes" with the flight of her arrow, even though it did not affect the modal features of her proficiency, is not to succeed "in the way characteristic of the competence"? I suggest that Gina★'s success *is characteristic* of her competence. Real-world performances are causally *messy*. I agree with Church: luck is *everywhere*. Luck runs through all of our performances—we are just often not cognizant of it. Watch the flight path of an arrow: it is not perfectly straight. The fletchings catch subtle changes in wind direction. Normally, the small, unpredictable changes in wind direction do not make a noticeable difference in outcome. But sometimes they do. And when the unpredictable eddies in air pressure do not appreciably affect the performance, even though they are present and constitute *some* small presence of luck, we are still happy to attribute "achievement" to the agent's performance.

In a sense, I do not disagree with Miracchi's account of achievement as competences where the manifestation conditions are satisfied. However, I do disagree with her application of "in the way characteristic of the competence." Performances of our competences are messy. Some luck in those performances is perfectly consistent with a robust sense of "achievement." And if Gina★ is a Gettier case, I do not see a principled distinction between Gina★ and Gina★★ such that the latter is *not* a Gettier case. But intuitions of Gina★★ seem to support viewing her success as an achievement. On pain of inconsistency, then, we should treat Gina★ just like Gina★★ and Gina: performances are messy, and the presence of some luck is not a problem. When is it not a problem? For Miracchi, when it satisfies the manifestation conditions. I take this to be consistent with my earlier (McKinnon 2013, 2014) views of the relationship between luck and performance normativity. And on my view, Gettier cases that satisfy these conditions constitute instances of achievement and are, thus, *knowledge*. Therefore, some Gettier cases are knowledge.

Finally, one might object that my view runs into an instance of the value problem: if I argue that performances are creditworthy irrespective of outcome, proportional to the agent's skill in their performance, how can I explain the strong, widespread intuition that we value successful skillful performances more than unsuccessful skillful performances (or, indeed, more than successful unskillful performances)? This is where connecting my EOV of luck to an account of achievement is helpful: achievement is a success term—one only achieves something (say, a home run) if one is successful in skillfully attaining one's goal. It is easy to see, then, why we value successful skillful performances more than unsuccessful but equally skillful performances: only the former gives us an *achievement*. It is quite consistent to think that we should evaluate performances qua skillful performance only in terms of the performance, irrespective of outcomes subject to luck, while maintaining the view that, nevertheless, we more highly *value* successful skillful performances.

In this chapter I have argued for an extension of my EOV of the metaphysics of luck, and its treatment of the normative evaluation of performances, by adding in an account of achievement. Achievements are, necessarily, *successful* skillful performances. And although I argue that we ought to normatively evaluate successful and unsuccessful performances the same qua skillful performance, irrespective of outcome, we value successful performances more. Why? Because we value *achievements*.

I have also applied this view to Gettier cases in epistemology, and elsewhere. On the traditional view of Gettier cases, they are instances of skillful (i.e., justified) true beliefs but do not amount to knowledge because the connection between the epistemic skill and the true belief do not have the "right" connection. I have argued that we must consider the nature of skillful performances—whether successful or not. When we do, we see that the presence of some degree of luck is unavoidable. But this does not deter us from thinking that agents deserve credit for their achievements through the successful exercise of a relevant skill. However, I have argued that if we want to continue to conceive of coming to know as a performance (whether "cognitive" or "epistemic"), then we must grant that some Gettier cases *are knowledge*. Full stop. Contra Church, who suggests that we avoid the ineliminability of luck by arguing for a certainty standard for knowledge, I argue that we must accept that knowledge, like all performances, is "messy" and shot-through with luck. If we are committed to the performance normativity of knowledge, by analogy with non-epistemic performances, then we can accept that luck does *not* always preclude knowledge.

I close with one observation: is it really better to be lucky than good? Of course, because our common use of "lucky" is in the sense of "good luck," which is a success term: one is only lucky when one succeeds. One can be skillful, though, and still fail. If I had to pick, I would take a life of luck. However, we do not get to pick, so we should aim to be skillful. All the same: I wish you good luck!

Notes

1 For example, Pritchard (2005, 2010, 2012, 2014) has named this project "anti-luck epistemology," which tends to be a form of virtue epistemology.
2 Zagzebski (1994); cf. Church (2013).
3 See also McKinnon (2015) for an extended discussion of performance normativity.
4 See also Hetherington (this volume) for an argument against what he calls the luck/knowledge incompatibility thesis.
5 See also Sosa (2007).
6 One might wonder how much work "fully enough" is doing for Sosa here. It is unclear. Sometimes he uses "fully enough" which suggests a non-binaristic view, but other times he suggests that some successful performances can be reached "just by luck." The latter, I argue, do not exist (when we are talking about something that an agent performed, like hitting a home run). What matters is not so much whether Sosa himself is a luck binarist; rather, what matters is my refutation of luck binarism as a viable view.
7 Pritchard (2005: 125, 132). It is worth noting that Pritchard has subsequently dropped L2 as a necessary condition.
8 See also Carter (2011) and Jarvis (2013).
9 To be fair, Church ultimately thinks that one must take an infallibilist account of knowledge *if we are to avoid Gettier cases*. However, he does not think that an infallibilist position is ultimately viable. See Church (this volume). I thank Church for pointing this out.

References

Bradford, G. (2013) "The Value of Achievements," *Pacific Philosophical Quarterly* 94(2), 204–224.
——. (2015) "Knowledge, Achievement, and Manifestation," *Erkenntnis* 80(1), 97–116.
——. (2016a) *Achievement*, Oxford: Oxford University Press.
——. (2016b) "Achievement, Wellbeing, and Value," *Philosophy Compass* 11(12), 795–803.
Carter, J. (2011) "A Problem for Pritchard's Anti-Luck Virtue Epistemology," *Erkenntnis* 78(2), 253–275.
Church, I. (2013) "Getting 'Lucky' with Gettier," *European Journal of Philosophy* 21(1), 37–49.
Jarvis, B. (2013) "Knowledge, Cognitive Achievement, and Environmental Luck," *Pacific Philosophical Quarterly* 94(4), 529–551.
McKinnon, R. (2013) "Getting Luck Properly Under Control," *Metaphilosophy* 44(4), 496–511.
——. (2014) "You Make Your Own Luck," *Metaphilosophy* 45(4–5), 558–577, and reprinted in Pritchard, D. & Whittington, L. (2015) *The Philosophy of Luck*, London: Wiley-Blackwell.

Luck and Norms

——. (2015) *The Norms of Assertion: Truth, Lies, and Warrant*, London: Palgrave Macmillan UK.
Miracchi, L. (2015) "Competence to Know," *Philosophical Studies* 172(1), 29–56.
Pritchard, D. (2005) *Epistemic Luck*, Oxford: Oxford University Press.
——. (2010) "Achievements, Luck, and Value," *Think* 9(25), 19–30.
——. (2012) "Anti-Luck Virtue Epistemology," *Journal of Philosophy* 109(3), 247–279.
——. (2014) "The Modal Account of Luck," *Metaphilosophy* 45(4–5), 594–619, and reprinted in Pritchard, D. & Whittington, L. (2015) *The Philosophy of Luck*, London: Routledge.
Sosa, E. (2007) *A Virtue Epistemology: Apt Belief and Reflective Knowledge*, Oxford: Oxford University Press.
——. (2011) *Knowing Full Well*, Princeton, NJ: Princeton University Press.
Turri, J. (2011) "Manifest Failure: The Gettier Problem Solved," *Philosophers' Imprint* 11(8), 1–11.
Zagzebski, L. (1994) "The Inescapability of Gettier Problems," *Philosophical Quarterly* 44(174), 65–73.

PART III

Moral Luck

17

THE DEFINITION OF "LUCK" AND THE PROBLEM OF MORAL LUCK[1]

Daniel Statman

In his seminal paper on moral luck, Bernard Williams announces that he will be using the notion of luck "generously [and] undefinedly" (Williams 1993: 37). Nagel does the same, using the notion of moral luck freely with no attempt to offer a precise definition. For both of them, luck has to do with lack of control, but what exactly this means and what the other conditions for luck are remain unclear. For 30 years or so, the questions raised by these two papers animated a lively discussion in ethics, in epistemology, and in the philosophy of religion,[2] by and large without anyone feeling that in order to make progress, a clear definition of luck was necessary. Recently, however, things have changed.[3] To refrain from exploring the general notion of luck is now considered by some writers as no less than philosophically "shocking."[4] In their view, progress in understanding what exactly we mean by "luck" can provide the key to understanding and potentially to solving the problem of moral luck or, at least, enabling it to be dismissed.

The purpose of this chapter is to reject this line of thought, namely, the belief that an analysis of what exactly we mean by the term "luck" might offer a way to solve the problem of moral luck. I do so by offering a critical examination of three papers on moral luck: by Duncan Pritchard (2006), and more recently by Steven Hales (2015) and Thomas and Jennifer Lockhart (2017) (hereafter 'the Lockharts'), respectively.

Pritchard argues that the two classical papers on moral luck, those of Williams and of Nagel, fail in offering a coherent account of the problem of moral luck. In his view, this failure arouses the suspicion that such an account cannot really be given. In the same vein, Hales argues that a proper understanding of the notion of luck yields the conclusion that there is no such thing as moral luck while the Lockharts make a more modest move in the same direction, one based on an analysis of the notion of control (the lack of which has always been seen as essential to luck). After dealing with all these papers in turn, I conclude with some general observations.[5]

Pritchard: Why the Standard Examples of Moral Luck Are Not Instances of Luck

In Pritchard's view, Williams and Nagel, the two philosophers who sparked off the moral debate, failed in putting forward even a partial account of luck, a failure that "disguises the fact that by the lights of any plausible account of this notion the examples of moral luck that they offer are ambiguous, to say the least" (Pritchard 2006: 1). This, by itself, does not show that there could be no coherent account of the problem of moral luck, but, in Pritchard's (2006: 1) view, it does point us toward this "grander claim." A proper understanding of the notion of luck is assumingly an important step in realizing that there is no genuine problem of *moral* luck. While Pritchard discusses both Nagel and Williams, I will limit my comments to his treatment of Nagel because it is the former's formulation of the moral luck problem that has dominated the philosophical debate rather than that of Williams.

Pritchard starts with the classic case of Nagel's pair of reckless drivers, one of whom hits a pedestrian while the other arrives at his destination unscathed. Pritchard concedes that the driver who killed the pedestrian would receive—and ought to receive—a harsher punishment than the lucky driver who did not, but, in his view, this does not show that his *moral* record is worse. Punishment does more than express moral disapproval, hence there is no inconsistency in saying that, on the one hand, the drivers are morally equal in the relevant respect, namely, equally blameworthy for their reckless behavior while, on the other, that they should receive different punishments:

> We might wish to punish one criminal more severely than another for committing the same crime for the sole reason that the one criminal's act, while otherwise identical, resulted in more suffering than the other's and we want our punishments (somehow) to represent this differing extent of suffering.
>
> *Pritchard 2006: 5*

However, as Pritchard rightly observes, this is a strategy often used by opponents of moral luck to object to the pairs of examples put forward by Nagel. They insist that the agents in these pairs are to be judged only by what is within their control, hence are morally equal in the relevant respects, and they then offer an argument to explain away the intuition that one offender is more blameworthy than the other. In Pritchard's version of this strategy, the source of the mistaken intuition lies in a failure to distinguish between moral opprobrium and legal punishment. Once the mistake is acknowledged, we can safely retain the correct, anti-luck, position. What Pritchard seeks to do is to strengthen this conventional criticism by a further argument that purportedly shows that Nagel's cases should not be taken as examples of moral luck in the first place.

How is this supposed to work? Pritchard assumes a modal account of luck according to which

> a lucky event is an event that occurs in the actual world but does not occur in most of the nearest possible worlds to the actual world where the relevant initial conditions for that event are the same as in the actual world.
>
> *Pritchard 2006: 3*[6]

Armed with this understanding, consider the case of a reckless driver who regularly risks harming pedestrians by his driving. If such a driver hits a pedestrian, it is not a case of *luck*; the event occurs in most of the nearest possible worlds to the actual world where the relevant initial conditions for that event are the same as in the actual one.

Pritchard makes a similar move with regard to Nagel's standard example of circumstantial luck in which a German who was an officer in a concentration camp is compared to a German who emigrated to Argentina in 1930 for business reasons but *would* have become a Nazi criminal had he stayed in Germany. If we suppose that the German expatriate was lucky not to have been in Germany in the 1930s, that would mean that there are many nearby possible worlds in which this agent lives in Germany and commits atrocities under the Nazi regime. But, says Pritchard, if this is taken at face value, there is indeed no moral difference between the actual Nazi officer and his German-Argentinian counterpart. If, however, we stipulate that the possibility that the German expatriate would have become a Nazi is remote, namely, that there are very few nearby possible worlds in which he would be obliged to commit such crimes, then, by definition, the fact that he leads a peaceful life in Argentina is not a matter of *luck*, hence not one of (good) *moral* luck.

Furthermore, it is hard to imagine two otherwise identical agents engaging in lifestyles that are so radically different from a moral point of view. That would be to say that two identical agents in nearby possible worlds, under the same initial conditions, would have radically different moral records, an assumption which seems impossible. Hence, once again, the fact that the German expatriate led a peaceful life in Argentina cannot be seen as a matter of luck, because that would imply the absurd result that, in some nearby possible world, *he* would be a Nazi murderer.

Let me now make some critical comments. First, I am not convinced that Pritchard offers a new argument against moral luck which is based on his general account (the "modal account") of luck. What seems to do the work in Pritchard's argument against Nagel is his firm conviction—shared by all opponents of moral luck—that (a) when two agents are identical in the relevant moral features, they should be seen as morally equal (again, in the relevant aspects) and (b) that these features do not include factors over which the agents do not have control. In this spirit, he says that, upon reflection, we would deny that the unlucky driver (who hit a pedestrian) committed a morally worse action than his counterpart, and deny that there is a moral difference between the actual Nazi and the would-be Nazi. Pritchard does not substantiate these assertions, which are at the very heart of the moral luck debate, he just invites the readers' agreement. But the important point for the present context is that these assertions in no way rely (or are presented as relying) on his (or any other) specific account of luck.

Pritchard realizes that his critique of Nagel follows the conventional strategy of simply denying the moral difference between the cases in each of the pairs mentioned by Nagel and, in order to show that he, nonetheless, adds to this critique, he says that his argument "supplements and strengthens" it. But the impression one gets from reading Pritchard is that the conventional critique is not only necessary for rejecting moral luck, but it is also sufficient; *it does all the required work.* And indeed, once one denies the moral difference between the two drivers or the two assassins, etc., how important can it be to go into an analysis of the notion of luck? This denial would immediately make the moral luck problem lose its sting.

Second, for the moral luck problem to emerge, it need not be the case that, strictly speaking, *both* the agents in the pairs of examples can be said to be subject to luck, only one of them need be. Assume, as Pritchard has it, that the reckless driver, the one who routinely endangers pedestrians, cannot conceptually be said to be *unlucky* if he hits one. Now think of a different driver (or of himself in a nearby possible world) who behaves in the same way but fortunately hits nobody. This other driver no doubt *can* be said to have been lucky in not hitting anybody. The question then is whether there is any moral difference between them, in particular, whether the latter is less blameworthy than the former. It is *this* question that Nagel wishes to raise and Pritchard has not shown how his (Pritchard's) general account of luck puts us in a better position to answer it (or to dismiss it).

Third, in Pritchard's view, it is hard, if not impossible "to imagine two otherwise identical agents engaging in lifestyles that, due to luck, are drastically divergent in their moral status" (2006: 9). That a vicious person engages in vicious activity is not a matter of luck; it is just playing out his character. *How* vicious his actions will turn out to be and what particular form they will take will depend on the contingent circumstances in which he finds himself, for example, growing up in Germany in the 1930s, but his moral status under these circumstances would not be drastically different from the one he would obtain under different circumstances.

But, as we learn from Milgram-like experiments, circumstances have a much more dramatic effect on the behavior of people than this argument assumes. Some would say that they are all that matter,[7] but even if one does not go that far, it is evident that many people who behaved very badly in the circumstances in which they were trapped would have led a completely normal life if the circumstances had been different, and the other way round; many people who led a normal life marked by no especially immoral behavior would have behaved very badly had they lived under different circumstances. Thus, the moral status of most people depends on the circumstances in which they find themselves, which are a matter of luck, both (and obviously) on the lack of control account and also on the modal one. There are nearby possible worlds where Hitler fails to come to power, in which Nagel's German citizen commits no atrocities and leads a peaceful life as a businessman in Berlin.

To conclude, then, Pritchard might be justified in rejecting moral luck (I leave that an open question), but his critique has a very loose connection, if any, to his general account of luck.[8]

Hales: "The Problem with Moral Luck is Luck Itself"[9]

In Hales's view, there are three different accounts of luck which usually overlap but, at times, part company. The first is the control account according to which an event is lucky (for some subject) if its occurrence is beyond her control. It is widely agreed that this is the most common understanding of "luck" in discussions of moral luck.[10] The second is the probability account, according to which an event is lucky (for some subject) if its occurrence is improbable. The third is the modal account which was introduced in the previous section. Since, in Hales's view, the notion of luck is unambiguous in ordinary language: there is no justification for assuming that it has a different meaning in the different philosophical contexts in which it is used, mainly in ethics vs. epistemology. That is to say, a constraint on any theory of the meaning of luck is that this meaning is held constant in more or less all contexts in which it is (properly) used.

The next step in Hales's argument is to argue that the first account—luck as lack of control—is the only one that could work in morality. If "luck" in "moral luck" referred to either of the other accounts (improbability or modal) then it would be impossible to make sense of some of the paradigmatic cases of moral luck mentioned by Nagel. However, argues Hales, if luck meant lack of control, it would lead to absurd results in epistemology, as it would make everything about knowledge a matter of luck (Hales 2015: 2395). Since we have only limited control over the beliefs that we hold, over the extent to which we are justified in holding them, and, quite obviously, over their truth, knowledge cannot be within our control, hence—on the control account—it is a matter of luck. Hales believes that this leads to an impasse:

> We can (1) reject the control theory of luck, which allows the preservation of epistemic luck but eliminates moral luck, or we can (2) accept the control theory, which lets us keep moral luck but botches epistemic luck entirely.
>
> *2015: 2396*

Hales believes that the way out of the impasse is to adopt option (1). The general lesson that follows from his analysis is that Williams, Nagel, et al. could have believed in the existence of moral luck only because they were somewhat confused about the meaning of "luck" in this expression. In Hales's view, once this term is properly defined, we can see that there is no such thing as moral luck; that it is not "a genuine thing of its own right" (2015: 2385). The celebrated problem of moral luck thus turns out to be one of those philosophical problems that rest on a conceptual confusion.

Or does it? I would like to raise three reasons against this conclusion. First, to get out of the above impasse, we are not forced to deny the reality of moral luck; we could just as well "botch epistemic luck entirely." Why would epistemic luck be botched? Because Hales understands its scope as relatively narrow, applying mainly to Gettier cases. Yet this distinctive interest of epistemic luck is not captured by the control account of luck which, as explained above, is very broad and encompassing.

But I see no reason to limit the meaning of epistemic luck in this way. Gettier-like cases are a great starting point to realize the effect of luck on (what is standardly believed to be) knowledge. Yet, once this is realized, the door is open to realizing that luck has a much broader effect on knowledge, one that ultimately undermines its very possibility. This is so because knowledge is traditionally regarded as distinct from true belief precisely by its resistance to luck. In this sense, epistemic luck is no different from moral luck. In both fields, supporters of luck start with paradigm examples—Gettier cases in epistemology, the pair of negligent drivers in ethics—and then move to more general and radical claims about the role of luck in the relevant field. In fact, both Nagel and Williams go this way in their original discussions. A more accurate formulation of option (2), consistent with Hales's argument, would therefore be that if the control account of luck is admitted (which would allow the preservation of moral luck), we would be forced to deny the very possibility of knowledge because "justified true belief is riddled with luck every step of the way" (Hales 2015: 2396).[11] But the wish to avoid the devastating effects of luck (under the lack of control account) in epistemology cannot by itself justify the rejection of this account and, consequently, is insufficient to reject the possibility of moral luck. Hales's main argument against the control account of luck, therefore, seems to fail. That this account leads to skepticism with regard to the very possibility of knowledge provides no reason to think that the account is mistaken. Maybe the contrary. We can now realize how widespread the illusion of control is and how important it is, intellectually and ethically, to expose it.

Second, it is rather unclear what Hales means in the conclusion of his paper when he says that moral luck is not a "real (or a 'genuine') thing in its own right" (2015: 2401). I do not see why supporters of moral luck should be committed to this rather obscure proposition. What they are committed to is something like the claim that factors beyond our control often determine our moral status, in particular influence our blame- and our praiseworthiness. To motivate this claim, they point to pairs of cases such as the negligent driver who got home safely vs. the one who hit a pedestrian. They contend that although the difference between them is a matter of luck (it is out of the driver's control that some pedestrian decided to cross the road at the wrong moment), holding different judgments for each of them is justified. Opponents of moral luck, by contrast, contend that the drivers are equally blameworthy. They are blameworthy for their negligent driving, which assumingly *was* under their control, not for hitting the pedestrian which was not. As explained above, according to Hales, the conceptual analysis of "luck" leads to the conclusion that moral luck is not a real thing. Does this mean that, in his view, the two drivers are equally blameworthy? This normative conclusion clearly does not follow from the above argument about the meaning of "luck." At most, what follows is that this word should not be used in any attempt to account for the apparent moral difference between the two drivers. But whether or not this advice should be adhered to (see below), it seems to make a rather minimal contribution to the question that is at the heart of what is known as the moral luck problem, namely, what role is played by what an agent *actually* does—in contrast to what she would have done based on her character, intentions, and efforts—in determining her moral status, in particular her praise- and blameworthiness.

Third, it seems false to contend that those who explicate moral luck in terms of (lack of) control have in mind a general *definition* of luck, such that an event or state of affairs, E, is a matter of luck for some subject, S, iff E's occurrence is not in S's control. Such a definition would immediately face the sunrise objection; the rise of the sun is good for us and also beyond our control, but it is surely not a matter of *luck*. But this objection is so obvious that we should refrain from ascribing the above definition to any serious philosopher. Indeed, in most cases in which participants in the moral luck debate assume a connection between luck and (lack of) control, it is obvious that they have in mind a one-way entailment (if E is a matter of luck for S, then S has no control over E)[12] and not a two-way one (adding that if S has no control over E, then E is a matter of luck for S).[13]

That many philosophers use "luck" in this sense without attempting a definition does not mean that they are using it as a "mere term of art" (Hales 2015: 2400). Lack of control captures a central aspect of what we mean by "luck"—albeit not *all* that we mean by it. So even if it is the case that "there is no philosophical compulsion to talk about luck at all in moral contexts" (ibid.), doing so might turn out to be quite helpful in grasping the philosophical problems that are raised by cases like those of the two negligent drivers, the criminal and the would-be criminal, and so on.

Finally, Hales believes that understanding "luck" in terms of lack of control does not enable a better grasp of the relevant philosophical issues. It is a case of *obscurum per obscuras*; replacing one obscure notion (luck) with an equally obscure one (control). But this assumed obscurity of control is inconsistent with Hales's strategy mentioned earlier in his chapter, where he concedes that although the control account of luck could explain the phenomenon of moral luck, it fails in accounting for epistemic luck. If the notion of control was so obscure, it would not be helpful in any context, either moral or epistemic.[14]

The Lockharts: Why Successful Attempts Are Not a Matter of Luck

For the purpose of their paper, Jennifer and Tom Lockhart subscribe to the common view that explicates luck in terms of lack of control (Lockhart & Lockhart 2017: 308). They agree, however, with Hales, that very little has been said to clarify what the notion of luck amounts to. In their view, once this notion is properly analyzed, many cases that are traditionally seen as cases of moral luck will be shown not to be so. Although they do not attempt to solve the problem of moral luck, they do regard their arguments as "largely in sympathy" with its denial. Thus, their paper serves as another example of an attempt to (at least partially) solve the problem of moral luck by a philosophical analysis of the concepts that underlie it, namely luck and control. In their case, too, I am skeptical as to how far this analysis can take us.

The Lockharts do not target all kinds of moral luck, only resultant luck, and, within this category, only intentional actions and not cases of negligence. The classic pair of cases that they start with is that of two assassins, Smith and Stith. Smith succeeds in killing her victim while Stith fails to do so because, at the crucial moment, a bird flies in the line of the bullet. The standard way to analyze this pair of cases by deniers of moral luck is as follows: if one accepts the Control Principle (CP), according to which "we are morally assessable only to the extent that what we are assessed for depends on factors under our control" (Nelkin 2013),[15] then there should be no moral difference in the assessment of the two assassins. In terms of what was under their control—their corrupt character, their decision to carry out the assassination, their actual attempt to do so (loading the gun, pointing it at the victim's head, pulling the trigger)—there is no difference between them. However, argue supporters of moral luck, we do assess them differently, which seems to yield the Morality Beyond Control Principle (MBC): "The scope of that for which we are morally assessable extends beyond that which is under our control" (Lockhart & Lockhart 2017: 308), or, put simply, luck plays a role in moral blameworthiness.

That Stith, the unsuccessful assassin, is (morally) lucky by the chance flight of the bird in the way of his bullet seems obvious. If it were not for that bird, he would be a *murderer*. An event that was completely beyond his control dramatically changed his moral status (and, in many countries, his legal status as well). But what about Smith, the successful assassin? Can he also be said to be subject to luck? The common wisdom in the field which derives from Nagel's own treatment of the case is that he can. If Stith's attempt was a matter of good (moral) luck, then so was that of Smith—though in the case of the latter it was bad (moral) luck. According to the CP, they should be equally assessable for the factors within their control (their decision to murder, their preparations, their actual attempt) and equally *un*assessable for what was beyond their control, namely, that the bullet they fired would have actually killed the victim—but clearly they are not. And this seems to lend support to the MBC principle.

As the Lockharts rightly note, proponents of the CP prefer to deal with cases like Smith and Stith by (a) claiming that upon reflection the moral difference between them disappears and (b) by offering an error theory about the source of the mistaken thought that they are morally different. The Lockharts believe that this strategy is misguided. It assumes that Smith was not in control of killing his victim and concludes from this assumption that, in accordance with the CP, we must assume that

Smith is not assessable for the killing, only (maybe) for those properties of his inner world that were causally related to the murder (and over which he could be said to have had control). As an alternative strategy to defending the CP (to which the Lockharts themselves are not committed—see Lockhart & Lockhart 2017: 324n2), they argue that Smith *was* in control of killing his victim, hence holding him blameworthy for doing so does not violate the CP and is not a case of luck affecting morality.[16] What underlies this strategy?

According to the Lockharts, the lesson that is usually inferred from the comparison between Smith and Stith is unwarranted. The inference goes as follows: Since Stith made the same effort as Smith to assassinate his victim but failed due to luck, Smith's *success* was similarly due to luck. He could have made the same effort he actually did without thereby killing his victim. Effort, therefore, is insufficient to produce the required intervention in the world, which is assumingly left for Fortuna to do. The problem with this line of thought is that it is based on the denial of agency. Agency, argue the Lockharts, "simply is the capacity to control what happens in the world" (2017: 318), a capacity that almost all persons enjoy. This capacity is imperfect, as we sometimes fail to change the world in the ways we attempt; we try to kill somebody and a bird blocks the bullet we fire. However, they argue:

> It does not follow from the *imperfection* of this capacity, from the fact that we may fail to exercise the capacity successfully, that what it is a capacity for is not *exercising* control. When the capacity is exercised successfully, therefore, in paradigmatic cases of action, the effort ensures that the agent will have performed the action.
>
> *Lockhart & Lockhart 2017: 318*

In other words, in paradigmatic cases of action (like that of Smith), the effort to φ *is* the performance of φ rather than something that merely prepares for it, so to say. It is, thus, false to say that Smith and Stith made the same effort (to assassinate their respective victims) and differed only in the way their efforts affected the world, efforts that were assumingly beyond their control (hence a matter of luck). Smith *was* in control of killing his victim, while Stith was not. Stith should be described as making a "mere effort" to kill his victim, while Smith's effort should be seen as identical to the act of killing his victim.

The Lockharts believe that the invalid inference mentioned above is parallel to a famous skeptical argument in epistemology that infers from the fallibility of our perceptual experience that such experience can never yield knowledge of the external world. McDowell's response to this argument that inspired the Lockharts in our context is that to have a perceptual capacity precisely *is* to have the capacity "to get into positions in which one has indefeasible warrants for certain beliefs," beliefs that transcend the subject's consciousness and capture something about the world "out there" (McDowell 2010: 245). The common fallacy in both fields is the thought that since we are imperfect in φ-ing (be it acting or perceiving) then even in paradigmatic cases of φ-ing we do not have the capacity *to* φ, only the capacity to *try* to φ.

To conclude, then, in the Lockharts' view, a proper understanding of what it means to be in control (of some action) leads to the conclusion that in paradigmatic cases of action, like that of Smith, it makes no sense to say that the agent's action was out of control, or (what amounts to the same thing) that it was a matter of luck.[17] Thus, examples like Smith and Stith do not lend support to the idea that the scope of the actions for which we are morally judged is beyond our control.

The Lockharts are clear about the modest goal of their paper. The paper does not presume to solve the problem of moral luck, they say, only to undermine a central motivation for assuming that such luck exists. Although they share with proponents of moral luck the intuition that Smith and Stith ought to be morally evaluated differently, they do not presume to provide an argument for this intuition. The point of their paper is to argue against *one* of the arguments that is supposed to undermine it, namely, that based on the assumed incompatibility of MBC with CP. Specifically, they seek to undermine the thought that Smith and Stith ought not to be assessed differently because what they were in control of was the same.[18]

Moreover, of the four types of moral luck listed by Nagel (resultant, circumstantial, constitutive, and causal[19]), the motivation on which they focus applies only to one, namely resultant luck. And even within this category they refer only to cases of intentional behavior, not to those of negligence. They would have to limit the type of luck that they are targeting even further to exclude what Nagel calls cases of decision under uncertainty, which are common in public and in private life (Nagel 1993: 61–62). For instance, a political leader signs a peace treaty with a former enemy. A year later it either turns out that this was a brilliant move, leading to peace, stability, and prosperity, or that it was a tragic decision, leading to yet another cycle of violence and bloodshed. With regard to cases like this, the Lockharts' strategy does not seem to work, probably because they are not "paradigmatic cases of *action*." They are best described as attempts (or "mere attempts") to achieve peace, the success of which, and hence the moral status of the relevant agents, clearly depend on factors beyond their control. Nobody would say that the effort to make peace, or the act of signing a peace treaty, is identical to the bringing about of a stable peace between two former enemy states.

In spite of these limitations, the Lockharts contend that their argument encourages resistance to the basic idea held by defenders of moral luck, namely, that people are sometimes morally assessable for factors beyond their control. I am not convinced, however, and in the remainder of this section I try to explain why.

The Lockharts concede that the moral evaluation of Smith and Stith will be, and *ought* to be, different. The common wisdom is that this shows how luck, understood in terms of lack of control, affects (or, if you wish, contaminates) moral judgments; it was Fortuna that turned Smith's effort, or bodily movement, into an act of murder while blocking Stith's effort from bringing about a similar result. By contrast, in the view put forward by the Lockharts, the different evaluation of Smith and Stith is no indication of the intervention of Fortuna. Consistent with the CP, both of these agents are assessed only for factors under their control. Smith was in control of the assassination that he carried out, hence he is evaluated for that. Stith was in control of forming the relevant intention and of attempting to carry it out, and he is morally evaluated for that. Neither illustrates a case of luck affecting morality.

I suspect that most readers would feel dissatisfied by this way of denying (or undermining) the effect of luck. This dissatisfaction has to do with a worry that the Lockharts themselves raise at the end of their paper, namely, that the inner state of Stith seems just as bad as that of Smith, hence they deserve the same level of blameworthiness. Why their inner states seem morally identical is obvious; they formed the same intention, made the same preparations, and in the end pulled their triggers with the purpose of killing—with Stith failing only because of factors beyond his control. That we nonetheless evaluate these agents differently—these *agents*, not (only) their *behavior*—shows that factors beyond our control, or, if you prefer, factors external to us, influence blameworthiness and praiseworthiness.

In other words, the normative question of whether Smith and Stith should be evaluated differently in spite of their inner world being relevantly similar (their intentions, desires, characters, and so on)—ultimately the central question in the moral luck debate—remains open however one analyzes the relation between efforts, attempts, and actions, and however one understands the notion of being-in-control.[20] The heirs of Kant propose that all we should care about in the moral evaluation of agents is their inner world, their good (or bad) will. To the extent that we care about actions, that is only because they typically express the will of the agents. Those in the other camp contend that what a person *actually* does is critical in morally evaluating her,[21] hence there is a moral distinction between the judge who took a bribe and the one who would have taken a bribe but was never offered one, and between the murderer who killed an innocent person and the one who would have done so if a bird had not shown up at the right moment to shield the victim.

Concluding Thoughts

Nagel and his followers point to pairs of cases that leave us deeply puzzled. On the one hand, we have the Kantian intuition that what matters morally is the inner world of agents, and this intuition makes us think that the agents in each of the pairs mentioned in the literature (Smith and Stith; the negligent drivers; the Nazi and the would-be Nazi; etc.) are morally equal. On the other hand, we have the intuition that the agents who actually cause bad results (through assassination, negligence, or mass murder) are morally worse—usually *much* worse—than their counterparts who do not. The way that Nagel sought to capture the puzzle was by talking about the role of *luck* in moral judgments, but the puzzle can be fully appreciated even without using this notion. Instead of luck, one can talk about lack of control which was Nagel's main intention in using this term in any case.[22]

Seeing control as the element that differentiates between the twin agents in the above cases does not necessarily mean that *neither* of them was in control of the relevant action/result (at least as far as resultant luck is concerned). To create the sense of puzzle (or paradox, as Nagel (1993: 66) has it), it is enough that *one* of them is judged for what was outside her control. On the Kantian view, that is sufficient to make it a mystery that the unlucky agent is evaluated better or worse than her twin-agent in spite of them having a relevantly similar inner world.

To conclude, then, achieving conceptual clarity is always a virtue in philosophy and this also applies to the central notions in the moral luck literature, those of luck and of control. Nonetheless, I am skeptical as to whether a better understanding of these notions will yield a solution to the problem or will even facilitate significant progress. Whatever labels we use, we cannot escape the sense of paradox that emerges when we face cases like Smith and Stith, the actual and the would-be Nazi, the negligent drivers, and so on. To overcome the paradox (if it *can* be overcome),[23] we must first realize how widespread it is and how diverse are the forms it takes, and second, we must develop a theory of blameworthiness. A central task of this theory will be to either provide a normative justification for the fact that "we judge people for what they actually do or fail to do, not just for what they would have done if circumstances had been different" (Nagel 1993: 66), or to explain why this practice is misguided. In the more conventional terms of this debate which still seem to me apt, such a theory will either justify the fact that luck plays a role in morality, or will explain it away.

Notes

1 Thanks to Bob Hartman for very helpful comments, to Tom and Jenn Lockhart for patiently clarifying their view to me, and to Oleg Krasnobayev for excellent research assistance.
2 See Zagzebski (1994) and Katzoff (2004).
3 Whittington (2014: 656) observes that "luck itself has for a long time been left undefined," but believes that it is now a better-defined notion, which helps to "get moral luck right," as the title of his paper suggests. Similarly, Pritchard (2006: 2) says that "what has been noticeably lacking in the literature is an assessment of the *manner* in which Williams and Nagel employ the concept of luck in their arguments."
4 See Hales (2015: 2386): "Shockingly under-examined is the genus of luck itself."
5 After I had started working on this chapter, I came across a footnote in Hartman (2016: 2846, n. 1) that makes a similar statement against Hales, namely, that "we do not need to know what luck is in order to inquire about relationship between control, praiseworthiness, and blameworthiness." In a sense, then, the current chapter can be seen as a footnote to that footnote.
6 See also Pritchard (2015: 147).
7 See, for instance, Harman (2000: 223–226).
8 See also Hartman (2017: 25–27) who argues that even if Pritchard was right about the nature of luck, the problem of moral luck would survive under a different name rather than be dissolved.
9 Hales (2015: 2385).
10 Hales (2015: 2387) notes that Peels is the only philosopher who explicitly does *not* adopt a straight control view; see also Pritchard (2006: n. 3).

11 I elaborate on the extent to which luck (in the sense of lack of control) undermines knowledge in Statman (1991).

12 See, for instance, the following citations which I borrow from Pritchard (2006: n. 3): "[S]omething which occurs as a matter of luck with respect to someone P is something which occurs beyond P's control" (Zimmerman 1993: 231); "[T]o say that something occurs as a matter of luck is just to say that it is not under my control" (Greco 1995: 83); "'As a matter of luck' here means: in a way that is beyond our control" (Moore 1990: 301); "By 'luck' I mean factors, good or bad, beyond the control of the affected agent" (Card 1990: 199).

13 I, therefore, do not share Whittington's assertion that "due to the more recent analysis of luck, LCAL [the lack of control account of luck] has been shown to be a flawed general account of luck" (Whittington 2014: 656). Within this account, lack of control is seen as a necessary condition for luck, not a sufficient one.

14 For a similar argument against Hales, see Hartman (2017: 29–31).

15 Dana Nelkin, "Moral Luck," in *The Stanford Encyclopedia of Philosophy*, cited by Lockhart and Lockhart (2017: 308).

16 The fact that Smith is blameworthy for the killing leaves open the possibility that he is *as* blameworthy as Stith, the would-be murderer, which is the position taken by Zimmerman (1993), Enoch & Marmor (2007), and others. However, the Lockharts make clear that in their view Smith ought to be judged morally more harshly than Stith.

17 That leaves open the possibility that some indirect results of the assassination, such as the depression that afflicts the son of the victim, are outside Smith's control and hence are a matter of (bad) moral luck. The Lockharts are, therefore, not committed to the denial of the common distinction between actions and results.

18 Thanks to the Lockharts for clarifying this point in correspondence.

19 The last two labels are mine, not Nagel's. See my Introduction in Statman (1993: 11).

20 The Lockharts concede that, for all they say, it might be true that because the inner states of Smith and Stith are morally identical, the correct moral evaluation of Smith and Stith is identical. Their point is just that one need not be forced to such a conclusion by Smith/Stith-like examples (email correspondence, January 2018).

21 See Nagel (1993: 66): "We judge people for what they actually do or fail to do, not just for what they would have done if circumstances had been different," and Driver (2012: 6) cited by Whittington (2014: 656): "When it comes to the significance of outcomes, people will frequently note that the agent's impact on the world is morally significant and to deny that significance encourages a kind of moral solipsism."

22 Here I am again walking in the footsteps of Hartman (2017: chapter 2).

23 Nagel believes that it cannot, that "in a sense the problem has no solution" (1993: 68).

References

Card, C. (1990) "Gender and Moral Luck," in O. Flanagan & A. Rorty (eds.) *Identity, Character, and Morality*, Cambridge: MIT Press, pp. 199–218.

Driver, J. (2012) "Luck and Fortune in Moral Evaluation," in M. Blaauw (ed.) *Contrastivism in Philosophy*, London: Routledge, pp. 154–172.

Enoch, D., & Marmor, A. (2007) "The Case against Moral Luck," *Law and Philosophy* 26, 405–436.

Greco, J. (1995) "A Second Paradox Concerning Responsibility and Luck," *Metaphilosophy* 26, 81–96.

Hales, D. (2015) "A Problem for Moral Luck," *Philosophical Studies* 172, 2385–2403.

Harman, G. (2000) "The Nonexistence of Character Traits," *Proceedings of the Aristotelian Society* 100, 223–226.

Hartman, R.J. (2016) "Against Luck-Free Moral Responsibility," *Philosophical Studies* 173, 2845–2865.

——. (2017) *In Defense of Moral Luck: Why Luck Often Affects Praiseworthiness and Blameworthiness*, New York: Routledge.

Katzoff, C. (2004) "Religious Luck and Religious Virtue," *Religious Studies* 40, 97–111.

Lockhart, J., & Lockhart, T. (2017) "Moral Luck and the Possibility of Agential Disjunctivism," *European Journal of Philosophy* 26, 308–332.

McDowell, J. (2010) "Tyler Burge on Disjunctivism," *Philosophical Explorations* 13, 243–255.

Moore, A.W. (1990) "A Kantian View of Moral Luck," *Philosophy* 65, 297–321.

Nagel, T. (1993) "Moral Luck," in D. Statman (ed.) *Moral Luck*, Albany: State University of New York Press, pp. 57–72.

Nelkin, D. (2013) "Moral Luck," in *The Stanford Encyclopedia of Philosophy* (Winter 2013 Edition), Edward N. Zalta (ed.) https://plato.stanford.edu/archives/win2013/entries/moral-luck/

Pritchard, D. (2006) "Moral and Epistemic Luck," *Metaphilosophy* 37, 1–25.

——. (2015) "The Modal Account of Luck," in D. Pritchard & L.J. Whittington (eds.) *The Philosophy of Luck*, New York: Wiley Blackwell, pp. 143–168.

Definition of "Luck"

Statman, D. (1991) "Moral and Epistemic Luck," *Ratio* 4, 146–156.

——. (1993) "Introduction," in D. Statman (ed.) *Moral Luck*, Albany: State University of New York Press, pp. 1–34.

Whittington, L.J. (2014) "Getting Moral Luck Right," *Metaphilosophy* 45, 654–667.

Williams, B. (1993) "Moral Luck," in D. Statman (ed.) *Moral Luck*, Albany: State University of New York Press, pp. 35–60.

Zagzebski, L. (1994) "Religious Luck," *Faith and Philosophy* 11, 393–413.

Zimmerman, Michael J. (1993) "Luck and Moral Responsibility," in D. Statman (ed.) *Moral Luck*, Albany: State University of New York Press, pp. 181–194.

18

KINDS OF MORAL LUCK

Carolina Sartorio

Nagel's Classification

There are different kinds of moral luck. Nagel (1979) famously identified four: resultant, circumstantial, constitutive, and causal. I start by explaining and discussing this classical taxonomy. In the rest of the chapter I focus on more recent developments and in potentially novel forms of moral luck.

Throughout the chapter, I will remain neutral on the question of whether there is, in fact, moral luck. So another way to describe my topic in this chapter is as follows: If we were to be committed to the existence of moral luck, what kinds of moral luck could we be committed to, as a result? Although this question is neutral on the existence of moral luck, thinking about it is a first important step toward taking a stand on that issue. For it can help us get clear on the full extent of the phenomenon, while at the same time helping us identify potentially relevant differences among the different kinds.

Let us start, then, with the classical taxonomy proposed by Nagel. We can illustrate Nagel's classification by focusing on a single example and considering different aspects of it at a time. I will use the example of a cold-blooded murderer who we blame for the shooting and killing of a victim on a certain occasion. According to Nagel, there is moral luck when the moral assessment of agents depends on factors that are beyond their control. Thus, the different kinds of moral luck in this case result from focusing on different kinds of factors that can be beyond the assassin's control and that can contribute to his assessment as a moral agent.

Note that this characterization of moral luck relies on an understanding of the concept of luck in terms of the lack of control of an agent (in our case, the assassin). I will follow Nagel and others in assuming this conception of luck. (Although this view is still quite standard in the moral luck literature, recently some philosophers have argued for alternative conceptions of luck; see, e.g., Pritchard (2005) and Levy (2011). But see Hartman (2017: ch. 2) for an argument that the standard lack-of-control conception is the one that is relevant to the problem of moral luck, even if it does not always match the ordinary usage of the word "luck.") Also, it is worth noting that Nagel's analysis focuses on a particular kind of moral assessment of agents: that of deserving blame (as in the case of the assassin) or praise. The literature on moral luck tends to follow Nagel on this point, so this will be my main focus here as well.

To motivate the different kinds of moral luck, consider, first, the *outcome* of the assassin's behavior: the victim's death. Note that many external factors contributed to that outcome coming about in the expected way. For example, imagine that a bird had flown by at the relevant time and had deflected the bullet away from its path. If such an event had happened, the victim would not have died. Hence the fact that this *did not* happen is one of the (many) factors that contributed to the outcome's occurrence. But whether such a bird flew by was, of course, not in the assassin's control. Still, had the bird flown by, we would have been inclined to blame the assassin less than in the actual case, because we would have blamed him for merely attempted murder instead of murder. Thus how blameworthy we are inclined to think the assassin is seems to depend on factors that are beyond the assassin's control: it seems to depend, in particular, on certain facts that helped determine the actual consequences of his behavior. This is *resultant* moral luck: moral luck about the outcomes or consequences of our behavior. (See also Williams (1981). The term "resultant moral luck" is from Zimmerman (1987).)

Next, note that the assassin only murdered somebody because he happened to be placed in circumstances where his violent tendencies were likely to be manifested. Had he never been placed in circumstances of that kind, he would not have shot anybody. To take an extreme case, imagine that he had been in a shipwreck and, as a result, had spent the rest of his adult life completely alone, as a castaway on a deserted island. In that case he would have escaped responsibility, not just for murder but also for attempted murder, since he would have never even attempted to murder anyone. Thus, how blameworthy we are inclined to think agents are also depends on other kinds of factors that are typically beyond their control, namely, the circumstances in which they find themselves and so the circumstances in which they act. This is *circumstantial* moral luck.

Next, note that yet another thing that had to happen for our assassin to shoot his victim is he had to have certain dispositions or character traits that would move him to perform that kind of act in the first place. Had he been placed in the relevant circumstances but lacked the relevant dispositions, he would not have performed or attempted to perform any murderous acts. For example, had he been born with very different (say, pacifist) tendencies, or, perhaps, had he been raised in a more loving environment, he would have never been moved to hurt anybody. Thus, how blameworthy we are inclined to think our assassin is also depends on other kinds of factors that are beyond his control: facts about his genes and the environment that contributed to his having a kind of internal constitution that led him to perform such a violent act. This is *constitutive* moral luck.

Finally, note that the assassin's behavior is also the result of more distant causes. In particular, if determinism is true, these causes are deterministic. This means that, given the laws of nature, and given the full state of the world at a time in the past (for example, some distant time before he was even born), there was only one possible way the world could have unfolded, and thus only one thing that the assassin could have done at the time. So, when we blame him for the murder, we are blaming him for the inevitable result of those remote causes, which were obviously outside his control. Had those causes been different in some relevant ways, he would not have committed the murder. But, as things stand, given the laws and the past, committing the murder was the only thing he could have done at the time. This is *causal* moral luck: moral luck about the causes of our behavior. According to Nagel, the problem of causal moral luck is just the classical problem of free will and determinism: the problem of whether acting freely and being morally responsible is compatible with living in a deterministic world.

So, on Nagel's view, there are four main kinds of moral luck. Changing the order slightly, these are: moral luck about the consequences of our behavior; its flipside: moral luck about the causes of our behavior; moral luck about the circumstances in which we act; and, finally, moral luck about our own constitution. In what follows I look a bit more closely at each category, by drawing attention to some recent developments.

Resultant Moral Luck

Let us start with resultant moral luck. The nature of this form of luck is, in fact, much richer than Nagel's discussion makes it seem. Here I will focus on just a few main points (for a more extended discussion, see Sartorio (2012)).

For starters, it is important to realize that the full nature of the phenomenon of resultant moral luck can only be seen in light of the concept of *derivative responsibility*. For resultant moral luck has to do with the consequences of our behavior and the conditions under which we can be morally responsible for them. And note that we are never directly or basically morally responsible for consequences. Instead, our responsibility in these cases is inherited from our responsibility for the behavior that led to those consequences. So this means that a closer investigation of the phenomenon of resultant moral luck will likely have to examine the conditions under which an agent's responsibility for a behavior makes him also responsible for the outcomes of that behavior, as well as the role played in this by factors that are beyond the agent's control.

To illustrate this point, consider the following variant on the assassin case. Imagine that when the assassin shoots he triggers a causal process that results in the victim's death but in a fully unexpected way. Imagine, for example, that when the bullet exits the gun a bird flies by and collides with the bullet, deflecting it away from its path but also seriously injuring the bird; however, when the victim, a *bird lover*, sees this, she is tremendously affected by the sight of the agonized bird and, as a result, dies of a heart attack in a matter of seconds. This is a case where the assassin's behavior causes the outcome, but the causal chain linking the behavior to the outcome is deviant (it departs from what was foreseeable or expected to happen in a substantial way). It is common to suggest that an agent cannot be morally responsible for the outcome in cases involving deviant causal chains (see, e.g., Feinberg 1970). If so, this suggests that what gives rise to the phenomenon of resultant moral luck is not *just* the fact that whether the act results in the outcome is partly due to factors beyond the agent's control, as Nagel's characterization makes it seem. Rather, or more precisely, it is the fact that what is beyond the agent's control is whether the act results in the outcome in the right kind of way. Thus, cases involving deviant causal chains point to an under-explored form of resultant moral luck. This is one where the relevant lack of control by the agent concerns not whether there is a causal link between the behavior and the outcome, but the form that such a causal link takes, or, in other words, the way in which the outcome is tied to the behavior.

Another important issue that has been the focus of some attention in recent years in the literature on moral responsibility is the phenomenon of resultant moral luck as it concerns "negative" agency: the omissions or non-doings of agents. Just like our positive actions, our omissions can have results and can make us responsible for those results. (This is so even if, for some, these are not causal results because omissions and other absences cannot have causal powers; see, e.g., Dowe (2001), who proposes a non-causal concept of consequence, "quasi"-causation, that applies to omissions and absences in general.) In many cases, whether our omissions result in outcomes is something that depends to a large extent on purely external factors. And these are factors that tend to be beyond our control.

To illustrate, imagine that you see a child drowning in the sea. Although you think you could easily save the child, you decide not to bother and the child dies. Now, imagine that, unbeknown to you, there were some hungry sharks swimming in the area that would have attacked you and killed you if you had attempted a rescue (this is a scenario discussed in Fischer and Ravizza (1998: ch. 5)). In this case, most think that, although you are blameworthy for not trying to save the child, you are not blameworthy for the child's death. Why are you not blameworthy for the child's death, if you are blameworthy for not trying to save him and he, in fact, died? The obvious answer seems to be: because, although he died, he did not die *as a result of* what you did. In other words: given the presence of the sharks, your behavior did not result in the child's death (see Sartorio 2016: ch. 2). If so, this is a case of resultant moral luck, one that involves an omission by an agent. In this case you are morally lucky because, due to the presence of external factors beyond your control (the sharks swimming in the water), your omission did not result in the expected outcome (although the outcome occurred); thus you are not blameworthy for the child's death. Had the sharks not been in the water, you would have been blameworthy for the child's death.

Scenarios of this kind are particularly interesting because they seem to show that the existence of the relevant kind of connection between the behavior and an outcome can depend on factors that are purely external in that they never actually come into play: they are not part of the process that leads to the child's death. Even if the sharks never intervene because you do not try to rescue the child, their mere presence seems enough to break the link between your behavior and the outcome, and to get you off the hook.

Note that this is a phenomenon that is likely to escape our attention if we are dealing just with positive acts. For example, in the assassin case, where the assassin shoots and kills his victim, it seems that all we have to look at to determine whether his behavior caused the outcome is the actual trajectory of the bullet (from the time it exits the gun until it hits the target) and any other factors that might have contributed to such a trajectory being what it is. Factors that are extrinsic to this process and that never come into play are just irrelevant. But, as we have seen, agents' omissions seem to be different in this respect. Thus, an investigation of omissions and the special conditions under which they can result in outcomes (thus making us responsible for those outcomes) seems important to understanding the full nature of the phenomenon of resultant moral luck and the different ways in which it can be manifested.

Circumstantial Moral Luck

Let us now turn to circumstantial moral luck. An interesting recent development concerning this category is the debate over "situationism" and its potential implications for our moral responsibility. Roughly, situationism is the claim that our behavior is heavily influenced by normatively irrelevant factors of the external circumstances ("situational factors"), in many cases without our being aware of such influence. Some argue that the surreptitious but pervasive influence of situational factors results in a special form of circumstantial moral luck ("situational" moral luck), and one that is particularly problematic (Herdova & Kearns 2015).

Consider, as an example, the "Good Samaritan" experiment in social psychology run by Darley and Batson (1973). Seminary students were asked to give a talk across campus. On the way there, they ran into a man who appeared to be (but was not really) in need of urgent medical care. The study found that whether the students were likely to help heavily depended on how much in a hurry they were: if they had been told that they had very little time to get to their lecture, they were much less likely to help than if they had been told that they had more time. Thus the study found that situational factors such as being in a rush and not being in a rush, which clearly make no difference to what one should do in these circumstances, heavily influence how people actually behave and how they respond to the reasons that they have.

More generally, studies of this kind suggest that agents can be held either blameworthy or praiseworthy for their acts depending on what kinds of situational factors influence their behavior, even if their being placed in those circumstances is outside their control, and even if they are completely unaware that they are being influenced by such factors. Note that in this case the difference in the moral assessment of agents is particularly significant because it is a difference in "valence" (blameworthy versus praiseworthy), and not just one in degree of responsibility (say, more blameworthy or less blameworthy, as in the case of the successful murderer versus the attempted murderer). Herdova and Kearns (2015) argue, for this and other reasons, that situational moral luck is an especially problematic form of moral luck.

Now, note that this also presupposes that agents in these scenarios retain a certain degree of control to be held morally responsible at all. This is an issue that has been the focus of some attention recently, especially within the context of theories that understand control in terms of responsiveness to reasons. (See, e.g., McKenna and Warmke (2017) and Sartorio (2018). Both are defenses of the idea that agents can be morally responsible in these scenarios because they retain a certain degree of reasons-responsiveness.)

Still, some argue that the influence of situational factors, if it were pervasive enough, would show that we are, in general, considerably less morally responsible than we typically think we are (see, e.g., Herdova & Kearns 2015, 2017). If so, this would result in a novel form of moral luck: one that concerns the degree or extent of our moral responsibility. I discuss another potential manifestation of this form of moral luck below. (For a development of a theory of moral responsibility that allows for degrees of responsibility, on the basis of degrees of reasons-responsiveness, see Coates and Swenson (2013).)

Constitutive Moral Luck

Let us now turn to constitutive moral luck. An important recent development that concerns this category is the debate between historical and non-historical theories of moral responsibility. Some theorists argue that the way in which agents come to acquire basic character traits and dispositions, which is something that tends to be outside of the agents' control, can matter to whether those agents are morally responsible for those dispositions or for the behavior that results from the exercise of the dispositions (this tracks the distinction between "direct" and "indirect" constitutive luck drawn by Enoch and Marmor (2007)).

Thus, *historical* views of responsibility are views that assign importance to the particular causal history of an agent's constitution. Historical views are sometimes motivated by considerations about luck that concern the "formative circumstances" of agents, which in some cases seem to act as exempting conditions (as suggested by Strawson (1962)). For example, drawing on Strawson's theory of responsibility, Watson (1987) discusses the example of Robert Harris, who brutally murdered two teenagers in order to use their car for a bank robbery. Watson points out that, although, on the face of it, Harris is a paradigmatic candidate for blame, our reactive attitudes toward him become more ambivalent once we find out about the history of neglect and abuse that led to a gradual change in his character and to his evil doings as an adult. The case of Harris is troubling, Watson also points out, because it brings out the important role that luck plays in the formation of our moral selves: it is unsettling to come to realize how incredibly fragile our moral selves are, and the fact that there is a sense in which we are all "potential evildoers" (Watson 1987: 132).

More recently, historical views have been motivated by appeal to scenarios of manipulation: scenarios where agents are manipulated into having and endorsing certain values, on the basis of which they then go on to act. Intuitively, we feel that, if an agent has been forcefully manipulated into having certain values on the basis of which she then acts, she cannot be morally responsible for what she does. Thus, some historical views aim to accommodate intuitive judgments of this kind (see, e.g., Mele 1995, 2006; Fischer & Ravizza 1998).

On the other hand, others have defended *non-historical* views of responsibility. These are views according to which, roughly, all that matters for responsibility is the satisfaction of certain instantaneous or internal conditions at the time when the agent acts (at least in cases of basic responsibility; see, e.g., Frankfurt 1988, 2002; McKenna 2004, 2012). On these views, how the agent came to have a certain constitution is irrelevant to her moral responsibility.

Thus, the debate between historical and non-historical views of responsibility is a debate about the kind of history that it is acceptable for our internal constitutions to have in order for us to be morally responsible agents. It is a debate that brings into sharper focus the fact that our constitutions are in big part a matter of luck (so much so that they can be brought about by, for example, the intervention of external manipulators), and the importance of considering the implications that this fact might have for our overall conception of ourselves as morally responsible agents.

It is also worth noting that some have thought that the problem of moral luck is so fundamental that it completely undermines the moral responsibility of agents. Notably, Levy (2011) defends a generalized form of skepticism about moral responsibility on the basis of considerations about luck, including, in particular, constitutive moral luck (see also Strawson 1994).

Causal Moral Luck

Finally, let us turn to causal moral luck. In contrast with the other categories, there has not been much work on causal moral luck as such (that is, as a specific form of moral luck). The reason is that, as anticipated at the beginning of this chapter, the problem of causal moral luck tends to be identified with the traditional problem of free will, which is of course a large topic deserving of its own consideration. Thus many think that it is best to set causal moral luck aside in order to distinguish the problem of moral luck from the more familiar skeptical worries embodied in the classical problem of free will (see, e.g., Hartman 2017: 5).

Still, arguably, thinking about the problem of free will in light of Nagel's taxonomy can be fruitful in that it can help us see the problem for what it really is. For it can help us identify the real threat to our free will as the one posed by, basically, the existence of causes beyond our control. Let me explain. Although Nagel himself sees the problem of causal moral luck in terms of just the potential truth of determinism, it is arguably broader than this. The deeper threat seems to be that, if our acts are the result of remote causes beyond our control, there seems to be an important sense in which we are not the *ultimate sources* of our acts. The existence of those antecedent causes beyond our control is what allegedly threatens our free will. Determinism is just one particular, and especially vivid, form that such a threat can take: if determinism is true, those remote causes also necessitate our acts. But, even if those causes are merely probabilistic, the fact that our behavior can be traced back to those causes that occur at a distant time beyond our control is, arguably, still enough to generate the worry that we are not the ultimate sources of our choices, and thus that we are not free. (On this point, see, e.g., Watson 1982: 9; Pereboom 2001: 47; Nelkin 2013; Sartorio 2015a: 261–262. For a discussion of ultimacy and the alleged threat to our free will, see, e.g., Strawson 1994; Smilansky 2000.)

In fact, many see the *lack* of determinism (the truth of *in*determinism) itself as a threat to our free will. For indeterminism seems to introduce randomness, and thus a problematic form of luck, into the etiology of action. In response, some libertarians argue that agents can be in control given the right kinds of indeterministic causal chains ("naturalistic" libertarians such as Kane (1996) and Balaguer (2010)). Other libertarians argue that agents can only be in control given certain special irreducible causal powers that they have qua substances, which guarantees that they are the true originators of their actions ("agent-causal" libertarians such as Chisholm (1966), O'Connor (2000), and Clarke (2003)).

New Forms of Moral Luck

In this final section I discuss potentially novel forms of moral luck that have been discussed in the recent literature on moral responsibility. By "novel" I do not mean to suggest that these are wholly new *categories* of moral luck, since Nagel's classification seems exhaustive in this regard (it seems to cover all the different dimensions relevant to the moral evaluation of agents: consequences, causes, circumstances, and constitutions). What I mean, instead, is that they are important potential new *sources* of moral luck, which could in principle crosscut the different categories.

One potentially novel form of moral luck has its source in a graded notion of moral responsibility. Moral responsibility is commonly regarded as coming in degrees. Consider, again, the case of the successful assassin who is blameworthy for murder as opposed to the unsuccessful one who is only blameworthy for attempted murder. If there is resultant moral luck, it is natural to think of this difference as a difference in the degree of the agent's responsibility: although both assassins are blameworthy for something (even if not the same thing), one is more blameworthy than the other. (In this section I focus mostly on responsibility for outcomes and resultant moral luck. But recall that above I discussed a potential connection between the idea that responsibility comes in degrees and a form of circumstantial moral luck, situational moral luck. In principle, this is an issue that could arise in connection with any form of moral luck.)

Now, imagine that causation *also* comes in degrees. That is to say, imagine that some causal factors can make a larger contribution than others to the occurrence of a given outcome (for a development of this idea, see, e.g., Braham and van Hees (2009) and Kaiserman (2016).) This is also a quite intuitive idea. In fact, we often seem to assume that it is true, for example, when we find ourselves trying to determine, among many causally contributing factors, which was the largest contributor to an outcome such as a traffic accident, or the result of a presidential election. This assumes that some events can make a larger causal contribution than others.

Now, if causation and moral responsibility both come in degrees, it is natural to expect that, when agents are morally responsible for outcomes, the extent of their responsibility will track the extent of their causal contributions to those outcomes, among other things. In particular, it is natural to expect that, other things being equal, the larger the actual contribution to an outcome, the larger the agent's responsibility for that outcome. (For a development of this idea, see Moore (2009: chs 5 and 6). Some just war theorists appeal to a similar idea to argue for a principle of civilian immunity, on the basis of the claim that the contribution of civilians to unjust threats is typically too small to make them liable; see, e.g., McMahan (2009: 225).) But note that, in general, the extent of an agent's contribution to an outcome will be just as dependent on external factors beyond the agent's control as the issue of whether the agent made any contribution at all. Thus this results in a new form of resultant moral luck, one that concerns the degree of an agent's responsibility for an outcome.

Let me illustrate this point with another variant on the assassin example. Imagine that when the assassin shoots at his victim the bird flies by and intercepts the bullet. However, imagine that this only manages to slow the bullet down a bit, so its momentum is no longer enough to cause serious harm by itself. Still, imagine that, when the victim (a bird lover) sees the bird getting hurt, she starts to have heart palpitations and this, together with the bullet entering her heart at the same time, is sufficient to bring about her death. (So what you have to imagine is that the bullet and the heart palpitations *jointly* bring about the victim's death because they are jointly sufficient for the death's occurrence.) If causal contributions come in degrees, then arguably the assassin makes a less significant contribution in this variant of the case than in the original case. If so, assuming that degrees of responsibility track degrees of causal contribution, it follows that the assassin is less blameworthy in this case than in the original case. But note that, here too, the difference between the two cases is due to factors beyond the assassin's control. So this results in a new form of resultant moral luck: one according to which the extent of the agent's responsibility for an outcome depends on the extent of the agent's contribution to that outcome, where this is something that is partly determined by factors beyond the agent's control. (For a discussion of this potential new form of moral luck, see Bernstein (2017). On the other hand, some argue against the underlying idea of degrees of causal contributions, and thus against the intelligibility of this form of moral luck; see Tadros (2018) and Sartorio Ms.)

Another potential new form of moral luck, and a particularly puzzling one, has its source in the fact that sometimes the moral responsibility of agents seems to be directly affected by the moral responsibility of other agents, that is to say, by the very fact that there exist other agents who are morally responsible. Let me illustrate with an example: the famous desert traveler case discussed in the literature on causation in the law (see, e.g., Hart & Honore 1985). The case goes like this: A man is about to go on a trip to the desert for which he will need his water canteen. The man has two enemies, X and Y, who want him dead and who independently carry out their secret plans to bring about his death. X first secretly drains the water out of the canteen and refills it with sand (so that the man will not notice the change in weight). Unaware of what X has done, then Y steals the canteen, thinking that it still contains water. Finally, not realizing that the canteen is gone, the man starts his journey without any water and dies of thirst in the desert.

This case gives rise to an interesting and difficult puzzle. The puzzle is that, on the one hand, we clearly want to blame someone for the man's death, but, on the other hand, it is not clear how we can blame anybody for it. For note that what X did was drain the water out of a canteen that was not going to be available to the man at the time he would need it, given that Y was going to steal it later.

Kinds of Moral Luck

And what Y did, in turn, was steal a canteen that no longer contained any water, given what X did. So neither behavior on its own seems to make a contribution to the man's death, given what the other agent did. But, again, surely somebody is to blame for the man's death!

Although this is not the place to discuss the puzzle in depth, I will just point out that the most promising answer seems to me to say that, although neither agent was an individual cause of the death, the behaviors by the two agents somehow collectively contributed to the man's death, and to then argue that this fact is sufficient for our being able to blame at least one of them (either X or Y or both) for the man's death. (For a development of this solution to the puzzle, see Sartorio 2015b.) But what is important for our purposes here is that blame seems appropriate in this case only because there is more than one morally responsible agent trying to cause harm: if there had been just one morally responsible agent and everything else remained the same, blame would no longer be appropriate.

Consider, for example, the following variants of the case:

> *Variant 1*: This time only one enemy is around: Y. Some fluky natural process results in the water being drained out of the canteen and its being replaced with sand. Not realizing this, Y then comes along and steals the canteen filled with sand. Everything else is the same as in the original case.

> *Variant 2*: This time only one enemy is around: X. After he drains the water out of the canteen and replaces it with sand, some unrelated and fluky natural process results in the canteen's being completely vaporized. Everything else is the same as in the original case.

Note that X no longer seems morally responsible for the man's death in Variant 2, and Y no longer seems morally responsible for the man's death in Variant 1. These scenarios appear to be more analogous to standard cases of resultant moral luck where an agent tries to cause harm but fails to do so, and thus is morally lucky because he does not end up being morally responsible for the harm. But note that the only thing that has changed from the original case is that one of the agents has been replaced by a natural phenomenon. So this means that, when the natural phenomenon results in the canteen being empty of water or in its being vaporized, we are tempted to not hold the remaining agent responsible; however, when it is the work of another morally responsible agent, we tend to hold the agent(s) (one or both of them) responsible (see Sartorio (2015b); but see Talbert (2015) for a response). Now, of course, this is very puzzling, for each agent's individual contribution is exactly the same in all of these cases. So, how can the *mere* fact that there is another morally responsible agent make a difference of this kind, if it does not make any difference to the agent's contribution?

Although this is indeed very puzzling, the phenomenon seems to generalize to other cases. Recall the case of the drowning child discussed above: if you do not attempt a rescue because you do not care about the child, but there were sharks in the water that would have stopped you if you had tried, you are not morally responsible for the child's death. In this case you are morally lucky. But now imagine that, unbeknown to you, some evil or incredibly negligent person was in the process of releasing the sharks into the water as you were making the decision not to help the child. So now the child dies because of a combination of your behavior and this other person's behavior. Surely, in this case we want to blame somebody for the child's death (either you or the other person or both), just like we wanted to blame somebody for the man's death in the original desert traveler scenario where X and Y attempt to cause his death. But note, again, that the only thing that has changed in this new variant of the case is that we have replaced a natural phenomenon with another morally responsible agent; your individual contribution remains exactly the same.

So this seems to be another instance of the same puzzling phenomenon, where the mere existence of another morally responsible agent can affect your moral responsibility, without affecting your own contribution in any way. Again, this is a quite atypical (and particularly puzzling) form of resultant moral luck. For what we see in standard scenarios of resultant moral luck is that a factor beyond the agent's control affects the agent's responsibility for an outcome, but only because it affects the agent's actual contribution to that outcome. (For a discussion of this potential new form of moral luck, and also of whether it extends to other kinds beyond resultant moral luck, see Sartorio (2015c).)

Acknowledgments

Thanks to the editors for the invitation to contribute to this volume, and to Michael McKenna and Robert Hartman for helpful comments on earlier drafts.

References

Balaguer, M. (2010) *Free Will as an Open Scientific Problem*, Cambridge, MA: MIT Press.
Bernstein, S. (2017) "Causal Proportions and Moral Responsibility," in D. Shoemaker (ed.) *Oxford Studies in Agency and Responsibility*, vol. 4, Oxford: Oxford University Press, pp. 165–182.
Braham, M., & van Hees, M. (2009) "Degrees of Causation," *Erkenntnis* 71(3), 323–344.
Chisholm, R. (1966) "Freedom and Action," in K. Lehrer (ed.) *Freedom and Determinism*, New York: Random House, pp. 11–44.
Clarke, R. (2003) *Libertarian Accounts of Free Will*, New York: Oxford University Press.
Coates, J., & Swenson, P. (2013) "Reasons-Responsiveness and Degrees of Responsibility," *Philosophical Studies* 165(2), 629–645.
Darley, J., & Batson, C. (1973) "'From Jerusalem to Jerico:' A Study of Situational and Dispositional Variables in Helping Behavior," *Journal of Personality and Social Psychology* 27(1), 100–108.
Dowe, P. (2001) "A Counterfactual Theory of Prevention and 'Causation' by Omission," *Australasian Journal of Philosophy* 79(2), 216–226.
Enoch, D., & Marmor, A. (2007) "The Case against Moral Luck," *Law and Philosophy* 26, 405–436.
Feinberg, J. (1970) "Sua Culpa," in *Doing and Deserving: Essays in the Theory of Responsibility*, Princeton, NJ: Princeton University Press, pp. 187–221.
Fischer, J.M., & Ravizza, M. (1998) *Responsibility and Control*, Cambridge: Cambridge University Press.
Frankfurt, H. (1988) *The Importance of What We Care About*, Cambridge: Cambridge University Press.
——. (2002) "Reply to John Martin Fischer," in S. Buss & L. Overton (eds.) *Contours of Agency*, Cambridge, MA: MIT Press, pp. 27–31.
Hart, H.L.A., & Honore, T. (1985) *Causation in the Law*, second edition, Oxford: Oxford University Press.
Hartman, R. (2017) *In Defense of Moral Luck: Why Luck Often Affects Praiseworthiness and Blameworthiness*, New York: Routledge.
Herdova, M., & Kearns, S. (2015) "Get Lucky: Situationism and Circumstantial Moral Luck," *Philosophical Explorations* 18(3), 362–377.
——. (2017) "This is a Tricky Situation: Situationism and Reasons-Responsiveness," *Journal of Ethics* 21(2), 151–183.
Kaiserman, A. (2016) "Causal Contribution," *Proceedings of the Aristotelian Society* 116(3), 387–394.
Kane, R. (1996) *The Significance of Free Will*, New York: Oxford University Press.
Levy, N. (2011) *Hard Luck: How Luck Undermines Free Will and Moral Responsibility*, Oxford: Oxford University Press.
McKenna, M. (2004) "Responsibility and Globally Manipulated Agents," *Philosophical Topics* 32, 169–192.
——. (2012) "Moral Responsibility, Manipulation Arguments, and History: Assessing the Resilience of Nonhistorical Compatibilism," *Journal of Ethics* 16, 145–174.
McKenna, M., & Warmke, B. (2017g) "Does Situationism Threaten Free Will and Moral Responsibility?" *Journal of Moral Philosophy* 14(6), 698–733.
McMahan, J. (2009) *Killing in War*, Oxford: Oxford University Press.
Mele, A. (1995) *Autonomous Agents: From Self-Control to Autonomy*, New York: Oxford University Press.
——. (2006) *Free Will and Luck*, New York: Oxford University Press.
Moore, M. (2009) *Causation and Responsibility: An Essay in Law, Morals, and Metaphysics*, Oxford: Oxford University Press.
Nagel, T. (1979) "Moral Luck," in *Mortal Questions*, New York: Cambridge University Press.
Nelkin, D. (2013) "Moral Luck," in *The Stanford Encyclopedia of Philosophy* (Winter 2013 Edition), Edward N. Zalta (ed.) https://plato.stanford.edu/archives/win2013/entries/moral-luck/.
O'Connor, T. (2000) *Persons and Causes: The Metaphysics of Free Will*, New York: Oxford University Press.
Pereboom, D. (2001) *Living Without Free Will*, Cambridge: Cambridge University Press.
Pritchard, D. (2005) *Epistemic Luck*, Oxford: Oxford University Press.
Sartorio, C. (2012) "Resultant Luck," *Philosophy and Phenomenological Research* 84(1), 63–86.

——. (2015a) "The Problem of Determinism and Free Will Is Not the Problem of Determinism and Free Will," in A. Mele (ed.) *Surrounding Free Will: Philosophy, Psychology, Neuroscience*, Oxford: Oxford University Press, pp. 255–273.

——. (2015b) "Resultant Luck and the Thirsty Traveler," *Methode* 4(6), 153–172.

——. (2015c) "A New Form of Moral Luck?" in A. Buckareff, C. Moya, & S. Rossell (eds.) *Agency, Freedom, and Moral Responsibility*, Basingstoke: Palgrave Macmillan, pp. 134–149.

——. (2016) *Causation and Free Will*, Oxford: Oxford University Press.

——. (2018) "Situations and Responsiveness to Reasons," *Noûs* 52(4), 796–807.

——. (Ms.) "More of a Cause?"

Smilansky, S. (2000) *Free Will and Illusion*, Oxford: Oxford University Press.

Strawson, G. (1994) "The Impossibility of Moral Responsibility," *Philosophical Studies* 75(1/2), 5–24.

Strawson, P. (1962) "Freedom and Resentment," *Proceedings of the British Academy*, reprinted in Watson (1982), pp. 59–80.

Tadros, V. (2018) "Causal Contributions and Liability," *Ethics* 128(2), 402–431.

Talbert, M. (2015) "Responsibility without Causation, Luck, and Dying of Thirst: A Reply to Sartorio," *Methode* 4(6), 173–184.

Watson, G. (ed.) (1982) *Free Will*, New York: Oxford University Press.

——. (1987) "Responsibility and the Limits of Evil: Variations on a Strawsonian Theme," in F. Schoeman (ed.) *Responsibility, Character, and the Emotions: New Essays in Moral Psychology*, Cambridge: Cambridge University Press, pp. 256–286.

Williams, B. (1981) *Moral Luck*, Cambridge: Cambridge University Press.

Zimmerman, M. (1987) "Luck and Moral Responsibility," *Ethics* 97, 374–386.

19

DENYING MORAL LUCK

Michael J. Zimmerman

The Nature of Moral Luck

The moral significance of luck has been debated since ancient times. (Two especially prominent figures in this debate are Aristotle (1941) and Kant (1964).) It is only in recent times, however, that philosophers have focused on what has come to be known as moral luck. The term "moral luck" was coined by Bernard Williams in a now-famous paper delivered at a meeting of the Aristotelian Society in 1976 (Williams 1993[1]), to which Thomas Nagel gave an equally famous reply (Nagel 1993). A minor industry was spawned. (It is important to note, however, that many of the issues with which Williams and, in particular, Nagel were concerned had been addressed more than a decade earlier by Joel Feinberg (Feinberg 1970: ch. 2).)

Moral luck is a species of luck. It is controversial just what luck is, although almost everyone agrees that it has three key components. (The controversy concerns just how these components are themselves to be understood.) First, luck typically pertains to personal welfare, and it is either good or bad. We normally do not cry out "What luck!" when what has happened carries no personal significance for anyone. Second, luck is typically a matter of chance. Although the odds are often high that *some* (un)lucky event will occur, an event will normally not qualify as (un)lucky if the odds were high that *it* would occur. Finally, luck is typically a matter of control—or, rather, the lack thereof. We normally do not declare someone (un)lucky if what happened was something over which he or she was in control.

We must now acknowledge an unfortunate, even if not unlucky, fact, and that is that, in almost all cases, discussion of what has been called moral luck has *not* been restricted to cases in which all three components just identified have played a role. Although Williams himself seems to have had all three components in mind, the matter is uncertain, since he never explicitly says so, remaining content simply with stating that he would "use the notion of 'luck' generously, undefinedly" (Williams 1993: 37). Nagel was not similarly noncommittal, but, in identifying what he meant by "luck," he explicitly stated that it was the third component in particular—lack of control—with which he was concerned (Nagel 1993: 59). He mentioned the first component only incidentally and the second not at all. The same is true of Feinberg (1970: 34 ff.) and of most, though not all, writers on moral luck since. Insofar as lack of control is typically insufficient for luck, this means that most discussions of so-called moral luck have been couched in misleading terms; for their specific target has been the moral significance of our lacking control over some state or event, *regardless* of whether its occurrence strictly qualifies as an instance of luck. (This means, in turn, that some critics of these discussions—e.g., Pritchard (2006)—have been off-target. Correctly pointing out that some of the discussions involve cases that are not strictly cases of luck, these critics have complained that these cases therefore do not speak to the moral significance of luck, overlooking the fact that the cases have simply been mislabeled and are really intended only to address the moral significance of the lack of control.) In keeping with most of the literature on moral luck, I will be construing luck liberally, and strictly inaccurately, as follows: someone S is lucky with respect to some proposition p just in case whether p is true is not within S's control. As we will see, p may concern either the occurrence of an event (such as the event of someone's dying) or the obtaining of some state (such as the state consisting of someone's being dead). If the state consists in some *moral* (or morally relevant) *fact about S* (such as the fact that S is morally obligated to prevent someone's dying, or the fact that S is morally responsible for someone's being dead), then it will qualify as an instance of *moral* luck in particular.

Given this stipulation about what luck in general and moral luck in particular come to, I must say something about how the relevant notion of control is to be understood. It is not only people that can control what happens (and thereby control whether some proposition is true). Thermostats control the temperature (and thereby control whether it is true that the ambient temperature is 68 °F); autopilots control the flight of airplanes; and so on. Indeed, people sometimes control what happens in much the same way as mere machines do. For example, by sweating or shivering, one controls one's body temperature. But people also often appear to exhibit a kind of control that mere machines cannot. A simple, mundane example is that of my raising my hand at will. The phrase "at will" is important. It is intended to convey the fact that whether I raise my hand is "up to me" (in a way in which maintaining or altering the temperature is not up to the thermostat), and if I raise my hand I thereby exercise the control I have over its being raised in a particular way; another particular way in which I might exercise this control is to *not* raise my hand but leave it at my side. Control, so understood, involves not only the possession of certain capacities but also the opportunity to exercise these capacities. Since I cannot run 100 meters in under 10 seconds, I am not in control of whether I do so. Usain Bolt can run 100 meters in under 10 seconds, but he too is not in control of whether he does so if he is asleep, or debilitated by illness, or bound to a chair.

It is important to recognize three distinct dimensions of the kind of personal control just sketched. For purposes of illustration, consider this well-known example (Davidson 1980: 4): "I flip the switch, turn on the light, and illuminate the room. Unbeknownst to me I also alert a prowler to the fact that I am home." As I construe this example, it is a certain executive decision of mine (a decision to do something "here and now") that sets a certain train of events in motion. We can picture the situation as shown in Figure 19.1.

The arrows represent causation. A, which consists simply of a, is the minimal action, if it can be called an action at all, constituted by my decision to act. B, which consists of my decision, a, causing the rising of my hand, b, is the action of my raising my hand. (In von Wright's terminology (von Wright 1971: 66), b is the "result" of B.) C, which consists of a's causing the change in position of the switch, c, is the action of my flipping the switch. D, which consists of a's causing the light's going on, d, is the action of my turning on the light. E, which consists of a's causing the room's illumination, e, is the action of my illuminating the room. And F, which consists of a's causing the prowler's

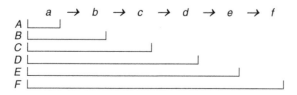

Figure 19.1 Alerting the prowler

being aware of my presence, f, is the action of my alerting the prowler. Note that, in light of the causal connections between a through f, I may be said to do F *by* doing E, E *by* doing D, D *by* doing C, and so on. In terminology that is familiar (but nonetheless sometimes used differently by different philosophers), A (or, possibly, B) is a *basic* action, while the others are *non-basic* actions. Figure 19.1 provides a graphic representation of this Russian-doll-like nesting of basic actions within non-basic actions within non-basic actions.[2]

As Figure 19.1 illustrates, an executive decision, as I conceive of it, occurs, not *prior to* the relevant action, but as *the initial part of* that action. In a typical case, the decision will be relatively close, in both causal and temporal terms, to the results of those actions of which it is a part, but it can on occasion be quite distant from such results. (Think of a killing in which the death occurs only months after the pertinent executive decision.) Moreover, an executive decision is typically one that the agent himself understands to constitute the initiation of action and to be the means by which he exercises control over consequent events.

The three dimensions of control illustrated in Figure 19.1 are these. First, control can be either *intentional* or *unintentional* (Mele 2003). The control I have over actions $A-E$ and their respective results $a-e$ is intentional, but the control I have over F and f is merely unintentional. Since I am wholly unaware of the prowler's presence, it no doubt sounds a little odd to say that alerting him is up to me. Nonetheless, it is clear that there is a genuine sense in which my alerting him is indeed within my control, precisely because the means of my doing so are within my control.

Second, control can be either *direct* or *indirect*. Whether the prowler is alerted is up to me, but only because I am in control of the room's being illuminated; moreover, I am in control of the room's being illuminated only because I am in control of the light's going on; and, of course, I am in control of the light's going on only because, ultimately, I am in control of my decision to act. It is a that is in my direct control; the other results of my actions, $b-f$, are in my control, but only indirectly so. (What of the *actions* $B-F$ themselves? Since they are composed of a combination of a, which is in my direct control, and some causal consequence of a, which is only in my indirect control, I think we should declare my control over them "*hybrid*.")

Finally, control can (in principle) be either *complete* or *partial*. One has complete control over something only if its occurrence is not contingent on anything that lies beyond one's control. Complete control is clearly unattainable by anyone at any time; any control that we ever have over anything is, at best, partial. For example, my control over any of $A-F$ and $a-f$, whether intentional or unintentional, direct or indirect or hybrid, can only be partial, since the occurrence of these events is contingent on the occurrence of a whole host of other events (such as my having been born, the earth's continuing to rotate on its axis, etc.) that lie and have always lain beyond my control.

One final preliminary point: Personal control of the kind at issue here is usually taken to be bilateral, in the sense that S has control over whether p is true just in case it is both the case that S can (i.e., has the capacity and opportunity to) see to it that p is true and the case that S can see to it that p is false. (For example, I have control over whether the light is on just in case I can both see to it that it is on and see to it that it is off.) Such control is now commonly called "regulative" control (Fischer 1994: 132). Appealing to cases in which a person can, allegedly, lack the option to do anything but what he in fact does and yet not be *compelled* to act as he does, some philosophers hold that there can also be a unilateral kind of control—"guidance" control—that S may have regarding p, even if S cannot see to it that p is false (Frankfurt 1969; Fischer 1994: 132). It is controversial just what guidance control is supposed to consist in and whether it is possible to have such control in the absence of regulative control. If mere guidance control is possible, then some of the remarks I make about moral luck below require qualification, but that is a complication that I will leave to one side. I will proceed under the assumption that, in all contexts, the kind of control at issue is regulative control.

I turn now to a discussion of four broad kinds of moral luck, the kinds differing according to the kinds of moral (or morally relevant) propositions at issue. The reason for this approach is straightforward. We should not assume at the outset that the affirmation or denial of one kind of moral luck requires the affirmation or denial of another kind.

Deontic Luck

Deontic propositions concern what one is *morally obligated* to do. Should we affirm or deny the existence of moral luck of *this* kind?

There is a well-known principle, often attributed to Kant (1965: A548/B576) and sometimes called OIC, that states that "ought" implies "can." The principle is controversial, in part because each of "ought" and "implies" and "can" is ambiguous. The principle is perhaps most often understood as holding that it is strictly impossible (either conceptually or metaphysically) for someone to be morally obligated to do something unless that person has both the capacity and the opportunity to do that thing. So understood, the principle comes close to the claim that moral obligation requires control—close, but not all the way. In order to get all the way there, the principle must be supplemented with the claim that "ought" also implies "can do otherwise." Let us label the principle, so supplemented, OIC★. I do not propose to inquire into whether OIC★ is true; I wish only to address its implications regarding the existence of deontic luck.

One puzzle that has preoccupied philosophers for centuries is the question of how moral responsibility is possible, given that it presupposes control and control seems to be impossible, in that it appears to be compatible with neither determinism nor indeterminism. I will return briefly to this puzzle later. A closely related puzzle, one that is noted not nearly so often (but see, e.g., Haji 2012: ch. 3), concerns the question of how moral obligation is possible. If OIC★ is true, and if control is impossible, being compatible with neither determinism nor indeterminism, then no one can ever be morally obligated to do anything. If so, it follows that, for each person S and action A, the proposition that S is not morally obligated to do A is both true and wholly beyond S's control. That would be a global form of deontic luck.

If, however, it is not only possible but in fact the case that we are sometimes in control of what we do, then OIC★ does not preclude our having moral obligations and this form of deontic luck does not exist. Nonetheless, it seems clear that some other forms do.

Suppose that you borrow a book from me at 9:00 a.m. with the promise to return it to me at noon. Noon arrives, and there is nothing preventing you from keeping your promise and nothing more important for you to do. It certainly seems reasonable to say that you have an obligation to return the book to me then—a claim that proponents of OIC★ are likely to endorse, and one that would seem to confirm the more general claim that whether we fulfill our moral obligations is up to us and so *not* a matter of luck. But two points should be noted.

First, even if you are in control of whether you return the book at noon, that control can again at best be partial, rather than complete, since your managing to return it will depend in part on events—such as your having been born, the earth's continuing to rotate, etc.—that lie beyond your control. Thus whether you fulfill your obligation will turn partly on factors that lie beyond your control and must still be declared lucky to *that* extent.

Second, it could happen that your obligation to return the book ceases to exist, in a way that lies beyond your control, prior to your having an opportunity to fulfill it. Suppose that I give you a call at 10:00 a.m., telling you that you need not return the book to me after all. "Keep it," I say, "it's yours." Then, arguably, although you did have an obligation to return the book, you no longer have this obligation. If so, your obligation has been extinguished in such a way that, even if I was in control of its ceasing to exist, you were not.

The forms of deontic luck just mentioned concern obligations that have already been incurred. Others concern their being incurred in the first place. Here again, there are two points to be noted.

First, whether the ground of an obligation exists might lie beyond one's control. Suppose, for example, that you are walking past a pond in which a small child is drowning (Singer 1972). It seems that you might well be obligated to save the child, even though the ground of this obligation—the fact that the child is drowning and only you can help him—is beyond your control. (Some will deny that you have this obligation, holding that any such "positive" obligation must be one that you have voluntarily undertaken (Lomasky & Tesón 2015: ch. 2). They will claim that, since you have no special relation to the child—he is not *your* child, you have made no promise to help him, etc.—he has no right to be saved by you, and that, since he has no right to be saved by you, you have no obligation to save him. Even if this were so, however, it would surely remain very plausible to think that the incurrence of "negative" obligations—e.g., the obligation not to push the child's head back under the water—need not depend on their having been voluntarily undertaken.)

Second, even if OIC★ is true and it follows that one cannot incur obligations that one cannot fulfill, the fact that one can fulfill them will *itself* often be beyond one's control. For example, the fact that you are strong enough to save the child is not within your control. (Or, at least, it is not *presently* within your control. Presumably, you could in the past have avoided being presently strong enough to save the child. You could, for example, have committed suicide yesterday. It might seem that in this way the incurrence of *any* obligation is ultimately in one's control. Maybe—but maybe not. Perhaps you have and always had an obligation not to commit suicide.) Similarly, the fact that the child will remain alive long enough for you to wade into the water and save him is also not within your control.

There is yet another important but seldom-noted form of luck that is not only consistent with but, in conjunction with another plausible thesis, implied by OIC★. That thesis is that someone cannot have a right against you that you do something unless you have an obligation to that person to do that thing. For example, your child cannot have a right against you that you take care of him unless you have an obligation to him to do so. We typically think that children do indeed have a right to be cared for by their parents. But suppose that you are unable to take care of your child. Then, given OIC★, you have no obligation to take care of him, and, given the thesis in question, he has no right after all to your care—an unfortunate fact that presumably lies beyond the control of either him or you.

Axiological Luck

Axiological propositions concern what is *good, neutral, or bad*. Such propositions might themselves be moral propositions—such as the propositions that Mother Teresa led a good (i.e., morally good) life and that Hitler led a bad (i.e., morally bad) life—but they might not be. Even if not moral propositions in their own right, however, they might be *morally relevant*. For example, the propositions that pleasure is good for its own sake and that pain is bad for its own sake do not seem to qualify as moral propositions, but many people take them to be highly relevant to determining what our moral obligations are.

It is plausible to think that some axiological propositions are within our (partial) control and thus (to that extent) not a matter of luck. For example, it seems reasonable to think that both Mother Teresa and Hitler were in control of their leading good and bad lives, respectively. Some axiological facts, however, such as the facts that pleasure is good and that pain is bad, seem to hold wholly independently of our control over anything and thus to qualify as a form of global moral luck.

What I have just said has been disputed. Ishtiyaque Haji (2012: ch. 4) has argued that, just as we cannot have an obligation to do something that we are not in control of doing, so too, more generally, we cannot have a reason to do something that we are not in control of doing. Moreover, something is good for its own sake only if we have a reason to take some positive attitude toward it, and something is bad for its own sake only if we have a reason to take some negative attitude toward it. It follows that nothing can be good or bad for its own sake unless we are in control of the relevant attitudes. If either determinism or indeterminism precludes our having control over anything, then, they also preclude anything's being good or bad for its own sake. If so, then, rather than the facts that pleasure is good and that pain is bad qualifying as a global form of moral luck, it would be the facts that pleasure is *not* good (or neutral, or bad) and that pain is *not* bad (or neutral, or good) that would qualify as such.

Aretaic Luck

Aretaic propositions concern *moral virtues and vices*. These involve such traits as compassion and pitilessness, kindness and cruelty, courage and cowardice, generosity and meanness, veracity and mendacity, and so on. To qualify as virtues and vices, these traits must, I think, be relatively deep-seated and enduring. A solitary impulsive act of kindness or cruelty, for example, does not itself suffice for the possession of the relevant virtue or vice.

The traits in question are traits of character. Some philosophers argue that, contrary to popular opinion, we have few, if any deep-seated and enduring traits of character (Doris 2002). If so, then we have few, if any moral virtues and vices. This fact, if it is a fact, presumably lies beyond anyone's control. It would count as a form of global aretaic luck.

But suppose that the view just mentioned is false, and that many of us do have deep-seated and enduring traits of character, some of which qualify as moral virtues and vices. Would our possession of these virtues and vices be a matter of luck? The answer depends on the answer to two further questions.

First, the traits at issue consist at least in part in dispositions to act in certain ways and/or think certain thoughts and/or experience certain emotions and/or have certain desires. Are we ever in control of having these dispositions? (Such control would have to be not only merely partial but also merely indirect.) I am inclined to think that the answer is that we never have intentional control over acquiring or retaining such dispositions, and also that we rarely have unintentional control over doing so (although we can forestall having or losing them by, e.g., committing suicide). This claim can of course be disputed (Aristotle 1941: bks II and III).

Second, is the possession of such dispositions sufficient for the possession of the relevant traits, or must these dispositions also be, at least sometimes, manifested in behavior in order for the traits to exist? If the dispositions must be so manifested, then, even if the possession of the underlying dispositions is a matter of luck, given that the manifestation is voluntary, the possession of the relevant traits will in that respect *not* be a matter of luck. (Even here, though, luck will have a role to play, insofar as the *opportunity* to manifest the traits lies beyond the agent's control. One cannot display compassion, for example, if one is marooned on a desert island.) I am inclined to think that such manifestation is not required. It seems possible that someone should have, for example, a cruel streak that is never manifested, precisely because the opportunity to manifest it never arises. (Think again of a desert island scenario.) Such a person would appear to have the vice of cruelty. Of course, if a disposition is never manifested, there might be no evidence of its existing, but that is consistent with its existing nonetheless. This is a tricky issue but, if I am right, then there would appear to be a great deal of a certain form of aretaic luck.

Hypological Luck

Hypological propositions concern what one is *morally responsible* for having done or brought about. It is this kind of moral luck in particular on which Nagel focused, and it is this kind that has been the focus of almost all discussions of moral luck since.

Consider the first puzzle mentioned in the section on deontic luck: If moral responsibility presupposes control, and control, being compatible with neither determinism nor indeterminism, is impossible, then no one is ever morally responsible for anything. This fact would constitute a global form of hypological luck.

It was not this puzzle that concerned Nagel, however; nor has it been the concern of those who have followed his lead. Their focus has been on a different form of hypological luck, one that there is reason to think exists *even if* we are sometimes in control of what we do. Before I discuss whether this form of luck does in fact exist, however, I should make explicit note of a presupposition that has commonly been made by all parties engaged in the debate about its existence.

That presupposition is that one cannot be morally responsible for having done or brought about something that was not in one's control. This claim, which I will call the Control Principle (cf. Nagel 1993: 58; Nelkin 2013), has traditionally been accepted by almost everyone, but in recent years opposition to it has mounted (see, e.g., Adams 1985; Smith 2005). If its opponents are correct, and we are often morally responsible for things (such as our beliefs, emotions, and other attitudes) that lie beyond our control, then of course hypological luck abounds. Typically, however, those who have argued explicitly for the existence of hypological luck have *not* done so on the basis of a rejection of the Control Principle. On the contrary, as I have just noted, they have accepted this principle and yet nonetheless claimed that such luck exists. But how is this claim *consistent* with the principle? *This* is the problem of moral luck (Nagel called it a paradox (1993: 68)) with which I will be concerned from this point on.

The short answer is that, once the distinction between complete and partial control is acknowledged, there is no paradox here at all. As noted earlier, complete control is impossible. Those who advocate the Control Principle while accepting the possibility of moral responsibility are therefore committed only to the claim that such responsibility requires partial control. But an agent's exercising merely partial control over an event is not only consistent with but *entails* that event's occurrence being to some extent a matter of luck for that person. To see this, consider the following pair of cases (Zimmerman 2002). Case 1: George shot at Henry, killing him in such a way that he satisfied whatever conditions (concerning both control and any other relevant matters) are necessary for his being morally responsible for Henry's death. Case 2: Georg shot at Henrik in circumstances (both "inside" his head and in the "outside" world) which were, to the extent possible, just like those of George, except for the fact that Georg's bullet was intercepted by a passing bird and Henrik remained unharmed. Is it not clear that, although George is morally responsible for Henry's death, Georg luckily escaped being morally responsible for Henrik's death, precisely because Henrik did not die? The luck in question stems from the fact that whether a passing bird intercepted his bullet was something that lay wholly beyond Georg's control.

Two responses are possible. The first is to accept that there is indeed a form of moral luck operating here (Moore 1997: ch. 5). Because of something not in his control, Georg is less to blame than George. This verdict is, in fact, perfectly consistent with the Control Principle. George is not being said to be to blame for anything that was not in his (partial) control; nor is Georg. Both men attempted to kill their respective targets, and both may be held responsible for doing so, but only because both were in control of making their respective attempts. Furthermore, since George was in (indirect) control of Henry's death, there is, as far as control is concerned, no reason not to hold him responsible for that, too; but, again, there is no death to pin on Georg.

The second response is to say that the foregoing position, while admittedly consistent with the Control Principle as that principle has been formulated, is *not* consistent with the key intuition that underlies that principle. This intuition rests on the idea that responsibility—whether in the form of blameworthiness or culpability, as in the present pair of cases, or in the form of praiseworthiness or laudability—comes in degrees, and it may be captured in what I will call the Extended Control Principle, according to which the degree to which one bears moral responsibility for having done or brought about something cannot be affected by anything that was not in one's control. Since the bullet's (not) being intercepted by a bird was something that was in neither George's nor Georg's control, the Extended Control Principle implies that there can be no difference in their degree of blameworthiness due to this difference between their cases. That George and Georg are, therefore, equally blameworthy is a verdict to which many people are drawn. Blameworthiness is the worthiness or desert of some kind of negative reaction, and, many would say, the presence or absence of a passing bird is irrelevant to what kind of reaction one deserves.[3]

This rejection of moral luck can be developed further in either of two ways. One way (Zimmerman 2002) is to draw a distinction between degree and scope of responsibility. On this approach, George and Georg are blameworthy to the same degree, but, since George is to blame for something (a death) that Georg is not, the scope of the former's blameworthiness is greater than that of the latter. That is, George is *to blame for more* than Georg is, even though this difference between them is not something that was in either agent's control. There is, therefore, a kind of moral luck at work here, but it is insignificant, in that what matters (for purposes of determining the kind of reaction that each agent deserves) is the fact that George is *no more to blame* than Georg is. In this respect, *no* moral luck is at work. The second way to develop the response (Khoury 2012) is to insist that scope cannot outstrip degree and hold that, since Georg is not responsible for any death, neither is George (contrary to the original description of Case 1). The upshot of this approach is a revised form of the Control Principle, according to which one cannot be morally responsible for having done or brought about something that was not in one's *direct* control.

The kind of luck at issue in the comparison of Cases 1 and 2 is often called resultant luck: luck with respect to what happens as a result of the decisions one makes. Everyone agrees that such luck is ubiquitous. The debate concerns whether there is any *moral* resultant luck. Those who claim that George is more to blame than Georg affirm the existence of such luck, whereas those who hold them equally blameworthy deny it.

Resultant luck is only one form of luck. Nagel distinguished three other forms, which he called constitutive luck, luck in one's circumstances, and luck in how one is determined by antecedent causes (Nagel 1993: 60). Since all three of these forms of luck concern, not what happens as a result of the decisions one makes, but rather (broadly speaking) the situations in which one makes these decisions, I will lump them all under the heading "situational luck." Again, everyone agrees that such luck is ubiquitous. The question is whether there is any *moral* situational luck.

Consider the following case, Case 3: Georg was in circumstances that were, to the extent possible, just like those of George (in Case 1), except that he sneezed just as he was about to make the decision to shoot at Henrik, and so Henrik remained unharmed. Those who say that, in Case 2, Georg is less to blame than George will of course not hesitate to say the same about Georg in Case 3. But what about those who say that, in Case 2, Georg is as much to blame as George? Whatever pressure there is to reach this verdict in Case 2 would seem also to apply to Case 3, and the Extended Control Principle confirms this. For just as the difference between Cases 1 and 2 was in neither George's nor Georg's control, so too the difference between Cases 1 and 3 was in neither agent's control.

This line of thinking can be taken still further. Consider the following case, Case 4: Georg was in circumstances that were, to the extent possible, just like those of George, except that Georg was too timid to pull the trigger, his timidity being attributable to factors wholly beyond his control. The Extended Control Principle implies, once again, that George and Georg are equally blameworthy.

"Absurd!" you might say. "This conclusion constitutes a *reductio* of this line of thinking. If this is where we end up when we apply the Extended Control Principle consistently to case after case, then we shouldn't apply it to begin with. We should declare Georg less blameworthy than George in *all* the cases that have been mentioned" (Moore 2009: 26, n. 22). But *is* this conclusion absurd? Again, many feel pressure to say that in Case 2 Georg is as much to blame as George and, although this same verdict might initially come as a bit of a surprise in Case 3 (not to mention Case 4), it might seem quite reasonable on reflection. It is a verdict that mandates a kind of *moral humility*, a stance whose fittingness is reflected in the popular saying, "There but for the grace of God go I."[4] The denial of all moral luck (of the form presently at issue), both resultant and situational, undeniably issues in a kind of egalitarianism. It has a great leveling effect, implying that, when it comes to moral praiseworthiness and blameworthiness, we are all pretty much alike (although some differences might remain, depending on just what is true of each person regarding what he or she would have done, but for some stroke of luck). Far from finding this view absurd, many will find it attractive (I do). It is important to note that this view does *not* imply that no one is morally responsible for anything. On the contrary, it comes closer to saying the converse, namely, that everyone is morally responsible for everything—but that, of course, is a grossly oversimplified characterization of it.

Michael J. Zimmerman

It might seem that I have set up a false dichotomy: either we should accept the presence of moral luck in all four cases or we should accept it in none. What of the possibility that Georg is as much to blame as George in some of Cases 2–4 but not in all of them? (The Extended Control Principle does not accommodate such a variation in verdicts, but perhaps another, more nuanced rendition of the underlying intuition would do so.) Why not, for example, draw the line between Cases 2 and 3, thereby denying the existence of moral resultant luck but affirming the existence of moral situational luck? This is the position advocated by Larry Alexander et al. in the following passage (2011: 190 f.):

> Ultimately, our position rests on the assumption that the control we have over our choices ... is immune to luck and is thus qualitatively and morally different from our control or lack thereof over our heredity and environment, the situations in which we find ourselves, and the causal consequences of our choices. No matter our past history, the options we confront, or the causal forces that will combine with those we initiate, what we choose is up to us in a way these other factors are not. It is not just that we have *more* control over our choices than over our constitution, our circumstances, and what we cause. Our control over our choices is different in kind, not different in degree. Bad luck before choice and bad luck after choice is just bad luck; unlike choice, it cannot affect our culpability.

I confess that I do not follow the reasoning here. I acknowledge that all control must be rooted in something, and I agree (although the matter is controversial) that it is rooted in our choices or decisions. It is over these events that we have and exercise direct control. But, again, any control that we have, whether direct or indirect, can only ever be partial, and so it seems to me simply to be a mistake to declare the control that we have over our choices immune to luck. This is a point made vivid in Case 3. Moreover, it is the fundamental similarity between Cases 2 and 3, not the differences between them, that would seem to justify reaching the same verdict about Georg in both. The reason for saying that in Case 2 Georg is as much to blame as George does not appeal to what was *in* Georg's control but to what lay *beyond* his control. The passing bird gives us no reason to think better of Georg than of George. In particular, it gives us no reason to declare Georg any less to blame than George. This kind of explanation bridges the divide between Cases 2 and 3, since the sneeze likewise gives us no reason to think better of Georg than of George. So, too, for Case 4: Georg's timidity gives us no reason to think better of him than of George.

None of this is to say that the transition from Case 2 to Case 3 is free of difficulty. One obvious point to note is that in Case 2, even if Georg is not to blame for killing anyone, still he is to blame for attempting to do so. In Case 3, though, the sneeze occurs before, indeed prevents, any such attempt, and so the question arises what he can be said to be to blame *for*. Here two answers are possible. One is to say that, although in Case 3 Georg is indeed as much to blame as George, nonetheless, unlike George, he is not to blame *for* anything. He is, as it might be put, blameworthy *tout court*, in virtue of the fact that he would have killed Henrik (just as George killed Henry), had he not been interrupted by the sneeze (Zimmerman 2002). (Note that since, as formulated above, the Extended Control Principle concerns itself only with responsibility *for* having done or brought about something, this principle would require some modification in order to accommodate this verdict.) Some find the idea of responsibility *tout court* incoherent (e.g., Peels 2017: 228). They would say that if Georg is as much to blame as George, there must be something for which he is to blame. What might this something be, given that Georg neither killed nor attempted to kill Henrik? One answer is that he is to blame for the very fact just mentioned, namely, that he would have killed Henrik had he not been interrupted by the sneeze. (Note that if this fact is not itself something that was in Georg's control, this answer would necessitate some modification to the Control Principle, as formulated above.)

Another way in which one might seek to endorse the verdict that in Case 2 Georg is just as much to blame as George, whereas in Case 4 he is not, is to draw the line, not between Case 2 and Case 3, but between Case 3 and Case 4. Such a position would affirm some instances of moral situational luck

Denying Moral Luck

while denying others. How might this position be defended? One suggestion is this (Peels 2017: 229 ff.). The proposition that, had he not sneezed, Georg would have killed Henrik involves a counterfactual scenario that is not far removed from the actual world, whereas the proposition that, had he not been timid, Georg would have killed Henrik involves a counterfactual scenario that is far removed from the actual world; and luck is a matter only of what happens in close or nearby worlds—distant worlds are irrelevant. I do not find this suggestion promising. Perhaps we are more likely to agree that Georg was (un)lucky to have sneezed than that he was (un)lucky to have been timid, but, if so, that has to do with the nature of *luck* in particular (regarding which see the first section above). The fact remains that Cases 3 and 4 are on a par with one another insofar as Georg's *lack of control* is concerned; he was not in control of his sneezing, and he was not in control of his timidity. The Extended Control Principle thus implies, once again, that in each case Georg is as much to blame as George.

Finally, it is very important to note that, as it stands, the Extended Control Principle is false! We have been assuming that it is possible to be morally responsible to some degree for having done or brought about something; yet this requires that one has been born and, as observed above, that is something that was not in one's control. It might seem that this simple point entirely vitiates the foregoing case against moral luck (of the form presently at issue), but that would be too hasty a conclusion. The intuition to which those who deny such luck seek to pay heed remains as compelling as ever, the present point notwithstanding. The lesson to draw is not that this intuition should be repudiated, but rather that any principle designed to capture it must be carefully formulated. It has been argued that no such principle will withstand scrutiny (Hanna 2014), but this argument has been rebutted in turn (Zimmerman 2015).

Summary

It is time to sum up.

I have construed luck as follows: someone S is lucky with respect to some proposition p just in case whether p is true is not within S's control. If p concerns some moral, or morally relevant, fact about S, then the luck in question is, more particularly, *moral* luck.

I have distinguished between three dimensions of control. Control can be either intentional or unintentional, either direct or indirect, and either complete or partial.

I have distinguished between four broad kinds of moral, or morally relevant, propositions: deontic propositions (having to do with moral obligation), axiological propositions (having to do with good and bad), aretaic propositions (having to do with moral virtue and vice), and hypological propositions (having to do with moral responsibility).

The fourfold distinction between moral, or morally relevant, propositions, when combined with the threefold distinction between dimensions of control, yields a wide variety of forms of moral luck. The question I have investigated is whether any of these forms of moral luck are actually instantiated. It seems clear that the answer is that some of them are, if only (but in fact not only) because no one is ever in complete control of anything. Yet it is also plausible to deny that some of these forms are ever instantiated. In this regard, two forms of moral luck strike me as especially significant: luck with respect to fulfilling one's moral obligations, and luck with respect to incurring moral responsibility. If OIC* is true, then no one can ever be morally obligated to do something that lies beyond his partial control, and so, in *that* respect and to *that* extent, there is no deontic luck. And if, in any of Cases 2–4, we should say that Georg is as much to blame as George is in Case 1, then again, in *that* respect and to *that* extent, there is no hypological luck.[5]

Notes

1 Williams 1993 is a revision of the original 1976 paper.
2 The kind of generation of non-basic actions out of a basic action represented in Figure 19.1 is causal. As Alvin Goldman notes, there are other kinds of generation that may relate non-basic to basic actions (Goldman 1970: ch. 2).

3 It is a further question just what kind of negative reaction it is of which George and Georg are supposed to be equally deserving. Does Georg deserve to be punished as severely as someone who is guilty of actual murder? Does George deserve to be punished only as severely as someone who is guilty of attempted murder? I will leave this question open.

4 At least, this constitutes one interpretation of the saying. Apparently some people, far from understanding the saying as a repudiation of moral luck, construe it as an affirmation of such luck. They interpret it as the claim that sometimes, through God's grace, not only do we avoid committing some sins, but we also thereby avoid incurring the guilt associated with the commission of those sins.

5 Many thanks to Ish Haji and Bob Hartman for comments on previous drafts.

References

Adams, R.M. (1985) "Involuntary Sins," *Philosophical Review* 94, 3–31.

Alexander, L. et al. (2011) *Crime and Culpability*, Cambridge: Cambridge University Press.

Aristotle (1941) "Nicomachean Ethics," in R. McKeon (ed.) *The Basic Works of Aristotle*, New York: Random House.

Davidson, D. (1980) *Essays on Actions and Events*, Oxford: Clarendon Press.

Doris, J. (2002) *Lack of Character*, New York: Cambridge University Press.

Feinberg, J. (1970) *Doing and Deserving*, Princeton, NJ: Princeton University Press.

Fischer, J.M. (1994) *The Metaphysics of Free Will*, Oxford: Blackwell.

Frankfurt, H.G. (1969) "Alternate Possibilities and Moral Responsibility," *Journal of Philosophy* 66, 829–839.

Goldman, A.I. (1970) *A Theory of Human Action*, Princeton, NJ: Princeton University Press.

Haji, I. (2012) *Reason's Debt to Freedom*, Oxford: Oxford University Press.

Hanna, N. (2014) "Moral Luck Defended," *Noûs* 48, 683–698.

Kant, I. (1964) *Groundwork of the Metaphysic of Morals*, H.J. Paton (trans.), New York: Harper and Row.

——. (1965) *Critique of Pure Reason*, N. Kemp Smith (trans.), New York: St. Martin's Press.

Khoury, A.C. (2012) "Responsibility, Tracing, and Consequences," *Canadian Journal of Philosophy* 42, 187–207.

Lomasky, L.E., & Tesón, F.R. (2015) *Justice at a Distance*, Cambridge: Cambridge University Press.

Mele, A.R. (2003) "Agents' Abilities," *Noûs* 37, 447–470.

Moore, M.S. (1997) *Placing Blame*, Oxford: Clarendon Press.

——. (2009) *Causation and Responsibility*, Oxford: Oxford University Press.

Nagel, T. (1993) "Moral Luck," in D. Statman (ed.) *Moral Luck*, Albany: State University of New York Press, pp. 57–71.

Nelkin, D.K. (2013) "Moral Luck," in *The Stanford Encyclopedia of Philosophy* (Winter 2013 Edition), Edward N. Zalta (ed.) https://plato.stanford.edu/archives/win2013/entries/moral-luck/

Peels, R. (2017) *Responsible Belief*, Oxford: Oxford University Press.

Pritchard, D. (2006) "Moral and Epistemic Luck," *Metaphilosophy* 37, 1–25.

Singer, P. (1972) "Famine, Affluence, and Morality," *Philosophy and Public Affairs* 1, 229–243.

Smith, A.M. (2005) "Responsibility for Attitudes: Activity and Passivity in Mental Life," *Ethics* 115, 236–271.

von Wright, G.H. (1971) *Explanation and Understanding*, Ithaca, NY: Cornell University Press.

Williams, B. (1993) "Moral Luck," in D. Statman (ed.) *Moral Luck*, Albany: State University of New York Press, pp. 35–55.

Zimmerman, M.J. (2002) "Taking Luck Seriously," *Journal of Philosophy* 99, 553–576.

——. (2015) "Moral Luck Reexamined," in D. Shoemaker (ed.) *Agency and Responsibility*, vol. 3, Oxford: Oxford University Press, pp. 136–159.

20

ACCEPTING MORAL LUCK[1]

Robert J. Hartman

Introduction

One way to frame the problem of moral luck is as a skeptical argument that rules out our being morally responsible agents. That is, no one is morally responsible for anything, because luck affects us in ways that universally preclude satisfying the control condition on moral responsibility. Another way to understand the problem of moral luck is as a contradiction in our commonsense ideas about moral responsibility. I take up the latter formulation.

In one strand of our thinking, we believe that a person can become more blameworthy by luck—that is, by factors beyond her control. Consider some examples to make that idea concrete. Two identical agents drive recklessly around a curb, and one but not the other kills a pedestrian (Nagel 1979: 29). Two identical corrupt judges would freely take a bribe if one were offered. By luck of the courthouse draw, only one judge is offered a bribe, and so only one judge takes a bribe (Thomson 1989: 214). Luck is the salient difference between the agents in each case pair. The location of the pedestrian is outside of each driver's control, and being offered a bribe is outside of each judge's control. But we blame the killer driver more than the merely reckless driver, and we blame the bribe taker more than the mere would-be bribe taker. This is because we believe that the killer driver and bribe taker are more blameworthy—that is, the killer driver and the bribe taker deserve more blame—than their counterparts.

Nevertheless, the idea that luck affects desert of praise and blame contradicts another feature of our thinking: We are praiseworthy and blameworthy only for what is within our control, and factors outside of our control cannot affect the praise and blame we deserve. After all, fairness requires that moral judgment is about the person and not what happens to her (Nagel 1979: 25). As Bernard Williams writes:

> There is pressure within it [our ordinary conception of morality] to require a voluntariness that will be total and will cut through character and psychological or social determination, and allocate blame and responsibility on the ultimately fair basis of the agent's own contribution, no more and no less.
>
> *1985: 194; cf. Williams 1981: 21–22; Williams 1993: 251*

Thus, according to this second strand of our commonsense ideas about moral responsibility, the drivers are equally blameworthy, because the salient difference between them is something outside of their control. The same is true for the judges.

To put the contradiction in terms of these examples, our ordinary thinking about moral responsibility implies that the drivers are and are not equally blameworthy. It also implies that the judges are and are not equally blameworthy.

My aim is to make progress in resolving this contradiction. I argue that certain kinds of luck can partially determine a person's praiseworthiness and blameworthiness, and so argue that the killer driver and bribe taker are more blameworthy than their counterparts.

Definitions and Dialectic

In terminology that is standard in the moral luck debate, I argue that various kinds of moral luck exist. *Moral luck* occurs when factors beyond an agent's control partially determine her positive praiseworthiness or blameworthiness (Hartman 2017: 2; cf. Nagel 1979: 26).

Two clarifications are in order about this standard account of moral luck. First, the term "positive" is introduced to rule out the idea that moral luck is responsibility-undermining luck. Second, the conception of luck implicit in that definition of moral luck is the lack of control conception. I recognize that the lack of control conception fails to capture at least some of our intuitions about which events are lucky or not lucky, and that this failure has led some philosophers to reject the standard account of moral luck (cf. Driver 2012; Hales 2015; Latus 2003; Levy 2011; Peels 2015; Pritchard 2005; Rescher 1995; Whittington 2014). For example, Andrew Latus (2003: 476) argues that lack of control cannot be a sufficient condition for an event to be lucky. After all, the lack of control view implies that it is lucky for me that the sun rose today, since it is outside of my control that it rose. Intuitively, however, it is not lucky for me that the sun rose today, and so the lack of control definition founders. Nevertheless, I argue in Hartman (2017: 23–31) that these philosophers miss what is important in an account of moral luck, because the moral luck debate is not about luck per se but about a contradiction in our ideas about moral responsibility. Here is a simple way to see the point. Even if an account of luck other than the lack of control account best captures our ordinary usage of the term "luck" or even if there is no good account of the way we use the word "luck," the puzzle to which Joel Feinberg (1962), Thomas Nagel (1979), and Williams (1981) point us remains, because ubiquitous lack of control continues to be in tension with the control condition that is part of our conception of morality (see also Anderson forthcoming; Statman this volume). (Of course, it might still be interesting to investigate alternative accounts of moral luck for one reason or another. Some of these alternative accounts might employ a different account of luck, or might investigate a different moral feature of our lives such as moral obligation or moral virtue, or both.)

Nagel's (1979: 28) taxonomy distinguishes between four kinds of moral luck—namely, resultant, circumstantial, constitutive, and causal moral luck. These kinds of moral luck are distinguished primarily by the type of factor that is beyond the agent's control. *Resultant moral luck* occurs when the consequence of an agent's action is beyond her control, and the consequence partially determines her positive praiseworthiness or blameworthiness. *Circumstantial moral luck* occurs when an agent faces a morally significant challenge that is outside of her control, and it affects her positive praiseworthiness or blameworthiness. *Constitutive moral luck* occurs when an agent's dispositions or capacities are not voluntarily acquired, and they affect her positive praiseworthiness or blameworthiness for a trait or an action. *Causal moral luck* occurs when the laws of nature and past states of affairs outside of a person's control causally determine her actions, and the laws and past affect her positive praiseworthiness or blameworthiness. The question of whether causal moral luck could exist is the same question as whether an action's having been causally determined is compatible with being morally responsible for that action, which is a standard topic in the free will literature.[2]

Let the *Moral Luck View* be the position that instances of resultant, circumstantial, and constitutive moral luck exist. It is noteworthy that the Moral Luck View is consistent with both compatibilism and incompatibilism about an action's having been causally determined and being morally responsible for that action.[3]

Before I make a case for accepting the Moral Luck View, it is important to take stock of two general considerations. First, I cannot advance the debate on behalf of the Moral Luck View by offering arguments that bottom out in standard pro-moral luck intuitions such as the intuition that the killer driver is more blameworthy, because the problem of moral luck is fundamentally a clash of intuitions. So, I will not rely on *standard pro-moral luck* intuitions even though I do appeal to intuitions at various places. Second, a systematic case for the Moral Luck View should include three kinds of arguments. It should include *indirect* arguments—namely, the kind of argument that renders implausible the denial of extant moral luck. It should include *direct* arguments—that is, the kind of argument that makes plausible the existence of moral luck. It should also include an *error theory* for the luck-free intuition; it should explain why we erroneously intuit that the drivers are equally blameworthy and that the judges are equally blameworthy.

My argument for the Moral Luck View will exemplify both methods to highlight a promising way to advance the debate. Given spatial limitations, however, I argue only for part of the Moral Luck View—namely, for extant circumstantial and resultant moral luck.[4] Along the way, I introduce four ways to resolve the contradiction in our thinking about moral responsibility that are opposed to the Moral Luck View to various degrees. I proceed as follows. First, I argue against one prominent way of denying that circumstantial moral luck exists. Second, I offer some evidence that resultant moral luck exists. Third, I explain why the errant luck-free intuition is widespread.

Against a Denial of Circumstantial Moral Luck

The denial of circumstantial moral luck amounts to the claim that the morally significant challenges a person actually faces outside of her control cannot affect her positive praiseworthiness and blameworthiness. For example, if there is no circumstantial moral luck in the judge case, then the judges must be equally blameworthy, because which of their possible circumstances are actual does not affect their overall degree of blameworthiness. There are three prominent approaches to the problem of moral luck that imply the denial of all or many cases of circumstantial moral luck.

The *Skeptical View* is the position that luck undermines moral responsibility (cf. Levy 2011; Strawson 1994; Waller 2011). If the Skeptical View is correct, neither judge is blameworthy for anything, because luck affects them both and luck undermines moral responsibility. So, because their circumstantial luck cannot positively affect their blameworthiness, no circumstantial *moral luck* exists in this case.

The *Character View* is the position that we are fundamentally praiseworthy and blameworthy for and only for our character traits (cf. Peels 2015; Rescher 1990; Richards 1986; Thomson 1989). Because the judges have the same corrupt character, they are thereby equally blameworthy even though only one of them takes a bribe. Thus, luck in actual opportunity cannot make a difference to their comparative degree of blameworthiness, and no circumstantial moral luck exists in this case.[5]

The *Counterfactual View* is the position that restricts the sphere of praiseworthiness and blameworthiness to actual and subjunctive exercises of agency, and so agents are praiseworthy and blameworthy not only *for* their actual free actions but also *in virtue of* what they would freely do in non-actual circumstances (Zimmerman 2002: 564–565; cf. Enoch and Marmor 2007: 420–425). On this view, the mere would-be bribe taker is blameworthy "tout court" or simpliciter in virtue of the fact that she would freely take the bribe if she were offered one (Zimmerman 2002: 564–565). Thus, on the Counterfactual View, the judges deserve the same degree of blame even though only the actual bribe taker is blameworthy *for* something in the actual world. The Counterfactual View, however, differs in part from the Character View, because a person's being praiseworthy or blameworthy in virtue of what she would freely do is not reducible to character evaluation. On Zimmerman's view, a person might be blameworthy for what she would freely do in a counterfactual circumstance in which she has *different* character traits.

My indirect argument for the Moral Luck View is an argument against the Counterfactual View's denial of circumstantial moral luck. It proceeds by way of the communicative function of blame. Angela Smith (2013: 41–42; cf. Macnamara 2015: 222–232) contends that moral protest is a function of blame.[6] What blame protests is the moral commitment implicit in the wrongdoer's behavior. Suppose that Paul gossips about Jennifer, and she finds out about it. When Jennifer reacts toward Paul with resentment or indignation, she challenges the moral presupposition implicit in Paul's behavior—namely, that it is acceptable to treat her in that way. This communicates to Paul that at least one person views his behavior as morally unacceptable, and it creates an opportunity for him to see himself through her eyes, which might elicit guilt, remorse, or regret. It could also be a catalyst for reconciliation.

The communicative function of blame reveals absurdities in the Counterfactual View's denial of circumstantial moral luck. Suppose that although Charles enjoys gambling, he has never been reckless. Suppose also that Charles loses his job in a non-actual circumstance in which he could easily have been, but that he does not actually lose his job. He would be devastated if he were to find himself in that non-actual circumstance, because his self-worth is bound up in that job. In fact, if he were in that circumstance, he would freely distract himself from his newfound emptiness by heading to the closest casino, and he would freely make a series of reckless bets and lose his life savings. Suppose that this kind of action is out of character for Charles and that Jan, Charles's wife, knows what Charles would freely do. It is revealed to her by God or by an angel. In any case, she actually blames Charles because of what he would freely do in a non-actual circumstance.

Has Jan done something wrong? By hypothesis, if she has done something wrong, it is not the case that she is blaming someone who is not blameworthy. After all, the Counterfactual View implies that Charles is blameworthy in virtue of its being true that he would freely risk the family savings. It appears in the right circumstances that the Counterfactual View implies the permissibility of *counterfactual-blaming*—that is, actually blaming someone because of what he would freely do in a circumstance that never becomes actual.

The difficulty for the Counterfactual View is that this case of counterfactual-blame lacks communicative value in a particular way. In blaming Charles, Jan protests the moral presupposition that gambling away the family's savings is an acceptable way to cope with loss, but Charles is neither theoretically nor practically committed to that presupposition. He is not theoretically committed to the presupposition, because he views the action of gambling his life savings as morally repugnant. That is, he believes that gambling one's life savings is morally wrong and ought not to be done. He is also not practically committed to the presupposition. For he performs no actual action that commits him to it, and he does not even form a distal intention to gamble his life savings in the case that he loses his job. We may even suppose that Charles's counterfactual reckless gambling is *out of character* to show that there is nothing in Charles's actual psychology to protest. It is only when Charles's slightly fragile dispositions, which he might or might not be morally responsible for, depending on how we fill in the details of the case, are coupled with a certain kind of non-actual emotional turmoil that there would be an exercise of agency to protest.

I contend, however, that Jan's actual blame would be a communicative failure, because anyone in Charles's position—namely, the position in which he is unaware of what he would freely do—would find being blamed bewildering and unintelligible. As a result, her blame cannot intelligibly function to invite Charles to feel remorse, repent, or make amends, which provides evidence that Charles is not blameworthy (cf. Watson 2004: 230). Jan also satisfies often-cited preconditions for having good standing to blame: (i) she knows that Charles is blameworthy, (ii) blaming Charles is not hypocritical, and (iii) she is relationally close to Charles. She also would have been harmed personally by the financial loss. If a person who possesses good standing to counterfactual-blame cannot meaningfully blame the blameworthy person, in what sense is this person worthy of blame at all? In other words, given Jan's good position to blame, the absurdity of her counterfactual-blaming Charles lends evidence that Charles is not blameworthy.[7] But then, Charles is both blameworthy and not blameworthy. Contradiction! Our initial assumption that the Counterfactual View is true turns out to be false, and so the way in which the Counterfactual View implies that denial of circumstantial moral luck is implausible.

For the sake of argument, we could even suppose that Charles is at least a little blameworthy for his dispositions that bind his self-worth to his job performance, but is *not* as blameworthy as he would have been if he had lost his job and gambled away his life savings. Importantly, even this supposition is incompatible with the Counterfactual View, because the Counterfactual View implies that Charles is *as blameworthy as* someone who freely gambles away their life savings. Thus, even in the case that Charles is only a little blameworthy, there exists at least some circumstantial moral luck. He is lucky to find himself in his actual circumstance instead of the circumstance in which he loses his job, and it affects his degree of blameworthiness.

If this argument against the Counterfactual View's denial of circumstantial moral luck is successful, it would support the claim that circumstantial moral luck exists, but it would not demonstrate that circumstantial moral luck exists. The same is true for other arguments against the Counterfactual View's denial of circumstantial moral luck (cf. Anderson 2011: 379; Brogaard 2003: 353–354; Hanna 2014; Hartman 2014: 83, 2017: 62–86, forthcoming-b; Rivera-López 2016: 419; Rosell 2015; Zagzebski 1994: 407).[8] The reason is that the Counterfactual View is not the only view that implies the denial of circumstantial moral luck. There are also the Skeptical and Character Views. For this reason, a complete indirect argument for extant circumstantial moral luck should target the Character, Counterfactual, *and* Skeptical Views.

For Resultant Moral Luck

The claim that circumstantial moral luck exists supports not only the Moral Luck View but also the *Asymmetry View*—namely, the view that we are praiseworthy and blameworthy to some degree for and only for our actions (and omissions). On the Asymmetry View, circumstantial and constitutive moral luck exist but resultant moral luck does not (cf. Rivera-López 2016). To put it in concrete terms, the Asymmetry View implies that the bribe taker is more blameworthy than the mere would-be bribe taker and that the reckless drivers are equally blameworthy. Thus, the Asymmetry View implies that there is a morally significant difference between the kind of luck that *rules out* two agents performing the same kind of action and the sort of luck that operates *after* two agents perform the same kind of action.[9] The Asymmetry View is the most popular response to the problem of moral luck (cf. Hartman 2017: 129–130; MacKenzie 2017: 96). In this section, I contend that we have reason to prefer the Moral Luck View over the Asymmetry View by arguing for the existence of resultant moral luck.

Michael S. Moore (1997: 233–246) offers an argument for resultant moral luck that appeals in part to the following *non-existence relation* between certain kinds of moral luck: If resultant moral luck does not exist, then circumstantial or constitutive moral luck do not exist either (cf. Zimmerman 2006: 605). Nevertheless, at least circumstantial or constitutive moral luck exists, which is a claim that a proponent of the Asymmetry View grants. Therefore, in the current argumentative context, it follows that resultant moral luck exists.

But why think that the non-existence relation is true? Moore (1997: 237) justifies it by appealing to this consideration: "Luck is luck, and to the extent that causal fortuitousness is morally irrelevant anywhere it is morally irrelevant everywhere." The problem, however, with this justificatory claim is that it is not obviously true (cf. Coffman 2015: 110–111), and it appears merely to restate the claim that it is supposed to justify. In fact, whether the non-existence relation is true is exactly what is at stake between proponents of the Asymmetry and Moral Luck Views! So, unless there is a good argument for the non-existence relation—and it is not clear to me what it might be—Moore's argument does not make progress in showing that resultant moral luck exists. There is room, then, to explore a new argument in the same neighborhood.

I propose that extant circumstantial moral luck provides analogical evidence for the existence of resultant moral luck.[10] I begin with a set of concrete examples involving three assassins, Sneezy, Off-Target, and Bullseye, and, subsequently, I argue for resultant moral luck in terms of those examples.

Sneezy, the first assassin, is hired for murder but has bad allergies. When the time comes to pull the trigger, she suffers a sneezing fit. The fit renders her incapable of taking the shot. If, however, Sneezy were to have found herself in the same circumstance except that her allergies fail to be triggered, she would have freely taken the shot. Off-Target, the second assassin, has allergies just the same as Sneezy, but her allergies are not triggered. As a result, she has an opportunity and takes the shot. She, however, is off-target, because a bird catches the bullet. The comparative case of Sneezy and Off-Target is a standard example of circumstantial luck. They each would freely perform the same kind of morally significant action if they were in the same circumstance, but they do not have the same opportunities. Bullseye, the third assassin, has typical luck. Her aim is not obstructed by an allergic reaction, and nothing blocks the path of the bullet. She has an opportunity, fires a shot, and kills her mark. The case of Off-Target and Bullseye is a standard example of resultant luck, because they freely perform the same kind of action but with different results.

The case of Sneezy and Off-Target is analogous to the case of Off-Target and Bullseye in at least three ways. First, the agents in both case pairs have identical agency in some sense and are distinguished at least partially by luck. Sneezy and Off-Target have *subjunctively* identical agency, because Sneezy would have freely taken the shot just as Off-Target does if she had been in Off-Target's circumstance. And Off-Target and Bullseye have *actually* identical agency, because they both actually freely take the shot in the same circumstance. Second, the actual mental states of Sneezy and Off-Target greatly resemble the actual mental states of Off-Target and Bullseye. All three assassins form the distal intention to kill the target, and they each carefully execute their meticulous assassination plan. Their actual mental states differ only by a moment, because only Off-Target and Bullseye have the final opportunity to sustain their intentions into overt actions. Third, the event of taking the shot and the event of killing the mark both depend on the agency of the relevant person. In the case of Sneezy and Off-Target, the unsuccessful attempt depends on Off-Target's voluntary choice, and, in the case of Off-Target and Bullseye, the successful assassination depends on Bullseye's voluntary choice. Plausibly, it is structural similarities of these kinds that lead David Enoch and Ehud Guttel (2010: 376) to assert that "The problem of moral luck seems to be the very same problem whether it is luck in consequences or in circumstances, and is typically so treated in the literature" (cf. Pritchard 2005: 261).

Furthermore, Off-Target is more blameworthy than Sneezy in a way that is partially determined by luck. For the sake of argument, we can assume that circumstantial moral luck exists, because the proponent of the Asymmetry View grants that assumption. Even outside of this dialectical context, however, there are good arguments for extant circumstantial moral luck. I mentioned one in the last section and provided references to others. So, because circumstantial moral luck plausibly exists, it is plausible that the difference in the morally significant challenges faced by Sneezy and Off-Target outside of their control can make a difference in their degree of blameworthiness. And since Off-Target sustains her distal intention into a bona fide assassination attempt and Sneezy does not, Off-Target is plausibly more blameworthy than Sneezy.

Here, then, is the *Parallelism Argument*. There are three important respects in which the case of Sneezy and Off-Target is analogous to the case of Off-Target and Bullseye—namely, the agents in both case pairs (i) have identical agency in some sense and are saliently distinguished by luck, (ii) have very similar actual mental states, and (iii) bring about morally significant events that depend on their voluntary actions. Additionally, Off-Target is more blameworthy than Sneezy in a way that is partially determined by luck, because only Off-Target actually executes her intention. But then, based on those similarities and on that difference in blameworthiness, we have good analogical evidence that Bullseye is more blameworthy than Off-Target in a way that is partially determined by luck. In other words, the fact that the sneezing fit makes a difference in blameworthiness between Sneezy and Off-Target provides good analogical evidence that the path of the bird makes a difference in blameworthiness between Off-Target and Bullseye.

How might one object to the Parallelism Argument? A minimally adequate response should identify a *relevant difference* between the cases of circumstantial and resultant luck such that the existence of circumstantial moral luck provides no evidence, or negligible evidence, for extant resultant moral luck.

Consider the following difference between the two case pairs: Sneezy and Off-Target do not actually perform the same kind of free action, but Off-Target and Bullseye do actually perform the same kind of free action. One might think that this difference between the two case pairs is a *relevant* difference, because one might think that praiseworthiness and blameworthiness supervene on actual free actions such that there can be no difference in degree of praiseworthiness and blameworthiness for two agents who perform qualitatively identical free actions. This *supervenience principle* implies that there can be no difference between the blameworthiness of Off-Target and Bullseye, because they perform qualitatively identical free actions. In other words, the supervenience principle implies that Off-Target and Bullseye are equally blameworthy with respect to their assassination escapades. Of course, the supervenience principle is compatible with there being a difference in the blameworthiness between Sneezy and Off-Target, because they do not actually perform qualitatively identical free actions. So, even if circumstantial luck can partially determine that Sneezy and Off-Target are blameworthy to different degrees, this fact does not provide evidence that resultant luck can partially determine that Off-Target and Bullseye are blameworthy to different degrees.

Unless the proponent of the Asymmetry View has a good reason to think that the supervenience principle is true, this objection begs the question against the proponent of the Parallelism Argument. In other words, we have no reason to think that a difference between the actual free actions of the agents in both case pairs is a *relevant* difference unless there is a reason for believing that the degree of praiseworthiness and blameworthiness supervenes on actual free actions. In view of the dialectical context, however, a proponent of the Asymmetry View cannot appeal merely to her intuition that the supervenience principle is true as a good reason for thinking that this difference is a relevant difference. After all, that kind of argument does not move past the basic conflict of intuitions between proponents of the Moral Luck and Asymmetry Views. And since I have provided the Parallelism Argument as an argument that does *not* bottom out in standard pro-Moral Luck View intuitions, no adequate reply to the Parallelism Argument can appeal merely to the basic intuition that motivates the Asymmetry View.

Are there other arguments for the supervenience principle? Perhaps there are, but it is not obvious to me what they might be. So, I leave the proponent of the Asymmetry View with a challenge to provide the argument. As it stands, however, we have good analogical evidence for extant resultant moral luck.

Error Theory for the Luck-Free Intuition

Suppose that we have before us a good cumulative case for the Moral Luck View—that is, for the claim that resultant, circumstantial, and constitutive moral luck exist and are everywhere. In that case, why is there a contradiction in our ordinary thinking about moral responsibility in the first place? Why do we mistakenly intuit that the drivers are equally blameworthy and that the judges are equally blameworthy? Let us refer to intuitions such as the drivers are equally blameworthy and the judges are equally blameworthy as the *luck-free intuition*. A good explanation for the widespread but errant luck-free intuition would reinforce the plausibility of the Moral Luck View. In this section, I offer such an explanation.

There are two broad ways to explain the prevalence of the luck-free intuition. On the one hand, one might attempt to explain it in a way that eliminates its moral value. For example, one might attribute the ubiquity of that intuition to the operation of a widespread cognitive bias. Let us refer to this kind of explanation as an *elimination error theory*. On the other hand, one might attempt to explain the luck-free intuition in a way that preserves a kernel of moral truth. For example, one might discover something insightful about the luck-free intuition and integrate it into moral evaluation. Call this kind of explanation an *integration error theory*.

Offering an integration error theory for a widely shared moral intuition is better than supplying an elimination error theory for two reasons. First, integration explanations are more charitable; they attribute at least a kernel of truth to the errant intuition. Second, widely shared moral intuitions very often provide at least some insight into morality. For these reasons, I maintain that we can satisfactorily explain the luck-free intuition with an elimination error theory only if no integration error theory can plausibly do so. There are at least three attempts by advocates of moral luck to integrate the luck-free intuition into moral evaluation (Brogaard 2003; Greco 1995; Otsuka 2009). In Hartman (2017: 119–127), I argue that John Greco's (1995) explanation for the luck-free intuition is superior to the others, and further develop Greco's explanation to increase its plausibility.[11]

Greco (1995: 82–83) distinguishes between two commonsense kinds of moral evaluation. *Moral record evaluation* pertains to being praiseworthy or blameworthy for an actual state of affairs such as a trait, an action, or a consequence, and *moral worth evaluation* pertains to being a good or bad person (Greco 1995: 90–91).[12] An agent's moral worth is a function of the voluntary actions that she actually performs as well as the voluntary actions that she would perform in a broad range of non-actual circumstances (Greco 1995: 91).[13]

These kinds of evaluation differ in the way that luck affects them. On the one hand, praiseworthiness and blameworthiness for states of affairs that we bring about in the world can be affected by certain kinds of luck. The only difference between the two drivers and the salient difference between the two judges is a matter of luck, and yet the killer driver and bribe taker are more blameworthy for a state of affairs than their counterparts. On the other hand, moral worth is luck-free in various respects. Since the drivers freely perform the same type of action and the judges would freely perform the same kind of action, the moral worth of the agents in each case pair is the same with respect to these events. That is, the killer driver's hitting the pedestrian reflects no worse on her as a person than the merely reckless driver's action, and the judge's actually taking a bribe reflects no worse on him as a person than its being true that the other judge would freely take a bribe in the same circumstance. Their actual and counterfactual free actions have the same impact on their moral worth. So, because moral worth is protected from luck in results and circumstances in these ways, this kind of moral evaluation preserves a kernel of truth from the luck-free intuition.

How, then, does the faulty luck-free intuition arise? It results from a conflation of these kinds of moral evaluation. We mistakenly infer *from* the claim that each reckless driver is no worse of a person than the other *to* the claim that each reckless driver is no more blameworthy than the other. And we errantly conclude *from* the claim that each corrupt judge is no worse of a person than the other *to* the claim that each corrupt judge is no more blameworthy than the other. But these inferences are mistaken precisely because being a good or bad person is not wholly determined by states of affairs for which one is praiseworthy and blameworthy. Greco, thus, solves the puzzle by adequately separating these two kinds of evaluation that we tend to conflate. And this explanation is compelling precisely because it appeals to modes of evaluation that are found in common sense, which explains why there is a contradiction in our commonsense ideas about moral responsibility.

One might worry, however, that Greco's solution is not plausible, because moral worth is not protected from all kinds of luck. An agent's non-voluntarily acquired character traits still significantly influence what she freely does and what she would freely do in a broad range of counterfactual circumstances. And so an agent is likely to have a better or worse moral worth depending on the non-voluntarily acquired dispositions with which she begins the moral life or non-voluntarily acquires sometime thereafter.[14] The worry, then, is that because moral worth is conditioned by constitutive luck, the scope of the error theory does not adequately explain the luck-free intuition.

To circumvent this explanatory shortcoming, Greco (1995: 94) introduces a distinction between two kinds of moral worth. *Actual moral worth* is a function of a person's actual free actions as well as her counterfactual free actions continuous with her actual history. In contrast, *essential moral worth* is a function of a person's actual free actions as well as her counterfactual free actions continuous with her actual *and* counterfactual histories. So, the difference between them is that only essential moral worth allows for what an agent would freely do in counterfactual circumstances continuous with counterfactual histories to count toward her being a good or bad person. To illustrate this difference, consider an example. Suppose that Henry has been habituated to be timid. When Tim insults him, Henry timidly walks away. If, however, Henry had a more raucous formative experience and was non-voluntarily confrontational instead of timid, he would have freely assaulted Tim. By hypothesis, the salient difference between Henry's choices traces back to the way in which he was habituated. Only Henry's walking away counts toward his actual moral worth, but both his walking away and his assaulting Tim count toward his essential moral worth. Greco (1995: 94) asserts that it is essential moral worth that is protected from luck in a way that provides the best error theory for the wide-spread luck-free intuition. After all, the error theory that explains the luck-free intuition in a greater range of cases is to be preferred, all other things being equal.

But even essential moral worth might not be entirely luck-free. If there are *essential* constitutive properties and if different constitutive properties are essential for at least some persons, then it is impossible for everyone to be in all the same counterfactual circumstances, which suggests that some agents might have a better or worse moral worth owing partly to which constitutive properties they have essentially.

Nevertheless, this kind of vulnerability to luck is not problematic. After all, it is incoherent to evaluate Tim as a good or bad person with respect to what he would freely do with different *essential* constitutive properties, because the object of evaluation would no longer be *Tim* (Greco 1995: 94–95). It would be someone else. Thus, the ambition to locate a moral self that is *entirely* luck-free is incoherent. Additionally, recall that our goal is to explain adequately the genesis and nature of a faulty intuition. One way in which an intuition might err is with respect to its scope. Given that the kind of agent evaluation that factors out *essential* constitutive luck is incoherent, it is plausible that the luck-free intuition is faulty at least with respect to its essential constitutive luck-free scope. Thus, we have a strong reason for thinking that the way in which essential constitutive luck shapes essential moral worth poses no difficulty for the error theory.[15]

Consider a different objection to the error theory. Essential moral worth is a counterintuitive standard by which to measure person-level goodness. More specifically, it is counterintuitive even partially to assess whether someone is a good or bad person by how she would freely act in a coun-terfactual circumstance with *contingent* constitutive properties that she *does not have* but *would have had* if she had a different history. In concrete terms, it is counterintuitive to think that what Henry would freely do given an alternative history in which he is non-voluntarily confrontational provides insight into whether he is a good or bad person.

The intuition behind this objection seems to me to be clearly right, and thus I think we should allow it to refine Greco's error theory. This intuition can help us to see that the essential moral worth error theory is a *hybrid* error theory; it is part *integration* error theory and part *elimination* error theory. To see which part is which, let us separate essential moral worth into three parts. Recall that essential moral worth is a function of an agent's

(i) actual free actions
(ii) counterfactual free actions in circumstances continuous with her actual history
(iii) counterfactual free actions in circumstances continuous with various counterfactual histories.

I contend that parts (i) and (ii) exhaust the integration part of the error theory. In other words, it is only a person's actual moral worth, parts (i) and (ii) of her essential moral worth, that provides insight into whether she is a good or bad person. Part (iii) is a problematic extrapolation from parts (i) and (ii), because part (iii) lacks even a kernel of moral truth with respect to person-level evaluation (cf. McKenna 1998: 139–141).[16] Even so, part (iii) of the error theory should not be jettisoned, because there is more explanatory work to be done concerning cases of constitutive luck. The explanation with respect to part (iii), however, is that the luck-free intuition is purely erroneous.

Conclusion

I have exemplified a general method that I take to be promising for advancing the moral luck debate—and in my case—for arguing that we should accept at least part of the Moral Luck View, which is the view that constitutive, circumstantial, and resultant moral luck exist. I offered an argument for circumstantial moral luck by arguing against the Counterfactual View. I also argued that we have good analogical evidence for resultant moral luck. Finally, I fortified these arguments by explaining away the intuitive appeal of the luck-free intuition as a confusion between moral record and moral worth evaluation.[17]

Notes

1   This chapter is based on my book *In Defense of Moral Luck: Why Luck Often Affects Praiseworthiness and Blameworthiness* (Routledge, 2017).
2   Paul Russell (2017) interestingly argues that the problem of moral luck supplies the best lens from which to view the free will debate.
3   It does not follow, however, that there is no interesting relationship between the Moral Luck View and compatibilism. I think that the Moral Luck View provides defeasible evidence for compatibilism, because if luck in results, circumstance, and constitution can positively affect moral responsibility, then there is at least some reason to think that luck in causal determination can also positively affect moral responsibility.
4   Elsewhere, I argue for the existence of constitutive moral luck. See Hartman (2017, Chs 3–6; forthcoming-a).
5   In Hartman (manuscript), I argue against the Character View.
6   Many philosophers take seriously the communicative function of blame. Michael McKenna (2012), for example, has a book-length account of blame modeled on communication.
7   Of course, there is a gap between the permissibility of blame and blameworthiness. So, it might be the case that it is not permissible for Jan to blame Charles even though Charles is blameworthy. Even so, that it is impermissible for Jan to blame Charles provides a defeasible reason to think that Charles is not blameworthy. I thank Dana Nelkin for pointing out the need for this footnote.
8   For replies to some of these objections, see Peels (2015) and Zimmerman (2015).
9   Both the Asymmetry and Character Views imply that resultant moral luck does *not* exist and that constitutive moral luck *does* exist. But only the Character View implies that *many* instances of circumstantial moral luck do *not* exist.
10 My argument, then, will differ from Moore's at least in two ways. First, my argument is an inductive argument. Second, I think that extant circumstantial moral luck provides the best case for the existence of resultant moral luck, whereas Moore appears to think, for example, that extant constitutive or causal moral luck offers just as powerful a case for resultant moral luck.
11 It is worth pointing out that proponents of the Skeptical, Character, Counterfactual, and Asymmetry Views have error theories for the intuition that the killer driver is more blameworthy than the merely reckless driver. For example, Zimmerman (2002: 560) contends that the killer driver is responsible for more things but that the killer driver is not more responsible—or more blameworthy. Richard Swinburne (1989: 42), R. Jay Wallace (1994: 128), and Brian Rosebury (1995: 521–524) suggest that the resultant moral luck intuition is the result of conflating legality and morality. The error comes from inferring from the claim that the killer driver merits greater legal punishment to the claim that she is more blameworthy. Richard Parker (1984: 271–273) offers the explanation that people confusedly equate causing greater harm with meriting greater blame. Henning Jensen (1984: 327) and Rosebury (1995: 513–514) submit that people mistakenly associate a greater negative emotional response to the killer driver with that driver's being more blameworthy. And Norvin Richards (1986: 201) suggests that people confuse greater evidence of an agent's blameworthiness with that agent's being more blameworthy. After all, the killer driver's recklessness is more evident to others than the merely reckless driver's recklessness. The list goes on (Cholbi 2014: 326–332; Domsky 2004: 446; Enoch 2012: 100–103; Jensen 1984: 325–328; Levy 2016; Martin and Cushman 2016; Royzman and Kumar 2004: 338–339; Scanlon 2015: 105; Thomson 1989: 208–210; Wolf 2001: 10–13). I do not assess any of these error theories, because error theories typically diminish the plausibility of a view only when we have independent reasons—that is, direct and indirect arguments—to think that the view is false. For this reason, I offer my error theory *after* my indirect and direct arguments for the Moral Luck View.

12 Greco's distinction roughly tracks the distinction between attributability and accountability moral responsibility. See Shoemaker (2015) and Watson (1996) for expositions of these purported kinds of moral responsibility.

13 In Hartman (2017: 133–135), I argue that whether compatibilism or libertarianism is correct, some or other suitable kind of counterfactual of freedom is true that fills out this account of moral worth.

14 Daniel Dennett (2015: 103–104) does not see a problem here, because he appears to think that constitutive luck averages out over the long run. It seems to me that Dennett's claim is implausible. As Bruce Waller (2011: 118) nicely recognizes, "The initial advantage [of good constitutive luck] is much more likely to be cumulative, rather than [to be] offset by subsequent bad breaks."

15 Proponents on both sides of the moral luck debate, including Zimmerman (2002: 575), agree that this aspiration is incoherent. At the very least, then, Greco's error theory does not face a *distinctive* difficulty due to the way in which essential moral worth is shaped by essential constitutive luck.

16 Not everyone agrees that part (iii) has no bearing on person-level evaluation (cf. Sorenson 2014: 309–310).

17 I am grateful to Ian Church, Michael McKenna, András Szigeti, and participants of the Summer Workshop on Moral Responsibility at the University of Gothenburg and the Linköping University Department Colloquium for comments and questions.

References

Anderson, M.B. (2011) "Molinism, Open Theism, and Soteriological Luck," *Religious Studies* 47(3), 371–381.
——. (forthcoming) "Moral Luck as Moral Lack of Control," *The Southern Journal of Philosophy*.
Brogaard, B. (2003) "Epistemological Contextualism and the Problem of Moral Luck," *Pacific Philosophical Quarterly* 84(1), 351–370.
Cholbi, M. (2014) "Luck, Blame, and Desert," *Philosophical Studies* 169(2), 313–332.
Coffman, E.J. (2015) *Luck: Its Nature and Significance for Human Knowledge and Agency*, New York: Palgrave Macmillan.
Dennett, D. (2015) *Elbow Room: The Varieties of Free Will Worth Wanting*, New Edition, Cambridge: MIT Press.
Domsky, D. (2004) "There Is No Door: Finally Solving the Problem of Moral Luck," *The Journal of Philosophy* 101(9), 445–464.
Driver, J. (2012) "Luck and Fortune in Moral Evaluation," in M. Blaauw (ed.) *Contrastivism in Philosophy: New Perspectives*, New York: Routledge.
Enoch, D. (2012) "Being Responsible, Taking Responsibility, and Penumbral Agency," in U. Heuer & G. Lang (eds.) *Luck, Value, and Commitment: Themes from the Ethics of Bernard Williams*, Oxford: Oxford University Press, pp. 95–132.
Enoch, D., & Guttel, E. (2010) "Cognitive Biases and Moral Luck," *Journal of Moral Philosophy* 7(3), 372–386.
Enoch, D., & Marmor, A. (2007) "The Case Against Moral Luck," *Law and Philosophy* 26(4), 405–436.
Feinberg, J. (1962) "Problematic Responsibility in Law and Morals," *The Philosophical Review* 71(3), 340–351.
Greco, J. (1995) "A Second Paradox Concerning Responsibility and Luck," *Metaphilosophy* 26(1), 81–96.
Hales, S. (2015) "A Problem for Moral Luck," *Philosophical Studies* 172(9), 2385–2403.
Hanna, N. (2014) "Moral Luck Defended," *Noûs* 48(4), 683–698.
Hartman, R.J. (2014) "How to Apply Molinism to the Theological Problem of Moral Luck," *Faith and Philosophy* 31(1), 68–90.
——. (2017) *In Defense of Moral Luck: Why Luck Often Affects Praiseworthiness and Blameworthiness*, New York: Routledge.
——. (forthcoming-a) "Constitutive Moral Luck and Strawson's Argument for the Impossibility of Moral Responsibility," *Journal of the American Philosophical Association*.
——. (forthcoming-b) "Moral Luck and the Unfairness of Morality," *Philosophical Studies*.
——. (manuscript) "Against the Character Solution to the Problem of Moral Luck."
Jensen, H. (1984) "Morality and Luck," *Philosophy* 59(229), 323–330.
Latus, A. (2003) "Constitutive Luck," *Metaphilosophy* 34(4), 460–475.
Levy, N. (2011) *Hard Luck: How Luck Undermines Free Will and Moral Responsibility*, Oxford: Oxford University Press.
——. (2016) "Dissolving the Puzzle of Resultant Moral Luck," *Review of Philosophy and Psychology* 7(1), 127–139.
MacKenzie, J. (2017) "Agent-Regret and the Social Practice of Moral Luck," *Res Philosophica* 94(1), 95–117.
Macnamara, C. (2015) "Blame, Communication, and Morally Responsible Agency," in R. Clarke, M. McKenna, & A. Smith (eds.) *The Nature of Moral Responsibility*, Oxford: Oxford University Press, pp. 211–236.
Martin, J.W., & Cushman, F. (2016) "The Adaptive Logic of Moral Luck," in J. Sytsma & W. Buckwalter (eds.) *A Companion to Experimental Philosophy*, Chichester: Wiley-Blackwell, pp. 190–202.
McKenna, M. (1998) "The Limits of Evil and the Role of Moral Address: A Defense of Strawsonian Compatibilism," *Journal of Ethics* 2(2), 123–142.

——. (2012) *Conversation and Responsibility*, Oxford: Oxford University Press.

Moore, M.S. (1997) *Placing Blame: A General Theory of Criminal Law*, Oxford: Oxford University Press.

Nagel, T. (ed.) (1979) "Moral Luck," in *Mortal Questions*, Cambridge: Cambridge University Press, pp. 24–38.

Otsuka, M. (2009) "Moral Luck: Optional, Not Brute," *Philosophical Perspectives* 23(1), 373–388.

Parker, R. (1984) "Blame, Punishment, and the Role of Result," *American Philosophical Quarterly* 21(3), 269–276.

Peels, R. (2015) "The Modal Solution to the Problem of Moral Luck," *American Philosophical Quarterly* 52(1), 73–87.

Pritchard, D. (2005) *Epistemic Luck*, Oxford: Oxford University Press.

Rescher, N. (1990) "Luck," *Proceedings and Addresses of the American Philosophical Association* 64(1), 5–19.

——. (1995) *Luck: The Brilliant Randomness of Everyday Life*, New York: Farrar, Straus, and Giroux.

Richards, N. (1986) "Luck and Desert," *Mind* 95(378), 198–209.

Rivera-López, E. (2016) "How to Reject Resultant Moral Luck Alone," *Journal of Value Inquiry* 50(2), 415–423.

Rosebury, B. (1995) "Moral Responsibility and 'Moral Luck'," *The Philosophical Review* 104(4), 499–524.

Rosell, S. (2015) "Moral Luck and True Desert," in A. Buckareff, C. Moya, & S. Rosell (eds.) *Agency, Freedom, and Moral Responsibility*, New York: Palgrave Macmillan.

Royzman, E., & Kumar, R. (2004) "Is Consequential Luck Morally Inconsequential? Empirical Psychology and the Reassessment of Moral Luck," *Ratio* 17(3), 329–344.

Russell, P. (2017) "Free Will Pessimism," in D. Shoemaker (ed.) *Oxford Studies in Agency and Responsibility*, vol. 4, Oxford: Oxford University Press, pp. 93–120.

Scanlon, T.M. (2015) "Forms and Conditions of Responsibility," in R. Clarke, M. McKenna, & A. Smith (eds.) *The Nature of Moral Responsibility: New Essays*, Oxford: Oxford University Press, pp. 89–111.

Shoemaker, D. (2015) *Responsibility from the Margins*, Oxford: Oxford University Press.

Smith, A. (2013) "Moral Blame and Moral Protest," in D. Justin Coates & Neal A. Tognazzini (eds.) *Blame: Its Nature and Norms*, Oxford: Oxford University Press, 27–48.

Sorensen, K. (2014) "Counterfactual Situations and Moral Worth," *Journal of Moral Philosophy* 11(3), 294–319.

Strawson, G. (1994) "The Impossibility of Moral Responsibility," *Philosophical Studies* 75(1–2), 5–24.

Swinburne, R. (1989) *Responsibility and Atonement*, Oxford: Oxford University Press.

Thomson, J.J. (1989) "Morality and Bad Luck," *Metaphilosophy* 20(3–4), 203–221.

Wallace, R.J. (1994) *Responsibility and the Moral Sentiments*, Cambridge, MA: Harvard University Press.

Waller, B.N. (2011) *Against Moral Responsibility*, Cambridge, MA: MIT Press.

Watson, G. (1996) "Two Faces of Moral Responsibility," *Philosophical Topics* 24(2), 227–248.

——. (ed.) (2004) "Responsibility and the Limits of Evil: Variations on a Strawsonian Theme," in *Agency and Answerability: Selected Essays*, Oxford: Oxford University Press, pp. 219–259.

Williams, B. (ed.) (1981) "Moral Luck," in *Moral Luck: Philosophical Papers 1973–1980*, Cambridge: Cambridge University Press.

——. (1985) *Ethics and the Limits of Philosophy*, Cambridge, MA: Harvard University Press.

——. (1993) "Postscript," in Daniel Statman (ed.) *Moral Luck*, Albany: State University of New York Press, pp. 1–34.

Whittington, L.J. (2014) "Getting Moral Luck Right," *Metaphilosophy* 45(4–5), 654–667.

Wolf, S. (2001) "The Moral of Moral Luck," *Philosophical Exchange* 31(1), 4–19.

Zagzebski, L. (1994) "Religious Luck," *Faith and Philosophy* 11(3), 397–413.

Zimmerman, M.J. (2002) "Taking Luck Seriously," *The Journal of Philosophy* 99(11), 553–576.

——. (2006) "Moral Luck: A Partial Map," *Canadian Journal of Philosophy* 36(4), 585–608.

——. (2015) "Moral Luck Reexamined," in David Shoemaker (ed.) *Oxford Studies in Agency and Responsibility*, vol. 3, Oxford: Oxford University Press, pp. 136–159.

21

LUCK AND LIBERTARIANISM

Laura W. Ekstrom

Libertarianism in metaphysics is traditionally characterized as the view that human free will is incompatible with causal determinism, coupled with the claim that human beings in fact have free will. The thesis of causal determinism is the thesis that every event is the causally necessary outcome of prior events, given the laws of nature. Alternatively expressed, the thesis of causal determinism is the claim that there is at every moment exactly one physically possible future, where a physically possible future is a future consistent with the past and the actual natural laws. In order not to make a presumption about the natural laws that in fact govern human deliberation and action, an agency theorist might pose what is termed a "libertarian account of free will," without making the further empirical claim that human beings in fact have free will of that sort. Such a theorist articulates what would need to be true in order for human beings to have free will. So as not to imply the further empirical thesis, such a theorist might call her account an "indeterminist" or "incompatibilist" account of free will.

Libertarian or indeterminist accounts of free will come in different varieties, including the broad categories of agent-causal accounts and event-causal accounts, among others. Influential agent-causal accounts were championed by, for instance, Thomas Reid, C.A. Campbell, and Roderick Chisholm, and in the contemporary literature such accounts have been articulated or defended by theorists including Helen Steward, Timothy O'Connor, Randolph Clarke, Meghan Griffith, and Derk Pereboom. Agent-causal theories characteristically maintain that, in accounting for free action, one must appeal to irreducible substance causation. As Griffith puts it, according to the agent-causalist, "the agent, the person, is a metaphysical substance whose causal activity grounds autonomous agency (and responsibility) … exercises of free will require something other than the usual causal story about actions flowing from mental states or events" (Griffith 2017: 73). When George freely flips on the light switch, for instance, according to the agent-causalist, essential to accounting for this free act is an irreducible causal relation between a substance, George, and some relevant event. (What the agent, as a substance, irreducibly causes varies by particular agent-causal account.)

Event-causal theorists, by contrast, suggest that, while we are perfectly sensible in making such statements as "George freely flipped on the light switch," nonetheless in such cases we are speaking in shorthand: what we really believe or ought to believe is that certain events involving George—events of which George is the subject—brought about the switch flipping. These events include, for example, George's coming to desire more light in the room and his forming the intention to flip the switch. On event-causal indeterminist accounts of free action, no appeal is

239

made to irreducible causal relations between substances and events; rather, preceding free action is a series of events that are causally connected. Event-causal indeterminist theories have been developed in recent literature by Robert Kane, Laura Ekstrom, Christopher Franklin, Alfred Mele, and David Hodgson.

A prominent charge against libertarian or indeterminist accounts of free will, as a bunch, is that they allegedly depict free agency in a way that is akin to positing something like a roulette wheel in the head. That is, some critics contend that on an indeterminist account of the nature of free agency, preceding a directly free act there is a bit of magic or randomness or perhaps some kind of metaphysically odd goings-on that any scientifically informed person ought to feel embarrassed to posit. Sometimes a charge in this neighborhood is expressed as the worry that libertarian or indeterminist accounts of free will succumb to a problem of luck, or that they depict agents as vulnerable to luck rather than as appropriately in charge of how they act.

In what follows, I reflect on instances of lucky and unlucky events, propose an account of the nature of luck, and address the charge that libertarian or indeterminist accounts of free will are undermined by a problem of luck.

On Luck

When we think carefully about the term "luck" and aim to capture examples commonly thought to count as instances of lucky and unlucky events, we arrive, I think, at something like the account I will set out below, which I call the SURE account of luck: a lucky event is a Significant, Uncontrolled, Risky Event.

Regarding the importance of the first condition, significance: Sometimes in speaking loosely we equate *luck* and *chance*. However, one feature that distinguishes between chance events and lucky ones is that a chance event—such as an electron's being in one place rather than another—might be of no significance to anyone. The event might not matter. An event can be chancy or a matter of chance and have no value. Lucky events, by contrast, are counted as lucky in part because they are significant to someone or to something about which someone cares—their occurring or not occurring is bad or good from someone's perspective.

To speak to the second condition, absence of control: In Thomas Nagel's categorization of kinds of luck in his influential article on moral luck—causal, circumstantial, resultant, and constitutive—the core notion is that of something's being uncontrolled, such that a circumstance, outcome, event, action, or trait is not "up to" someone, not sufficiently or wholly within the sphere of his agency. For instance, one's choices might put in motion a series of events that snowball for good: One might play a part in initiating a social movement that results in positive legislative change. Or one's choices could be part of a series of events that work together for ill: One's vote might help to elect a leader whose actions lead to a devastating war. These results are, with respect to the agent in question, lucky or unlucky, as the case may be. Likewise, many of the circumstances we face in our lifetimes are not up to us: whether or not we live through an economic depression, for instance, and whether or not we are betrayed by someone we love. Some aspects of our own constitution as persons are (at least apparently) under our control. For instance, I can work on my patience and compassion, and I can take steps to alter my physical attributes by diet and exercise, coloring my hair, and so on. It is not up to us, though, that we have certain natural endowments, including some physical features, such as natural hair color and height, and some psychological traits, such as natural curiosity and a tendency toward introversion. What concerns Nagel in thinking about luck is the absence of agent control.

To speak to the third condition, risk: In accounting for luck in terms of both significance and absence of control, some theorists take their work to be completed. John Greco, for instance, claims: "To say that something occurs as a matter of luck is just to say that it is not under my control" (Greco 1995: 83). Similarly, Daniel Statman writes:

Luck and Libertarianism

> Let us start by explaining what we usually mean by the term "luck." Good luck occurs when something good happens to an agent P, its occurrence being beyond P's control. Similarly, bad luck occurs when something bad happens to an agent P, its occurrence being beyond his control.
>
> *Statman 1991: 146*

Consider the following examples of events and states of affairs, however, which serve as challenges to an account of luck requiring only absence of control and significance: the Sun's rise tomorrow; the non-occurrence of an attack on the nuclear power plant near my home; the forces of gravitation continuing to hold; the emergence of clean drinking water from my kitchen faucet; your seeing what is before you when you open your (uncovered) eyes upon awaking; no one having murdered you in your sleep last night; the continued beating of your heart; and my house not having been flooded in a tsunami.

Each one of these cases is something that is significant for me or for you. Each is out of our control. However, none of these cases would typically be described as "lucky." More carefully, given the filling in of some relevant facts—such as that there *never* have been threats to the power plant near my home; scientists have not announced a finding that the laws of gravitation will suddenly cease to hold; no alerts have been sounded concerning the tainting of my drinking water, which has always been clean in the past; you have no medical condition that makes your vision unreliable; you live in a safe area, and there have been no threats against your life; you have no unusual heart condition; I live nowhere near a flood zone—none of the cases given in the previous paragraph would be accurately described as "lucky."

You might remark, of course, "I'm lucky no one murdered me in my sleep last night," but ordinarily this makes sense only against a background of facts about your beliefs concerning your circumstances and other matters, such as that you spent the night last night in a motel in a particularly dangerous area, or that there have been a string of unsolved murders in your neighborhood. If we take it that you have held in mind a thought such as one of these as you made your remark, then typically we do not think you have misused the term "lucky;" rather, in such a context, we see that your not having been murdered in your sleep last night was not, from your perspective, virtually certain. To the contrary, it seemed to you to be something that might well not have occurred. In other words, you took there to be a real risk that you might have been murdered.

The sun's rising tomorrow, your heart's continuing to beat, and so on—these, to many of us, in usual circumstances, are expected as part of the ordinary routine. By contrast, the notion of something's happening by luck is typically associated with its occurring such that there was, prior to its occurrence, a perceived significant chance that it might not have occurred. Its non-occurrence was a *genuine risk*.

On this approach to understanding luck, then, the term "lucky event" can be defined by the following necessary conditions, which are jointly sufficient. The articulation of each condition is an attempt to make more precise the relevant notions of significance, lack of control, and risk.

1. *Significance*: An event E is lucky for an agent S—that is, is a matter of good luck or bad luck for S—only if (i) E is significant to S, as judged by S, or (ii) E is significant to S, as judged by a rational informed evaluator, T, or (iii) E would be assessed as significant to S by a (hypothetical) rational informed evaluator, T*, were T* to (exist and) learn of the relevant features of E and S.
2. *Lack of Control*: An event E is lucky for an agent S—that is, is a matter of good luck or bad luck for S—only if the occurrence of E is not fully under S's control.
3. *Risk*: An event E at t is lucky for an agent S—that is, is a matter of good luck or bad luck for S—only if (i) S rationally takes there to be (or to have been) a considerable risk [substantial chance] that, given the circumstances in the temporal interval just prior to t, E will not occur at t (or might not have occurred at t, if E has already occurred) or (ii) S would rationally take there to be (or to

241

have been) a considerable risk [substantial chance] that, given the circumstances in the temporal interval just prior to t, E will not occur (or might not have occurred, if E has already occurred) were S rationally to assign a subjective probability to the occurrence of E [or were S rationally to assess (or to have assessed) the risk of the non-occurrence of E] or (iii) in a case in which S is incapable of forming probability judgments [assessments of risk], a rational informed proxy for S takes (or would take) there to be (or to have been) a considerable risk [substantial chance] that, given the circumstances in the temporal interval just prior to t, E will not occur (or might not have occurred, if E has already occurred).[1]

Indeterminist Free Will and Luck

Suppose that we adopt the SURE account, or some suitably amended related account, as an account of a lucky event.

One pertinent question is this: Is it *important* that we have a detailed account of the nature of luck, when our aim is to assess indeterminist accounts of free will with respect to concerns about luck? If we want to be careful in our accusations against types of theories of free agency and in our responses to those charges, it would seem to be important. That is, when theorists use the term "luck" as a weapon against certain theories of free will, it would seem to be helpful to pin down what luck is, so as to be clear about what intuitions are or are not, and should or should not be, doing crucial work.

However, it is evidently the case, as will become clearer further on, that the debates concerning "luck" and free will truly rest, at base, on varying understandings of *control* and *abilities*, as well as background intuitions concerning causation, explanation, and selection.

On the event-causal indeterminist account of free will I have defended (Ekstrom 2016), in a case of directly free action, the act is caused non-deviantly and indeterministically by certain kinds of agent-involving events—that is, attitudes of hers, such as preferences, convictions, desires, values, and beliefs, which provide a reasons explanation of the act—and the act is not the result of compulsion, manipulation, or coercion for which the agent herself has not freely arranged.[2] An act counts as a directly free act just in case it is an act the freedom of which does not derive from earlier free acts. Up until the directly free act is performed, there remains a chance that the agent will do otherwise.

If our decisions and other acts are indeterministically caused by the relevant kinds of prior agent-involving events, rather than deterministically caused by such events, then those decisions and other acts have seemed to some people to be random or accidental or "a matter of luck." According to Neil Levy, for instance, standard versions of both event-causal libertarianism and agent-causal libertarianism "introduce a degree of luck into free action, which is unacceptable" (Levy 2011: 41). Both kinds of libertarian accounts of free action, Levy contends, "fail because on either kind of libertarianism, it is a matter of luck that the agent chooses, or is the source of, the action he actually performs" (Levy 2011: 42).

However, I think such concerns can be successfully answered. First, a free act, as the event-causal libertarian depicts it, is not *random*, since it is caused and justified by reasons. It does not happen magically or for no reason at all; it has a causal history and a reasons explanation. Furthermore, a free act on the event-causal libertarian account is not *accidental*; instead, it is something the agent does on purpose. But do event-causal libertarian accounts of free action leave an agent *vulnerable to luck* in what she decides to do?

Consider, for instance, a decision concerning whether or not to make an offer to purchase a particular house. For some people this is an easy decision: the house is clearly the best among a range of attractive options, exactly suited to one's needs and in just the right location. But suppose that Mary has been on a house hunt for a few years in a down market: the inventory of available homes for sale is low, and few of those that come available meet the various needs of members of the family, including a location in the same school district so that the teens in the family can finish their remaining years of high school with known peers and teachers, as well as all or most of the home being on one level in order to accommodate a family member's joint problems, and few or no stairs at the entrances of the house for the same reason. Suppose Mary has found a house that is in the right school district and mostly on one level, but that there are multiple stairs at each entrance. She has investigated various options for addressing the accessibility problem—ramps, lifts, and so on—and adding the cost of these to the asking price of the house puts it significantly above what she had wanted to spend. But the house has a sufficient number of bedrooms and other positive features: good layout, natural light, convenience to shopping. Mary's question is whether or not the improvement in lifestyle that would come with the purchase of the house is worth the increase in costs over the home in which the family currently lives. The potential new home is bigger, but more expensive. It is less accessible, but more suitable for entertaining. Mary is a cautious deliberator, torn between a move up in living space and, on the other hand, the freedom to travel, dine out and such that comes with the current lower mortgage.

On the event-causal indeterminist account of free action mentioned above, in a case of directly free action, the act is caused non-deviantly and indeterministically by particular sorts of agent-involving events—attitudes of hers, which provide a reasons explanation of the act—and the act is not the result of compulsion, manipulation, or coercion for which the agent herself has not freely arranged. In the present case, suppose that Mary decides to make an offer to purchase the house. Her decision is a free act just in case she has not been the victim of manipulation, compulsion, or coercion as she made it, and the relevant considerations, many of which are enumerated above, have non-deviantly and indeterministically caused the decision to make an offer.

In supposing that the various reasons Mary has cause the decision indeterministically rather than deterministically, have we turned the decision to make an offer to purchase the house into a lucky event? That is, is it a matter of *luck* that Mary has decided to make a purchase offer?

The decision is significant, and it is risky in the sense specified. So the question rests on the condition of lack of control. The answer to our question concerning the luckiness or non-luckiness of Mary's decision depends on what it means for an event to be fully under a person's control. And in attempting to unpack this meaning, we find ourselves in a discussion of agents' powers, abilities, skills, and opportunities—right in the thick of things in the debate over the nature of free action.

On a natural account of what it is for an event to be fully under a person's control, an event E is under S's full control just in case S can voluntarily and rationally make it the case that E occurs and S can voluntarily and rationally prevent the occurrence of E. On this account, an event E is *not* fully under S's control, then, just in case either (i) S cannot voluntarily and rationally make E occur or (ii) S cannot voluntarily and rationally prevent E's occurrence. Does an agent's having full control over an event on this account require the falsity of the thesis of determinism? Compatibilists might maintain that, in the case of a free decision, the agent *can* make it the case voluntarily and rationally that the decision occurs simply by using her skills for coming to a decision for reasons that cause and justify it, and the agent *can* voluntarily and rationally prevent the occurrence of the decision, since she possesses the skills either to not make a decision at all at the time or to make a different decision for reasons that would cause and justify it (or both).

By contrast, incompatibilists might maintain that it is only if determinism is false and indeterminism is appropriately located within an agent's decision process that an agent has both the relevant powers and the opportunities to exercise them, since at the time of the decision over which she has full control, the past and the natural laws *leave room for* her abilities to be exercised in either one of more than one way. From the perspective of the incompatibilist, then, provided that the decisions in question are significant ones and that the agents in question prior to their decisions take there to be a significant chance (risk) that they will not make those particular decisions, causally determined compatibilist-free decisions meet the conditions of the account of luck, in being out of the agent's full control. In a case in which the causally determined compatibilist-free agent decides to do the right thing, she is lucky that the past and the natural laws led to her deciding in that way. Such an agent was lucky to make the right decision because it was not under her full control that she decided as she did, since being under her full control has incompatibilist conditions.

Arguably, then, the control that an agent with event-causal-libertarian freedom has is "enhanced" over that had by an agent with compatibilist freedom in that it is only the first who has full control over her free decisions: she can voluntarily and rationally make them occur and she can voluntarily and rationally prevent them, in the circumstances. And for this reason the free decisions as depicted by the event-causal indeterminist account are not lucky. Free acts on the event-causal indeterminist account are not out of the agent's control.

The critic will object that this does not work. The event-causal-libertarian free agent, the objector might contend, cannot *select which* of the potential decision outcomes is the actual outcome of her deliberation over what to do. The problem is alleged to be this: if some of her reasons incline toward one decision outcome and other of her reasons incline toward a different decision outcome (or toward not making a decision in the circumstances), then which way it turns out is not up to her or is not under her full control and so is lucky.

Take again our case about deciding whether or not to make an offer to purchase a particular house. Suppose that the agent is in motivational equipoise. As Derk Pereboom presses the problem, we could now ask this: with this motivational equipoise in place, what is it that *settles* whether the decision to make the offer occurs or the decision not to make an offer occurs (Pereboom 2001, 2014a, 2014b)? It might seem that the event-causal libertarian can only say that when one of the decisions occurs, it does so without anything about the agent settling that it did. Why might one think so? Because the extent to which the agent is involved is, at this point, allegedly exhausted by the preceding considerations, which by hypothesis are in equipoise. One might doubt that this picture allows sufficient agential control for free agency. Here, one might suggest, the agent-causalist has an apparent advantage, since she can say that the agent, as substance, settles which outcome occurs.

At this point it is crucial to ask the following question. What does it mean for an agent to "settle" a matter? It seems to me that it means that the agent decides what to do. She settles the matter at hand by making a decision concerning what to do in the circumstances. If the notion of settling in the luck objector's objection means "causally determines," then it is true indeed that nothing settles which outcome occurs, on the event-causal libertarian model of free action. If the allegation is that it takes causal determination of a choice in order for that choice to be free, then one can simply and plausibly deny the allegation. To merely make the allegation is to beg the question against all incompatibilist accounts of free agency.

It is important to notice that indeterministic causes *bring about* their effects (Anscombe 1981). The causal events—in this case the agent's attitudes or considerations—do not simply sit around, inert, waiting for someone to give them causal power. The event-causal libertarian maintains that, when the agent makes the free decision, her decision is caused and justified by her reasons, and at the time of making it she had the power to do otherwise by making a different decision (or not deciding at all) for reasons that would have caused and justified that outcome. Thus the decision she made was up to her.

Thus, it *is* something about the agent that settles which decision occurs: the agent exercises her will in making a decision for reasons. To exercise one's will is to use one's ability to choose. From my point of view, it is not true that an agent-causalist has an advantage in being able to say that the agent, as substance, settles which decision occurs, for that requires a substance to stand in a causal relation with an event, a notion I (though not others) find to be opaque and to raise more problems than it is meant to solve. The event-causal libertarian has the advantage in being able to say that events—the occurrence of certain of an agent's attitudes, which are considerations relevant to the decision—cause the event of the decision. That is what it *is* for an agent to exercise her ability to make a decision for reasons.

The critic might reply: but what explains or accounts for or caused the fact or state of affairs that there was the particular decision outcome there was, rather than a different outcome? The event-causal libertarian, the critic might charge, cannot offer an explanation or an account for (or name the cause of) this fact of A rather than B. If the answer is simply, "that is the way the indeterministic deliberative or decision process happened to turn out," then does this not show that, on the event-causal libertarian model, the agent is not fully in control of her free decisions and hence that those decisions, so long as also significant and risky, are lucky events?

Recall what it is for an event to be lucky: it is for it to be a significant, uncontrolled, and risky event. The free (significant and risky) decision of an event-causal libertarian free agent is not a lucky event. When she freely decides to do A, she thereby decides to do A rather than B, and her decision to do so is under her control. If she had freely decided to do B, then she would have thereby decided to do B rather than A, and her decision to do so would be under her control. In neither case of decision-making is she passive—pushed about by some magical force called Luck—and in neither case is the decision uncaused or rationally inexplicable or arbitrary or random or a matter of luck.

To pursue the matter further, consider Peter van Inwagen's case (van Inwagen 2002) of Alice, who is deciding whether to lie or to tell the truth. Van Inwagen has argued that, if agents such as Alice are free with respect to their decisions, then the thesis of causal determinism must be false. Consider the following way of expressing a "luck problem" for an event-causal indeterminist account of free action, posed with respect to this case:

> We assume, now, that Alice has the ability to tell the truth and the ability to lie. This seems insufficient, however, because it seems to remain a matter of luck (or chance) whether Alice *exercises* her abilities *in one way rather than another*. This is just another way of saying that Alice lacks the power or control to exercise either one of the two abilities *such that* she can *select* which alternative to pursue.
>
> *Schlosser 2014: 381*

Suppose that Alice is free with respect to her decision concerning whether to lie or to tell the truth, and suppose that causal determinism is false. My response to the challenge posed in the quoted passage is as follows. When Alice exercises her abilities in one way, she thereby exercises them in one way rather than another. In making a decision concerning which alternative to pursue she has thereby selected which alternative to pursue. The luck objector, in this case Marcus Schlosser, contends that "it remains a matter of luck (and insufficient control) which alternative Alice will choose." However, the alternative Alice chooses is not a lucky event on the plausible account of luck described above.

Further on, Schlosser writes:

> [T]raditional libertarians hold that having free will consists in having a kind of control that cannot be had by agents in a deterministic world. Since neither non-deviant causation by reason-states nor the biasing of choices by reason-states requires genuine indeterminism, it seems that there is something missing in the event-causal account of libertarianism. Intuitively, what seems to be missing is the power or control over which alternative to pursue—the power or control to select one alternative rather than another ... proponents of the luck argument could not coherently give an account of this kind of control under the assumption that free choices are undetermined. They argue, in effect, that it is impossible to have this kind of control over undetermined choices.
>
> *Schlosser 2014: 384*

It is true that non-deviant causation by reason-states does not require genuine indeterminism. But it does not follow from this that something is missing in the event-causal libertarian account. Contrary to Schlosser's assertion, the event-causal libertarian free agent *does* have the power to select one alternative rather than another, and she selects one in deciding. The power to select one alternative (over another) is the ability to decide to act in that way such that one's decision to act in that way is caused but not determined by the inputs into one's decision process. On the event-causal libertarian account of free action, what we have is an agent who makes a decision for reasons that cause and justify the decision and who is not coerced, manipulated, or compelled in doing so and who could have instead done otherwise, by making a different decision or by not deciding at all. It is not as if something has happened here leaving the agent passive with respect to it. Rather, she decided at a time when she also could have done otherwise: she had the ability to do otherwise and the opportunity to exercise her ability to do otherwise afforded by the non-necessitation of a unique outcome by past events given the natural laws.

In sum, an event-causal indeterminist account of free will such as the one I have described above withstands objections in the neighborhood of "the problem of luck" alleged by various theorists to afflict libertarian accounts of free will. As has become clear in the course of the argument above, a plausible account of luck—one that captures our intuitions concerning a range of cases of lucky and unlucky events—has conditions that are not fully pertinent to the core issue in the debate over free agency and causal indeterminism: namely, the sort of agent control over an action that makes that action count as free. Nonetheless, I think it is important to pin down what luck is and is not, so as to make clear to "luck objectors" that they ought to put their charges in appropriate terms.

Notes

1 Compare a related account of luck in Levy 2011.
2 I defend an earlier event-causal indeterminist account on free action in Ekstrom (2000, 2003, 2011).

Bibliography

Anscombe, E. (1981) "Causality and Determination," in *The Collected Philosophical Papers of G.E.M. Anscombe*, vol. 2, Minneapolis: University of Minnesota Press, pp. 133–147.
Chisholm, R. (1964) "Human Freedom and the Self," The Lindley Lecture, University of Kansas.
Clarke, R. (2003) *Libertarian Accounts of Free Will*, Oxford: Oxford University Press.
Ekstrom, L. (2000) *Free Will: A Philosophical Study*, Boulder, CO: Westview Press.
———. (2003) "Free Will, Chance, and Mystery," *Philosophical Studies* 113, 153–180.
———. (2008) "Review of *Free Will and Luck*, by Alfred Mele," *Philosophical Books* 49, 71–73.
———. (2010) "Volition and the Will," in Timothy O'Connor & Constantine Sandis (eds.) *The Blackwell Companion to the Philosophy of Action*, Malden, MA: Wiley-Blackwell, pp. 99–107.
———. (2011) "Free Will Is Not a Mystery," in Robert Kane (ed.) *The Oxford Handbook of Free Will*, second edition, Oxford: Oxford University Press, pp. 366–380.
———. (2016) "Toward a Plausible Event-Causal Indeterminist Account of Free Will," *Synthese*, first online 4 July 2016, doi: 10.1007/s11229-016-1143-8.
———. (forthcoming) "Conscious Gestalts, Apposite Responses and Libertarian Freedom," in Michael Sevel & Allan McCay (eds.) *Free Will and The Law: New Perspectives*, New York: Routledge.
Franklin, C. (2013) "How Should Libertarians Conceive of the Location and Role of Indeterminism?" *Philosophical Explorations* 16, 44–58.
Greco, J. (1995) "A Second Paradox Concerning Luck and Responsibility," *Metaphilosophy* 26, 81–96.
Griffith, M. (2017) "Agent Causation," in Kevin Timpe, Meghan Griffith, & Neil Levy (eds.) *The Routledge Companion to Free Will*, New York: Routledge, pp. 72–85.
Hitchcock, C. (1999) "Contrastive Explanation and the Demons of Determinism," *British Journal for the Philosophy of Science* 50, 585–612.
Hodgson, D. (2012) *Rationality + Consciousness = Free Will*, Oxford: Oxford University Press.
Kane, R. (1996) *The Significance of Free Will*, Oxford: Oxford University Press.
———. (ed.) (2002) *Oxford Handbook of Free Will*, first edition, Oxford: Oxford University Press.
———. (ed.) (2011) *Oxford Handbook of Free Will*, second edition, Oxford: Oxford University Press.
———. (2011) "Rethinking Free Will: New Perspectives on an Ancient Problem," in Kane (ed.) *Oxford Handbook of Free Will*, second edition, Oxford: Oxford University Press, pp. 381–404.
Levy, N. (2011) *Hard Luck: How Luck Undermines Free Will and Responsibility*, Oxford: Oxford University Press.
Mele, A. (1995) *Autonomous Agents: From Self-Control to Autonomy*, Oxford: Oxford University Press.
———. (2006) *Free Will and Luck*, Oxford: Oxford University Press.
Nagel, T. (ed.) (1979) "Moral Luck," in *Mortal Questions*, Cambridge: Cambridge University Press, pp. 24–38.

O'Connor, T. (2000) *Persons and Causes: The Metaphysics of Free Will*, New York: Oxford University Press.

Pereboom, D. (2001) *Living Without Free Will*, New York: Cambridge University Press.

——. (2014a) "The Disappearing Agent Objection to Event-Causal Libertarianism," *Philosophical Studies* 169, 59–69.

——. (2014b) *Free Will, Agency, and Meaning in Life*, Oxford: Oxford University Press.

Schlosser, M. (2014) "The Luck Argument Against Event-Causal Libertarianism: It Is Here to Stay," *Philosophical Studies* 167, 375–385.

Statman, D. (1991) "Moral and Epistemic Luck," *Ratio* 4, 146–156.

Steward, H. (2012) *A Metaphysics for Freedom*, Oxford: Oxford University Press.

van Inwagen, P. (1983) *An Essay on Free Will*, Oxford: Oxford University Press.

——. (2002) "Free Will Remains a Mystery," in Robert Kane (ed.) *Oxford Handbook of Free Will*, first edition, pp. 158–179.

22

LUCK AND COMPATIBILISM

Mirja Pérez de Calleja

Free Will, Determinism, and the Luck Objection to Libertarianism

An old question in philosophy is whether free will is compatible with determinism. The two main positions in this debate are *compatibilism*, which says that free will and determinism are compatible, and *incompatibilism*, which says that they are incompatible. *Libertarians*, in the free will literature (unlike in political philosophy), are incompatibilists who claim that some people have free will and hence the world is indeterministic at some level.

Compatibilists and incompatibilists usually agree on understanding free will as the control condition on moral responsibility, namely whatever kind and amount of control one must have over one's will and behavior to qualify for being justly blamed and praised. Thus, obstacles to free will are influences and conditions that undermine a person's control in a way that might be—depending on the details of the case—sufficient to excuse or exempt her from moral responsibility. Compatibilists and incompatibilists might agree that several factors undermine people's free will independently of whether determinism does. Popular candidates include physical force, serious threats and coercion, debilitating mental disorders, brain tumors that significantly affect desires and tendencies, phobias, compulsions, addictions, and different forms of manipulation, such as brainwashing, social conditioning, and indoctrination.

The kind of determinism at issue here is physical determinism, to be distinguished from psychological, social, and evolutionary determinism, respectively. Physical determinism would affect each and every physical event, and not only general facts about some subset of phenomena, such as people's psychology, social dynamics, or evolutionary trends.

Peter van Inwagen's now standard definition of determinism says that determinism is "the thesis that there is at any instant exactly one physically possible future" (van Inwagen 1983: 3). In other words, if determinism is true, then at any point in the history of the universe, exactly one future in all its physical details is compatible with the past up to that point and the laws of nature. Thus, if the world is deterministic, so is the whole history of the universe down to every microphysical detail, and hence each human thought and action was already guaranteed to happen billions of years ago (presumably just after the Big Bang, if the laws of nature were fixed then). We do not know if determinism is true or false, but there are physicists and philosophers who bet either way (and some who claim that we know that it is true, or that it is false).

Note that determinism is not fatalism. The truth of determinism would not mean that we are destined to do all we do in the way in which Oedipus was doomed to kill his father and marry his mother. Oedipus was destined to kill his father and marry his mother no matter what else he did. If he had taken another course of action, he would have ended up killing his father anyway, a bit sooner or later, and in some different way than how he actually killed him. In contrast, if determinism is true, we are determined to think and do *all* we think and do, in the perfectly specific way in which we do. Arguably, whether or not the world is deterministic, our actions causally depend on our deliberations and decisions and, in general, events causally depend on prior events, in such a way that, had those causes not happened, those effects would not have happened either.[1]

Compatibilism is consistent with the thesis that we do not have free will, say because the world is indeterministic in a way that precludes free will, or because our actions are too strongly influenced by unconscious tendencies and attitudes that we do not identify with, or because our character traits, motives, and reactions are completely determined by our genes and early environment. However, most compatibilists claim that some people do have free will, and that acting freely is just acting knowingly and voluntarily, free from our list of standard excuses and exemptions.[2]

Incompatibilists, in contrast, claim that, if everything that happens, including each and every one of our traits, thoughts, choices, and bodily actions, was determined since billions of years ago to happen exactly as it does, then it is not *up to us* what we want and care for, what we think, nor, perhaps most importantly, what we choose. If determinism is true, what anyone chooses now was really *settled* billions of years ago. Thus, a typical incompatibilist condition for freedom of choice is that, until the agent chooses, it must remain *nomologically possible* (namely, compatible with the past up to that point and the laws of nature) that they will choose otherwise or refrain from choosing instead. For most incompatibilists, this is required for the agent to have been and remained able to choose otherwise, or to postpone decision, up to the moment of choice, and this ability is essential to free will.

This incompatibilist condition on free choice is what generates the luck objection to libertarianism.[3] If what I choose remains undetermined right until the moment I decide, in such a way that, just before that moment, both choosing to lie and choosing to tell the truth at the next moment are nomologically possible, then it is just a matter of chance that I choose as I do instead of otherwise. (The same problem arises if refraining from choosing at that moment is nomologically possible: then it is just a matter of chance that I choose as I do instead of choosing otherwise or refraining from choosing.) If my choice meets this incompatibilist condition on free choice, then it is nomologically possible for me to choose otherwise after going through exactly the same deliberation (if there is deliberation) and in exactly the same state of mind about the matter, without a change in my beliefs about my circumstance, the general reasons I take myself to have for each option, and so on. Thus, the luck objection goes, if my choice is undetermined in the way required by incompatibilists, then my choosing as I do instead of otherwise is just a matter of chance, and I am either lucky to choose the right thing or unlucky to choose the wrong thing, as the case may be.[4] This luck—luck about choosing as one does instead of otherwise at a certain point in time—is known in the free will literature as *present luck*.

It has typically been understood that present luck raises a problem only for incompatibilism, because this luck is entailed by incompatibilists' indeterminism condition on free choice, but it is not entailed by any necessary condition that compatibilists postulate. However, this assumption has recently been challenged in the literature. Several authors[5] have independently argued that the luck objection applies to compatibilism too. The present chapter explores two versions of what has come to be known as the *luck objection to compatibilism*, and some possible flaws of these objections. But first, a few words about the question of whether chance and determinism might be compatible.

Chance and Luck in a Deterministic World?

Many philosophers think that, even if determinism is true, some counterfactual conditionals[6] are true, such that if the past or the laws had been somewhat different, a different outcome would have ensued. For instance, determinism is compatible with its being true that, if it had not rained so much, the river would not have flooded—because if the river had not flooded due to the heavy rain, nothing else would have caused it to flood.

Taking this line of reasoning a bit further, several philosophers[7] have recently offered accounts of luck—the kind of luck that involves[8] chance present in lottery winnings and lightning strikes—on which determinism is compatible with chance and luck. According to these philosophers, what characterizes lucky events[9] is that they could easily have failed to occur, and what this requires is *not* that a different outcome might easily have ensued from *exactly* identical initial conditions, but rather from *relevantly* identical conditions that might themselves easily have been actual—possible conditions that differ from the actual conditions only in intuitively small and trivial respects. In a nutshell (and leaving aside the differences between these accounts), the claim is that, if determinism is true, there are still things that might *easily* have turned out differently than they actually did because, if the initial conditions had been only *slightly* different in intuitively unimportant respects, the outcome would have been different.

A further question is whether it is the case that, even if determinism is true, many things that happen might just have failed to happen (not for all we can tell, but objectively speaking), *given exactly similar initial conditions*. If determinism is true, might lottery winnings, lightning strikes, and similar events really be (and not merely appear) chancy, even if chance does require that a different outcome might have ensued *from identical initial conditions*? There is a growing body of work in philosophy of science that argues that determinism is compatible with objective chance.

It is standard to classify objects, properties, events and facts into different *levels*[10] that are ordered roughly like a layered cake, with the bottom layer corresponding to the most basic or fundamental microphysical level. Thus, we can say that the social and economic evolution of a country is settled by a huge number of mental and bodily actions and their consequences, which are in turn settled by neural, biological and mechanical events, which depend on chemical processes, which depend on molecular processes, which depend on atomic processes, which in turn depend on sub-atomic processes, and so on down to the most fundamental microphysical level. The economic development of a given society would not be different if, say, one person took a different route to the bank one day; but all the economically significant actions of a certain people within a certain period, in all their details, settle a specific set of economic developments. What goes on at each level is fully settled by what happens at the next level or levels[11] down, but not the other way around.

If determinism is true, then presumably the laws that govern the lowest microphysical level are deterministic. And it has traditionally been assumed that, if the lowest level is deterministic, then all the other levels are too, since they ultimately depend on the lowest level in the way just described. However, some philosophers[12] claim that determinism is compatible with objectively chancy events at higher levels, because whether or not an outcome is a matter of chance depends on the level of description at which the event is singled out and inserted into a web of causal relations.[13] Thus, even if the lowest-level microphysical processes that underpin an injection's stopping a malaria attack are deterministic, the injection's working instead of failing may be under-determined by the whole set of biochemical factors and conditions from which it ensues—namely, the injection's chemical content, the attack's severity, the person's health condition before the attack, and so on.

Whether or not determinism and objective chance are compatible, what seems clear is that, independently of determinism's truth, some very useful causal explanations are probabilistic. Probabilistic reasoning and explanation—and hence, *arguably*, chance—are essential in economics, decision theory, population statistics, evolutionary theory, the biology of diseases and their treatments, quantum mechanics, and (against popular opinion) even classical mechanics. And none of these disciplines assumes either the truth or the falsity of determinism.

Neil Levy's Luck Objection to Compatibilism

According to Neil Levy (2011, 2016), the truth of determinism is compatible with present luck, because determinism is compatible with choices being significantly influenced by events that happen by chance just a few moments before choice and, bypassing the agent's rational control, make a difference to what option the agent chooses. In particular, Levy (2011: 90–91; 2016: 4–5) says, even if determinism is true, our choices might be influenced by our mood swings, by what considerations come to mind during deliberation, by the force with which different considerations strike us, by the weight we give to each of the considerations that come to mind, by when and where our attention wanders, by how our deliberation is "primed by chance features of our environment" (Levy 2011: 91), and the like, in such a way that, if the chancy event occurs, the agent will choose one option, and if it does not occur, she will choose a different option. In sum, events such as considerations coming to mind, distractions, and so on are chancy and affect our choices in a way we do not control, whether determinism is true or false. So there is present luck under determinism as well. Thus, present luck is not only a problem for libertarians who endorse the typical libertarian indetermination condition on free choice; there is a luck problem for compatibilists too (Levy 2011: 91).

The response that both Alfred Mele (2006, 2015) and Ishtiyaque Haji (2016: 619) give to Levy's argument is that, even though, whether determinism is true or false, chancy events may affect our decisions in a way that bypasses our rational control, how these chancy events affect our deliberations and choices is in part up to us. For instance, it is within our power to either attend or fail to attend to considerations that come to mind, to assess these considerations with diligence and thoroughness or do exactly the opposite, and so on.

Levy's response to this objection is that considerations that come to mind chancily not only might *affect* deliberation; they might *make the difference* (holding fixed all the other considerations) to what outcome deliberation has—for instance, to whether someone chooses a prima facie laudable action or a censurable one instead. On Levy's view, despite people's control over whether and how they attend to considerations that come to mind, it is not fair to blame someone if they chose a bad action instead of a good one because they happened to have bad luck in what considerations struck them during deliberation.

However, for Levy, present luck is only half of the luck problem that compatibilists have. On Levy's view, there are two kinds of luck that undermine responsibility: present luck, and a kind of luck that Levy calls *constitutive luck*, following Thomas Nagel (1976, 1979).[14] Levy defines constitutive luck as "luck in the traits and dispositions that make one the kind of person one is" (Levy 2011: 29), which include, among other things, one's values and commitments (see Levy 2016: 6). Relatedly, Levy (2011: 88) defines an agent's *endowment* as the set of traits and dispositions that, due to being a product of her genes and early environment, is "the direct product of constitutive luck" (p. 88). During our lives, we often reflect, choose, and act in ways that modify our endowment, and hence some of the traits and dispositions that we have as adults are not part of our endowment, but rather part of our *modified endowment* (p. 88).

On Levy's view, not all luck involves chance: there is "chancy luck" (2011: 36) and "non-chancy luck" (pp. 24, 29, 36). Present luck is always chancy, but there is both chancy and non-chancy constitutive luck (pp. 30–32). For example, some personal traits are chancy because they might have been different if the person's environment during her formative years had been different, and because this formative environment might very well have been different (p. 31). But other personal traits are not chancy, because they are ensured by stable features of the person's environment and culture (pp. 31–32).

A paradigmatic example of a chancy lucky event is a given number's winning a lottery. This event meets Levy's three conditions to be chancy lucky for an agent (the lottery winner, in this case): (i) the event is significant (good or bad) for the agent; (ii) the agent lacks direct control over the event; and (iii) the event might easily have failed to occur, in the sense that it would, or would likely, have failed to occur if the actual conditions had been only slightly different in intuitively unimportant respects (Levy 2011: 36).[15] With this third condition, Levy intends to capture the fact that the event happened by chance without implying that the event was undetermined.

As to *non-chancy luck*, such as one's luck about some of the genes with which one is born, Levy (2011: 36) argues that it requires the satisfaction of four conditions. The first two conditions are exactly the same as the first two conditions for chancy luck. The third and fourth conditions capture the fact that the event or state of affairs is unusual in its kind, where the kind under which the event or state of affairs is classified is determined in each case by the context of interest (pp. 7, 33–34, 36). For instance, when someone says that a genius is lucky to be so clever, the relevant reference group is the group of humans, and not the group of mammals: the genius counts as lucky because he is cleverer than most people, and not because he is cleverer than his dog.[16]

Levy argues that present luck and constitutive luck *together* pose a fatal problem for compatibilism.[17] In particular, Levy thinks that the problem of constitutive luck might have had a solution if it had been possible to *take ownership* of one's endowment, by reflecting, choosing, and acting along the years in ways that contribute to strengthening, modifying, or dropping traits and dispositions that one was merely lucky (or unlucky) to get from one's genes and early environment.

But, Levy argues, any of these purported acts of self-formation will itself be either subject to present luck, or to constitutive luck, or to both, and hence one's modified endowment is also the result of luck (2011: 96). This is because choices made in a motivationally divided state are subject to present luck, while the rest of choices, namely the ones that are settled by whatever traits and dispositions the agent has at the time of choice, are either subject to constitutive luck or subject to both constitutive and present luck, since the agent's traits and dispositions at the time of choice will be either the result of her endowment, or the combined result of her endowment and of presently lucky and constitutively lucky actions that modified her endowment. So the problem of constitutive luck has no solution, because choices that are not settled by the agent's traits and dispositions are subject to present luck (pp. 87–89).

Similarly, the problem of present luck might have had a solution if there had been no constitutive luck; but, since acts that are not subject to present luck are subject to constitutive luck, present luck has no solution (pp. 87–89).

Thus, Levy's conclusion is that every choice and bodily action is, "(directly or indirectly) *either* the product of constitutive luck *or* of present luck, or both" (2011: 94, emphasis in the original; see also 2011: 8). Levy's luck objection to compatibilism is that

> the only plausible solution to the problem of constitutive luck, namely agents' taking responsibility for their initial endowment from their genes and formative environments, is vitiated by luck (since the acts whereby agents would take such responsibility themselves either *express* their constitutive luck, or are subject to present luck).
>
> *2011: 12*

Taylor Cyr (2017: 8–10) argues that Levy's luck objection to compatibilism is unsuccessful because, if the world were deterministic, not all actions of *taking ownership* of one's traits and dispositions would be subject to present luck. To illustrate this, Cyr (pp. 8–9) considers Charles, an agent in a deterministic world, who hears a dog yelp in pain and, thinking that it might be his neighbor's dog and reflecting that he wants to be the type of person who helps friendly dogs, decides to stop what he is doing and check if he can help. Cyr notes that Charles's decision is not subject to present luck on Levy's account, because, given Charles's appreciation of dogs, his habit to help dogs, and other relevant values and dispositions, his decision does not depend on the considerations that occur to him, the mood he happens to be in, his attention not wandering at the time, or the like. He was overwhelmingly likely to decide to look for the source of the yelp, independently of these chancy factors in the causal antecedents of his decision.

But Charles's decision, being an easy choice for him (which is what saves it from present luck), would count for Levy as an action that is settled by Charles's traits and dispositions at the time,[18] and hence an action that is subject either to constitutive luck, or to present luck, or to both, directly or indirectly. Pace Cyr (2017: 8, n. 21), Levy's luck objection to compatibilism does not succeed only if it is the case that, if determinism were true, all actions through which we might take responsibility for our endowments would be subject to present luck.[19] Again, Levy's premise is, rather, that all such actions—and all actions in general—would be either presently lucky, or constitutively lucky, or both. (See, for instance, Levy 2011: 94.) However, this claim has also been contested. Robert Hartman (2017: 47–48) has offered three classes of counterexamples to it. (Hartman's complete criticism of Levy is significantly more complex than his attack of this claim, and it centrally involves arguing against Levy's claim that present and constitutive luck necessarily undermine moral responsibility (see Hartman 2017: ch. 3). But, for reasons of space, I chose to focus on Hartman's counterexamples to Levy's claim that all actions are subject to either present luck, or constitutive luck, or both.)

First, Hartman (2017: 47–48) considers actions that are settled by the agent's modified endowment but fail to meet Levy's lack of direct control condition on constitutive (and present) luck. His example features Jane, who, brought up to be a thief in a family of thieves, progressively endorses her lifestyle and the values that come with it. One day, as an adult, she sees an opportunity to easily steal a wallet, and her modified endowment settles her deciding to steal it. "Plausibly," Hartman writes, "the event of Jane's stealing the wallet is an event over which she has direct control, because reaching out and grasping the wallet is a basic action that Jane can perform that will probably bring about the event of her stealing the wallet and because she realizes that this is the case" (p. 48). According to Levy (2011: 19), an agent has direct control over an event if she can bring about its occurrence by performing some basic action that she knows will probably bring about the event. Thus, given Levy's own conditions for direct control, Jane's stealing the wallet is under her direct control, and hence the act fails to meet Levy's conditions for constitutive luck. (The act also fails to meet Levy's conditions for present luck, both because it is under Jane's direct control, and because it is settled by Jane's traits and dispositions, rather than depending on chancy events that immediately precede it.)

Second, Hartman (2017: 48) considers actions that are settled by the agent's endowment but fail to meet Levy's significance condition for constitutive luck, and also the unlikeliness and uncommon instantiation conditions for chancy and non-chancy constitutive luck, respectively. As a result of an inherited disposition to be kind, Jeff holds the door open for a neighbor who is carrying boxes, in spite of the fact that he does not care about helping her on that occasion. Jeff's action is not presently lucky, since it is settled by his dispositions at the time of action. And it is not constitutively lucky either, because it stems from a disposition that he is not lucky to have, since it is a common one among people within Jeff's culture and it was unlikely for Jeff to have grown without developing it. Moreover, the action does not meet Levy's significance condition on either present or constitutive luck, because Jeff acts just out of habit, without caring about being kind on that occasion. Thus, the action is settled by Jeff's *endowment*, but is not constitutively (or presently) lucky.

Finally, Hartman (2017: 48) considers actions that are not constitutively lucky because they are not settled by the agent's traits and dispositions (neither by her endowment, nor by her modified endowment), but are not presently lucky either, because they are neither significant for the agent nor chancy. Hartman imagines Nathan, who is sure to vote for someone but is not inclined toward any candidate in particular. Just before he gets to the voting booth, three of his friends call him, independently but simultaneously, all to tell him to vote for Bernie Sanders. Nathan gets one of these calls and this settles his voting for Sanders. Even though Nathan's vote depends on a last minute call, it does not meet Levy's chanciness condition on present luck, because if Nathan had not received a call from that friend, he would have received a call (to the same effect) from either of the other two friends who called him. Moreover, Nathan's voting for Sanders does not meet Levy's significance condition on present luck, because Nathan does not care which candidate he votes for (he just cares about voting rather than abstaining).

Thus, Hartman has identified three classes of actions that are neither presently nor constitutively lucky according to Levy's own criteria. Arguably, however, the problem of luck for compatibilists that Levy identifies does not depend on the fact that he defines a lucky event's significance for an agent in terms of what that agent happens to care about at the time of action. Levy could, alternatively, understand a lucky event's being significant for an agent simply in terms of the event's being good or bad for the agent, whether or not she then cares about, or even properly understands, that event's implications and consequences for her own well-being and moral goodness.[20] On this account, being kind to his neighbor is good for Jeff just because doing morally good things is good for one, even on occasions when one does not care about that. But this only relieves a small part of the pressure of Hartman's counterexamples.

Mirja Pérez de Calleja's Luck Objection to Compatibilism

Mirja Pérez de Calleja's (2014) luck objection to compatibilism is, in a nutshell, that present luck is compatible with determinism because the chanciness that is inherent to present luck is independent of determinism's truth or falsity. Pérez de Calleja's argument starts by considering an indeterministic case of present luck, introduced by Mele (2006: 73–74) to illustrate that present luck is a problem for libertarians. Bob is a normal, healthy agent (with no mental disorders, addictions, etc.) who lives in an indeterministic world. At a given point in time, and after deliberating about the matter, Bob chooses to cheat on a bet, because he wants the money. Up to the time of decision, it was nomologically possible (i.e., compatible with the past and the laws of nature) for Bob to decide at that time not to cheat instead, for moral reasons that incline him against cheating. Thus, Bob's choice meets libertarians' indeterminism condition on freedom of choice, and it is subject to present luck.

Pérez de Calleja (2014: Section 2) argues that just making Bob's world deterministic—without changing his character traits, reasons, habits, desires, inclinations, deliberation, or state of mind about the matter at issue—would not change the fact that there is no explanation for why Bob chooses to cheat *instead of* choosing to do the right thing. This is because such an explanation would have to adduce some difference in high-level causal factors that can explain the fact that Bob chooses the option he chooses (namely, his reasons, motives, character traits, way to deliberate, and so on). For instance, Bob's remembering that he needs to pay a certain debt would explain why he chooses to cheat instead of choosing to refrain from cheating, if it were the case that, had he not remembered his debt (and holding fixed all the other high-level factors), he would have refrained from cheating. But we are assuming that no high-level factor makes the difference to what Bob chooses at the time in question. Bob is psychologically able to either cheat or refrain from cheating, given the way he is and his state of mind at the time of choice. That is why, in Mele's original indeterministic scenario, either choice is nomologically possible at the same point in time, after exactly the same past.

It follows from determinism's definition that, if determinism is true, then what actually happens at each point in time is the only nomologically possible continuation of the past. Thus, Pérez de Calleja grants that, if Bob's world were deterministic, then the past up to the time he chooses to cheat, given the deterministic laws of nature, would be compatible only with Bob's deciding to cheat at that moment, in the perfectly specific way in which he does down to every microphysical detail. Nothing else would be compatible with the past and the laws of nature, not even Bob's deciding to cheat in ways that differ only microphysically from how he actually decides to cheat. Thus, Pérez de Calleja grants that, if Bob's world were deterministic, there would be some explanation (possibly one too long for humans to comprehend) for why the perfectly specific microphysical process that underpins Bob's decision to cheat happens at that exact time instead of *anything else* happening then. But, according to Pérez de Calleja, this would *not* be an explanation for why Bob chooses to cheat instead of choosing to refrain. Again, such an explanation would have to adduce high-level factors, such as the reasons that Bob recognizes as relevant to choose either way, the weight he gives to different considerations during deliberation, or the like. Consider a roughly analogous fact: while a rock's exact shape and location on a mountain slope helps explain why an avalanche hits a mountain cabin in the perfectly specific way in which it does instead of hitting the cabin in some other way, the rock does not explain why the avalanche hits the cabin instead of missing it; had the rock not been there, the avalanche would still have buried the cabin.

Hence, Pérez de Calleja argues, determinism would not eliminate the chanciness in Bob's choosing to cheat instead of choosing to refrain from cheating, because determinism's truth would not change the fact that Bob is motivationally divided about what to do, and psychologically able both to cheat because he wants the money and (alternatively) to refrain from cheating because of moral reasons. Therefore, the chanciness in Bob's decision-making is not due to the fact that Bob's decision is undetermined.

More generally, according to Pérez de Calleja, the truth of determinism is independent of the fact that it is very likely that, in some cases where the agent is motivationally divided about what to do, there are small periods of time in which whether the agent decides to A or decides to B is a matter of chance, given a past identical in all *relevant* respects (where the aspects of the past that are relevant to explain a decision's content are all high-level factors concerning the agent's condition and state of mind). Therefore, she concludes, compatibilists and libertarians have the same problem of present luck: either they accept that lots of presently lucky decisions are free (despite how unintuitive this claim might be for some); or they accept that present luck precludes or at least undermines freedom of choice, and hence that many decisions that we ordinarily blame and praise are actually not free and responsible, or that they are not as free and responsible as we ordinarily take them to be.

Mele (2015: 13) grants that the truth of determinism is compatible with Bob's decision being chancy and subject to present luck. But, he argues, the dialectical implications of this are not as favorable to libertarians as Pérez de Calleja claims. While *typical libertarians* (p. 7)—i.e., libertarians who hold that an action is directly[21] free only if its non-occurrence remains nomologically possible until the time of action—must accept that every directly free action is presently lucky, compatibilists do not have to accept this, since no necessary condition on directly free action that compatibilists postulate implies present luck.

Mele (2015) acknowledges that many compatibilist accounts do in fact leave room for present luck in directly free action. But he notes that, unlike typical libertarians, compatibilists need not say that choices that are subject to present luck are free. If a compatibilist becomes convinced that present luck undermines freedom of choice, she can harden her conditions on free choice to rule out present luck, thus building a picture on which the only free choices are choices that are settled by the agent's state of mind at the time, and hence are not chancy. Alternatively, a compatibilist might claim that only motivationally settled choices are *directly* free, and that the freedom and moral responsibility of presently lucky choices is inherited from the freedom of settled choices that contributed to forming the moral character and reasons on which agents act on occasions in which they are motivationally divided about what to do. Importantly, the compatibilist can make her conditions on freedom of choice more demanding in either of these ways without abandoning compatibilism or the claim that we are free and responsible.

In contrast, Mele (2015) argues, a typical libertarian cannot accept that the motivationally divided decisions in question are too chancy to be directly free and responsible, without substantially changing her account of free will. She would have to limit the indeterminism required for direct freedom of choice to events that happen before choice (such as better judgments, the formation of preferences, or the like), or else become a compatibilist, an impossibilist (namely someone who claims that free will is impossible), or an agnostic about free will.

A Difference between Levy's and Pérez de Calleja's Views on Deterministic Present Luck

Both Levy and Pérez de Calleja claim that determinism is compatible with present luck, but they think this for different reasons. Levy (2011: 14) thinks that indeterminism is not necessary for chanciness. But, on his picture of deterministic present luck, what happens by chance is not the choice itself (which is antecedently settled), but rather some event in its causal antecedents that makes a difference to what the agent chooses. In contrast, undetermined presently lucky choices do themselves happen by chance on Levy's view. Thus, Levy believes that determinism is compatible with less chance than indeterminism is compatible with, and he concedes that the indeterminism required by libertarians diminishes the agent's degree of control (pp. 50–51).

But it is not clear why Levy does not apply his account of the chanciness that is compatible with determinism to choices themselves. Levy (2011: 3) says that we know that Megan is lucky to win the lottery even though we do not know if the world is deterministic or indeterministic, because we know that "had the balls rotated for microseconds longer, or if they had microscopic differences in curvature or roughness, different numbers would have been drawn" (see also Levy 2016: 4, n. 9.) Why does Levy think that, while events such as people winning lotteries and considerations coming to mind may happen by chance whether determinism is true or false, events such as choices may be chancy only if determinism is false? Levy does not explain on what criterion he makes this distinction.

It seems that, if an account of chance along the lines of Levy's (or Pritchard's, or Coffman's) applies to some mental events that happen in a deterministic world, then it applies also to choices performed in a deterministic world by an agent who is in a truly motivationally divided state of mind. Thus, it is unclear why Levy does not say, for instance, that a choice performed in a deterministic world is chancy if the agent might easily have chosen otherwise in a relevantly identical state of mind about the matter. (Perhaps Levy might want to add some further initial conditions that must be relevantly identical, such as the agent's unconscious desires and tendencies, her physical condition at the time, and so on. But this does not change the present point.)

Thus, one difference between Levy's and Pérez de Calleja's luck objections to compatibilism is that, on Levy's version of deterministic present luck, a deterministic agent would have decided otherwise only after deliberating differently (or, if there is no deliberation, only in a different state of mind about the matter on which she decides), due to some chancy factor in the decision's causal antecedents, such as a consideration's coming to mind or a mood change. In contrast, Pérez de Calleja claims that determinism's truth would not mean that no decisions are such that the agent might just have chosen otherwise after deliberating in the same way and while being in the same state of mind about the matter, including the considerations that she was taking into account, the mood she was in, and so on. So far, no argument in the literature has tried to show that determinism's truth would make a difference to which events are chancy and which ones are not, assuming that determinism is compatible with chance in the first place.

Questions for Future Research

One potentially fruitful avenue of research is the question of deterministic chance. Is objective chance really compatible with determinism, or is all chance in deterministic worlds merely epistemic (namely, a mere appearance of chance, due to our ignorance about hidden difference-makers)?

Another important question is whether luck requires objective chance or can be grounded just on epistemic chance. One possibility is that determinism is incompatible with objective chance but compatible with luck.

On the other hand, even if determinism is compatible with both luck and objective chance, an independent question with obvious dialectical implications is whether it matters or not that the alternative possibilities that compatibilists and libertarians may agree matter for free will are ever nomologically possible. We will not settle the compatibility debate until we settle this question, but it is hard to know how to address it directly.

Acknowledgments

I am very grateful to Bob Hartman for extremely useful comments and suggestions on previous drafts of this chapter.

Notes

1 On the difference between determinism and fatalism, see Hobart (1934: 16–17) and van Inwagen (1983: ch. 2).
2 See Strawson (1962) for a very influential argument in favor of the conclusion that determinism's truth makes no difference to moral responsibility: the conditions that ground moral responsibility are independent from whether determinism is true or false.
3 The reason why the luck objection is usually aimed at libertarians and not at incompatibilists is that an incompatibilist might say that free will is incompatible with the falsity of determinism too, and hence that free will is impossible.
4 The luck problem is most intuitively a threat to responsibility when the alternative decisions and ensuing actions have different moral values.
5 For reasons of space, this chapter does not discuss Seth Shabo's (Manuscript) elegant version of the luck objection to compatibilism. His objection is, in a nutshell, that compatibilist accounts according to which free will is independent of determinism's truth or falsity offer purportedly sufficient conditions on free choice that do not rule out the kind of indeterminism that brings about present luck.
6 A counterfactual conditional is a conditional whose antecedent, or if-clause, states something contrary to fact. Counterfactual conditionals have the form *If p had been the case, then q would have been the case*, or *If p were the case, then q would be the case*.
7 See, for instance, Driver (2013), Coffman (2007), and Pritchard (2005).
8 Not all chancy events are lucky. For a person to count as lucky (or unlucky) about a given chancy event, that event must matter, or be significant (good or bad) for that person (see Coffman (2007), Levy (2011), Mele (2006), and Pritchard (2005), to name just a few sources; Pritchard (2014) abandons this view).
9 Following convention, I use "lucky event" to refer to events about which someone is lucky or unlucky.
10 Whether these levels are levels of description or rather *ontological levels* (i.e., levels of being), and indeed whether there is a difference between these two possibilities, are difficult philosophical questions.
11 Again, the layered cake is only a rough analogy. The levels are not supposed to form a linear order.
12 To mention just a few: Glynn (2010), List and Pivato (2015), Loewer (2001), Sober (2010), and Strevens (2011). For arguments against the compatibility of determinism and objective chance, see Lyon (2011) and Schaffer (2007).
13 The arguments that these philosophers give for the compatibility of chance and determinism are interestingly diverse.
14 See also Bernard Williams (1976, 1981).
15 Levy does not use the notion of outcomes that might easily have failed to occur, but rather puts condition (iii) using a possible-worlds analysis of counterfactuals, largely following Pritchard's and Coffman's accounts of chancy events that occur in a deterministic world (see Levy 2011: ch. 2). The above formulation of Levy's condition in terms that avoid possible-worlds talk is controversial, and Levy does not (to my knowledge) subscribe to any such translation in particular.
16 These explications of Levy's conditions for chancy and non-chancy luck leave out important complexities that are not directly relevant to the present discussion.
17 More precisely, for historical compatibilism, namely the variety of compatibilism that claims that the history of an agent, and in particular the way they came to have the character and motives that they presently have, is relevant to whether they now act freely and responsibly.
18 Levy writes: "Decisions are easy for compatibilist agents when their dispositions and values render them easy; that is, when the pre-existing background of reasons (desires, attitudes, beliefs, and values) against which they deliberate decisively supports one course of action over alternatives" (2011: 94).
19 Cyr's idea seems to be that the agent has taken responsibility for that part of his modified endowment, but he provides no response to Levy's argument that it is not possible to take ownership for one's modified endowment.
20 See Coffman (2007) for an argument in favor of a significance condition along these lines.
21 A directly free action is one whose freedom does not derive from the freedom of actions in its causal antecedents.

References

Coffman, E.J. (2007) "Thinking about Luck," *Synthese* 158(3), 385–398.
Cyr, T. (2017) "Moral Responsibility, Luck, and Compatibilism," *Erkenntnis*: DOI 10.1007/s10670-017-9954-7.
Driver, J. (2013) "Luck and Fortune in Moral Evaluation," in M. Blaauw (ed.) *Contrastivism in Philosophy*, New York: Routledge, pp. 154–172.
Glynn, L. (2010) "Deterministic Chance," *British Journal for the Philosophy of Science* 61, 51–80.

Haji, I. (2016) "Luck, Compatibilism, and Libertarianism," *Dialogue* 54, 611–631.

Hartman, R. (2017) *In Defense of Moral Luck: Why Luck Often Affects Praiseworthiness and Blameworthiness,* New York: Routledge.

Hobart, R.E. (1934) "Free Will as Involving Determination and Inconceivable Without It," *Mind* 43, 1–27.

Levy, N. (2011) *Hard Luck: How Luck Undermines Free Will and Moral Responsibility,* Oxford: Oxford University Press.

———. (2016) "Luck and Manipulation Cases: A Response to Professor Haji," *Dialogue* 54, 633–646.

List, C., & Pivato, M. (2015) "Emergent Chance," *Philosophical Review* 124(1), 119–152.

Loewer, B. (2001) "Determinism and Chance," *Studies in History and Philosophy of Modern Physics* 32, 609–620.

Lyon, A. (2011) "Deterministic Probability: Neither Chance nor Credence," *Synthese* 182, 413–432.

Mele, A.R. (2006) *Free Will and Luck,* New York: Oxford University Press.

———. (2015) "Libertarianism, Compatibilism, and Luck," *The Journal of Ethics* 19(1), 1–21.

Nagel, T. (1976) "Moral Luck," *Proceedings of the Aristotelian Society* 50, 137–151.

———. (1979) "Moral Luck," in *Mortal Questions,* Cambridge: Cambridge University Press, pp. 24–38.

Pérez de Calleja, M. (2014) "Cross-World Luck at the Time of Decision Is a Problem for Compatibilists as Well," *Philosophical Explorations* 17(2), 112–125.

Pritchard, D. (2005) *Epistemic Luck,* Oxford: Clarendon Press.

———. (2014) "The Modal Account of Luck," *Metaphilosophy* 45, 594–619.

Schaffer, J. (2007) "Deterministic Chance?" *British Journal for the Philosophy of Science* 58, 113–140.

Sober, E. (2010) "Evolutionary Theory and the Reality of Macro Probabilities," in E. Eells & J. Fetzner (eds.) *Probability in Science,* La Salle, IL: Open Court, pp. 131–161.

Strawson, P.F. (1962) "Freedom and Resentment," *Proceedings of the British Academy* 48, 1–25.

Strevens, M. (2011) "Probability out of Determinism," in C. Beisbart & S. Hartmann (eds.) *Probabilities in Physics,* Oxford University Press, pp. 339–364.

van Inwagen, P. (1983) *An Essay on Free Will,* Oxford: Clarendon Press.

Williams, B. (1976) "Moral Luck," *Proceedings of the Aristotelian Society* 50, 115–135.

———. (1981) *Moral Luck: Philosophical Papers 1973–1980,* Cambridge: Cambridge University Press.

PART IV

Epistemic Luck

23

THE GETTIER PROBLEM

Ian M. Church

In Plato's *Theaetetus*, we are asked to consider the difference between *knowledge* and *mere opinion*. Knowledge, we learn, must be about something that is true. While you might have a false *opinion*, you cannot be said to properly *know* something when it is false. And drawing from imagery in the *Meno*, we might add that knowledge is "tied down" in a way that a mere opinion is not—if you know that *p* then you have reason or justification for believing *p*. Mere opinions are fragile in a way that knowledge is not. Mere opinions might be swayed via rhetoric or persuasion. Knowledge, it is thought, is gained via education and is far less fragile. In sum, then, mere opinions are beliefs that are supported by little or at least insufficient justification and might or might not be true. And knowledge, in contrast, is a belief that is true and sufficiently justified. Belief, sufficient justification, and truth were considered, since time immemorial (or so the story goes), to be necessary conditions on knowledge.

In his seminal 1963 article, "Is Justified True Belief Knowledge?," Edmund Gettier argued that, while justification, truth, and belief might be *necessary* for knowledge, such conditions are not (when taken together) *sufficient* for knowledge. In other words, Gettier argued that a belief could be justified and true and yet fail to be an instance of knowledge.

> CLASSIC CASE: Smith and Jones are applying for the same job. Smith has very strong evidence for thinking that Jones will get the job (e.g., the employer tells Smith that he will hire Jones, etc.), and for thinking that Jones has ten coins in his pocket (e.g., Jones emptied his pockets in front of Smith and then clearly, slowly, in good lighting, and perhaps even counting out loud, placed ten coins in his pocket). As such, Smith forms a belief in the general proposition that "the man who gets the job has ten coins in his pocket." As it turns out, however, Smith gets the job and he happens to also have ten coins in his pocket.
>
> *paraphrased from Gettier 1963: 122*

In this case, Smith seemingly has a justified true belief that "the man who gets the job has ten coins in his pocket," but, as almost everyone agrees, surely Smith's belief is not knowledge.[1] Again, while justification, truth, and belief might be *necessary* for belief, such conditions do not seem to be jointly *sufficient* for knowledge.

261

The project of trying to define knowledge in terms of necessary and jointly sufficient conditions—conditions that are assumed to be conceptually more primitive than the concept of knowledge—is what I will call in this chapter *the reductive analysis project*.[2] And the specific reductive analysis in terms of justification, truth, and belief is sometimes called *the traditional analysis of knowledge* or *the tripartite analysis of knowledge*.

For philosophers who were interested in giving a reductive analysis of knowledge, Gettier's counterexamples posed a serious problem. As such, epistemologists quickly tried to find ways to save or repair the traditional analysis of knowledge—typically by trying either to strengthen the justification condition or by adding more conditions (i.e., justified true belief plus some fourth condition). What ensued was a wide array of theories of justification (e.g., justification as evidence, justification as reliability, internalist justification, externalist justification, etc.) and additional conditions on knowledge (e.g., safety conditions, sensitivity conditions, defeasibility conditions, etc.). All of this sought to understand knowledge via reductive analysis, all of which assumed something like a *warranted true belief* analysis of knowledge (where "warrant" stands for "whatever turns true belief into knowledge"). Unfortunately, none of these proposals (in any combination) seemed to achieve lasting success against Gettier counterexamples—either falling into further Gettier-style counterexamples or leading to unpalatable conclusions (such as radical skepticism). After over 50 years of proposed solutions being met with serious challenges, a viable reductive analysis of knowledge, it might seem, is a Sisyphean endeavor.

At heart of the problem posed by Gettier is the incompatibility of a certain species of epistemic luck with knowledge. Consider again the CLASSIC CASE above: The truth of the target belief is incredibly *lucky*, given the way it was formed, and as such that belief is precluded from being rightly called knowledge. Epistemic luck, at least of a certain sort, seems to be incompatible with knowledge. And almost every proposed solution to the Gettier Problem has tried to develop a viable analysis of knowledge that is immune to that kind of epistemic luck. *In this chapter, we will explore the luck at issue in Gettier-styled counterexamples and the subsequent problem it poses to any viable reductive analysis of knowledge.* In the first section, we will consider the specific species of luck that is at issue in Gettier counterexamples, then, in the next section, I will briefly sketch a diagnosis of the Gettier Problem and try to explain why the relevant species of luck has proven to be extremely difficult to avoid. And finally, I will consider a prominent objection to the proposed diagnosis of the Problem.

Understanding the Luck at Issue in Gettier Counterexamples

As Duncan Pritchard noted in his seminal book, *Epistemic Luck* (2005), there seemed to be a near universal intuition within the contemporary epistemological literature "that knowledge excludes luck"—what he calls the "epistemic luck platitude"—however, as Pritchard is quick to point out, we have to be careful here; not all instances of luck preclude knowledge (2005: 1). In this section, we are going to briefly elucidate the different kinds of epistemic luck identified by Pritchard so as to better understand the specific kind of luck at issue in Gettier cases.[3] Once we know what kind of luck plays a role in Gettier cases, we will hopefully be better positioned to diagnose the Gettier Problem.[4]

Let us start by considering the kind of luck that is not at issue in Gettier counterexamples by considering some species of luck that are epistemically benign, that do not preclude knowledge. Although it is almost universally agreed that the lesson to be learned from Gettier cases is that knowledge is incompatible with luck—that luck is the central and fundamental component of all Gettier cases—Pritchard goes on to show that there are at least four species of epistemic luck that do not preclude knowledge. The first of these is:

Content Epistemic Luck: It is lucky that the proposition is true.

Pritchard 2005: 134

For example, Eli is walking down Placid Lane, a calm suburban road, and sees a car crash into a tree. To be sure, there are hardly ever car accidents on Placid Lane. It might be a matter of luck that a given car accident occurred; this, however, does not prevent agents from knowing that it occurred. Eli's belief that the accident occurred is warranted and only luckily true, but the luck at issue is epistemically inconsequential.

Pritchard identifies the second species of benign luck as:

Capacity Epistemic Luck: It is lucky that the agent is capable of knowledge.

Pritchard 2005: 134

If it is somehow lucky that a given agent has the capacity to know a given belief, this does not prevent that agent from knowing it. Using Pritchard's example, say Jones is walking through the forest and only narrowly avoids being smacked in the face with a branch that would have blinded him (perhaps he bent down to tie his shoe right when the branch swung by); it is, therefore, lucky that Jones has the capacity to see, but this luck does not thwart Jones's future perceptual beliefs from being known (Pritchard 2005: 135).

The third species of benign epistemic luck that Pritchard identifies is called:

Evidential Epistemic Luck: It is lucky that the agent acquires the evidence that she has in favour of her belief.

Pritchard 2005: 136

Smith just so happens to walk by his employer's door and overhear that he is going to be fired, which, let us say, is true. It is, then, a matter of luck that Smith has the evidence that he has in favor of his belief that "I am going to be fired," but such luck does not preclude Smith from knowing such a belief.[5]

Finally, the fourth species of benign epistemic luck that Pritchard identifies is:

Doxastic Epistemic Luck: It is lucky that the agent believes the proposition.

Pritchard 2005: 138

Not only is it lucky that Smith overhears that he is going to be fired when he just so happens to walk by his employer's door, it is also lucky that he forms the belief that he is going to be fired. He would not have formed the belief that he is going to be fired in relevant nearby possible worlds. As Pritchard notes, it does not look like a given event can exhibit Evidential Epistemic Luck without exhibiting Doxastic Epistemic Luck and vice versa, at least not without being contentious.[6] As with Evidential Epistemic Luck, Doxastic Epistemic Luck, too, seems epistemically benign—Smith can know he is going to be fired even if he exhibits Doxastic Epistemic Luck.

Gettier cases, according to Duncan Pritchard and many others, are caused by a specific species of luck (see Pritchard 2005: 145–148). As such, the lesson to be learned from Gettier cases is not so much that knowledge is incompatible with luck simpliciter, but rather that knowledge is incompatible with a particular *species* of it. By these lights, any successful analysis of knowledge, therefore, must (at the very least) track knowledge ascriptions in accord with this species' absence. Pritchard calls this species of luck that is behind Gettier cases "Veritic Epistemic Luck." According to Pritchard, a given agent's belief exhibits Veritic Epistemic Luck when the following description is met:

Veritic Epistemic Luck: It is a matter of luck that the agent's belief is true.

Pritchard 2005: 146

To be sure, Veritic Epistemic Luck is *not* meant to refer to cases where it is a matter of luck that *the propositional content* of an agent's belief is true. Certainly, such luck *is* compatible with knowledge;

for example, we can have knowledge of who won the lottery, where lightning struck, what number rolling a die produced, etc. Pritchard goes on to elucidate what Veritic Epistemic Luck demands, namely, that

> the agent's belief is true in the actual world, but that in a wide class of nearby possible worlds in which the relevant initial conditions are the same as the actual world—and this will mean, in the basic case that the agent at the very least *forms the same belief in the same way* as in the actual world—the belief is false.
>
> Pritchard 2005: 146, emphasis mine

So in order for something to be an instance of Veritic Epistemic Luck, not only does it have to be a matter of luck that the agent's belief is true, but it has to be lucky *given the way it was formed*.

There are, to be sure, two sub-species of Veritic Epistemic Luck, *environmental luck* and *intervening luck*, and only the latter is considered to be relevant to Gettier counterexamples. A classic example of environmental luck is found in the fake barn case:

> FAKE BARNS: Henry is driving in the country with his son. For the boy's edification Henry identifies various objects on the landscape as they come into view. "That's a cow," says Henry, "That's a tractor," "That's a silo," "That's a barn," etc. Henry has no doubt about the identity of these objects; in particular, he has no doubt that the last-mentioned object is a barn, which indeed it is. Each of the identified objects has features characteristic of its type. Moreover, each object is fully in view, Henry has excellent eyesight, and he has enough time to look at them reasonably carefully, since there is little traffic to distract him … Suppose we are told that, unknown to Henry, the district he has just entered is full of papier-mâché facsimiles of barns. These facsimiles look from the road exactly like barns, but are really just façades, without back walls or interiors, quite incapable of being used as barns. They are so cleverly constructed that travelers invariably mistake them for barns. Having just entered this district, Henry has not encountered any facsimiles; the object he sees is a genuine barn. But if the barn on that site were a facsimile, Henry would mistake it for a barn.
>
> Goldman 1976: 772–773[7]

In such a case, it is a matter of luck, given the way the belief was formed, that Henry's belief is true—satisfying my gloss of Pritchard's definition of veritic luck. And even though Henry saw a real barn and formed a true belief based on that perception, he fails to know, because his reasons for thinking "that's a barn" are not sufficient in such an environment—where, by hypothesis, he is unable to distinguish real barns from fake barns. Given the environment, his reasons for thinking that "that's a barn" could have very easily led to a false belief, if he just so happened to be looking at one of the facsimiles.[8]

Gettier cases are different. Recall the CLASSIC CASE from the beginning of this chapter. In such a case, it is a matter of luck, given the way the belief was formed, that Smith's belief is true—satisfying the definition of veritic luck—because his reasons for thinking that "the man who gets the job has ten coins in his pocket" do not rightly capture why the belief is true. *The protagonist in Gettier cases, is the victim of double luck.*[9] Due to some bad luck, Smith's reason for believing that "the man who gets the job has ten coins in his pocket," in the CLASSIC CASE, are significantly undermined: Smith heard from the employer that Jones was going to be hired and saw that Jones had ten coins in his pocket, leading to the belief in question; however, Jones does not get the job, undermining Smith's belief. Thanks to some countervailing good luck, however, Smith's belief turns out to be true *for other reasons*: unbeknownst to Smith, he gets the job, and he also has ten coins in his pocket. The reasons for Smith's belief are not insufficient due to an unfavorable environment (as in cases like FAKE BARNS). Smith's reasons for his belief are insufficient because they are significantly undermined as a result of bad luck, and would have led to a false belief if it had not been for the countervailing or intervening luck making Smith's belief true for significantly different reasons. This sub-species of veritic luck, which Pritchard calls *intervening luck*, is the luck involved in Gettier cases.

The Gettier Problem is not simply the problem of developing a viable analysis of knowledge that precludes luck. Some types of luck are epistemically benign. The Gettier Problem, as we are discovering, is the problem of developing a viable analysis of knowledge that precludes luck that, roughly speaking, comes between the reasons for a given belief and the truth of that belief. More precisely, the Gettier Problem is the problem of developing a viable analysis of knowledge that precludes a sub-species of veritic luck, *intervening luck*: luck where a given belief is true but for reasons not captured by the given agent's reasons. And already, I think, we can begin to see why the Gettier Problem has been so resilient for over 50 years. Based on our understanding of intervening luck in this section, we might predict that a given theory of warrant cannot avoid Gettier counterexamples unless it guarantees the truth of the belief in question, because otherwise the belief might be true for reasons not captured by the warrant which would "Gettierize" the belief. But given that the warrants we have for our beliefs rarely, if ever, guarantee our beliefs' truth, we might worry that any theory of warrant that makes such a requirement will only lead us to radical skepticism. We might already see the worry that no reductive analysis of knowledge can viably solve the Gettier Problem, that the Gettier Problem might be inescapable.

A Diagnosis of the Problem

As noted at the beginning of this chapter, recent history has shown us that it is notoriously diffi-cult to develop a viable reductive analysis of knowledge in terms of necessary and jointly sufficient conditions that can avoid Gettier counterexamples. It is extremely difficult to develop a theory of knowledge that is not vulnerable to intervening luck. And in response to this somber history, many epistemologists have started to avoid Gettier problems altogether. Some have simply decided to talk about other epistemic goods—such as justification, warrant, understanding, etc.—to avoid the whole Gettier Problem rigmarole.[10] Others have simply put the problem on the shelf; developing reductive accounts of knowledge that simply include a caveat, "Gettier problems aside" or "barring Gettier counterexamples."[11] And others still have given up on the reductive analysis project—the project of analyzing knowledge in terms of necessary and jointly sufficient conditions that are taken to be conceptually primitive—opting, instead, to treat knowledge itself as an unanalyzable primitive.[12] But before we shift focus to other epistemic goods, or to non-reductive models, or before we put Gettier problems on the shelf, it is important for us to understand and diagnose why the Gettier Problem is so problematic. And that is the goal of this section.

According to Linda Zagzebski's article, "The Inescapability of Gettier Problems" (1994), she proposed a diagnosis of Gettier problems where, if whatever we take to bridge the gap between true belief and knowledge (i.e., warrant) bears some violable relationship to truth, then it will be possible for that belief to be so warranted and true for reasons unrelated to the warrant. That is to say, so long as we reasonably assume that warrant is neither divorced from truth nor inseparable from it, Gettier cases are "inescapable." The worry, however, is that if we assume that warrant is indeed inseparable from truth, then we might never actually be in possession of such warrant.[13] We might think then that the Gettier Problem has proven to be so very problematic because it faces a dilemma: either (i) assume that warrant bears a close but not inviolable relationship to truth and face Gettier counterexamples or (ii) assume that warrant bears an inviolable relationship to truth and risk skeptical conclusions. In this section, I will try to very briefly lend credence to such a diagnosis of the Gettier problem.

Again, taking "warrant" to be whatever bridges the gap between true belief and knowledge, the starting place that almost everyone seems to agree on is that if it is possible to have a warranted, false belief, then it is possible for such a belief to be so warranted and true for reasons not captured by the warrant. In other words, if we assume that warrant is fallible, then Gettier problems will be unavoidable.[14] So, if we are going to try to avoid Gettier counterexamples, whatever bridges the gap between true belief and knowledge must be infallible.[15]

But what is perhaps less appreciated in the literature is just how strong this claim is. If a given account of warrant does not make it impossible for a belief to be so warranted and false, then that account of warrant cannot avoid Gettier counterexamples. For example, if a given account of warrant rules out the possibility of a warranted false belief in all *close* possible worlds—which is already a strong account of warrant—it can still be vulnerable to Gettier counterexamples, since it has not ruled out the possibility of a warranted false belief in *distant* possible worlds. A distant possible world could obtain, and the belief could be so warranted and true for other reasons. In other words, the belief could still be Gettiered.[16] Continuing with the modal example, any truly infallible account of warrant aimed at avoiding Gettier counterexamples must preclude the possibility of a warranted false belief *in all possible worlds*. That said, if a given belief is warranted and if it is impossible for it to be so warranted and false, then there is a real worry that we might never have a warranted belief, and so never have knowledge. It looks like radical skepticism might be looming on the immediate horizon.

A possible worry: Some theories of warrant—for example, causal theories and achievement theories—seem to necessitate truth but without leading to radical skepticism. For example, consider the following account of knowledge: *S knows p iff S's belief that p is caused by the fact that p.* Here, it looks like truth is built *into* the account of knowledge such that it is not possible to have a warranted false belief, yet it is not obvious that it leads to skeptical conclusions. As such, the above diagnosis of the Gettier Problem seems incorrect; an account of warrant can entail truth without leading to skepticism.

A response: While such an account might *appear* to be infallibilistic about warrant, it is easy to see that such an account of knowledge is actually fallibilistic upon closer inspection. First of all, note that it is easy to generate a Gettier case against it. Consider the following:

> SPRING: While visiting a local children's museum, S looks across a room to see what looks like a spring in a large box and forms the belief "There's a spring in that box!" What S sees, however, is a mere hologram of a spring generated by a series of mirrors within the box, which reflect the actual spring, which (luckily) is elsewhere within the box. (Given the current setup, the hologram of the spring could not be there if the actual spring was not elsewhere in the box.)

S's belief that "There's a spring in that box" is caused by the fact that there is indeed a spring elsewhere in the box (being reflected by the mirrors). The aforementioned definition of knowledge seems to be satisfied, though the belief is Gettiered. Seeing the way in which such an account can be Gettiered helps us see that it employs a fallibilistic account of warrant. Critically for the proposed diagnosis of the Gettier Problem, we need to know the following: if *S knows p iff S's belief that p is caused by the fact that p*, then what bridges the gap between the true belief and the knowledge? In other words, what is functioning as *warrant* in such an account of knowledge? Answer: It is the sort of causal relationship that stands between *p* and the corresponding belief. And what cases like SPRING show is that it is possible to be in *the very same sort of relationship* without having a true belief. The hologram of the spring—the very same causal source—could have, with a different configuration of mirrors, just as easily caused a false belief (if, for example, the actual spring was not in the box but was being reflected from somewhere else, perhaps the floorboards). Being false, such a belief is clearly not knowledge; however, the *warrant* seems to remain intact. As such, the theories of warrant, in such cases, are fallibilistic; and, as expected, they lead to Gettier counterexamples.

The Gettier Problem

But what is more, the only way such an account could truly avoid Gettier counterexamples, is if it was impossible for a given causal relationship to lead to anything other than a true belief. If we assumed that *S knows p iff S's belief that p is caused by the fact that p*, and we assumed that any given cause had to guarantee the truth of *p* (the same sort of cause could not have produced a false belief), then Gettier problems can indeed be avoided. But now it looks like skepticism is looming on the horizon. Very few (if any) of our beliefs have causes that could not have possibly led to a false belief. And as such, it seems like such an account of knowledge, as predicted, is extremely difficult to satisfy. So, the Gettier Problem leaves us with a dilemma. Either assume a fallibilistic account of warrant and face Gettier counterexamples or assume an infallibilistic account of warrant and risk radical, intractable skepticism. And insofar as neither leg of this dilemma is attractive, the Gettier Problem seems unsolvable.

Let us put this a bit more formally. Let us start, again, with the widely agreed upon claim that fallibilist accounts of warrant will always face Gettier counterexamples:

1. If it is possible for a warranted belief to be false ($\Diamond(Wb \cdot \neg b)$), then it is possible for a belief to be so warranted and true for reasons not captured by the warrant.

Add to this, the strong intuition that Gettier cases are incompatible with knowledge, which effectively forces us to deny 1's consequent.

2. Knowledge precludes the possibility of warranted belief that is true for reasons not captured by the warrant (i.e., Gettier cases are not instances of knowledge).

And by denying 1's consequent, we have to also deny its antecedent via *modus tollens*, which is the denial of fallibilism:

3. It is not possible for a warranted belief to be false.

    ($\neg\Diamond(Wb \cdot \neg b)$).

And that is logically equivalent to the following:

4. It is necessarily the case that: if a belief is warranted, then it is true ($\Box(Wb \rightarrow b)$).

Starting with the modest assumption that fallibilistic accounts of warrant will always be vulnerable to Gettier counterexamples (1) and the intuition that Gettier cases are incompatible with knowledge (2), we are straightforwardly led to infallibilism (4). But if warrant sufficient for knowledge *necessarily* entails the truth of the given belief, then it is not clear that an infallibilistic account of warrant could ever be met; leaving infallibilism under the threat of radical skepticism.

In sum, then: The Gettier Problem is the problem of developing a reductive analysis of knowledge that viably precludes the intervening luck at work in Gettier counterexamples. At the start of this section, we set out to consider why the Gettier Problem has proven to be so very problematic, seemingly evading a viable solution for over 50 years. Now, perhaps, we are in a better position to see why the Problem is so very problematic. Any viable reductive analysis of knowledge faces a dilemma between being vulnerable to Gettier counterexamples or risk collapsing into radical skepticism. In keeping with Zagzebski's (1994) diagnosis, the only way to avoid intervening luck, it seems, is to assume an infallible theory of warrant, to require a given theory of warrant to guarantee the truth of the belief in question, ruling out the possibility of the belief being true for reasons not captured by the warrant. Ruling out the possibility of intervening luck, however, seems to require a theory of warrant that guarantees the truth of the belief in question; and given that we rarely possess enough warrant to guarantee the truth of our beliefs, then we are left with the worry that we might not ever have enough warrant for knowledge, leaving us with skepticism.

There are, of course, a few ways to object to this diagnosis. One possibility that we have already very briefly considered is the possibility of rejecting the second horn of this dilemma, rejecting the idea that infallible theories of warrant will lead to skepticism.[17] But there is another way to object to the proposed diagnosis, and that is by rejecting the starting premise (and the first horn of the dilemma) that fallible theories of warrant are vulnerable to Gettier counterexamples. If it is possible to give a viable analysis of knowledge that avoids Gettier counterexamples without requiring an infallible theory of warrant, then we do not need to worry about whether infallibilism about warrant leads to skepticism. The proposed diagnosis would be dead in the water. This is the kind of objection we will consider in the next section.

An Objection

In their paper, "Infallibilism and Gettier's Legacy" (2003), Daniel Howard-Snyder, Frances Howard-Snyder, and Neil Feit consider what they call three nonpartisan arguments against fallibilism and contend that each is lacking. Most importantly for our purposes, however, they contend that an argument for infallibilism based on the sort of diagnosis of the Gettier Problem proposed in the previous section is simply flawed. Contra the proposed diagnosis, Howard-Snyder et al. argue that the Gettier Problem can indeed be solved fallibilistically, while assuming that warrant bears a close but not inviolable relationship to truth. In this section, we will briefly consider Howard-Snyder et al.'s opposition to the proposed diagnosis, and I will argue that their opposition fails—and does so precisely along the lines predicted by the proposed diagnosis of Gettier problems in the previous section.

According to Howard-Snyder et al., the following (purportedly) fallibilism-friendly condition on warrant viably avoids Gettier counterexamples:

> S's belief that p is warranted only if S's belief that p would not be accidentally true for S, if it were true.
>
> *Howard-Snyder et al. 2003: 309*

"[T]he distinctive feature of standard Gettier cases," according to Howard-Snyder et al., "is that the reason [S] believes p or the processes involved in his believing p are not properly related to those facts that render p true" (2003: 308). As such, what Howard-Snyder et al. have done is to convert their diagnosis of Gettier counterexamples into an anti-Gettier condition on warrant; interpreting this latter condition as simply demanding that "S's belief that p" will only be warranted if "the following subjunctive conditional is true: if S's belief that p were true, then it would also be true that what makes p true is properly related to the reasons for, or the processes involved in, S believing p" (Howard-Snyder et al. 2003: 309). And, according to Howard-Snyder et al., there is no reason to think that this condition precludes the possibility of a warranted false belief; they have seemingly provided us with a fallibilism-friendly way to circumvent the Gettier Problem, without, so they would hold, sacrificing feasibility.

Ignoring the worry that such a condition is ad hoc, I want to argue that, based on two plausible readings of their condition, it runs into precisely the sort of dilemma predicted by the diagnosis of the Gettier Problem offered in the previous section. No matter how we understand Howard-Snyder et al.'s condition, it will either run into Gettier counterexamples or lead to radical skepticism through infallibilism.

The first plausible reading of Howard-Snyder et al.'s proposed condition of warrant is one where it prohibits luckily true beliefs, where the luck at issue is presumably veritic (in general) or intervening (in particular) epistemic luck. I think it is fairly clear that Howard-Snyder et al. could easily be conflating "X is lucky" with "X is accidental" such that when they prohibit accidentally true beliefs (or beliefs whose reasons are not properly related to the belief's truth), they are really prohibiting something like luckily true beliefs of the relevant sort. What is more, given their extrapolation of their account, it also seems fairly clear that when they prohibit accidentally true beliefs they are really prohibiting something very much like veritically lucky true beliefs as understood in the first section of this chapter.

In other words, it seems like Howard-Snyder et al. could easily be read as prohibiting beliefs that, given the way they were formed, are luckily true. Now, if this is right, the problems they run into are straightforward. Plausibly, almost every belief we hold is at least minutely (veritically) lucky, almost every belief we have could have been false given the way in which it was formed; as such, Howard-Snyder et al.'s only hope for avoiding Gettier counterexamples is to make their condition prohibit even marginally lucky beliefs; in so doing, however, they would likely be committing themselves to radical skepticism—seemingly, very few of even our most secure beliefs are completely luck-free. Given that an all-out ban on lucky beliefs would effectively make it impossible for a belief to be warranted and false, ironically, it seems as though the only way Howard-Snyder et al.'s condition, so understood, can *really* avoid Gettier counterexamples is if it commits to infallibilism.

But perhaps that is not the way to read Howard-Snyder et al.'s condition after all. Perhaps, instead, when they prohibit accidentally true beliefs (i.e., beliefs whose reasons do not properly relate to the truth), they are prohibiting beliefs that are somehow true for the wrong reasons (whatever precisely that means)—beliefs that are true for reasons that *your* reasons, evidence, or cognitive processes would not have predicted. Surely this is precisely what is at issue in Gettier counterexamples, so perhaps *this* is the way to read their proposed condition on warrant. Sadly, however, this is going to run into similar troubles as the previous reading. Surely being "true for the right reasons" or being "true for reasons my evidence would predict" is a matter of degree. And, seemingly, the vast majority of our beliefs are, to at least some minute extent, going to be true for reasons we could not have predicted. For example, my secure belief that, as I am writing this, I am working at Hillsdale College is surely knowledge, but it is probably true, at least in part, for reasons my evidence does not account for—reasons like, such and such a form was filled out (which I had nothing to do with) making my employment at Hillsdale official, etc.

So surely Howard-Snyder et al. would not want to establish an all-out prohibition on beliefs that are not *entirely* true for the right reasons, reasons predicted by my evidence, because such a prohibition would seemingly push us toward radical skepticism. But unless Howard-Snyder et al. make such a prohibition, it looks as though Gettier counterexamples are going to be inevitable. Consider the following example:

THE HORTICULTURALIST: David is an expert horticulturalist, able to competently distinguish between the some 20,000 different species of orchid. David is presented with an orchid and asked to identify its species. Using his amazing skill, he can clearly tell that this particular orchid is either going to be an X-species or a Y-species (which look quite similar), and upon even further expert analysis, he comes to the conclusion that it is an X-species of orchid, which it is. However, Kevin, David's nemesis and an expert horticulturalist in his own right, decided the night before to, using his skill as a horticulturalist, make the X-species of orchid look like a Y-species of orchid. Thankfully, however, Alvin, David's other expert horticulturalist nemesis (who is conveniently not on speaking terms with Kevin), decided to try to trick David in the same way—arriving shortly after Kevin left, perceiving that the orchid was a Y-species, and cleverly making it look, once again, like an X-species. As such, while David's belief that the given orchid is an X-species of orchid is largely for the right reasons (he was, after all, able to narrow down the possibilities from over 20,000 to just two), he does not ultimately *know* that it is an X-species of orchid since he was effectively Gettiered by the combined efforts of Kevin and Alvin.

Howard-Snyder et al. could always object that the relevant belief of protagonists like David is not true enough for the right reasons, but strengthened cases can always be produced. As such, given the right-reasons reading, it once again looks as though the only way for Howard-Snyder et al.'s proposed condition on warrant to completely avoid Gettier counterexamples is if it prohibits any belief from being knowledge that is true for any reason not predicted by the given agent's evidence, reasons, or cognitive processes. As such, if Howard-Snyder et al.'s condition is to avoid Gettier counterexamples, it will, in accord with our diagnosis, seemingly lead us to radical skepticism. And insofar as it is not possible for a warranted belief to be false while satisfying "true for the *completely* right reasons" reading of their condition, it looks again as though, ironically, the only way for their condition to surmount the Gettier Problem is to acquiesce to infallibilism.

Conclusion

The Gettier Problem has been a perennial problem in epistemology for over 50 years, and it has been a driving force behind the growing body of research on epistemic luck. However, as more and more proposed solutions have been developed in an attempt to save the reductive analysis project, just as many Gettier-styled counterexamples or worries facing those solution have been noted. The goal of this chapter has been to better understand what the Gettier Problem is and propose an answer as to why it has proven to be so very problematic, why a viable reductive analysis of knowledge in terms of warranted true belief has been so elusive. And after considering a taxonomy of luck that identifies the specific species of luck at issue in Gettier cases, we began to see why the Gettier Problem is so problematic: it is inescapable.[18] According to our proposed diagnosis, any given reductive analysis of knowledge faces a dilemma: either assume that warrant is fallible and face Gettier counterexamples or assume that warrant must be infallible and risk falling into radical skepticism. In sum, fallible theories of warrant will always face Gettier counterexamples, because if a warranted belief can be false then it can also be true for reasons not captured by the warrant (true via intervening luck). And infallible theories of warrant risk skepticism, because if a given theory of warrant is to avoid Gettier counterexamples then it needs to guarantee the truth of the belief in question. Given that few of our beliefs ever enjoy that much warrant—where they could not have gone wrong—there is a real worry that we are left with skepticism. Plato's insights into the nature of knowledge, that it requires truth, belief, and justification or warrant, might very well be correct; however, if the proposed diagnosis is correct, then maybe we were wrong to assume that such conditions could amount to a viable reductive analysis of knowledge.[19]

Notes

1 For discussions on how widespread this agreement might be, see Milburn and Machery's chapter in this *Handbook*.
2 The reductive analysis project treat "knowledge" as akin to terms like "bachelor." "Bachelor" does yield a definition in terms of necessary and jointly sufficient conditions that are conceptually more primitive: namely, in terms of *unmarried* and *male*. The hope, then, is that "knowledge" too will yield a similar in analysis, traditionally in terms of truth, belief, and justification.
3 To be sure, the goal in this section is not to propose a *theory* regarding the nature of luck. In the second part of this *Handbook*, a number of different theories regarding the nature of luck are proposed—lack of control theories, modal theories, risk theories, etc.—but our goal here is to simply give a taxonomy of the different kinds of epistemic luck. Such a taxonomy, it is assumed, will be relevant regardless of what particular theory of luck we might want to endorse.
4 In this chapter, I will be assuming—along with most of the contemporary philosophical literature on the Gettier Problem—that the kind of luck at issue in Gettier cases is incompatible with knowledge. That said, however, such an intuition can be and has been challenged. See Stephen Hetherington's chapter in this *Handbook*.
5 A version of this example was developed in Unger (1968: 159) and was referenced by Pritchard (2005: 136).

6 For example, we might say that perception immediately forms beliefs, such that an agent who luckily perceived some evidence might be evidentially lucky but not doxastically; however, such a model only seems compatible with an externalist point of view. Conversely, we might say that a given agent had all the evidence needed for such and such a belief but did not believe it until by luck some non-evidential stimulus caused the agent to draw the appropriate conclusion; however, can evidence for X count as evidence for X if the agent fails to recognize it as such? It is not at all clear. See Pritchard (2005: 136–141).

7 Also see Zagzebski (1994: 66). Duncan Pritchard notes that cases like FAKE BARNS are not Gettier cases, because the protagonist does not make a "cognitive error" (Pritchard *et al.* 2010: 35–36).

8 For more on environmental luck, see Ben Jarvis's chapter in this *Handbook*.

9 See Zagzebski (1996: 295–299).

10 See Kvanvig (1992).

11 John Greco has occasionally expressed a "Gettier problems aside" view (1993: 413). That said, however, this is not all indicative of Greco's approach to the Problem; in fact, he has proposed, arguably, some of the most sophisticated solutions to the Gettier Problem in the literature.

12 See McDowell (1995) and Williamson (2000).

13 To be sure, Zagzebski does not make this point, but, as I will argue in this section, it seems to naturally follow from such a diagnosis.

14 This point is also highlighted in Chisholm (1982); Dretske (1971); Goldman (1986); Howard-Snyder et al. (2003); Nozick (1981); and Sturgeon (1993). To be sure, Howard-Synder et al. (2003) highlight this agreement in the literature and try to suggest that it is misplaced; we will consider Howard-Synder et al.'s objection later in this chapter.

15 Now, to be sure, this all assumes that warrant bears some close, if not infallible, relationship to the truth. Some epistemologists (e.g., Hetherington (2001) and Hetherington in this volume) have denied this—denied that warrant needs to bear any relationship to the truth. While such views have been powerfully argued for, they are nevertheless outliers in the literature; unfortunately, we will not have time to address them in this chapter.

16 This is a point I made in "Getting 'Lucky' with Gettier" (Church 2013a).

17 No doubt, a great deal more needs to be said on this score. Arguably, many contemporary accounts of virtue epistemology endorse an infallible theory of warrant without leading to skepticism in any obvious way. Unfortunately, we do not have the space to consider such objections here; however, I have responded to one such objection elsewhere (see Church 2013b).

18 At least within a viable reductive analysis of knowledge. Plausibly, one might "escape" the Gettier Problem by abandoning the project of defining knowledge in terms of a reductive analysis.

19 I am enormously grateful to Bob Hartman for his detailed feedback on an earlier draft of this chapter. I am also thankful to John Greco for arguing with me about many of the ideas presented here and for putting up with my stubbornness! This research was made possible by the generous support of the John Templeton Foundation.

References

Chisholm, R.M. (1982) *The Foundations of Knowing*, Brighton, UK: The Harvester Press.

Church, I.M. (2013a) "Getting 'Lucky' with Gettier," *European Journal of Philosophy* 21, 37–49.

——. (2013b) "Manifest Failure Failure: The Gettier Problem Revived," *Philosophia* 41, 171–177.

Dretske, F.I. (1971) "Conclusive Reasons," *Australasian Journal of Philosophy* 49(1), 1–22.

Gettier, E. (1963) "Is Justified True Belief Knowledge?" *Analysis* 23, 121–123.

Goldman, A.I. (1976) "Discrimination and Perceptual Knowledge," *The Journal of Philosophy* 73, 771–791.

——. (1986) *Epistemology and Cognition*, Cambridge, MA: Harvard University Press.

Greco, J. (1993) "Virtues and Vices of Virtue Epistemology," *Canadian Journal of Philosophy* 23, 413–432.

Hetherington, S. (2001) *Good Knowledge, Bad Knowledge: On Two Dogmas of Epistemology*, Oxford: Oxford University Press.

Howard-Snyder, D., Howard-Snyder, F., & Feit, N. (2003) "Infallibilism and Gettier's Legacy," *Philosophy and Phenomenological Research* 66, 304–327.

Kvanvig, J.L. (1992) *The Intellectual Virtues and the Life of the Mind: On the Place of the Virtues in Epistemology*, Savage, MD: Rowman & Littlefield Publishers.

McDowell, J.H. (1995) "Knowledge and the Internal," *Philosophy and Phenomenological Research* 55, 877–893. https://doi.org/10.2307/2108338

Nozick, R. (1981) "*Philosophical Explanations*," Oxford: Oxford University Press.

Pritchard, D. (2005) *Epistemic Luck*, Oxford: Oxford University Press.

Pritchard, D., Millar, A., & Haddock, A. (2010) *The Nature and Value of Knowledge: Three Investigations,* Oxford: Oxford University Press.

Sturgeon, S. (1993) "The Gettier Problem," *Analysis* 53, 156–164.
Unger, P. (1968) "An Analysis of Factual Knowledge," *The Journal of Philosophy* 65, 157–170.
Williamson, T. (2000) *Knowledge and Its Limits*, Oxford: Oxford University Press.
Zagzebski, L. (1994) "The Inescapability of Gettier Problems," *The Philosophical Quarterly* 44, 65–73.
——. (1996) *Virtues of the Mind: An Inquiry into the Nature of Virtue and the Ethical Foundations of Knowledge.* Cambridge: Cambridge University Press.

24

THE PROBLEM OF ENVIRONMENTAL LUCK

Benjamin Jarvis

Introduction

The topic of this chapter is *environmental luck*, a condition that beliefs very often exhibit when they are true even though the subject has come to have them in contexts where the subject's usual ways of thinking typically result in beliefs that are false. In the first section, I will sketch briefly what environmental luck is before pivoting, in the next section, to philosophical questions surrounding it. I will propose that the central question about environmental luck is not the question that a number of philosophers have, in fact, taken up—which is whether knowledge precludes it—but, rather, why it is a feature of any epistemic significance. In the remainder of the chapter, I outline a possible answer to this question. I suggest that area under the receiver operator curve—a metric commonly used to assess categorization models in practical contexts—can be applied in the case of belief. This metric makes it easier to see that beliefs exhibiting environmental luck are not quality beliefs in an important sense to be defined. I end by suggesting that this conection between (generalized) environmental luck and quality seems to indicate that the former does matter for epistemology.

What is Environmental Luck?

Environmental luck is a condition of beliefs. Intuitively, a lucky outcome is good by chance. What is good about a case of environmental luck is fairly straightforward—the belief exhibiting the condition is true, which also entails that a false belief with the same content has been avoided.[1] However, the "by chance" part of environmental luck is more nuanced.[2] Environmental luck entails that true belief has come about by chance in a particular way.

Occasionally, even an unreasonably held belief is true. These beliefs are lucky to be sure, but a need for luck to avoid believing a falsehood is owed to the unfavorable conditions created by the thinker. Reasonable thinking would have avoided a belief altogether—and, thus, a need for luck for the belief to be true. "Environmental luck" is typically understood to preclude these cases where a need for luck is created by the subject in this way. For the sake of having a label, we might call this contrasting condition "undeserved luck."

However, environmental luck is not merely the contrasting condition of "deserved" luck. Reasonable thinking is at least generally fallible, and when it errs, luck is again required to put it right. Technology can be used to create an elaborate illusion that makes it reasonable for someone to believe that she is looking in the direction of a dog. Here, a reasonable response to her senses is likely to lead her astray. To avoid the falsehood, she needs luck—a real dog in the same direction as the illusory one. In some sense, the need for luck stems from the environment—in this example, the technological ruse. But, this too is not environmental luck in the standard sense. This is "intervening luck." Intervening luck appears in classic Gettier cases.[3]

To understand environmental luck, we need to make a further distinction between cases where, because of the environment, reasonable thinking errs and cases where, because of the environment, odds merely favor that it will. Intervening luck is restricted to (and typically occurs in) the former, but environmental luck only occurs in the latter. We might set up our ruse—with illusory dogs in nearly every direction—but what if our intended victim only looks in the one direction we did not plan on? There, it so happens, is a dog. She does not err in taking her sense at face value—the path from the dog to her belief about the dog is just as it would be in a more normal case. But, she very easily might have erred if things had turned out slightly differently, that is had she merely looked in a different direction. In cases of environmental luck such as this, the need for luck stems from the fact that reasonable thinking is not well suited for one's immediate surroundings.

This final observation helps us see that, in ways that matter, environmental luck is more similar to "undeserved luck" than it is to intervening luck. Unreasonable thinking is very often not well suited for harvesting truths from one's environment. Reasonable thinking differs in that it ordinarily is. However, even then—assuming that this way of thinking is fallible—there will be immediate environments in which it is not well suited. And, whether one's thinking is reasonable or unreasonable, if one finds oneself in an immediate environment where that thinking is not well suited and yet it produces a belief, one's going to need a lucky break to avoid falsehood. Standardly, the belief counts as exhibiting environmental luck only if one gets this lucky break and one's thinking was reasonable. Arguably, though, whether one's thinking was reasonable or not, the lucky breaks are of the same kind. Call this more general kind "generalized environmental luck."

One way to appreciate that generalized environmental luck might be the more important kind is to consider a theoretical possibility in which there is not a principled distinction between reasonable and unreasonable thinking. Although I would not endorse this theoretical possibility, I consider it plausible, particularly if one thinks that reasonableness inherently comes in degrees. The idea would be that different ways of thinking might lead to beliefs that are more or less reasonable depending on how prone they are to error, but any threshold or division demarcating reasonableness *tout court* is arbitrary (unless it be perfection, which seems too much to ask for a belief to be reasonable in any ordinary sense). Assuming this idea is true, there is no principled distinction between undeserved and environmental luck either. But, we can still make sense of generalized environmental luck.

What is the Problem of Environmental Luck?

Typically, cases of environmental luck have come up in the context of the theory of knowledge.[4] In this context, the question is whether it is possible for a belief exhibiting environmental luck to qualify as knowledge. A basic rationale for thinking knowledge precludes intervening but not environmental luck goes something as follows:

1. Knowledge requires more than merely believing reasonably and truly—it requires some connection between the two.
2. If a cognitive process leading to a belief irreparably involves erring in some way, then the needed connection is broken.
3. However, no such erring need occur in cases of environmental luck, so the requirement for knowledge can be met.[5]

Nevertheless, it is easy enough for an opponent to deny (3) on the grounds that environmental luck too breaks the required connection (albeit in a different way).[6] Arguably, a belief that qualifies as knowledge should be a manifestation—or "proof of concept"—of how a certain way of thinking leads to the truth. However, an instance of environmental luck no more proves out the reasonability of a way of thinking than undeserved luck does. By way of example, suppose Sam blows money previously earmarked for rent in Las Vegas but happens to meet rent through a lucky happenstance. It would be foolish of him to claim that this outcome "proves out" the way of thinking that led to his belief that gambling rent money in Vegas would not prevent him from meeting rent. Contrast Samantha who deposits her money earmarked for rent in a safe deposit box. Unfortunately, nearly all of the safe deposit boxes in Samantha's bank are robbed that month. Fortunately for Samantha, hers is one of the very few that isn't. Samantha might well have been reasonable in coming to believe that depositing rent money in the safe deposit box would not prevent her from meeting rent. However, it would still be foolish of her to claim that this outcome proves out her way of thinking.

Whether or not environmental luck is compatible with knowledge, there is a more fundamental question as to why environmental luck should matter for epistemology. An epistemologist might be of the opinion that it is of interest whether a thinker is doing her part to get at the truth and does get to the truth without being especially concerned about any further details, including whether intervening or environmental luck comes into play. This is, in principle, compatible with thinking that knowledge precludes both of these species of "deserved" luck so long as knowledge too matters little per se for epistemology. For instance, speaking of any knowledge-incompatible case of "deserved" luck, Schechter (2017: 139) suggests:

> [W]hen we focus on the details of the case, the fact that the subject doesn't count as knowing is of little intuitive significance. We are used to talking in terms of knowledge and treating knowledge as the most significant epistemic status. But this may be more an accident of human language and psychology than a guide to the epistemological joints of nature.

Notably, Schechter does not deny that knowledge and environmental luck are incompatible. He merely suggests that, even if they are, knowledge too does not matter. Arguably, then, the principal problem of environmental luck is not understanding whether it precludes knowledge but instead understanding why it matters for epistemology. Call this "Schechter's challenge."

For my part, I might be willing to concede that environmental luck per se does not matter much, if only because generalized environmental luck subsumes its importance. An account of why generalized environmental luck matters might not strictly meet Schechter's challenge, but I think it comes close enough to move the dialectic further. I will focus on sketching this account in the remaining sections of this chapter.

Why Generalized Environmental Luck Matters

To a first approximation, generalized environmental luck matters at least because it is important to take it into account when measuring the effectiveness of a subject's ways of thinking in the natural world (or, for that matter, in alien contexts). As a first qualification, "effectiveness" here is restricted to effectiveness at believing truths and not believing falsehoods. For the sake of elegance, I will use "quality" as a stand-in for this restricted "effectiveness" henceforth. However, it would be wrong to confuse "quality" so understood with reasonableness, justification, or anything similar. It is an open question to what extent ways of thinking that are effective at yielding true beliefs and avoiding false ones are reasonable ways of thinking that generate beliefs that are justified.[7]

So, why should generalized environmental luck matter for quality? Improving the quality of one's thinking reduces the number of cases where significant luck is required in order for it to turn out that one's belief is true. This tends to reduce instances of generalized environmental luck as a proportion of one's true beliefs. To put it differently, the quantity of generalized environmental luck among a subject's beliefs is generally inversely related to the quality of the subject's thinking.[8] The result is that a proper measure of quality should discount cases of generalized environmental luck.

By way of illustration, consider a counterfactual doppelganger of Samantha who exhibits higher quality thinking. Whereas Samantha was aware of a very small number of safe deposit box robberies in the region, Samantha's doppelganger additionally recognized a pattern among these robberies that suggested her bank was a more likely target. As a result, counterfactual Samantha's doppelganger did not come to believe that money in her safe deposit box would be available to pay rent at the end of the month; she cleared out her safe deposit box as a precaution instead. The upshot is that, in virtue of her higher quality thinking, Samantha's doppelganger lacks a true belief that Samantha has. At first, this result might seem puzzling. Lacking a true belief can indicate a deficit of insight, especially when others in similar conditions are in a position to know. In this case, however, Samantha's true belief exhibits generalized environmental luck. And, beliefs that exhibit generalized environmental luck manifest a deficit in the quality of one's thinking, though these beliefs are true.

To be clear, this deficit in the quality of one's thinking need not be a deficit of insight. In Samantha's case, perhaps better pattern recognition would prevent generalized environmental luck (whether or not Samantha's belief counted as reasonable or justified). However, in some cases, there is no improvement in the subject's rationality, creativity, ingenuity, etc. that could help avoid generalized environmental luck. In these cases, the problem is that, while the subject's way of thinking is very reasonable, it is nonetheless fallible—meaning there are contexts in which it works less well. In some (inevitable) cases of generalized environmental luck, the subject is in just such a context.

Area Under the Receiver Operator Curve

Whether to believe or not is fundamentally a categorization task—at least if the belief in question is understood to be a dichotomous state. In the current era of "big data," it is very common to use data to build models geared to handle categorization tasks.[9] For instance, a business might build and use a model to categorize potential customers into those who (possibly) will respond to an advertisement and those who (probably) won't. There are standard ways of evaluating the quality of such models.[10] It is enlightening to see how a standard performance metric deals with what is, in effect, generalized environmental luck. Given how models are very typically scored, cases of generalized environmental luck are treated as indicating weakness in the model. These cases are to be avoided, if possible, by using better categorization models. The fact that the standard formal approach to categorization treats cases of generalized environmental luck as negative outcomes to be avoided if possible lends credence to the idea that this is also true in the case of belief. It also suggests that the distinction between cases that do and do not exhibit generalized environmental luck is one that matters.

First, it is important to appreciate that generalized environmental luck is something that can be extended beyond the case of belief. The simple way to do that is to realize that it usually makes perfect sense to think about the outputs of a model as the model's "beliefs." For instance, the model might "believe" that Jane Smith (possibly) will respond to the advertisement while Joe Jones (probably) won't. And, of course, just as with beliefs there are facts that determine whether these outputs are correct. Models give outputs systematically on the basis of underlying features of a case. This systematic processing is analogous to a "way of thinking," and both are subject to failure in similar manners. For instance, it might be that the model has categorized Jane Smith as a good prospect in part because of her zip code. But, it might be that, unknown to the model, the people living on certain streets in the zip code—including perhaps Jane Smith—are different from the rest. Given that somebody lives on those streets, they might, in fact, be less likely to respond to the advertisement than the general population. It could be that Jane Smith (given her other characteristics) will respond anyway when

The Problem of Environmental Luck

the advertisement is sent, but here the model is lucky and the luck looks exactly like generalized environmental luck.

Standard categorization models—including decision trees and logistic regression[11]—do not output a category per se so much as a score, generally interpreted as a probability. Categorizations are typically made using a score threshold. However, often modelers want to get a sense about how the model performs across different thresholds. A simple metric for this purpose is *area under the receiver operator curve* (AUC).[12]

To understand AUC, we must first understand what a receiver operator curve is. A receiver operating characteristic curve (ROC curve) plot depicts what percentage of truths the model is able to deliver (as a percentage) on the y-axis for a given level of error tolerance (as a percentage) on the x-axis. Put another way, it depicts the model's true positive rate—probability that the model outputs a verdict given that it is true—for a given false positive rate—probability that the model outputs a verdict given that it is false. A higher true positive rate is always better, while a higher false positive rate is always worse. However, the two are generally related. It is always possible to achieve a perfect true positive rate of 100% if one accepts a perfectly poor false positive rate of 100%—the model just has to categorize everything positively. Similarly, it is always possible to achieve a perfect false negative rate of 0% if one accepts a perfectly poor true positive rate of 0%—the model just has to categorize nothing positively.

Probability in this context generally has a "frequentist" interpretation—meaning, it is the limit of a proportion of cases where the event happens as the number of trials of some real-world process goes to infinity. In a business context, what the "real-world" process is tends to be much better defined than it might be with any belief-forming process. Even so, because probabilities are limits, the ROC curve for a model is usually known only to a certain level of approximation by applying the model to a set of test data originating from the "real-world" process. For instance, suppose that we send the advertisement in question to 20 people from our population. We have our model score these 20 people as prospects; then, we observe whether the people in question do or do not respond. To plot our best approximation of the "true" ROC curve, we order these people by their scores. To get our false positives rates for the x-axis, we add a column with the running total of the number of people who did not respond. The false positive rates for our plot are these running totals as a percentage of those who did not respond. Similarly, to get our true positive rates for the y-axis, we add a column with the running total of the number of people who have responded. The true positive rates for our plot are these running totals as a percentage of the total number of people who responded. Table 24.1 is a concrete example of a table this process might produce. Figure 24.1 is the ROC curve approximation that we would plot from this table.

Note that each of the points in the ROC curve plot corresponds to using a particular threshold for categorization. For instance, the fifth point on the table—for Diane—corresponds to the point on the plot at $x = 6.7\%$, $y = 80\%$. The corresponding threshold for categorization is the model score on the row—in this case, 0.42. So, in plotting the point for that threshold, persons are categorized as ones who will respond if they receive a model score greater than or equal to 0.42. In our table, that is Diane and everyone above her—Jane, Henry, Luke, and Juan. Of these five, four did in fact respond to the advertisement—Jane, Henry, Luke, and Juan. Since only one other responded, this group is 80% of the total that responded, meaning that our best estimate for the true positive rate for the model with this threshold is 80%. On the other hand, the one who did not respond is one out of 15 total, meaning that our best estimate for the false positive rate is 6.7%. This is why the point appears at $x = 6.7\%$, $y = 80\%$. Notice, though, that these are probably not good estimates of the true and false positive rates. The model scores for Jane, Henry, Luke, Juan, and Diane are 0.77, 0.73, 0.60, 0.53, and 0.42, respectively. If these are indeed good estimates for the probabilities of responding given their respective features, then it is a bit fortuitous that four of them in fact responded. The approximation should get better as we collect more data, but 20 points is probably not enough.

Benjamin Jarvis

Table 24.1 Example data for ROC curve

Person	Model score	Response	Running "no" count	Running "yes" count	False positive rate %	True positive rate %
Jane	0.77	Yes	0	1	0.0	20.0
Henry	0.73	Yes	0	2	0.0	40.0
Luke	0.60	Yes	0	3	0.0	60.0
Juan	0.53	Yes	0	4	0.0	80.0
Diane	0.42	No	1	4	6.7	80.0
John	0.30	No	2	4	13.3	80.0
Patrick	0.28	No	3	4	20.0	80.0
Karen	0.22	No	4	4	26.7	80.0
Anne	0.21	No	5	4	33.3	80.0
Trevor	0.19	No	6	4	40.0	80.0
Rachel	0.17	Yes	6	5	40.0	100.0
Allison	0.13	No	7	5	46.7	100.0
Cesar	0.11	No	8	5	53.3	100.0
Georgina	0.09	No	9	5	60.0	100.0
Isabella	0.09	No	10	5	66.7	100.0
Mark	0.07	No	11	5	7.3	100.0
Mary	0.07	No	12	5	80.0	100.0
Aurora	0.05	No	13	5	86.7	100.0
Jason	0.04	No	14	5	93.3	100.0
Martina	0.04	Yes	15	5	100.0	100.0

Counts	
"Yes"	5
"No"	15
Total	20

Still, we can learn the general shape of ROC curve from looking at this example. They begin in the lower left-hand corner and generally travel to the upper right-hand corner. This reflects the previously mentioned relationship between true and false positive rates: the greater the tolerance for error—the higher the false positive rate allowed in categorization—the greater the potential to yield correct categorizations—the higher the true positive rate. In fact, ROC curves are monotonic increasing. The true positive rate cannot decrease when the false positive rate increases because (1) additional false categorizations from the model do not change the true positive rate and (2) additional true categorizations only raise the proportion of potential true categorizations the model is realizing.

Area under the ROC curve—AUC—is the measure of the area between the ROC curve and the x-axis. To appreciate the significance of this measure, consider that a perfect ROC curve would jump straight up to $x = 0\%$, $y = 100\%$ before traveling straight across to $x = 100\%$, $y = 100\%$. Perfection entails that the model is perfectly separating correct categorizations from incorrect categorizations by always scoring the former higher than the latter. The better a model's scoring—in terms of scoring correct categorizations higher than incorrect ones—the more the model's ROC curve approaches this perfect ROC curve. Notice that area between the perfect ROC curve and the x-axis is one (because it is a one by one square). The area under any imperfect ROC curve will be less than one because it will leave out some of the upper left-hand corner, but the closer it is to perfection, the

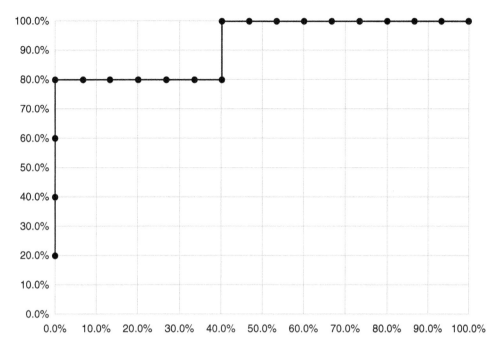

Figure 24.1 Example ROC curve

closer the AUC will be to one. This is part of the reason why AUC is a reasonable metric for assessing model scores.

The "perfectly imperfect" AUC would, of course, be zero—that is, no area at all. Here, the ROC curve would be a line that begins at $x = 0\%$, $y = 0\%$ and extend to $x = 100\%$, $y = 0\%$ before jumping up to $x = 100\%$, $y = 100\%$. The obvious way to create an ROC curve of this sort is simply to reverse all of the verdicts from a perfect model. A model creating an ROC curve with AUC equal to zero has to be exceptionally good at delivering the wrong answer, doing so with perfect reliability. Of course, this also means that a model of this sort is very useful; one can recover the truth by accepting the reversed verdict. In fact, it is as hard to find a model with an AUC of zero as it is to find a model with an AUC of one. If one has one, one effectively has the other—although possibly one might not know which is which.

The truly bad outcome, then, is not a model with an AUC of zero—since that provides a path to an AUC of one—but one that produces an ROC curve that corresponds exactly to the diagonal line from $x = 0\%$, $y = 0\%$ to $x = 100\%$, $y = 100\%$ (see Figure 24.2). A model with this performance delivers no information because the outputs are effectively random noise. In fact, it is easy to construct a model that will approximate this performance simply by randomly assigning scores. Return to our previous example of responding to a given advertisement and suppose, for purposes of illustration, that the base rate of response among the relevant population is 30%. Notice that it would be very easy to get a true positive rate of 50% simply by randomly assigning scores above the categorization threshold for 50% of the population. When we do this, we should expect that about 30% of that 50% categorized as responders—or 15% of the total population—will, in fact, respond to the advertisement. This is out of a possible 30% of the total population who are potential responders—so the true positive rate should indeed be close to 50%. At the same time, 70% of that randomly assigned 50%—or 35% of the population—will have been categorized as responders even though they will not respond. These are the false positives. 70% of the population would not respond if targeted—these are the potential false positives. So, the false positive rate is also 50% (= 35%/70%). Notice that nothing especially hinges on the choice of 50% as the true positive rate that we are trying to achieve,

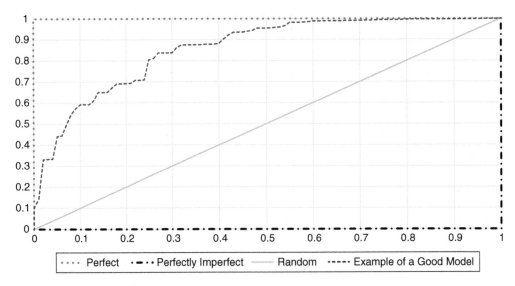

Figure 24.2 Illustration of AUC curves

or, for that matter, 30% as the base rate (so long as it is between zero and one). We can always achieve an approximate true positive rate of q% simply by randomly assigning scores above our categorization threshold for q% of the population. The resulting false positive rate will also be approximately q%. We can do this for all possible thresholds at once just by having our "model" randomly assign scores from the start. When we draw the ROC curve for this "model by random assignment," it will be at least approximately the diagonal line from $x = 0\%$, $y = 0\%$ to $x = 100\%$, $y = 100\%$.

Note that the AUC of this diagonal line is exactly one half even though the model for this diagonal line is exhibiting poor performance at every threshold. One lesson here is that a good AUC generally should be more than one half. However, a corollary is that some correct categorizations do not really contribute to having a good AUC. Any correct categorization causes an ROC curve to "step up"—and so, strictly speaking, pushes AUC higher. Nevertheless, some correct categorizations are doing this in a way that merely keeps up with the performance of a model delivering random outputs while others constitute genuine insights that help a model exceed mediocre performance of that sort.

The idea that a correct categorization could cause the ROC curve to "step up" without really contributing to a good AUC might sound paradoxical, but the net effect of making correct categorizations can, in fact, be mediocre depending on which other model outputs they accompany. Consider again the model that categorizes Jane Smith as a good prospect in part because of her zip code even though people living on certain streets in the zip code—including Jane Smith—are different from the rest in a way that makes them generally much less responsive to the advertisement. Note that if we restricted the model's application to people living on just those streets, the model is effectively acting like a model that simply categorizes everyone as a good prospect. This means that when the overall ROC curve steps up because the model outputs all the possible true positives among this subpopulation, it also likely makes a step to the right because the model outputs all the possible false positives among that subpopulation as well. More importantly, the step to the right must be greater in magnitude to the step up because of the particulars of the situation. By assumption, the people living on those streets are less receptive to the advertisement, meaning the ratio of potential true positives (receptive people) to potential false positives (non-receptive people) in this subpopulation is less than the same ratio in the general population. This guarantees that the increase in the false positive rate from adding all the possible false positives from this population matches or exceeds the increase in the true positive rate from adding all of the possible true positives. The net effect of the total movement is mediocre since it is more to the right than up. Indeed, that kind of move in the ROC curve cannot be responsible for driving a higher AUC even though it is partly the result of some correct categorizations.

In fact, for the model to make a genuine improvement here, it must begin to score people living in Jane Smith's part of the zip code differently from the rest of the zip code—and possibly also begin to score any responsive people in that part of the zip code differently from the rest of the people there. If the model is able to reduce the score of most of the people in that part of the zip code while keeping the score of the more receptive people like Jane up, AUC should improve because the ROC curve no longer has to go so far to the right when it goes up. Notice, though, that when this happens, the categorization of Jane Smith as a good prospect when correct no longer looks to be analogous to a case of generalized environmental luck. The model is now tuned to a more nuanced pattern. The disappearance of anything analogous to generalized environmental luck is, of course, not an accident. Cases analogous to generalized environmental luck are antithetical to good AUC scores; improving an AUC score requires making such cases go away.

AUC and Generalized Environmental Luck

In theory, there is nothing preventing someone from using AUC as a metric for evaluating agents. Whether the agent believes $<p>$ or not is effectively a categorization of whether or not the proposition $<p>$ is true, and the process by which an agent comes to believe or not believe is effectively a model. It is possible that agents do not assign fine-grained score propositions by assigning probabilities to propositions, but believing versus not believing effectively qualifies as at least a coarse-grained scoring.[13] All that is left to get an AUC score is to determine the false positive rate for belief—the percentage of beliefs that $<p>$ that are false—and the true positive rate for belief—the percentage of $<p>$'s being true that are believed. This is a bit tricky to do in full generality. However, we might do this for a restricted range of conditions. For instance, if $<p>$ is $<There's\ a\ barn\ in\ front\ of\ me>$, we might calculate the false positive and true positive rates for relevantly similar conditions—ones where the subject has similar background beliefs, a similar perspective with similar lighting in roughly the same region, etc. Let us suppose that once all the factors are specified, the false positive rate is 0.01 and the true positive rate is 0.98. The area under the curve is the rectangle with height equal to the true positive rate and the width equal to one minus the false positive rate. So, in this particular case, AUC is 0.9702.

The interesting question for our purposes is how cases of generalized environmental luck bear on this AUC. In order to improve AUC, a model has to better separate truths from falsehoods—i.e., it has to do better at scoring the former higher than the latter. In terms of our agent in this example, that means she either (1) must believe $<There's\ a\ barn\ in\ front\ of\ me>$ in more of the circumstances in which it is true (holding all else equal) or (2) must believe $<There's\ a\ barn\ in\ front\ of\ me>$ in fewer of the circumstances when it is false (again, holding all else equal). Suppose we hold the agent's true positive rate fixed—so (1) is no longer an option. What does accomplishing (2) require in practical terms? It requires being fooled less often by barn façades, barn facsimiles, barn illusions, and all other manner of fake barns. That means either believing less often in circumstances where one is likely to be fooled or becoming harder to fool even in those circumstances. Either way diminishes the number of cases of generalized environmental luck. Conversely, assume that the subject has diminished cases of generalized environmental luck without lowering the true positive rate. This means either believing less often in circumstances where one is likely to be fooled or becoming harder to fool even in those circumstances. Either result pushes the agent's AUC down by lowering the false positive rate.

The result, then, is generalized environmental luck is inversely related to AUC. Indeed, AUC provides a formal way of fleshing out what it means to say that beliefs exhibiting generalized environmental luck do not manifest quality thinking. These beliefs might be good in the sense that they are true, but they are not quality in the sense that the agent only has them due to her natural deficiencies.

In fact, they are part of the chaff of mostly false beliefs that the agent cannot separate from the grain of truth. They exist not because of the agent's cognitive abilities but only because any way of coming to beliefs, as the result of baseline rate of truth within a population of potential beliefs, will result in some true beliefs. Moreover, a goal of inquiry is often to find ways to eliminate the beliefs of this sort by better avoiding the need for luck in the first place—whether by figuring out how to be more cautious in contexts where luck is required or becoming more skilled at believing in these contexts.

Conclusion

These final points bring us back to Schechter's challenge. Supposing knowledge does preclude generalized environmental luck, might this not just be because knowledge is not an especially natural kind? This seems to me rather unlikely. It is plausible that knowledge is a belief that is reasonable but also exhibits *quality*. Quality here means that the belief is a manifestation of quality ways of thinking, which in turn means that the ways of thinking are suited to get to the truth in the agent's environment. It is quality (as an attribute of belief) that precludes (generalized) environmental luck; beliefs that exhibit (generalized) environmental luck diminish the quality of thinking as measured by AUC or other similar metrics. Moreover, the inclusion of quality as a constraint on knowledge does not appear to be a mere accident in the evolution of one of our most central epistemic concepts. Quality is, in fact, a sought-after feature in the current development of models used in real business contexts to categorize faster or more accurately than a human can. The reality is that practitioners try to build models to ensure that model categorizations will be quality so that business success will be more systematic. What matters to practitioners is not so much any particular categorizations but rather what these individual cases reveal about the model. Agents should prefer that their beliefs be quality—and not exhibit (generalized) environmental luck—for analogous reasons. What matters is not so much the beliefs themselves but what beliefs exhibiting (generalized) environmental luck indicate about how well the agent's thinking is tuned to the environment.

Notes

1 On the value of true belief, see Lynch (2004) and McHugh (2012). I suspect it makes little difference in this context whether the good in question is having a true belief or avoiding a false one. Cf. Whiting (2013).
2 For a detailed discussion on the relevant distinctions, see Pritchard (2005) or Pritchard (2007). For my purposes, a short summary will suffice.
3 Gettier (1963). Again, for more details, see Pritchard (2005) or Pritchard (2007).
4 For example, see not only Pritchard (2005) and Pritchard (2007), but also Turri (2011, 2012, 2013).
5 For a detailed attempt to make out an argument in this spirit using the ability framework from Sosa (2007), see Turri (2011).
6 For instance, see Jarvis (2013).
7 The question here essentially concerns the extent to which something in the spirit of the reliabilism of Goldman (1979) might be true.
8 Cf. Carter et al. (2013).
9 On the era of "big data," see Manyika et al. (2011).
10 Standard does not mean without controversy or to be applied in all circumstances. For discussion of some of the standard metrics used to assess models (including the F-score mentioned later), see Powers (2011).
11 See Provost and Fawcett (2013: chs 3 and 4). For a more technical treatment, see Hastie et al. (2017: chs 4 and 9).
12 For a discussion of ROCs and AUC, see Provost and Fawcett (2013: ch. 8).
13 When a binary coarse-grained scoring is involved, practitioners may use some version of the F-score rather than AUC. An F-score is AUC divided by a weighted average of the true positive rate and one minus the false positive rate. (The exact weights determine which version of the F-score is used.) For further discussion, see van Rijsbergen (1979: 133–134). However, AUC might be an appropriate choice if one prefers to control for the false positive rate, i.e. optimize subject to the constraint that the false positive rate be no greater than some number, rather than accept some trade-off between the true positive rate and false positive rate.

References

Carter, J.A., Jarvis, B., & Rubin, K. (2013) "Knowledge and the Value of Cognitive Ability," *Synthese* 190(17), 3715–3729.

Gettier, E. (1963) "Is Justified True Belief Knowledge?" *Analysis* 23(6), 121–123.

Goldman, A.I. (1979) "What Is Justified Belief?" in G. Pappas (ed.) *Justification and Knowledge*, Dordrecht: Reidel, pp. 29–49.

Hastie, T., Tibshirani, R., & Friedman, J. (2017) *The Elements of Statistical Learning*, 2nd edition, New York: Springer.

Jarvis, B. (2013) "Knowledge, Cognitive Achievement, and Environmental Luck," *Pacific Philosophical Quarterly* 94(4), 529–551.

Lynch, M. (2004) "Minimalism and the Value of Truth," *The Philosophical Quarterly* 54(217), 497–517.

Manyika, J. et al. (2011). "Big Data: The Next Frontier for Innovation, Competition, and Productivity," McKinsey Global Institute. [Online] Available from: www.mckinsey.com/business-functions/digital-mckinsey/our-insights/big-data-the-next-frontier-for-innovation [Accessed 26 November 2017]

McHugh, C. (2012) "The Truth Norm of Belief," *Pacific Philosophical Quarterly* 93(1), 8–30.

Powers, D.M.W. (2011) "Evaluation: From Precision, Recall and F-measure to ROC, Informedness, Markedness & Correlation," *Journal of Machine Learning Technologies* 2(1), 37–63.

Pritchard, D.H. (2005) *Epistemic Luck*, Oxford: Oxford University Press.

——. (2007) "Anti-luck Epistemology," *Synthese* 158(3), 277–297.

Provost, F., & Fawcett, T. (2013) *Data Science for Business*, Sebastopol, CA: O'Reilly Media.

Schechter, J. (2017) "No Need for Excuses," in J.A. Carter et al. (eds.) *Knowledge-first: Approaches in Epistemology and Mind*, Oxford: Oxford University Press, pp. 132–162.

Sosa, E. (2007) *A Virtue Epistemology*, Oxford: Oxford University Press.

Turri, J. (2011) "Manifest Failure: The Gettier Problem Solved," *Philosopher's Imprint* 11(8), 1–11.

——. (2012) "Is Knowledge Justified True Belief?" *Synthese* 184(3), 247–259.

——. (2013) "Knowledge as Achievement, More or Less," in M.A. Fernandez (ed.) *Performance Epistemology*, Oxford: Oxford University Press, pp. 124–136.

van Rijsbergen, C.J. (1979) *Information Retrieval*, 2nd edition, London: Butterworths.

Whiting, D. (2013) "The Good and the True (or the Bad and the False)," *Philosophy* 8(2), 219–242.

25

ANTI-LUCK EPISTEMOLOGY

Tim Black

Gettier Cases and Anti-Luck Epistemology

Philosophers were once under the impression that one's being justified in believing that something is true is sufficient for one to know that it is true. However, with the help of Edmund Gettier's (1963) "Is Justified True Belief Knowledge?," philosophers became aware of a weakness in this, for knowledge is susceptible to luck in ways that justification is not: my belief's being true simply as a matter of luck can keep my belief from amounting to knowledge even when it has no effect on whether I am justified in holding that belief. Gettier's counterexamples, which involve epistemic agents whose justified beliefs are true simply as a matter of luck, exploit this in undermining the tripartite account of knowledge, according to which to know is to have a justified true belief. His counterexamples are widely and perhaps even unanimously thought to show that cases in which one's belief is true simply as a matter of luck illustrate that one's having a justified true belief that p is not sufficient for one's knowing that p.

In one of Gettier's counterexamples, Smith is justified in believing both that Jones will get the job and that Jones has ten coins in his pocket. From these two beliefs, Smith justifiedly infers that

(C) the man who will get the job has ten coins in his pocket.

Let us suppose that Smith's belief that C is true. Still, Smith's belief does not count as knowledge: although Jones will *not* get the job, "by the sheerest coincidence, and entirely unknown to Smith," *he* (Smith) will get the job, and *he* has ten coins in his pocket (Gettier 1963: 123). Although Smith comes to hold his belief that C in a way that is reliable and that provides him with reasons that would in normal circumstances be identical to the reasons why his belief is true, his belief is based in this instance on reasons that are *different* from those that make it true. Smith's belief that C is true simply as a matter of luck, and it therefore fails to count as knowledge. Given Gettier's counterexamples, and the dozens of other counterexamples that highlight the susceptibility of knowledge to luck, it has become a bit of orthodoxy in contemporary epistemology to hold that no belief that is true simply as a matter of luck can amount to knowledge, even if it turns out that we are justified in holding that belief. A main goal of contemporary epistemology is to theorize a remedy for this problem by providing a set of conditions the satisfaction of which will keep knowledge from being vulnerable to luck.

284

There are at least two things these conditions might target: *epistemic agents*, where the conditions would attempt to specify something *we* can do to ensure that our beliefs amount to knowledge; or the conditions might specify things that must be true of *our beliefs themselves* if those beliefs are to amount to knowledge. Gettier's counterexamples seem to highlight a failure on the part of epistemic agents (see Lowy 1978), and we will consider anti-luck conditions that target epistemic agents later in this chapter. We will turn now, however, to conditions that target our beliefs themselves, since most epistemologists now focus on this, trying to identify conditions that our beliefs can satisfy in order to keep them safe from luck and to ensure that they amount to knowledge.

For epistemologists in this camp, what exactly does it mean to say that our beliefs are true simply as a matter of luck? Duncan Pritchard identifies a notion of luck that might help to answer this question, *veritic epistemic luck*, which he characterizes as follows: "It is a matter of luck that the agent's belief is true," where

> this demands that the agent's belief is true in the actual world, but that in a wide class of nearby possible worlds in which the relevant initial conditions are the same as in the actual world—and this will mean, in the basic case, that the agent at the very least forms the same belief in the same way as in the actual world [...]—the belief is false.
>
> *Pritchard 2005: 146*

So, for example, Smith's belief that C is veritically epistemically lucky because while it is true in the actual world, it is false in too many of the nearby possible worlds in which Smith forms that belief in the same way as in the actual world. To avoid being veritically epistemically lucky, Smith's belief must be true not only in the actual world, but also in a sufficient proportion of nearby possible worlds in which he forms the belief that C in the same way as in the actual world. Theories that address the issue of veritic epistemic luck in this way are *modal* epistemologies, according to which a belief counts as knowledge only if there is a modal connection—that is, a connection not only in the actual world, but also in other non-actual possible worlds—between the belief and the facts of the matter. A modal epistemology might say, more specifically, that a belief counts as knowledge only if it is true both in the actual world and in a certain proportion of worlds within a specified set or range of non-actual possible worlds.

The trouble here, of course, is with "a sufficient proportion": in order to eliminate veritic epistemic luck, in *what* proportion of the relevant nearby possible worlds must Smith's belief that C be true? In trying to answer this question, epistemologists start from at least two places. Each of these places corresponds to a distinct way of giving expression to our anti-luck intuition about knowledge. First, to say that Smith's belief is true simply as a matter of luck might be to say that there is nothing about Smith's circumstances, in which his belief happens to be true, that ensures that he will believe that C—even if C had been false, Smith might still have believed that C. This way of giving expression to our anti-luck intuition corresponds to epistemologies known as *sensitivity* theories, which we will consider in the next section. Next, to say that Smith's belief is true simply as a matter of luck might be to say that there is nothing about that which led Smith to believe that C that guarantees that C will be true—it might have been that Smith's circumstances are just as they actually are, but that his belief that C is *false*. This way of giving expression to our anti-luck intuition corresponds to epistemologies known as *safety* theories, which we will consider later in the chapter.

Sensitivity Theories

Robert Nozick (1981) famously suggests that S knows that p only if S's belief that p is sensitive to the truth, that is, only if S would not believe that p if p were false (see also Dretske 1971). In evaluating sensitivity's counterfactual condition, we consider the nearest possible world in which p is false—that is, the state of affairs, or the world, in which p is false, but that is otherwise as similar to the actual state of affairs as it can be—and then determine whether, in that world, S believes that p. If S does believe that p in that world, then her belief that p is insensitive, and she does not know that p. If S does not believe that p in that world, her belief is sensitive, which means that her knowing that p is not ruled out.

As Nozick points out, sensitivity theories, unlike the tripartite account, allow us to get the right result in Gettier cases. According to sensitivity theories, Smith does not know that C because it is simply a matter of luck that his belief that C is true: In the nearest possible world in which the man who will get the job does *not* have ten coins in his pocket—in which, let us suppose, Jones has ten coins in his pocket but Smith, who will get the job, has only nine—Smith nonetheless believes that the man who will get the job *does* have ten coins in his pocket (see Nozick 1981: 173).

Sensitivity theories almost immediately face a problem, however, due to their treatment of a certain anti-skeptical argument:

1. I know that I have hands.
2. I know that my having hands entails that I am not a handless brain-in-a-vat (that is, a handless brain floating in a vat of nutrients and electrochemically stimulated so as to generate perceptual experiences that are exactly similar to those that I am now having in what I take to be normal circumstances).
3. If I know both that I have hands and that my having hands entails that I am not a handless brain-in-a-vat, then I know that I am not a handless brain-in-a-vat.
4. Therefore, I know that I am not a handless brain-in-a-vat.

Sensitivity theories have trouble with this argument in two ways. First, there is the complaint that while sensitivity theories allow us to say that (1) is true, they force us to deny (4). (1) is true because my belief that I have hands is both true and sensitive—the nearest possible world in which I have no hands is a world in which, let us say, I lost my hands in some unfortunate accident; but I do not believe in that world that I have hands, for I clearly see there that I have no hands. (4) is false, however, because even if my belief that I am not a handless brain-in-a-vat is true, it is *insensitive*: in the nearest possible world in which I *am* a handless brain-in-a-vat, I still believe that I am *not* a handless brain-in-a-vat, since in that world everything appears to me just as it does in this world.

This sort of result suggests that sensitivity theorists will reject (3), which is an instance of an epistemic closure principle:

If S knows that p and that p *entails* q, then S knows that q.

We feel the pull of this principle in cases like the present one. For if I know that I have hands, should I not also know that certain incompatible skeptical hypotheses are false? Should I not also know that I am not a handless brain-in-a-vat? Since sensitivity theories seem to lead to the rejection of a compelling closure principle, and since they seem to offer no direct response to the skeptic, no response that explains how we know that certain skeptical hypotheses are false, many epistemologists are reluctant to adopt them.

Yet this is not the end of the story, for Nozick revises his theory in order "to take explicit account of the ways and methods of arriving at belief" (Nozick 1981: 179), relying on a standard taxonomy of methods that includes perception, memory, testimony, and intuition:

S knows that p if and only if

a. p is true;
b. S believes, via method or way of coming to believe M, that p;
c. if p weren't true and S were to use M to arrive at a belief whether (or not) p, then S wouldn't believe, via M, that p; and

d. if p were true and S were to use M to arrive at a belief whether (or not) p, then S would believe, via M, that p.

Nozick provides the following example in support of this revision: "A grandmother sees her grandson is well when he comes to visit; but if he were sick or dead, others would tell her he was well to spare her upset" (Nozick 1981: 179). When her grandson is well, the grandmother believes on the basis of seeing him that he is well. But if he were not well, she would use another method—testimony, Nozick stipulates—in forming a belief as to whether her grandson was well. In that case, however, her belief would be *false*. Yet, as Nozick says, the fact that she *would* use another method "does not mean that she doesn't know he is well (or at least ambulatory) when she sees him" (Nozick 1981: 179). This suggests that the only worlds that are relevant to S's knowing that p are worlds in which, in arriving at the belief that p, she forms her belief in the same way as in the actual world.

Moreover, given Nozick's revised sensitivity condition, although Nozick himself failed to notice this, worlds in which I am a handless brain-in-a-vat need not be relevant to whether I know that I am not a handless brain-in-a-vat. In those worlds, one might argue, my belief is produced by a method that is different from the one that produces my belief in the actual world (see Black 2002). Thus, Nozick's revised sensitivity condition gives us room to say that I know both that I have hands and that I am not a handless brain-in-a-vat. Sensitivity theories, at least those willing to make the sort of revision recommended by Nozick, need neither embrace skepticism nor deny the epistemic closure principle.

Safety Theories

The anti-luck intuition that we have in response to Gettier cases might also take the following form: to say that S's belief that p is true simply as a matter of luck is to say that there is nothing about that which led S to believe that p that guarantees that p will be true—it might have been that S's circumstances are just as they actually are, but that her belief that p is *false*. This way of giving expression to the anti-luck intuition corresponds to epistemologies known as *safety* theories. Ernest Sosa, who introduced a safety condition on knowledge, puts it like this:

> Call a belief by S that p "safe" iff: S would believe that p only if it were so that p. (Alternatively, a belief by S that p is "safe" iff: S would not believe that p without it being the case that p; or, better, iff: as a matter of fact, though perhaps not as a matter of strict necessity, not easily would S believe that p without it being the case that p.)
>
> *Sosa 1999: 142*

Pritchard, whose anti-luck epistemology revolves around a safety condition, provides some of the details that are left implicit in Sosa's formulation: If S knows a contingent proposition, p, then in most nearby possible worlds, S believes that p only when p is true (see, e.g., Pritchard 2005: 71). In evaluating S's belief against a safety principle, we consider all of the nearby possible worlds in which S believes that p. If in most of those worlds p is true, then S's belief that p is safe. If, on the other hand, S's belief that p is false in too many of those worlds, S's belief is not safe.

Like sensitivity accounts, safety accounts yield the right result in Gettier cases. Suppose once again that although Smith is justified in holding the true belief that C, he does not *know* that C. Smith's belief is true simply as a matter of luck since "by the sheerest coincidence, and entirely unknown to Smith," *he* (Smith) will get the job, and *he* has ten coins in his pocket (Gettier 1963: 123). The safety condition yields the right result here: Smith does not know that C because C is false in too many nearby possible worlds in which he believes that C.

But there are cases that suggest that the safety condition, as it is formulated above, is inadequate.

FELON: A man has been accused of murder. The man's mother holds the true belief that her son is innocent, and she holds this belief on the basis of excellent evidence in its favor, including reliable forensic evidence about the cause of the victim's death. It seems, then, that the mother knows that her son is not the murderer.

Yet while her son is not in fact the murderer, he very nearly was—he intended to murder the victim but before he could act on his intention, the victim, let us say, died of a heart attack. Moreover, in too many of the nearby worlds in which the man's mother believes that he is not the murderer, he *is* the murderer and her belief that her son is innocent is generated simply by her intense love for her son (see Pritchard 2005: 153; Armstrong (1973: 208–209) discusses a similar case, attributing it to Gregory O'Hair.)

Again, our intuition here is that the mother knows that her son is innocent. After all, she is well aware of excellent forensic evidence in favor of the claim that he is innocent. According to safety, however, at least as it is formulated above, the mother does *not* know that her son is innocent, for in too many of the nearby possible worlds in which she believes that her son is innocent, her son did in fact commit murder.

This sort of case highlights the need to make it more difficult for a world to count as one of the relevant nearby possible worlds. In particular, it suggests that the safety condition ought to make additional demands that concern the methods that epistemic agents use in forming their beliefs:

> (Safety II) If S knows a contingent proposition, p, then in most nearby possible worlds *in which S forms her belief about p in the same way as she forms her belief in the actual world*, S believes that p only when p is true.

Safety II handles FELON, for in most of the nearby possible worlds in which the mother forms her belief about her son's innocence *on the basis of excellent evidence in favor of that belief*, her son did not commit murder.

Yet Safety II faces difficulties of its own. Suppose that S holds a ticket in a fair lottery with a large number of participants. We are reluctant to say of S that she knows that her ticket is a loser. Nonetheless, S's belief satisfies the conditions set out in Safety II—in *most* nearby possible worlds in which she believes that her ticket is a loser and in which she forms her belief as she does in the actual world, namely on the basis of her belief that it is highly likely that her ticket is a loser, her ticket is in fact a loser. "The problem," Pritchard (2005: 163) says

> seems to be that the agent's belief, whilst meeting [Safety II], is still veritically lucky since, given the nearness of the possible worlds in which the agent wins the lottery (and thus where forming her belief on the basis of the odds leads her astray), it is still a matter of luck that her belief happens to be true.

What is now required, Pritchard suggests, is an even stronger version of the safety principle, one that further increases the proportion of the relevant nearby possible worlds in which S's belief must be true:

> (Safety III) If S knows a contingent proposition, p, then in *nearly all (if not all)* nearby possible worlds in which S forms her belief about p in the same way as she forms her belief in the actual world, S believes that p only when p is true.

Safety III handles the lottery case. S fails to know that her ticket is a loser, according to Safety III, because in too many of the nearby possible worlds in which she believes that her ticket is a loser and in which she forms her belief in the same way she does in the actual world, her ticket is *not* a loser.

Pritchard's main argument for Safety III—and for its "nearly all (if not all)" qualification—comes in terms of the lottery puzzle:

> The agent who forms her belief that she has lost the lottery purely on the basis of the odds involved lacks knowledge because her belief, whilst true and matching the truth in most nearby possible worlds in which she forms her belief in the same way as in the actual world, does not match the truth in a *small cluster* of nearby possible worlds in which what she believes is false (i.e., where she wins the lottery).
>
> *Pritchard 2005: 163; emphasis added*

But what if her belief fails to match the truth in an *even smaller cluster* of nearby possible worlds? In such a case, Safety III might count her as knowing that she has lost the lottery. But this is counter-intuitive, perhaps because we are reluctant to count the agent as knowing if there is *even one* nearby possible world in which her belief fails to match the truth.

Considerations like this might push us away from Safety III and toward the final version of the safety principle that we will see here:

> (Safety IV) S's belief is safe if and only if in most nearby possible worlds in which S continues to form her belief about the target proposition in the same way as in the actual world, and in all very close nearby possible worlds in which S continues to form her belief about the target proposition in the same way as in the actual world, the belief continues to be true (see Pritchard 2007: 290–292).

Safety IV handles the lottery case in what seems to be a fairly unobjectionable way.

But the worry remains, at least in the abstract, that Safety IV is not sufficiently strong. It might be that we want a guarantee that the relevant belief continues to be true even beyond the very close nearby possible worlds. Perhaps there is a case in which S's belief is false in some nearby worlds that are very close to the worlds that are very close—just outside the sphere of very close nearby worlds, let us say, but so close as to touch it. Maybe this sort of case could be used in pointing out a weakness in Safety IV, one that calls for an even stronger version of the safety principle.

So, while sensitivity theories and safety theories do a lot to let us know what it means for a belief to be true simply as a matter of luck and what needs to be the case in order to eliminate this sort of luck, it might be that what we really want from an anti-luck condition for knowledge is a *guarantee* that our beliefs will be true when the specified conditions are met. Perhaps there are modifications of the sensitivity theory or of the safety theory that would get us closer to this sort of account, but we should also be willing, it seems, to see what we might find when we look in other directions.

Internalist Anti-Luck Epistemology

We have said that a main goal of contemporary epistemology is to provide a set of conditions the satisfaction of which will keep knowledge from being vulnerable to luck, and we have been discussing theories that hold that these conditions should target *our beliefs themselves* and specify what must be true of our beliefs if those beliefs are to amount to knowledge. Having examined such conditions and discovered that it might repay our efforts to see what lies in the other direction, we now turn our attention to conditions that target *epistemic agents*, that is, conditions that attempt to specify something *we* can do to ensure that our beliefs are not true simply as a matter of luck.

The initial thought here is that justification—that is, the kind of justification that epistemic agents have for holding beliefs—is epistemically significant and, as such, should have a place in our epistemological theorizing. We might even think that justification, seen in this way, is necessary for knowledge: if S knows that *p*, she is justified in believing that *p*. This will work, however, only if we can theorize this conception of justification as being immune to luck. The sort of luck that is relevant here—the sort of luck to which this conception of justification would need to be immune—is, very roughly, this:

S's belief that p is true simply as a matter of luck if and only if [a] S is justified in believing that p, [b] p is true, and [c] S's justification for believing that p is true is distinct from that which makes p true.

One might hope to eliminate this sort of luck by making sure that one's justification for believing that p is true is *not* distinct from that which makes p true. Yet, for just those reasons uncovered by Gettier, it has proven notoriously difficult to specify conditions that allow us to do this. Indeed, some have been led to conclude that we can specify no such conditions.

Still, there are those who maintain that epistemic agents might be able to do something to ensure that their beliefs are not true simply as a matter of luck. So, for example, virtue responsibilists note that in doxastic endeavors, epistemic agents can exercise intellectual virtues such as epistemic conscientiousness, which involves a desire to believe what is true and to avoid believing what is not true (see Montmarquet 1993), and open-mindedness, which involves an honest consideration of alternatives to one's own view as well as a willingness to see things from perspectives that are different from one's own (see Baehr 2011). To allow us to avoid epistemic luck, it seems that in forming or holding certain beliefs, exercises of intellectual virtue should guarantee the truth of those beliefs, especially in light of the results of the discussion in the previous section of this essay. But exercises of intellectual virtue do not seem up to this task, for it seems plausible to say that the protagonists of at least some Gettier-style cases exercise intellectual virtues in forming beliefs, but then end up with beliefs that are nevertheless true simply as a matter of luck.

In an effort to bridge this gap, some virtue responsibilists maintain that it is necessary for knowledge that we believe the truth *because of* an exercise of intellectual virtue (see Sosa 1991: 277; Zagzebski 1996: 270–271). One potential worry with this sort of strategy is that it provides no mechanism for allowing us to see or to make sure that we do in fact believe the truth because of an exercise of intellectual virtue. Imagine a case that involves an exercise of intellectual virtue and in which I hold the true belief that p because of that exercise of intellectual virtue. We can also just as easily imagine a case that involves an identical exercise of intellectual virtue and in which I hold the true belief that p, not because of that exercise of intellectual virtue, since a bit of bad luck prevents it from leading me to the truth, but only because a stroke of good luck ensures that my belief is nevertheless true. It might very well be that I cannot discriminate between these two cases, and this points to the lack of a mechanism that would let us see that we believe the truth because of exercises of intellectual virtue.

Perhaps there is a more promising avenue to pursue here. John McDowell, for the past three decades or so, has been calling our attention to a view on which exercises of rational perceptual capacities can allow us to see that we believe the truth because of those exercises of rational perceptual capacities. His thought is that epistemologists have been blind to a certain theoretical space, a space occupied by an overlooked view concerning perceptual justification—or perceptual *warrant*—and perceptual knowledge. This view regards perception as a capacity "to get into states that consist in having a certain feature of the objective environment perceptually present to one's self-consciously rational awareness" (McDowell 2011: 37), so that "in non-defective exercises of a perceptual capacity subjects get into perceptual states that provide *indefeasible* warrant for perceptual beliefs" (McDowell 2011: 38). And perceptual beliefs that enjoy indefeasible warrant are immune to luck.

McDowell finds this way of thinking about observational knowledge in Wilfrid Sellars' influential "Empiricism and the Philosophy of Mind." On a Sellarsian approach to observational knowledge, an instance of observational knowledge is "an act of reason," where this means, at least in part, that when someone has a bit of observational knowledge, "she can state not only what she knowledgeably believes, but also how her believing it is rationally grounded in a way that shows the belief to be knowledgeable" (McDowell 2011: 10). In addition to being able to state what one knowledgeably believes, there are two conditions on this sort of observational knowledge. First, "a report [of such knowledge] must have an authority that consists in its issuing from a reliable capacity," such as "the capacity to know the colours of things by seeing them" (McDowell 2011: 11). Second, as Sellars says, that authority must "be recognized by the person whose report it is" (Sellars 1997: 74).

This approach to observational knowledge is epistemologically internalistic: "the warrant by virtue of which a belief counts as knowledgeable is accessible to the knower," as McDowell (2011: 17) puts it. But this seems to be vulnerable to a troubling objection: McDowell's Sellarsian view seems to require that one has the ability not only to cite a perceptual state as an epistemic warrant but also to say why the warrant that state provides is not undermined or defeated. McDowell puts the objection, as he finds it in the work of Tyler Burge (Burge 2003, in particular), as follows:

> One would need to argue that, though the warrant provided by the perceptual state is defeasible, it is not defeated on this occasion. That would require working with some notably sophisticated concepts: defeasible warrant, defeating conditions, considerations that warrant one in discounting the possibility that one's perceptual warrant is defeated in the present circumstances.
>
> *McDowell 2011: 28–29*

And it is implausible to demand this sort of conceptual sophistication from ordinary epistemic agents, who, after all, have plenty of observational knowledge.

McDowell maintains, however, in defense of his Sellarsian approach, that this objection depends "on the assumption that the warrant a perceptual state provides for a belief cannot guarantee the truth of the belief" (McDowell 2011: 30). McDowell's approach to observational knowledge denies this crucial assumption. He maintains that perceptual states can provide *indefeasible* warrant for beliefs; there is an "indefeasible connection" (McDowell 1998: 385) between one's being in a certain perceptual state—for example, one's seeing that something is green—and things being a certain way in the objective environment—for example, something's being green. This makes it natural to say that when one is in a certain perceptual state, one thereby knows how things are in the objective environment.

But why do epistemologists maintain that perception provides only defeasible warrant for beliefs? The first step in this direction is the recognition that perceptual capacities are *fallible*: each such capacity sometimes fails to do what it is specified as a capacity to do. From this claim, McDowell suggests, Burge and others conclude that "perceptual states, in themselves, can provide only defeasible warrant for beliefs" (McDowell 2011: 34). McDowell maintains, however, that if we make this inference, we are making a mistake about the notion of fallibility: although we certainly ought to see perception as fallible, it is nevertheless the case that "when all goes well in the operation of a perceptual capacity of a sort that belongs to its possessor's rationality, a perceiver enjoys a perceptual state in which some feature of her environment is *there* for her, perceptually *present* to her rationally self-conscious awareness," in which case "the warrant for belief that the state provides is indefeasible; it *cannot* be undermined" (McDowell 2011: 30–31). That is, the fallibility of our perceptual capacities is consistent with the fact that certain perceptual states provide indefeasible warrant.

McDowell also suggests that we sometimes mistake *bad* cases—cases that reveal the fallibility of a perceptual capacity, cases, that is, in which *not* all goes well in the operation of a perceptual capacity—for *good* cases. There are, McDowell grants, bad cases that we cannot distinguish from good cases. Given this, some have complained that for McDowell each and every perceptual state provides warrant for believing *only* that "either one is in the good case," in which some feature of the objective environment is there for the perceiver, "or one is in the bad case and so being undetectably deceived" (Pritchard 2009: 472). The complaint, then, is that the warrant provided for a belief by a perceptual state can never be "better than it would be in the bad case, even if one is in fact in the good case"

(Pritchard 2009: 472): if some bad cases are indistinguishable from good cases, then perceptual states can only ever provide defeasible warrant for beliefs, making them vulnerable to luck.

Those who take this kind of route to defeasibility will in all likelihood deny that perceptual capacities themselves put us in a position to know "that it is through perception that one knows whatever it is that one knows about the environment" (McDowell 2011: 41–42). For these theorists, if perception works to give us knowledge of the objective environment, it does so on something like the following model:

> [W]hen I see that things are thus and so, I take it that things are thus and so on the basis of having it look to me as if things are thus and so. And it can look to me as if things are thus and so when they are not; appearances do not give me the resources to ensure that I take things to be thus and so, on the basis of appearances, only when things are indeed thus and so. If things are indeed thus and so when they seem to be, the world is doing me a favour.
>
> *McDowell 1998: 396*

To say, on this model, that some bad cases are indistinguishable from good cases is to say something like this: perceptual appearances, even when I am as careful as I can be in using my perceptual capacities, do not ensure that things are indeed as I perceptually take them to be. From this, it does indeed seem to follow that our perceptual capacities can provide only defeasible warrant for beliefs.

According to McDowell, however, the inference to defeasibility from indistinguishability—that is, the indistinguishability of some bad cases from good cases—does not work: even though some bad cases are indistinguishable from good cases, it is nevertheless true that there are perceptual states that provide indefeasible warrant for beliefs. McDowell claims, in fact, that the inference from indistinguishability to defeasibility can work only if it is made against the backdrop of the assumption that perception is *not* the sort of capacity McDowell takes it to be. McDowell's view is one according to which perceptual capacities are capacities "to get into states that consist in having a certain feature of the objective environment perceptually present to one's self-consciously rational awareness" (McDowell 2011: 37). Through such capacities, we know certain things about the objective environment and we know that it is through those very capacities that we know whatever it is we know about the objective environment. The inference from indistinguishability to defeasibility works only when we ignore this plausible view.

Having denied the inference from fallibility to defeasibility, as well as the inference from indistinguishability to defeasibility, McDowell has done a great deal to show that his view deserves consideration and attention. It is a view that we should by no means ignore in our epistemological theorizing. Still, some feel that something is missing, namely, a positive account of how perceptual capacities operate so as to provide indefeasible warrant for beliefs, warrant that is not vulnerable to luck. Pritchard, for example, notes that

> McDowell himself never explicitly offers [a] supporting argument [for his anti-skeptical strategy], and rests content instead to offer his view in a broadly quietistic manner (as if simply outlining the main contours of the position would suffice for his audience to recognise its truth, and thereby exit the fly-bottle of scepticism).
>
> *Pritchard 2009: 478*

An Alternative Strategy

There is a virtual consensus among contemporary epistemologists that the aim of believing is to believe what is true. This aim is external to the activity of believing, in that it is separate and distinct from the activity itself. Søren Kierkegaard maintains that activities with external aims are *aesthetic* activities (see Kierkegaard 1987, vol. 2: 174, 179, 190–191, 254). Such activities are susceptible to luck, where, in spite of our best efforts to control the outcome, the world can interfere with the activity so as to keep it from achieving its aim. As we have seen, a main goal of contemporary epistemology is to theorize a prophylactic against this sort of luck by providing a set of conditions the satisfaction of which will guarantee that we believe only what is true. But this can seem futile, because when an activity has an external aim, it seems that there is always space between the activity and its aim into which the world can make its way and, once there, seize the movements of the activity and "digest" them, as Kierkegaard's pseudonym Judge William puts it (Kierkegaard 1987, vol. 2: 174). The possibility of luck can seem unavoidable when the activity of believing has the external aim of truth, and this is something that seems to be confirmed by the persistent difficulties faced by strategies like those we have been discussing in this essay.

Suppose, on the other hand, that the activity of believing has an *internal* aim, one that is neither separate nor distinct from that activity itself. The thought here is that the aim of the activity of believing is to engage in that activity in a particular way, specifically, as my ideal self would engage in that activity. Activities with internal aims are, for Kierkegaard, *ethical* activities (see, for example, Kierkegaard 1987, vol. 2: 256, 259, 264). Ethical activities have internal aims and a structure of inwardness, in that a person who is engaged in those activities "wants to actualize [...] his ideal self" (Kierkegaard 1987, vol. 2: 259). Moreover, when the activity of believing has this internal aim and this structure of inwardness, there is no possibility of luck, for the aim of the activity is *to believe as my ideal self would believe*, and I achieve that aim when I *believe as my ideal self would believe*. There is no room here for luck, no room for the world to intervene in the affairs of the activity of believing.

So the aim of what we might call the ethical activity of believing is to believe what my ideal self would believe. A part of this aim, of course, is to believe in this moment what my ideal self would believe in this moment. And so now the question is this: what do I believe when I successfully pursue this aim? The answer is that I believe in this moment what my ideal self would believe in this moment. This is fully generalizable: When I successfully pursue the aim of the ethical activity of believing, namely, to believe at t what my ideal self would believe at t, I believe at t what my ideal self would believe at t. There is no space here—no space at all—between the aim of the ethical activity of believing and the results of my successful pursuits of that aim. This means that the ethical activity of believing is one in which there is no possibility of luck.

Now, in believing—that is, in believing as my ideal self would believe—it might very well be the case that I end up with beliefs that are true, for there are circumstances in which my ideal self would hold beliefs that are true rather than false. It is just that when I am engaged in the ethical activity of believing, I am oriented inward as I engage in that activity: I engage in that activity for the sake of becoming my ideal self and not for the sake of anything outside of that, neither to hold beliefs that are true, nor to hold beliefs that will be beneficial, nor to hold beliefs that are gratifying, nor to hold beliefs that are convenient. I hold the beliefs that I hold because they are the beliefs my ideal self would hold; I hold them in order to become my ideal self.

And so it seems that an epistemology of this sort, in addition to eliminating the possibility of luck, can accommodate the fact that truth is often the result of the activity of believing. Indeed, it seems compatible with the fact that *knowledge* is often the result of that activity. An epistemology of this sort, which I will call a Kierkegaardian epistemology, which sees the activity of believing as having an internal aim, has the resources both to eliminate the possibility of luck and to make room for the fact that we know a great many things. This gives it an advantage over epistemologies that see the activity of believing as having an external aim and that therefore leave themselves vulnerable to luck.

References

Armstrong, D.M. (1973) *Belief, Truth and Knowledge*, Cambridge: Cambridge University Press.
Baehr, Jason (2011) *The Inquiring Mind: On Intellectual Virtues and Virtue Epistemology*, Oxford: Oxford University Press.
Black, Tim (2002) "A Moorean Response to Brain-in-a-Vat Scepticism," *Australasian Journal of Philosophy* 80, 148–163.

Burge, Tyler (2003) "Perceptual Entitlement," *Philosophy and Phenomenological Research* 67, 503–548.

Dretske, Fred I. (1971) "Conclusive Reasons," *Australasian Journal of Philosophy* 49, 1–22.

Gettier, Edmund (1963) "Is Justified True Belief Knowledge?" *Analysis* 23, 121–123.

Kierkegaard, Søren (1987) *Either/Or*, 2 vols. trans. Howard V. Hong & Edna H. Hong, Princeton, NJ: Princeton University Press.

Lowy, Catherine (1978) "Gettier's Notion of Justification," *Mind* 87(345), 105–108.

McDowell, John (1998) "Criteria, Defeasibility, and Knowledge," in *Meaning, Knowledge, and Reality*, Cambridge, MA: Harvard University Press, pp. 369–394.

———. (2011) *Perception as a Capacity for Knowledge*, Milwaukee, WI: Marquette University Press.

Montmarquet, James A. (1993) *Epistemic Virtue and Doxastic Responsibility*, Lanham, MD: Rowman and Littlefield.

Nozick, Robert (1981) *Philosophical Explanations*, Cambridge, MA: Harvard University Press.

Pritchard, Duncan (2005) *Epistemic Luck*, Oxford: Clarendon Press.

———. (2007) "Anti-Luck Epistemology," *Synthese* 158, 277–297.

———. (2009) "Wright *contra* McDowell on Perceptual Knowledge and Scepticism," *Synthese* 171, 467–479.

Sellars, Wilfrid (1997) [1956] *Empiricism and the Philosophy of Mind*, Cambridge, MA: Harvard University Press.

Sosa, Ernest (1991) *Knowledge in Perspective*, Cambridge: Cambridge University Press.

———. (1999) "How to Defeat Opposition to Moore," in James E. Tomberlin (ed.) *Philosophical Perspectives 13, Epistemology*, London and Malden, MA: Blackwell, pp. 141–153.

Zagzebski, Linda Trinkaus (1996) *Virtues of the Mind: An Inquiry into the Nature of Virtue and the Ethical Foundations of Knowledge*, Cambridge: Cambridge University Press.

26

THE LUCK/KNOWLEDGE INCOMPATIBILITY THESIS

Stephen Hetherington

An Older Luck/Knowledge Incompatibility Thesis

Much modern epistemological reflection on the nature of knowledge is still being shaped by its ancient roots. In particular, these words—from Socrates in Plato's dialogue *Meno* (97e–98a)—continue to influence epistemology:[1]

> To acquire an untied work of Daedalus is not worth much, … for it does not remain, but it is worth much if tied down, for his works are very beautiful. What am I thinking of when I say this? True opinions. For true opinions, as long as they remain, are a fine thing and all they do is good, but they are not willing to remain long, and they escape from a man's mind, so that they are not worth much until one ties them down by (giving) an account of the reason why. And that, Meno my friend, is recollection, as we previously agreed. After they are tied down, in the first place they become knowledge, and then they remain in place. That is why knowledge is prized higher than correct opinion, and knowledge differs from correct opinion in being tied down.

Socrates' picture is metaphorical, somewhat generic, and very programmatic. It is metaphorical, with its invocation of Daedalus' statues—famous for their ability, and indeed tendency, to run away when not tethered. In this respect, these statues are being said to be like our true beliefs.[2] They have the potential to be distinctively valuable, as does a true belief. But this potential is realized only once they are tied down (and thereby held in place)—a process and result that is claimed to mirror a true belief's becoming *knowledge*. Thus, it seems, we are meant to infer that knowing includes an element akin to that tethering. And in this respect Socrates' picture is less generic than it might have been. For he suggests that what thereby needs to be present, as part of the knowing, is a *logos*—which is present, he also suggests, through *recollection*. In that way, the believer would bring to mind an *account* (this being the translation here of "*logos*") of how her belief is true. We might describe this as her *understanding*, well enough, that the belief is true; which could be a matter of her understanding, well enough, *how* the belief is true. Even this is a quite programmatic description, though: Socrates is proposing just one from among the possible ways in which we might claim to understand his metaphor.

Was epistemological progress thereby made by Socrates? Most post-1963 epistemologists will say that most pre-1963 epistemologists would have taken from that Platonic portrayal this seemingly Socratic moral (a moral emerging from Socrates' words):

> A belief is not knowledge simply in virtue of being true (its being accurate). The belief's being knowledge requires also its being *tethered* for the believer, such as by her having good evidence for the belief's being true. This good evidence might include an account of *how* the belief is true.

What else might epistemologists claim to learn from Plato's account? Socrates and Meno were discussing whether, in undertaking a journey to Larissa, one needs only a *true belief* as to the correct direction, or whether something relevantly stronger—specifically, *knowledge*—is needed. The two of them agree that knowledge is preferable; why, though? For example, was Socrates telling Meno that a true belief is knowledge only if, by possessing an associated account of the belief's being true, the believer would not be relying upon *luck*, in traveling to Larissa? Not in those words. But others— contemporary *anti-luck* theorists of knowledge—could well wish to place that interpretive sheen upon Socrates' words. They might claim to see an *incompatibility* thesis about knowing and luck as being embedded, even if inchoately, within his words. Accordingly, their accompanying interpretive thinking could proceed along these lines:

> Even a true belief is not knowledge if the believer has not done enough to eliminate some significant element of *luck* in the presence of that true belief. This could encompass both the true belief's coming to exist in the first place and its then staying in place (its being maintained). The true belief's merely *happening* to stay in place, for instance, would not be enough for it still to be knowledge, because even its continued presence might be due merely to luck; in which event, the belief—regardless of its being true and regardless of how non-luckily it originally came into existence—is not as *dependable* a guide as is needed, if it is to be knowledge.

A Newer Luck/Knowledge Incompatibility Thesis

Recent epistemology has not rested content with the aforementioned version of a luck/knowledge incompatibility thesis—a Socratic one. Epistemologists have enriched that thinking, largely as a move within what is often called *post-Gettier* epistemology.

Edmund Gettier (1963) made his mark within contemporary philosophy with a challenge to what he saw (ibid.: 121n1) as "perhaps" a version of the Socratic account of knowing. Because Gettier's challenge has attained the status of epistemological orthodoxy, I will not repeat or evaluate it here in detail.[3] But I will outline the basic idea, with an eye on how this has led to a newer luck/knowledge incompatibility thesis than the one prompted by the Socratic thinking in the *Meno*.

Gettier directed our attention to a putative philosophical *definition* of knowledge. It was a definition that he thought of as encompassing the Socratic picture (in the previous section) of knowing's nature. Should we regard that picture as relevantly *complete*—albeit generic and programmatic—in its portrayal of the state of having some knowledge? Is knowledge *nothing beyond* how it is portrayed by Plato—namely, as a true belief that is well supported (epistemically justified, to use the usual epistemological jargon), such as by good or even excellent evidence for its being true? In short, is knowledge *definable*—albeit generically and programmatically—as a justified true belief?

Not if Gettier was right; and, according to most epistemologists, he *was* right in his key move. He gave us two imagined *counterexamples* to the knowledge-equals-justified-true-belief definition. These counterexamples are descriptions of possible situations where someone has a justified true belief that

The Luck/Knowledge Incompatibilty Thesis

falls short of being knowledge—and hence is *not* equal to justified-true-belief. So said Gettier, in interpreting his imagined situations. Other philosophers immediately concurred with him; and thus began a vast post-1963 epistemological enterprise—post-Gettier epistemology.

Gettier's own two counterexamples, along with the many similar ones that have since been imagined, are generally called *Gettier cases*. And such cases have seemed to many recent epistemologists to be describable in anti-luck terms. Those descriptions have taken two forms—sometimes being offered simply as *intuitive*, sometimes receiving more *technical* treatments.

I will explain all of that in a moment. For specificity, here is a famous and representative Gettier case:[4]

> *The sheep-in-the-field*. Looking on at a field, you see what looks like a sheep. You form the belief, "There is a sheep in that field." You are correct—yet not because what you are seeing is a sheep. Rather, it is a disguised dog. But there is a sheep in the field anyway, feeding peacefully behind a slight hill, hidden from your gaze. Your belief is therefore true. So, it is a belief that is true and supported by evidence with many features that good evidence typically has. Is the belief knowledge? Presumably not.

Yet why would that belief not be knowledge? Here is a supposedly *intuitive* anti-luck answer:

> *Only luckily* is your belief true, given its being guided into existence by that particular sensory evidence (which makes no mention of the actual sheep, whose existence is why your belief is actually true).

Here is a more *technical* anti-luck answer:[5]

> Your belief is true only in a *veritically* lucky way. In order to understand this failing, consider the possible worlds most like this one from among those where again you form a belief as you do here within that same perceptual situation—standing outside that field, using your senses as you do here, being guided by seemingly identical sensory evidence to what you have used here. In many of those possible worlds, we assume, your belief is false; for the *actual* sheep (or its counterparts within those worlds) not being in the field is not precluded by what your senses are telling you. Hence, even though your belief is true within this world, *only luckily* is it true within this world.

Epistemological Significance

Gettier's challenge has thus prompted increased acceptance among epistemologists of some form of luck/knowledge incompatibility thesis. In Gettier cases (we are told by epistemologists in general), the central belief—the Gettiered belief—is not knowledge; and this (we are told by anti-luck epistemologists) is *because* the Gettiered belief is true only luckily, in spite of its being supported by good evidence. The claim that no Gettiered belief is knowledge has been widely embraced by epistemologists. This claim has attracted such attention due to the epistemologically widespread belief that it provides real insight into knowledge's nature, by taking us forensically into the heart of an otherwise perplexing piece of philosophy.

So, if a luck/knowledge incompatibility thesis can unravel the complexities—as epistemologists have long taken to be latent—within Gettier's challenge, then the thesis is not only true but *helpfully* true. It is standardly proffered, therefore, as a thesis that assists us in *understanding* something important about knowledge—something close to the center of the web of features that are constitutive of whatever knowing is, most fundamentally characterized. In that respect, we are being enjoined to treat any luck/knowledge incompatibility thesis as epistemologically significant because it has purportedly *explicative* import, revealing something significant about knowledge's nature.

297

The post-Gettier version of the luck/knowledge incompatibility thesis is thus said to point to the luck present within any Gettier case as sufficing to *explain why* the case's central belief, although true and well justified, fails to be knowledge. The more general moral thereby being grounded is that any true belief—even when well justified—fails to be knowledge *if* there is significant luck in how it has come into existence, or in how it is being maintained, as a true belief. The latter luck would be taken to explain the former failure.

Critical Evaluation

How should we approach the challenge of evaluating the truth and explanatory potential of a luck/knowledge incompatibility thesis?

First, for simplicity we can talk of *the* luck/knowledge incompatibility thesis, allowing it to be the post-Gettier version, which in the following sense incorporates the older, Socratic version. If there can be knowledge-precluding luck even when a belief is true *and* justified, then—a fortiori—there can be knowledge-precluding luck when a belief is true without also being justified.

So, how are we to decide whether the post-Gettier version of the luck/knowledge incompatibility thesis is true, let alone true and explanatorily useful? We will make little if any epistemological progress with this issue by simply exchanging supposed intuitions (even if these are in agreement with each other).[6] Equally, insofar as there is intuitive support for the thesis, our relying too much upon a specific technical formulation of it will risk our not doing justice to the thesis, especially if that formulation has its own problems. Accordingly, we should seek a middle evaluative path: the language used in the rest of this section will therefore be only slightly technical. (Yet, even thus constrained, we will uncover a simple reason why the luck/knowledge incompatibility thesis—*even* if true—cannot play the explicative role, described in the previous section, of helping us to understand knowledge's nature.)[7]

Consider, then, a generic version of the luck/knowledge incompatibility thesis. We may avoid any very specific assumptions about the nature of the luck being discussed.[8] Nonetheless, one general feature must be mentioned, since it would be part of any specific version of the thesis. We need to note that, whenever the luck/knowledge incompatibility thesis alerts us to a particular belief's being luckily true, the thesis is saying that, somehow and somewhere in that belief's coming into existence or being maintained as a true belief, there was a significant and marked possibility of this particular combination of belief-plus-truth *not* coming into existence or being maintained. Because the belief *is* true, that particular combination *has* in fact eventuated, perhaps due to a role played by some supportive evidence; even so (as at least a minimal aspect of the luck pertaining to how that belief is both present and true), that particular combination *might well not* have eventuated.

We could also parse that point in this way:

> Even when what could otherwise be some *good* luck is bringing about or maintaining the belief—in that the belief is present or maintained as a *true* belief—a correlative kind of bad luck instead *could easily* (even with all else being equal) have been bringing about or maintaining a belief—so that a false belief would instead have been present or maintained (even with all else being equal). The latter luck—the bad luck, that "could easily" have been the only luck operative in the situation—is enough to prevent the former luck—the good luck—from crowning the resulting true belief as an instance of knowledge.

Thus, we can appreciate an essential element of the spirit underlying the luck/knowledge incompatibility thesis. But that reasoning in support of that thesis also directs us (as the rest of this section will show) toward a reason why the luck/knowledge incompatibility thesis *cannot* ever help us to understand or explicate knowledge's absence from a situation.

From the previous section, the luck/knowledge incompatibility thesis purports to be *explicating* a way—specifically, due to the presence of a pertinent form of luck—in which even a true belief that

The Luck/Knowledge Incompatibilty Thesis

is evidentially supported (let alone a true belief lacking such support) can fail to be knowledge. This failure to be knowledge is supposedly being *explained* by the former state of affairs—that is, by the true, and perhaps justified, belief's being present only in a relevantly lucky way, which prevents even the belief's being true and justified from sufficing to make the belief knowledge.

Yet already we can begin to appreciate why this explicative aim will never be satisfied. Consider the following exchange:

> [spoken by me, S.H.] *Within* any possible situation where a given true belief is present only luckily, there is no accompanying failure of the belief—due to the luck—in the sense of its also being false within that possible situation. (This is trivially so: in no possible situation is a belief both true and false.)

> [spoken by a proponent of the luck/knowledge incompatibility thesis] That trivially true point is irrelevant. A given true belief can be present luckily in *this* world—and is therefore not knowledge in this world—in part because that same belief (with all else being equal) is false in various *other* relevant possible worlds. In those *further* possible worlds, the belief is false, hence immediately not knowledge in those worlds. (I say "immediately" because it is manifest that, in any possible world, if a belief is knowledge then it is true.) And the belief is thereby—even if not immediately—also not knowledge in this world (because, given the relevance of those other worlds, the belief is *thereby only luckily* true in this world).

> [spoken by me, S.H.] But that reasoning by a proponent of the luck/knowledge incompatibility thesis, although epistemologically familiar, remains irrelevant to her explicative challenge—a challenge to which my first point in this exchange, although trivially true, *is* relevant. The luck/knowledge incompatibility thesis envisages a modal state of affairs—constituted by those further possible worlds, in which the belief reappears, although not always as a true belief. But that envisaged modal state of affairs literally constitutes only *the belief*—but not therefore *the luckily true belief*—being *tracked or re-identified across* those various possible worlds. Accordingly, the modality that is literally being *constituted* by that envisaged state of affairs—the modality, after all, *is* that pattern of possible worlds and their contents—is at most *about* the recurring belief as such that is present within each of those worlds. It is not thereby *about* the (luckily, and perhaps justified) true belief as such—since this true (and perhaps justified) belief as such is *not* reappearing within all of those possible worlds. For we are explicitly told that the belief is not true within all of those worlds; hence, we are *im*plicitly told that those worlds are not jointly constituting a modal state of affairs including the justified and (luckily) true belief as such. However (from the previous section), our guiding epistemological challenge right now is that of understanding how *even a true* belief could fail—even when supported by good evidence—to be knowledge, due to some kind and degree of luck in how that combination of truth and belief (and perhaps evidence) is present or maintained. Correlatively, the challenge right now is not to understand merely how *a belief* could fail to be knowledge, in virtue of the fact that, although it is true, it need not have been (even with all else being equal). Yet *that* understanding is the most that could be articulated by talking in that standardly proposed way of that range of worlds, in some of which the belief is false.

This does not prove immediately that the luck/knowledge incompatibility thesis is false. But it *does* tell us that this pessimistic view of the thesis should be considered seriously—now, all the more so. What we have found so far is that the thesis—even *if* true—lacks the explicative power attributed to it by its proponents. And perhaps this is at least partly because the thesis is *not* true. How might that be so? Here is a stark thought: perhaps the thesis is not true, because each and any true belief *is* knowledge—regardless, therefore, of whether or not it is luckily true.[9] If so, then accompanying luck even in how a given true belief is true would never be a reason why that true belief—let alone if it is also justified—is *not* knowledge.

299

Stephen Hetherington

Examples

The line of thought in the previous section is epistemologically heterodox. It is rather abstract, too. So, we might usefully test it on our two earlier examples—each of which is taken by many epistemologists to motivate some version of a luck/knowledge incompatibility thesis.

First, let us rejoin Socrates and Meno as they contemplate that journey to Larissa. If we wish to parse their conversation in terms of a concern about some pertinent kind of luck, it is clear what the luck in question would be. If they set out on the journey equipped only with a *true belief* as to the correct direction to follow—thus lacking anything epistemically stronger than that true belief—then it seems that Socrates and Meno would regard it as lucky if the true belief is *maintained* along the way. They agree that the true belief is no less helpful than knowledge would be, *provided* that the true belief stays in place. But will it do so? Tethering is therefore proposed by Socrates as a way of accomplishing that outcome. Tethering thereby sets aside any *need* for there to be continued good luck in the true belief's somehow being maintained.

Notice, though, how tethering is thus *not* an action or state of affairs with independent merit—an action or state of affairs possessing a point in this setting *beyond* its setting aside that need for continuing good luck. Hence, the thinking by Socrates and Meno falls short of establishing as strong a commitment about knowledge's nature as is expressed by the luck/knowledge incompatibility thesis. Seemingly, Socrates and Meno's thinking tells us that if we *could* maintain the true belief, this would be enough also to maintain all of the relevant merits that are being expected of the corresponding instance of knowledge over that same time period (insofar as a conception of knowledge's nature is to be motivated by this discussion between Socrates and Meno). Significantly, however, this in turn suggests that the true belief on its own is *already* an instance of that knowledge *at* a time: if *maintaining* the true belief is enough to accomplish whatever it is that the knowledge would be expected to accomplish over that period, then perhaps *having* the true belief now is sufficient for already having the knowledge—having it *now*, at any rate.[10]

Of course, having the true belief now is no guarantee that the true belief *will* be maintained. Yet even that cautionary observation does not entail that the true belief is *not* knowledge now. Such an entailment obtains only if the belief's being knowledge now awaits, or at least ensures, its continuing to be knowledge. No wonder, then, that tethers are envisaged by Socrates as being needed from the outset: the tether is supposedly what, by its being present now, will maintain the true belief in place.

But that view—of all synchronic knowledge (knowledge-at-a-particular-time) as needing to be diachronic knowledge (knowledge-held-from-one-time-to-the-next)—is highly questionable[11]: knowing now does *not* await or ensure knowing later, for example. Nor is that entailment guaranteed by tethers anyway; for tethers can slip or be damaged. To put the same point less metaphorically: having evidence in support of a true belief as to the direction to follow in undertaking a journey will not guarantee a successful arrival, even with all else being equal. Like the belief in question, the supportive evidence *itself* must be maintained—alongside the belief, just as firmly present *as* the belief. Holding it, too, in place could even *distract* one from holding in place the initial true belief: now there is *more* material—there are *more* beliefs—that must be maintained, rather than merely the initial true belief. In practical terms—remember that we are talking about an *action* of traveling to Larissa—what matters most is the maintenance of the true belief. Having a back-up power supply or generator—which is what the evidence or tether amounts to—is thus not *essential*. It might be helpful. Then again, it might not. So, it should not be assumed to be *needed* as an essential condition or part of the pertinent knowledge's being present.

Let us revisit also our earlier Gettier case—the field containing that dog disguised as a sheep (along with a real but hidden sheep). As ever, there are different ways of trying to explicate the supposedly knowledge-precluding luck present within this situation. But each of them will instantiate a more generic and underlying idea—to the effect that there was a *real possibility of you not* forming a true belief (as you have actually done), relevantly restricted as you are in responding to the evidence with which you are being presented while standing outside that field. We will be assured (as part of telling us why your belief, although true and justified, is not knowledge) that there are many possible variations on the case, in enough of which various important aspects of your epistemic perspective are being maintained—yet where there is *no* sheep in that field.

Now, along some such lines, maybe there is indeed luck in your sheep-in-the-field belief's being present and true. Yet even to understand this is not to understand, in addition, how the true belief is too luckily present to be knowledge. Basically, in order to have the former understanding, we need to imagine simply a range of possibilities where *the belief* reappears, presumably sometimes true, definitely sometimes not. Even basically, however, in order to have the latter understanding we need to imagine a range of possibilities where *the true belief* reappears, at least sometimes failing to be knowledge (in spite of never also failing to be true).

And *is* the latter imaginable? Whether it is depends ultimately on how we should evaluate the previous test case—the philosophically famous journey to Larissa. And that case, we have seen just now, might *not* be providing good support even for the older and simpler—Socratic—luck/knowledge incompatibility thesis. In any event, we face the new point (from the previous paragraph) that we should not react to the sheep-in-the-field case by confusing (i) the question of whether *the belief* is luckily *true*, with (ii) the question of whether *the true belief*, by being *luckily* true-or-false-or-whatever, is not *knowledge*.

An Objection and a Reply

The previous two sections imply that to describe a belief as luckily true is never a way of explicating its not being knowledge. For a necessary condition of having that sort of understanding is failed, perhaps surprisingly so, by any attempt to apply the luck/knowledge incompatibility thesis.

Let us now consider an objection to that way of doubting the explanatory power of that thesis. This objection asks (as follows) whether a focus on belief-forming or belief-maintaining *methods* can restore the standardly claimed explanatory power to that thesis:

> Above, we have talked of evaluating a particular belief—the one that is claimed to be true only luckily—across possible situations or worlds. But we need not apply the luck/ knowledge incompatibility thesis in that way. We can evaluate instead a belief-forming or -maintaining *method*. A particular belief could then be deemed only luckily true, because it is present and true only as the product of a *generally* poor belief-forming or -maintaining method—so that one has formed or maintained the particular true belief via a method that would *most likely* have given one a false belief instead. Using a method like that is no way to gain or maintain knowledge: the belief is true only luckily, hence is not knowledge.

Yet such reasoning is weaker than would standardly be believed by epistemologists. Here is an alternative interpretation of the epistemic impact of using an unreliable belief-forming or -maintaining method to form or maintain a true belief.

A method's being generally poor (unreliable in this world and/or across possible worlds) entails at least that it is not *inherently* knowledge-producing or knowledge-maintaining—because it is not inherently at-least-true-belief-producing or -maintaining. This tells us that citing the use of that method is at least not enough in itself to stamp, as being knowledge, a belief produced or maintained via the method. Accordingly, we may also grant that one could well need to be lucky if one is to gain or maintain even a true belief by using such a method. Yet this concession need not then be interpreted as entailing that one *never* gains or maintains knowledge in that way—unless, of course, we have independently shown that a true belief produced or maintained in a lucky way is not knowledge. And this, from earlier sections, is not something that we have already shown. Perhaps, therefore, we have the interpretive license to say the following:

Suppose that the method is far from reliable at producing or maintaining true beliefs. Suppose that this is at least a lack of reliability in producing or maintaining knowledge: whenever it does produce or maintain a false belief, it is thereby *manifesting* that unreliability (given that any instance of knowledge needs to be true). Even so, that lack of reliability in producing or maintaining knowledge—manifested in those actual or possible failures to produce or maintain a true belief—might be because knowledge *is nothing more than* true belief.

Again, until this is independently shown not to be so, we should not assume that the former unreliability is *in itself* a reason to deem—as falling short of being knowledge—even any true belief that is produced or maintained by the belief-forming or -maintaining method.[12]

A Luck/Knowledge Compatibility Thesis?

We have found that epistemologists might be unable to call upon the luck/knowledge incompatibility thesis to *explicate* there being a sense of "luckily" in which a belief's being formed or maintained luckily precludes its being knowledge. Two earlier sections ("Critical evaluation" and "An objection and reply") ended by suggesting briefly the possibility that a belief's being luckily true is in fact *not* a barrier to its being knowledge: perhaps any true belief, let alone any justified true belief, *is* knowledge. That suggestion amounts to the idea of replacing the luck/knowledge incompatibility thesis with a more heterodox luck/knowledge *compatibility* thesis.

Unlike the luck/knowledge incompatibility thesis, which would point to luck's presence to explain why some particular belief, although true and even justified, is not knowledge, a luck/knowledge compatibility thesis need only be saying that the luck's presence does not *prevent* a belief (all else being equal) from being knowledge. This compatibility thesis would regard the luck as being explanatorily epiphenomenal in that respect. By all means (the thesis might continue), tell us what makes a belief luckily true, since this might be a feature with some significance for how we could wish to view that belief's epistemic dimensions. Yet do not assume (we will then be advised) that the significance has to include the belief's *thereby failing* to be knowledge.

Could we even talk usefully—and still in a compatibilist vein—of a belief's *luckily being* knowledge? At the very least, we could do so by applying Duncan Pritchard's (2005) notion of *evidential* luck, whereby a person can be lucky to gain some specific evidence in the first place, only then to use it aptly—and luckily—in forming what is thereby a well justified true belief and even perhaps knowledge. As this chapter's discussion has exemplified, however, evidential luck is not what epistemologists have in mind when endorsing the luck/knowledge incompatibility thesis. They generally have in mind something like Pritchard's concept of *veritic* luck (mentioned above, in the second section of the chapter). Yet even the presence of this sort of luck, we have seen, cannot be *shown*—and hence should not be *assumed*—to be incompatible with a true belief's being knowledge. Again, therefore, the question arises of whether it is possible that a belief *could* be knowledge even while being true in a veritically lucky way, for example. Can we make sense of this idea, at least in an initial or prima facie way?

I believe so, although here I will offer only a few programmatic remarks in support of this view.

Recall our discussion of Socrates and Meno—their pondering the respective merits of a true opinion that is, and a true opinion that is not, knowledge. We might take from their discussion a pragmatist moral about what knowledge can be enough for (as in: what must we expect *of* knowledge?)—and hence what can be enough for knowledge (as in: what must we expect if there is to *be* knowledge?). The point of contention between Socrates and Meno concerned what would hold in place a particular true opinion, enabling it to guide its holder through to Larissa. If a tether is added, this guidance will indeed be accomplished, we are told by Socrates. But even if we grant the claimed need for guidance if there is to be knowledge, and even if we interpret such guidance via the Socratic metaphor of a sustained tether, we should acknowledge that a tether with this pragmatic power need

The Luck/Knowledge Incompatibilty Thesis

not be *evidential*. More generally, it need not even be epistemic—in the sense of being a feature with a special link to truth as such.[13] Rather, it might be merely *psychological*: for instance, it need not be anything beyond an effective state of one's being *determined* to hold in place what seems to one to be a true opinion worth holding in place. Once an opinion is true, what matters most in a tether is simply *that* it hold the opinion in place. What is less important is *how* this is achieved. For example, what is not also needed is that the tether allow the person to *explain, to herself or others, why* she has and is maintaining that opinion. Such an ability could well be *welcome* in many a piece of knowledge: clearly, there are settings where this *is* expected of knowledge. (Philosophical settings themselves come readily to mind here.) That capacity, however, is not always *needed* in a piece of knowledge—needed, that is, simply in order *for there to be* the piece of knowledge at all. Indeed, this discussion between Socrates and Meno is itself one that should help us to see—along the lines outlined just now—why knowledge per se does not have that need. That is so, in spite—ironically—of the fact that this classic discussion between Socrates and Meno has often been cited by epistemologists as an argument *for* knowledge's needing to include something of an evidential, but at least of an epistemic, nature.

We should thereby be encouraged to think more broadly about knowledge's nature. And then the encouraging thought might occur to us that even a true belief's being luckily maintained *is* a tether. This tether *can* possess all of the power that Socrates and Meno would ask it to have, if it is to guide one effectively onwards to Larissa. A true belief is being maintained simpliciter, after all, if it is being luckily maintained. And what holds in that way of a true belief's being maintained holds also of its being formed in the first place: if one is to head toward Larissa, then forming a belief that represents accurately—even if luckily so—the direction to follow is all that one could want of knowledge *at that initial time* as to the direction to follow. Obviously, one could be concerned that, without an evidential tether, one might forget the path to take. (And so we find Socrates stressing the potential importance of recollection.) But in that respect there is nothing special about having an *epistemic* tether, such as evidence pointing to the pertinent truth that is being represented. All that is needed is *any* sort of tether, including one that is a tie simply to the belief's staying—once the belief is present, once it is representing what is true. And luck can be just such a tether. Truth-directed luck in particular can be so.

We thus return to a compatibilist conjecture. Perhaps it is possible to know luckily, even in a veritically lucky way. Perhaps it is possible, similarly, to know dogmatically, as one remains tethered by one's obstinacy to what is in fact a true opinion. And so on. In this structurally allowed sense, there might be many ways to know—more of them than epistemologists usually acknowledge. We should at least not cast aside such possibilities prematurely; what might well be a mistaken allegiance to the luck/knowledge *in*compatibility thesis could incline us toward performing that dismissive action.

Notes

1 The translation here is from Grube (1981: 86).
2 Although Socrates talks, in this translation, of *opinions*, I will follow contemporary epistemological practice by writing mainly of *beliefs*, as being the identifiable units within, or aspects of, a person, some of which might collectively be all of her knowledge.
3 For extensive discussion of it, see Shope (1983), Lycan (2006), and Hetherington (2016).
4 It comes from Chisholm (1966: 23n22; 1977: 105; 1989: 93), although I am not using Chisholm's own words in presenting it.
5 This technical way of thinking originates with Engel (1992, 2011). In recent years, it has been associated especially with Pritchard (e.g., 2005).
6 In fact, many epistemologists have claimed—and still claim—to be accepting the thesis on the basis of an intuition that it is true. Nonetheless, the epistemic strength of any such reliance upon appeals to intuition has been questioned increasingly in recent years, particularly with the rise of experimental philosophy—a development initiated especially by Weinberg, Nichols, and Stich (2001). For further discussion of this issue, see Deutsch (2015) and Hetherington (2016: ch. 6).
7 Elsewhere (Hetherington 2016: ch. 3), I show in detail why the concept of veritic luck (mentioned above)—like its close cousin, the concept of epistemic safety (e.g., Sosa 1999)—provides no explicative insight into

303

why the epistemologically standard interpretation of Gettier cases is true, if indeed it is. The argument that I am about to present is a more general one. For a still fuller version, see Hetherington (2016: ch. 2).

8 For some extended discussions of this, see Levy (2011) and Coffman (2015).

9 Have any epistemologists not only hypothesized, but actually argued for, this view of knowledge? How *could* it be that any true belief is knowledge? Generically, two paths have been followed toward that view. Either (i) we argue that all and only instances of true belief are instances of knowledge (e.g., Sartwell 1991, 1992; Hetherington 2018). Or (ii) we argue just that all true beliefs are knowledge—leaving open whether there are or might be instances of knowledge that also have something more, such as evidence, within them (e.g., Hetherington 2001, 2011; Foley 2012). This "something more" might *improve* an instance of knowledge as knowledge (e.g., in accord with how strong the included evidence is), even without having been part of what *makes* that instance of knowledge knowledge at all. The final section of this essay will comment further upon alternative (i).

10 I should note that this is my interpretive suggestion. It is not the interpretation of this passage that is standardly offered by epistemologists.

11 For a more detailed critical discussion of it, see Hetherington (2011: ch. 4).

12 For more on this reasoning, see Hetherington (1998, 2013).

13 Talk of a tether can be evidential—as pre-1963, pre-Gettier, epistemology would presumably have taken it to be. It can equally well be more generally epistemic, by being about what Plantinga (1993a, 1993b) calls *warrant*. Inspired especially by post-Gettier epistemology, Plantinga was designating *whatever* else is (epistemic and) needed if a true belief is to be knowledge. See Hetherington (2016: 153–154).

References

Chisholm, R.M. (1966) *Theory of Knowledge*, Englewood Cliffs, NJ: Prentice-Hall.
——. (1977) *Theory of Knowledge*, 2nd edn, Englewood Cliffs, NJ: Prentice-Hall.
——. (1989) *Theory of Knowledge*, 3rd edn, Englewood Cliffs, NJ: Prentice Hall.
Coffman, E.J. (2015) *Luck: Its Nature and Significance for Human Knowledge and Agency*, Basingstoke: Palgrave Macmillan.
Deutsch, M. (2015) *The Myth of the Intuitive: Experimental Philosophy and Philosophical Method*, Cambridge, MA: The MIT Press.
Engel, M. (1992) "Is Epistemic Luck Compatible with Knowledge?" *The Southern Journal of Philosophy* 30, 59–75.
——. (2011) "Epistemic Luck," *The Internet Encyclopedia of Philosophy*, www.iep.utm.edu/epi-luck.
Foley, R. (2012) *When Is True Belief Knowledge?* Princeton, NJ: Princeton University Press.
Gettier, E.L. (1963) "Is Justified True Belief Knowledge?" *Analysis* 23, 121–123.
Grube, G.M.A. (trans.) (1981) *Plato: Five Dialogues*, Indianapolis: Hackett Publishing.
Hetherington, S. (1998) "Actually Knowing," *The Philosophical Quarterly* 48, 453–469.
——. (2001) *Good Knowledge, Bad Knowledge: On Two Dogmas of Epistemology*, Oxford: Clarendon Press.
——. (2011) *How To Know: A Practicalist Conception of Knowing*, Malden, MA: Wiley-Blackwell.
——. (2013) "Knowledge Can Be Lucky," in M. Steup, J. Turri, & E. Sosa (eds.), *Contemporary Debates in Epistemology*, 2nd edn, Malden, MA: Wiley Blackwell, pp. 164–176.
——. (2016) *Knowledge and the Gettier Problem*, Cambridge: Cambridge University Press.
——. (2018) "The Redundancy Problem: From Knowledge-Infallibilism to Knowledge-Miminalism," *Synthese* 195(11), 4683–4702.
Levy, N. (2011) *Hard Luck: How Luck Undermines Free Will and Moral Responsibility*, New York: Oxford University Press.
Lycan, W.G. (2006) "On the Gettier Problem Problem," in S. Hetherington (ed.) *Epistemology Futures*, Oxford: Clarendon Press, pp. 148–168.
Plantinga, A. (1993a) *Warrant: The Current Debate*, New York: Oxford University Press.
——. (1993b) *Warrant and Proper Function*, New York: Oxford University Press.
Pritchard, D. (2005) *Epistemic Luck*, Oxford: Clarendon Press.
Sartwell, C. (1991) "Knowledge Is Merely True Belief," *American Philosophical Quarterly* 28, 157–165.
——. (1992) "Why Knowledge Is Merely True Belief," *The Journal of Philosophy* 89, 167–180.
Shope, R.K. (1983) *The Analysis of Knowing: A Decade of Research*, Princeton, NJ: Princeton University Press.
Sosa, E. (1999) "How Must Knowledge Be Modally Related to What Is Known?" *Philosophical Topics* 26, 373–384.
Weinberg, J.M., Nichols, S., & Stich, S. (2001) "Normativity and Epistemic Intuitions," *Philosophical Topics* 29, 429–460.

27

LUCK AND SKEPTICISM

John Greco

Contemporary epistemology includes a variety of approaches to the analysis of knowledge. For example, knowledge is variously characterized as requiring good evidence, reliable formation, virtuous formation, safety from falsehood, and sensitivity to truth. One way to understand these various characterizations is as attempts to explicate the anti-luck condition on knowledge. That is, assuming that knowledge is incompatible *in some sense* with merely lucky true belief, these various characterizations can be understood as articulating just what that sense is. For example, evidentialists can be understood as arguing that knowledge is not just luckily true, because it is grounded in good evidence. Likewise, reliabilists can be understood as arguing that knowledge is not just luckily true, because it is reliably formed. Other approaches to knowledge in the history of epistemology can be understood this way as well. For example, we can understand Plato as arguing that knowledge is less lucky than true opinion, because only knowledge is backed up by an account regarding why something is true. Put differently, in cases of knowledge it is "no accident" that the knower hits upon the truth, insofar as that person has good evidence for her belief, or forms her belief in a reliable way, or has an explanation regarding why it is true.

Understood this way, various approaches in the theory of knowledge are trying to explicate the anti-luck or "no accident" condition on knowledge. Likewise, various skeptical arguments can be understood as attempting to exploit that condition. That is, various skeptical arguments can be understood as challenging our claims to knowledge in some domain, precisely because our beliefs there are, even if true, only luckily true. This explains why skeptical arguments do not typically claim that our beliefs are *false*. That is not their point. Rather, skeptical arguments claim that our beliefs do not amount to knowledge *even if true*. Even if our beliefs are true, the skeptic argues, they are only luckily true.

The following well-known skeptical argument, inspired by Descartes' *Meditations*, illustrates the point.

Skeptical Argument

1. S knows that p only if S can rule out all possibilities that are incompatible with p.
2. It is *possible* that I am asleep and dreaming, and not actually sitting by the fire. It is also *possible* that I am deceived by a powerful demon, and that all my beliefs about the material world are false.[1]
3. But I cannot rule out these alternative possibilities—things might appear to me just as they do, even if these possibilities are true.

305

Therefore,

4. I do not know that I am sitting by the fire, or that any of my beliefs about the material world are true.

The point is now easy to see. Nothing in the skeptical argument above claims that our beliefs about the material world are *not true*. The idea, rather, is that it is *possible* that they are not true. But even that possibility, if not somehow ruled out, is enough to undermine our knowledge. One plausible interpretation of this last idea is this: Even if our beliefs are true, we are *just lucky* that they are true. For all we know, they might not be true.

Understood this way, there are two strategies available for responding to the skeptical argument. The first is to deny that we cannot rule out alternative possibilities. This first strategy agrees with the skeptic that the anti-luck condition on knowledge is to be understood in terms of ruling out alternative possibilities, but disagrees that our beliefs about the material world do not meet that condition. The second available strategy is to disagree with the skeptic regarding how to characterize the anti-luck condition. That is, one might deny that knowledge requires ruling out alternative possibilities, in favor of some other characterization of the anti-luck condition, such as that knowledge must be reliably formed, or virtuously formed, or appropriately safe or sensitive. The present point generalizes. In general, there are two broad strategies for responding to skeptical arguments: (i) deny that our beliefs are "just lucky" in the sense that the skeptic claims that they are, or (ii) deny that knowledge cannot be "just lucky" in the sense that the skeptic claims that it cannot be. This second strategy will accept that knowledge cannot be "just lucky" in *some* relevant sense. But it attempts to replace the skeptic's characterization of the anti-luck condition with a more adequate one.

The remainder of the chapter will proceed according to the above understanding of contemporary theories of knowledge and skeptical challenges to our knowledge. The first section returns to the skeptical argument above, understood as arguing that our beliefs are too lucky to count as knowledge. One major claim of Part One is that **Skeptical Argument** trades on "internalist" characterizations of the anti-luck condition on knowledge. Put differently, the argument limits the resources for warding off luck to factors "internal" to the knowing subject. The second section develops this theme by arguing that internalist conceptions of the anti-luck condition have analogs in moral theory, and especially Platonic and Kantian restrictions against moral luck. In both cases, it is argued, internalist characterizations of the anti-luck condition are grounded in dubious ideals of self-sufficiency and invulnerability.

The third section looks at three approaches in contemporary epistemology that argue for alternative characterizations of the anti-luck condition on knowledge: sensitivity theories, safety theories, and virtue epistemology. These theories reject the skeptic's characterization of the anti-luck condition in favor of one that more adequately characterizes the way in which knowledge is incompatible with lucky true belief. One major claim of this section is that a safety condition on knowledge is better motivated than a sensitivity condition. A second major claim is that virtue-theoretic considerations further motivate a safety condition on knowledge, and also help to make the characterization of that condition more precise. In effect, the virtue condition on knowledge, properly understood, entails a safety condition on knowledge, properly understood. Finally, all of this is in service of anti-skeptical results. That is, once the anti-luck condition on knowledge is properly characterized in terms of safety and virtue, the skeptical argument reviewed in the first section does not get off the ground. Put differently, we are left with no good reasons for thinking that our beliefs are generally "too lucky" to count as knowledge.[2]

The Skeptical Argument

As was suggested above, several well-known skeptical arguments can be understood as exploiting the anti-luck condition on knowledge. More specifically, such arguments can be understood as

Luck and Skepticism

characterizing that condition in a particular way, and then claiming that our beliefs in some domain are, even if true, too lucky to count as knowledge. In this section we will look at one skeptical line of argument that employs this strategy to challenge our knowledge of the material world.

To begin, return to the skeptical argument that we considered above. That argument operated on an initially plausible understanding of the anti-luck condition on knowledge, articulated in its first premise:

1. S knows that p only if S can rule out all possibilities that are incompatible with p.

The idea behind that premise was interpreted as follows: If there are alternative possibilities to p that S cannot rule out, then S's belief that p is too lucky to count as knowledge. Even if p is in fact true, for all S knows, p could be false.

We can see the plausibility of this idea by considering an example (Stroud 1984). Suppose that you claim that you see a goldfinch in the garden, based on your observation that the bird is of a particular size and color, and with a tail of a particular shape. Suppose now that a friend challenges your claim to know, pointing out that woodpeckers also are of that size and color, and also have tails with that shape. This seems to be a legitimate challenge to your claim to know that the bird is a goldfinch. More generally, if one's evidence for one's belief that the bird is a goldfinch is consistent with the possibility that it is in fact a woodpecker, then one does not know on the basis of that evidence that it is a goldfinch.[3]

The second major premise of the skeptical argument simply points out some possibilities that we might not ordinarily consider, but that remain possibilities nonetheless.

2. It is *possible* that I am dreaming, and not actually sitting by the fire. It is also *possible* that I am deceived by a powerful demon, and that all my beliefs about the material world are false.

The third premise of the argument claims that I cannot rule out these possibilities, and points to a reason for accepting that claim. Namely, if those possibilities were actual, things would appear to me just as they do now. Put differently, I have no *basis* or *grounds* for ruling out one possibility in favor of another, since the way things appear—the ways things seem to me—is the same in all the cases. Accordingly, the argument concludes, I do not know that I am sitting by the fire, or that any of my beliefs about the material world are true.

Clearly enough, the force of the argument depends a great deal on what we mean by "rule out," when the skeptic claims that we cannot rule out alternative possibilities to what we believe. In fact, the skeptic needs a sense of this notion on which it is plausible *both* that (a) knowledge requires that one can rule out alternative possibilities in that sense, and (b) we are typically not in a position to rule out alternative possibilities in that sense.

One powerful way to understand this crucial notion is in terms of a capacity for discrimination. In particular, it seems plausible to think of perceptual knowledge as involving an ability to discriminate actual word states of affairs from other perceptual possibilities. The skeptical argument, then, points out that our beliefs about the material world seem not to satisfy the anti-luck condition when understood this way. We can see this skeptical line of reasoning clearly by reinterpreting **Skeptical Argument** as follows.

No Discrimination

1. S knows that p only if S has the ability to discriminate the fact that p from alternative possibilities.
2. It is *possible* that I am dreaming, and not actually sitting by the fire. It is also *possible* that I am deceived by a powerful demon, and that all my beliefs about the material world are false.
3. But I have no ability to discriminate between the fact that p and these alternative possibilities. For example, I have no ability to *perceptually* discriminate between the fact that p and these

alternative possibilities—things would appear to me just as they do, whether p is true or one of these other possibilities is true.

Therefore,

4. I do not know that I am sitting by the fire, or that any of my beliefs about the material world are true.

Is there a way to respond to the argument when it is understood this way? I want to suggest that we look closer at premise 3 of the argument, and the claim that we lack any ability to discriminate between real-world facts and alternative possibilities. The reason given for this claim is that "things would appear to me just as they do, whether p is true or one of these other possibilities is true." Accordingly, the present argument is thinking of our perceptual abilities in terms of reflectively accessible or "internal" mental states. Specifically, "to discriminate" is here understood as "to discriminate on the basis of appearances," and in this respect we seem to be working with an internalist picture.

Be that as it may, it is hard to see where the argument goes wrong, once the picture is granted. For it does seem to be the case that sensory appearances would be the same—things would appear to me just as they do—whether my beliefs about the world are true or one of the skeptical possibilities is true. That is, in fact, how the skeptical scenarios have been designed. But then, if knowledge really does require that I can discriminate real-world facts from alternatives on the basis of sensory appearances, then it seems that I do not have knowledge about the material world.

The moral of the story is that skepticism about the material world looks good on an internalist reading of the anti-luck condition. Is there a principled way to reject that understanding of the anti-luck condition?

Internalist Ideals, Epistemic Luck, and Moral Luck

In the next section we will turn to some anti-internalist understandings of the anti-luck condition on knowledge. Before doing so, I want to explore the relation between internalism in epistemology and an analogous anti-luck stance in moral theory.[4]

We can define internalism more precisely as a supervenience thesis:

(I) The facts about an individual's epistemic status (of one sort or another) supervene on facts that are appropriately "internal" to the individual.

We get different versions of internalism depending on how the notion of "internal to the individual" is understood. One important version of internalism is "privileged access internalism": The facts about an individual's epistemic status supervene on facts to which the individual has privileged access—facts that she can know "by reflection alone" (Alston 1986). A different way to understand the notion of "internal to the knower" is due to Conee and Feldman: "internalism is the view that a person's beliefs are justified only by things that are internal to the person's mental life ... the things that are said to contribute to justification are in the person's mind" (Connee and Feldman 2004: 55). Accordingly, we can define "mental state internalism" as follows: The facts about an individual's epistemic status supervene on facts about the individual's mental life.

Understood this way, internalism entails a kind of epistemic individualism. Epistemic individualism makes epistemic status supervene on the cognitive resources of the individual. Internalism restricts that further, making epistemic status supervene on resources that are *internal* to the individual. In this way, internalism endorses an ideal of self-sufficiency in the intellectual realm—one's epistemic status is entirely a function of one's own resources, and, in particular, resources that are appropriately internal to the self. In fact, internalism can be viewed as a kind of epistemic individualism on steroids. We can think of epistemic individualism as embracing a kind of independence from *other persons*. In effect, internalism embraces a kind of independence from *the world in general*.

Internalism and Skepticism

It is widely acknowledged that internalism at least threatens to be a skeptical view. Specifically, internalists incur the burden of showing how such restricted epistemic resources can account for adequate epistemic standing vis-à-vis beliefs about the external world, other minds, the past, laws of nature, etc.[5] Sometimes the problem is characterized, as we did above, in terms of evidential support: How can the meager evidence that the internalist allows herself support beliefs about external objects, the past, etc.? Other times the problem is characterized in terms of circularity: How can the internalist satisfy herself that her perception is reliable, without using her perception to do so? More generally, how can the internalist validate to herself that she has any reliable grasp on external world facts, using only the resources she has allowed herself, and without falling into circularity, which validation cannot tolerate? (Fumerton 1995; Greco 2000).

To the extent that internalism fails to answer these worries, the non-skeptical internalist will be characterized by illusions of self-sufficiency. Suppose the internalist gives up on answering these worries and embraces skepticism. Then she will have given up the illusion of self-sufficiency, but she will still be embracing the ideal.

An Analogy to the Practical Realm

In *The Fragility of Goodness*, Martha Nussbaum (1986) characterizes Greek thought as preoccupied with the vulnerability of human excellence and happiness to the contingencies of good fortune. According to Nussbaum, this preoccupation motivated a retreat in *value* to what can be guaranteed by one's own agency. For example, she argues, Platonic conceptions of virtue and happiness, centered as they are around reason and contemplation, are primarily motivated by a strategy to distance human excellence and good from what cannot be controlled. In this regard, Nussbaum cites Plato's defense in the *Phaedo* and *Republic* "of a life of self-sufficient contemplation, in which unstable activities and their objects have no intrinsic value" (Nussbaum 1986: 9).

A similar dynamic is played out in the Kantian retreat to a realm of pure agency. Consider the following oft-cited passage from Kant's *Groundwork*.

> A good will is not good because of what it effects or accomplishes—because of its fitness for attaining some proposed end … Even if, by some special disfavor of destiny … this will is entirely lacking in power to carry out its intentions; if by its utmost effort it still accomplishes nothing, and only good will is left … then it would still shine like a jewel for its own sake as something which has its full value in itself.
>
> *Kant 1964: 62*

This conception of the agent is both endorsed and lamented by modern-day Kantians such as Thomas Nagel. In a now famous discussion, Nagel notes the various ways in which a human life is subject to luck, and concludes that, in this light, the sphere of "genuine agency" seems to disappear.

> If one cannot be responsible for consequences of one's acts due to factors beyond one's control, or for antecedents of one's acts that are properties of temperament not subject to one's will, or for the circumstances that pose one's moral choices, then how can one be responsible even for the stripped-down acts of the will itself, if *they* are the product of antecedent

John Greco

circumstances outside of the will's control? The area of genuine agency, and therefore of legitimate moral judgment, seems to shrink under this scrutiny to an extensionless point.

Nagel 1979: 35

Importantly, Nagel is willing to give up the illusion of pure agency but not the ideal. Rather than rejecting a notion of agency that makes moral responsibility and moral value impossible, he accepts the skeptical conclusion.

In a sense, internalism does for intellectual evaluation what Plato and Kant do for practical evaluation—it retreats to a sphere, or tries to retreat to a sphere, where the agent and her success are beholden to nothing and no one. Clearly enough, this is a sphere in which the agent is largely protected from the contingencies of luck. It is less than clear, however, whether this conception of the agent, together with its attendant ideals of self-sufficiency and invulnerability, make for an adequate understanding of the anti-luck condition on knowledge. In the next section we explore some externalist alternatives.

Safety, Sensitivity, and Virtue

In the first section, we said that various skeptical arguments can be understood as exploiting the anti-luck condition on knowledge. We have also shown how a family of skeptical arguments employs an internalist understanding of the anti-luck condition to argue against our knowledge of the world. This suggests that a good strategy for replying to these arguments is to challenge their understandings of the anti-luck condition in favor of an alternative. In fact, we may understand a variety of externalist theories in contemporary epistemology as doing just that. Such theories have sometimes been accused of "changing the subject" of traditional epistemology. A better way to characterize externalist theories, I suggest, is that they are challenging traditional epistemology's understanding of the anti-luck condition on knowledge.

We defined epistemic internalism as follows:

(I)   The facts about an individual's epistemic status (of one sort or another) supervene on facts that are appropriately "internal" to the individual.

Epistemic externalism simply denies epistemic internalism. Thus, on an externalist view, the facts about an individual's epistemic status are not wholly determined by facts that are internal to the individual. What kinds of facts might matter? Most notably, these will be causal and other modal facts, describing relations between the individual and the world. For example, facts about the reliability of one's cognitive faculties, facts about the proper functioning of one's cognition, and, more generally, facts about causal and modal relations between the individual and her environment.[6] These are all paradigmatically external facts, in that they are neither facts to which one has privileged access nor are they facts about one's mental states.

As such, externalism replaces the notion of a pure agent operating in an internal realm, with that of an embodied agent operating in the world. What matters for intellectual status is a function *both* of (a) what goes on internal to cognition and (b) how that cognition relates to the world; e.g., whether the agent's environment is enabling or undermining. In this way, externalism makes epistemic status depend partly on an environment that is not of the agent's own making. In doing so, it also makes epistemic status, and the agent herself, vulnerable to contingencies and to what she cannot control.

In this section, we look at three externalist theories (or better, families of theories) that can be fruitfully understood this way. In particular, we will see how sensitivity theories, safety theories, and virtue theories can be understood as rejecting traditional conceptions of the anti-luck condition on knowledge. In the course of discussion, I will argue that, although all three approaches succeed in yielding anti-skeptical results, safety theories are better motivated than sensitivity theories, and that virtue theories further motivate a safety condition on knowledge. Moreover, a virtue-theoretic approach yields insights regarding just how the safety condition should be characterized.

Sensitivity Conditions and Their Anti-Skeptical Implications

The spirit of a sensitivity condition is that, in cases of knowledge, one would notice if things were different. This sort of "epistemic sensitivity" is similar to other kinds of sensitivity in important ways. More generally, when one is sensitive to some state of affairs (for example, allergens in the air), one reacts in a particular way, and would react another way if things were different (if allergens were not in the air).

Sensitivity conditions are standardly presented by means of subjunctive conditionals. For example,

S's belief that p is *sensitive* just in case: If p were false, then S would not believe that p.

More formally,

$\sim p \Rightarrow \sim B(p)$

Sensitivity is thus a modal notion, and as such it is standardly interpreted by means of a possible worlds heuristic. For example,

Sensitivity. S's belief that p is *sensitive* just in case: (a) S believes that p, and (b) In the closest possible world where p is false, S does not believe that p.

Think of a space of possible worlds centered on the actual world and branching out according to some appropriate similarity ordering. S's belief that p is sensitive just in case: in the closest world where p is false, S does not believe that p. Put differently, the closest not-p world is also a world where S does not believe that p.

It is well known that the sensitivity condition is implausible when stated in its simplest form, as it is above. The most common complication is to make a distinction between "outright" sensitivity and "relative" sensitivity. For example, Nozick famously defended a version of the sensitivity condition that makes sensitivity relative to a method (Nozick 1998: ch. 4).

Hence,

Method-relative Sensitivity. S's belief that p is *method-relative sensitive* just in case: (a) S believes p using method M, and (b) In the closest possible world where p is false and S forms her belief using M, S does not believe that p.

We can think of methods as corresponding to sources of belief, such as perception, memory, and reasoning. Suppose S believes that there is a cup on the table, forming her belief on the basis of visual perception. The present idea is that S's belief is sensitive, in the relevant sense, just in case, if the cup were not on the table (if it were on the floor, for example) and S employed her visual perception, S would not believe that the cup is on the table. As before, S's perceptual belief is thus "sensitive" as to whether the cup is actually on the table or not.

Clearly enough, this understanding of the anti-luck condition has anti-skeptical implications. For in most cases where we think we have knowledge, our beliefs are indeed sensitive in the relevant sense. Perceptual knowledge that there is a cup on the table is a case in point. Consider another everyday case: inferring that it has recently rained, on the basis of seeing that the streets and trees are wet. This seems like a fine piece of reasoning on the basis of adequate evidence—good enough, in fact, to yield knowledge in the typical case. The present understanding of the anti-luck condition explains this. For if it were not true that it recently rained, I would not have evidence that it did, and so would not have inferred that it did.

Another way to appreciate the anti-skeptical implications of the sensitivity condition is to see how it interacts with **No Discrimination**. The first premise of that argument was as follows:

1.   S knows that p only if S has the ability to discriminate the fact that p from alternative possibilities.

Sensitivity theories allow us to deny this premise. This is so, even though the notion of sensitivity is quite close to the notion of discrimination. For example, to say that one can perceptually discriminate between the cup's being on the table and its being on the floor is close to saying that one's perceptual beliefs are sensitive to these different states of affairs. But here is the crucial difference: a sensitivity condition requires that, in cases where one knows that p, one can discriminate p's being the case from the *closest* possibilities where p is not the case, as opposed to *all* possibilities where p is not the case. This alternative characterization of the anti-luck condition allows us to retain the intuitive idea that knowledge requires discrimination of a sort, while rejecting the much stronger version of this idea employed in **No Discrimination**.

Safety Conditions and Their Anti-Skeptical Implications

Safety theories offer yet another understanding of the anti-luck condition. The spirit of a safety condition is that, in cases of knowledge, S would not easily go wrong by believing as she does. This sort of "epistemic safety" is similar to other kinds of safety in important ways. More generally, when one is safe, one would not easily go wrong. That is, when one is safe, one is not actually going wrong, and would not easily go wrong, either (Williamson 2000: 123–124).

Like sensitivity conditions, safety conditions can be interpreted using a possible worlds heuristic.

> **Safety**. S's belief that p is *safe* just in case: In close possible worlds where S believes that p, p is true.

Think of a space of possible worlds centered on the actual world and branching out according to some appropriate similarity ordering. S's belief that p is safe just in case: there are no close worlds where both S believes that p, and p is false. Put differently, we would have to go a long way off from the actual world to find a world where both S believes that p and p is false.

Also like the sensitivity condition, a simple safety condition is known to be inadequate, and is therefore standardly replaced by relative safety conditions. For example, Sosa has defended a version of the safety condition that makes safety relative to a *basis* (Sosa 1999a, 1999b, 2000), and Sosa and Greco have defended versions that make safety relative to an *ability* (Sosa 2007, 2015; Greco 2012, 2016, forthcoming-b).

Hence,

> **Basis-relative Safety**. S's belief that p is *basis-relative safe* just in case: (a) S believes that p on basis B, and (b) In close worlds where S believes that p on B, p is true.
>
> **Ability-relative Safety**. S's belief that p is *ability-relative safe* just in case: (a) S's belief that p is produced by cognitive ability A, and (b) In close worlds where S's belief that p is produced by A, p is true.

Finally, safety theories have clear anti-skeptical implications. In most cases where we think we have knowledge, our beliefs are safe in the relevant sense. Perceptual knowledge that there is a cup on the table is again a case in point. Likewise, not easily would one go wrong by inferring that it has rained on the basis of wet streets and trees. That is, throughout the space of close worlds where one reasons this way, one will be right in reasoning this way. That is, of course, consistent with there being possible worlds where the streets and trees are wet, and yet it has not recently rained. That would be the case, for example, in worlds where there is an elaborate hoax by a movie production company, or an elaborate deception by an evil demon. The point that safety theories exploit is that these possible worlds are not close worlds, and therefore do not undermine the safety of our beliefs in the actual world.

Accordingly, safety theories, like sensitivity theories, provide a resource for denying essential premises of skeptical arguments. In particular, safety theories allow us to deny the first premise of **No Discrimination**. In short, a safety condition requires that, throughout the space of close worlds, one would not easily go wrong by employing one's perceptual abilities. This, in turn, requires that one can perceptually discriminate between perceivable facts and a host of alternatives. For example, perceptual knowledge that the cup is on the table requires being able to discriminate between the cup's being on the table and the cup's being on the floor. What it does not require is that one can discriminate the perceptual facts from far off possibilities, such as that one is the victim of a Cartesian demon.

Better Safe or Sensitive?

We have now seen how both sensitivity and safety theories deliver anti-skeptical results. In particular, they do so by replacing a traditional internalist understanding of the anti-luck condition with an externalist modal condition. But which modal interpretation of the anti-luck condition is preferable?

One way to get traction on that question is to consider the "point and purpose" of the concept of knowledge (Craig 1990; Henderson and Greco 2015). That is, we might ask what is the point or purpose of using knowledge language and making knowledge-related evaluations in the first place. An important suggestion by Edward Craig is that one central purpose is to identify good informants:

> [A]ny community may be presumed to have an interest in evaluating sources of informa-
> tion; and in connection with that interest certain concepts will be in use … [The] concept
> of knowledge is one of them. To put it briefly and roughly, the concept of knowledge is used
> to flag approved sources of information.
>
> *Craig 1990: 11*

Suppose that Craig is correct in at least this much—that one important role that the concept of knowledge plays is to identify good informants and good information. If that is so, then we should expect that knowledge requires a strong modal relation between knower and world. That is, a *good* informant will be a person who *reliably* believes the truth, or who believes the truth *dependably*. Put differently, a good informant will be someone who does not believe the truth *just by accident*. Given this important relation between being a knower and being a reliable informant, what sort of modal relation should we expect knowledge to require?

Answering this last question, I want to argue, speaks decisively in favor of a safety condition over a sensitivity condition. The central idea is this: We want our informants to be reliable (or dependable) across close counterfactual situations—we want them to be keyed in to how things actually are, and to how things might easily be, in the contexts in which their information is needed. The other side of that coin is this: It does not matter whether our informants are sensitive to far-off counterfac- tual situations. That is, it does not matter whether they are reliable or dependable in situations vastly different from the contexts in which their information is needed. Accordingly, the concept of a good informant requires a safety condition rather than a sensitivity condition.

Consider an example to illustrate the point (Craig 1990). Suppose that I am standing on an African plain and you are high up in a tree. I need information about whether there are predators in the area, and I look to you as my informant. What condition must you satisfy to be a *good* informant?

Presumably it is something like this: You are reliable on the question whether there are any predators out there! But what does *that* require? Presumably this: Not only that you have a true belief about whether there are predators nearby, but that you would not easily have a false belief about this. In other words, your being a good informant requires that you satisfy a safety condition.

What is *not* required, however, is that you are sensitive to the relevant facts out to far-off worlds. Suppose, for example, that you are insensitive to whether you are being deceived about predators in the area by an evil demon, or by futuristic anthropologists who have the technology to so deceive you. That does not in the least affect your being a good informant for me here and now. Again, what matters is that you are reliable in the situation we are actually in.

But isn't it plausible that being a good informant requires sensitivity in *close* counter-factual situations. For example, you would not be a good informant for me if you believed that there are no predators around, but would still believe that if one came along. And this is clearly the case if one could *easily* come along. Plausibly, it is just this sort of consideration that makes a sensitivity requirement on knowledge so attractive in the first place.

Let us call a modal relation along these lines "close sensitivity," defined more precisely as follows:

Close Sensitivity. Within some restricted space of possible worlds RSW, if p were false, S would not believe that p. Alternatively: Inside RSW, in the closest world where p is false, S does not believe that p.[7]

Think of a space of possible worlds centered on the actual world and branching out according to some appropriate similarity ordering. We may define a *restricted space of worlds* by drawing a circle (or a globe) some distance out from, and centering on, the actual world. Any possible world so captured will be inside the restricted space. Again, the intuitive idea that we are trying to capture here is that S's belief might be sensitive *within some space of close counterfactual situations*. Accordingly, our close sensitivity condition does not speak to what happens in "far-off" counterfactual situations, but only in ones relevantly close to the situation that S is in.

Our Close Sensitivity condition accommodates the idea that sensitivity out to far-off worlds is irrelevant to being a good informant. Nevertheless, Close Sensitivity fails to accommodate the idea that we want informants to be reliable *across* or *throughout* a space of close counterfactual situations. An example will illustrate the point.

> *Assassins.* Suppose that there are ten assassins, each of whom is not in fact among us, but could easily be among us. Suppose also that the ten could not *equally* easily be among us. That is, one of the assassins (Mr. Near) could *very* easily be among us, but each of the others would have to do somewhat more to get himself into our midst. Suppose also that you are aware that Mr. Near is an assassin and could easily identify him if he were among us. However, the other nine assassins are unknown to you.

Now consider the proposition *There are no assassins among us.* Even if that proposition is true and you believe that it is true, clearly you are not a good informant in this regard. That is because there are many close worlds where there is an assassin among us but where you do not notice that there is. However, your belief that there are no assassins does satisfy Close Sensitivity. This is because the *closest* world in which there is an assassin among us is a world where Mr. Near is among us, and you *do* recognize him.

The example shows that Close Sensitivity does not capture the idea of sensitivity *throughout* a space of worlds, and so does not accommodate the idea that we want our informants to be reliable *across* a range of close counterfactual situations, or *throughout* a relevant space. Insofar as we take knowers to be good informants, Close Sensitivity does not specify a condition on knowledge, either. At least as far as that kind of consideration is concerned, the advantage goes to safety theories.[8]

Luck and Skepticism

Virtue Epistemology

Return to the internalist conception of agency that we saw earlier in the chapter, and to the analog that we saw attributed to Plato and Kant in the domain of *moral* agency. In moral theory, those looking for a corrective to Plato and Kant often invoke Aristotle and his virtue-theoretic approach.[9] Aristotle's virtue theory would clearly count as externalist on the present understanding, since virtuous performance is tied up with paradigmatically externalist properties and relations, such as the agent's dispositions, the etiology of action in proper motivation and deliberation, causal and other relations to the external world, and the agent's relations to the social world. Accordingly, Aristotle and other virtue theorists see various external factors as relevant to practical agency and the evaluation of performance in the practical-moral realm.

Ernest Sosa and Linda Zagzebski, among others, have argued for a similar corrective in epistemology (Sosa 1991; Zagzebski 1996). That is, each has argued that a turn to virtue theory in epistemology would have similar benefits as in ethics and moral theory. More specifically, a number of virtue epistemologists have argued that knowledge is fruitfully conceived as a kind of success from virtue. Put differently: In cases of knowledge, the knower's getting things right can be attributed to her own virtuous thinking.[10]

The next thing to see is that virtue-theoretic considerations motivate a particular kind of safety condition on knowledge. More exactly, the idea that knowledge is a kind of success from virtue *entails* an ability-relative safety condition (Greco 2016, forthcoming-b). First, we can understand abilities in general as reliable dispositions to achieve a kind of success, when in relevant conditions and in an appropriate environment. For example, José Altuve has the ability to hit baseballs in fair weather and in a normal baseball environment. A cognitive ability, then, is a reliable disposition to believe truths in some relevant range, when in relevant conditions and in an appropriate environment. It is in this sense that perception, for example, is a cognitive ability. Moreover, the relevant notion of reliability is modally strong: a reliable disposition *would* produce true belief, in appropriate conditions and environments, with a high degree of regularity. Accordingly:

> S's belief p is produced by cognitive ability A *only if*: in most close worlds where S's belief p is produced by A (in appropriate conditions and environment), p is true.

But, of course, that just is the ability-relative safety condition from above.

> **Ability-relative Safety**. S's belief that p is *ability-relative safe* just in case: (a) S's belief that p is produced by ability A, and (b) In close worlds where S's belief that p is produced by A, p is true.

The fact that a virtue condition on knowledge entails this safety condition is a significant theoretical advantage of that account. After all, the debate among safety and sensitivity theorists is a debate over what modally strong relation between mind and world is required by knowledge. Likewise, the debate over different *kinds* of safety condition is a debate about that issue. What all parties to these debates agree on, though, is that knowledge does require some such modal relation or another. The foregoing discussion shows that a virtue-theoretic account *motivates* just such a condition on knowledge. In that sense, a virtue-theoretic approach *explains why* knowledge requires a modally strong relation between mind and world, and explains in some detail just how that relation should be characterized.

Another way to make the same point, also in keeping with the discussion above, is to say that a virtue-theoretic account explains why knowledge is inconsistent with certain kinds of luck, and explains in some detail just what kind of luck knowledge cannot tolerate. Specifically, *knowledge excludes luck in just the way that success from virtue in general excludes luck.*

John Greco

In sum, the anti-luck condition on knowledge captures a highly intuitive idea: that in cases of knowledge, it is "no accident" that S believes the truth. A virtue-theoretic approach gives a fairly precise explication of that intuitive idea: In cases of knowledge, S believes from cognitive ability, and in most close worlds where S believes from cognitive ability (in appropriate conditions and environment), S believes the truth.[11]

Notes

1 Beliefs about the material world are here juxtaposed to beliefs about my own mental states—in particular, how things seem or appear to me. Doubts about our knowledge of the material world is sometimes called "external world skepticism," the idea being that objects and events in the material world are "external" to our minds. In this chapter I will use the terms "material world skepticism" and "external world skepticism" interchangeably.
2 Of course, this is not to say that our beliefs are *never* too lucky to count as knowledge. The point, rather, is that they are not *generally* too lucky, or in any principled way too lucky, in the way they would need to be to issue in broad skeptical results.
3 Further support for premise 1 comes from reflection on scientific enquiry. Suppose that there are several competing hypotheses for explaining some phenomenon, and suppose that these various hypotheses are "live" in the sense that current evidence does not rule them out as possibilities. It would seem that one cannot know that one of the hypotheses is true until further evidence rules out the remaining ones.
4 For a more extended discussion of the argument in the second section of this chapter, see Greco (forthcoming-b).
5 For an extended argument that internalism entails broad skeptical results, see Greco (2000). For similar worries on behalf of an internalist, see Fumerton (1995).
6 Examples of externalist views include Dretske (1970), Goldman (1976), Plantinga (1993), Nozick (1998), Sosa (2007), and Greco (2010).
7 Thanks to Duncan Pritchard for suggesting a sensitivity condition along these lines.
8 For a more extended argument along these lines, see Greco (2012).
9 For example, see Nussbaum (1986) and Anscombe (1958).
10 Intellectual virtues (or excellences) are here understood as abilities to reliably get things right, relative to some field or subject-matter, and under appropriate conditions. For example, visual perception is an ability to form true beliefs about various features of middle-sized objects (e.g., color, size), under appropriate lighting conditions, with an unobstructed view, etc. A number of authors have argued that knowledge is a kind of success from ability, including Zagzebski (1996), Riggs (2002, 2007, 2009), Greco (2003, 2010), and Sosa (2007, 2015).
11 Thanks to Ian Church, Robert Hartman, Duncan Pritchard and John Putz for comments on earlier drafts.

References

Alston, W.P. (1986) "Internalism and Externalism in Epistemology," *Philosophical Topics* XIV, 179–221. Reprinted in Alston, *Epistemic Justification*. Ithaca, NY: Cornell University Press.
Anscombe, E. (1958) "Modern Moral Philosophy," *Philosophy* 33, 1–19.
Connee, E., & Feldman, R. (2004) *Evidentialism: Essays in Epistemology*, Oxford: Oxford University Press.
Craig, E. (1990) *Knowledge and the State of Nature*, Oxford: Oxford University Press.
Dretske, F. (1970) "Epistemic Operators," *The Journal of Philosophy* 67, 1007–1023.
Fumerton, R. (1995) *Metaepistemology and Skepticism*, Lanham, MD: Rowman and Littlefield.
Goldman, A. (1976) "Discrimination and Perceptual Knowledge," *Journal of Philosophy* 73, 771–791.
Greco, J. (2000) *Putting Skeptics in Their Place: The Nature of Skeptical Arguments and Their Role in Philosophical Inquiry*, Cambridge: Cambridge University Press.
——. (2003) "Knowledge as Credit for True Belief," in Michael DePaul & Linda Zagzebski (eds.) *Intellectual Virtue: Perspectives from Ethics and Epistemology*, Oxford: Oxford University Press, pp. 111–134.
——. (2010) *Achieving Knowledge: A Virtue-theoretic Account of Epistemic Normativity.* Cambridge: Cambridge University Press.
——. (2012) "Better Safe than Sensitive," in Kelly Becker & Tim Black (eds.) *The Sensitivity Principle in Epistemology*. Cambridge: Cambridge University Press, pp. 193–206.
——. (2016) "Knowledge, Virtue and Safety," in Miguel Ángel Fernández (ed.) *Performance Epistemology*, New York: Oxford University Press, pp. 51–61.

Luck and Skepticism

——. (forthcoming-a) "Intellectual Humility and Contemporary Epistemology: A Critique of Epistemic Individualism, Evidentialism and Internalism," in Mark Alfano, Michael P Lynch, & Alessandra Tanesini (eds.) *The Routledge Handbook on the Philosophy of Humility.*

——. (forthcoming-b) "Safety in Sosa," *Synthese.*

Henderson, D., & Greco, J. (eds.) (2015) *Epistemic Evaluation,* Oxford: Oxford University Press.

Kant, I. (1964) *Groundwork of the Metaphysics of Morals,* H.J. Paton (trans.), New York: Harper and Row Publishers.

Nagel, T. (1979) "Moral Luck," in *Mortal Questions,* Cambridge: Cambridge University Press, pp. 24–38.

Nozick, R. (1998) *Philosophical Explanations,* Cambridge, MA: Harvard University Press.

Nussbaum, M. (1986) *The Fragility of Goodness: Luck and Ethics in Greek Tragedy and Philosophy,* Cambridge: Cambridge University Press.

Plantinga, A. (1993) *Warrant and Proper Function,* Oxford: Oxford University Press.

Riggs, W. (2002) "Reliability and the Value Knowledge," *Philosophy and Phenomenological Research* 64(1), 79–96.

——. (2007) "Why Epistemologists Are So Down on Their Luck," *Synthese* 158, 329–344.

——. (2009) "Luck, Knowledge, and Control," in D. Pritchard, A. Haddock, & A. Millar (eds.) *Epistemic Value,* Oxford: Oxford University Press, pp. 204–221.

Sosa, E. (1991) "The Raft and the Pyramid: Coherence versus Foundations in the Theory of Knowledge," in *Knowledge in Perspective: Selected Essays in Epistemology.* Cambridge: Cambridge University Press, pp. 165–191.

——. (1999a) "How Must Knowledge Be Modally Related to What Is Known?" *Philosophical Topics,* 26, 373–384.

——. (1999b) "How to Defeat Opposition to Moore," *Noûs,* 33, 141–153.

——. (2000) "Skepticism and Contextualism," *Philosophical Issues* 10, 1–18.

——. (2007) *A Virtue Epistemology: Apt Belief and Reflective Knowledge, Volume 1,* Oxford: Oxford University Press.

——. (2015) *Judgment and Agency,* Oxford: Oxford University Press.

Stroud, B. (1984) *The Significance of Philosophical Skepticism,* Oxford: Oxford University Press.

Williamson, T. (2000) *Knowledge and Its Limits,* Oxford: Oxford University Press.

Zagzebski, L. (1996) *Virtues of the Mind: An Inquiry into the Nature of Virtue and the Ethical Foundations of Knowledge,* Cambridge: Cambridge University Press.

28

EPISTEMIC LUCK AND THE EXTENDED MIND

J. Adam Carter

Epistemic Luck, Knowledge and Cognitive Internalism

Most contemporary epistemologists accept the following anti-luck platitude:

Anti-luck platitude: For all S, p, if S knows a proposition, p, then S's belief that p is not (in some to-be-specified sense) "true by luck."

Something like the anti-luck platitude was arguably the key take-away lesson from Gettier's (1963) counterexamples, which showed (*contra* the JTB theory) that a belief could be justified and true, and yet, true by luck in a way that seems intuitively incompatible with knowledge.[1]

But the platitude needs some sharpening. In what sense, exactly, does knowledge require that a belief not be true by luck? We know of some very chancy events *that* they occurred, and so the anti-luck platitude must be unpacked in a way that is reconcilable with this fact.[2] Also, we sometimes know things (improbable or not) on the basis of evidence that we could have very easily not have come across. The detective who just happens to catch a piece of very compelling evidence blowing in the wind can come to *know* that a suspect is guilty—even when it was just a matter of luck that the evidence was acquired in the first place.[3]

According to Duncan Pritchard (2005), the way forward is to model the crux of the anti-luck platitude modally, in terms of a *safety condition*. This strategy, while popular, is not the only way to do things.[4] But it is the strategy I will focus on here. Doing so will, I hope, most clearly help to reveal how our views about the bounds of cognition can affect our thinking about epistemic luck.

First though, some quick review. Pritchard's safety strategy takes as a starting point a *modal account of lucky events* generally speaking.[5] This account says that if any event is lucky, then it is an event that occurs in the actual world but which does not occur in a wide class of the nearest possible worlds where the relevant conditions for that event are the same as in the actual world. A fair lottery win counts as lucky on the modal account because in a wide class of the nearest possible worlds where the initial conditions (i.e., you buy a ticket) are the same as in the actual world, you lose.

One kind of event is true belief formation. On the modal account, S's true belief that p is lucky in a way that is incompatible with knowledge (what Pritchard calls *veritically lucky*) if and only if S's belief that p is true in the actual world α but false in nearly all nearby possible worlds in which S forms the belief in the same manner as in α.[6]

318

A belief is defined as "safe" when the truth of the belief is not (veritically) lucky in this way—namely, when in the nearest possible worlds in which S continues to form her belief about the target proposition in the same way as in the actual world, it continues to be true. We can now unpack the anti-luck platitude in terms of the notion of safety: if S knows a proposition, p, then S's belief cannot be "true by luck" in the sense that S's belief that p must be safe; put colloquially, if S knows that p, then *S couldn't easily have been incorrect* given the relevant way that S in fact forms her belief about whether p.

So far, so good. But what should count as the relevant way the individual forms the belief in the actual world? This matters. It affects what we will end up "holding fixed" about the process employed in the actual world, when going out to nearby worlds and assessing whether the belief is true.

According to a rather naive way of thinking about this, the way you form a belief in the actual world, for the purposes of assessing the safety of a belief, is just a matter of whatever evidence for that belief you have in your possession in the actual world.[7] On reflection, though, this is not enough to hold fixed when looking out to other worlds. After all, the mental processes that one deploys in evaluating one's evidence could vary in reliability (perhaps dramatically[8]) across cases where the evidence one has remains exactly the same. Accordingly, if on the safety account we do not at least hold fixed the mental processes one employs in the actual world in forming a belief, when moving out to possible worlds, we would have no way of accounting for why (for example), for two individuals who have the same evidence, the person who haphazardly evaluates that evidence but luckily draws the right conclusion fails to know, while the person who reads the evidence unimpeachably and draws the right conclusion does not.

The foregoing suggests a plausible corollary to a safety condition on knowledge—call it the *cognitive fixedness thesis*.

> **Cognitive fixedness thesis**: For all S, p, and cognitive process ϕ, if ϕ is a cognitive process that S employs in the actual world in forming her p-belief, then, in evaluating the safety of S's p-belief, ϕ must be held fixed when we go out to nearby possible worlds to assess whether S's p-belief remains true.

For example, in Figure 28.1, suppose AW is the actual world, and let A, B, C, and D be close nearby worlds to the actual world AW. Cognitive fixedness tells us that if an individual S at AW employs a cognitive process (CP) in her belief that p in AW, then when we look to A, B, C, and D to assess whether S's belief remains true in these nearby worlds, we must also suppose that CP is the cognitive process that S employs in A, B, C, and D, rather than any other cognitive process.

Crucially, *without* cognitive fixedness assumed to be in play, the safety account would be open to allowing cases where the cognitive process that is *actually* used by an agent in forming the target belief

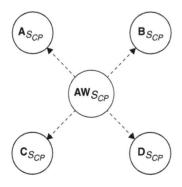

Figure 28.1

is treated as not part of the relevant way she forms her belief in the actual world, and consequently, the account would end up generating implausible results—e.g., that whether one was drunk when drawing an inference could potentially not matter for determining whether her belief is safe.

Interestingly, there are potentially conflicting ways to interpret the cognitive fixedness thesis, depending on how we think about what actually *counts* as the cognitive process one employs. The received view on this matter, *cognitive internalism* (e.g., Adams & Aizawa 2001, 2008, 2010) says the following:

> **Cognitive internalism**: An individual's mind is (in short) in her head; cognitive processes (e.g., memory, inference, introspection, etc.) are exclusively intracranial processes, which play out inside the head.

The cognitive fixedness thesis, paired with a background commitment to cognitive internalism, gives us a more explicit version of the cognitive fixedness thesis, according to which:

> **Cognitive fixedness thesis (internalism)**: For all S, p, and *intracranial cognitive process* ϕ_i, if ϕ_i is a cognitive process that S employs in the actual world in forming her p-belief, then, in evaluating the safety of S's p-belief, ϕ_i must be held fixed when we go out to nearby possible worlds to assess whether S's p-belief remains true.

Cognitive internalism, however, has become increasingly controversial in recent philosophy of mind and cognitive science.[9] In the next section, I will briefly sketch a more inclusive picture of a cognitive process—one that owes in a large part to work by Clark and Chalmers (1998)—and on this basis, consider an "extended mind friendly" interpretation of the cognitive fixedness thesis and show how this thesis interfaces in surprising ways with knowledge, luck, and safety.

Safety, Cognitive Fixedness and Active Externalism

Consider at this point the following case, due to Clark and Chalmers (1998):

> Otto suffers from Alzheimer's disease, and like many Alzheimer's patients, he relies on information in the environment to help structure his life. Otto carries a notebook around with him everywhere he goes. When he learns new information, he writes it down. When he needs some old information, he looks it up. For Otto, his notebook plays the role usually played by a biological memory.

Upon considering such a case, one might be inclined to think something along the following lines: "It's almost as if Otto's memory is in his notebook, not his head!" After all, Otto in the above case is using the notebook to store and retrieve information, which is what we ordinarily use our biomemory to do.

What proponents of the EMT insist is that Otto's memory really is outside his head—*literally*—namely, that his memory process criss-crosses the boundaries between Otto's brain and the world, so as to include the notebook as part of the memory process. As Clark and Chalmers put it, in terms of a parity insight:

> **Parity principle**: If, as we confront some task, a part of the world functions as a process which, were it to go on in the head, we would have no hesitation in accepting as part of the cognitive process, then that part of the world is part of the cognitive process.
>
> *Clark & Chalmers 1998: 8*

Clark and Chalmers' rationale for this inclusive way of thinking about what to include as part of a cognitive process is aimed at safeguarding against bioprejudice—namely, giving undue consideration to things such as material constitution and location when delineating cognitive processes. As they put it:

> [T]he notebook plays for Otto the same role that memory plays for Inga; the information in the notebook functions just like the information [stored in Inga's biological memory] constituting an ordinary non-occurrent belief; it just happens that this information lies beyond the skin.[10]
>
> *Clark & Chalmers 1998: 13*

As Clark and Chalmers appraise the situation, Otto's memory process is a transcranial process that includes his notebook; and furthermore, Otto's memories are stored in his notebook no less than our memories are stored in biomemory. And just as, in ordinary circumstances, we are credited with non-occurrent beliefs in virtue of information that is stored in biomemory, Otto is credited with non-occurrent beliefs in virtue of information that is stored in his extended memory, i.e., the notebook. In this respect, Otto's mind is literally extended; it supervenes on parts of the world outside his skin and skull.

Clark and Chalmers' embracing of the extended mind is, of course, at tension with cognitive internalism. Call the denial of cognitive internalism *cognitive externalism*—namely, the denial of the claim that (in short) necessarily, cognitive processes have intracranial material realisers. Clark and Chalmers' EMT entails cognitive externalism, though this entailment is asymmetrical.[11]

For our purposes, what matters presently is this: if we think about what literally *counts* as part of a cognitive process in an externalist rather than an internalist fashion, then the familiar internalist unpacking of the cognitive fixedness thesis is no longer viable. Rather, what will be needed is an externalist gloss of the cognitive fixedness thesis, according to which:

> **Cognitive fixedness thesis (externalism)**: For all S, p, and *transcranial cognitive process* ϕ_T, if ϕ_T is a cognitive process that S employs in the actual world in forming her p-belief, then, in evaluating the safety of S's p-belief, ϕ_T must be held fixed when we go out to nearby possible worlds to assess whether S's p-belief remains true.

To get a feel for how the externalist cognitive fixedness thesis will have a bearing on which beliefs count as safe, consider the following variation on Clark and Chalmers' case of Otto, due to Carter (2013):

> *Notebook Jokester*: Otto consults his notebook to determine when his doctor's appointment was today, and finds the correct time, noon, written in the book. Unbeknownst to Otto, his notebook had been stolen by a jokester, who fudged with the times of Otto's other appointments that day, changing them all back an hour. The jokester, however, overlooked the doctor's appointment, leaving the original and correct time intact.[12]

Against a background commitment to cognitive internalism, the state and qualities of Otto's notebook (e.g., what is written in the book, whether certain pages are missing) are the sort of things that could vary across possible worlds along with other aspects of Otto's environment. After all, by the internalist cognitive fixedness thesis, what we are obligated to hold fixed across worlds is just the intracranial cognitive process Otto employs in the actual world, a process that does not include the qualities of the notebook he consults. The safety theorist operating with an internalist fixedness principle accordingly can allow that in some nearby worlds, the jokester changes the entry in Otto's notebook that corresponds with his doctor's appointment. And this, indeed, seems like a prima facie good outcome. After all, by supposing that in some nearby worlds the jokester changes the time of the doctor's appointment (rather than overlooking just this one entry) we can straightforwardly account for the strong intuition in *Notebook Jokester* that the unsafety of Otto's belief undermines his knowledge; his belief could easily have been incorrect because the jokester could easily have tinkered with, rather than left alone, the doctor's appointment entry.

Things are interestingly different in *Notebook Jokester* for the "extended mind" safety theorist who operates with a Clark/Chalmers-style externalist rather than internalist cognitive fixedness principle. Because the state of Otto's notebook is literally the state of Otto's memory, given the EMT, the state of Otto's notebook *must* be exported to all possible worlds, when—in evaluating the safety of Otto's belief—we assess whether his target belief remains true in these worlds.

But once *this* point is appreciated, a strange result materializes. Since by stipulation the jokester leaves intact Otto's correct entry specifying his doctor's appointment, the *correct entry* for the doctor's appointment is (as part of the state of the notebook, namely, the state of Otto's memory) itself exported to all worlds for the purposes of evaluating the safety of the target belief in the actual world. But this means Otto's belief in the actual world is safe! After all, in the nearest worlds (i.e., in Figure 28.2, *A*, *B*, *C*, and *D*) where Otto (O) consults his notebook as he does in the actual world, he is consulting a notebook (NB) with the *correct* time written for his doctor's appointment. And those are worlds where Otto believes truly the time of his appointment—i.e., he looks right at the correct entry[13].

I noted that this is a strange result because Otto's belief is *obviously* unsafe—structurally very similar to a barn façade case. *Ex hypothesi*, in *Notebook Jokester*, the jokester really could have easily tinkered with the entry for Otto's doctor's appointment just as the jokester did with the other entries in the notebook, which would have led Otto to believe incorrectly what time the doctor's appointment was. And yet, with the externalist cognitive fixedness principle in play, the safety theorist seems forced into the awkward position of saying otherwise. As with any puzzle, something has to be rejected, but it is not clear what. To appreciate why, consider three potential salient options and their respective drawbacks:

> Option 1. *Reject the EMT*. Rationale: Otto's belief is clearly unsafe. But, since safety theorists who embrace EMT should accept the extended cognitive fixedness principle, and this principle generates the results that Otto's belief is not unsafe, the EMT should go. A drawback is that this will plausibly be the last option that one already friendly to the EMT would be inclined to pursue. But more importantly, this route seems to sidestep rather than really engage with the puzzle.
>
> Option 2. *Reject that EMT proponents should embrace the externalist cognitive fixedness principle*. Rationale: this allows one to hold on to the EMT while at the same time avoiding the unpalatable result that Otto's belief is safe. A drawback, though, is that it would be unprincipled at best

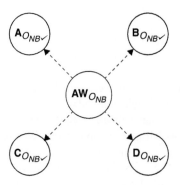

Figure 28.2

for the safety theorist who embraces EMT to advert to the internalist version of the cognitive fixedness principle just to achieve the result that Otto's belief comes out unsafe. After all, the internalist version of the cognitive fixedness thesis simply makes explicit that what should be held fixed (when evaluating for safety) under the description of a "cognitive process" are exclusively intracranial cognitive processes. But embracing this line, for the EMT theorist, is tantamount to purporting to embrace a position while theorizing in a way that suggests otherwise.

Option 3. *Deny that Otto's belief in Notebook Jokester is unsafe*. Rationale: like Option 1, this is a quick way out of the puzzle. However, this line is really a nonstarter; at least, to pursue this line, one would need to defend the position that Otto could not easily have been wrong, given the relevant way he formed the belief, while maintaining that (for example) in paradigmatic instances of unsafe belief which seem closely structurally similar—for example, barn façade cases—the protagonists have unsafe beliefs.

"Extended" Epistemic Luck: New Philosophical Problems

In this section, I want to suggest why cases like *Notebook Jokester* raise some additional perplexities for traditional thinking about knowledge, luck, and safety, beyond the puzzle sketched in the previous section. In particular, in the next subsection, I will show how such "extended luck" challenges the familiar intervening/environmental luck distinction; I will then raise and reply to an objection to the epistemic significance of such cases as raised in recent work by Benjamin Jarvis (2015), and finally, I will close by outlining a further kind of problem brought about by the interfacing of epistemic luck and the extended mind, which I call the retroindication problem.

Taxonomising Epistemic Luck

In the mainstream literature on epistemic luck, there is a distinction due to Pritchard (2005) between two *kinds* of knowledge-undermining (i.e., veritic) epistemic luck: *intervening* and *environmental*. This distinction is useful in marking two structurally different kinds of Gettier cases.[14] "Intervening luck" undermines knowledge when the unsafety of the target belief is due to luck intervening "between the agent and the fact" in a way that is not present in cases where the unsafety of a target belief is simply a matter of her being in an environment where she easily could have been mistaken. For example, in Gettier's (1963) famous original cases, there is a disconnect between the justification the agent has for the target belief and what causes the belief to be true, a disconnect that is then regained by luck.[15] By contrast, in barn-façade-style cases (e.g., Ginet 1975; Goldman 1976), the unsafety of the target belief does not owe to any such disconnect. For instance, in Ginet's (1975) original case, nothing goes ostensibly awry. The hero in question forms a perceptually grounded belief that there is a barn in front of him, having looked directly at a genuine barn. The source of the unsafety of the belief is just down to the individual being in the environment she is in, one in which she is surrounded by fakes. In nearby worlds, she looks at a fake rather than a real barn and believes falsely.

Question: in *Notebook Jokester*, is the truth of Otto's unsafe belief about his doctor's appointment a matter of intervening or environmental luck? As it turns out, neither answer is wholly satisfying.

In one respect, the answer seems to be *environmental*. Consider that in the barn façade case—the paradigmatic environmental luck case—the hero looks at an actual barn in a circumstance under which he easily could have looked at a fake and believed falsely. And Otto's situation in *Notebook Jokester* is arguably very similar. Because the jokester overlooks Otto's doctor's appointment belief, leaving it intact and accurate, this particular piece of information is much like the "real barn" in the barn façade case—i.e., with some abstraction: one looks to something accurate which is surrounded by what is inaccurate and which one easily could have looked to. The setback, however, with this diagnosis, is this: while the safety theorist adverting to a cognitive internalist cognitive fixedness thesis can unproblematically help herself to it, the proponent of EMT cannot. After all, if you are an EMT theorist, it is hard to see why Otto should be described as in a bad *environment*. Unlike barns, the entries in his notebook—no matter what their state—are internal to his cognitive life.

The alternative, of course, is to think of the case instead as one where the unsafety of Otto's belief is more akin to a case of intervening luck. However, this description is problematic as well; it is not the case that there is a disconnect between the justification the agent has for the target belief and what causes the belief to be true, as is characteristic of intervening luck cases. In this respect, unsafe beliefs, in extended mind cases, would appear to require some kind of modification for a taxonomy of kinds of knowledge-undermining luck proposed initially against a tacit commitment to cognitive internalism.

Jarvis's (2015) Bio-jokester

Consider the following "bio-twist" on *Notebook Jokester*, due to Benjamin Jarvis (2015: 468):

> **Bio-Jokester**: Otto★ (without Alzheimer's) has a normally functioning biological memory, which he consults to determine when his doctor's appointment was today, and finds the correct time, noon, is what he (at least seems) to remember. Unbeknownst to Otto★, his memory has been systematically altered by a jokester, who used pharmaceuticals and sub-liminal suggestion to plant false memories about his other appointments that day, making Otto★ inclined to believe that they are an hour earlier than he used to believe. The jokester, however, overlooked the doctor's appointment, leaving the original and correct time registered in Otto★'s memory.

With reference to this creative "intracranial twist" on the case, Jarvis casts doubt on whether cases like *Notebook Jokester* point to any special epistemological significance of extended mind cases, per se. In particular, Jarvis questions whether the fact that *Notebook Jokester* is an extended mind case is itself relevant either to the kind of puzzle proposed at the end of the second section or to the taxonomical problem concerning environmental and intervening luck canvassed above. He reasons, with reference to his *Bio-Jokester* case, that cases that do not feature radically extended cognition (i.e., by the lights of the EMT) should generate the same kinds of epistemological issues. This is because Jarvis says that he does not see "any reason to think that there should be a difference in verdict between JOKESTER and BIO-JOKESTER" (2015: 468).

While I am sympathetic to some extent with Jarvis's worry, I want to explain why I think the thrust of the worry can be resisted. Let me now be clear about what I grant and do not grant. I grant that that Jarvis's case appears to have as much import as *Notebook Jokester* does for our theorizing about the environmental/intervening distinction, as per the previous section. In short, and for reasons that mirror what was noted about *Notebook Jokester*, if the target belief is unsafe, in Jarvis's *Bio-Jokester* case, it does not fit neatly in either the environmental or the intervening category. This is, I think, additional evidence for supposing that views that advert to this distinction (for instance, as it plays an important role in recent debates about knowledge-how and understanding[16]) will need to clarify exactly how it is to be drawn.

However, I want to now pose a dilemma to Jarvis's diagnosis of *Bio-Jokester*. The dilemma, in short, is this: First, there is reason to reject Jarvis's conclusion that the cases are in fact epistemically sym-metrical, because there are reasons to suppose that Otto's belief in *Notebook Jokester* is unsafe (this was, to be clear, something that I argued that the EMT theorist who adverts to an externalist fixedness principle cannot account for) whereas Otto★'s belief in *Bio-Jokester* is (despite initial appearances) very plausibly *actually* safe. However—and here is the crux of the dilemma—if one were to adjust the details of the *Bio-Jokester* case so as to control for this epistemic difference, then *Bio-Jokester* comes apart from *Notebook Jokester* in a different epistemic respect—namely, it will (more so than *Notebook Jokester*) be plausibly diagnosed as a case of an unsafe belief due to intervening luck.

Epistemic Luck and the Extended Mind

In order to defend this dilemma, it is important to see why, despite initial appearances, Otto⋆'s belief in *Bio-Jokester* is plausibly actually safe and in this respect differs from *Notebook Jokester*, whose belief ought to be diagnosed as unsafe. Consider that Otto⋆'s belief in his doctor's appointment in *Bio-Jokester* is unsafe only if Otto really would (given the description of his belief forming in the actual world) believe falsely in nearby worlds. But it is this point that is dubious in a way that it is not in *Notebook Jokester*. Remember that, in *Bio-Jokester*, it is a feature of the case that Otto⋆ is storing the information relevant to organizing his life in biomemory. Operating under the assumption that Otto⋆ is appropriately epistemically vigilant, he will—like other individuals in normal circumstances—rely on *metacognitive virtues* (see, for instance, Morton 2004; Sosa 2015), in light of which Otto will be sensitive to certain kinds of abberations and incoherences. For instance, we can assume that in the default case, if Otto⋆ attempts to retrieve one of the memories that was altered by pharmaceuticals and subliminal suggestion, he will (upon locating the memory) be sensitive to how this fails to cohere with his other beliefs; normally functioning metacognitive faculties will plausibly "flag" such beliefs, so that the individual does not simply automatically endorse it. This fact militates against the "unsafety" verdict for the doctor's appointment belief in *Bio-Jokester*; even if Otto⋆'s doctor's appointment belief is affected by the jokester in nearby worlds, it is not clear that (with properly functioning metacognitive virtues) in those worlds if Otto⋆ retrieved that entry, he would actually endorse its content, and thereby, believe falsely. Whereas, the same is not the case in *Notebook Jokester*, where, if the content of the doctor's appointment entry was altered by a jokester, it is hard to see how Otto would be in any position to flag this in a relevantly analogous way that would prevent him from automatically endorsing its content.

Of course—and here is the rest of the dilemma—one might suppose this disanalogy could be controlled for. Simply revise the case of *Bio-Jokester* so that the pharmaceuticals and subliminal inception have further deleterious effects on Otto⋆'s memory—namely, effects that undermine not just some of his diary entries. Rather, we could suppose the pharmaceuticals and subliminal messages disable his meta-cognitive virtues so that Otto⋆ is in no position anymore to spot incoherences between the beliefs that are tampered with by the jokester and other beliefs he holds.

This move attains the result that Otto⋆'s belief in *Bio-Jokester* will be unsafe. But it gets this result at the cost of raising a further disanalogy: as soon as we revise *Bio-Jokester* in the fashion just described, *Bio-Jokester* (unlike *Notebook Jokester*) begins to look like a pretty clear case of intervening epistemic luck. Otto⋆ after all would be using a now thoroughly defective cognitive process, one riddled pretty comprehensively with pharmaceuticals and sublimation, which happens to issue a true belief on a particular occasion. In light of this dilemma, I think *Notebook Jokester* continues to raise philosophical problems for the safety theorist which cannot so easily be mimicked by intracranial analog cases.

Luck, Fixedness, and the Retroindication Problem

I want to now briefly sketch a final philosophical issue relevant to anti-luck epistemology—what I call the retroindication problem—which is uniquely raised by extended luck cases. The details of the retroindication problem might be easiest to appreciate by running a "high-tech" variation on *Notebook Jokester*; call this "Glitchy iCloud":

> **Glitchy iCloud**: Otto⋆⋆ consults his iPhone's Apple Calendar to determine when his doctor's appointment was today, and finds the correct time, noon, written in the online diary. Unbeknown to Otto⋆⋆, an iCloud glitch has affected all of Otto⋆⋆'s Apple Calendar entries; however, a further glitch which counteracts the original glitch prevents the original glitch from tampering with just the doctor's appointment entry.

Provided Otto's notebook is part of his extended cognitive process in *Notebook Jokester*, so is Otto⋆⋆'s iPhone in *Glitchy iCloud*—and indeed, high-tech formulations of Otto are standard fare in the extended cognition literature.[17] With reference to the extended cognitive fixedness principle, which safety theorists inclined to the EMT should embrace, the extended cognitive process that Otto★★ employs in the actual world—namely, a process that includes the iPhone—must be held fixed in all worlds when we assess whether Otto★★'s belief continues to be true. The retroindication problem is that, even if we hold this fixed, certain *other* things could happen in such worlds which, if these things were to happen, would cause Otto★★'s relationship with the iPhone to *no longer count as an extended cognitive process*, by the lights of extended cognition, thus retroindicating that the process that includes the iPhone should not be held fixed in such worlds. This is a problem for evaluating safety that is unique to extended mind cases.

To make the retroindication problem more concrete, just add some further detail to *Glitchy iCloud*. Consider that, for the purpose of evaluating the safety of Otto★★'s belief in the actual (*Glitchy iCloud*) world, some worlds will be worlds where the following is true: the glitch (which we hold fixed, as is, as part of the state of Otto★★'s mind) will cause a media campaign against Apple, one which has as a consequence that Otto★★ (in such worlds) is constantly exposed to news stories and testimony according to which he is told *not* to trust any information on an Apple device. In such worlds, Otto★★ subjects all entries on his iPhone calendar to intense critical scrutiny and does not automatically endorse the information stored in the calendar.

But in worlds where Otto★★ fundamentally mistrusts his iPhone, Otto★★'s interaction with it *no longer qualifies* (at least, by Clark's lights) as an extended cognitive process; Otto★★ will be, in short, not relying on the device anymore in a way that is analogous to the way we rely on biomemory in the intracranial case. But if this is right, then it retroindicates that Otto★★'s extended process (from the actual world) should *not* (and contrary to the externalist cognitive fixedness thesis) be assumed to be the cognitive process that he employs at such worlds; the entries in the online calendar, in such worlds, are no longer part of a *cognitive* process.

The retroindication problem, thus, calls into question the coherence of maintaining the externalist cognitive fixedness principle, by revealing how what counts (by the lights of EMT) as an extended cognitive process in the actual world might not be exportable to all worlds *as* an extended cognitive process. This is a further issue, generated by extended mind cases, that I think deserves attention by philosophers interested in the anti-luck ramifications of radically extended cognition.

Concluding Remarks

The connections between the EMT, in the philosophy of mind and cognitive science, and mainstream epistemology, are still in early days.[18] Here my aim has been to raise what I think are some of the more interesting philosophical issues the EMT poses for the specific area of epistemology concerned with the relationship between knowledge and luck. I have argued that on at least one natural way of thinking about this relationship, in terms of safety, the EMT generates some new perplexities. In particular, I have argued that EMT proponents ought to, when assessing the safety of a target belief, embrace a version of the cognitive fixedness thesis that comports with the EMT conception of what should be held fixed under the description of a cognitive process in the actual world.

However, I have shown that once a suitably "externalist" fixedness principle is in play, it is hard to maintain intuitive judgments about safety, and furthermore, it becomes less clear how we should distinguish between environmental and intervening epistemic luck, a distinction that is much more straightforward in cases where what is fixed under the description of a cognitive process is the intracranial cognitive process employed in the actual world. I have considered and responded to some challenges to the significance of the kind of puzzles I have raised, and I concluded by raising yet another problem—the retroindication problem—with which I think extended mind friendly safety theorists must grapple. I have not attempted to solve the problems I have raised here. I am, as yet, not convinced what the right way forward will be to address them. My more modest aim is to show that extended mind cases have important and interesting import for how we theorize about knowledge and luck, and to make explicit where some of these points of interest lie.

Acknowledgments

I am especially grateful to Ian Church for helpful comments on a previous version of this chapter. I am also thankful to Andy Clark, Bolesław Czarnecki, Emma C. Gordon, Benjamin Jarvis, Jesper Kallestrup, Duncan Pritchard, and Orestis Palermos for many fruitful discussions about issues at the intersection of epistemology and the extended cognition and mind theses.

Notes

1 For discussion on this point, see Church (2013), Pritchard (2015a), Carter and Broncano-Berrocal (2017: sec. 1), and Broncano-Berrocal (2016: sec. 1c).

2 Consider one very liberal reading of "true by luck": *S*'s belief that *p* is true by luck iff it is a matter of luck *that p is true*. The anti-luck platitude, unpacked in this way, says that if *S* knows a proposition, then it is not a matter of luck *that p is true*. But this is obviously false given that we know all sorts of improbable propositions. Let *p* be the proposition *I was just dealt a royal flush in Texas Hold 'Em poker!* Suppose *p* is true, and thus that you were dealt a hand of cards the probability of which was just 0.0032%, a frequency of 1 in 4,324 hands. After the cards are all dealt and the royal flush sits clearly on the table, you obviously *know* it is a royal flush. Its improbability or disconnection from your skill is by the by.

3 See here Engel (1992: 66–72), Pritchard (2005: 136) and Greco (2004: 398).

4 The modal account is not uncontroversial. For example, according to the lack-of-control account of luck, an event is lucky for a given agent just when it is significantly enough beyond that agent's control (see, for example, Broncano-Berrocal 2015; Coffmann 2007; Riggs 2009; Zimmerman 1987). While the modal account will be helpful for illustrative purposes, in light of the points that will be made here about the cognitive internalism and the EMT, similar conclusions to those I will draw below could be reframed in terms of the lack-of-control account of luck. For some recent skepticism about either of these accounts of luck, see Lackey (2008) and Hales (2014).

5 E.g., Pritchard (2014). For a recent modification of this account in light of some objections raised to previous formulations, see Carter and Peterson (2017). See also (Pritchard 2015b, 2016) for presentations of Pritchard's recent transition from anti-luck epistemology to anti-risk epistemology.

6 See also Pritchard (2013).

7 For a more detailed discussion of evidence and luck, in connection with the propositional/doxastic justification distinction, see Bondy and Pritchard (2016).

8 Sherlock, for example, could evaluate evidence against Moriarty in normal conditions, or he could evaluate this evidence while under the influence of crystal DNT, a drug that causes generally reliable but believable hallucinations. If the hallucination-infused evaluation of the evidence led Sherlock to believe Moriarty was guilty, then (unlike in the normal good case) Sherlock would be in no better a position, epistemically, than the Duke of Devonshire who, in a case noted by Moore (1993: 189), "once dreamt that he was speaking in the House of Lords and, when he woke up, found that he was speaking in the House of Lords."

9 For a sample of some recent challenges to cognitive internalism, see for example Clark and Chalmers (1998), Clark (2008), Sutton (2010), Hutchins (1995), Palermos (2011), Menary (2006), and Wilson (2000).

10 Clark (2008) grants that, just as in the case of ordinary biological memory, the availability and portability of the resource of information should be crucial (see for discussion also Carter et al. 2015). Accordingly, Clark provides a set of functionalist criteria that must be satisfied by non-biological candidates for inclusion into an individual's mind: (1) "That the resource be reliably available and typically invoked." (2) "That any information thus retrieved be more-or-less automatically endorsed. It should not usually be subject to critical scrutiny [...] It should be deemed about as trustworthy as something retrieved clearly from biological memory." (3) "That information contained in the resource should be easily accessible as and when required" Clark (2008: 46).

11 Not all strategies of resisting cognitive internalism involve endorsing the full EMT. For example, the embedded cognition thesis is arguably more conservative than the EMT while nonetheless parting ways with cognitive internalism. For a taxonomy of various varieties of cognitive (and epistemic) externalism and their relationship to one another, see Carter et al. (2014).

12 Note that we can abstract from this case to form a kind of recipe for generating similar cases, including "high tech" versions of the case. For instance, just suppose Otto is storing his information not in a notebook but in his Apple Calendar on his iPhone; further, suppose a computer glitch affects all of his entries but, due to a further glitch which counteracts the original glitch, prevents the original glitch from tampering with the doctor's appointment entry. I consider a case of this sort below.

13 After all, in most worlds where Otto consults his notebook, replete with the correct entry, he believes truly. This much is part and parcel with the thought that Otto is simply a vigilant user of his notebook (as

is necessary to meet Clark's glue and trust conditions—see, for example, Pritchard (2010)), one who by stipulation is using his notebook in a way that is analogous to the way we store and retrieve information in biomemory.

14 See, for example, Pritchard (2015a), Carter and Broncano-Berrocal (2017: sec. 1), and Broncano-Berrocal (2016: sec. 1c). The distinction has theoretical importance in debates about understanding and knowledge-how, standings that have been argued to be compatible with environmental but not epistemic luck, unlike propositional knowledge which is incompatible with both varieties. To the extent that this is right, it would count against proposals that identify understanding and knowledge-how with knowledge-that. See, for example, Carter and Pritchard (2015b) for a presentation of this kind of argument.

15 In Gettier's Smith/Jones case, the justification Smith has for the proposition "The man who will get the job has 10 coins in his pocket" is justification Smith has for the proposition that "Jones will get the job and has ten coins in his pocket." But what makes the target proposition true has nothing to do with Jones whatsoever. It is that Smith got the job and had ten coins in his pocket. Note that this regained disconnect that typifies intervening luck should not be conflated with the more general phenomenon described by Zagzebski (1994) as "double luck," which is general enough to subsume both intervening and environmental cases. After all, it is bad luck that the protagonist in a barn façade case happens to be in an epistemically inhospitable environment but good luck that perception issues a true belief on the particular occasion that it does. But this does not mean that the source of the justification for the target proposition and what causes it to be true are disconnected in the way we find it to be in intervening luck cases.

16 For an overview of how the intervening/environmental luck distinction has import for these debates, see for example Carter and Pritchard (2015a, 2015b).

17 See, for example, Clark (2003) for a range of such cases.

18 For a forthcoming volume of essays on the relationship between active externalist approaches in the philosophy of mind and cognitive science and mainstream epistemology, see Carter et al. (2018).

References

Adams, F., & Aizawa, K. (2001) "The Bounds of Cognition," *Philosophical Psychology* 14(1), 43–64.

———. (2008) *The Bounds of Cognition*, Oxford: Blackwell.

——— (2010) "Defending the Bounds of Cognition," in R. Menary (ed.) *The Extended Mind*, Cambridge, MA: MIT Press, pp. 67–80.

Bondy, P., & Pritchard, D. (2016) "Propositional Epistemic Luck, Epistemic Risk, and Epistemic Justification," *Synthese* 195(9), 3811–3820.

Broncano-Berrocal, F. (2015) "Luck as Risk and the Lack of Control Account of Luck," *Metaphilosophy* 46(1), 1–25.

——— (2016) "Epistemic Luck," *Internet Encyclopedia of Philosophy*.

Carter, J.A. (2013) "Extended Cognition and Epistemic Luck," *Synthese* 190(18), 4201–4214.

Carter, J.A., & Broncano-Berrocal, F. (2017) "Epistemic Luck," in Tim Crane (ed.) *Routledge Encyclopedia of Philosophy*, 1–15. Routledge.

Carter, J. Adam, & Peterson, M. (2017) "The Modal Account of Luck Revisited," *Synthese* 194(6), 2175–2184.

Carter, J. Adam, & Pritchard, D. (2015a) "Knowledge-How and Cognitive Achievement," *Philosophy and Phenomenological Research* 91(1), 181–199.

——— (2015b) "Knowledge-How and Epistemic Luck," *Noûs* 49(3), 440–453.

Carter, J.A., Clark, A., Kallestrup, J., Palermos, S.O., & Pritchard, D. (eds.) (2018) *Extended Epistemology*, Oxford: Oxford University Press.

Carter, J.A., Gordon, E.C., & Palermos, S.O. (2015) "Extended Emotion," *Philosophical Psychology* 29(2), 198–217.

Carter, J.A, Kallestrup, J., Palermos, S.O., & Pritchard, D. (2014) "Varieties of Externalism," *Philosophical Issues* 24(1), 63–109.

Church, I.M. (2013) "Getting Lucky with Gettier," *European Journal of Philosophy* 21(1), 37–49.

Clark, A. (2003) *Natural-Born Cyborgs: Minds, Technologies and the Future of Human Intelligence*. Oxford: Oxford University Press.

———. (2008) *Supersizing the Mind: Embodiment, Action, and Cognitive Extension*. Oxford: Oxford University Press.

Clark, A., & Chalmers, D. (1998) "The Extended Mind," *Analysis* 58(1), 7–19.

Coffmann, E.J. (2007) "Thinking about Luck," *Synthese* 158(3), 385–398.

Engel, M. (1992) "Is Epistemic Luck Compatible with Knowledge?" *Southern Journal of Philosophy* 30(2), 59–75.

Gettier, E. (1963) "Is Justified True Belief Knowledge?" *Analysis* 23(6), 121–123.

Ginet, C. (1975) *Knowledge, Perception and Memory*. Dordrecht: D. Reidel Publishing Company.

Goldman, A. (1976) "Discrimination and Perceptual Knowledge," *Journal of Philosophy* 73(20), 771–791.

Greco, J. (2004) "A Different Sort of Contextualism," *Erkenntnis* 61(2–3), 383–400.

Hales, S.D. (2014) "Why Every Theory of Luck Is Wrong," *Noûs* 50(3), 490–508.

Epistemic Luck and the Extended Mind

Hutchins, E. (1995) *Cognition in the Wild*, Cambridge, MA: MIT Press.

Jarvis, B. (2015) "Epistemology and Radically Extended Cognition," *Episteme* 12(4), 459–478.

Lackey, J. (2008) "What Luck Is Not," *Australasian Journal of Philosophy* 86(2), 255–267.

Luper-Foy, S. (1984) "The Epistemic Predicament: Knowledge, Nozickian Tracking, and Scepticism," *Australasian Journal of Philosophy* 62(1), 26–49.

Menary, R. (2006) "Attacking the Bounds of Cognition," *Philosophical Psychology* 19(3), 329–344.

Moore, G.E. (1993) *G.E. Moore: Selected Writings*. London and New York: Routledge.

Morton, A. (2004) "Epistemic Virtues, Metavirtues, and Computational Complexity," *Noûs* 38(3), 481–502.

Palermos, S.O. (2011) "Belief-Forming Processes, Extended," *Review of Philosophy and Psychology* 2(4), 741–765.

Pritchard, D. (2005) *Epistemic Luck*, Oxford: Oxford University Press.

—— (2007) "Anti-Luck Epistemology," *Synthese* 158(3), 277–297.

—— (2010) "Cognitive Ability and the Extended Cognition Thesis," *Synthese* 175(1), 133–151.

—— (2013) "There Can Not Be Lucky Knowledge," in Matthias Steup & John Turri (eds.) *Contemporary Debates in Epistemology*, Oxford: Blackwell, pp. 152–164.

—— (2014) "The Modal Account of Luck," *Metaphilosophy* 45(4–5), 594–619.

—— (2015a) "Anti-Luck Epistemology and the Gettier Problem," *Philosophical Studies* 172(1), 93–111.

—— (2015b) "Risk," *Metaphilosophy* 46(3), 436–461.

—— (2016) "Epistemic Risk," *Journal of Philosophy* 113(11), 550–571.

Riggs, W. (2009) "Luck, Knowledge, and Control," in D. Pritchard, A. Haddock, & A. Millar (eds.) *Epistemic Value*, Oxford: Oxford University Press, pp. 204–221.

Sainsbury, R.M. (1997) "Easy Possibilities," *Philosophy and Phenomenological Research* 57(4), pp. 907–919.

Sosa, E. (1999) "How to Defeat Opposition to Moore," *Noûs* 33(13), 141–153.

—— (2015) *Judgment and Agency*, Oxford: Oxford University Press.

Sutton, J. (2010) "Exograms and Interdisciplinarity: History, the Extended Mind, and the Civilizing Process," in Richard Menary (ed.) *The Extended Mind*, Cambridge, MA: MIT Press, pp. 189–225.

Williamson, T. (2000) *Knowledge and Its Limits*, Oxford: Oxford University Press.

Wilson, R.A. (2000) *The Mind Beyond Itself*, New York: Oxford University Press.

Zagzebski, L. (1994) "The Inescapability of Gettier Problems," *The Philosophical Quarterly* 44(174), 65–73.

Zimmerman, M.J. (1987) "Luck and Moral Responsibility," *Ethics* 97(2), 374–386.

PART V

The Psychology of Luck

29

COGNITIVE BIASES AND DISPOSITIONS IN LUCK ATTRIBUTIONS

Steven D. Hales and Jennifer Adrienne Johnson

Luck is a deep current in human culture. In ancient Greece and Rome luck was personified as a fickle and indifferent deity. Astride the wheel of fortune, she would raise those at the bottom of society to the top and capriciously drop those at the pinnacle of success back down to penury. The ancients approached luck in one of three ways. The first was to propitiate Fortuna or redirect her ill luck to others and capture her good fortune for ourselves, through charms, curses, or talismans. Petronius, a Roman courtier during the reign of Nero, described a dinner party at which a small statue with an amulet around its neck was placed on the table to bring the diners good luck.[1] Sigmund Freud, as one might expect, claimed that lucky charms are all easily recognized as genital or sexual symbols.[2]

The second approach was the Stoic strategy of defying the power of Fortuna by refusing to recognize things in the outside world as having any hold over us. A Stoic sage is insulated from misfortune because he does not value the objects of the external world, and believes it is virtue alone that ensures the good life. In his *Moral Epistles* Seneca advised that

> the wise man is sufficient unto himself for a happy existence, but not for mere existence. For he needs many helps towards mere existence; but for a happy existence he needs only a sound and upright soul, one that despises Fortuna.
>
> *Seneca 1917: IX*

The final ancient tactic was to deny the power of luck by insisting that all is fated to occur. The idea that we are powerless to avoid our ineluctable destiny is a theme seen in *Oedipus Rex*, the prophesied betrayal of Jesus, and the myth of Sisyphus, among other places. If everything happens by design, then nothing happens by luck.

Little advance was made in the mastery and understanding of luck until the Renaissance and the invention of probability theory. Gambling was directly responsible for the development of probability theory—if there is anyone who wants to subjugate luck, it is gamblers. Numerous mathematicians, including Cardano, Pascal, Fermat, de Moivre, and Bernoulli developed the mathematics of probability in order to solve gambling puzzles. By the 18th century they declared victory over luck. Pierre Rémond de Montmort wrote in his *Analytical Essay on Games of Chance* (1708):

> [Most men] believe that it is necessary to appease this blind divinity that one calls Fortune, in order to force her to be favorable to them in following the rules which they have imagined. I think therefore it would be useful, not only to gamesters but to all men in general, to know that chance has rules which can be known.
>
> *David 1962: 144*

Montmort and others were sure that they had worked out these rules and there was little more to be said on the topic.

By the 20th century it became clear that the mathematicians might not have the final word on luck,[3] and that such a ubiquitous and multifaceted concept is best approached with tools from several disciplines. Our interest is in how psychology and philosophy can work together to help explain the nature of luck. Previous psychological work on luck has tended to be somewhat piecemeal, even venturing into pop-psych/self-help territory. For example, Richard Wiseman's *The Luck Factor: Changing Your Luck, Changing Your Life: The Four Essential Principles* promises "a scientifically proven way to understand, control, and increase your luck" (Wiseman 2003: xiii). His four principles are maximize your chance opportunities, listen to your lucky hunches, expect good fortune, and turn your bad luck into good (Wiseman 2003: 161–162).

When people think of luck, they generally think of good luck. The line "Lord, if it wasn't for bad luck, I wouldn't have no luck at all" from Lightnin' Slim's 1954 song "Bad Luck Blues" is clever because it draws attention away from the familiar dichotomy of good vs. bad luck to the contrast between any kind of luck vs. no luck at all. In what follows, we will argue that there are results from experimental psychology that show that ordinary people are systematically irrational in how they interpret the same event as being a bit of good luck or bad luck. We show first that framing effects strongly determine the assignment of good luck or bad, and second we show that one's personal inclinations toward optimism or pessimism also affect whether one interprets an event as being lucky or unlucky. Philosophical theories of luck have two aims: (1) to properly delineate between good/bad luck and non-luck, and (2) to correctly distinguish between events that are lucky (in the sense of good luck) and unlucky. We argue that, due to the results of our psychological studies, no theory of luck is able to achieve the second aim.

Scholarly work has investigated the connection between study subjects' beliefs in luck and various psychological traits such as depression, anxiety, optimism, neuroticism, attribution style, self-esteem, and irrational beliefs. Day and Maltby (2003) measured subjects' beliefs in luck and found a significant correlation between a belief in personal good luck and optimism and the holding of irrational beliefs. In particular, they argue that a belief in one's own luckiness produces optimistic traits and a reduced level of irrational beliefs. Depressed, anxious people tend to have irrational beliefs that diminish their self-worth. Believing that one is lucky counteracts those tendencies. Other work has focused on the psychology of gamblers. The more subjects believe in luck as a fungible quality or personal power, the more they will gamble. Their belief in this kind of luck tends to lead to an illusion of control over gambling results and thence to gambling addiction (Lim & Rogers 2017; Kim et al. 2015; Wohl & Enzle 2002).

Pritchard and Smith (2004) survey the psychological literature on luck and conclude that it has been hampered by insufficient clarity about the nature of luck. While Pritchard and Smith's literature review is a bit dated, their conclusion remains current. Karl Teigen is one of the few psychologists whose work bears on understanding luck itself. He has supported a modal account of luck, arguing that people view themselves as lucky or unlucky based upon counterfactual outcomes that they see as salient alternatives to their actual histories (Teigen 2005; Teigen & Jensen 2011). Near disasters trigger feelings of good luck and near successes lead to feelings of bad luck. In our own work, we have conducted studies that aim to move the ball downfield to a more satisfactory theory of the nature of luck. Unless we understand what luck is—and what it is not—luck research risks resembling alchemy more than chemistry. Both philosophy and psychology can contribute to this understanding.

Cognitive Biases and Dispositions

In the past several years we have specifically investigated how cognitive biases, or systematic errors in thinking, influence people's attributions of good and bad luck. By better understanding how cognitive biases influence luck attributions, we hope to contribute to contemporary philosophical theories of luck and introduce the possibility that luck does not exist but is instead a cognitive illusion. In our studies, we present participants with scenarios (e.g., "A severe snowstorm hit the town. Half of the town's residents never lost their power") and ask the participants to judge the luckiness of the scenario on a scale with four options: *unlucky, somewhat unlucky, somewhat lucky, lucky*. In our first study, we investigated how framing affects luck attributions (Hales & Johnson 2014).

The influence of framing in human decision making was made famous through the studies of Amos Tversky and Daniel Kahneman (1981, 1986). Framing refers to how a situation is presented; for example, a single situation can be framed as a gain or as a loss, a positive outcome or a negative outcome. Framing has been shown to influence a variety of human judgments in experimental settings including purchasing choices, gambling risks, and medical decisions. In a typical research study, a problem is presented to participants who are then offered two possible solutions to the problem. Statistically speaking, the two solutions are identical. Therefore, if respondents show systematic patterns in choosing one option over another, the framing of the outcome has led to a cognitive bias in decision making.

Below is an example Tversky and Kahneman (1986) borrowed from McNeil and colleagues regarding lung cancer treatment options. Participants were asked to choose either the surgery or the radiation therapy based on the statistical information provided below.

Surgery Option:
Of 100 people having surgery, 90 live through the post-operative period, 68 are alive at the end of the first year, and 34 are alive at the end of five years.

Radiation Therapy Option:
Of 100 people having radiation therapy, all live through the treatment, 77 are alive at the end of one year and 22 are alive at the end of five years.

When given the treatment options in a *survival* frame, as shown above, only 18% of respondents preferred the radiation treatment. It seems that most participants were swayed by the 34% five-year survival rate offered by the surgery over the 22% five-year survival rate offered by the radiation therapy. This was in spite of the immediate and one-year survival rates being higher for the radiation therapy.

When the statistically identical treatment options were presented in a *mortality* frame, as shown below, participants' preferences shifted.

Surgery Option:
Of 100 people having surgery, 10 die during surgery or the post-operative period, 32 die by the end of the first year, and 66 die by the end of five years.

Radiation Therapy Option:
Of 100 people having radiation therapy, none die during treatment, 23 die by the end of one year, and 78 die by the end of five years.

Compared to the 18% who chose the radiation therapy when presented in the survival frame, 44% favored the radiation treatment when presented in the mortality frame. In this case, the surgery's heightened chance of immediate death compared to the radiation therapy (10% versus 0%) and death within one year (32% versus 23%) seemed to convince more people to choose the latter option. Even when these scenarios were presented to experienced physicians and business students knowledgeable in statistics the same framing effect was found. This example and many like it show just how pervasive and robust this cognitive bias is in human decision making.

To our knowledge, no one had determined if framing influences attributions of good or bad luck. If we could show that luck attributions were susceptible to this cognitive bias, we thought we could provide evidence that might challenge contemporary philosophical theories of luck. We first created hypothetical scenarios that we deemed had a luck component to them. Examples of the scenarios included hitting five out of six numbers in a lottery, losing power after a storm, walking away from a life-threatening car accident, and just missing hitting a pedestrian with one's car (Hales & Johnson 2014). We first pilot tested the scenarios to make sure that other people considered them lucky or unlucky; they did. Then we set out to determine if people's attributions of good or bad luck to the scenarios could be influenced by framing.

To do this, we presented each of the hypothetical scenarios in either a positive frame or negative frame such as the example below.

Positive Frame:
A severe snowstorm hit the town. Half of the town's residents *never lost* their power.

Negative Frame:
A severe snowstorm hit the town. Half of the town's residents *lost* their power.

It is important to note that just as Tversky and Kahneman's survival-framed and mortality-framed treatment options were statistically identical, the outcomes of the positively and negatively framed luck scenarios were likewise identical. That is, in both versions of the scenario there was a 50% chance that a town resident lost his or her power. Yet we found that participants' luck attributions were significantly influenced by the framing. Sixty-eight percent of the participants who were presented the positively framed outcome judged it as *lucky* or *somewhat lucky* while only 4% of the respondents who were presented the negatively framed outcome judged it as *lucky* or *somewhat lucky*. This pattern was not unique to this particular scenario. Here is another that we presented to participants in our study.

Positive Frame:
Tara Cooper *hit five* out of six numbers in the Megabuck$ lottery.

Negative Frame:
Tara Cooper *missed one* out of six numbers in the Megabuck$ lottery.

In this case, 84% of the participants who were presented the positively framed scenario judged Cooper to be lucky; only 40% of respondents presented the negatively framed version judged Cooper to be lucky. Because the statistical probability of both occurrences is identical, differences in luck judgments must be attributed to the framing.

In total we presented participants with eight different luck scenarios; half of our participants judged the positively framed version and the other half judged the negatively framed version. We found a significant framing effect for each scenario with an average shift in luckiness of about 40%. That is, positively framed versions were judged lucky by 40% more of the participants compared to the statistically identical negatively framed versions. Attributions of good and bad luck are susceptible to framing just as we have seen in purchasing choices, gambling risks, and medical decisions in the work of Tversky and Kahneman (1981, 1986).

This pattern of findings was also evident when we presented the framed event in the context of longer stories such as those below (Hales & Johnson 2014).

Cognitive Biases and Dispositions

Positive Frame:

"*I hit five out of six! I've never come anywhere close to hitting the big jackpot before!* It was just unbelievable," Cooper exclaimed, still stunned. Berwick bakery worker Tara Cooper stopped off at her usual place for a breakfast coffee and bagel, Brewed Awakening, and decided to pick up a lottery ticket before heading to first shift. "I don't usually play Megabuck$, and don't know why I did today." After work, she checked her numbers online. "I was like, oh my God!"

Negative Frame:

"*I missed the jackpot by one lousy number! Story of my life.* It was just unbelievable," Cooper exclaimed, still stunned. Berwick bakery worker Tara Cooper stopped off at her usual place for a breakfast coffee and bagel, Brewed Awakening, and decided to pick up a lottery ticket before heading to first shift. "I don't usually play Megabuck$, and don't know why I did today." After work, she checked her numbers online. "I was like, oh my God."

In fact, the pattern of results for this long version of the Cooper scenario was nearly identical to that seen for the short version. Eighty-four percent of respondents who were presented the positively framed story, whether long or short, judged her to be lucky; 41% of respondents who were presented the negatively framed long story judged her to be lucky (it was 40% of respondents who judged her to be lucky in the short version).

The same was true of the long version of the snowstorm scenario shown below.

Positive Frame:

"Half of the residents *never lost* their power," reported the mayor. "It *could have been a lot* worse. We *dodged a* bullet." Roads were slick for morning commuters and icy trees knocked out electrical lines after a major winter storm blanketed the area in snow and ice this past weekend. Forecasters had predicted that the town would take the brunt of the worst storm of the season.

Negative Frame:

"Half of the residents *lost* their power," reported the mayor. "It *can't get much* worse. We *weren't able to dodge this* bullet." Roads were slick for morning commuters and icy trees knocked out electrical lines after a major winter storm blanketed the area in snow and ice this past weekend. Forecasters had predicted that the town would take the brunt of the worst storm of the season.

Sixty-one percent of participants who were presented the positively framed long version considered the town's residents lucky (it was 68% of those presented the short version), while only 9% who were presented the negatively framed long version considered the residents lucky (it was 4% in the short version). When combining the results from all eight of the long versions of the luck scenarios, we observed an average shift in luckiness of about 55%. That is, positively framed long versions were judged lucky by 55% more of the participants compared to the statistically identical negatively framed long versions.

In the same study, the long versions of the luck scenarios offered us an opportunity to test the influence of another cognitive bias, the serial position effect. The serial position effect is a memory processing bias which states that information presented first (primacy effect) and information presented most recently (recency effect) benefits from better recall (Ebbinghaus 1885; Rundus 1971). For example, when reading a story, a person might better remember the beginning (primacy effect) and end (recency effect) compared to the middle of the story. We reasoned that if the beginning and end of a story benefit from a memory boost, placing the key component of the luck scenario in those positions would lead to the greatest framing effect.

We used the long versions of the luck scenarios but varied the placement of the positively or negatively framed portion of the event. That is, the framed portion of the event occurred at the beginning of the story for some participants, the middle of the story for other participants, and at the end of the story for the remaining. Below are examples of a positively framed event from our study.

Positive Frame at the Beginning:
"I hit half my shots from the free throw line! Not bad for a beginner, huh?" Mark exclaimed with a grin. Even though he was one of the tallest kids in his class, Mark Zabadi had never picked up a basketball before. "I dunno," he said, "Guess I'm more of a gamer—not much of a team sports guy." But when some of his friends found themselves short a player for a pickup game, they convinced Mark to play.

Positive Frame in the Middle:
When some of his friends found themselves short a player for a pickup game, they convinced Mark to play. "I dunno. Guess I'm more of a gamer—not much of a team sports guy. *But I hit half my shots from the free throw line! Not bad for a beginner, huh?" Mark exclaimed with a grin.* Mark Zabadi had never picked up a basketball before even though he was one of the tallest kids in his class.

Positive Frame at the End:
Even though he was one of the tallest kids in his class, Mark Zabadi had never picked up a basketball before. "I dunno," he said, "Guess I'm more of a gamer—not much of a team sports guy." But when some of his friends found themselves short a player for a pickup game, they convinced Mark to play. *"I hit half my shots from the free throw line! Not bad for a beginner, huh?" Mark exclaimed with a grin.*

Interestingly, the location of the positively framed portion of the event did not significantly affect luck attributions; the scenario was considered lucky across all three versions. For example, the percent of respondents who rated Mark as lucky was 92% for the beginning version, 84% for the middle version, and 88% for the end version. When combining the results of all eight scenarios from our study, luck ratings when the event was at the beginning (86% judged lucky), middle (85% judged lucky), and end (88% judged lucky) did not significantly differ. Such consistency could be due to the Pollyanna principle (i.e., positivity bias), which is the tendency for people to generally recall positively valenced events better than negatively valenced events (Matlin & Stang 1978). Positivity bias could mean that the location of the positive event had no influence on recall because positive events are recalled well regardless of their serial position.

On the other hand, the location of the negatively framed portion of the event did significantly affect luck attributions. Below are examples.

Negative Frame at the Beginning:
"Yeah, I missed half my shots from the free throw line. Not great, huh?" Mark said with a frown. Even though he was one of the tallest kids in his class, Mark Zabadi had never picked up a basketball before. But when some of his friends found themselves short a player for a pickup game, they convinced Mark to play. "I dunno," he said, "Guess I'm more of a gamer—not much of a team sports guy."

Negative Frame in the Middle:
When some of his friends found themselves short a player for a pickup game, they convinced Mark to play. "I dunno," he said, "Guess I'm more of a gamer—not much of a team sports guy. *Yeah, I missed half of my shots from the free throw line. Not great, huh?" Mark said with a*

frown. Mark Zabadi had never picked up a basketball before even though he was one of the tallest kids in his class.

Negative Frame at the End:
Even though he was one of the tallest kids in his class, Mark Zabadi had never picked up a basketball before. "I dunno," he said, "Guess I'm more of a gamer—not much of a team sports guy." But when some of his friends found themselves short a player for a pickup game, they convinced Mark to play. *"Yeah, I missed half of my shots from the free throw line. Not great, huh?" Mark said with a frown.*

We found that the closer the negatively framed portion of the event was to the end of the story, the less luck was attributed by the participants. For example, the percent of respondents who rated Mark as lucky was 52% for the beginning version, 32% for the middle version, and 24% for the end version. When combining the results of all eight scenarios, the pattern remained. In particular luck ratings were similar when the negatively framed portion was at the beginning (35% judged lucky) and in the middle (30% judged lucky), but decreased when it was at the end (21% judged lucky). The effect was significant and suggested that the recency effect might have influenced respondents' luck attributions.

Overall, regardless of the length of the luck scenario or the order in which the scenario was presented, we found that framing caused robust and consistent changes in people's judgments of good and bad luck. This demonstrated that luck attributions, like many other human judgments, are affected by cognitive biases.

In more recent work we sought to determine if dispositional optimism plays a role in people's luck attributions (Hales & Johnson 2018). We presented participants with scenarios that involved luck but it was unclear whether the scenarios were instances of good or bad luck (i.e., the scenarios were ambiguous in regard to luck). For example, take the following true story that was presented to participants in our study.

Channing Moss was a US soldier serving in Afghanistan. His unit was attacked by Taliban insurgents, who fired a rocket propelled grenade (RPG) into Moss's abdomen. The unexploded but live warhead stuck out of his left side and the rocket fins stuck out of his right. After a very risky operation, the RPG was removed. Several surgeries later, Moss is home with his family.

Overall, should Channing Moss be considered unlucky because he was hit with an RPG, or should he be considered lucky because he survived? We reasoned that optimistic people would be drawn more to the bright side of the situation and thereby judge Channing Moss as more lucky than pessimistic people who would be swayed more by the negative part of the scenario. Optimism is commonly—and properly—considered a personality trait. It is relatively stable over time, differs across humans, and is at least in part heritable (Carver et al. 2010). But more specifically, optimism is a trait that reveals one's cognitive expectation for future events. That is, an optimist has the expectation that good things will happen in one's future, while a pessimist has the expectation that bad things will happen in one's future. Given the fact that optimism is inherently cognitive in nature made it of particular interest to us as we continued our journey to discover how cognitive biases and expectations influence the interpretation of luck events as good or bad luck.

In our first study, we presented participants with five ambiguous luck vignettes that were all based on true stories. They included the story of Channing Moss surviving the RPG, Tsutomu Yamaguchi surviving the atomic bombings of Hiroshima and Nagasaki, Bill Morgan surviving a near-fatal car accident, Eduardo Leite surviving a head-first 5th story fall, and Roy Sullivan surviving seven lightning strikes. Participants were asked to judge the luckiness of the person in each story (i.e., was the person *unlucky, somewhat unlucky, somewhat lucky, lucky*?). Then participants completed the 10-item Life Orientation Test (LOT-R), the most common measure of dispositional optimism (Scheier et al. 1994). The LOT-R requires participants to state their agreement with statements such as "I am always optimistic about my future" and "Overall, I expect more good things to happen to me than bad."

Scores on the LOT-R provide a continuum of optimism with no criterion for what score constitutes the cut-off between an optimist and a pessimist. Therefore, to test our hypothesis we examined the correlation between luck judgments of the ambiguous vignettes and scores on the LOT-R. We found a significant positive correlation between one's level of optimism and one's luckiness ratings of the vignettes. That is, the more optimistic a person, the more likely they were to judge people in the vignettes as lucky. Likewise, the more pessimistic a person, the more likely they were to judge the people in the vignettes as unlucky. The findings seemed to suggest that a person's cognitive expectation that good or bad events should happen to *them* (i.e., their level of optimism) influenced their judgments about the luckiness of *others* (i.e., the people in the vignettes).

One concern with these findings is the possibility that the subjects were effectively ignoring half of the information they received. Perhaps the optimists were just setting aside the negative component of the case and focusing solely on the good aspect, and the pessimists were doing the same by focusing on the bad portion and ignoring the positive features of the vignette. If that was going on, then the optimists and pessimists were essentially talking past each other; they were not really assessing the *total* situation for luck. To obviate this concern we designed a follow-up study.

In the second study, a new group of participants was presented the same vignettes that we used in our first study, but the "good" and "bad" parts of the vignettes were presented separately to ensure that optimists could not just ignore the negative component of the case and pessimists could not ignore the positive component. Below is an example of how we presented Tsutomu Yamaguchi's case as two parts.

- In 1945, Tsutomu Yamaguchi was on business in Hiroshima when the first atomic bomb hit and in his hometown of Nagasaki in the second-ever nuclear attack. Tsutomu Yamaguchi was: (circle one): *unlucky, somewhat unlucky, somewhat lucky, lucky*
- Tsutomu Yamaguchi survived both nuclear attacks and lived until he was 93. Tsutomu Yamaguchi was: (circle one): *unlucky, somewhat unlucky, somewhat lucky, lucky.*

Overall, optimistic and pessimistic participants were largely in agreement regarding the luckiness of the "good" and "bad" events. Ninety-seven percent of participants rated the good events as *lucky* or *somewhat lucky*, and all participants rated the bad events as *unlucky* or *somewhat unlucky*. Optimists and pessimists can clearly agree upon what constitutes good versus bad luck. However, optimists and pessimists varied in their judgments of the severity of the bad luck components. The more pessimistic the person, the more unlucky she considered the bad luck component. The more optimistic the person, the less unlucky she considered the bad luck component. This was not the case for the good luck component; level of optimism did not significantly predict attributions of luckiness to the good luck component.

We think the results of our second study help explain the findings of our first study. We posit that when people judged the ambiguous luck scenarios in their entirety in our first study, optimists were seeing the bad luck component of the event as unlucky but not as unlucky as pessimists deemed it to be. This could explain why optimists judged the scenario in its entirety as more lucky than pessimists.

What are the philosophical implications of these psychological findings? The apposite solution to other cases of cognitive biases is to disregard the error-prone System 1 intuitions in favor of the reflective theorizing of System 2. For example, if you know that you are subject to the Gambler's Fallacy, then a careful application of probability theory when gambling is the cure. If you know that you keep falling for the Availability Error (considering only recent or psychologically salient events) when calculating future risk, then the right response is a close examination of risk statistics. Given the fact that optimists view events as luckier than pessimists do, or the result that luck attributions are strongly determined by framing and salience effects, perhaps the correct thing to do is revert to a theory of luck that will tell us how to accurately decide whether someone is lucky or not. Then we will be able to avoid the erroneous biases or personality traits that distort our perceptions of luck.

There are three major theories of luck: the probability, modal, and control theories. According to the probability theory, an occurrence is lucky (or unlucky) only if it was improbable that it would occur. The modal theory of luck maintains that an event is lucky only if it is fragile—had the world been very slightly different it would not have occurred. The third theory of luck is the control view, which states that if a fact was lucky or unlucky for a person, then that person had no control over whether it was a fact. To these necessary conditions for luck, nearly everyone (Pritchard (2014) being the lone exception) adds a significance condition: for someone to be lucky (or unlucky) that an event has occurred, that event must in some way be of significance to that person. All other more sophisticated versions are variants or elaborations on these ideas.[4]

Unfortunately, the hope of a bailout by theory is in vain. The available theories of luck are incapable of solving the problems raised in our studies. To settle the framing cases here is what we want: a defensible theory of luck to tell us whether Tara Cooper really is lucky or whether she really is unlucky. Then we could dismiss one frame as misleading and accept that the other frame is better at leading us to the truth. Consider first the probability theory of luck. According to it, something's luckiness is a function of its importance and probability of occurrence. Under the probability theory, Tara is lucky to hit five out of six numbers in the Megabuck$ lottery if and only if (1) hitting five numbers mattered to her in a positive way and (2) it was improbable that she would hit five of six numbers. Let us suppose that those conditions were satisfied. Thus Tara *was* lucky to hit five numbers in the lottery. Also according to the probability theory, she was *unlucky* to miss one of six numbers in the Megabuck$ lottery if and only if (1) missing one of the numbers mattered to her in a negative way, and (2) it was improbable that she would hit all six numbers. Assuming those conditions were satisfied, it follows that she was unlucky to miss one of the six numbers.

We get the same result under the modal theory. According to the modal theory, a very small change in the world, such as one ball in the Megabuck$ lottery hopper rotating an extra 20 degrees, would have meant that Tara Cooper did not hit five of six numbers in the lottery, and so her hitting those numbers was modally fragile. Thus her success in getting five out of six was lucky. It is also the case that a very small change in the world would have meant that she got all six numbers right in the lottery, and she was unlucky not to find herself in this very close possible world instead. Again, Tara Cooper is both lucky and unlucky for the same thing.

The control theory lines up with the others. The fact that Cooper got five of six lottery numbers correct was wholly outside her control. Coupled with the fact that getting those numbers mattered to her, under the control theory she was lucky to get five of six numbers in the lottery. However, it was also not within her control to hit all six numbers, although she would have surely loved to. Thus the fact that she missed one number was a case of bad luck. While Tara Cooper was lucky to have hit five out of six numbers in the lottery, she was unlucky to have missed one number.

Tara Cooper was not simultaneously lucky and unlucky for the exact same event. In the snowstorm example, the town's residents were not both lucky and unlucky; those are contrary properties in the same way that *being red all over* and *being blue all over* are contraries, or *skydiving* and *swimming* are contraries. No one can skydive and swim simultaneously, and no one can be both lucky and unlucky for the same thing in the same way. An adequate theory of luck should tell us, in any given case, whether the subject of luck is objectively lucky or objectively unlucky, just as probability theory tells a gambler whether he is objectively likely to be dealt good cards after a run of bad ones, or not. If probability theory could not do that, we would still be stuck with the Gambler's Fallacy. If a theory of luck cannot render a consistent, univocal, and objective decision about a putative case of luck, then we have no solution to cognitive bias. In fact, it suggests that there might be no more to luck than cognitive bias.

Luck defenders might rejoin that it is not the probability, modal, or control elements of a theory of luck that are meant to parse good luck from bad. Rather, it is the significance condition that does that work. It is not enough to know that an event is chancy, or that a chancy event affects someone; we need to know whether it affects them in a good or bad way. The way that we do that is to consider for whom the event is significant, and the manner in which it matters. For example, if Bertrand and Dora are playing blackjack against each other, and Dora is dealt Jack-Ace, that is very improbable (about 0.5%) and certainly matters for Dora. Obviously it matters just as much for Bertrand too, just inversely. Without establishing that not only is the low chance of Jack-Ace significant for both Dora and Bertrand, but that it affects her in a good way and him in a bad way, it cannot be sorted out who is lucky and who is unlucky.

Coffman has recently argued that an event is a stroke of good (or bad) luck for an agent only if it is in some respect good (or bad) for that agent (Coffman 2015: 34). Ballantyne has similarly argued that an individual is lucky with respect to some event only if the putatively lucky event has an objectively positive or negative effect on an interest of that agent (Ballantyne 2012: 331). Whittington maintains that "significance … is … objective, in the sense that it does not depend entirely on the desires of perceptions of the agent in order to count as significant for that agent. Furthermore, the value of the significance may well be the opposite of what the agent perceives" (Whittington 2016: 1616–1617).

For Coffman, Ballantyne, and Whittington, an event can be simultaneously lucky and unlucky for the same person, as when a lottery win makes one luckily rich but unluckily a prime target for swindlers. In this sense a lottery win is a double-edged sword. Their idea is consonant with the cases we presented in the first optimism/pessimism study which contained a compound event composed of both lucky and unlucky parts. As in those cases, presumably there is also an *overall* assessment about whether an event is lucky or unlucky. For example, a lottery winner could plausibly judge that despite some downsides, taken all in, winning was a lucky event. Ballantyne and Whittington also concur that the subject of luck could be mistaken about whether an event is lucky or unlucky. Ballantyne offers an example of a person with anorexia who vows to drink only water in order to shed pounds, but nonetheless maintains a healthy weight because the water supply is unknowingly connected to a nutritional supplement. Ballantyne argues that the person with anorexia is objectively lucky, even though she might not see it that way (Ballantyne 2012: 322).

Grant for the sake of argument that an event is lucky or unlucky for an agent only if it is positively or negatively significant for them. Also grant that no one is infallible about the manner in which an event is significant and, like the person with anorexia, could be mistaken. Even these strong assumptions about a significance condition do not ameliorate or help with interpreting the results of our studies.

In our second optimism/pessimism study, participants recognized that getting impaled with an RPG was an event significant to Channing Moss and it was bad luck. Study participants also saw that receiving successful surgeries and surviving the RPG attack was a significant event and an instance of good luck. Optimists and pessimists agreed on these points, and they are surely reasonable views, not at all like Ballantyne's reasoning-impaired person with anorexia. The key finding in the second study was that the more optimistic participants rated the bad luck events as being *more* positive than the more pessimistic participants did. Even optimists acknowledge the bad luck events are unlucky, they just do not see them *as* unlucky as the more pessimistic people do. In our view, it is this difference that serves to explain participants' assessments of the compound events of the first optimism/pessimism study. When Channing Moss had an RPG embedded in his abdomen, that was unlucky (the significance condition gets this right). When he survived the whole ordeal, that was lucky (the significance condition gets this right too). However, for optimists, getting impaled with an RPG was not all *that* bad so it made the getting-impaled-and-surviving event a luckier one than the pessimists believed. For pessimists, his getting skewered with an RPG was so unlucky that it diminished the good fortune of his survival. Here the significance condition cannot sort out who is correct.

Overall, Channing Moss was either lucky or unlucky. Optimists think he was luckier than the pessimists do, because they disagree with the pessimists about just how bad Moss's bad luck really was. Barring relativism about luck, the pessimists and the optimists cannot both be right. The significance condition on luck was supposed to determine just who is lucky or unlucky, and to what extent. As

Cognitive Biases and Dispositions

we have seen, though, it fails to provide a principled way to adjudicate between the varying luck judgments of persons at different locations on the optimism/pessimism scale.

The framing and recency effects are cognitive biases in the perception of luck, and lead to inconsistent judgments as to whether a person or an event is lucky or unlucky. Luck attributions also vary by the personality traits of optimism and pessimism. No doubt there are other cognitive peculiarities or psychological qualities that affect our observations and assignments of luck as well. Why does this matter? A kayak paddle half in the water looks bent, and out of the water it does not. Parallel train tracks disappearing into the distance appear to converge. It is when we have perplexing, inconsistent perceptions like these that we turn to a theoretical explanation to sort things out. A decent theory should (1) tell us that in fact the paddle is not really bent and the tracks do not truly converge and (2) explain away the competing perceptions. A theory of optics that could not do those things would be rejected as inadequate for that very reason. No theory of luck is able to tell us that Tara Cooper or Channing Moss really is lucky (or unlucky), much less offer an explanation as to why the alternative interpretation is mistaken. The popular ideas of probability, modality, lack of control, and significance not only fall short, but there is no clear way to see how they might be improved. When theories of luck fail to do their job, a plausible stance is that—like bent paddles and converging tracks—luck is a cognitive illusion. At the very least, "luck" is not a harmless and anodyne concept to which philosophers should blithely help themselves in thinking about morality, epistemology, or free will.

Notes

1 Petronius (1960) ch. 60.
2 "Let us study such a collection, worn in the form of little silver pendants: the four-leaf clover, a pig, a mushroom, a horseshoe, a ladder, and chimney-sweep. The four-leaved clover has taken the place of the three-leaved one which is really suited to be a symbol. The pig is an ancient fertility symbol. The mushroom is an obvious penis-symbol: there are mushrooms which owe their systematic name (*Phallus impudicus*) to their unmistakable resemblance to the male organ. The horseshoe copies the outline of the female genital orifice, and the chimney-sweep, who carries the ladder, appears in this company on account of his activities, with which sexual intercourse is vulgarly compared" (Freud 1917: 64).
3 Although mathematicians tend not to have noticed. See Bewersdorff (2005), Mazur (2010), and Smith (2016).
4 For example, Coffman (2015) and Levy (2011).

References

Ballantyne, N. (2012) "Luck and Interests," *Synthese* 185(3), 319–334.
Bewersdorff, J. (2005) *Luck, Logic, and White Lies: The Mathematics of Games*, Wellesley, MA: A. K. Peters.
Carver, C.S., Scheier, M.F., & Segerstrom, S.C. (2010) "Optimism," *Clinical Psychological Review* 30(7), 879–889.
Coffman, E.J. (2015) *Luck: Its Nature and Significance for Human Knowledge and Agency*. New York: Palgrave Macmillan.
David, F.N. (1962) *Games, Gods, and Gambling*. New York: Hafner Publishing Co.
Day, L., & Maltby, J. (2003) "Belief in Good Luck and Psychological Well-Being: The Mediating Role of Optimism and Irrational Beliefs," *The Journal of Psychology* 137(1), 99–110.
Ebbinghaus, H. (1885) *Memory: A Contribution to Experimental Psychology*, Leipzig: Duncker & Humblot.
Freud, S. (1917) *Introductory Lectures on Psychoanalysis*, New York: Penguin.
Hales, S.D., & Johnson, J.A. (2014) "Luck Attributions and Cognitive Bias," *Metaphilosophy* 45(4–5), 509–528.
———. (2018) "Dispositional Optimism and Luck Attributions: Implications for Philosophical Theories of Luck," *Philosophical Psychology* 31(7), 1027–1045.
Kim, S.-R., Kwon, Y.-S., & Hyun, M.-H. (2015) "The Effects of Belief in Good Luck and Counterfactual Thinking on Gambling Behavior," *Journal of Behavioral Addictions* 4(4), 236–243.
Levy, N. (2011) *Hard Luck: How Luck Undermines Free Will and Moral Responsibility*. Oxford: Oxford University Press.
Lim, M.S.M., & Rogers, R.D. (2017) "Chinese Beliefs in Luck Are Linked to Gambling Problems via Strengthened Cognitive Biases: A Mediation Test," *Journal of Gambling Studies* 33(4), 1325–1336.
Matlin, M.W., & Stang, D.J. (1978) *The Pollyanna Principle: Selectivity in Language, Memory, and Thought*, Boston, MA: Schenkman Publishing Company.

Mazur, J. (2010) *What's Luck Got to Do with It? The History, Mathematics, and Psychology of the Gambler's Illusion*, Princeton, NJ: Princeton University Press.

Petronius (1960) *Satyricon*, W. Arrowsmith, trans., New York: New American Library.

Pritchard, D. (2014) "The Modal Account of Luck," *Metaphilosophy* 45(4–5), 594–619.

Pritchard, D., & Smith, M. (2004) "The Psychology and Philosophy of Luck," *New Ideas in Psychology* 22, 1–28.

Rundus, D. (1971) "Analysis of Rehearsal Processes in Free Recall," *Journal of Experimental Psychology* 89(1), 63–77.

Scheier, M.F., Carver, C.S., & Bridges, M.W. (1994) "Distinguishing Optimism from Neuroticism (and Trait Anxiety, Self-Mastery, and Self-Esteem): A Re-evaluation of the Life Orientation Test," *Journal of Personality and Social Psychology* 67, 1063–1078.

Seneca, L.A. (1917) *Moral Epistles*, R.M. Gummere, trans., Cambridge, MA: Harvard University Press.

Smith, G. (2016) *What the Luck?* New York: The Overlook Press.

Teigen, K.H. (2005) "When a Small Difference Makes a Large Difference: Counterfactual Thinking and Luck," in D.R. Mandel, D.J. Hilton, & P. Catellani (eds.) *The Psychology of Counterfactual Thinking*, London: Routledge, pp. 129–146.

Teigen, K.H., & Jensen, T.K. (2011) "Unlucky Victims or Lucky Survivors? Spontaneous Counterfactual Thinking by Families Exposed to the Tsunami Disaster," *European Psychologist* 16, 48–57.

Tversky, A., & Kahneman, D. (1981) "The Framing of Decisions and the Psychology of Choice," *Science* 211(4481), 453–458.

——. (1986) "Rational Choice and the Framing of Decisions," *The Journal of Business* 59(4), S251–S278.

Whittington, L. . (2016)."Luck, Knowledge, and Value," *Synthese* 193(6), 1615–1633.

Wiseman, R. (2003) *The Luck Factor: Changing Your Luck, Changing Your Life: Four Essential Principles*. New York: Miramax.

Wohl, M.J.A., & Enzle, M.E. (2002) "The Deployment of Personal Luck: Sympathetic Magic and Illusory Control in Games of Pure Chance," *Personality and Social Psychology Bulletin* 28, 1388–1397.

30

LUCK AND RISK

Karl Halvor Teigen

On December 30, 2006, a pickup driver on State Route 59, Utah, lost control over his car, probably speeding. The car broke the guardrail, flipped over a drainage outlet, and landed on all four wheels outside the road facing the wrong direction. A close-up photo, originally published by CNN and later displayed on several internet sites, showed the car precariously balanced on the hillside (Mikkelson & Mikkelson 2007). In a subsequent study (Teigen 2011), this picture was shown to a large class of students who were asked to evaluate five headlines: "An unlucky driver"; "An unusual U-turn"; "With the guardrail as springboard"; "Incredible luck"; "Can thank higher powers." All suggested headlines were rated on scales from 1 to 10. The *guardrail as springboard* received the highest mean score (6.87), but interestingly, *incredible luck* (5.71) was rated much higher than *an unlucky driver* (2.61). After all, the driver had only suffered minor injuries in this dramatic event.

The class was then presented with another, bigger picture of the same event. A photo taken from a distance showed that the truck is standing on the edge of a 200-feet vertical drop. The sight of the abyss made the audience gasp, and when allowed to revise their headline ratings, the students gave *incredible luck* top scores ($M = 8.48$), closely followed by *can thank higher powers* ($M = 8.02$).

The morals to be drawn from this little experiment are threefold: (1) An "incredibly lucky" event is not necessarily attractive, or pleasant. One can safely assume that the driver on State Route 59 wished the accident had never happened. (2) The "luckiness" of an event is crucially dependent upon what did *not* happen, rather than the factual circumstances. Both pictures showed the same factual outcome of the accident, but the second picture made the counterfactual appear far more disastrous and perhaps more salient. (3) When luck intensifies, the step from luck as accidental to luck as magical becomes a small one. Higher powers (God, fate, guardian angels) are summoned in matters of life and death (Pepitone & Saffiotti 1997), and, curiously enough, they tend to arrive on the scene in the last minute, just in time for saving lives, but too late to prevent the accident from happening. It appears, in line with the previous point, that what matters is not so much that lives are saved, but that death is imminent (Pritchard & Smith 2004).

In what follows, I will develop these three observations further, drawing on results from psychological research that examines under which circumstances people are inclined to describe themselves or others as lucky or unlucky. In this chapter we are not concerned either with the reality of luck or with how the concept should ideally be used and understood, but how this term (and its cognates) is used in daily life and in everyday language.

From the opening example and other experimental findings, it appears that luck attributions are particularly frequent in situations involving *risks*. This is based on two central features, which will be examined in turn below, namely the contrastive nature of luck, and the prominence of close counterfactuals in risky situations. People are lucky when an outcome turns out better than one might have feared. The third theme to be developed in this chapter is how people make sense of such events that takes place seemingly outside one's control. Should they be regarded as random, or is there an element of personal or even magical causality involved?

Something Worse Could Have Happened

We examine in this section the contrastive nature of luck (Driver 2012). Events are not lucky or unlucky just in and by themselves, but in comparison to a counterfactual or hypothetical outcome that did *not* occur. When people consider themselves "lucky," they always have such alternative possibilities in mind. They compare themselves to other people (those that are "not so lucky"), or to how their own life would have been "if not for ...." In other words, they imagine what has been called *downward counterfactuals.* If they compare themselves *upwards*, to more enviable others or to something that could have turned out better "if only ...," they might feel unlucky and will speak of their bad luck.

In the simplest case, events are contrasted with a neutral baseline or default, as when an unexpected gift, a lottery prize, a job offer, or a romantic proposal arrive "out of the blue." In such case, the "worse" counterfactual alternative is no gift, no prize, no offer, no proposal, or in other words: business as usual, an uneventful life. Such incidents, where people are surprised by an obviously nice event that did not have to happen, could be called instances of *pure* luck. Similarly, losses and accidents that clearly represent a negative deviation from normalcy, with which they are compared, can be considered pure bad luck. In these cases, the contrasting counterfactuals are often not highlighted, but implied.

But other cases are more mixed, by allowing bad events to be compared with something even worse (and sometimes, good outcomes to be contrasted with outcomes that are even better). In the face of risks and threats, preservation of the status quo can be turned into a lucky event. People will describe a drunk driver as lucky to avoid a collision and a fare dodger fortunate not to be caught by a ticket inspector. Once the damage is done, as with the driver in our opening vignette, one might think that the consequences could have been dramatically worse, making actual accidents appear lucky. Lucky individuals in the media often come in this category, as can be testified by YouTube videos of so-called "lucky people," "lucky drivers," and even "the world's luckiest squirrel" (surviving a 100 mph run-in with a Lamborghini). Use of the term luck to describe such happenings might appear paradoxical, but follow the same logic. Both pure luck and mixed luck incidents compare what happened to a potentially worse alternative, which might be status quo (in the pure case) or something still worse (in the mixed case).

Health personnel conducting open-ended, in-depth interviews with Norwegian tourists coming back from South East Asia after the 2004 tsunami disaster were surprised to find that nearly all (90.6%) interview protocols contained terms designating good luck, often several times in each open-ended interview. In contrast, only five instances of bad luck concepts were found, mostly describing the plight of other people (Teigen & Jensen 2011). In a follow-up study two years later, more than 95% said they had been more lucky than unlucky, the remaining 5% expressed a mix of both. What appeared, from people at home, as the most unlucky Christmas holiday imaginable, became for the survivors a series of lucky coincidences, because it was for them so easy to imagine something even more catastrophic. Their stories were replete with counterfactual statements. "Just incredible luck that we did not live somewhere on the beach" (as originally intended). "This is what we are left with: What *could* have happened. Because we were so insanely lucky when the wave came" (p. 52).

Similar results were obtained from interviews of residents affected by bushfires in Australia (Eriksen & Wilkinson 2017). Nearly all of them (85%) included spontaneous, unsolicited references to good luck, with a mean of 3.05 occurrences per interview. Such terms were almost ten times more frequent than references to bad luck (or bad fortune).

One might think that those least afflicted saw themselves especially lucky. True enough, participants in the tsunami study had all survived. But those most directly exposed to the disaster used the term "lucky" twice as often than those who had been less affected. The bushfire study included "lucky" residents who had their houses burned. In both these studies, nearness to complete disaster was more important than actual damage.

To simplify, people appear (and feel) lucky whenever they obtain an unexpected gain, or when they avoid an expected loss. In this context expected does not mean foreseeable, as counterfactual successes or disasters can be *postcomputed* (Kahneman & Miller 1986), that is, imagined post hoc, as the full picture unfolds and more details of the situation become known. To quote one tsunami survivor: "It became only worse and worse. One felt luckier and luckier all the time" (Teigen & Jensen 2011: 52).

On this background, even good luck experiences can become a mixed blessing. For all we know, "pure" and unequivocal good luck experiences might be less frequent than the mixed ones, as nice events are less effective in instigating counterfactual thinking (Roese 1997). This contrasts with Rescher's (1995) claim that good and bad luck, by definition, represents "a good or bad result, a benefit or a loss. If X wins the lottery, it is good luck; if Z is struck by a falling meteorite, that is bad luck" (p. 32). Now these are pure cases. But in the same author's opening chapter, good luck is illustrated by a very mixed case—namely, the non-bombing of Kokura in World War II. This Japanese city was the original target of the second atomic bomb. But due to accidental weather conditions: haze over Kokura, the bomb was dropped over Nagasaki instead. "And what was an incredible piece of good luck for the inhabitants of Kokura turned equally bad for those of Nagasaki" (Rescher 1995: 3). Here we have an incredible piece of good luck in a city where nothing happened out of the ordinary.

Luck stories in the media are often of the mixed kind. The Croatian music teacher Frane Selak (n.d.) has been called "the world's luckiest man" after cheating death seven times (before winning in the lottery). The same honorary title has been bestowed on Tsutomu Yamaguchi (n.d.), who survived both Hiroshima and Nagasaki. Anat Ben-Tov, survivor of two bus bombings in Tel Aviv, was keenly aware of the mixed nature of luck when interviewed in her hospital bed. "I have no luck, or I have all the luck," she told reporters. "I am not sure which" (Perspectives 1995).

Luck in daily life is of a less dramatic kind. Norwegian students who were asked to describe a recent lucky episode from their own life included some pure positive instances, like finding money in the streets, guessing the right exam questions, or meeting a good friend by chance. But an even greater number of instances were mixed, including risky situations in traffic and sports which had taken a fortunate turn, lost objects that were recovered, ferries and trains that were almost lost, but caught in the last minute, and so on (Teigen 1995: Study 1). Participants in this study also rated their stories for attractiveness ("Is this an experience you would like to have repeated?"). Their ratings formed a bimodal distribution. Only half of the lucky episodes were worth being relived. This ambivalence was confirmed by a second group that read 30 vignettes based on the original stories. They would generally prefer *not* to experience these lucky situations themselves. What mattered was clearly not the valence of the factual outcome by itself, but rather the *difference* in valence between the factual outcome and the imagined counterfactuals. The larger the difference in attractiveness, the luckier the actor was judged to be ($r = .71$).

Good luck and good experiences are, accordingly, not the same. People who were simply asked to tell about *positive* episodes, happy moments, from their daily life, reported incidents of a different nature. Many were of an interpersonal character (receiving a hug, being invited for dinner). Such incidents are nice per se, and need not be contrasted with worse counterfactuals. Stories about *negative* experiences and bad luck episodes were more alike (Teigen 1995: Studies 3 and 4). Why? We can assume that people generally strive for, and achieve, an acceptable state of normalcy or status quo. Bad things that happen will automatically be compared with this default. It has been claimed that counterfactual thinking typically occurs whenever people experience adverse events (Roese 1997), precisely because such events are construed as deviant or "abnormal" (Kahneman & Miller 1986). Their deviance is, accordingly, in need of being examined and explained (Weiner 1985). Thus, negative events and unlucky episodes are similar as both generate "upward" counterfactuals, that is, thoughts about a better outcome than the one that actually occurred. We ask how failures could have been avoided, and blame ourselves and others for not taking preventive measures and "allowing" an accident to occur. In other words, we compare what happened with counterfactuals that "should" or "ought" have been. Such thoughts can be adaptive. According to the "Functional theory of counterfactual thinking" (Epstude & Roese 2008; Roese & Epstude 2017), they play an important role in motivating behavior and preparing for the future.

Close Calls

We observed in the previous section that luck depends on counterfactuals, but these can go both ways. When will a situation be compared with something better, and when will thoughts of worse outcomes be particularly prominent? Epstude and Roese (2008) claimed that counterfactuals are mostly of an "upward" nature, and for good reasons, as thoughts about a better life can help us to achieve it. If they are right, why should we sometimes bother with downward counterfactuals and imagine life as worse? Yet such "downward" thoughts were, in our studies, a prerequisite for feeling lucky, rather than just feeling good.

It has been argued that downward comparisons can also be adaptive, as they make people more content with their lot ("we did not win, but at least we made it to the podium"; "the car is wrecked, but at least we are alive"). Such thoughts apply especially to situational features that cannot be changed, and to people that will not be given another chance, but have to rest content with whatever they have got (Markman et al. 1993).

But downward thoughts need not be driven by a motive to feel better or to be preserved by their adaptive functions. Sometimes they occur as the result of a purely cognitive or attentional process that makes dangers "pop up" in the perceptual field. Thus, downward counterfactuals emerge spontaneously whenever worse outcomes are perceived as *close*.

Participants in the studies cited above were asked to evaluate not only the attractiveness, but also the closeness of the counterfactual event. How *easily* could the alternative outcome have happened? "I dropped a pot of potatoes onto the kitchen floor—boiling water splashing all around—but I was not hurt." This was, somewhat paradoxically, presented as a good luck incident, the reason being that the actor could easily imagine being scalded in a situation that was already out of control. Degree of closeness (ratings of how easily the alternative outcome could have happened) turned out to be highly correlated ($r = .63$) with ratings of degree of luck. The protagonist in the potato incident seemed to have accepted the dropping of the pan as a fact and being splashed with boiling water as a close, readily imaginable possibility. Similarly, the tourists in the tsunami study must have felt that they were closer to disaster than to safety. The emphasis on closeness as a gradable determinant of luck seems to agree well with the central role of modal nearness (as opposed to objective probabilities) in Pritchard's (2014) modal account of luck.

Counterfactual closeness can be achieved in different ways. Depending upon the domain in question, a real or imagined alternative can be spatially, temporally, socially, or conceptually close. According to Construal Level Theory (Trope & Liberman 2010), all these distances are subjectively exchangeable in the sense that they have similar psychological effects. Closeness to a negative event can, accordingly, be conceived in terms of perceived spatial or temporal distance, as when you are "lucky" to catch the last bus seconds before it leaves, or the car just in front of you is singled out for police control. But closeness can also be achieved in a more dynamic sense, as when a series of events describe a discernible upward or downward trend, pointing toward a specific outcome that might seem "doomed" to occur unless diverted. Participants who were asked to illustrate their good luck experiences as a cartoon in three frames, produced stories where the two first scenes typically indicated a downward trajectory, which took a sudden upward turn in the last scene (Teigen, Evensen, Samoilow, & Vatne 1999).

This implies that the same outcome might illustrate good or bad luck according to the order in which events take place. A player winning, and then losing, the same amount of money is considered unlucky. But if he wins back an initial loss, people will consider it an example of good luck. Similar effects can be obtained from the way a tale is told (Hales & Johnson 2014). Good news after bad news gives a luckier impression than bad news after good, regardless of the chronological order of events (Teigen, Evensen, Samoilow, & Vatne 1999). Sometimes, two misfortunes can appear luckier than one. A traveller, who had to cancel his trip because of illness, was judged to feel "a little lucky" when his flight was cancelled anyway. This would make his illness less critical, by turning the counterfactual into a semifactual: "Even without the illness, my trip would have to be called off."

Luck has, by some authors (e.g., Rescher 1995; Wagenaar 1988), been related to perceived probability, suggesting that a positive outcome is perceived as luckier when it is believed to be improbable, or rare. Our studies indicate that high probability of the counterfactual outcome is even more crucial than low probability for what actually took place. To estimate probabilities in retrospect of something that did not happen might seem odd. Yet people do it on a regular basis. After a game, a player might say: "We had a good chance of winning the match." From this, most listeners will infer that the team did not win, despite the "good chance" (Teigen 1998a).

How are such post-hoc probabilities assessed? Studies indicate that probability estimates of what happened and what did not happen will be estimated in different ways. To assess the chances for the actual outcome, most people attempt to turn the clock back and try to remember or imagine what the chances looked like beforehand. The probabilities for the counterfactual outcome can be assessed in a different and more direct way through a simple closeness judgment. Imagine that Ivan and Boris play Russian roulette with two bullets (to enhance excitement). Both players survive. It turns out that Ivan's six-chambered revolver has stopped spinning wedged in between the two bullets, whereas the spinning barrel in Boris' revolver came to rest between two empty chambers. When asked who had the better chances of survival (the factual outcome), most people said that chances were the same (4/6) for both players. But when asked who was more likely to be killed (the counterfactual), a majority agreed with Ivan, who claimed he had been close.

This *closeness heuristic* for assessing probabilities of outcomes that did not happen can lead to elevated risk judgments. In one study, Norwegian students (attending classes in law and economics) were asked whether they had ever been in a life-threatening situation. Of 146 students, 80 (55.8%) said yes. Traffic accidents and near-misses were common. Other situations ranged from mountain climbing, parachuting, and violent assaults, to incidents of choking and poisoning. Illnesses were rarely mentioned. They were then asked to estimate their probability of being killed and finally to rate how "close" they had been to death on a scale from 0 to 10 (Teigen 2005: Experiment 2). Estimated probabilities of death ranged from 10% to 100% (*sic*), with a mean of 55.9%. If we take these figures literally, one would expect a third of the Norwegian population to be lost before the age of 25. But these probabilities were not derived from frequencies. Instead they were strongly correlated ($r = .84$) with closeness ratings, indicating that proximity and probability were, in this study, almost interchangeable concepts.

When Risk Breeds Luck

The studies reported in the previous sections demonstrate that luck in daily life typically occurs in situations where worse outcomes are perceived as close. Such incidents have much in common with situations involving risks. We now take this observation further by discussing the role of risks and hazards in generating lucky incidents (in addition to producing, sometimes, unlucky ones).

A risk is usually defined as the probability for an aversive event. In high-risk domains, or high-risk environments, probabilities are high, or the consequences are severe, or both. In the risk management literature, risks are often color-coded from green (acceptable risk), through yellow/orange (moderate risk) to red (high risk) in a diagram with frequency or probability on the vertical axis and amount of damage along the horizontal axis. In these charts, we find a green area in the lower left corner, red risk in the upper right, and moderate risks along the diagonal, indicating that risks can be regarded as moderate with frequent, but minor accidents, or with more severe consequences occurring rarely. In other domains, for instance in medicine, the consequences are typically specified (e.g., death risks, or risks of specific side effects); degree of risk and the probability of this specific outcome will then become synonymous concepts. In business and gambling contexts, "risky" prospects refer more commonly to those with highly variable outcomes, with opportunities for big losses as well as for substantial gains. When lay people are asked to explain the meaning of risk, they produce definitions similar to these, although in practice they seem to attend more closely to outcome magnitudes than to the probability dimension (Huber 2012; Teigen, Brun, & Frydenlund 1999). Despite the fact that risks seem to be ubiquitous, and are discussed to an extent that have made some scholars speak about modernity as a "risk society" (Beck 1992; Giddens 1999), the probabilities associated with most risks are, in a Western society, quite low. Substances, activities, or technologies with, say, more than a 10% chance of causing severe damage would soon be avoided or banned. With even lower probabilities, the probabilistic side of risk becomes more difficult to process and grasp. In an attempt to standardize verbal descriptions of risk, it has been suggested that adverse responses in a medical context that exceeds 1 percent should be labeled "high risk" (Calman 1996). But most people expect "high risk" to denote much higher chances, perhaps around 60% (Berry 2004). The gap between objectively measured and subjectively perceived risks indicate that people will see dangers around and feel they are substantial, even in a relatively safe environment. From this, we can infer that most people who find themselves exposed to risks (as they define it) will escape unharmed. Still, they might feel the presence of close and worse counterfactuals. In other words, they might feel lucky.

If luck depends on close and worse counterfactuals, as discussed above, risky or hazardous situations should have the potential of generating luck. Such situations might be considered *dangerous*. In one study (Teigen 1998b), student participants were asked to briefly describe incidents from last year that they had experienced as dangerous or risky, regardless of actual outcome. They were further asked to rate the degree of good or bad luck involved, and to what extent the event had been a pleasant or unpleasant one. In addition to describing what happened, they were also asked to indicate whether something else could "easily" have happened, and how pleasant or unpleasant that could have been.

Almost half of the stories turned out to be about risky traffic situations, ranging from collisions and vehicles out of control, to careless crossing of the road on foot. Other risky incidents involved leaking boats, diving, parachuting, skiing, climbing, falling, and assaults. Most incidents (87%) were described as unpleasant. Yet a majority (70%) declared themselves as more lucky than unlucky. The explanation of this apparent paradox lies in the fact that (a) something else could easily have happened (in nine out of ten stories), and (b) that this alternative outcome would have been even more disastrous.

The stories were subsequently distributed to a new group for obtaining a "second opinion" from outsiders. This panel of peers perceived the original situations as very unpleasant but also quite lucky. They also judged an alternative, worse outcome as having been close. Moreover, ratings of good luck correlated strongly with ratings of counterfactual closeness ($r = .76$) and counterfactual aversiveness ($r = .78$). So, for instance, the situation judged to be most "lucky"—a driver miraculously avoiding a head-on collision with two trucks racing side by side on a narrow road—was also given top scores for dangerousness, closeness of counterfactual, and potential aversive consequences. In contrast, the most "unlucky" person—who had spoken to some strangers in the street and received an unexpected blow to his head—was among the few who had been in a dangerous situation that turned out worse than could have been expected.

Two separate studies (Teigen 1998b: Experiments 1 and 2) showed high correlations between judged dangerousness and perceived luck (r = .69 and r = .87). Perhaps the very concept of "danger" implies, for some people, situations that end well, but *could* be disastrous (even if the instructions asked participants to report situations that had been dangerous regardless of consequences). To make sure that negative consequences would be included, participants were, in a third experiment, asked to report incidences in which they had behaved in a careless or negligent way. They were again asked to rate their own and other people's stories for degree of carelessness and degree of good or bad luck. How pleasant/unpleasant were the incidents, how easily could they have led to a different outcome, and, in that case, how pleasant/unpleasant would this counterfactual outcome have been.

Stories about carelessness ranged from thoughtless behavior in traffic to poor exam preparation, spilled coffee, and unprotected sex. Careless episodes were generally viewed as more unpleasant than pleasant, and could easily (in 83% of the cases) have led to outcomes that were even worse. As a result, people regarded both their own and others' incidents of careless behavior as more lucky than unlucky, with good luck being positively related to degree of carelessness. The most careless participant had jumped with a paraglider without taking instructions, plummeted to the ground, and was only saved by a thin layer of snow. He was also the luckiest one. In contrast, another participant had dined without making use of the table napkin and had spilled brown sauce on her white sweater. Not so thoughtless, but not very lucky, either.

These studies lead to the perhaps paradoxical conclusion that people who are committed to safety and prepare themselves for all eventualities will rarely experience good luck. By shielding themselves from bad luck they have fewer close calls to celebrate. They might enjoy safety and be better off than the careless and the unprepared, but also less lucky.

Random vs. Personal and Magical Luck

A lucky turn of events, a lucky coincidence, a lucky free kick in a football game, could easily, almost by definition have been less lucky. The notion of *random* luck, or luck "by chance" seems primarily applicable to unlikely incidences, or rather, to situations where a worse outcome is deemed more likely than the factual one. By attributing an outcome to random luck, we claim that it is not predictable or controllable, and seem to deny that a simple causal explanation can be found. Yet this does not always stop people from going a step further and asking for principles or forces "behind" the good or bad luck. By doing so, they frequently overstep the boundaries of science, and "misattribute" (Wiseman & Watt 2006) phenomena that they find remarkable and strange to paranormal powers, which scientists find even more remarkable and strange. Instead of giving an unlikely outcome (to be saved "against all odds"), a likely explanation (it happened by chance) they invent an *unlikely* explanation (for instance, supernatural intervention), which makes the outcome appear more likely (Griffiths & Tenenbaum 2007). Some survivors of the tsunami disaster seemed torn between a mundane and a paranormal luck concept, as put by one: "It is not luck, it is more than luck. It is a very strong feeling" (Teigen & Jensen 2011: 52), perhaps indicating that miracles cannot be explained by chance alone. The tension between random luck and magic luck has been observed by several authors (Cohen 1960).

To illustrate, individuals who claim that they *believe* in luck do not simply mean that they have realized the role of chance in life (Bandura 1998; Mlodinow 2008; Taleb 2007), but indicate a conviction that outcomes of a certain kind are governed by occult, non-material forces. This became evident in Wagenaar and Keren's (1988) studies of gamblers and football fans. When asked to estimate the role of chance vs. skill in blackjack, or for the outcome of a football game, they argued that luck should be included as an important third factor. Luck was considered similar to chance in some respects, for instance by being unpredictable, but was in other respects more similar to skills, by being causal and operating over a stretch of time (not unlike a resource that can be exploited and consumed).

Beliefs in magic luck can take many forms. Perhaps most popular is the belief that some people are more disposed for good luck outcomes than others. In a Japanese survey, 79.6% answered affirmatively to the statement: "There are individual differences in the strength of luck" (Murakami 2014). Perceived individual differences also form the basis for Darke and Freedman's (1997a) *Belief in Good Luck Scale*. This scale measures agreement with statements like "Some people are consistently lucky and others are unlucky" and "I consider myself to be a lucky person." Agreement with such items seems to imply both a belief in the existence of luck as an individual characteristic and being personally favored by it. North American students tended to agree rather than to disagree with both these items. In a different study, Darke and Freedman (1997b) found that high believers (according to this scale) tended to take more risks after winning a gamble, while low scorers risked less after winning. Perhaps they fell prey to a different superstition, namely a belief in *fleeting luck*, or a belief that good and bad events tend to take turns and alternate in periods and perhaps cancel each other out. This view of luck as a changeable state rather than a trait characterizing certain individuals has been incorporated in more recently developed scales of belief in luck (Öner-Özkan 2003; Young et al. 2009). Other scales have been developed to distinguish other aspects of perceived luck, such as luck in gambling (Wohl et al. 2011), belief in bad vs. good luck (André 2009), and beliefs in personal luck vs. fortunate circumstances (André 2009; Thompson & Prendergast 2013).

It might, however, be misguided to dismiss all such beliefs as evidence of magical thinking, as they can partly reflect folk theories of randomness, rather than paranormal views. Moreover, it is not necessarily irrational to regard good and bad luck as associated with individual differences, as some people might make better use of random happenings than others. Thus "lucky" people do not have to possess a magical ability to bend chance in their favor, but may be skilful at arranging conditions for luck to occur and be quick in seizing the opportunities that arise. Occasions for luck come to those that lead an active and eventful life, do not give up easily, keep their eyes open, and expose themselves to serendipitous happenings. From these observations, psychologists have even claimed that people can be taught to be luckier (Wiseman 2003). As for bad luck, the controversial notion of *accident proneness* implies that some people experience more than their share of unlucky incidents (Day et al. 2012; Visser et al. 2007). There need not be a mystery involved; it suffices to think that some people are more inattentive and commit more mistakes, than do others (Broadbent et al. 1982; Wallace et al. 2002). From the study of careless episodes (Teigen 1998b) reported above, one might perhaps predict that mindless and accident-prone people experience both more bad luck and more good luck events in their lives.

Beliefs in oneself as a lucky or unlucky person can further be based on personal memories of fortunate or unfortunate episodes in one's own life, without assumptions of hidden forces or a continued future luck (Thompson & Prendergast 2013). Interestingly, the relevance of such events depends critically on counterfactuals rather than what really happened. Participants in one study (Teigen, Brun, & Frydenlund 1999: Study 1) were asked to judge their degree of good or bad luck in life after recalling autobiographical incidents where something clearly positive or negative had happened to them. Both groups rated themselves as more lucky than unlucky, regardless of the type of incidents they had recalled. Two other groups were asked to describe incidents where something clearly positive or negative could "easily" have happened, but did not happen after all. These participants rated themselves as very lucky after considering bad things that had not happened, and more unlucky after recalling opportunities they had missed. So, looking back upon your luck in life: do not count your blessings, count your risks.

Close calls work for gamblers, as well. Wohl and Enzle (2003) found that gamblers rated themselves as luckier on the Belief in Good Luck Scale after being near a big loss than when being close to winning. It worked prospectively as well: Those near a big loss bet more on a subsequent game of roulette than did those who had been close to winning. More recently, Wu, van Dijk, Li, Aitken, and Clark (2017) found that near-loss players felt luckier than near-winners on a spinner task; they felt especially lucky when the spinner stopped just after passing through a region of losses, compared to when it stopped just before. The players who had managed to pass "unharmed" through the loss sections were also willing to bet more.

The boundary line between the mundane and the mysterious, the normal and the paranormal is, in this area, a hazy one. Related to the belief in personal luck, people tend to appreciate a risk-taking manager (who succeeds by chance) as equally competent as a manager who succeeds without taking risks, and both are seen as much more competent than a manager who takes a chance, but fails (Dillon & Tinsley 2008). Related to beliefs about fleeting luck, people will adopt procedures and rituals designed to make good luck stay longer and chase bad luck away. Xu, Zwick, and Schwarz (2012) observed that people who recalled or experienced bad luck took more risks in a new gamble after wiping their hands, as if they were afraid that their bad fortune would stick. Those with good luck became more cautious after wiping their hands, as if they felt their good luck would be washed away. Situations where risks and uncertainties abound (sports, exams, travels, health) can easily become a hotbed for even more elaborate magical rituals to invoke good luck and ward off misfortunes. Survivors of still greater risks are more disposed to attribute their luck to divine intervention. The opening example of this chapter—the pickup on the edge of an abyss—was on one internet site introduced with the prophetic words: "I bet this guy will be in church Sunday" (Mikkelson & Mikkelson n.d.). Not a poor bet.

Conclusions

Luck and risk are intimately related, perhaps more closely than most people think. Regardless of one's views on luck, as random, personal, or magic, people are considered *lucky* when escaping risks unharmed, and *unlucky* when harmed. Degree of good luck depends on closeness and on severity of this implied or imagined harm, degree of bad luck upon the severity of harm as well as closeness of a (missed) escape. Since most situations have a potential of a better ending but also for ending worse, it is reasonable to conclude that luck primarily exists not in the outside world, but in the minds of men. Hales and Johnson (2014) called luck accordingly "a cognitive illusion," but, as such, one with tangible consequences. Take a risky decision or a hazardous maneuver that went well "by chance." Contemplating the alternative, one might conclude that luck is on our side, and feel protected. Alternatively, one might see the closeness as a wake-up call, a disaster averted this time by sheer luck, and feel alarmed. Dillon, Tinsley, and Burns (2013) distinguish between *resilient* near-misses (in the first case) and *vulnerable* near-misses (in the second). They observe that individuals who experience resilient near-misses also miss an opportunity for learning. They will be more likely to ignore hazard warnings and be less prepared for a future disaster.

People are not only lucky when they run objective risks and are physically close to disaster. When questioned about their luck in life, people often bring up themes of a more existential character, like being lucky to have a family, to have good health, or to live in a peaceful society (Teigen 1997). Such descriptions of more permanent aspects of their luck are almost identical to stories about what they are *grateful* for in life. Although not endangered, these assets become only lucky by being contrasted with a downward counterfactual. When people are asked *why* they feel lucky, and grateful, for having a good life, they go to the opposite extreme and claim they "could" have lived in poverty or war. People have powerful imaginations. While closeness is essential for spontaneous counterfactuals, it is less critical for people's deliberate assessments of their luck in life. When students who are "lucky" to be born in Norway, are asked to consider "what could have been different in your life?"—they go to the other extreme and suggest a third world country. They never say: "I could have lived in Sweden."

References

André, N. (2009) "I Am Not a Lucky Person: An Examination of the Dimensionality of Beliefs around Chance," *Journal of Gambling Studies* 25, 473–487.

Bandura, A. (1998) "Exploration of Fortuitous Determinants of Life Paths," *Psychological Inquiry* 9, 95–99.

Beck, U. (1992) *Risk Society: Towards a New Modernity*, London: Sage.

Berry, D. (2004) *Risk, Communication, and Health Psychology*, London: Open University Press.

Broadbent, D.E., Cooper, P.F., Fitzgerald, P., & Parkes, K.R. (1982) "The Cognitive Failures Questionnaire (CFQ) and its Correlates," *British Journal of Clinical Psychology* 21, 1–16.

Calman, K.C. (1996) "Cancer; Science and Society and the Communication of Risk," *British Medical Journal* 313, 802–804.

Cohen, J. (1960) *Chance, Skill, and Luck: The Psychology of Guessing and Gambling*, Harmondsworth, UK: Penguin Books.

Darke, P.R., & Freedman, J.L. (1997a) "The Belief in Good Luck Scale," *Journal of Research in Personality* 31, 486–511.

———. (1997b) "Lucky Events and Belief in Luck: Paradoxical Effects on Confidence and Risk Taking," *Personality and Social Psychology Bulletin* 23, 378–388.

Day, A.J., Brasher, K., & Bridger, R.S. (2012) "Accident Proneness Revisited: The Role of Psychological Stress and Cognitive Failure," *Accident Analysis and Prevention* 49, 532–535.

Dillon, R.L., & Tinsley, C.H. (2008) "How Near Misses Influence Decision Making Under Risk: A Missed Opportunity for Learning," *Management Science* 54, 1425–1440.

Dillon, R.L., Tinsley, C.H., & Burns, W. (2014) "Near Misses and Future Disaster Preparedness," *Risk Analysis* 34, 1907–1922.

Driver, J. (2012) "Luck and Fortune in Moral Evaluation," in Martijn Blaauw (ed.) *Contrastivism in Philosophy: New Perspectives*, New York: Routledge, pp. 154–172.

Epstude, K., & Roese, N.J. (2008) "The Functional Theory of Counterfactual Thinking," *Personality and Social Psychology Review* 12, 168–192.

Eriksen, C., & Wilkinson, C. (2017) "Examining Perceptions of Luck in Post-bushfire Sense-making in Australia," *International Journal of Disaster Risk Reduction* 24, 242–250.

Frane Selak (n.d.) *Wikipedia*, https://en.wikipedia.org/wiki/Frane_Selak

Giddens, A. (1999) "Risk and Responsibility," *Modern Law Review* 62, 1–10.

Griffiths, T.L., & Tenenbaum, J.B. (2007) "From Mere Coincidences to Meaningful Discoveries," *Cognition* 103, 180–226.

Hales, S.D., & Johnson, J.A. (2014) "Luck Attribution and Cognitive Bias," *Metaphilosophy* 45, 509–528.

Huber, O. (2012) "Risky Decisions: Active Risk Management," *Current Directions in Psychological Science* 21, 26–30.

Kahneman, D., & Miller, D.T. (1986) "Norm Theory: Comparing Reality to its Alternatives," *Psychological Review* 93, 136–153.

Markman, K.D., Gavanski, I., Sherman, S.J., & McMullen, M.N. (1993) "The Mental Simulation of Better and Worse Possible Worlds," *Journal of Experimental Social Psychology* 29, 87–109.

Mikkelson, D.P., & Mikkelson, B. (2007) "Livin' on the Edge," *Snopes.com*. www.snopes.com/photos/accident/culvert.asp

Mlodinow, L. (2008) *The Drunkard's Walk: How Randomness Rules our Lives*, Harmondsworth, UK: Penguin Books.

Murakami, K. (2014) "Absolute and Relative Judgments in Relation to Strength of Belief in Good Luck," *Social Behavior and Personality* 42, 1105–1116.

Öner-Özkan, B. (2003) "Revised Form of the Belief in Good Luck Scale in a Turkish Sample," *Psychological Reports* 93, 585–594.

Pepitone, A., & Saffiotti, L. (1997) "The Selectivity of Nonmaterial Beliefs in Interpreting Life Events," *European Journal of Social Psychology* 27, 23–35.

"Perspectives '95" (1995) *Newsweek* 42, December 25.

Pritchard, D. (2014) "The Modal Account of Luck," *Metaphilosophy* 45, 594–619.

Pritchard, D., & Smith, M. (2004) "The Psychology and Philosophy of Luck," *New Ideas in Psychology* 22, 1–28.

Rescher, N. (1995) *Luck: The Brilliant Randomness of Everyday Life*, New York: Farrar, Straus and Giroux.

Roese, N.J. (1997) "Counterfactual Thinking," *Psychological Bulletin* 121, 133–148.

Roese, N.J., & Epstude, K. (2017) "The Functional Theory of Counterfactual Thinking: New Evidence, New Challenges, New Insights," *Advances in Experimental Social Psychology* 56, 1–79.

Taleb, N.N. (2007) *The Black Swan: The Impact of the Highly Probable*, New York: Random House.

Teigen, K.H. (1995) "How Good is Good Luck? The Role of Counterfactual Thinking in the Perception of Lucky and Unlucky Events," *European Journal of Social Psychology* 25, 281–302.

———. (1997) "Luck, Envy, and Gratitude: It Could Have Been Different," *Scandinavian Journal of Psychology* 38, 313–323.

———. (1998a) "When the Unreal Is More Likely Than the Real: Post Hoc Probability Judgments and Counterfactual Closeness," *Thinking and Reasoning* 4, 147–177.

———. (1998b) "Hazards Mean Luck: Counterfactual Thinking and Perceptions of Good and Bad Fortune in Reports of Dangerous Situations and Careless Behaviour," *Scandinavian Journal of Psychology* 39, 235–248.

——. (2005) "The Proximity Heuristic in Judgments of Accident Probabilities," *British Journal of Psychology* 96, 423–440.

——. (2011) "Flaks og uflaks—bare tilfeldigheter?" [Good and Bad Luck: When the Incidental Looks Intentional], *Tidsskrift for Norsk Psykologforening* 48, 1072–1079.

Teigen, K.H., Brun, W., & Frydenlund, R. (1999) "Judgments of Risk and Probability: The Role of Frequentistic Information," *Journal of Behavioral Decision Making* 12, 123–139.

Teigen, K.H., Evensen, P.C., Samoilow, D.K., & Vatne, K.B. (1999) "Good and Bad Luck: How to Tell the Difference," *European Journal of Social Psychology* 29, 981–1010.

Teigen, K.H., & Jensen, T.K. (2011) "Unlucky Victims or Lucky Survivors: Spontaneous Counterfactual Thinking by Families Exposed to the Tsunami Disaster," *European Psychologist* 16, 48–57.

Thompson, E.R., & Prendergast, G.P. (2013) "Belief in Luck and Luckiness: Conceptual Clarification and New Measure Validation," *Personality and Individual Differences* 54, 501–506.

Trope, Y., & Liberman, N. (2010) "Construal-level Theory of Psychological Distance," *Psychological Review* 117, 440–463.

Tsutomo Yamaguchi (n.d.) *Wikipedia*, https://en.wikipedia.org/wiki/Tsutomo_Yamaguchi

Visser, E., Pijl, Y.J., Stolk, R.P., Neeleman, J., & Rosmalen, J.G.M. (2007) "Accident Proneness, Does it Exist? A Review and Meta-analysis," *Accident Analysis and Prevention* 39(3), 556–564.

Wagenaar, W.A. (1988) *Paradoxes of Gambling Behaviour*, Hove, UK: Lawrence Erlbaum.

Wagenaar, W.A., & Keren, G.B. (1988) "Chance and Luck Are Not the Same," *Journal of Behavioral Decision Making* 1, 65–75.

Wallace, J.C., Kass, S.J., & Stanny, C.J. (2002) "The Cognitive Failures Questionnaire Revisited: Dimensions and Correlates," *The Journal of General Psychology* 129, 238–256.

Weiner, B. (1985) "'Spontaneous' Causal Thinking," *Psychological Bulletin* 97, 74–84.

Wiseman, R. (2003) *The Luck Factor: Changing Your Luck, Changing Your Life, the Four Essential Principles*, London, UK: Miramax.

Wiseman, R., & Watt, C.A. (2006) "Belief in Psychic Ability and the Misattribution Hypothesis: A Qualitative Review," *British Journal of Psychology* 97, 323–338.

Wohl, M.J.A., & Enzle, M.E. (2003) "The Effects of Near Wins and Near Losses on Self-perceived Personal Luck and Subsequent Gambling Behavior," *Journal of Experimental Social Psychology* 39, 184–191.

Wohl, M.J.A., Stewart, M.J., & Young, M.M. (2011) "Personal Luck Usage Scale (PLUS): Psychometric Validation of a Measure of Gambling-related Belief in Luck as Personal Possession," *International Gambling Studies* 11, 7–21.

Wu, Y., van Dijk, E., Li, H., Aitken, M., & Clark, L. (2017) "On the Counterfactual Nature of Gambling Near-misses: An Experimental Study," *Journal of Behavioral Decision Making*. doi: 10.1002/bdm.2010

Young, M.J., Chen, N., & Morris, M.W. (2009) "Belief in Stable and Fleeting Luck and Achievement Motivation," *Personality and Individual Differences* 47, 150–154.

Xu, A.J., Zwick, R., & Schwarz, N. (2012) "Washing Away Your (Good or Bad) Luck: Physical Cleansing Affects Risk-taking Behavior," *Journal of Experimental Psychology: General* 141, 26–30.

31

EMOTIONAL RESPONSES TO LUCK, RISK, AND UNCERTAINTY

Sabine Roeser

Introduction

"I am so lucky"—that is a statement that typically also involves an emotional experience, such as relief, gratefulness, bliss, happiness, depending on the situation and the specific circumstances. Can our emotions tell us anything meaningful about our experience of luck? And what about notions that are related to luck, such as risk and uncertainty? This chapter explores these questions. I argue that luck, risk, and uncertainty are closely intertwined, and that emotions can provide us with important insights into the evaluative aspects of these notions.

Luck, Risk and Uncertainty

The notions luck, risk, and uncertainty are closely related. We are and feel lucky when an uncertain development that involved a risk or chance of a negative outcome turns out well. If the probability of a positive outcome was high from the start, our feeling of "being lucky" will be less strong than in the case of a low probability of a positive outcome. Furthermore, the importance of the outcome will also play a role in how much weight we attach to our experience of being lucky. In other words, the probability as well as the importance of the possible positive or negative outcome will play a role in our evaluation and experience of being lucky. In the literature on risk and uncertainty, the notion risk is usually used in contexts where probabilities are known and uncertainty in contexts where probabilities are unknown. Based on this terminology, we can say that in situations of uncertainty, the variable that matters for our assessment and experience of being lucky is then the importance we assign to the possible positive or negative outcome. This is a first crude characterization of the inter-relation between the notions luck, risk, and uncertainty. Further on, I will also examine the relevance of counterfactual and modal accounts of luck.

I have mentioned the notions of feeling, assessment, and experience. The question arises what the relation and relevance of these notions is in the context of luck, risk, and uncertainty. In the following sections, I will explore this by examining the role of emotions for our assessment and experience of risk, uncertainty, and luck, respectively. I start with risk, because the field of risk assessment and the role of emotions therein is more well-studied at this point than the role of emotion in the contexts of uncertainty and luck. I will develop my arguments for the latter contexts based on my examination of emotions in the context of risk.

356

Emotions and Risk

Risks can relate to a variety of issues, for example, technological risks, health risks, or risks related to important life goals; such as the risk of a plane crash, of a nuclear meltdown, of contracting a deadly disease, or of being rejected for a research grant application. Risks give rise to emotional responses, most typically to fear of the unwanted and uncertain consequences, but also to indignation in case of unwanted exposure to negative effects or feelings of responsibility in case oneself has a role in creating or mitigating risks. Emotions are usually met with suspicion in public decision making as they are seen as a threat to rationality. Policy makers and scientific experts typically emphasize the need for objective, rational information and methods of risk assessment.

This is also reflected in mainstream academic research on risk. Emotions have been an important topic in research on risk perception (Slovic 2010). Such research shows that emotions play an important role in laypeople's risk perception. Usually, risk scholars see emotions as contrary to reason or rationality. This is based on the highly influential "Dual Process Theory" (DPT), developed most famously by Nobel Prize winner Daniel Kahneman (2011). According to DPT, our mental capacities fall into two different systems: system 1 is considered to be intuitive and emotional and works fast, but is prone to biases, system 2 is taken to be rational and normatively superior to system 1 but comes at the cost of being slow and requiring more mental effort. This has led scholars to draw a variety of conclusions: to argue that in decision making about risk rational approaches should overrule emotions (Sunstein 2005), to accept and follow supposedly irrational emotions for democratic (Loewenstein et al. 2001) or pragmatic (De Hollander & Hanemaaijer 2003) reasons. Slovic et al. (2002, 2004) and Kahan (2008) see emotions as indications of what people value; still, Slovic et al. (2002, 2004) argue that emotions should be checked by analytical methods.

However, there are other theories of emotions, which see them not so much as contrary to rationality but rather as a specific form of rationality, namely *practical rationality*. For example, the neuropsychologist Antonio Damasio (1994) has shown that people with brain defects who lose their capacity to feel emotions also lose their capacity to make practical and moral judgments in concrete circumstances, while their IQ remains unaffected. Furthermore, these patients make risk judgments that deviate significantly from those of others (Damasio 1994).

Furthermore, numerous emotion scholars from philosophy and psychology have developed so-called "cognitive theories of emotions" (e.g. Frijda 1986; Lazarus 1991). Some of these theories hold that emotions are *based* on cognitions (appraisal theory, Scherer 1984), others even see emotions as a *form* of cognition (Solomon 1993). Several philosophers have argued that paradigmatic emotions are affective and cognitive at the same time (Nussbaum 2001; Roberts 2003; Zagzebski 2003; Roeser 2011).

Philosophers have argued that there is a large variety of affective states, such as feelings, moods, and cognitive emotions (Ben Ze'ev 2000; Griffith 1997). While many social psychologists and decision theorists focus on non-cognitive states such as feelings and spontaneous gut reactions, philosophers are often more interested in cognitive emotions that have a narrative structure and are relevant for moral reflection (cf. Roberts 2003). It is important to be aware of this heterogeneity of affective states, as presumably they can play different roles and have different distinctive features. Importantly, while unreflective gut reactions might indeed be highly susceptible to biases, cognitive, narrative, and moral emotions can play an important role in moral judgment (Roeser 2011). Emotions are an important source of insight into moral values (Goldie 2000; Brady 2013; Roeser & Todd 2014).

These ideas can also shed different light on the role of emotions in the context of risk. As has been argued by ethicists and social scientists, risk is not a purely technical notion, but it also entails ethical and societal aspects (Fischhoff et al. 1981; Shrader-Frechette 1991; Krimsky & Golding 1992; Asveld & Roeser 2009; Roeser et al. 2012). The standard definition of risk as used by quantitative risk scholars, engineers, risk analysts, and risk managers is in terms of the probability of an unwanted effect, and they use quantitative approaches such as (risk) cost benefit analysis in order to decide which of different risky options is preferable. However, as risk ethicists and social scientists have pointed out, this is highly problematic. First of all, there are methodological complications, such as how to measure and compare risks and benefits, and they might be incommensurable (Espinoza 2009). Furthermore, what counts as an "unwanted effect" already entails a value judgment. The most common measure is in terms of human fatalities. But what about people who get injured due to an accident, or who have long-term negative health effects due to a polluting factory? And what about negative effects for animals and the environment? In the standard accounts of risk, they are only included to the extent that they also affect human wellbeing, but this implies an anthropocentric stance that is far from value neutral and should be made explicit and be the subject of moral evaluation. Different kinds of ethical values can be included in mathematical models of risk, but this *presupposes* an ethical evaluation, it cannot *replace* it (Roeser 2018). Furthermore, it is questionable whether the same model can hold for different contexts, or whether one might need context-specific evaluations, given insights from context-sensitive approaches to ethics such as developed by Ross (1967[1930]), Dancy (2004), and in medical ethics by Beauchamp and Childress (2006). Yet another problem is that cost benefit analysis is based on expected utility theory, which is a consequentialist approach. In ethics, well-known objections against pure forms of consequentialism are that it does not acknowledge considerations of justice, fairness, equity, and autonomy. Concerning justice, fairness, and equity, important questions are: who undergoes the risks, and who reaps the benefits? Concerning autonomy, important questions are: do people have a say concerning the risks to which they are exposed? Who is included in the decision making process? These are important ethical considerations that do not play a role in quantitative approaches to risk (Hansson 2004; Asveld & Roeser 2009; Roeser et al. 2012; Roeser 2018). For these reasons, Möller (2012) argues that risk is a "thick concept," i.e. a concept that has descriptive and ethical aspects.

Based on these considerations concerning the ethical dimension of risk, in combination with an understanding of emotions as an important source of ethical insight, it is possible to come to a different view of the role of emotions in the context of risk. Rather than seeing them as a source of irrationality, we can see emotions as a source of ethical sensitivity in the context of risk (Roeser 2018). Psychological research by Paul Slovic has shown that laypeople have a broader conception of risk that includes important considerations (Slovic 2010). These considerations of laypeople indeed correspond with the ethical considerations such as the ones discussed above (Roeser 2007). Slovic has also done numerous studies that show that emotions play an important role in laypeople's risk perceptions (Slovic et al. 2002; Slovic 2010). Slovic, who works within the framework of Dual Process Theory, argues that "risk as feeling" needs to be corrected by "risk as analysis" (Slovic et al. 2004). This challenges his earlier work that saw laypeople's risk perceptions as providing legitimate considerations. However, based on an alternative, cognitive theory of emotions, the fact that laypeople's risk perceptions are grounded in emotions does not threaten their legitimacy. To the contrary, such a theory allows for the interpretation of Slovic's empirical data as follows: laypeople have a broader, more ethically sensitive perception of risk because their risk perceptions are also grounded in emotions (Roeser 2018). Of course, this does not mean that laypeople's emotional responses cannot be biased, but they are not necessarily so. Instead, these responses are an important source of ethical sensitivity. Emotions such as care, concern, indignation, and feelings of responsibility can make us more sensitive to ethical aspects of risk such as justice, fairness, and autonomy which get overlooked by quantitative approaches (for all this, see Roeser 2018). This does not mean that emotions are infallible; like all other mental capacities they are fallible, which means that emotions need to be the object of ethical reflection, which can involve factual information, rational argumentation as well as emotional capacities such as sympathy, compassion, and imaginatively engaging with different viewpoints (Roeser 2009).

Acknowledging the importance of ethics and emotions in evaluating risks does not mean that scientific, descriptive, and technical information can be neglected. That kind of information is *necessary* for an evaluation of risk, but it is not *sufficient*. Evaluating risks also requires ethical insight, for which emotions are an indispensable source (Roeser 2018). In the next section, I will discuss how these ideas can shed light on emotions in the context of uncertainty, and I will then proceed to discuss the role of emotions in the context of luck.

Emotions and Uncertainty

In the academic literature on risk and uncertainty, these notions are typically distinguished as follows: in the case of risk, the possible outcomes and their probabilities are known, in the case of uncertainty, the probabilities are unknown. Some scholars additionally distinguish a further notion, namely ignorance, to refer to situations where the kind of possible outcomes are also unknown. The precautionary principle is an ethical approach to deal with situations of uncertainty and ignorance. It states that the burden of proof for the safety of a new technology lies with the party that introduces the new technology, rather than requiring opponents of a technology to prove that the technology is not safe (cf. Ahteensuu & Sandin 2012). So there are ethical considerations that are specific for situations of uncertainty. The question arises whether this also means that people have emotions that are specific for such situations.

Indeed, people can have different emotional responses to risk, but also to uncertainty. For example, some people are uncertainty averse (e.g. Epstein 1999; also cf. literature on the Ellsberg paradox and ambiguity aversion, Ellsberg 1961). If we define risk as at least the possibility of an unwanted effect (plus possible ethical considerations as discussed above), then people might have negative emotional responses not only toward the unwanted effect, but also to the uncertainty. Typical emotional responses to uncertainty are fear and anxiety. These are also emotions that are discussed in the academic literature on risk and emotion, and they are usually seen as a threat to decision making (Sunstein 2005). However, in the previous section, I argued that emotions can shed important light on ethical aspects of risk. In this section, I will examine whether emotions can also be a source of insight concerning uncertainty.

Uncertain risks that give rise to strong emotional responses usually involve important possible outcomes where a lot is at stake, but where the timing and the exact outcome are uncertain. Examples can concern the result of a medical examination, a job application, or a possible natural or technological disaster, such as an earthquake or a nuclear meltdown (Roeser 2014).

When faced with uncertainty, people typically experience a lack of control. Indeed, the various kinds of risks that I mentioned, concerning health, a job application, and natural or technological disasters are, to some extent, beyond our control, but in different ways. Whether we are prone to certain health risks can be a matter of genetics, environmental circumstances as well as lifestyle, and our lifestyle is largely affected by socioeconomic variables. Natural risks can be independent of human activity, but they can also be the result of human-induced pollution, which typically results from collective actions where our individual contribution might not be directly visible to us. This relates to technological risks. Technologies can have negative environmental impacts, such as climate change, but such impacts might not always be known, either because there is no conclusive evidence (uncertainty), or because people are not aware of existing evidence. People can contribute to negative environmental impact and climate change out of ignorance, negligence, or free rider behavior. Their ignorance might or might not be culpable (Robichaud 2017). Free rider behavior can be based on selfish emotions, and negligence can be based on being careless and on lacking feelings of responsibility. These examples illustrate that while some emotions might lead us to morally problematic behavior in the case of uncertainty, other, particularly moral emotions can help us to act more responsibly (Roeser 2012).

In the previous section, I have discussed ethical aspects of risk that are left out of quantitative approaches to risk as well as to uncertainty, such as justice, fairness, and voluntariness. Feelings of care, responsibility, and sympathy with possible victims of our behavior can make us more aware of the moral impact of our actions. Furthermore, these emotions can also provide us with motivation to act more responsibly, for example concerning protecting the climate, as motivation is seen as an inherent aspect of paradigmatic emotions (Roeser 2012). Such emotions might even motivate us to act responsibly when probabilities are not known or certain, by applying the precautionary principle to ourselves: rather than giving oneself the benefit of the doubt, feelings of care and responsibility can make us more aware of our responsibilities for others and motivate us to reduce our environmental impact by choosing less convenient but environmentally more friendly options, such as public transportation and consuming less energy.

Emotions and Luck

In the previous sections I have reviewed the literature on risk and emotion as well as the more limited literature on emotions and uncertainty. Hardly anything has been published on luck and emotions. So in this section, I will largely discuss hitherto unexplored territory, drawing on my previous discussion in this chapter as well as touching on a variety of possibly relevant issues. My discussion is hence highly speculative and exploratory and by no means complete. Hopefully, the topics I identify in what follows can serve as input for further academic research on this important and interesting topic.

I have discussed in the previous sections that the standard approach to risk sees risk as a product of a chance of a negative effect; conversely, luck can be understood as a (small) chance of something happening that we evaluate as positive and important. As I argued previously, emotions can help to experience and assess something as risky because emotions can point out what matters to us. Analogously, emotions can help us to evaluate something as lucky. This can concern the evaluation of the importance dimension of luck. Emotions can also concern the assessment of the probability dimension, namely concerning how to appreciate a small or large chance.

Furthermore, in the literature on luck there are counterfactual (Kahneman & Varey 1990) and modal accounts (Pritchard 2004; Pritchard & Smith 2004). On a counterfactual account of luck, one feels lucky because things could have easily been worse, so it involves a comparison with a likely scenario. This is also captured on the modal account of luck: in a broad class of nearby possible worlds, things are worse. The reverse holds concerning the experience of being unlucky: in a different yet likely scenario (in terms of probabilities), or in nearby possible worlds (in terms of a modal account), things could easily have been better. This also concerns a near miss or hit: we can experience stronger feelings of bad luck in case of a near miss or near hit than if we are far away from gaining. For example, when we are rejected for a job application, this can be even more painful when one hears that one had almost got the job. At the same time, knowing that it was a near miss or near hit can also be comforting. In other words, in a nearby possible world one could have been the "lucky one," which can be painful: "I almost got it!"; as well as comforting: "Apparently I was a serious candidate." This also holds for a probabilistic account of luck: the same probability can be assessed as good luck as well as bad luck, depending on our point of reference.

In principle, every situation could potentially be interpreted and evaluated in either way, as there will always be nearby possible worlds or counterfactual yet likely alternative scenarios in which things could have been better but also worse. Pritchard and Smith (2004) refer to an example by Heider (1989) concerning a survivor of a car accident who praises his luck at "only having broken his arm," where things could easily have turned out even worse, for example, he could also have been more severely injured or even dead. Of course, a different and also legitimate and understandable assessment of the situation would have been if the person were to say "I had bad luck because I got into a car accident and broke my arm." In other words, our emotions and feeling of being lucky or unlucky involve a comparison with how well or badly things could have worked out in a nearby possible world, or in a likely but different scenario.

This is also reflected in the famous metaphor of seeing the glass half full or half empty. This can be a matter of personality trait, where some people have the tendency to focus on how things could have been better, such as the notorious "greener grass of the neighbor," whereas others praise their life in terms of all the things that have worked out. This difference in evaluation can also be variable and depend on situational factors, such as mood, mental and physical health, etc.

This difference in *evaluation* of something in terms of good or bad luck also relates to the question how we *cope* with good luck and bad luck. People differ in the way in which they cope and persevere in case of bad luck, versus how easily they give up. This gives rise to the question: How much luck is involved in how one copes with luck? Genetic, psychological, and external (socio-economic and cultural) factors probably play a role here, but this question also relates to intricate questions concerning free will and responsibility: To what extent is it in our hands to "get our act together" and try to approach our lives more optimistically (cf. Hartman 2017)? This relates to discussions of desert, which also touches on discussions in political philosophy: To what extent are people responsible for how they deal with obstacles in life (i.e., "bad luck"), and which role should the government have in compensating for circumstances that make it harder for people to cope with and overcome obstacles?

Next to these political issues and implications, luck and emotion give rise to questions related to rational behavior. A famous saying is that pessimists are more realistic than optimists. However, the problem is that pessimism is a self-fulfilling prophecy: a coherent pessimist will not try to reach a far-away goal, but if we do not try we are certain not to succeed. On the other hand, being optimistic and hence motivated to try is no guarantee of success. That is why the pessimistic person will be easily confirmed in their pessimistic worldview, whereas it is much harder for optimists to find confirmation for their efforts by experiencing good luck. Achieving something that is hard to get usually requires trying over and over again and being able to cope with failures. Trying to achieve a difficult goal is not a deterministic endeavor, where one is bound to succeed if one tries hard enough. While this can be discouraging, overcoming failures and being lucky can also be a source of value and of a blissful experience that one might not have had if things had been too easy. Indeed, various authors argue that good luck involves something positive the occurrence of which is beyond our control (Nagel 1979; Statman 1991; Latus 2000).

This can be illustrated by a famous thought experiment in philosophy, namely Robert Nozick's idea of an "experience machine" (Nozick 1974: 42–45). Hooking on to his machine would mean that our brain-states would be manipulated in a way that we experience whatever we want as real, meaning that all our dreams would come out in our experience in exactly the way we would want them. However, typically people do not find this idea appealing for a number of reasons, for example concerning the genuineness and authenticity of our experiences and efforts. For the context of luck and emotion, this thought experiment is also informative: it seems like nothing matters anymore if everything is too easy. There is no nearby possible world in which things would have been significantly (and genuinely) worse. Too much undeserved good luck might result in feeling empty and as if everything is arbitrary; in that sense, too much undeserved good luck could even result in existential despair (for a philosophical elaboration of existential despair, see Ratcliffe (2014)). In such a setting, we would miss a certain resistance of the world that we would need to overcome with our own efforts and in which we deserve a good outcome. Furthermore, in the experience machine everything is certain, as the machine will adapt entirely to one's wishes. Even if one would wish for uncertainty and ask for random events, they would be based on one's own command, and they would not reflect any genuine effort, overcoming obstacles, "fate" or other uncertain aspects that can make life events meaningful and important.

Another issue concerns our long-term experiences of emotions as a result of good or bad luck. For example, in case of illness one longs back to the "normal days" that seem to be utterly happy in hindsight but at that time one was not aware of. There is evidence that people adapt to good or bad situations. For example, a lottery winner might not be able to feel lucky and happy for long (cf. Brickman et al. 1978). A person gets used to the new status quo and cannot appreciate her luck anymore. One might be tempted to conclude from this that, in the end, external, material, and societal circumstances do not matter and people adapt to a specific set point of happiness that is hardwired or dependent on irrelevant conditions. However, Lucas (2007) provides for more nuanced evidence on this; he argues that happiness levels can change and that adaptation varies depending on external circumstances. Furthermore, Veenhoven (1991) has argued that one should be careful to not confuse contentment and happiness. While contentment is very adaptive, happiness is less so:

> It is argued that the theory happiness-is-relative mixes up "overall happiness" with "contentment". Contentment is indeed largely a matter of comparing life-as-it-is to standards of how-life-should-be. Yet overall happiness does not entirely depend on comparison. The overall evaluation of life depends also on how one feels affectively and hedonic level of affect draws on its turn on the gratification of basic bio-psychological needs. Contrary to acquired "standards" of comparison these innate "needs" do not adjust to any and all conditions: they mark in fact the limits of human adaptability. To the extent that it depends on need-gratification, happiness is not relative.
>
> *Veenhoven 1991: 1*

This is an important nuance to avoid relativistic and cynical conclusions, such as that we do not need to help people in dire or unlucky circumstances, as they will adapt to their situation. Indeed, they might adapt, and they might even be content, but happiness requires a more substantive satisfaction of objective needs. This also resonates with different approaches in ethics concerning basic needs and capabilities: while some philosophers argue that needs and capabilities are relative, others argue for a so-called objective list account of moral values and capabilities to which all human beings are entitled in order to live a fulfilling life (cf. Nussbaum 1994). Nussbaum (1994: 83) has identified being able to avoid pain and have pleasurable experiences as a basic capability.

A lot of luck is involved concerning which part of the world and society one is born into, which determines one's chances to be lucky or unlucky to a large extent, and henceforth also one's chances to not only be content but also happy. It seems to be a matter of justice and fairness that people have equal chances to experience good emotions rather than bad ones. Those of us who are more lucky should cultivate their feelings of responsibility and care to contribute to the circumstances of those who are less lucky.

Conclusion

In this chapter I have discussed the role of emotions in the contexts of risk, uncertainty, and luck. I have first discussed how the concepts of risk, uncertainty, and luck are related. I have then discussed the role of emotions in each of these contexts. While there is substantial research on risk and emotion, and limited research on uncertainty and emotions, there is hardly any conceptual or empirical research on luck and emotions. Therefore, my discussion of luck and emotion has been speculative and explorative, but hopefully my discussion has highlighted relevant topics for further research. I have identified links with important discussions in philosophy and in the social sciences: concerning modal and counterfactual accounts of luck, concerning free will and responsibility, implications for political theory and rational behavior, concerning the nature of our experiences and the possibility of adaptation to a status quo, and concerning research on basic needs and wellbeing. A lot more needs to be said on all these topics; hopefully this essay can provide for a starting point for further research. Given the importance of luck (good and bad luck) for our lives and our emotional experiences, this is a topic that deserves more thorough investigation.

Acknowledgment

I would like to thank Robert Hartman for his very helpful comments.

References

Ahteensuu, M., & Sandin, P. (2012) "The Precautionary Principle," in S. Roeser, R. Hillerbrand, P. Sandin, & M. Peterson (eds.) *Handbook of Risk Theory*, Dordrecht: Springer, pp. 961–978.

Asveld, L., & Roeser, S. (eds.) (2009) *The Ethics of Technological Risk*, London: Earthscan.

Beauchamp, T., & Childress, J. (2006) *Principles of Biomedical Ethics*, Oxford: Oxford University Press.

Ben-Ze'ev, A. (2000) *The Subtlety of Emotions*, Cambridge, MA: MIT Press.

Brady, M. (2013) *Emotional Insight: The Epistemic Role of Emotional Experience*, Oxford: Oxford University Press.

Brickman, P., Coates, D., & Janoff-Bulman, R. (1978) "Lottery Winners and Accident Victims: Is Happiness Relative?" *Journal of Personality and Social Psychology* 36(8), 917–927.

Damasio, A.R. (1994) *Descartes' Error: Emotion, Reason and the Human Brain*, New York: G.P. Putnam.

Dancy, J. (2004) *Ethics without Principles*, Oxford: Oxford University Press.

De Hollander, A.E.M., & Hanemaaijer, A.H. (2003) *Nuchter omgaan met risico's*, Milieu—en natuurplanbureau (MNP)—RIVM, Bilthoven: RIVM.

Ellsberg, D. (1961) "Risk, Ambiguity, and the Savage Axioms," *Quarterly Journal of Economics* 75(4), 643–669.

Epstein, L.G. (1999) "A Definition of Uncertainty Aversion," *Review of Economic Studies* 66(3), 579–608.

Espinoza, N. (2009) "Incommensurability: The Failure to Compare Risks," in L. Asveld & S. Roeser (eds.) *The Ethics of Technological Risk*, London: Earthscan/Routledge, pp. 128–143.

Fischhoff, B., Lichtenstein, S., Slovic, P., Derby, S.L., & Keeney, R. (1981) *Acceptable Risk*, Cambridge: Cambridge University Press.

Frijda, N. (1986) *The Emotions*, Cambridge: Cambridge University Press.

Goldie, P. (2000) *The Emotions: A Philosophical Exploration*, Oxford, New York: Clarendon Press.

Griffith, P.E. (1997) *What Emotions Really Are: The Problem of Psychological Categories*, Chicago: University of Chicago Press.

Hansson, S.O. (2004) "Philosophical Perspectives on Risk," *Techné* 8, 10–35.

Hartman, R.J. (2017) *In Defense of Moral Luck: Why Luck Often Affects Praiseworthiness and Blameworthiness*, New York: Routledge.

Heider, F. (1989) "The Notebooks: Vol. 4. Balance Theory," M. Benesh-Weiner (ed.), München-Weinheim, Germany: Psychologie Verlags Union.

Kahan, D.M. (2008) "Two Conceptions of Emotion in Risk Regulation," *University of Pennsylvania Law Review* 156(3), 741–766.

Kahneman, D. (2011) *Thinking Fast and Slow*, New York: Farrar, Straus and Giroux.

Kahneman, D., & Varey, C.A. (1990) "Propensities and Counterfactuals: The Loser that Almost Won," *Journal of Personality and Social Psychology* 59, 1101–1110.

Krimsky, S., & Golding, D. (1992) *Social Theories of Risk*, Westport, CT: Praeger Publishers.

Latus, A. (2000) "Moral and Epistemic Luck," *Journal of Philosophical Research* 25, 149–172.

Lazarus, R. (1991) *Emotion and Adaptation*, New York: Oxford University Press.

Loewenstein, G.F., Weber, E.U., Hsee, C.K., & Welch, N. (2001) "Risk as Feelings," *Psychological Bulletin* 127, 267–286.

Lucas, R.E. (2007) "Adaptation and the Set-Point Model of Subjective Well-Being: Does Happiness Change after Major Life Events?," *Current Directions in Psychological Science* 16(2), 75–79.

Möller, N. (2012) "The Concepts of Risk and Safety," in S. Roeser, R. Hillerbrand, P. Sandin, & M. Peterson (eds.) *Handbook of Risk Theory*, Dordrecht: Springer, pp. 55–85.

Nagel, T. (1979) "Moral Luck," in *Mortal Questions*, Cambridge, UK: Cambridge University Press.

Nozick, R. (1974) *Anarchy, State, and Utopia*, New York: Basic Books.

Nussbaum, M.C. (1994) "Human Capabilities, Female Human Beings," in M.C. Nussbaum & J. Glover (eds.) *Women, Culture, and Development: A Study of Human Capabilities*, Oxford: Oxford University Press, pp. 61–85.

———. (2001) *Upheavals of Thought: The Intelligence of Emotions*, Cambridge: Cambridge University Press.

Pritchard, D.H. (2004) "Epistemic Luck," *Journal of Philosophical Research* 29, 193–222.

Pritchard, D., & Smith, M. (2004) "The Psychology and Philosophy of Luck," *New Ideas in Psychology* 22, 1–28.

Ratcliffe, M. (2014) "Evaluating Existential Despair," in S. Roeser & C. Todd (eds.) *Emotion and Value*, Oxford: Oxford University Press, pp. 229–246.

Roberts, R.C. (2003) *Emotions: An Essay in Aid of Moral Psychology*, Cambridge, UK, New York: Cambridge University Press.

Robichaud, P. (2017) "Is Ignorance about Climate Change Culpable?" *Science and Engineering Ethics* 23(5), 1409–1430.

Roeser, S. (2007) "Ethical Intuitions about Risks," *Safety Science Monitor* 11, 1–30.

———. (2009) "The Relation between Cognition and Affect in Moral Judgments about Risk," in L. Asveld & S. Roeser (Eds.) *The Ethics of Technological Risks*, London: Earthscan, pp. 182–201.

———. (2011) *Moral Emotions and Intuitions*, Basingstoke: Palgrave Macmillan.

——. (2012) "Emotional Engineers: Toward Morally Responsible Engineering," *Science and Engineering Ethics* 18(1), 103–115.

——. (2014) "The Unbearable Uncertainty Paradox," *Metaphilosophy* 45(4–5), 640–653.

——. (2018) *Risk, Technology, and Moral Emotions*, New York: Routledge.

Roeser, S., & Todd, C. (eds.) (2014) *Emotion and Value*, Oxford: Oxford University Press.

Roeser, S., Hillerbrand, R., Sandin, P., & Peterson, M. (eds.) (2012) *Handbook of Risk Theory*, Dordrecht: Springer.

Ross, W.D. (1967 [1930]) *The Right and the Good*, Oxford: The Clarendon Press.

Scherer, K.R. (1984) "On the Nature and Function of Emotion: A Component Process Approach," in K.R. Scherer & P. Ekman (eds.) *Approaches to Emotion*, Hillsdale, London: Lawrence Erlbaum Associates, pp. 293–317.

Shrader-Frechette, K.S. (1991) *Risk and Rationality: Philosophical Foundations for Populist Reforms*, Berkeley: University of California Press.

Slovic, P. (2010) *The Feeling of Risk: New Perspectives on Risk Perception*, London: Earthscan.

Slovic, P., Finucane, M., Peters, E., & MacGregor, D.G. (2002) "The Affect Heuristic," in T. Gilovich, D. Griffin, & D. Kahnemann (eds.) *Heuristics and Biases: The Psychology of Intuitive Judgement*, Cambridge: Cambridge University Press, pp. 397–420.

Slovic, P., Finucane, M., Peters, E., & MacGregor, D.G. (2004) "Risk as Analysis and Risk as Feelings: Some Thoughts about Affect, Reason, Risk, and Rationality," *Risk Analysis* 24(2), 311–322.

Solomon, R.C. (1993) *The Passions: Emotions and the Meaning of Life*, Indianapolis: Hackett Publishing Company.

Statman, D. (1991) "Moral and Epistemic Luck," *Ratio* 4, 146–156.

Sunstein, C.R. (2005) *Laws of Fear*, Cambridge: Cambridge University Press.

Veenhoven, R. (1991) "Is Happiness Relative?" *Social Indicators Research* 24, 1–34.

Zagzebski, L. (2003) "Emotion and Moral Judgment," *Philosophy and Phenomenological Research* 66, 104–124.

32

THE ILLUSION OF CONTROL

Anastasia Ejova

The term "illusion of control" was proposed by the Harvard experimental psychologist Ellen Langer (1975) after she observed a peculiar pattern of behavior in an experiment staged around a real office lottery. Tickets were cards with pictures of American Football players, and the ticket seller was secretly instructed by Langer to draw a ticket out of a hat for half of the ticket purchasers while giving the other purchasers the opportunity to see all the cards on offer and select one. Subsequently, the seller approached all ticket-holders, informing them that, even though all tickets had been sold, people in another office where some of the tickets had been sold were interested in buying more. When asked about the amount of money for which they would be willing to resell their ticket, ticket-holders who had personally selected a ticket named a larger amount, on average. To Langer, this finding suggested that people can fall under the illusion that the probability of winning a lottery or any other game against a random-outcome generator can be increased by taking strategic action, such as picking one's favorite ("lucky") football player. In the 40 years since Langer published her study, experimental psychologists have replicated her finding while further testing her hypothesis that behaviors indicative of an illusion of control (e.g., the patterns of quoted resale prices) become more pronounced the more the game against a random-outcome generator resembles a game of skill. In support of this hypothesis, the follow-up studies have suggested that the illusion of control increases with the number of available response options, the degree to which symbols on the lottery tickets (or their equivalents in the given game of chance) are familiar, and the frequency of wins experienced over a number of playing rounds. These findings have been reviewed in papers by Presson and Benassi (1996), Thompson, Armstrong, and Thomas (1998), and Stefan and David (2013).

The first section of this chapter focuses on defining the illusion of control. Four short sections follow, in which the chapter develops an explanation of the illusion of control—namely, that it is a reflection of an ongoing problem-solving process aimed at winning in games of chance. Later sections consider the proposed explanation's implications for theory and research on human concepts of luck, as specified by the modal account of luck. It is argued that the background beliefs that generate candidate solutions to the problem of how to win in games of chance—beliefs about randomness and the supernatural—also shape human concepts of luck both within and outside of games of chance. In both cases, the background beliefs motivate conceptions of luck as a predictable supernatural force, personal quality, or personal quality conferred by a supernatural force.

Anastasia Ejova

A Definition of the Illusion of Control (in Games of Chance)

In the paper describing the office lottery experiment, Langer effectively defined the illusion as

> the belief that, in a game against a random-outcome generator, it is possible to perform better than the average person by approaching the game as though it were a game of skill. The skilled approach involves taking time to determine which possible strategies are most appropriate based on some combination of task-relevant background knowledge and simple trial-and-error.
>
> *Langer 1975: 313*

In three particular types of gambling—lotteries, roulette, and slot-machine gambling—the probability of winning is completely independent of all prior events, including the player's choices, so Langer's definition can readily be applied to distinguish as an illusion of control any behavior or survey response pattern indicative of belief in a non-zero contingency between actions and game outcomes.

While the illusion of control has predominantly been studied in the context of lotteries, roulette, and slot-machine gambling, references have been made to the illusion of control over health (Langer 1983), investments (De Carolis & Saparito 2006), driving (Stephens & Ohtsuka 2014), and other kinds of gambling (e.g., Keren & Wagenaar 1985). All these activities involve a degree of skill—a non-zero contingency between actions and outcomes—so taking a "skilled approach" during these activities does not constitute an illusion or error. However, many gambling activities feature a random-outcome generator, and—with the exception of poker and pari-mutuel race- and sports-betting[1]—all gambling activities provided commercially (outside the home) are losing games, in which it is an error to assume that optimal strategizing can generate anything but loss minimization. In these losing games, the gambling provider is like a thrower of a coin who charges 10 cents per guess but unfairly only pays back 19 cents for each correct guess (Bjerg 2010). Given the frequency of random-outcome generators and beliefs in the possibility of winning through a skilled approach in commercial gambling, it is implicit in many discussions of the illusion of control that the phenomenon additionally encompasses *the erroneous belief that it is possible to use the skilled approach to consistently win money in commercial gambling games* (Walker 1992: 141). The explanation of the illusion of control put forward in the next section accommodates both the narrow and broad definitions of the illusion.

Overall, the presented definition of the illusion of control, implies that attempts at strategizing count as illusions of control only when the strategist is aware that task outcomes are generated randomly (or at least with very high uncertainty) by a wheel, lottery, computer, or race-and-sports-betting system.[2] In experiments examining the effects of win-frequency—or, more broadly, success-frequency—on the illusion of control, this aspect of the definition has not been recognized. The experiments (e.g., Alloy & Abramson 1979; Thompson et al. 2007) have examined ratings of perceived control (from "no control" (0) to "complete control" (100)) depending on whether participants experienced "successes"—more specifically, onsets of a light—in a random 75 percent of rounds or a random 25 percent. In each trial, participants could press or not press a button, and they were instructed to test the controllability of outcomes by refraining from pressing in approximately 50 percent of rounds. Critically, participants were not told that the outcome-generating mechanism was random, since such information would have likely influenced their answers to the control-rating question.

The problem with revealing nothing about the random outcome-generating mechanism when studying the illusion of control is that, in doing so, one assumes that judgments about the potential causal consequences of personal actions in games of chance are made following the same process as judgments about the potential causal consequences of any event about which one has no background knowledge. Three main theories have been developed for how people make causal judgments when presented with no information except how often the candidate cause and candidate effect co-occur and occur in isolation. For various reasons, none of the theories are able to make predictions about conclusions drawn at the end of a game of chance. The theories, effectively, generate predictions about human judgments for various datasets, such as those examined in an experiment by Griffiths and Tenenbaum (2005: Experiment 1). In this experiment, participants viewed 14 tables, each with four cells of data relevant to describing the relationship between injection with a chemical and the expression of a particular gene in mice. Cell 1 indicated the number of injected mice found to have the gene, Cell 2—the number of non-injected mice found to have the gene, Cell 3—the number of injected mice found not to have the gene, and Cell 4—the number of non-injected mice in the lab found not to have the gene. Participants then rated, on a scale from "not at all" (0) to "every time" (20), the extent to which they believed that the chemical caused the gene to be expressed. Notably, in experiments on human causal reasoning, presenting data in tables is equivalent to presenting it as it would appear in a game of chance—sequentially, rather than in a summary table (e.g., separately for each mouse). According to one theory of human causal reasoning—Jenkins and Ward's (1965) ΔP model—people's causal judgments for each condition are proportional to the ΔP index: the probability of the effect occurring in the presence of the cause (Cell 1 value divided by the total number of data points in which the cause occurred) minus the probability of the effect occurring in the cause's absence (Cell 2 value divided by the total number of data points in which the cause was absent). The ΔP measure, effectively, captures the counterfactual interpretation of "causality" as the change in the probability of the effect occurring as a consequence of the occurrence of the cause. Critically, neither the ΔP model, nor a second prominent model of human causal reasoning (Cheng 1997), predicts that, when the contingency between the candidate cause and candidate effect is zero, causal contingency ratings increase in line with the value of Cell 1—the frequency with which the candidate cause and candidate effect co-occur. Yet this is precisely what was observed by Griffiths and Tenenbaum, similar preceding studies, and the light-onset studies of the illusion of control described above.

Griffiths and Tenenbaum's own "causal support" model of human causal reasoning—described in the same 2005 paper as their large experiment and in a 2009 review paper—predicts increased contingency judgments with increasing confirming cases in the zero-contingency genetics scenario. Moreover, unlike the other two models, it can accommodate the fact that, in most games of chance, the value of Cell 2 is always zero, as players must act in every round, and thus do not have an option equivalent to not injecting a chemical. However, an issue for the causal support model (and other models of causal inference) in attempting to account for the illusion of control is that, in the context in which the illusion of control has tended to be documented—games against random-outcome generators—there is extensive evidence that people have expectations about *series* of random outcomes (e.g., Nickerson 2002; Scheibehenne & Studer 2014). More specifically, the evidence suggests that people believe each loss in games of chance to be an indication that the action preceding the loss is more likely to generate a win in the next round. This expectation has been termed the "gambler's fallacy," along with the analogous expectation that each win with a certain action reduces that action's likelihood of producing a win in the next round. Meanwhile, all three of the discussed models of human causal reasoning make predictions about situations in which people encounter *mutually independent* outcomes that amass into a dataset. Overall, then, current theories of human causal reasoning do not permit us to meaningfully attribute the illusion of control wholly to the normal way in which humans reason about any cause-and-effect relationship, regardless of context. In the case of the illusion of control, the context is that the candidate effects are randomly generated outcomes.

A Proposed Explanation for the Illusion of Control: Problem-solving Based on Background Knowledge

Armed with a definition of the illusion of control, we are able to consider, over the next four sections, an explanation for the phenomenon. Indeed, in mentioning background knowledge and trial-and-error, the discussed definition of the illusion of control already contains a hint of the explanation. Under this explanation, the illusion of control involves being in the midst of applying a problem-solving approach to a game of chance. Problem-solving consists of physically trialling or mentally simulating actions in an iterative manner to determine whether they achieve the goal state or bring the goal state closer (Anderson 1993). The goal state in the game-of-chance context is a monetary or honorary win. The problem-solving approach is taken by some game-of-chance participants for two reasons. First, games of chance feature visible action alternatives, including buttons on slot machines, the grid of possible bets in roulette, and number options for lottery tickets. Because the action alternatives and potential monetary prize are among the only visible design features of these games, at least some players are likely to conclude that the two features might be causally connected. Second, games of chance are defined as "games," which, in other domains, such as sports and multi-player card games, involve a causal connection between available actions and the prize on offer.

As an illustration of the problem-solving process at work in a game of chance, consider an example where a person contemplates three actions for bringing about an overall monetary win in slot-machine gambling: (1) selecting machines that have not produced a win for some time, (2) not playing on popular days for gambling (e.g., weekends) to avoid being tricked by venue owners, who, he believes, re-program machines to pay out less on such days, and (3) taking a lucky charm to the venue. All three strategies have been widely documented in interviews with slot-machine players (King 1990; Livingstone et al. 2006). In a search through physical trial, the person might perform the first action for some number of sessions. Should he find his bank balance to be rapidly shrinking rather than growing, he is likely to switch to performing one of the other two contemplated actions. He could also conceive of other potentially effective actions or action combinations. Any strategic action conceived of during this iterative search process represents an illusion of control. Upon running out of action alternatives to trial, the person would cease solving the problem of how to obtain gambling wins and, with that, cease experiencing an illusion of control. He could continue playing to keep friends company or to avoid some personal issues, but the illusion of control would no longer be a feature of his play.

In mentioning "background knowledge," our definition of the illusion of control pre-empts the fact that, both in terms of content and quantity, contemplated actions in any problem-solving situation depend, at least in part, on the individual's background beliefs. Effectively, background beliefs are internally represented theories of the world that generate possible problem solutions for evaluation, directing attention to particular aspects of the problem (Murphy & Medin 1985; Thagard 1992). Generative beliefs vary in generality, such that all but the most situation-specific beliefs are theories capable of generating more specific theories or beliefs. Theories across levels are adjusted based on both data from the environment and constraints from more general theories, meaning, of course, that people differ in terms of the theories they hold, perhaps at all but the most general levels (Tenenbaum et al. 2007). In the above example, the slot machine player's second belief that venue managers re-program slot machines to provide a lower return on popular days for gambling is among the less general theories generated by the *theory of mind*—one of the most general theories available to humans (e.g., Wellman & Gelman 1992). According to the theory of mind, all human beings, including oneself, act according to certain beliefs and desires (i.e., goals), which are, in turn, influenced by relevant states of the world. One of the theories following from the theory of mind is that, in business settings, a common goal is to maximize profit, taking into account current states of the world, which include business cycles. The more situation-specific theory that the owners of commercial gambling venues make changes to equipment in response to the business cycle follows.

Based on the proposed account of how background knowledge influences the problem-solving process underlying the illusion of control, it is possible to explain Langer's findings and the results of other interview-based and experimental research on the illusion of control by appealing to literature on the content of relevant background beliefs. The next two sections propose that beliefs indicative of an illusion of control (i.e., of ongoing problem-solving) are constrained, not only by the same theories of mind and mechanics that humans apply in everyday functioning, but also by theories of randomness and supernatural forces.

Problem-solving Based on a Universal Theory of Randomness

Suggestions are emerging that the "gambler's fallacy"—the aforementioned expectation that sequences produced by a random-outcome generator are highly unlikely to feature overly long runs of any one possible outcome—is a universal theory of randomness. The universality of the theory is attributed to limitations in human short-term memory capacity. One variant of this proposal about the shaping role of memory-capacity limitations was put forward by Hahn and Warren (2009; see Rapoport & Budescu (1997) for a slightly different account). Simulations conducted by these authors revealed that *short* sequences of chance-determined outcomes (that is, sequences of up to 50 random outcomes) have a certain property. This is the property that, if any set of six consecutive outcomes is selected from the sequence, uniform runs (e.g., six tails following the toss of a coin) and perfect alternations (e.g., the sequence *tails-heads-tails-heads-tails-heads*) are the least likely outcome combinations. The property is even more pronounced in sequences of 20 outcomes but does not hold in longer sequences of 500, or even 100, outcomes. In a typical board game or game of heads-or-tails, people experience chance outcomes in sequences of no more than 50. Over the course of those 50-outcome-long playing sessions, they are likely to notice structure across only five or six outcomes at a time, as that is the capacity of human short-term memory (Miller 1956). Thus, in attending to fragments of what are already short random sequences, people learn that chance, as they experience it, is a process that is unlikely to generate uniform runs and perfect alternations.

As a generative background theory, the gambler's fallacy is likely to motivate a behavior often reported by participants in games of chance: persistence with a chosen strategy (e.g., a particular number in roulette or a particular line on a slot machine) for longer than one would in a non-chance game (Steenbergh et al. 2002). The persistence is driven by the expectation that, with every losing round (every missed equal chance at success compared to other strategies), the chosen strategy becomes increasingly more likely to succeed. Slot-machine players might similarly expect that the machines, which can, effectively, produce only two outcomes—wins and losses—become more likely to pay out with each additional losing outcome. Like the player in our problem-solving example, these players will begin their gambling sessions by looking out for machines that have produced long losing streaks for other players. Think also of a classic case of the illusion of control, documented by a sociologist among craps players (Henslin 1967) and consistently observed during board-games: the tendency to throw dice harder to obtain higher outcomes. A hypothesis testable with any device capturing hand-motion-strength (e.g., Lang et al. 2015) is that harder pre-throw shakes of dice and harder throws tend to follow throws of low numbers on previous turns. Arguably, the more effortful shakes and throws are aimed at making the die as random as possible, so that—as is expected from all random-outcome generators—preceding trends (of low throws, in this case) are reversed.

Problem-solving Based on a Universal Theory of Supernatural Entities

Theories in the cognitive science of religion point to a general belief structure that generates all variants of religious belief (Atran & Norenzayan 2004), including less doctrine-specific supernatural beliefs about supernatural agents such as fate and karma (Wilson et al. 2013). The religious belief structure has three components: belief in the existence of supernatural agents (gods, ghosts, angels, etc.), belief in the power of supernatural agents to avert life-threatening events (usually for "deserving" individuals), and belief in rituals as a means of appealing to supernatural agents. The universality of this belief set has been attributed to the fact that it is a by-product of evolved cognitive mechanisms, including fear of illness and death, the tendency to react to every rustling of leaves as though it might signal the approach of a predator, and the tendency to hold separate theories about "substances," "plants," "animals," and "humans." Arguably, theories of supernatural entities are relevant in games of chance because the outcomes in these games are visibly outside of natural (e.g., human) influence. Another reason for why people might be tempted to attribute chance outcomes to the intentions of supernatural agents is that these outcomes are infinitely complex in that they do not follow rules (Nickerson 2002). As pointed out famously by philosopher Daniel Dennett (1987), there is often processing effort to be saved and predictive power to be gained from conceiving of complex systems, such as computers, as intentional agents with beliefs and goals. The next section suggests that luck is conceived of by some as a fickle supernatural force—an intentional version of chance, which, under the gambler's fallacy, likewise does not favor any one outcome for long. A further reason for why supernatural beliefs are readily applied in games of chance is that, card-decks and other random-outcome generators that feature in many modern gambling games, have, traditionally, due to their visible independence from natural forces, been used for communicating with supernatural forces for the purposes of fortune-telling, property division and enforcement of criminal justice. For example, property left in a will was often divided among remaining family members through the drawing of lots (Aubert 1959; Reith 2002).

An illusion of control involving persistent gambling due to a belief in an imminent win as a just reward for charitable behavior during the week (a belief documented by Henslin (1967), for example) is among the phenomena that can be explained if the described belief structure is assumed to be a relevant background theory in games of chance. In line with the broader belief that supernatural agents are responsive to rituals, participants in games of chance also, as mentioned earlier, widely report using "lucky charms" and various rituals aimed at obtaining good outcomes. Before examining the connection between the proposed explanation of the illusion of control and human concepts of luck, let us briefly consider the evidence for the explanation.

Evidence for the Proposed Explanation

In a recent demonstration of problem-solving during gambling, Ejova, Navarro, and Delfabbro (2013) conducted an experiment in which participants in a slot-machine-like task experienced wins primarily at the beginning of 48 rounds of play, primarily at the end, or spread evenly throughout. Reports of strategy effectiveness were found to be higher in the late-wins condition compared to the early-wins condition, suggesting that participants were expecting to discover the correct strategy through trial-and-error—a component of problem-solving. Meanwhile, evidence of a cluster of supernatural gambling strategies has emerged in studies examining which statements expressing gambling strategies attract similar responses in surveys asking respondents to indicate how much they agree (or disagree) with each statement (for a review, see Ejova, Delfabbro & Navarro (2015)).

Human Concepts of Luck Within and Outside of Games of Chance: Questions Raised by the "Modal Account" of Luck

In defining what is common in vignettes about "lucky events" in psychology and philosophy, the "modal account" of luck (Chapter 10 in this volume) and elaborated by Pritchard (2014; Pritchard & Smith 2004) and Levy (2011) provides insight into human concepts of luck—that is, into how the word "luck" is understood in everyday settings. According to Pritchard and Smith's (2004) account, a lucky event has two defining features:

(1) It occurs in the actual world but does not occur in most of the nearest possible worlds to the actual world (worlds that most resemble the actual world).
(2) It is significant to the agent concerned.[3]

The "actual world" in this case is the complete description of the physical environment in which the event occurred, while "possible worlds" are counterfactual (that is, hypothetical) environments where at least one feature is different. The more features a possible world has in common with the actual world, the "nearer" it is to that world. A typically cited example of a lucky event (e.g., Pritchard

& Smith 2004) is the story of a massive landslide that bypasses just one unremarkable house in a settlement—Jack's family home. In most possible worlds involving a landslide of the same magnitude affecting the same settlement, Jack's house in particular would not survive, and, given that homes are of great personal significance for most people, the event is, in the minds of those who hear the story, and, presumably, in Jack's mind, a lucky one for Jack. Degrees of perceived luckiness can vary. Greater luckiness is perceived with increases in the number of nearby possible worlds not featuring the event, or with increases in the event's personal significance.

Experimental evidence for the modal account of luck comes from studies that, effectively, test the predictions of the modal account in games of chance. Under the modal account, favorable outcomes of games of chance are lucky by default (and unfavorable outcomes—losses—are unlucky), providing they are of personal significance. This is because chance outcomes, by definition, occur in environments with many nearby possible worlds in which the significant event does not occur: worlds that differ from the actual world only in terms of the outcome produced by the random-outcome generator. In support of this hypothesis, two studies examining ratings of luckiness after each outcome in a game of chance observed that luckiness ratings were not zero. Instead, in line with the notion of increasing perceived luckiness with increasing event significance, luckiness ratings increased with increasing win amounts and decreased with increasing loss amounts (Wu et al. 2015, 2016). In what, incidentally, constituted a test of the modal account's first tenet, the authors additionally examined luckiness ratings following near-losses (i.e., rounds where participants neither won nor lost money, but where a spinning arrow fell close to a losing outcome). It was found that luckiness ratings increased as the amount nearly lost increased, and as the amount nearly won decreased. These findings suggest that increased awareness of nearby possible worlds with more negative (or positive) outcomes affects perceived luckiness.

With its clear specification of how humans might conceive of luck and how luck and chance might be conceptually connected, the modal account of luck provides a foundation for discussing connections between concepts of luck and the illusion of control, as explained by the problem-solving account. A necessary preliminary step is to outline the questions raised about human concepts of luck by the modal account and psychological research on luck. One question is whether luckiness is something that can be ascribed to an event only after the event has occurred. Effectively, the question is whether humans conceive of luckiness as something that can be predicted.

If the answer to the first question is "yes," a second question is whether predictions are made on the basis of concepts of luck as an external force or a quality of the person. Across two very similar experiments, Wohl and Enzle (2009) observed behavior that suggested that people make predictions about luck as a personal quality (i.e., a "trait" that people possess to varying degrees). The experiments were staged around an online roulette game in which participants were instructed to choose between spinning the wheel in person and delegating the task to an unseen (online) partner—a person who was actually in league with the experimenters. Prior to the spinning-role decision, while the participants were casually chatting online, the confederate participant described himself, to half the participants, as believing himself lucky on account of having enjoyed consistent gambling success. To the other half of participants, he did not mention luck or gambling. Wohl and Enzle found that the probability of delegating the wheel spin was higher when the confederate described himself as lucky. There is, however, also evidence that at least some people believe luck to be predictable while being external to the person. More specifically, these people see value in performing rituals to summon luck or a higher force capable of influencing luck. Wohl and Enzle conducted a third experiment in which half of the participants, before making a decision about whether or not to delegate the drawing out of a scratch-lottery ticket to a confederate partner, were told by the confederate that he (the confederate) had enjoyed uninterrupted gambling success ever since touching a well-known sports memento—the Canadian National Hockey Team's "Lucky Loonie"—during a visit to a museum. Participants hearing this from the confederate were, again, more likely to delegate ticket choice, as compared to participants who heard a version of the story in which the confederate made no mention of touching the lucky object or subsequent gambling success. Beliefs related in interviews about gambling experiences, and, indeed, in surveys about exam and sports preparation, are replete with further examples of ritualistic actions and objects (i.e., "lucky charms") used in persuading luck (or, presumably, an external force that influences luck) to produce a favorable outcome (Felson & Gmelch 1979; Keren & Wagenaar 1985; Ohtsuka & Chan 2009).

As will become clear in the next two sections, the problem-solving explanation of the illusion of control can be extended to generate a number of hypotheses regarding the extent to which luck is conceived of as a predictable personal quality, external force, or trait-force combination—both, within games of chance and more generally.

The Problem-solving Explanation's Implications for Concepts of Luck in Games of Chance

The first set of hypotheses based on the problem-solving explanation of the illusion of control concern luck specifically in games of chance. According to the problem-solving explanation, the gambler's fallacy and a notion of justice-wielding supernatural forces are general belief structures that generate strategies for benefiting from—and, as part of that, predicting—randomly generated events. Among these randomly generated events are emotionally significant ones that, according to the modal account of luck, can be termed "lucky." Thus, one sense in which luck is predictable is that, in games of chance, it is thought about in terms of the gambler's fallacy—that is, as a cyclical phenomenon. Bingo and blackjack players have, in interviews, reported that they do not expect "lucky streaks" to continue endlessly, or lucky charms to remain lucky forever (Keren & Wagenaar 1985; King 1990). A related sense in which luck is predictable is that, in games of chance, it is thought about in supernatural terms—that is, as subject to the control of a justice-wielding supernatural power responsive to rituals, or as, in itself, a supernatural power responsive to rituals and concerned with moral justice. Arguably, in games of chance, if either luck or chance are to be attributed the status of a supernatural force, luck is given the honor because chance has a clear physical basis—the random-outcome generator. Critically, regardless of whether luck is conceived of as a justice-enforcing supernatural force or a state subservient to such a force, it follows from descriptions of human supernatural beliefs as being concerned with justice that people can think about lucky (or unlucky) events as the results of an external force and a personal quality *acting in concert*. That is, regardless of how exactly one might conceive of luck in line with broader supernatural beliefs, one would believe good luck to be a reward for displaying admirable personal qualities. There is experimental evidence that, after reading short stories about beneficiaries of uncontrollable good events and victims of uncontrollable bad events, American and Japanese primary-school-aged children reported liking the beneficiaries more than the victims (Olson et al. 2006, 2008).

The Problem-solving Explanation's Implications for Concepts of Luck Outside of Games of Chance

With respect to concepts of luck outside of games of chance, the problem-solving explanation of the illusion of control hints at reasons for why the gambler's fallacy and beliefs in the supernatural continue to be relevant constraints, producing beliefs in cyclical luck and beliefs in the pairing of good luck with good personal qualities. Both reasons are based on the explanation's implications for why supernatural beliefs are relevant to predicting the output of random-outcome generators. One reason offered as part of the problem-solving explanation is that randomly generated sequences are complex and people might have a tendency to think about complex systems as having intentions, including, for example, divine intentions. Under the modal account, lucky events are similarly complex, in that they are uncontrollable. In having the property that they do not occur in most nearby counterfactual worlds, they cannot be planned based on counterfactual reasoning—that is, based on considerations about what could hypothetically happen (e.g., Coricelli et al. 2007). Thus, if Jack's home happens to not be destroyed in a landslide because Jack had earlier purposefully chosen a piece of land and architectural design that would withstand landslides, Jack would not consider the survival of his home a lucky event. It follows that, as complex events, lucky events even outside of games of chance, are amenable to being thought about as events intended by supernatural agents (who desire to bring about moral justice).

Concepts of luck as cyclical (or "fickle;" Díaz 2006), even outside of games of chance, can be explained by borrowing from one of the problem-solving explanation's proposals regarding the universality of the gambler's fallacy, as well as its suggestion that "the will of the gods" and random-outcome generators are conceptually connected due to age-old traditions. Throughout history, random-outcome generators have, due to their imperviousness to human control, been used in fortune-telling. One can extend this reasoning to suggest that luck and randomly generated outcomes are traditionally conceptually connected because the significant but uncontrollable events that the modal account of luck defines as lucky would have been a major topic of interest in fortune-telling. Remembering only some six randomly generated foretold outcomes at a time, fortune-tellers and their clients would have observed the same lack of perfect repetitions and perfect alternations that Hahn and Warren (2009) observed in simulated short random sequences. Thus, consistent good luck, consistent bad luck, and perfect alternations between good and bad luck would have come to be deemed impossible.

Overall, the problem-solving account of the illusion of control hints that, both within and outside of games of chance, luck—as defined by the modal account—is conceived of as being predictable in line with the tenets of two broader belief structures. According to one structure—the universal gambler's fallacy—luck comes in waves and is therefore predictable (to some degree) based on the recent history of lucky and unlucky outcomes in the task or more generally. According to the other belief structure—a universal structure of beliefs about supernatural entities—luck plays a part in the supernatural mechanisms by which good things happen to good people. Under this belief structure, lucky outcomes are predictable based on how deserving—how moral—one considers oneself to be.

Conclusions and Future Research

The proposed explanation of the illusion of control (a phenomenon for which we also arrived at a disambiguated definition) posits that strategies in games of chance and concepts of luck even outside of games of chance are constrained by standard theories of the natural world and two additional general belief structures. The first is the gambler's fallacy that random-outcome generators do not produce long streaks of neat patterns, and the second is a belief in justice-enforcing supernatural forces responsive to rituals. While serving as a basis for defining points of difference and intersection between human concepts of luck and typical strategies in games of chance, the proposed explanation of the illusion of control can also be drawn upon to address questions that follow from the modal account of human concepts of luck. More specifically, the problem-solving explanation provides insight into why luck appears to be thought of as a predictable state that reflects, simultaneously, personal qualities and the activity of supernatural forces.

Given that the illusion of control is specific to games of chance and that chance outcomes are lucky under the modal account if they are significant to the player, it is worth considering the implications of the discussion in this chapter for all types of research on gambling (experimental, survey-based, and interview-based). Some recent experiments examined the effects of wins and near-losses (instances of good luck if money is significant to the participant), as well as of losses and near-wins (instances of bad luck), on the brain activation patterns of people who gamble regularly or have problems with gambling (Chase & Clark 2010; Sescousse et al. 2016). This chapter's proposal that randomly generated outcomes, including lucky outcomes, are conceived of as having no lasting local patterns suggests that participants' brain activation patterns additionally depended on series of outcomes. Moreover, average levels of activation over the course of the playing session are likely to have been influenced by the combination of two factors that could have been assessed through surveys prior to the playing session: the degree to which participants endorsed supernatural beliefs about ultimate justice and the degree to which they considered themselves deserving of a sizeable win.

Notes

1 In poker and pari-mutuel betting, the gambling provider simply takes a fixed proportion of the total amount bet by the pool of players prior to close of betting (Bjerg 2010; Griffith 1949).
2 In race- and sports-betting, the "system" generating uncertainty is a combination of the factors governing competitor performance and patterns of betting among other bettors (Walker 1992: 20).
3 Pritchard (2014) abandoned this as a necessary condition for luck, but Levy (2011) endorses it.

References

Alloy, L.B., & Abramson, L.Y. (1979) "Judgment of Contingency in Depressed and Nondepressed Students: Sadder but Wiser?" *Journal of Experimental Psychology: General* 108(4), 441–485. https://doi.org/10.1037/0096-3445.108.4.441

Anderson, J.R. (1993) "Problem Solving and Learning," *American Psychologist* 48(1), 35–44. https://doi.org/10.1063/1.3183522

Atran, S., & Norenzayan, A. (2004) "Religion's Evolutionary Landscape: Counterintuition, Commitment, Compassion, Communion," *Behavioral and Brain Sciences* 27(6), 713–770.

Aubert, V. (1959) "Inquiry: Chance in Social Affairs," *Inquiry: An Interdisciplinary Journal of Philosophy* 2(1–4), 1–24.

Bjerg, O. (2010) "Problem Gambling in Poker: Money, Rationality and Control in a Skill-Based Social Game," *International Gambling Studies* 10(3), 239–254. https://doi.org/10.1080/14459795.2010.520330

Chase, H.W., & Clark, L. (2010) "Gambling Severity Predicts Midbrain Response to Near-Miss Outcomes," *Journal of Neuroscience* 30(18), 6180–6187. https://doi.org/10.1523/JNEUROSCI.5758-09.2010

Cheng, P.W. (1997) "From Covariation to Causation: A Causal Power Theory," *Psychological Review* 104(2), 367–405. https://doi.org/10.1037//0033-295X.104.2.367

Coricelli, G., Dolan, R.J., & Sirigu, A. (2007) "Brain, Emotion and Decision Making: The Paradigmatic Example of Regret," *Trends in Cognitive Sciences* 11(6), 258–265. https://doi.org/10.1016/j.tics.2007.04.003

De Carolis, D.M., & Saparito, P. (2006) "Social Capital, Cognition, and Entrepreneurial Opportunities: A Theoretical Framework," *Entrepreneurship: Theory and Practice* 30(1), 41–56. https://doi.org/10.1111/j.1540-6520.2006.00109.x

Dennett, D. (1987) *The Intentional Stance*, Cambridge, MA: MIT Press.

Díaz, J.C. (2006) "Tuchē and Technē: An Archaeology of Luck and Poetic Art in Greek Thought," *International Studies in Philosophy* 38(1), 31–43. http://dx.doi.org/110.5840/intstudphil200638114

Ejova, A., Delfabbro, P.H., & Navarro, D.J. (2015) "Erroneous Gambling-Related Beliefs as Illusions of Primary and Secondary Control: A Confirmatory Factor Analysis," *Journal of Gambling Studies* 31(1), 133–160. http://dx.doi.org/10.1007/s10899-013-9402-9

Ejova, A., Navarro, D.J., & Delfabbro, P.H. (2013) "Success-Slope Effects on the Illusion of Control and on Remembered Success-Frequency," *Judgment and Decision Making* 8(4), 498–511. http://journal.sjdm.org/12/12912/jdm12912.pdf

Felson, R.B., & Gmelch, G. (1979) "Uncertainty and the Use of Magic," *Current Anthropology* 20(3), 587–589.

Griffith, R.M. (1949) "Odds Adjustments by American Horse-Race Bettors," *The American Journal of Psychology* 62(2), 290–294.

Griffiths, T.L., & Tenenbaum, J.B. (2005) "Structure and Strength in Causal Induction," *Cognitive Psychology* 51(4), 334–384. https://doi.org/10.1016/j.cogpsych.2005.05.004

———. (2009) "Theory-Based Causal Induction," *Psychological Review* 116(4), 661–716. https://doi.org/10.1037/a0017201

Hahn, U., & Warren, P.A. (2009) "Perceptions of Randomness: Why Three Heads are Better than Four," *Psychological Review* 116(2), 454–461. https://doi.org/10.1037/a0015241

Henslin, J.M. (1967) "Craps and Magic," *American Journal of Sociology* 73(3), 316–330. https://doi.org/10.1086/224479

Jenkins, H.M., & Ward, W.C. (1965) "Judgment of Contingency Between Responses and Outcomes," *Psychological Monographs* 79, 231–241.

Keren, G., & Wagenaar, W.A. (1985) "On the Psychology of Playing Blackjack: Normative and Descriptive Considerations with Implications for Decision Theory," *Journal of Experimental Psychology* 114(2), 133–158. https://doi.org/10.1037/0096-3445.114.2.133

King, K.M. (1990) "Neutralizing Marginally Deviant Behavior: Bingo Players and Superstition," *Journal of Gambling Studies* 6(1), 43–61. https://doi.org/10.1007/BF01015748

Ladouceur, R., Sylvain, C., Boutin, C., & Doucet, C. (2002) *Understanding and Treating the Pathological Gambler*, London: Wiley.

Lang, M., Krátky, J., Shaver, J.H., Jerotijevič, D., & Xygalatas, D. (2015) "Effects of Anxiety on Spontaneous Ritualized Behavior," *Current Biology* 25(14), 1892–1897. https://doi.org/10.1016/j.cub.2015.05.049

Langer, E.J. (1975) "The Illusion of Control," *Journal of Personality and Social Psychology* 32(2), 311–328.

——. (1983) *The Psychology of Control*, Beverly Hills, CA: Sage Publications Inc.

Levy, N. (2011) *Hard Luck: How Luck Undermines Free Will and Moral Responsibility*, Oxford: Oxford University Press.

Livingstone, C., Wooley, R., & Borrell, J. (2006) *The Changing Electronic Gambling Machine (EGM) Industry and Technology*, Melbourne, Australia: Australian Institute of Primary Care. Available online: http://apo.org.au/node/3198

Miller, G.A. (1956) "The Magical Number Seven, Plus or Minus Two: Some Limits on Our Capacity for Processing Information," *Psychological Review* 63(2), 81–89. http://dx.doi.org/10.1037/h0043158

Murphy, G.L., & Medin, D.L. (1985) "The Role of Theories in Conceptual Coherence," *Psychological Review* 92(3), 289–316.

Nickerson, R.S. (2002) "The Production and Perception of Randomness," *Psychological Review* 109(2), 330–357. https://doi.org/10.1037//0033-295X.109.2.330

Ohtsuka, K., & Chan, C.C. (2009) "Donning Red Underwear to Play Mahjong: Superstitious Beliefs and Problem Gambling Among Chinese Mahjong Players in Macau," *Gambling Research* 22(1), 18–33.

Ohtsuka, K., & Ohtsuka, T. (2010) "Vietnamese Australian Gamblers' Views on Luck and Winning: Universal Versus Culture-Specific Schemas," *Asian Journal of Gambling Issues and Public Health* 1(1), 34–46. https://doi.org/10.1007/BF03342117

Olson, K.R., Banaji, M.R., Dweck, C.S., & Spelke, E.S. (2006) "Children's Biased Evaluations of Lucky Versus Unlucky People and Their Social Groups," *Psychological Science* 17(10), 845–846. https://doi.org/10.1111/j.1467-9280.2006.01792.x

Olson, K.R., Dunham, Y., Dweck, C.S., Spelke, E.S., & Banaji, M.R. (2008) "Judgments of the Lucky Across Development and Culture," *Journal of Personality and Social Psychology* 94(5), 757–776. https://doi.org/10.1037/0022-3514.94.5.757.Judgments

Presson, P.K., & Benassi, V.A. (1996) "Illusion of Control: A Meta-Analytic Review," *Journal of Social Behavior & Personality* 11(3), 493–510.

Pritchard, D. (2014) "The Modal Account of Luck," *Metaphilosophy* 45(4–5), 594–619. doi:10.1111/meta.12103

Pritchard, D., & Smith, M. (2004) "The Psychology and Philosophy of Luck," *New Ideas in Psychology* 22(1), 1–28. https://doi.org/10.1016/j.newideapsych.2004.03.001

Rapoport, A., & Budescu, D.V. (1997) "Randomization in Individual Choice Behavior," *Psychological Review* 104(3), 603–617. https://doi.org/10.1037/0033-295X.104.3.603

Reith, G. (2002) *The Age of Chance: Gambling and Western Culture*, London: Routledge.

Scheibehenne, B., & Studer, B. (2014) "A Hierarchical Bayesian Model of the Influence of Run Length on Sequential Predictions," *Psychonomic Bulletin & Review* 21(1), 211–217. https://doi.org/10.3758/s13423-013-0469-1

Sescousse, G., Janssen, L.K., Hashemi, M.M., Timmer, M.H.M., Geurts, D.E.M., ter Huurne, N.P. et al. (2016) "Amplified Striatal Responses to Near-Miss Outcomes in Pathological Gamblers," *Neuropsychopharmacology* 41(10), 2614–2623. https://doi.org/10.1038/npp.2016.43

Steenbergh, T.A., Meyers, A.W., May, R.K., & Whelan, J.P. (2002) "Development and Validation of the Gamblers' Beliefs Questionnaire," *Psychology of Addictive Behaviors* 16(2), 143–149. https://doi.org/10.1037/0893-164X.16.2.143

Stefan, S., & David, D. (2013) "Recent Developments in the Experimental Investigation of the Illusion of Control: A Meta-Analytic Review," *Journal of Applied Social Psychology* 43(2), 377–386. https://doi.org/10.1111/j.1559-1816.2013.01007.x

Stephens, A.N., & Ohtsuka, K. (2014) "Cognitive Biases in Aggressive Drivers: Does Illusion of Control Drive Us Off the Road?" *Personality and Individual Differences* 68, 124–129. https://doi.org/10.1016/j.paid.2014.04.016

Tenenbaum, J.B., Griffiths, T.L., & Niyogi, S. (2007) "Intuitive Theories as Grammars for Causal Inference," in A. Gopnik & L. Schulz (eds.) *Causal Learning: Psychology, Philosophy, and Computation*, Oxford: Oxford University Press, pp. 301–322.

Thagard, P. (1992) "Adversarial Problem Solving: Modeling an Opponent Using Explanatory Coherence," *Cognitive Science* 16(1), 123–149. https://doi.org/10.1016/0364-0213(92)90019-Q

Thompson, S.C., Armstrong, W., & Thomas, C. (1998) "Illusions of Control, Underestimations, and Accuracy: A Control Heuristic Explanation," *Psychological Bulletin* 123(2), 143–161. https://doi.org/10.1037/0033-2909.123.2.143

Thompson, S.C., Nierman, A., Schlehofer, M.M., Carter, E., Bovin, M.J., Wurzman, L., et al. (2007) "How Do We Judge Personal Control? Unconfounding Contingency and Reinforcement in Control Judgments," *Basic and Applied Social Psychology* 29(1), 75–84. https://doi.org/10.1080/01973530701331189

Walker, M.B. (1992) *The Psychology of Gambling*, Oxford: Pergamon Press.

Wellman, H.M., & Gelman, S.A. (1992) "Cognitive Development: Foundational Theories of Core Domains," *Annual Review of Psychology* 43, 337–375. http://dx.doi.org/10.1146/annurev.ps.43.020192.002005

Wilson, M.S., Bulbulia, J., & Sibley, C.G. (2013) "Differences and Similarities in Religious and Paranormal Beliefs: A Typology of Distinct Faith Signatures," *Religion, Brain & Behavior* 4(2), 104–126. http://dx.doi.org/10.1080/2153599X.2013.779934

Wohl, M.J.A., & Enzle, M.E. (2009) "Illusion of Control by Proxy: Placing One's Fate in the Hands of Another," *British Journal of Social Psychology* 48(1), 183–200. https://doi.org/10.1348/014466607X258696

Wu, Y., Van Dijk, E., Aitken, M., & Clark, L. (2016) "Missed Losses Loom Larger Than Missed Gains: Electrodermal Reactivity to Decision Choices and Outcomes in a Gambling Task," *Cognitive, Affective, & Behavioral Neuroscience* 16(2), 353–361. https://doi.org/10.3758/s13415-015-0395-y

Wu, Y., van Dijk, E., & Clark, L. (2015) "Near-Wins and Near-Losses in Gambling: A Behavioral and Facial EMG Study," *Psychophysiology* 52(3), 359–366. https://doi.org/10.1111/psyp.12336

33

POSITIVE PSYCHOLOGY AND LUCK EXPERIENCES

Matthew D. Smith and Piers Worth

Introduction

The idea of luck is ubiquitous but by no means simple, in the sense as it means precisely the same to everyone, everywhere. Expressions for "luck" in different languages introduced nuances that are difficult if not impossible to capture in any particular tongue. And even those who speak the same language do not necessarily use the word "luck" in the same sense.

Cohen 1960: 114

As is apparent from the range of perspectives that are being presented in this volume, the concept of "luck" is not an easy one to pin down. With six separate clusters of chapters it is evident there are many views of luck. Even when we focus our attention on how psychologists have worked with the concept of luck, different approaches have highlighted some of the nuances alluded to by Cohen (1960). For example, research has revealed: how people view luck as a cause of an event (e.g., Weiner 1985); that people often distinguish luck from chance (e.g., Wagenaar & Keren 1988); the nature of individual differences in people's beliefs about luck (e.g., Darke & Freedman 1997; Smith 1998), and how people often view events as "lucky" or "unlucky" by comparison to imagined alternatives (e.g., Teigen 1995).

In some of this work, researchers have often made implicit assumptions about the nature of luck. Most notable is the work of attribution theorists, who have sought to understand how we typically think about causes for events, in particular how we might ascribe causes for successes and failures (e.g., Weiner 1985; Weiner et al. 1971). This approach has suggested that causal factors of any event might be conceived as either (a) internal or external, (b) stable or unstable, and (c) controllable or uncontrollable. In this framework, luck is typically treated as an external, unstable, and uncontrollable factor to which we might attribute our successes or failures (e.g. Weiner 1985). For example, passing an exam could either be explained in terms of one's own hard work (an internal, stable, and controllable cause) or because one was fortunate that the "right" questions came up on the exam (an external, unstable, and uncontrollable cause).

In this chapter, we seek to build on previous attempts to examine the way in which luck is conceived in our daily lives, and to some extent challenge the extent to which luck is appropriately seen as an external and uncontrollable factor when making sense of events. A central part of this discussion is based around the argument that many events in everyday life are difficult, if not impossible, to clearly delineate as exclusively within or outside of our personal control. That is, events are typically derived through a subtle and complex mixture of both controllable and uncontrollable factors. We further argue that by exploring luck alongside positive psychology concepts such as gratitude, positive emotions, and optimism, it is possible to add to the understanding of luck and its potential place and contribution in our perceptions and overall health.

We will explore how ideas that sit within the emerging discipline of positive psychology might impact upon individuals' perception and experience of luck. In this way, we will draw upon, and contribute to, the discourse on psychological wellbeing. It is also in our focus on the *experience* of luck that we perhaps differentiate the aim of this work from some of the other theoretical approaches to luck. In this regard, we are perhaps less concerned with understanding what luck "is" and more with the experiences we might typically align with luck and how our perceptions of luck might impact us.

There has been a small amount of work to date within psychology that has explored luck from this angle (e.g., Smith 1998; Wiseman 2004). This work has started to show how people's perceptions of luck are varied and nuanced, and these lay perceptions allow "luck" to be something that we can influence or regulate through psychological and behavioral principles. For example, Smith (1998) interviewed people about their thoughts and beliefs about luck and how they saw luck as playing a role in different parts of their lives. In broad terms, three general views of luck emerged. First, some tended to view luck as synonymous with chance in that it referred to a cause, or set of causes, that was largely random. A second view of luck conceived of it as relating to causes that did have some "design" to them, though they were outside of our control. In this way, luck was aligned to notions such as fate or destiny. A final view of luck resonated with a perspective that luck was something over which one could exert some control. This view was reflected in notions such as how one could engage in behaviors that might bring good luck, as well as the notion that we can make our own luck.

Wiseman (2004) built on this latter idea in work that continued to explore the differences between "lucky" and "unlucky" people, or at least people who perceived themselves in this way.[1] The essence of this work was to draw out the kinds of behaviors and thought processes that self-perceived "lucky" people tended to engage in that their "unlucky" counterparts did not. These were organized into four general *principles*. The first of these notes how "lucky" people were more likely to maximize chance opportunities. This might manifest in a number of ways, such as giving attention to building and maintaining a strong "network of luck" through developing and nurturing social relationships. "Lucky" people were also more likely to display a relaxed attitude and be open to experience, meaning that they were more likely to notice and be open to opportunities as and when they arose.

The second principle linked luckiness to a willingness to listen to, and even develop, one's intuitive impressions. "Lucky" people were more likely to pay attention to their "gut" feelings about a situation and make decisions about how to act in accordance with these hunches. The suggestion was that our better decisions are often ones that feel right and that trusting our instincts can be a route to experiences of good luck.

The third principle evoked the power of expectation. If we expect good things to happen, if we expect to experience good fortune, then this will likely have an impact on the likelihood of indeed experiencing good fortune. This might be a simple direct consequence of having the positive expectation of success as such expectations mean one is more likely to attempt to achieve one's goal in the first place. One is also more likely to persevere in the face of challenges if one is working with an expectation that things are going to work out for the best.

Wiseman's fourth principle focuses on ways of dealing with "bad luck." Again, working from the perspective of what distinguishes "lucky" people from "unlucky" people, he notes that even "lucky" people experience their share of bad luck. It is not as if they go through their lives without bad things happening. The essence of Wiseman's fourth principle is to find ways of "turning bad luck into good." This might include changing one's perspective so as to be able to see some part of what has happened as positive.

We seek to build on the work started by Wiseman (2004) by exploring more deeply how these and other psychologically based ideas might impact on people's experience of luck. We do this by explicit reference to ideas that now sit within the discipline of "positive psychology."

Introducing "Positive Psychology"

The historical advocacy for positive psychology occurred in the work of humanistic psychologists Abraham Maslow (e.g., 1954/1970) and Carl Rogers (e.g. 1967/2004). Following a modern day proposal for a discipline of positive psychology by Martin Seligman in his Presidential address to the American Psychological Association in 1998, he and Mihalyi Csikszentmihaly (2000: 5) suggest

> positive psychology at the subjective level is about valued subjective experiences: well-being, contentment, and satisfaction (in the past); hope and optimism (for the future); and flow and happiness (in the present). At the individual level, it is about positive individual traits: the capacity for love and vocation, courage, interpersonal skill, aesthetic sensibility, perseverance, forgiveness, originality, future mindedness, spirituality, high talent and wisdom. At the group level, it is about civic virtues and the institutions that move individuals toward better citizenship: responsibility, nurturance, altruism, civility, moderation, tolerance and work ethic.

While many definitions of positive psychology exist, we believe this is an original and comprehensive one.

Exploring the Links between Positive Psychology and Experiences of Luck

In the discussion that follows, we consider some key concepts and research topics that now sit within positive psychology and how they potentially might play a role in our understanding of luck experiences. We see this discussion as a re-examination of the *psychology* of luck, so as to better understand how events and experiences that are typically aligned with luck might be impacted by our thoughts and feelings and actions, as well as how our approach to luck might, in turn, impact our psychological experience and wellbeing.

We begin with "gratitude" as a topic that has been well researched within positive psychology and already been the subject of research exploring its link with perceptions of luck (e.g., Teigen 1997). We then focus our attention on the role of positive emotions (of which gratitude may be regarded as one), with emphasis on the "broaden and build" theory of positive emotions (Fredrickson 1998). We then explore links between optimism and luck experiences, before examining an aspect of psychological wellbeing referred to as "environmental mastery" (Ryff 1989).

Gratitude

Gratitude has been, and continues to be, a key topic for positive psychology research, with much of the focus on exploring its relationship with wellbeing (e.g., Emmons & Shelton 2002; Lomas et al. 2014). In this work, gratitude has been conceptualized in a variety of ways such as "a felt sense of wonder, thankfulness, and appreciation for life" (Emmons & Shelton 2002: 460) or simply as "the positive recognition of benefits received" (Emmons 2004: 5).

The links between gratitude and luck have been explored by several researchers. This work tends to highlight how perceptions of being lucky are often associated with perceptions of being grateful. For example, Teigen (1997) presented students with a series of statements that were either "luck statements" (e.g., "it is lucky that I have a family") or "good statements" (e.g., "it is good that I have a family") and asked them to give a brief explanation of the meaning behind each statement, especially in terms of to what extent the "luck statements" communicated anything different from, or in addition to, the "good statements." The primary finding here was that the luck statements, in contrast with the good statements were more likely to be seen as implying comparison with others. A follow-up study, reported in the same paper, directly asked participants to rate the statements in terms of the extent to which they related to expressions of gratitude, as well as expressions of sympathy or care, envy, and comparison with others. Luck statements received higher ratings of implied gratitude than good statements, when these described a positive state of affairs (e.g., "it is lucky I have job"; "it is lucky I have good health"). In a third study, participants were instead asked to describe a situation from their own life in which they felt grateful. The majority of these accounts described a situation in which they had felt grateful toward a specific person (referred to as "personal" gratitude), with a minority describing a more general gratitude toward "life" or a "high power" (which Teigen referred to as a type of "existential" or "impersonal" gratitude). Participants who had described an instance of "personal" gratitude were prompted to also provide an account of "impersonal" gratitude, and vice versa. Participants were then asked to rate their stories along a number of dimensions, including how lucky and how unlucky they considered themselves to be. Both personal and impersonal gratitude stories received high ratings of luckiness, confirming a link between perceptions of luck and perceptions of gratitude.

Teigen's emphasis throughout this work has been on the role of "counterfactual thinking" in people's ascriptions to luck. Counterfactual thinking refers to how we often compare events or situations with imagined alternatives (e.g., Epstude & Roese 2008; Roese 1997). Such thinking seems to be central to how people often view events as lucky or unlucky, by imagining possible outcomes that might have easily happened that were either more attractive than what actually happened (in the case of events perceived as unlucky) or less attractive than what happened in reality (in the case of events perceived as lucky) (e.g., Teigen 1995). When faced with events that are readily acknowledged as involving luck, at least in part, people seem to spontaneously engage in counterfactual thinking and it is this that may serve as the basis of the links between luck and gratitude. For example, Teigen and Jensen (2011) conducted interviews with 85 Norwegian tourists who had been exposed to the tsunami disaster that struck Southeast Asia in December 2004. The majority of the sample had been in life-threatening situations. Others had been close witnesses and suffered some kind of hardship as a consequence of the disaster. A first round of interviews took place between nine and 11 months after the tsunami, in which interviewees were asked to reflect on their experience of the tsunami and its consequences. While the interviewers did not directly ask questions about luck, there was one question that was included toward the end of the interview that asked whether they had thought if there was something they might have done differently. Nearly all interviewees spontaneously, i.e., without being prompted, included reference to luck concepts (e.g., Norwegian terms such as "hell"/ "uhell" [meaning lucky/unlucky] and "heldig"/"uheldig" [fortunate/unfortunate]), with the vast majority making reference to good luck rather than bad luck.

On the face of it, this might seem surprising that interviewees were typically referring to how lucky they had been as opposed to how unlucky they might have regarded themselves to have been caught up in the disaster. It seems they were spontaneously comparing their experience to an imagined counterfactual scenario where things could have been much worse. As many thousands of people lost their lives in the disaster, it is easy to see how such tragic counterfactual outcomes might be easily imagined for these interviewees, and therefore they see themselves as being lucky or fortunate by comparison.

Gratitude, both of the "personal" and "impersonal" kind described above, was mentioned in a smaller proportion, around a quarter, of the interviews, often in connection to luck. The personal gratitude was directed toward people who had given them help during the disaster, whereas the impersonal gratitude, according to the authors "comes close to suggesting a belief in fate or higher powers, as the feeling of gratefulness seems to ask for someone to be thanked" (Teigen & Jensen 2011: 52). A separate analysis searching for occurrences of counterfactual thinking revealed the predominance of downward counterfactual thinking (comparing to worse possible outcomes) over upward counterfactual thinking (comparing to better possible outcomes). While not all of the expressions of counterfactual thinking were directly linked to expressions of luck, many were. The preponderance of feelings of good luck rather than bad luck, and downward counterfactual comparisons rather than upward comparisons, might be taken as further signs of the link between perceptions of luckiness and imagining how things might have been worse. Feelings of gratitude could play a part in this link.

It is therefore apparent that perceiving oneself as lucky can at least imply feelings of gratitude that involve appreciating the way an event might have turned out in comparison to a less attractive imagined possible alternative. As we have seen, even if the set of events in and of themselves are not attractive (such as being in a life-threatening situation caused by a tsunami), one might still consider oneself as being fortunate by comparing to how things might have easily been worse (a lucky survivor). One might feel gratitude for this state of affairs, and this might be a general gratitude that is not directed to any particular person or group of people, but instead a more "impersonal" feeling of being thankful. Thus, gratitude might serve a purpose that helps us to cope with negative experiences, by allowing us to reappraise them with reference to imagined worse alternatives.

A separate, yet related, question concerns the role that gratitude might play in *creating* experiences that could be perceived as "good luck" experiences. The argument here is less concerned with how gratitude reflects, or engenders, counterfactual thinking, and is more concerned with how a grateful attitude to life in general might play a role in bringing about experiences that are deemed fortunate. The discussion above suggests that an appreciative or grateful mindset might, at the very least, mean that more events in general will be *perceived* as lucky if one is able to readily bring to mind less attractive alternatives in contexts that we typically take for granted. For example, most people living in the developed world might get up in the morning and have a wash or take a shower with hot running water. It is something we take for granted. However, in some parts of the world hot running water cannot be taken for granted and, when we remind ourselves of this, we might more readily appreciate what we have access to that others do not.

In addition to this widening of what we might classify as lucky or fortunate, we might ask how gratitude could actively have an impact on the creation of luck experiences. Here we are drawing on work on gratitude that has examined the impact of keeping a regular gratitude journal, e.g., daily or once a week, in which one makes a note of things in one's life that have happened over that day or week for which one is grateful. Such work has highlighted how cultivating gratitude in this way can not only have a positive impact upon wellbeing, but also appears to have interpersonal benefits in that people indicate they are more likely to engage in prosocial behaviors such as helping someone with a personal problem or offering emotional support (Emmons & McCullough 2003).

We speculate that a further positive consequence of cultivating gratitude that might be mediated through its interpersonal benefits is an increased possibility of what might be referred to as "interpersonal luck." That is, prosocial behavior toward others could have a reciprocal effect, meaning a rise in experiences of being the benefactor of unrequested, and perhaps unexpected, good deeds of others. Indeed, it might be through a process of this kind, at least in part, that one develops the kind of social "network of luck" to which Wiseman (2004) refers. He describes how self-perceived lucky people tended to have a larger social network than self-perceived unlucky people that they often built through seeking and creating opportunities to connect with others. The expression of gratitude to others, and the prosocial consequences of this, might be one way such a network is built, echoing the suggestions by Steindl-Rast (1984, 2013) that gratitude promotes an expanded and stronger sense of social links and cohesion. This is something we will explore more fully below in relation to the "broaden and build" theory of positive emotions (e.g., Fredrickson 1998).

Positive Emotions

As we have noted above, gratitude might at the very least confer emotional benefits or might be conceived as an emotion itself. The work of Barbara Fredrickson has taken the latter approach and has argued how this, alongside other "positive" emotions, could have what she has termed a "broaden and build" effect upon psychological processes and subsequent physical, intellectual, and social resources (Fredrickson 1998). The theory is predicated on the question of what purpose do positive emotions serve. Fredrickson (1998) argued that existing theories of emotion were largely, if not fully, focused on emotions that might be typically regarded as "negative" emotions, such as anger or fear. She therefore argued that theories to date did not sufficiently account for the range of positive emotions, especially in terms of the relationship between such emotions and our thought processes and actions. In an attempt to redress the balance and bring a clearer focus on those emotions that are typically regarded as positive (e.g., amusement, awe, joy, serenity), Fredrickson reassessed the claim that emotions lead to what theorists referred to as "specific action tendencies" (e.g., Frijda et al. 1989; Levenson 1994). This term refers to the idea that emotions lead to "urges to act in a particular way" (Fredrickson 1998: 302), such as anger might lead to attack, or fear might lead to escape. Fredrickson argues that it is clear how this might apply to these kinds of negative emotions, but less so in the context of positive emotions where any urge to act is not so specifiable. As a way of resolving this disparity between positive and negative emotions, she proposed instead that it might be more helpful to consider how emotions lead to "thought-action tendencies," in which negative emotions would typically be associated with a narrowing of the thought-action repertoire, and positive emotions with a broadening of the thought-action repertoire. From this perspective, we still might see fairly specific action tendencies associated with emotions such as anger and fear, whereas positive emotions such as joy or amusement might lead to a wider range of ways of thinking and acting that are more open and playful. She goes on to propose that this broadened way of thinking and acting might, over time, serve to build a range of resources that can be subsequently drawn upon. Thus, playful behavior might develop intellectual resources as we often learn through play, and may develop social resources as we seek to connect with others through play.

Fredrickson and her colleagues have undertaken a number of studies examining different aspects of this theory that have broadly supported the possible broadening and building effects of emotions (e.g., Fredrickson & Branigan 2005; Fredrickson 2013).

In the context of the present discussion, the question is to what extent might this model impact upon our understanding of "luck" experiences? We speculate that to the extent that the model accurately explains some of the consequential thoughts and actions of positive emotions, then a mechanism might exist by which positive emotions are an antecedent of experiences that might be attributed to luck. Let us consider first the proposed broadening effects of positive emotions upon the scope of one's attention, thinking, and action. A broadening effect on attention might mean that the focus of attention is softened, and our peripheral attention is widened, meaning that we might become more aware of our wider environment and therefore notice stimuli and opportunities that were previously "hidden" to us, or outside of our awareness. Daniel Simons and colleagues' work on inattentional blindness reveals how we can often be "blind" to stimuli that should be quite obvious if our attention was not narrowly focused on some other task (e.g., Simons & Chabris 1999). We might hypothesize that broadening effects of positive emotions on attention would result in a lessening of susceptibility to such inattentional blindness.

Assuming our broadened attention allows us to increase our awareness of possible opportunities in our environment, a broadening effect on how we *process* such opportunities might result in us being more likely to recognize these as opportunities that are relevant and potentially beneficial to us (i.e., as possible sources of fortuitous events). One way this might manifest itself is that broadened thinking processes lead to us being more willing and able to make connections between events and therefore increase the incidences of what appear to be meaningful occurrences and coincidences. If all this also leads to broadened action then we have a greater chance of action that capitalizes on the opportunity that has presented itself and been interpreted as an opportunity.

We can therefore see that any possible broadening effects of positive emotions could have consequences for how we make sense of, and interact with, our environment. We speculate that these could be instrumental in creating circumstances that form the basis of experiences that many of us might describe as lucky or fortunate.

If we turn to the second part of the proposed broadening and building consequences of positive emotions, we might further elucidate how these might lead to luck experiences. Fredrickson (1998) argues that the broadening effects of positive emotions serve to also build lasting resources. As noted above, these resources may be drawn upon some time after the initial experience of the emotion itself. For example, social resources, in the form of friendships and acquaintances are ones that might be borne out of somewhat fleeting shared emotional experiences, yet they become a long-term feature of one's life that can be the source of comfort, support, and love. They might also be the source of unexpected opportunities (e.g., job offers) that some would see as strokes of luck. As these kinds of benefits are not likely to be perceived as being overtly connected with the original emotion then their occurrences are, instead, likely to be construed as "merely" fortuitous.

Optimism

Psychological work on optimism has tended to conceive of optimism in the context of either having favorable generalized expectancies about the future (e.g., Carver et al. 2010) or making adaptive attributions about how events have turned out in the past (e.g., Seligman 1991).

While it might be that both conceptions of optimism have relevance in our discussion of "luck" experiences, our focus here is on optimism for future events. When considering our expectations about how a future event might turn out, where there is some degree of uncertainty and we are not fully in control of the outcome, we might adopt an optimistic outlook that is characterized by an expectation that we could "be lucky," in that we expect things will work out well. Smith (1998) found a link between perceived luckiness and optimism. Participants were administered a "Perceived Luckiness Questionnaire" that allowed respondents to rate themselves in terms of how lucky or unlucky they perceived themselves to be, alongside an established measure of dispositional optimism, the Life Orientation Test (LOT) (Scheier & Carver 1985). This latter measure aims to assess people's general expectancies about the future by having respondents rate their agreement with statements such as "In uncertain times, I usually expect the best" and "I rarely count on good things happening to me" (reverse scored).

Not too surprisingly, perceived luckiness was found to be strongly positively correlated with optimism, with the participants classified as "lucky" on the PLQ obtaining significantly higher scores on the LOT than participants classified as "unlucky." This pattern tells us that perceived luckiness and optimism are related, though it tells us little about any possible *causal* relationship between them. Is it that a broadly optimistic disposition, as reflected in higher scores on the LOT, might lead one to develop a perception of oneself as a lucky person? Alternatively, is the causal relationship the reverse, with a personal belief in one's own luckiness being a *cause* of an optimistic outlook? This view seemed to be an underlying assumption behind the development of the LOT, with the authors suggesting that "a person may hold favorable expectancies for a number of reasons—personal ability, because the person is lucky, or because he is favored by others" (Scheier & Carver 1985: 223). A further possibility is that there is some other factor that influences both perceived luckiness and optimism. For example, there might be an underlying aspect of personality that is at least partly responsible for both of these. A separate line of work has explored the relationship between beliefs about luck, optimism, and psychological wellbeing, suggesting that believing luck to be a positive and stable influence in one's life might have adaptive consequences for wellbeing, and that this relationship is mediated by optimism (Day & Maltby 2003).

The focus here has been on the relationship between optimism and *perceived* luckiness and *beliefs* about luck. In the context of the present discussion, we wish to go a step further to propose how optimism might play a role in *creating* luck experiences. We see this working in the way proposed by Wiseman (2004), in that a positive expectation about a future event, perhaps manifesting as a belief that one will be lucky, might play a role in bringing about the very event that one expects. In this regard it becomes a self-fulfilling prophecy: a belief in being lucky leads to the experience of being lucky.

Environmental Mastery

The concept of "environmental mastery" features within one of the major theoretical approaches to psychological wellbeing (Ryff 1989; Ryff & Keyes 1995). It is presented as one of six distinct key dimensions of psychological wellbeing or positive functioning and is defined as a "capacity to manage effectively one's life and surrounding world" (Ryff & Keyes 1995: 720).

Environmental mastery, as conceived by Ryff and Keyes (1995), relates, in part, to the extent to which we are able to exert some kind of control over our environment, and includes how we might be able to take advantage of or create environmental opportunities. We must also ask whether the notion of environmental mastery also involves, to some extent, our willingness and capacity to seek influence and be open while relinquishing control? We note that many aspects of our environment are indeed beyond our control (e.g., traffic, the weather) and other aspects of our environment might be potentially controllable, yet we question whether they are aspects that we *need* to seek control over (e.g., other people's actions).

Researchers have long understood many aspects of the psychology of the extent to which we perceive personal control over our environment. Rotter's early work on locus of control revealed individual differences in how we tend to perceive the extent of control we have over what happens to us in our lives (Rotter 1966). He argued that some of us have a tendency to perceive ourselves as instrumental in bringing about events (internal locus of control), while others might have a tendency to regard events as being due to factors that are beyond their control (external locus of control). His work heralded a wealth of research around the locus of control construct, much of which focused on specific contexts, such as health or occupational settings (e.g., Wallston et al. 1978; Spector 1988). One theme of this body of work was to examine the relative benefits of an internal vs. external locus of control, with a consensus emerging that an internal locus of control was preferable, especially in the context of health outcomes, as this was associated with health-promoting behaviors over which each of us as individuals do have control, such as diet and exercise. In this context, it therefore seems that a bias in which our focus is toward seeing outcomes as something within our control is likely to be beneficial to our health. This might be especially true when we take into account that some people have a greater "desire" for control than others, and when a high desire for control is combined with a tendency to perceive events as beyond one's control (i.e., an external locus of control) then this can have detrimental implications for mental health and has been found to be linked to proneness to depression (e.g., Burger 1984).

However, it seems likely that one would not want to be exclusively focused on our own agency in terms of bringing outcomes about, including health outcomes. There is value in being aware of when events are beyond our control and that we must accept them as such.

Acting as though we have control over an environment or events that are objectively beyond our control is, to some extent, human nature. Indeed, this "illusion of control" has been observed in dice players who throw dice hard for a high number and more softly for a low number (Henslin 1967). In a series of classic studies, people were consistently found to act as though they were exerting skill and control in a situation that was objectively determined by chance (e.g., Langer 1975; Langer & Roth 1975).

This apparent confusion or ambiguity with what we regard as potentially within or outside of our personal control is, in fact, central to our discussion of positive psychology in relation to luck experiences. It is the essence of why we believe that these ideas have relevance to the broader theoretical discussion surrounding luck in the first place: events that appear out of our control might, in reality, at least in part, be influenced by our interactions with the world. The perhaps surprising aspect of this, we argue, is that this influence might be brought about most effectively by our willingness to relinquish any direct attempts to exert control over these events. Instead, it is through practices such as cultivating gratitude, positive emotions, and an optimistic outlook that allow the space for us to recognize and appreciate the role of luck in our lives.

Conclusion

In this chapter we have attempted to draw out possible links between theoretical and research approaches that currently sit within positive psychology and how these might aid our understanding of luck experiences. Our focus has been on links between luck and gratitude, positive emotions, optimism, and environmental mastery, with an emphasis on how these might increase what might typically be described as "good luck" experiences. Before we leave this discussion, it is important to note how these ideas might play a role in how we deal with "bad luck" experiences. For example, an illness or an accident that leaves us restricted in how we go about our business might be construed by many as a case of bad luck. Losing one's job through redundancy might be another common experience that would often be characterized as something that is bad luck.

Ways of coping with adversity have been explored by researchers whose focus has been on processes associated with resilience (e.g., Masten 2001; Luthar et al. 2000). In the context of this work, Lyubomirsky and Della Porta (2010) have argued in favor of proactively adopting the kinds of approaches outlined in this chapter, such as cultivating gratitude or optimism, as a way of developing a resilience toward adversity. If we see experiences of misfortune as one form of adversity, then this approach reflects our own in terms of highlighting the role that positive psychology can play in how we cope with (bad) luck.

It is an approach that throws into question whether luck is indeed the untameable beast it might first appear. As we noted earlier, our everyday lives consist of myriad events that are, to some extent, within our control and to some extent beyond our control. Our acceptance and appreciation of this at a fundamental psychological level could be an important first step in bringing luck on our side. Further, when we start to consider the relationship between luck and the discipline of positive psychology, not only do we see how positive psychology might add to our understanding of luck experiences, we also see how introducing luck to the discipline of positive psychology might allow for a deeper awareness of the relationship between luck and psychological wellbeing. As reflected in the words of Cohen (1960) that opened this chapter, luck is experienced personally, not in the abstract, and the influences on our lives have personal nuances and locations and the meaning attributed to it reflects personal stories and lives. If we bear this in mind, then further psychological assessments of luck have the capacity to more fully unpack the link between luck, psychology, and health.

Note

1 Wiseman simply refers to these groups as lucky and unlucky people. In our discussion of this work we will put the terms "lucky" and "unlucky" in inverted commas to illustrate that these terms, used in this context, reflect their *perceptions* of themselves as lucky or unlucky.

References

Burger, J.M. (1984) "Desire For Control, Locus of Control, and Proneness to Depression," *Journal of Personality* 52, 71–89.

Carver, C.S., Scheier, M.F., & Segerstrom, S.C. (2010) "Optimism," *Clinical Psychology Review* 30, 879–889.

Cohen, J. (1960) *Chance, Skill and Luck: The Psychology of Guessing and Gambling*, London: Pelican.

Darke, P.R., & Freedman, J.L. (1997) "The Belief in Good Luck Scale," *Journal of Research in Personality* 31, 486–511.

Day, L., & Maltby, J. (2003) "Belief in Good Luck and Psychological Well-being: The Mediating Role of Optimism and Irrational Beliefs," *Journal of Psychology* 137, 99–110.

Emmons, R.A. (2004) "The Psychology of Gratitude: An Introduction," in R.A. Emmons & M.E. McCullough (eds.) *The Psychology of Gratitude*, New York: Oxford University Press, pp. 3–16.

Emmons, R.A., & McCullough, M.E. (2003) "Counting Blessings Versus Burdens: An Experimental Investigation of Gratitude and Subjective Well-being in Daily Life," *Journal of Personality and Social Psychology* 84, 377–389.

Emmons, R.A., & Shelton, C.M. (2002) "Gratitude and the Science of Positive Psychology," in C.R. Snyder & S.J. Lopez (eds.) *Handbook of Positive Psychology*. Oxford: Oxford University Press, pp. 459–471.

Epstude, K., & Roese, N. (2008) "The Functional Theory of Counterfactual Thinking," *Personality and Social Psychology Review* 12, 168–192.

Fredrickson, B.L. (1998) "What Good Are Positive Emotions?" *Review of General Psychology* 2, 300–319.

——. (2013) "Positive Emotions Broaden and Build," in E. Ashby Plant & P. Devine (eds.) *Advances in Experimental Social Psychology*, vol. 47, Burlington: Academic Press, pp. 1–53.

Fredrickson, B.L., & Branigan, C. (2005) "Positive Emotions Broaden the Scope of Attention and Thought-action Repertoires," *Cognition and Emotion* 19, 313–332.

Frijda, N.H., Kuipers, P., & Schure, E. (1989) "Relations among Emotion, Appraisal, and Emotional Action Readiness," *Journal of Personality and Social Psychology* 57, 212–228.

Henslin, J.M. (1967) "Craps and Magic," *American Journal of Sociology* 73(3), 316–330.

Langer, E.J. (1975) "The Illusion of Control," *Journal of Personality and Social Psychology* 32 (2), 311–328.

Langer, E.J., & Roth, J. (1975) "Heads I Win, Tails It's Chance: The Illusion of Control as a Function of the Sequence of Outcomes in a Purely Chance Task," *Journal of Personality and Social Psychology* 32(6), 951–955.

Levenson, R.W. (1994) "Human Emotion: A Functional View," in P. Ekman & R. Davidson (eds.) *The Nature of Emotion: Fundamental Questions*, New York: Oxford University Press, pp. 123–126.

Lomas, T., Froh, J.J., Emmons, R.A., Mishra, A.J., & Bono, G. (2014) "Gratitude Interventions: A Review and Future Agenda," in A.C. Parks & S.M. Schueller (eds.) *The Wiley Blackwell Handbook of Positive Psychological Interventions*, Chichester: John Wiley & Sons, pp. 3–19.

Luthar, S.S., Cicchetti, D., & Becker, B. (2000) "The Construct of Resilience: A Critical Evaluation and Guidelines for Future Work," *Child Development* 71, 543–562.

Lyubomirsky, S., & Della Porta, M.D. (2010) "Boosting Happiness, Buttressing Resilience: Results from Cognitive and Behavioural Interventions," in J.W. Reich, A.J. Zautra, & J.S. Hall (eds.) *Handbook of Adult Resilience*, London: Guildford Press, pp. 450–464.

Maslow, A.H. (1954/1970) *Motivation and Personality*, 3rd edition, London: Harper Collins.

Masten, A. (2001) "Ordinary Magic: Resilience Processes in Development," *American Psychologist* 56, 227–238.

Roese, N.J. (1997) "Counterfactual Thinking," *Psychological Bulletin* 121, 133–148.

Rogers, C. (1967/2004) *On Becoming a Person*, London: Constable and Company Ltd.

Rotter, J.B. (1966) "Generalized Expectancies for Internal versus External Control of Reinforcement," *Psychological Monographs* 80(1), 1–28.

Ryff, C.D. (1989) "Happiness Is Everything, Or Is It? Explorations on the Meaning of Psychological Well-being," *Journal of Personality and Social Psychology* 57, 1069–1081.

Ryff, C.D., & Keyes, C.L.M. (1995) "The Structure of Psychological Well-being Revisited," *Journal of Personality and Social Psychology* 69, 719–727.

Scheier, M.F., & Carver, C.S. (1985) "Optimism, Coping, and Health: Assessment and Implications of Generalized Outcome Expectancies," *Health Psychology* 4, 219–247.

Seligman, M.E.P. (1991) *Learned Optimism*, New York: Alfred A. Knopf.

Seligman, M.E.P., & Csikszentmihalyi, M. (2000) "Positive Psychology: An Introduction," *American Psychologist* 55, 5–14.

Simons, D.J., & Chabris, C.F. (1999) "Gorillas in Our Midst: Sustained Inattentional Blindness for Dynamic Events," *Perception* 28, 1059–1074.

Smith, M.D. (1998) *Perceptions of one's own luckiness: The formation, maintenance, and consequences of perceived luckiness.* Unpublished Ph.D. thesis. Hatfield: University of Hertfordshire.

Spector, P.E. (1988) "Development of the Work Locus of Control Scale," *Journal of Occupational and Organizational Psychology* 61, 335–340.

Steindl-Rast, D. (1984) *Gratefulness, the Heart of Prayer*. New York: Paulist Press.

——. (2013) *A Good Day: A Gift of Gratitude*. New York: Sterling Ethos.

Teigen, K.H. (1995) "How Good Is Good Luck? The Role of Counterfactual Thinking in the Perception of Lucky and Unlucky Events," *European Journal of Social Psychology* 25, 281–302.

——. (1997) "Luck, Envy and Gratitude: It Could Have Been Different," *Scandinavian Journal of Psychology* 38, 313–323.

Teigen, K.H., & Jensen, T.K. (2011) "Unlucky Victims or Lucky Survivors? Spontaneous Counterfactual Thinking by Families Exposed to the Tsunami Disaster," *European Psychologist* 16, 48–57.

Wagenaar, W.A., & Keren, G.B. (1988) "Chance and Luck Are Not the Same," *Journal of Behavioural Decision Making* 1, 65–75.

Wallston, K.A., Wallston, B.S., & DeVellis, R. (1978) "Development of the Multidimensional Health Locus of Control (MHLC) Scales," *Health Education & Behavior* 6, 160–170.

Weiner, B. (1985) "An Attributional Theory of Achievement Motivation and Emotion," *Psychological Review* 92, 548–573.

Weiner, B., Frieze, I., Kukla, A., Reed, L., Rest, S., & Rosenbaum, R. (1971) *Perceiving the Causes of Success and Failure*, New York: General Learning Press.

Wiseman, R. (2004) *The Luck Factor*. London: Random House.

PART VI

Future Research

34

LUCK IN SCIENCE[1]

J.D. Trout

The role of luck in science is a popular but complex topic, for at least two reasons. First, it is not easy to arrive at a common conception of luck. Is it chance? Randomness? Uncontrollability of outcome? Contingency? Second, whatever luck is, its sources seem to differ in kind and magnitude, making general lessons difficult to extract. Particular kinds of luck mattered more or less to scientific advance across history and across the globe. Lucky access to waterways might have mattered more to scientific progress in Europe in 1600 than in China in 850. A lucky or contingent idiosyncratic personality trait might prompt a discovery for one science at one moment in history, and might not even merit notice in another science at another geographic location or moment in history. Even when a role for luck in science is established, it is especially difficult to assess its general impact or significance.

The important role of luck and contingency in scientific advance has been much neglected in contemporary philosophy of science, a philosophical atmosphere that favors a narrative of deliberate and controlled scientific experimentation and investigation. But the historical record of scientific progress documents the opposite: Many advances in the history of science result from lucky events and shocking contingencies. Once we recognize this fact as part of the historical record, we can offer a more unified explanation for scientific progress. Ironically, the type of scientific realism that celebrates a persistently upward trend of theoretical progress in science also documents a chancy path, cut by luck and contingency.

Interest in the role of luck in science, and in many other drivers of the fate of science, begins with the observation that the treasures of scientific wisdom are not evenly distributed across civilizations. Wherever a scientific outlook (or at least engineering and practical achievements) seemed to take hold, we are often told that it was the result of the scientific method, a deliberate and sometimes drab mix of experimental design, observation, and record-keeping. But this explanation for the rise of modern science will not do. After all, the learned investigators in ancient China, ancient India, and early Islam were no strangers to the discipline of experimentation. To take just one example, recorded astronomical observations by the ancient Chinese are still used to fix the orbits of long-period comets (Marsden 1983: 60). Success in science, then, is unevenly distributed and not reducible to proper application of the scientific method. The reasons for this uneven distribution of successes are many—differences in resources, individual intellect, cultural orientation, exposure to trade routes, environmental challenges, and so on. So many of the reasons are contingent, the effects of chance or luck.

391

In addressing the role of luck in scientific advance, I do not propose to argue for a particular conception of science, but we surely won't mean by "science" whatever the respected leaders and intellectual authorities of a culture counted as successful inquiries into the world. If that were our measure, we would be including humoral theories, theories of balance of yin and yang, all variants of alchemy, and race-based theories of human development and behavior, to name a few. The systematic and successful study of nature began at different times, at different places, with different approaches, across the globe. Ancient Indian, Chinese, and Arabic societies had troubled metaphysical views that hampered scientific traditions, but excelled at mathematical theorizing. All had ingenious paths to finding, securing, and distributing water and other natural resources. Many had impressive technologies—achievements of timekeeping, engineering, and, occasionally, practical medicine—but none had good theories, and some are still dogged by traditions of folklore dominated by narrative and anecdote.

There were many contingencies in the history of science that no doubt set us on the right metaphysical path, but not all contingencies are equally influential, of course. In *Wondrous Truths* (Trout 2016), I argue that later alchemy was an important factor in the rise of modern science. But we routinely ask questions about other events in the history of science that also seem lucky or contingent. These questions can mark causes big and small. What if the Paris Academy's norm of coordinating vocabulary, or of peer review, had not arisen when, or where, it did? What if the concentration of wealth in Europe in the 1700s had been different? What if Japan's samurai culture had not discouraged the use of gunpowder and firearms?

The Many Senses of "Luck"

We describe many different kinds of events as lucky, such as choices, lives, soccer goals, guesses, and marriages. While each of these events is deemed lucky because its outcome is a success, each of these "lucky" events can have a different kind of cause. Sometimes we highlight a "lucky" event's chanciness, or its fleeting nature. We might say that a gambler makes a lucky bet on a longshot that won, or that advocates of the Copenhagen interpretation of quantum mechanics were lucky that a broadly empiricist conception of knowledge won out over competing accounts in the 1930s.

If examples of actual use are a representative guide, chanciness alone does not make an outcome lucky; it is not a sufficient condition for luck, as it is broadly conceived in philosophy in the English-speaking world, and in non-academic parlance. The outcome could be bad or good, but its level of uncertainty, like getting the one green marble in a single blind draw from an urn of 20, is a descriptive statistical fact about the possible outcomes of random draws. Results that are the result of chance are not always "lucky" outcomes in the way we actually use the term.

It is tempting to treat luck (Broncano-Berrocal 2015) or contingency, as anything that is beyond, or not under, the agent's control (Nagel 1979; Williams 1981; Card 1993; Latus 2003). But just as the adage says that we make our own luck, we might have a hand in determining what is within our control.[2] In a way, it is lucky that you had a successful audition, landing the leading soprano role. But then again, you have spent 5,000 hours practicing. Indeed, there may be different kinds of luck. Recent accounts canvass chance or probability (Rescher 1995), modal non-robustness (Pritchard 2005, 2014; Whittington 2014; Carter and Peterson 2016), or lack of control (Mele 2006). More peripheral, but worth noting, is the descriptive fact that we tend to evaluate as "lucky" only those events significant to the attributor.

Luck has the ring of contingency. In general, a contingent outcome in a system can result from a tiny and perhaps unidentifiable feature of initial conditions (such as the rise of human life from the Earth's early suitability to shallow marine environments, or from a large and identifiable factor in a process, such as the extinction of the dinosaurs from an asteroid strike. In some sense, each of these events is contingent, accidental, or lucky. We might not care to call such an outcome "lucky," because we do not want to judge the outcome as good or bad. But for the purposes of the meaning of luck

Luck in Science

in science, these are all relevant sources of, or influences on, luck in science.[3] Our purpose is not to stipulate lexical use, but to capture often surprising, typically unpredictable, or unappreciated phenomena that influence noteworthy outcomes.

When contingent facts such as inclement weather, an unplanned meeting, or a serendipitous chemical mixture, drive a scientific advance, the target hypothesis receives especially potent confirmation, because the measuring techniques instrumental in securing confirmation could not possibly have conspired to produce the same outcome. After all, the introduction of different techniques was unplanned and unguided, perhaps even accidental. It might be that the history of science is highly contingent, but that scientific success is all but inevitable. Perhaps scientific genius, human persistence, or the canons of experimental method virtually guarantee scientific success. Events could have turned out in any number of ways, but (almost) all of them involve great success in one form or another. Therefore, my thesis needs to identify events not simply where the history of science is contingent, but where its success itself is contingent. Success itself is contingent when a chance event made the difference between progress and stagnation or failure.

History and Contingency

The hindsight bias prevents us from appreciating the power of contingency: when progress is undeniable, as it is in every area of developed science, it is easy to believe that it was also inevitable. In science, the sentiment proceeds, nothing is left to chance: project a hypothesis, manipulate a variable, record the outcome, and then repeat with a slight variation. But this incremental image of the history of science obscures its most exciting features. The truth is, progress was driven by contingencies of creative talent, geographic location, social affiliation with the right people, the purposes of patronage, access to raw materials, and the needs of industry or the military. To spin the history of science into a story of rational development, you need an unscientific tolerance for inaccuracy, an aversion to uncertainty, and a compulsive need for narrative closure. The reality, however, is far messier. This view of history as contingent has precedent elsewhere: cultural history, unlike the history of science, is much more comfortable with assertions of accident and contingency, but they are still jarring and dramatic. For example, in his magisterial *Guns, Germs and Steel*, Jared Diamond (1999) asks why Europe emerged as the dominant power in the world. His answers often cite accidents—contingencies of history or geography—rather than the unfolding of a plan or policy. Military might is always an obvious cause of domination, because it is always the consequence of a carefully executed plan. But military might is not the whole story. For example, while the domestication of animals reaches back at least as far as Jericho, medieval Europeans were the first to live in close proximity to the animals they bred. This specifically European variation of domestication was, amazingly, a certain entrée to world domination: enemies, and potential enemies, were wiped out by the germs incubated in Europeans after the microbes made the jump from the animals they domesticated. And while it was not the sole cause of European dominance, it was a beefy contributor. European germs wiped out nonresistant populations even before they could become enemies of the Europeans (Diamond 1999).

If historical contingencies caused the rise of colonialism, why couldn't the same be true for the rise of science? But ask anyone on the street about how science originated, and if you get an answer it will likely be a fanciful story that begins with the experimental method, drab and uninspired. According to that narrative, only after the method's introduction could science be done in earnest. Francis Bacon (1561–1626) formulated a handful of canons for experimentation that will grind a passable meal out of any intellectual ingredients (Bacon 1620/2000). The experimental story is soothing for a number of reasons. The view that advances are ground out by sheer earnestness and dutiful application of existing knowledge assures people that, no matter how imagination might fail us, there are still great discoveries to come. Progress requires no grand theoretical landscape. By simply and faithfully applying the canons of experimental method, we can produce better hybrid plants, create stronger bridges, design better sewerage systems, and breed better mice.

393

The problem with this generalization about the origin of modern science is that, like most generalizations, it leaks. Rather badly. The experimental method preceded Bacon by at least 400 years, and by itself had little power to transform a bad science into a good one. Explanations of success that invoke the rise of the experimental method, though comforting, are feeble and limited. So the answer must lie elsewhere. The truth is, given the huge lurches of theoretical progress documented in the historical record, the only way to explain the spectacular success of modern science is to assign a major role to contingent or serendipitous discovery and advance. Once we give due weight to contingency in scientific progress, we can for the first time give a more accurate account of the history of science.

All historians of science acknowledge the influence of contingency when it suits their purpose. In fact, the contingency of scientific progress explains otherwise inexplicable findings. Thomas Kuhn emphasizes the contingency in every theoretical movement: "An apparently arbitrary element, compounded of a personal and historic accident, is always a formative ingredient of the beliefs espoused by a given scientific community at a given time" (Kuhn 1962/1996: 19–20). When a theory lacks the fertile body of beliefs that press the advance, "it must be externally supplied, perhaps by a current metaphysics, by another science, or by personal and historical accident" (Kuhn 1962/ 1996: 31–32).

Modern textbooks also do not ignore the creative aspect of science altogether, nor the routine leaps that we make in our ordinary theoretical investigations. One chemistry textbook notes simply that hypotheses are "derived from actual observation or from a 'spark of intuition'" (Silberberg 2000: 12). A representative, topical biology textbook observes that, in addition to using both deductive and inductive reasoning, hypotheses can also be generated in other ways, namely, by "(1) intuition or imagination, (2) aesthetic preferences, (3) religious and philosophical ideas, (4) comparison and analogy with other processes, and (5) serendipity." That is, "hypotheses are formed by all sorts of logical and extralogical processes" (Minkoff & Baker 2001: 6). Similarly, a biology textbook notes that "there is considerable creativity within the boundaries of these investigative processes. Insights can result from accident, from sudden intuition, or from methodical research" (Starr & Taggart 1984: 21). Yet these insights, apparently, are still within the boundaries of a method. As we will see, the role contingency plays in the advance of science is far greater than even Kuhn and the textbooks give it credit for.

The beginning of science itself benefited from this sort of fortuitous contingency. The very best practices of proto-science amounted to the routine reliance on alchemical adepts (many of whom were frauds),[4] instruments that were poorly made or applied to the wrong phenomena, theories of mystical or occult origin, theological conceit, and/or ideological imposition, all mistaken to their core. Science advanced despite its dependence on overwhelmingly false scientific theories of yore, the misleading feeling of fluency and understanding conveyed by bad explanations, the inefficiencies of human exploration, political and religious campaigns against science, and the world's complexity. Yet despite all of these obstacles, engineering exploits such as bridge building, feats of practical medicine such as the treatment of digestive ailments, and theoretical speculations about the underlying composition of the physical world bred a modern science that, together with democracy, must be counted as the greatest accomplishments of human civilization.

In the grand scheme of things, science happened virtually all at once. Human civilizations emerged in the last 15,000 years in Africa, Eurasia, and the Americas, and yet modern science was born and took shape in a brief period from 1640 to 1730, within a slender band of Europe. Why then? Why there? Why so successful?

For animals like us, it could be a crushing discovery that progress is often irreducibly fluky. It is disturbing, or at least a little unsettling, to recognize that one of your greatest achievements issued from sheer luck, from the spinning wheel of office mates, a casual conversation, or a weather pattern. Under an ideology that equates science with prediction and control, the role of luck or fortune seems incompatible with great discovery. We desire to find something out and, having gathered and evaluated the evidence, we have the feeling that the evidence is now under our cognitive control—that we understand. We try to fit all of the pieces of a process into a coherent explanation or unified picture. If we prefer to see ourselves as the custodians and beneficiaries of a just world, we need to tell ourselves that hard work is rewarded, success is not arbitrary, and competence comes from intellectual authority—we understand that which is under our cognitive control. But having looked at the biological underpinnings of explanation and understanding, we now sadly know that, in telling themselves a story of incremental and methodological progress, people create in themselves a feeling of understanding *that might or might not be accurate.*

After more than three centuries of post-Newtonian rhetoric about the bracing merits of doing experimental duty, it is time to examine the forces we cannot control. Let us celebrate the importance of unplanned, unguided, and occasionally uninterested theorizing not as a dignified alternative to experimental reasoning, but as essential to it. Theory construction makes clear that real, lived science is chancy and haphazard, unpredictable and downright fluky.[5] This makes scientific progress historically contingent when the reasons for its occurrence were, from the point of view of some intelligible image of development, accidental.

Sources of Contingency

If scientific talent and resources were everywhere the same, the rate and character of scientific discovery might be more uniform. The high steppes of central Asia might have been the site of the first effective germ theory of disease. But it wasn't. In 1800, the electric-chemical discoveries made by Berzelius in Stockholm might have been made by people living in Constantinople, Tokyo, or any of the largest cities in Africa. But they weren't. The pattern is decidedly nonrandom. All possible discoveries are not equipossible. The aspects of a scientist's conceptual world that produce departures from equipossible discovery may concern history, culture, climate, financial sponsorship—whatever facts support ingenuity, sustain hard work, or impose disciplined training. But, importantly, none of these features get traction unless the discovery promotes a theory or theoretical outlook that actually captures the causal structure of the world.

History is not an experimental science, and so we cannot nail down that a scientific success is genuinely contingent rather than, say, inevitable because redundantly determined. But there are signposts when an event that can be tied to a theoretical advance occurs against a background of a normal or routine course of events. For example, further examples of small contingencies, of unplanned advance, can arise from factors beyond the internal sources of scientific investigation. The brewery next door prompted Joseph Priestley to mull over apparently "heavier air" emanating from that location, and that became an occasion to study the features of carbon dioxide. Priestley was especially interested in its ability to extinguish glowing embers, while at the same time he uncovered the powerful combustive forces of oxygen largely by chance. As he characterized the contingency: "If, however, I had not happened, for some other purpose, to have had a lighted candle before me, I should probably never have made the trial."[6]

In fact, Priestley offers a lovely general description of contingency:

> The contents of this section will furnish striking illustration of the truth of a remark which I have more than once made in my philosophical writing and which can hardly be too often repeated, as it tends greatly to encourage philosophical investigations; viz. that more is owing to what we call chance, that is, philosophically speaking, to the observation of events arising from unknown causes, than to any proper design, or preconceived theory in this business.
>
> For my own part, I will frankly acknowledge, that, at the commencement of the experiments recited in this section, I was so far from having formed any hypothesis that led to the discoveries I made in pursuing them, that they would have appeared very improbable to me had I been told of them; and when the decisive facts did at length obtrude themselves

upon my notice, it was very slowly, and with great hesitation, that I yielded to the evidence of my senses.

Priestley 1775: 29

Some contingencies vault an entire field forward. Of course, this all didn't just "happen." Lucky breaks must be coupled with minds able to realize their importance. Pasteur was deeply engaged in the science of his time, and when you are busily employed in the business of inquiry, you are in a position to benefit from fortuitous opportunities. Pasteur modestly, but probably accurately, put his discoveries down to this benefit. In his words: "*Dans les champs de l'observation, le hazard ne favorise que les esprits préparés.*" ("In the field of observation, chance favors only the prepared mind" (Pasteur 1854). This is a common theme that acknowledges contingency. Joseph Henry, the distinguished American physicist, said, "The seeds of great discoveries are constantly floating around us, but they only take root in minds well-prepared to receive them."[7] Good scientists often feel most keenly that they are responsible for their discoveries. But even the most gifted and successful scientists recognize the role of contingency/luck in scientific advancement.

Types of Contingency

The success of modern science does not issue from only the most deliberate methods of investigation; if that were true, science would have taken off when we developed mathematics and had the resources to perform voluminous observation. But it didn't. Instead, our explanations succeeded because our background theories were very good, when we made the right leaps. And we can arrive at those theories for many reasons, not all of them "rational."

There are at least six kinds of contingency familiar in human history: psychological, environmental, timing, historical, cultural, and biological.

1. *Psychological Contingencies (Idiosyncrasy).* Scientific advances sometimes originate from personal variables—if not outright idiosyncrasies. And this fact can have confirmatory value. As noted earlier, it is a tenet of experimentation that evidence is more secure when established by diverse means. Idiosyncrasy is one source of diversity in testing, a source of unplanned variation. Thus, idiosyncratic concepts and practices serve the purposes of intellectual foraging. The influence of idiosyncrasy should not be surprising, because little is known about the discovery process. What do such individual accidents look like? Philosopher of mind Jerry Fodor captures perfectly the experience of unexpected insight:

> The ways that people do this are notoriously idiosyncratic. Some go for walks. Some line up their pencils and stare into the middle distance. Some go to bed. Coleridge and De Quincy smoked opium. Hardy went to cricket matches. Balzac put his nightgown on. Proust sat himself in a cork-lined room and contemplated antique hats. Heaven knows what De Sade did.
>
> *Fodor 1974: 202*

People clearly do things they believe will put them in creative moods. The techniques are as varied as personality. Indeed, there are many subjective reports of moments of insight in the history of science that have no detectably objective or rational basis. Instead, it is largely based on a person's quirks—his or her peculiar sleeping habits, social incompetence, unusual training, and so forth. Kuhn, for example, claims that Kepler was a sun worshipper, and this eased his transition to a sun-centered Copernicanism (Kuhn 1962/1996: 152–153). As in this case, these idiosyncrasies translate into success only when they reliably connect to theoretical features of the world, and conversely, personal quirks could just as easily cause people to *miss* opportunities to develop accurate theoretical views. The important point is that success, like failure, can have a chancy and personal beginning, and it is no

Luck in Science

argument against a given theoretical view whether it began with either a dutiful experiment or a hallucination.

2. *Environmental Contingencies*. So much of the history of science is told as a character narrative, a study in how intellect bent the world toward progress. But just as often, scientific progress occurred because the world was already bent. Environmental contingencies are geographic features of the world that made science and its discoveries possible or likely. Scientific advance awaited leisure and concentration of resources, and this required civilization. But the rise of dense civilizations normally depended on not one but many factors, not all of which are environmental. The presence of local water might be one of many properties that contributed to a thriving civilization, even if the civilization would not have failed without it. And its presence might be an environmental contingency. The proximity of water is often thought to be a necessary condition for a civilization's prosperity, but the abundance of water is only an occasional presence in rising flourishing civilizations. Many great civilizations, such as Athens and Constantinople, were not near substantial bodies of fresh water. Sometimes access to abundant water contributes to a civilization's success as much for trade as for agriculture and drinking. In this way, scientific development depended on distinctly geographical, practical contingencies. This is not to say that all scientific centers were near significant waterways. Some civilizations near water have not made scientific advances, and some cultures not near significant water sources, such as Madrid, had flourishing science. It is to say that the presence of water typically plays a potent causal role in producing the growth of scientific culture. Nor is abundant water sufficient for a flourishing civilization. Witness that the largest US cities are not near the largest US rivers (measured by discharge), and relatively few are, like Chicago, on a lake. The ultimate success of a large, civilized center can depend on a vast variety of factors—geographic, cultural, economic, and theoretical. This is precisely the multicausal path that contingent processes follow.

3. *Contingencies of Timing*. Of course, not all guesses, accidents of history, and chance meetings result in a theoretical advance. More often than not, they lead to false belief and missions down rabbit holes. And it is the causal structure of the world that determines which cases of scientific serendipity result in findings that are durable and unifying. In fact, we assign more confirmatory weight when a serendipitous or unexpected event connects unrelated theories. Some of them concern uncanny timing. Usually these lucky events are treated as mere intellectual curiosities, sources of amusement. We benefit from these fortunate happenings, but precisely because these events are so chancy and unexpected, no one can hope to *use* (or even rely on) fluky timing as a reliable pivot point to produce discoveries. But when the effects of contingent timing are beneficial, it is an especially powerful form of confirmation. A typical case of fortunate timing occurred when, in 1846, Claude Bernard solved the mystery of the carnivorous rabbits. Puzzled one day by the chance observation that some rabbits were passing clear—not cloudy—urine, just like meat-eating animals, he inferred that they had not been fed and were subsisting on their own tissues. He confirmed his hypothesis by feeding meat to the famished animals. An autopsy of the rabbits yielded an important discovery concerning the role of the pancreas in digestion: the secretions of the pancreas broke down fat molecules into fatty acids and glycerin. Bernard then showed that the principal processes of digestion take place in the small intestine, not in the stomach as was previously believed (Rogers 2011: 65). Had Bernard not noticed the clear rabbit urine, he never would have asked the question of why they were passing clear urine. Had he not known about carnivore urine, he would have never pursued his explanation. Had the rabbits not been denied food, he would not have asked whether digestion occurs beyond the stomach. And importantly, if Bernard had seen the rabbit urine *before* having the background knowledge, the discovery might not have occurred.

4. *Sweeping Effects of Simple Historical Contingencies*. Some tiny events have unexpectedly large consequences when, for independent reasons, geographic or political conditions align. Or so it has been claimed. Lynn White spelled out the important, yet contingent, consequences of the stirrup for Europe.[8] There, the introduction of the simple stirrup changed military history, and thus the history of a continent. Soldiers on horseback no longer fell from missing a blow, and so could swing their

swords more frequently and with greater abandon. This new-found stability on horseback gave them a decided advantage over their less wieldy opponents. No matter what one thinks about this particular case, there are large historical impacts from local events, such as the Venetian Navy's decision to pursue the use of telescopes for early detection of enemy ships. This might, at first, appear to be an insignificant decision, but it prompted Galileo's refinement of lenses, and his use of them together in more powerful arrangements in telescopes.[9] At that point, they were easily and fruitfully turned to the sky, for celestial observation.

5. *Unintended Cultural Side Effects*. Culture is dynamic, and its developments can throw off powerful side effects, such as pollution or processed foods. An example of unintended cultural side effects comes from the Islamic world, in which timekeeping was crucial to prayer. Not surprisingly, resources, attention, and ingenuity were applied to the challenge of accurate timekeeping. But it was, of course, a contingent fact that a religion arose that placed such a priority on accurate timekeeping.[10] That is, timekeeping was not developed for its own sake, no matter how useful it might actually be. Only in service of a religion was such an important advancement achieved. Another example is the Industrial Revolution and the rise of thermodynamics—the steam and the internal combustion engine, as well as electric generators, all were developed to assist in the push toward industrialization, rather than for their own sake.

6. *Biological Contingency and Cognitive Limits*. Another kind of contingency is biological, and it comes from the distinctive limits of a species' brain—its computational power. These computational limits are analogous to an animal's "*Umwelt*"—the environment as it is experienced by a particular animal. While there is a particular number corresponding to the insects a spider catches in its web every day, it will never know it; spiders have no concept of number. Yet it is a fact that there is a concrete number, and that number has causal consequences. This number is a part of an explanation of the spider's continued health—its adequate nutrition—that is a true explanation that the spider will never know. Just because it is correct does not mean the spider has access to it. Like the spider, we too might be ignorant of some facts about ourselves—such as the causes of human consciousness—that we might never be able to appreciate. There are also experiences had by other species that are closed off to us. While we know what it is like to feel jealous, to get angry, or to experience joy, we haven't a clue about the feeling of the lungfish's first breaths out of water, or the feeling that draws a lemming into group behavior. When an organism's experience is so remote from our own experience that we cannot understand what it is like to be that thing, we are perceptually or cognitively sealed off from it. While we are aware we do not share other species' *Umwelts*, that knowledge alone gets us no closer to understanding their experiences. Given that there are things we *know* we don't know (e.g., how consciousness works) and that there are things we know we will *never* know (e.g., other species' *Umwelts*), it is clear that humans cannot be the pinnacle of *possible* intelligence, understanding, or computational power.

Together with an account of progress, this conception of luck in science unifies luck or contingency with an account of explanation whose goodness is determined by an explanation's truth rather than its perspectival virtues such as intelligibility or objective features such as conformity with a formal structure (like Hempel's Deductive-Nomological Model) (Hempel 1965). In terms of advances in our scientific understanding, it is a contingent fact that humans have rigid neurological limits on how much we can remember, how quickly we process information, how much information we can process at once, and the complexity of ideas that we are able to entertain. The contingency of cognitive limitations is important because it suggests strongly that there are true explanations that we cannot understand. But I do not have to defend this strong claim. It is enough to argue that there are explanations that we do not understand at the moment. If we characterize explanation as a description of underlying factors that bring about an effect, then it is possible to have explanation without understanding, because it is possible to accurately describe causal factors without a receptive audience, or any audience at all. In fact, this ontic conception of explanation, the

Luck in Science

idea that there can be explanations that are true even though no one understands them, is marked by its insensitivity to audience.

This ontic conception of explanation fits nicely with the nature of luck or contingency. This fit is important because, when explaining the many features of science—its practical success, its predictive accuracy, its power to unify disparate domains, etc.—luck is essentially an explanatory notion. If an explanation's goodness is dependent on its accuracy or truth, not on whether anyone does or will understand it, then it also does not rely for its truth on its pedigree, or where it came from. A good explanation can have its origin in luck. Or in dutiful lab work. Or in mad excogitation. Or in vast resources devoted to competitive discovery. Or in all of these states and activities. The ontic view is not about the origin of *explanation* or about a recipe to make one; it is a view about what makes an explanation *good*.[11] In keeping with this ontic view, there are perfectly good explanations that might *never* be understood, and might not be produced in a way that can be repeated. Certainly, there are some that *are not* understood or repeated. And this cluster of issues raises questions about the metaphysical status of such explanations. Are they abstract objects? Creatures in Plato's heaven? But these challenges are no greater than the ones that naturalistic philosophers, and so materialist philosophers, face elsewhere.

Because the criteria for *good* explanations (i.e., truth and accuracy) are ontic and not constituted by or dependent upon the standards of human assessment, it can be (and often is) a piece of luck or contingency that we acquire a good explanation. Including a lucky source of an explanation is a description, and not a demotion, of it. It is a matter for historians and philosophers of science to identify these episodes. Pedigree is not constitutive of good explanation; explanations survive because they are true or accurate, no matter how haplessly they might have been arrived at. They do not, after all, result chiefly from the work of the scientific method or an attempt to understand, both willful and controlled efforts. Therefore, luck must play a role in science in order to explain how people sometimes *stumble* onto good explanations when easily understood bad explanations are so common, especially in a bad theory. Not everyone is similarly moved by the evidence that the history of science provides. Some philosophers are still committed to the project of rational reconstruction. Committed to presenting scientific progress as the result of a rational process—like the deliberate and controlled steps of the experimental method—some philosophers might be uneasy with luck as a benefactor of science. But a descriptively accurate history of science authenticates that science also flourishes when scientists are constrained and influenced by forces not immediately within their control. We can trace these influences in each of the sources of contingency I have discussed. If this stumbling, lucky arrival of an explanation implies a process not under our immediate control, this is an explanation that nevertheless unifies disparate observations in the history and context of science. The kind of unifying power that the luck-explanation provides is precisely what we expect from good explanations. Of course, when it arrives, contingency can surprise. But *that* it sometimes arrives to our great benefit is not unexpected.

Notes

1 I want to thank Marcella Linn for helping me to think about the issue of luck generally, and Abram Capone for very useful comments on this chapter.
2 There are, of course, hybrid accounts. (See Latus 2003; Levy 2011; Riggs 2009; Broncano-Berrocal 2015).
3 Recent discussions of contingency and luck in science can be found in Sterelny (2016) and Trout (2016).
4 See Nummedal (2007: 1–2) for her account of later 16th-century alchemist Philipp Sömmering.
5 For one example in which contingency plays a role, see Kitcher (1990).
6 (Priestley 1775: 114); Page numbers found at http://books.google.com/books?id=gB0UAAAAQAAJ&prin tsec=frontcover#v=onepage&q&f=false.
7 From his presidential address (November 24, 1877) to the Philosophical Society of Washington. Reprinted in Bauer (1908).
8 This form of argument is widely called path dependent.
9 Galileo tells this story in more detail in his "The Assayer" (1623/1957).

10 I am not arguing that the existence of any specific religion is a contingent fact. Instead, I am making the point that, in regard to the science of timekeeping, religion is a contingent factor. That is, certain scientific discoveries might have depended on the existence and development of a particular religious or cultural view.

11 For another pleasingly ontic account that complements the one in Trout (2002), see Craver (2007: esp. p. 200): "I advocate an ontic view of explanation according to which one explains a phenomenon by showing how it is situated in the causal structure of the world." A brief philosophical digression. It is reasonable to wonder whether the view I have proposed is really a theory of explanation. If the ontic view is one about the very nature of explanation, then it is an open question how true a schema has to be in order to be an explanation. On the other hand, if it is a view about what makes an explanation good, then one might object that I have not really provided an account of what explanations are. I prefer the latter. I do not think I have offered a theory of explanation, but I am not sure that counts as an admission, or if so whether it is damaging. I think we can say, at most, only a few things about common practices associated with what we tend to call "explanations." I think explanation is an important but informal affair. I doubt we can lay down many general rules that are true of all and only explanations.

References

Bacon, F. (1620/2000) *The New Organon*, L. Jardine & M. Silverthorne (ed.). Cambridge: Cambridge University Press.

Bauer, L.A. (1908) "The Instruments and Methods of Research," *Philosophical Society of Washington Bulletin* 15, 103–126.

Broncano-Berrocal, F. (2015) "Luck as Risk and the Lack of Control Account of Luck," *Metaphilosophy* 46(1), 1–25.

Card, C. (1993) "Gender and Moral Luck," in O. Flanagan & A. Rorty (eds) *Identity, Character, and Morality*, Cambridge, MA: The MIT Press, pp. 199–218.

Carter, J.A., & Peterson, M. (2016) "The Modal Account of Luck Revisited," *Synthese* 1–10.

Craver, C. (2007) *Explaining the Brain*, New York: Oxford University Press.

Diamond, J.M. (1999) *Guns, Germs, and Steel: The Fates of Human Societies*, New York: W.W. Norton & Company.

Fodor, J. (1974) *The Language of Thought*, New York: Crowell.

Galilei, G. (1623/1957) *The Assayer*, in *Discoveries and Opinions of Galileo*, S. Drake (trans), New York: Doubleday Anchor.

Hempel, C. (1965) *Aspects of Scientific Explanation and Other Essays in the Philosophy of Science*, New York: Free Press.

Kitcher, P. (1990) "The Division of Cognitive Labor," *Journal of Philosophy* 87, 5–22.

Kuhn, T.S. (1962/1996) *The Structure of Scientific Revolutions*, 3rd ed., Chicago, IL: University of Chicago Press.

Latus, A. (2003) "Constitutive Luck," *Metaphilosophy* 34(4), 460–475.

Levy, N. (2011) *Hard Luck: How Luck Undermines Free Will and Responsibility*, New York: Oxford University Press.

Marsden, B. (1983) *Catalogue of Cometary Orbits*, Hillsdale, NJ: Enslow.

Mele, A. (2006) *Free Will and Luck*, New York: Oxford University Press.

Minkoff, E.C., & Baker, P.J. (2001) *Biology Today: An Issues Approach*, New York: Garland Publishing.

Nagel, T. (1979) "Moral Luck," reprinted in D. Statman (ed.) *Moral Luck* (1993), New York: SUNY Press, pp. 57–72.

Nummedal, T. (2007) *Alchemy and Authority in the Holy Roman Empire*, Chicago, IL: University of Chicago Press.

Pasteur, L. (1854, December 7) Lecture, University of Lille.

Priestley, J. (1775) *Experiments and Observations on Different Kinds of Air*, vol. II, London: J. Johnson.

Pritchard, D. (2005) *Epistemic Luck*, Oxford: Oxford University Press.

———. (2014) "The Modal Account of Luck," *Metaphilosophy* 45(4–5), 594–619.

Rescher, N. (1995) *Luck: The Brilliant Randomness of Everyday Life*, New York: Farrar, Straus and Giroux.

Riggs, W. (2009) "Luck, Knowledge, and Control," in A. Haddock, A. Millar, & D. Pritchard (eds.) *Epistemic Value*, Oxford: Oxford University Books, pp. 204–221.

Rogers, K. (2011) *Medicine and Healers through History*, New York: Encyclopedia Britannica, pp. 204–221.

Silberberg, M.S. (2000) *Chemistry: The Molecular Nature of Matter and Change*, New York: McGraw-Hill.

Starr, C., & Taggart, R. (1984) *Biology: The Unity and Diversity of Life*, 3rd edition, Belmont, CA: Wadsworth.

Sterelny, K. (2016) "Contingency and History," *Philosophy of Science* 83 (October), 521–539.

Trout, J.D. (2002) "Scientific Explanation and the Sense of Understanding," *Philosophy of Science* 69 (June), 212–233.

———. (2016) *Wondrous Truths: The Improbable Triumph of Modern Science*, New York: Oxford University Press.

Whittington, L. (2014) "Getting Moral Luck Right," *Metaphilosophy* 45(4–5), 654–667.

Williams, B. (1981) "Moral Luck," reprinted in D. Statman (ed.) *Moral Luck* (1993), New York: SUNY Press.

35

THE PHILOSOPHY OF LUCK AND EXPERIMENTAL PHILOSOPHY

Joe Milburn and Edouard Machery

In this chapter, we discuss the contributions experimental philosophy can make to the philosophy of luck. The philosophy of luck covers a diverse range of topics, as the content of this volume indicates. To make things more manageable we will focus on contributions experimental philosophy can make to anti-luck epistemology (for discussion of moral luck and experimental philosophy, see Kneer & Machery ms).

The chapter will proceed as follows. In the first section, we will introduce the notion of anti-luck epistemology. In the second section, we will cover experimental philosophy and note some of the ways that it can be brought to bear on questions pertaining to anti-luck epistemology. There we distinguish between negative and positive approaches in experimental philosophy. Finally, in the third section, we review some of the work in which experimental philosophy and anti-luck epistemology intersect. There we will argue that while there has been enlightening work done bearing on weak anti-luck epistemology, there has been very little experimental work that bears directly on strong anti-luck epistemology. We end by sketching some of the ways in which experimental philosophers can more directly engage strong anti-luck epistemology.

Anti-Luck Epistemology

We can distinguish between two versions of anti-luck epistemology. We can call the first weak anti-luck epistemology and the second strong anti-luck epistemology. Weak anti-luck epistemology is synonymous with what Stephen Hetherington (2016) has called Gettierism, or what others have called Gettierology. It is committed to two theses. The first is that knowledge is something different from defeasibly justified true belief. The second is that reflecting on Gettier cases can provide insights into the nature of knowledge.

Gettier cases are so-called, because of their appearance in Edmund Gettier's (1963) paper, "Is Justified True Belief Knowledge?" While the exact nature of Gettier cases is controversial (e.g., Weatherson 2013), we can treat any putative example of defeasibly justified true belief that falls short of knowledge as being a Gettier case. Consider the following version of one of Gettier's original cases.

401

Ford Case
Smith has been told by Jones that Jones has just bought a Ford. Jones is typically a reliable informant. Smith has no idea where his old friend Brown is. However, he knows about disjunction introduction. On the basis of Jones's testimony, he forms the following belief: Either Jones owns a Ford, or Brown is in Barcelona. As it turns out, Jones was lying about buying the Ford but Brown *is* in Barcelona.

Presumably, Smith possesses defeasible justification for his belief. His belief is also true. But it seems that Smith does not have knowledge.

Since Gettier's paper, philosophers have provided a number of such cases, which have been grouped into two broad classes. The first class are sometimes called "helpful Gettier cases" because a helpful turn of events makes one's belief true; the second are sometimes called "dangerous Gettier cases" because in these cases one is in danger of forming a false belief (Hetherington 1999; Sosa 2007).

Perhaps the best known of these latter sorts of cases is the following, originally published in Goldman (1976), though attributed to Carl Ginet.

Fake Barn Case
Henry is driving unawares through Red Barn Façade County, a county so-named because it contains many more red barn façades than real red barns. In fact, while there are hundreds of red barn façades, there is only one real red barn. These barn façades are made so that they always fake unsuspecting people into believing that they are actually real barns. Henry happens to drive past the only red barn in the county and forms the true belief that there is a red barn in front of him.

In this case, Henry forms a true belief, though he is in danger of forming a false belief.

Other familiar helpful Gettier cases include the Sheep Case and the Bic Pen Case.

Sheep Case
Roderick sees a dog in a field that is cleverly disguised as a sheep and on this basis forms the belief that a sheep is in the field. As it turns out, there is a sheep in the field beyond his view.

Bic Pen Case
Heather places a Bic pen on her table and goes away; on this basis she believes that there is a Bic pen on the table; a thief enters the room and takes the Bic pen off the table; however, in doing so the thief drops another Bic pen *onto* the table.

In these cases, a helpful turn of events allows Roderick's and Heather's belief to be true, beliefs that would have otherwise been false.

The literature on Gettier problems is immense and highly contentious. Perhaps the only thing approaching a consensus that has arisen from this literature is that JTB accounts of knowledge—accounts that understand knowledge to be (defeasibly) justified true belief—are untenable. This is exactly one of the claims of weak anti-luck epistemology, and in general we can take weak anti-luck epistemology to be the dominant contemporary position (but see Sartwell 1991; Weatherson 2003; Hetherington 2016).

Strong anti-luck epistemology agrees with weak anti-luck epistemology that knowledge is something different from defeasibly justified true belief, and it agrees that reflection on Gettier cases can provide insights into the nature of knowledge. However, it goes beyond these claims. Strong anti-luck epistemology centers its reflections on knowledge around what Pritchard (2005, 2012) calls the *anti-luck intuition* or the *anti-luck platitude*.

Anti-Luck Platitude

If S knows that p, then it is not a matter of luck (in some particular sense) that S's belief that p is true.

According to anti-luck epistemologists, the anti-luck platitude is one of the core platitudes concerning knowledge. The program of anti-luck epistemology is to use the anti-luck platitude as a springboard to better understand knowledge. This is done by first providing an account of luck in general, and then by specifying the exact sense(s) in which its being a matter of luck that one's belief is true is incompatible with knowledge.

We can identify two main approaches in strong anti-luck epistemology. The first is Pritchard's modal approach (Pritchard 2005, 2007, 2009, 2015). Pritchard starts with a modal account of luck. Simplifying a bit, his account of luck in general is as follows:

Modal Luck: MLE An event is lucky *iff* (i) it obtains in the actual world but does not obtain in a wide class of nearby possible worlds in which the relevant initial conditions for that event are the same as in the actual world, or (ii) it obtains in the actual world but does not obtain in some of the nearest possible worlds in which the relevant initial conditions for the event are the same as in the actual world.

Pritchard then understands knowledge precluding luck as particular species of luck. According to Pritchard,

Modal Epistemic Luck: MEL An individual S's belief that p is lucky to be true in a way incompatible with knowledge just in case, there are a wide class of nearby worlds in which S forms the belief that p on the same basis as in the actual world, but p is not true, or in some of the nearest possible worlds in which S forms the belief that p on the same basis as in the actual world, p is not true.

A competitor to Pritchard's modal approach to epistemic luck is an ability approach advocated by John Greco and John Turri among others (Greco 2010, 2012; Turri 2011, 2016). Here luck is understood not in modal terms, but in terms of ability and/or virtue.[1]

Ability Luck: ALS An agent S's success is lucky just in case the success is not attributable to S's ability.

Knowledge precluding luck is then understood as follows:

Ability Epistemic Luck: AEL An agent S's true belief that p is lucky to be true (in a way incompatible with S knowing that p) *iff* S's believing truly that p is not attributable to S's ability.

It should be clear that strong anti-luck and weak anti-luck epistemology are distinct from each other. Nevertheless, they are clearly related. One of the burdens of weak anti-Gettier epistemology is to explain why possessing defeasibly justified true belief is insufficient for possessing knowledge. One way of understanding the appeal of strong anti-luck epistemology, then, is to understand it as providing such an explanation. We can have defeasibly justified true beliefs and still lack knowledge, because it can be a matter of luck that our defeasibly justified beliefs are true. The anti-luck platitude and the various ways of spelling out this platitude explain why individuals in Gettier cases fail to have knowledge.

Experimental Philosophy

Experimental philosophers are committed to appealing to and acquiring experimental evidence that bears on the relevant philosophical issues (O'Neill & Machery 2014). To the extent that a philosophical issue has empirical implications, the importance of the relevant experimental data will be obvious. In the limiting case, we might be able to settle a philosophical issue merely by settling the empirical facts.

We should expect philosophical claims concerning concept possession and linguistic practice to have empirical implications. The empirical implications of philosophers' claims in metaphysics or in normative fields such as ethics or epistemology, however, are less obvious. Because the core claims of anti-luck epistemologists are metaphysical and normative, it is not obvious whether the claims of anti-luck epistemology have empirical implications, and one might doubt that experimental philosophy can contribute to the debates surrounding them.

These doubts, we think, can be allayed. Experimental evidence can be relevant to philosophical issues even if it cannot directly confirm (or disconfirm) some philosophical theory; in what follows we consider a variety of ways that experimental evidence can be relevant to anti-luck epistemology.

One way that experimental evidence might be relevant to anti-luck epistemology is that it might *debunk* the grounds that anti-luck epistemologies are built upon. Consider the standard method employed by anti-luck epistemologists, taking Pritchard as a test case.

Pritchard's strategy in arguing for modal epistemic luck (MEL) is to show how MEL can explain the truth of our judgments concerning a number of distinct cases. So for instance, Pritchard's claim is that MEL can explain why it is that we fail to have knowledge in cases in which we make a lucky guess or in Gettier cases. In those sorts of cases there is a wide range of nearby possible worlds in which we form a belief about the same target proposition and in which the belief turns out to be false. For instance, in the Ford case, we can imagine a wide range of nearby possible worlds in which Brown is not in Barcelona, and so Smith's belief turns out to be false. Likewise, if one merely guesses that, for example, the next flip of a coin will land heads, it is true that in a wide range of nearby possible worlds in which one forms their belief in the same way, it will be false. Pritchard also thinks that MEL can explain why it is that we cannot know that a given ticket will lose the lottery on the basis of its long odds of winning; in some of the nearest possible worlds, that ticket will win. At the same time MEL does not seem to rule out clear cases of knowledge in that it does not require that we have indefeasible evidence for our knowledgeable beliefs or that they arise from infallible processes of belief formation. So Pritchard's defense of MEL rests on judgments about particular cases (or kinds of cases) and its ability to explain the truth of our judgments concerning these cases.

We can call this method for defending and criticizing philosophical positions *the method of cases* (e.g., Machery 2017). There is an intense, multi-layered controversy about the exact description of the method of cases (Williamson 2007; Malmgren 2011; Cappelen 2012; Deutsch 2015; Horvath 2015; Colaço & Machery 2017; Machery 2017), but one plausible way of describing the method of cases is as follows. In employing the method of cases we take as our starting points our judgments regarding a range of real and hypothetical cases. We then generate general principles that in some ways explain why our judgments regarding the various cases are correct. These general principles can, in turn, be criticized for failing to conform with our judgments regarding other (hitherto) unconsidered cases.

The method of cases is a reliable method only if our starting points (i.e., our judgments concerning real and hypothetical cases) are reliable. But plausibly, empirical data can give us reason for doubting the reliability of our judgments.

There are two main ways that this can be done. First, there can be empirical evidence that large groups of people who are prima facie our epistemic peers fail to share our spontaneous judgments about cases (Machery 2017: ch. 4). Given certain assumptions, this gives us reason for doubting that *our* judgments are reliable. If there are many others whose judgments disagree with ours, why should we suppose that we are reliable instead of them?

Second, there can be empirical evidence that judgments about the relevant cases are shaped by non-epistemic factors such as ethnicity, gender, personality, or age. Again, given certain assumptions, this can give reason for believing that our judgments are unreliable. If people's judgments are generally shaped by non-epistemic factors, why should we take ours seriously?

We can call this use of empirical evidence to weigh in on philosophical positions "negative" or "restricting." The negative approach in experimental philosophy is highly controversial. Even if philosophers' judgments about cases disagree with the general public's or if people's judgments about certain cases are influenced by non-epistemic factors, the skeptical conclusions regarding the method of cases do not immediately follow. On the one hand, the general public's judgments might not be of the same evidential value as philosophers' (e.g., Williamson 2011). And even if this is not the case, still, controversial assumptions concerning peer disagreement might be needed to generate a skeptical conclusion. Furthermore, philosophers and non-philosophers might be making spontaneous judgments regarding different things; that is, it might be that philosophers and non-philosophers are using different concepts of knowledge or justified belief when they attribute knowledge or justification (e.g., Sosa 2007). On the other hand, that people's judgments are biased by non-epistemic factors does not imply that philosophers' judgments are biased by non-epistemic factors, and *a fortiori* it does not imply that a particular philosopher's judgments are biased by non-epistemic factors. Nevertheless, we can take empirical results to give us at least prima facie reasons for doubting the reliability of the method of cases in certain instances.

There are also positive approaches in experimental philosophy. One positive approach that is relevant to anti-luck epistemology is what we can call the supplementary approach. On this approach, the method of cases is not challenged by empirical evidence; instead, empirical evidence about the general public's judgments regarding the relevant cases is added to the initial data for constructing general principles. On this approach, the method of cases is not rejected, but supplemented. It should be noted that just as experimental results can call into question the reliability of philosophers' judgments, it is also possible for experimental results to partially vindicate the reliability of philosophers' judgments. If philosophers' judgments are shown to be consistent with the judgments of the majority people throughout a wide range of cultures, this convergence gives us some reason for accepting these judgments as reliable.

In what follows we will assume that there is nothing, in principle, that keeps empirical evidence of the relevant kind from bearing on questions in anti-luck epistemology in the ways mentioned above; instead we will judge the particular merits of the arguments.

Experimental Philosophy and Anti-Luck Epistemology

In this section we review the work in experimental philosophy that bears on anti-luck epistemology and we provide suggestions for further research. We argue that while much illuminating work has been done on issues pertaining to weak anti-luck epistemology, there is need for more work that directly engages strong anti-luck epistemology. For while there has been a significant body of work dealing with Gettier cases, no work has been done to test whether the anti-luck platitude is widely shared, and how central it is in determining knowledge attributions. Furthermore, more work needs to be done on whether we should understand the anti-luck platitude primarily in modal terms or in terms of ability.

The Negative Program

Almost all of the work in experimental philosophy that bears on anti-luck epistemology has focused on judgments about Gettier cases (for review, see Turri 2016). This is not surprising given the role that Gettier cases have played in theories of knowledge in 20th-century analytic philosophy, and in the way that Gettierology exemplifies the method of cases. Some of this work has been negative.

Experimental philosophers have presented data suggesting that philosophers' judgments about Gettier cases do not match the general public's, that these intuitions vary across demographic groups, and that, furthermore, irrelevant demographic variables affect judgments regarding these cases. This evidence can be interpreted as threatening the method of cases underlying anti-luck epistemology.

Divergence between Lay People and Philosophers

If the general public ascribes knowledge to protagonists in Gettier cases, this would put significant pressure on anti-luck epistemology, since both weak and strong anti-luck epistemology presuppose that Gettier cases provide examples of defeasibly justified true belief that falls short of knowledge.

As it happens, Starmans and Friedman (2012) give evidence that Americans tend to ascribe knowledge in some helpful Gettier cases, except in cases that are structurally similar to the Sheep Case given above.[2] This finding has been extensively discussed (e.g., Nagel et al. 2013a; Starmans & Friedman 2013; Turri 2013). Starmans and Friedman hold that lay people react differently to two different kinds of helpful Gettier cases (see also Turri 2013: fn. 8; Blouw et al. 2017): those based on "authentic evidence" and those based on "apparent evidence." In the former type of helpful Gettier cases, the protagonist originally forms a belief on the basis of evidence that makes the belief based on it true; by contrast, apparent evidence is "evidence that appears to be informative about reality, but is not really" (Starmans & Friedman 2012: 9). Machery et al. (2015) and Machery et al. (2017) have shown that across cultures a justified belief formed on the basis of apparent evidence is not taken to be an instance of knowledge even when it is true (see also Nagel et al. 2013b).

But what about "Gettierized" justified true beliefs formed on the basis of authentic evidence, for example, beliefs like those in the Bic pen case? Starmans and Friedman's work suggests that, contrary to philosophical orthodoxy, the general public tends to attribute knowledge in such cases.

Turri (2013) has presented evidence that the general public attributes knowledge in these sorts of cases, because they are not paying attention to the relevant aspects of the case.[3] Turri's hypothesis is that what underlies philosophers' judgments concerning Gettier cases is an awareness of the "double-luck" structure in the cases. On this view, Gettier cases arise when one experiences a stroke of bad luck that threatens to make their defeasibly justified belief false, which is then canceled by a stroke of good luck. He notes that the vignettes participants were invited to read in Starmans and Friedman's study did not make the double luck structure of the cases perspicuous, and hypothesized that it was a failure to notice the double luck structure that led participants to ascribe knowledge in these cases. To test this hypothesis, Turri first replicated Starmans and Friedman's findings when people were presented with Gettier cases that did not make the double luck structure perspicuous. He then presented the relevant Gettier cases to participants in distinct stages, starting with the presentation of a justified belief, then introducing an element of bad luck that would typically prevent the belief from being true, and finally introducing an element of good luck that makes the belief turn out to be true after all. Turri does this by presenting participants with the three stages of the Gettier case on three distinct screens and asking a comprehension question on each screen. When presented with the cases in this way, participants denied knowledge to protagonists in Gettier cases. In some of Turri's experiments, in fact, 100% of the participants denied knowledge to protagonists in these kinds of helpful Gettier cases.

Colaço et al. (2014) offer evidence that the general public tends to ascribe knowledge in fake barn cases, the most famous kind of dangerous Gettier cases, and that the number of fake barns that the protagonist has been exposed to does not have a significant effect on knowledge attribution. More recently, Turri et al. (2015) and Turri (2017) found no difference in lay knowledge attribution in fake barn cases and paradigmatic instances of knowledge.

The interesting twist here is not that lay people differ from philosophers in ascribing knowledge when the protagonist forms a true belief when she could have so easily formed a false one, but rather that the common view that philosophers tend to deny knowledge in this kind of scenario appears to

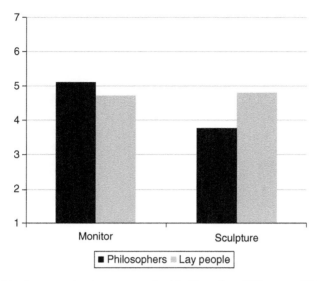

Figure 35.1 Two of the dangerous Gettier cases examined in Horvath and Wiegmann (2016)

be mistaken. It is well known that at least some influential philosophers ascribe knowledge in fake barn cases: While Goldman and Lewis think that the protagonist does not know the relevant proposition, Millikan and Lycan think that she does. But what about philosophers in general? Horvath and Wiegmann (2016) have, however, recently shown that on average philosophers and lay people make the same kind of judgment about a range of fake barn cases (Figure 35.1).

If in fact, one does not possess knowledge in fake barn cases, then it seems that both lay people *and* philosophers are mistaken.

Cultural Variation and Gettier Cases

Weinberg, Nichols, and Stich's (2001) article has been extremely influential in the experimental study of knowledge ascription. In it they provided evidence that East Asians tend to ascribe knowledge in cases that are structurally similar to the Bic pen case, whereas Westerners tend to deny knowledge in these cases (Figure 35.2). It would thus seem that Westerners and East Asians disagree about whether individuals in some helpful Gettier cases possess knowledge. This cultural diversity puts some pressure on the idea that Western philosophers' judgments regarding these cases are reliable.

However, Weinberg et al.'s results have not been replicated. Nagel et al. (2013b), Seyedsayamdost (2015a), and Kim and Yuan (2015) provided evidence that both Westerners and Eastern Asians tend to deny knowledge to protagonists in cases structurally similar to the Bic pen case.

More recently, empirical evidence has accumulated that judgments elicited by at least some helpful Gettier cases are cross-culturally stable. Machery et al. (2015) collected evidence that individuals from Brazil, India, Japan, and the USA tend to ascribe knowledge at a significantly lesser rate in helpful Gettier cases than in paradigmatic cases of knowledge. Machery et al. (2017) have dramatically extended this body of research. They collected data from 2,838 participants in 24 sites, located in 23 countries (counting Hong-Kong as a distinct country) and 17 languages. For 23 out of 24 sites and 16 out of 17 languages a large majority of people (between 70 and 90%) judged that a Gettierized belief was not an instance of knowledge (Figure 35.3).

The only exception to this pattern was the Bedouins in Israel, but the number of Bedouin participants was very small and a replication is called for before drawing any conclusion from their answer. In the meantime, we view these results as providing convergent evidence that people do not view subjects in helpful Gettier cases to possess knowledge.

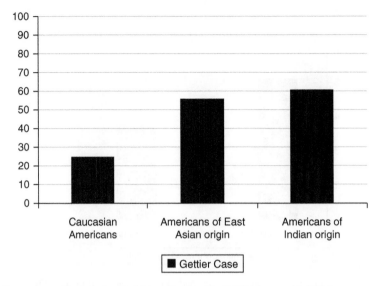

Figure 35.2 Proportion of knowledge denial in a Gettier case in Weinberg et al. (2001)

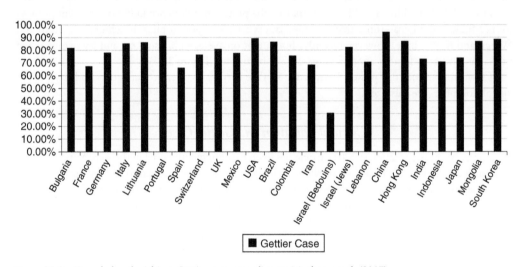

Figure 35.3 Knowledge denial in a Gettier case according to Machery et al. (2017)

Further Demographic Variation and Gettier Cases

Colaço et al. (2014) report that *age* affects knowledge attributions in fake barn cases (a dangerous Gettier case), with younger people more likely to ascribe knowledge than older people, but it is unclear whether this finding replicates (Machery 2017). Buckwalter and Stich (2015) report that judgments about helpful Gettier cases vary across *gender*, but that finding too fails to replicate (Adleberg et al. 2015; Seyedsayamdost 2015b; Machery et al. 2017).

More recently, Holtzman (2013) and Machery et al. (2017) have independently shown that personality correlates with the judgments made in response to helpful Gettier cases. In both papers, people who are more open to experience are more likely to judge that, in a helpful Gettier case, the Gettierized belief is not an instance of knowledge. That is, people who tend to seek new experiences

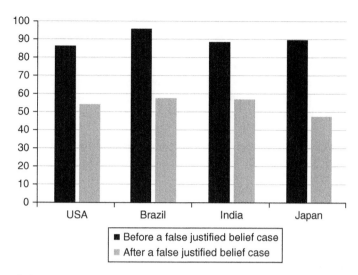

Figure 35.4 Knowledge denial in a Gettier case before and after a false justified belief case according to Machery et al. forthcoming

and engage in creative ventures are more likely to judge that a justified belief that is made true by luck is not an instance of knowledge.

Influence of Irrelevant Factors

Across four countries that are characterized by very different cultures and languages—the USA, Brazil, India, and Japan—Machery et al. (2018) found that people express very different judgments about helpful Gettier cases when a Gettier case is read first or when it follows a case describing a justified, but false belief. In the four countries, people were much more likely to judge that a justified belief made true by luck fails to be an instance of knowledge in the former situation than in the latter (Figure 35.4).

People are nearly twice as likely to judge that a justified belief made true by luck fails to be an instance of knowledge when it is read first compared to when it follows a case describing a justified, but false belief.

The Positive Program of Experimental Philosophy

Sixty years ago, Austin (1956) argued that everyday uses of concepts such as the concept of an excuse were extremely subtle, and that philosophers might be prone to ignore this subtlety. As he put it (Austin 1956: 11):

> If a distinction works well for practical purposes in ordinary life (no mean feat, for even ordinary life is full of hard cases), then there is sure to be something in it, it will not mark nothing. (…) Certainly ordinary language is not the last word: in principle it can everywhere be supplemented and improved upon and superseded. Only remember, it is the first word.

Experimental philosophers might reveal that lay knowledge ascriptions are differently sensitive to variations in Gettier cases and that philosophers have not paid sufficient attention to such subtle distinctions. Turri et al. (2015) provide evidence that lay knowledge ascription is sensitive to distinctions in helpful Gettier cases that have been ignored by philosophers (see also Blouw et al. 2017). Their findings suggest the following. First, people ascribe knowledge to a protagonist when a threat (i.e., a situation that would make her belief false) fails to materialize, as happens in dangerous Gettier cases. Second, when a threat becomes actual, but is somehow compensated by another event ("the back up"), as happens in the sheep and Bic pen cases, people are less likely to ascribe knowledge than in a clear case of knowledge. However, how less likely they are to do so depends on the "similarity" between the back up and the threat. As they put it,

> For example, consider our shopper, who believes that she has a diamond in her coat pocket, but whose diamond is stolen before she leaves the store. People are more inclined to attribute knowledge if her belief is true because the thief felt guilty and slipped the diamond back into her pocket than if it is true because her grandmother long ago sewed a diamond into the coat pocket.
>
> *Blouw et al. 2017: 387*

Limitations of Past Experimental Philosophy and Recommendations

From the preceding it should be clear that experimental philosophers have made important contributions to debates concerning weak anti-luck epistemology. First, experimental philosophers have provided evidence that lay people tend *not* to attribute knowledge in helpful Gettier cases in which the protagonist's belief is based on apparent evidence. At the same time, they have provided evidence that lay people tend to attribute knowledge in so-called dangerous Gettier cases. Finally, they have provided evidence that lay people are sensitive to variations in helpful Gettier cases, variations that have typically been ignored by philosophers. This work both confirms weak anti-luck epistemology's distinction between defeasibly justified true belief and knowledge, and it provides further grist for the weak anti-luck epistemologist's mill.

These findings also bear on strong anti-luck epistemology but not in a direct way. Recall that strong anti-luck epistemology presupposes weak anti-luck epistemology and that one of the motivations for it is its ability to provide an explanation for why certain cases of defeasibly justified true belief fall short of knowledge. Thus, given that experimental philosophy confirms weak anti-luck epistemology, it gives some support to strong anti-luck epistemology.

At the same time, it is unclear the extent to which previous experimental work bears upon strong anti-luck epistemology, and this is for three reasons. First, the experimental findings do not indicate whether individuals tend to accept or reject the anti-luck platitude. Remember that strong anti-luck epistemology is to start with the anti-luck platitude as a springboard to better understand the nature of knowledge. If the general public accepted or rejected the anti-luck platitude, this could give us evidence whether anti-luck epistemology was on the right track. As of now, however, there is no empirical data to suggest that the anti-luck platitude is widely shared.

Second, if the program of strong anti-luck epistemology is to show the promise that philosophers like Pritchard believe it does, then luck ascriptions should play an explanatory role in denying knowledge. Again, strong anti-luck epistemologists hold that the anti-luck platitude is one of our core presuppositions about knowledge, so that understanding luck in general is important for understanding knowledge. It would be hard to accept this if, in general, people were uninfluenced by considerations about luck in making knowledge ascriptions. But current experimental findings do not indicate whether considerations of luck influence how and when individuals attribute knowledge. So while there is evidence that individuals tend to not attribute knowledge in certain kinds of helpful Gettier cases, there is no evidence that this is *because* they accept the anti-luck platitude.

Even Turri's (2013) work that was designed to show that individuals tend not to attribute knowledge when they are aware of the "double luck" structure of Gettier cases does not directly bear on the viability of strong anti-luck epistemology. To see this consider a double abnormality account of

Gettier cases. In this account, Gettier cases are understood to involve two distinct kinds of abnormality. First, there is an abnormal circumstance that normally would result in one holding a false belief despite the belief's being defeasibly justified; second, there is another abnormal circumstance that cancels out the first, resulting in one holding a true belief after all. Turri's findings do not favor the hypothesis that considerations of luck determine knowledge ascriptions over the hypothesis that considerations of normality determine such ascriptions.

Third, the experimental findings do little to favor one account of knowledge precluding epistemic luck over another. Consider, again, the two main accounts of knowledge precluding epistemic luck. The first is Pritchard's modal account; the second is the ability account favored by Greco. Both of these accounts seem consistent with the experimental work done on Gettier cases. On the one hand, both have the resources to exclude helpful Gettier cases (and especially those that are dependent on apparent evidence) as cases of knowledge. On the other hand, both have the resources to exclude fake barn cases as cases in which the protagonist has knowledge. Consider again Pritchard's modal account of epistemic luck. According to this account, an individual S's belief that p is subject to knowledge precluding epistemic luck, just in case in some of the nearest possible worlds, or in a sufficient number of nearby possible worlds in which initial conditions are the same as the actual world, S's belief that p is false. Notice that nothing is said to specify what counts as the relevant initial conditions. Are the relevant initial conditions just that one is in, for example, Red Barn Façade County (i.e., an environment in which one is likely to be fooled)? Or is the relevant condition that one is having a veridical perception of a red barn (or some other relevant object)? Depending on which of these is the case, Pritchard's modal account of knowledge precluding epistemic luck will either count fake barn cases as instance of knowledge precluding epistemic luck or not.

Similarly, consider a virtue theoretic account of knowledge precluding luck, such as John Greco's. According to his account of knowledge precluding epistemic luck, an individual S's true belief that p is lucky in a way incompatible with knowledge just in case S's having the true belief that p is not attributable to S. In general, however, whether S's truly believing that p is attributable to S will depend on whether S is in the right kind of environment and conditions. As virtue theorists often point out; one might have the ability to hit a bull's-eye with a bow and arrow from far away, but not when there is a violent storm, or when they are stone-drunk. But depending upon whether the relevant environment or conditions in the Fake Barn cases includes only the immediate environment, or if it includes all of, for example, Red Barn Façade County will change whether or not the subject in these cases has the relevant ability.

Conclusion

In this chapter we have distinguished between two types of anti-luck epistemology: weak anti-luck epistemology and strong anti-luck epistemology. We have also distinguished a number of ways that experimental philosophy can contribute to anti-luck epistemology. We have suggested that the findings of experimental philosophy are in line with weak anti-luck epistemology, showing that individuals throughout different cultures tend to recognize cases in which one has defeasibly justified true belief but not knowledge. Finally, we have argued that more experimental work is needed to deal directly with strong anti-luck epistemology.

Notes

1   It is unclear that Greco and Turri would accept the label of strong anti-luck epistemologist. Their work focuses more on the notion of ability rather than luck. However, aspects of their work can be appropriated by strong anti-luck epistemology.
2   Starmans and Friedman do not take this work to necessarily undermine the method of cases; instead, they offer a range of explanations for the differences in judgments between the general public and philosophers regarding these cases.

3 However, Turri also acknowledges that people are more likely to ascribe knowledge in this kind of Gettier cases (Turri 2013: fn. 8).

References

Adleberg, T., Thompson, M., & Nahmias, E. (2015) "Do Women and Men Have Different Philosophical Intuitions? Further data," *Philosophical Psychology* 28, 615–641.

Austin, J.L. (1956) "A Plea for Excuses: The Presidential Address," *Proceedings of the Aristotelian Society* 57, 1–30.

Blouw, P., Buckwalter, W., & Turri, J. (2017) "Gettier Cases: A Taxonomy," in R. Borges, C. de Almeida, & P. Klein (eds.) *Explaining Knowledge: New Essays on the Gettier Problem*, Oxford: Oxford University Press, pp. 242–252.

Buckwalter, W., & Stich, S. (2015) "Gender and Philosophical Intuition," in J. Knobe & S. Nichols (eds.) *Experimental Philosophy*, vol. 2, Oxford: Oxford University Press, pp. 307–346.

Cappelen, H. (2012) *Philosophy without Intuitions*, Oxford: Oxford University Press.

Colaço, D., & Machery, E. (2017) "The Intuitive Is a Red Herring, *Inquiry* 60(4), 403–419.

Colaço, D., Buckwalter, W., Stich, S.P., & Machery, E. (2014) "Epistemic Intuitions in Fake-barn Thought Experiments," *Episteme* 11, 199–212.

Deutsch, M. (2015) *The Myth of the Intuitive: Experimental Philosophy and Philosophical Method*, Cambridge, MA: MIT Press.

Gettier, E. (1963) "Is Justified True Belief Knowledge?" *Analysis* 23, 121–123.

Goldman, A. (1976) "Discrimination and Perceptual Knowledge," *The Journal of Philosophy* 73, 771–791.

Greco, J. (2010) *Achieving Knowledge: A Virtue-Theoretic Account of Epistemic Normativity*, Cambridge: Cambridge University Press.

——. (2012) "A (Different) Virtue Epistemology," *Philosophy and Phenomenological Research* 85, 1–26.

Hetherington, S. (1999) "Knowing Fallibly," *Journal of Philosophy* 96, 565–587.

——. (2016) *Knowledge and the Gettier Problem*, Cambridge: Cambridge University Press.

Holtzman, G. (2013) "Do Personality Effects Mean Philosophy is Intrinsically Subjective?" *Journal of Consciousness Studies* 20, 27–42.

Horvath, J. (2015) "Thought Experiments and Experimental Philosophy," in C. Daly (ed.) *The Palgrave Handbook of Philosophical Methods*, London: Palgrave Macmillan UK, pp. 386–418.

Horvath, J., & Wiegmann, A. (2016) "Intuitive Expertise and Intuitions about Knowledge," *Philosophical Studies* 173, 2701–2726.

Kim, M., & Yuan, Y. (2015) "No Cross-cultural Differences in the Gettier Car Case Intuition: A Replication Study of Weinberg et al. 2001," *Episteme* 12, 355–361.

Kneer, M., & Machery, E. (ms) "No Luck for Moral Luck."

Machery, E. (2017) *Philosophy within its Proper Bounds*, London: Oxford University Press.

Machery, E., Stich, S. P., Rose, D., Alai, M., Angelucci, A., Berniunas, R., et al. (2017) "The Gettier Intuition from South America to Asia," *Journal of Indian Council of Philosophical Research* 34, 517–541.

Machery, E., Stich, S.P., Rose, D., Chatterjee, D., Karasawa, K., Struchiner, N., et al. (2015) "Gettier across Cultures," *Noûs*. doi:10.1111/nous.12110.

Machery, E., Stich, S.P., Rose, D., Chatterjee, A., Karasawa, K., Struchiner, N., et al. (2018) "Gettier was Framed!" in M. Mizumoto, S.P. Stich, & E. McCready (eds.) *Epistemology for the Rest of the World*, Oxford: Oxford University Press, pp. 123–148.

Malmgren, A.S. (2011) "Rationalism and the Content of Intuitive Judgements," *Mind* 120, 263–327.

Nagel, J., San Juan, V., & Mar, R.A. (2013a) "Authentic Gettier Cases: A Reply to Starmans and Friedman," *Cognition* 129, 666–669.

——. (2013b) "Lay Denial of Knowledge for Justified True Beliefs," *Cognition* 129, 652–661.

O'Neill, E., & Machery, E. (2014) "Experimental Philosophy: What Is it Good For?" in E. Machery & E. O'Neill (eds.) *Current Controversies in Experimental Philosophy*, New York: Routledge, pp. vii–xxix.

Pritchard, D. (2005) *Epistemic Luck*, Oxford: Oxford University Press.

——. (2007) "Anti-luck Epistemology," *Synthese* 158, 277–297.

——. (2009) "Safety-Based Epistemology: Whither Now?" *Journal of Philosophical Research* 34, 33–45.

——. (2012) "Anti-Luck Virtue Epistemology," *The Journal of Philosophy* 109, 247–279.

——. (2015) "Anti-Luck Epistemology and the Gettier Problem," *Philosophical Studies* 172, 93–111.

Sartwell, C. (1991) "Knowledge is Merely True Belief," *American Philosophical Quarterly* 28, 157–165.

Seyedsayamdost, H. (2015a) "On Normativity and Epistemic Intuitions: Failure of Replication," *Episteme* 1, 95–116.

——. (2015b) "On Gender and Philosophical Intuition: Failure of Replication and Other Negative Results," *Philosophical Psychology* 28, 642–673.

Sosa, E. (2007) *A Virtue Epistemology: Apt Belief and Reflective Knowledge*, New York: Oxford University Press.

Starmans, C., & Friedman, O. (2012) "The Folk Conception of Knowledge," *Cognition* 124, 272–283.

——. (2013) "Taking "Know" For an Answer: A Reply to Nagel, San Juan, and Mar," *Cognition* 129, 662–665.

Turri, J. (2011) "Manifest Failure: The Gettier Problem Solved," *Philosophers' Imprint* 11, 1–11.

——. (2013) "A Conspicuous Art: Putting Gettier to the Test," *Philosophers' Imprint* 13, 1–16.

——. (2015) "From Virtue Epistemology to Abilism: Theoretical and Empirical Developments," in C.B. Miller, R.M. Furr, A. Knobel, & W. Fleeson (eds.) *Character: New Directions from Philosophy, Psychology, and Theology*. Oxford: Oxford University Press, pp. 315–322.

——. (2016) "Knowledge Judgments in 'Gettier'Cases," in J.M. Systma & W. Buckwalter (eds.) *A Companion to Experimental Philosophy*, Malden, MA: Wiley Blackwell, pp. 337–348.

——. (2017) "Knowledge Attributions in Iterated Fake Barn Cases," *Analysis* 77, 104–115.

Turri, J., Buckwalter, W., & Blouw, P. (2015) "Knowledge and Luck," *Psychonomic Bulletin & Review* 22, 378–390.

Weatherson, B. (2003) "What Good Are Counterexamples?" *Philosophical Studies* 115, 1–31.

——. (2013) "Margins and Errors," *Inquiry* 56, 63–76.

Weinberg, J., Nichols, S., & Stich, S. (2001) "Normativity and Epistemic Intuitions," *Philosophical Topics* 29, 429–460.

Williamson, T. (2007) *The Philosophy of Philosophy*, Oxford: Blackwell.

——. (2011) "Philosophical Expertise and the Burden of Proof," *Metaphilosophy* 42, 215–229.

36

LEGAL LUCK

Ori J. Herstein

What Is Legal Luck?

Subject to some qualifications (discussed in the closing section), "legal luck" obtains where one's legal status—such as legal rights, obligations, liabilities, and culpability—turns on facts not under one's control (Enoch 2008: 28).[1] A full account of "control" is beyond our scope but basically the idea is that we are often in control of conduct and of outcomes that we bring about when acting in our capacity as practical agents.

The two instances of legal luck most explored in the literature critical of legal luck involve the tort of negligence (Feinberg 1962; Waldron 1995; Schroeder 1997) and the criminal law of attempts (Feinberg 1962; Davis 1986; Lewis 1989; Kessler 1994; Kadish 1994; Alexander 1994).

The classic scenario for exploring luck in negligence involves two equally negligent drivers. While both are driving carelessly, one accidently hits a pedestrian who, as luck would have it, happens to cross the road at that exact moment, while the other driver hits no one. It is stipulated that while failing to pay attention to the road was within the control of both drivers, the consequences of their respective failures to do so were not. In terms of what was under the drivers' control, it was similarly a matter of luck whether anyone crossed the road at the same moment of their carelessness. Now, although the two drivers are alike with regard to what is within their control, tort law judges them very differently. The unlucky driver is held liable for hitting a pedestrian, while the second driver—who was equally negligent yet fortunately hit no one—is not liable at all. To recover damages in negligence, it is not enough to prove that the defendant's negligent behavior put one at unreasonable risk of harm; the law also requires that the plaintiff prove that the defendant's risky conduct actually harmed one. Accordingly, the stark difference in the legal statuses of the two drivers turns on facts similarly outside of their control, entailing that legal liability for negligence can turn on luck.

On to the law of criminal attempts. In many jurisdictions, punishment for a completed crime is more severe than it is for a failed attempt at completing the same crime. And whether an attempt is successful often turns, at least to a degree, on facts beyond one's control. For example, if a sudden gale serendipitously alters the trajectory of an assassin's bullet thereby saving the target's life, the would-be assassin is guilty of attempted murder, even though the charge would have been full-fledged murder but for the unexpected gust of wind. Accordingly, differences in legal culpability and punishment between the successful and the unsuccessful criminal may turn on facts similarly beyond their control, thereby grounding the extent of criminal culpability in luck.

414

Having detailed two of the literature's specific examples of legal luck, there are three general types of legal luck. Thomas Nagel offers a taxonomy of morally salient types of luck (Nagel 1993). Although Nagel is focused on "moral luck" (a concept explained below), his categories are helpful for conceptualizing different types of legal luck. Most prominent in the literature on legal luck is "resultant luck,"[2] which involves legal liability for certain uncontrolled outcomes of one's conduct. Another form of luck is "circumstantial," which is luck in the circumstances of conduct where those circumstances are both beyond one's control and influence what one does. Accordingly, circumstantial legal luck involves legal status turning on circumstances rather than on agency. Nagel also explores what is known as "constitutive luck." Often our actions are influenced by our character traits, dispositions, capacities, talents, and natural inclinations, none of which are subject to our control, at least not readily, and which are often molded by forces also largely beyond our control, such as our genes and the circumstances of our upbringing. Constitutive legal luck involves legal status turning on facts arising out of such constitutive features.

Regardless of the type of legal luck involved, the literature is mostly myopic to the variance in degrees in legal luck. Much of the literature on luck and the law comes from moral philosophy, which tends to view law as a reservoir of examples of moral luck, often glossing over the legal details. Yet ignoring the law's nuances might result in an inflated conception of the extent of legal luck.

Legal luck admits degrees. Control is a matter of degree—one can have more or less control over her actions and their outcomes. And given that legal luck involves legal status turning on facts beyond one's control, it follows that one's legal status might involve more or less legal luck based on the given level of one's control over the relevant facts, such as the extent to which one can raise or reduce the probability of an occurrence.

As reflected in the paradigmatic examples of legal luck presented above, the type of legal luck most often explored is the resultant luck found in legal causation. Causation in law is normally predicated on a conjunction of two tests. Typically, first comes what is known as the "but for test" which asks whether X would have transpired but for the defendant's conduct. If the answer is "no," then the defendant's conduct did not—as a matter of law—cause X. If, however, the answer is "yes," then the defendant's conduct is what lawyers call a "factual cause" of X. Yet in order to prove as a matter of law that the defendant caused X, the plaintiff must also establish that the defendant's conduct was a "proximate cause" of X.

The tests for proximate causation are several and still evolving, and can vary in nuance among different branches of the law. Yet they all function to pick out from the vast chains of factual causes leading up to X those causes that warrant legal liability. Presently the most common test for determining proximate causation is the "reasonable foreseeability" test, which asks whether a reasonable person under similar circumstances would have foreseen X as a likely outcome of said conduct. Other tests turn on whether an outcome is too "remote" or "accidental" to count as legally caused by the defendant's conduct.

Accordingly, the law of causation removes from the scope of liability most instances of potential resultant legal luck. As a matter of factual causation, our legally wrongful (or otherwise liability grounding) conduct invariably contributes to numerous causal chains leading to any number of harmful or otherwise destructive outcomes—most of which are too remote to imagine, let alone control. Were we liable for the unforeseeable or remote factual outcomes of our legal wrongs, the extent of luck's role in determining our liability would be crushing. Thankfully liability does not extend to all such outcomes.

Important for our purposes is that tests such as the foreseeability test have a measure of control built into them. Ability to foresee an outcome provides the opportunity not only to learn of the likelihood of the outcome but often also thereby provides the opportunity to take action to avoid that outcome or, at least, to reduce the probability of it occurring, thereby providing for a measure of control over that outcome. This suggests that the luck inherent in legal causation involves a relatively lower degree of resultant luck than might seem at first blush, especially given that most people have a predictive capacity approximating what the courts normally determine as "reasonable foreseeability." Accordingly, by limiting liability to what we can reasonably foresee, the law at least often significantly diminishes luck's role in determining liability.

Another often discussed instance of legal luck involves the constitutive luck found in tort law's "reasonable person standard." Legal negligence involves a breach of a duty of care which then causes harm to the person to whom that duty was owed. Courts normally construe "care" as what a reasonable person would have done under the same circumstances. Thus, if one causes (foreseeable) harm to a person to whom one owes a duty of care one is normally liable for the harm, provided that one caused it while acting unreasonably.

Now, what of people whose capacities and abilities fall short of the capacities and abilities of the "reasonable person," making it much harder or even nearly impossible for them to meet the law's standard of conduct? Are such people liable for harms they cause while acting "unreasonably"? But for a handful of exceptions, such as children and people with physical disabilities, the answer is "yes." The reasonable-person standard is what the law calls an "objective standard," applying to everyone regardless of idiosyncrasies. In the words of Oliver Wendell Holmes:

> If, for instance, a man is born hasty and awkward, is always having accidents and hurting himself or his neighbours, no doubt his congenital defects will be allowed for in the courts of Heaven, but his slips are no less troublesome to his neighbours than if they sprang from guilty neglect. His neighbours accordingly require him, at his proper peril, to come up to their standard, and the courts which they establish decline to take his personal equation into account.
>
> *Holmes 1881: 86–87*

One could scarcely imagine a starker rendition of a rather strict version of constitutive legal luck.

Then again, like in the case of legal causation, here too the literature at times gives an exaggerated impression of the extent of legal luck. When determining the contours of the reasonable person's reasonableness, courts typically take a variety of considerations into account, including not only social policy and judges' objectives for how people should behave, but also social custom and approximations of the actual abilities and limitations of the citizenry. Rarely does the law adopt a standard so aspirational that most people would find it highly difficult let alone nearly impossible to follow. As described in a leading treatise, the reasonable person "has not the courage of Achilles, the wisdom of Ulysses or the strength of Hercules" (Rogers 2010: 93).

Thus, although the reasonable-person standard is normative rather than sociological, frequently it is designed to approximate—at least partially—the abilities of the common person. This is quaintly reflected in a classic description of the reasonable person as "[t]he man on the Clapham omnibus … The man who takes the magazines at home, and in the evening pushes the lawn mower in his shirt sleeves" (*Hall* v *Brooklands Auto Racing Club* 1933).

Accordingly, while the law of negligence involves the potential for rather harsh constitutive legal luck, in practice such luck mostly arises in the fringe cases of people lacking the full capacities ascribed to the reasonable person.

At times, however, law does wholeheartedly adopt higher degrees of legal luck. An example is the "thin skull" exception to the rule of proximate causation, according to which liability may attach to those who cause others personal injury even if the *extent* of the injury was not reasonably foreseeable. This doctrine applies if the (extra) unforeseen harm resulted from a concealed frailty in the victim. The classic example is of a victim with a latent medical condition—such as haemophilia—suffering serious injury as the result of a minor battery. Given that such (extra) harm is considered too remote to reasonably foresee, causing it is largely beyond one's control. This is because control has epistemic conditions as well as metaphysical ones, and the foreseeability test speaks to the former. Holding one liable under such circumstances for unforeseeable harms involves, therefore, a significant measure of resultant legal luck.

Regimes of "strict liability" also involve a high level of legal luck. Strict liability is liability for what one does or causes faultlessly. In other words, it is liability for conduct and outcomes that might have been *un*reasonable to avoid or prevent. For instance, the doctrine of "respondent superior" holds faultless employers liable for harms resulting from their employees' negligence when performed within the scope of the employment. "Product liability" is another example. In many jurisdictions, manufacturers are liable for harms caused by a defect in their product, even when faultless in making the product defective. The tort of trespass to land also turns on strict liability, imposing liability even on unintentional trespassers who took all reasonably available precautions to avoid encroaching upon another's property.

Now that we have a sense of what legal luck is, we turn to the matter of its justification.

What Is Moral Luck?

The literature on legal luck is often intertwined with the philosophical literature on "moral luck," a term referring to luck's putative role in determining a person's moral record, including blameworthiness, praiseworthiness, accountability, and culpability (Statman 1993: 1–35; Nelkin 2013). In fact, the notion of legal luck is very much the legal corollary of moral luck. Moral luck negates what is known as the "control principle," under which what goes on a person's moral record is conditioned on what is under that person's control. Accordingly, one is not appropriately subject to moral assessment for that which is beyond her control. Moral luck is, therefore, at odds with the control principle. Now, whether there really is moral luck is a contested matter. For every supporter of moral luck there are at least as many detractors. Luckily, litigating the matter is not central to understanding *legal* luck. What is important for our purposes are the implications of whether or not moral luck exists on the justification of legal luck. To which we turn next.

Moral Luck and Legal Luck

For those accepting the existence of moral luck there appears nothing problematic in legal luck per se. This remains the case even when one's legal status ought to somehow track one's moral record. Because if one accepts moral luck, then the mere fact that one's legal status is not fully sensitive to what is under one's control does not necessarily entail that the law does not track one's moral record. In fact, as explained below, accepting moral luck might yield an argument in favor of instances of legal luck.

In contrast, for those denying the existence of moral luck—thereby holding the view that a person's moral record is necessarily grounded in control—legal luck raises potential moral concerns. These arise in cases in which one's legal status ought to somehow track one's moral record. Because given that legal luck entails legal status divorced (at least to an extent) from control, and given the premise that control grounds moral record, it follows that legal luck involves legal status divorced (at least to an extent) from moral record.

As explored below, whether one's legal status ought to somehow track one's moral record is a normative question touching on the moral grounds of law. In this section, it is assumed that there are some instances of legal status in which moral record ought to have such a role. Notice that the locution "somehow track one's moral record" is purposely vague. One's legal status in relation to Y could track one's moral record in relation to Y in more than one way: explicitly turning on moral record; turning on the same facts that ground moral record; coincidentally corresponding to moral record; and so on. For our purposes, it is enough that some such tracking relation ought to obtain to raise concerns with legal luck.

Returning to the example of the two drivers, in the eyes of those rejecting resultant moral luck the unlucky driver is not blameworthy or culpable for the *outcomes* of his driving, as they are outside of his control. Now, if in such cases one's legal liability for the outcomes of one's conduct ought to track one's moral record vis-à-vis those outcomes, then the luck inherent to legal causation in such cases seems wrongful, because such luck involves legal liability divorced from moral record.

Yet notice that even for hardened devotees of the control principle, the measure of wrongness of different instances of legal luck may differ. Under the control principle—in those cases where one's legal status ought to somehow track one's moral record—more legal luck is worse than less. Given that control and, therefore, luck come in degrees, and given that moral record turns on control, it follows that cases of less legal luck involve more control and, therefore, more sensitivity to moral record than cases of more legal luck involving less control. Thus, assuming the control principle and rejecting moral luck, all else being equal, legal doctrines of strict liability are typically morally worse than doctrines such as legal causation and negligence—at least when legal status ought to track moral record.

Is Legal Luck *Pro Tanto* Wrong?

David Enoch argues that for those rejecting moral luck *any* instance of legal luck is *pro tanto* wrong (Enoch 2008: 31–38). Here is why. Legal luck entails legal status wholly or partially divorced from control. Assuming that moral record is grounded in control, and further assuming that one's moral record in relation to certain facts is always relevant for what one's legal status ought to be in relation to those facts, it follows that legal luck is always *pro tanto* wrongful. This does not entail that all cases of legal luck are, all things considered, wrong, but does entail that there is always some reason counting against legal luck. Whether any instance of legal luck is *all things considered* wrongful turns also on various other potentially competing reasons germane to the particular case and to the type of legal status at hand.

Key to Enoch's argument is that one's moral record vis-à-vis Y is always a reason for what one's legal status ought to be vis-à-vis Y. As Enoch writes:

> [I]t just seems basically unfair to have one's interests influenced profoundly by the law in ways that have nothing to do with one's (relevant) moral status ... The way the law treats me (with regard to a certain incident, or case, or action, or whatever) should be sensitive, it seems to me, to what my moral status is (with regard to that incident, case, action, or whatever).

> *Enoch 2008: 36–37*

For Enoch's argument to work, *all* legal luck must impact its subjects. And for his argument to escape the charge of negligibility that impact must often be significant, otherwise other considerations for and against legal luck would regularly drown out Enoch's *pro tanto* reasons.

Yet not all possible instances of one's legal status impact one's interests—for example, culpability under an unenforceable and little-known law or a legal entitlement that is more bother pursuing than it is worth. And whether there is something specific to the type of legal statuses involved in cases of legal luck necessarily impacting one's interests is unclear. What is clear is that the definition of legal luck as legal status turning on facts beyond one's control does not establish such a necessary relation between legal luck and interests. And to make his argument Enoch must establish such a connection.

Thus, as it stands, the view that there is an ever-present reason counting against any instance of legal luck proves too broad. That said, even if legal luck's obliviousness to moral record does not *always* count against it, obviously often it does. As reflected in much of the literature referenced above, legally caused deprivation not grounded in fault often seems deeply unfair.

Legal Luck and Agency: Is Legal Luck *Pro Tanto* Justified?

Counting in favor of accepting luck as a part of the moral landscape is the fact that the control principle seems to entail a diminished human agency (Nagel 1993: 66; Walker 1993: 239–247; Williams 1993; Statman 2014: 103–107). If true, this line raised by proponents of the view that moral luck exists might help bolster an argument in favor of certain instances of legal luck.

As stipulated at the outset, controlled action is the type of action that one performs as an agent. The view that moral record turns on control is based on the view that agency grounds moral record, that is, we are only blameworthy, praiseworthy, or culpable for that which we do or bring about as agents. Now people are part of a complex causal web, inhabiting a world governed by the natural laws of cause and effect. Thus, much of what we appear to do or bring about is, in fact, not under our control, either wholly or partially, and, therefore, does not seem to involve our agency—at least not entirely. Thus, purifying the moral record of luck threatens shrinking agency to an "extensionless point" (Nagel 1993: 66). Even our will and intentions—seemingly inhabiting agency's inner citadel—are not always entirely free of causal determinants (Feinberg 1962, 349–350). Accordingly, agency without moral luck seems largely inert. That is, most of what we imagine as *our* actions—in the sense that we are accountable, blameworthy, and praiseworthy for them—are in fact events in which our agency is affected by factors outside of our control, at least to a substantial degree. This entails that while our lives are ours in the sense that we live them, they are far less *ours* in the sense of active practical agents.

Relatedly, purifying agency from luck entails a highly contracted and faded self. Bernard Williams puts the point well:

> One's history as an agent is a web in which anything that is the product of the will is surrounded and held up and partly formed by things that are not, in such a way that reflection can go only in one of two directions: either in the direction of saying that responsible agency is a fairly superficial concept, which has a limited use in harmonizing what happens, or else that it is not a superficial concept, but that it cannot ultimately be purified—if one attaches importance to the sense of what one is in terms of what one has done and what in the world one is responsible for, one must accept much that makes its claim on that sense solely in virtue of its being actual.
>
> *Williams 1993: 44–45*

This truncated picture of the self is troubling. To use Williams's terms, we do attach importance to what we are in terms of what we have done. We experience ourselves and give meaning to our lives as active agents. Accordingly, what we do as agents—our choices, failures, successes—and what credit and blame we deserve for them, take part in forming our life story and "who we are." Purifying agency from any luck leaves us, therefore, with very little agency, thereby shrinking our existence as fully fledged active selves as well as dissolving much of the meaning that we find in that existence.

If these reflections are broadly correct, adopting the control principle and rejecting moral luck clash with rather basic conceptions and premises that we hold true about the nature and parameters of agency and the self, which, according to proponents of the idea of moral luck, gives reason for believing in moral luck and for rejecting the veracity of the control principle. It is the fact of moral luck that enables the type of agency that can robustly exist in the actual world—recognizing that some of our conduct and some of its outcomes are ours as agents, thereby influencing our moral record, even though they arise out of luck and are fully, or at least partially, beyond our control.

Given all this, building on Honore's ideas on luck in tort law and assuming, for the sake of argument, that moral luck exists, I submit that moral luck's purported role in forming agency and the self is relevant to the justification of legal luck. Writing on resultant luck, Honore claims that society's norms allocate accountability according to the luck-dependent outcomes of our conduct. And we are in effect forced to "bet" on those outcomes when we act, without certainty as to whether things will end up to our credit or discredit (Honore 1988: 540). Moreover, Honore believes that we are better off living with a luck-infused moral record, because although it might entail discredit for failures and misdeeds that we are not (at least not fully) responsible for, it also credits us with our many successes for which we are similarly not morally responsible. And, in the process, we gain a fully fledged self (Honore 1988: 542–543).

How do we come to know the scope of our actions, successes, failures, praiseworthiness, and culpability? Relatedly, how do we come to appreciate and live by the parameters of our agency and self? The answer is that these occur—to a significant degree—through the inculcation of social norms. Law is central to such social norms. Perhaps more than any other social institution it is the law that directs us on matters of accountability, instructing us on what we are credited with and discredited for, how far our culpability extends, what we deserve, and to what we are entitled given our conduct. The law thereby contributes to forming and to informing our sense of the breadth of agency and of where our self begins and where it ends.

To perform this task, the law must incorporate luck into the conditions of legal status, mirroring our luck-infused moral records. Were legal status devoid of luck—turning purely on what is within our control—the law would have painted a faded and inert picture of agency and conveyed a narrow conception of the self. Now the law of course never entirely mirrors moral record—nor should it. Even at the price of projecting a false image of the breadth of agency. My point is only that in incorporating luck into legal status, the law can and often does perform this task. And that this counts in favor of the law incorporating a measure of legal luck. Notice that none of this, of course, establishes that legal luck is *pro tanto* justified. Even assuming moral luck exists, legal luck neither necessarily reflects moral record nor necessarily captures the nature of agency.

Justifying Legal Luck

Having explored reasons for and against legal luck in general, we now turn to the justification of legal luck as it appears in specific branches of the law. When reflecting on the justification of an instance of legal luck, the key issue is whether the law—in that instance—ought to track one's relevant moral record.

Let us begin with tort law. Much of the literature on luck in tort law attempts to vindicate legal luck, arguing that personal moral record—such as fault and desert—are just not part of the grounds and logic of tort law. Working within a Kantian paradigm, Arthur Ripstein views law as a systematic realization of equal freedom guaranteed by reciprocal (and coercive) limits. The role of tort law under this picture is to protect people's reciprocal rights in their "means," such as in their person and property (Ripstein 2008: 69). Oriented toward rights, tort law therefore typically ought to respond to violation of such rights, whether or not such violations spring from moral fault (Ripstein 2008, 2016). John Goldberg and Benjamin Zipursky view tort law as devoted to securing victims of certain wrongs a legal recourse for responding to, and for extracting a remedy from, those who wronged them. Focused more on wrongs to victims, this goal does not turn on whether or not the wrongdoing, which ought to trigger a legal right of action, involved fault (Goldberg & Zipursky 2007; Zipursky 2008). Gregory Keating views accident law as ideally devoted to the fair and favorable balancing of liberty and personal security (Keating 2006). Pursuant to this Rawlsian view, tort liability ought to spring from accidental disruptions to that balance, whether negligent or faultless.

Moreover, whether or not explicitly engaging the issues of legal and moral luck, there are still other accounts of the grounds of tort law that are also potentially hospitable to legal luck, such as the view that tort law ought to maximize social wealth and, accordingly, function to impose liability in ways that minimize the costs of accidents (Calabresi 1970) and incentivize economically optimal conduct (Posner 1972; Landes & Posner 1987). Under such views, so long as torts of strict liability and negligence deliver economic efficiency, their incorporation of luck is immaterial and even desirable.

Even in criminal law—wherein moral desert is undoubtedly a central consideration—the case against legal luck is not clear cut. The strongest case against incorporating legal luck in criminal punishment is predicated on retributive justice. Retributivism is the view that punishment ought to be meted out to fit people's just deserts. That is, punishment should be meted out for the relevant aspects of defendants' moral record. Accordingly, for those rejecting moral luck—thereby adopting the control principle for moral record—retributive justice counts against legal luck in punishment because legal luck entails punishment regardless of moral desert. And, were retribution the *sole* consideration animating the justness of punishment, it would follow that legal luck in punishment is wrong. Even those who are not retributivists (that is, do not view desert as reason in favor of punishing) yet do view desert as a necessary condition for, or a "side-constraint" on, just punishment (Hart 1968), would deem legal luck wrong when prescribing punishment beyond the constraints of desert.

Yet not everyone is a retributivist, and even among retributivists retribution does not necessarily stand alone among the grounds of just punishment. And these other grounds do not necessarily cut against legal luck in punishment. Thus, at least for some, just punishment is not necessarily incompatible with legal luck, even if we were to reject moral luck.

For instance, removing dangerous recidivist criminals from society is a goal of punishment oblivious to whether or not the crime is within a defendant's control (Eisikovits 2005; Kadish 1994: 685–686). Deterrence is another often-mentioned goal of punishment, which also does not necessarily count against legal luck (Lewis 1989: 55–56; Kadish 1994: 685–687; Eisikovits 2005). For example, while attempting to deter people from doing what is out of their control might seem futile, sometimes punishing those lacking in control could serve to deter others who do possess the requisite control (Shavel 1990).

There are still other efforts to justify legal luck in punishment (Hart 1968; Davis 1986; Kenny 1988; Moore 1997: 192–247; Katz 2000; Ripstein 2008). I will mention two. Arguing noncommittedly from the value of fairness, David Lewis suggests lessening the sting of the luck inherent to the criminal law of attempts (Lewis 1989). According to Lewis, when attempting to commit a crime one effectively enters a lottery for what punishment one will face if caught and convicted—if successful one will face harsher punishment than if one's attempt falls short. Given that only the attempt is under one's control and given that whether or not one's attempt succeeds is a matter of luck, whether or not one will face a harsher sentence is also a matter of luck. Yet this type of legal luck is putatively fair because anyone who attempts to commit a crime is subjected to the same lottery.

Another argument in favor of different punishment for failed and successful attempts involves criminal law's purported communicative goal (Duff 2001). Some argue that criminal punishment is and ought to be a vehicle of condemnation, wherein the community expresses its values and censure to criminals as well as to their victims and to the general citizenry. Arguing from the expressivist paradigm, Antony Duff believes it important for the law to communicate that a completed crime is worse than a failed attempt at the same crime, because only then does law communicate the added disvalue of completed crime. Equal punishment for successful and for failed attempts would signal that the law—and thereby the community—is oblivious to such added disvalue, such as the harm to the victims and the costs to society at large (Duff 1990: 31–37).

The Bounds of Legal Luck

I close with the question with which we began: What is legal luck? Conceiving of legal luck as we have thus far solely in terms of "facts beyond one's control affecting one's legal status" is too expansive. Numerous facts that are beyond our control impact our legal rights and obligations. Construing "legal luck" to encompass them all seems to dilute the category, losing sight of the type of cases that have drawn the scholarly attention enumerated above. For example, the contractual right for payment that a lottery ticket holder has against the lotto company only vests once she wins the lottery, which is clearly beyond her control. Is hers really a case of what we have in mind when thinking of "*legal* luck"? Or, is my status as a murderer a matter of "*legal* luck" given that numerous circumstances not under my control contributed to my success in killing my victim? Such as, once I aimed and pulled the trigger my pistol did not jam or misfire, my target did not bend over to tie his shoelaces just as I fired, and a flock of birds did not fly by just in time to absorb my fire. Yet, although I might be a "lucky murderer," am I *legally* lucky? Seems not. At least not in the sense of the literature we are trying to understand here. Accordingly, if we took "legal luck" to mean only "facts outside of one's control affecting one's legal status," then given that most of life's circumstances involve a measure of lack of control, it would follow that the category of "legal luck" is ubiquitous, including numerous cases that seem outside the scope of the literature on legal luck.

This raises two related challenges. One is to better delineate the bounds of "legal luck," capturing those instances of luck that have drawn philosophical attention and differentiating them from other less relevant cases of luck impacting legal status. A second challenge is normative—explaining whether this tighter conception of "legal luck" warrants the special scholarly attention it has received. Does the category of "legal luck," as distinguished from other cases of luck impacting legal status track anything of distinct moral significance or concern, such as the fairness concerns explored above?

Setting out to delineate the bounds of legal luck, Enoch draws a distinction between legal luck and what he calls "plain luck that carries legal implications" (hereinafter "plain luck") (Enoch 2008: 38–44). According to Enoch, the "luck" in "legal luck" is internal to the law. It is, if you will, luck that the law itself creates. In contrast, where plain luck is at issue, the law is merely sensitive to non-legal circumstances that involve luck, thereby making the law indirectly susceptive to the effects of luck that already exist regardless of the law. Another way Enoch puts the distinction is that legal luck is luck that the law creates intentionally, while plain luck is luck that the law merely foresees or allows to have legal implications. For example, whether or not an attempt at X succeeds in X-ing is often a matter of resultant luck. Given that law draws a legal distinction—explicitly turning on the outcomes of actions—between the crime of X-ing and the crime of attempted X-ing, the law intentionally creates (in Enoch's terms) a legal distinction turning on resultant luck. Or, assuming that people's natural capacities and inclinations, such as intelligence, carelessness, accuracy, etc., are a matter of constitutive luck, if the law then draws a legal distinction that explicitly turns on such capacities and inclinations—as in the legal distinction between a "reasonable person" and an "unreasonable person"—the law is actively and intentionally determining legal status based on luck.

Yet, Enoch's distinction does not help us with the two challenges set out above. As for the normative challenge, Enoch explains that his distinction between legal luck and plain luck does not track any intrinsically morally significant difference (Enoch 2008: 53). And as for delineating "legal luck," the distinction between plain luck and legal luck does not always comfortably fit all clear-cut cases of "legal luck." Here is an example. A recent election for a seat on the Virginia State Legislature was ruled a tie, and, pursuant to Virginia law, a lottery decides the winner. I take this as a clear-cut case of luck affecting legal status that is not a case of what the literature on "legal luck" has in mind (perhaps because the Virginia law seems fair). Nevertheless, the Virginia example is, I think, exactly what Enoch has in mind by "legal luck," as it is a case of the law actively and intentionally creating a lottery to determine legal outcome.

Moreover, Enoch's distinction between "legal luck" and "plain luck" is brittle. For one thing, as Enoch himself concedes, the distinction is vague. For instance, considering that different judges sometimes rule differently on similar cases, does the fact that judges are often assigned cases randomly not suggest that judicial rulings can turn not on one's relevant actions but rather on which judge one was assigned (Waldron 2008)? In such cases does the law foresee/allow luck to determine legal status or does it intend/make it so? It seems unclear. In addition, often the distinctions between what the law does or allows and between what the law intends or foresees seem mostly a matter of description. At least to me, it rings just as true to say that the tort of negligence allows rather than makes it so that constitutive luck in one's natural capacities has legal implications. After all, any time a fact affects one's legal status it does so due to the law, as it is always and only law that vests facts with legal significance. And whether this is something that the law does/allows or intends/foresees often seems mostly due to framing. Relatedly, law neither intends nor foresees; neither does law act nor allow things to happen, at least not in any straightforward way. The law is a system of norms and institutions, and although the law necessarily involves people who act, omit, and have mental states, such as intending and foreseeing, the law itself is not an agent. Moreover, even when we can claim in some sense that law intends or acts—be it through the law's human organs or otherwise—this is surely not true of all laws involving luck.

Yet, but for Enoch's essay, there is a dearth of scholarship on delineating the parameters of legal luck. One possible avenue forward is to find inspiration in attempts to draw the bounds of *moral* luck. I will close with a suggestion.

Robert Hartman argues that delineating the bounds of moral luck is best achieved looking not to the concept of "luck," but rather to the tension in our beliefs out of which the notion of "moral luck" was born (Hartman 2017: 23–31). As Williams and Nagel point out (Williams 1993; Nagel 1993), on the one hand we believe that people's moral record is not impacted by that which is not under their control. Yet on the other hand, purifying moral record from all that is not under one's control entails unintuitive conclusions about our agency and moral records. Under Hartman's approach, the question of moral luck therefore arises when this tension manifests—that is, when facts outside of one's control seem, nevertheless, to impact one's agency and moral record.

When is that the case? According to Barbara Herman not all facts that are outside of one's control—even if influencing one's actions and/or their outcomes—impact moral record. Herman believes that lack of control does not influence moral record when the facts outside of one's control are abnormal or irregular (Herman 1995: 147), a view she shares with Michael Moore (1997: 211–218). Herman explains that we assume a baseline of effective control that includes much that we do not control, making normal action—performed against the backdrop of that baseline—a matter of course, even though what we control is never in and of itself sufficient to effect our ends. According to Herman:

> Whether or not the world cooperates in our efforts is out of our control, but it is not a matter of luck, if luck marks the introduction of something arbitrary from the moral point of view. It is an ordinary component of rational agency that we act on the assumption that things are as they seem. That we are not, say, in an environment where ordinary causal connections are disrupted … Because it is reasonable to trust that normal actions will not misfire, we are not lucky when they succeed, even though, as we know, there may be a littered field of "almost mishaps" in our wake.
>
> *Herman 1995: 147*

Perhaps something similar is true for delineating the breadth of legal luck. Possibly it is only when law holds that irregular occurrences—that are outside of one's control—affect one's legal status, that the phenomenon scholars have labelled "legal luck" arises. This would explain why, for example, if one's natural capacities are under the reasonable-person standard it seems like a case of constitutive legal luck, while the normal case of falling within the standard does not. Or why a would-be assassin missing his target due to a mosquito landing on his nose—causing him to flinch—seems a case of resultant legal luck, while the normal cases in which no mosquito unexpectedly appears to save the day are not discussed as involving luck at all. Or why proximate causation—turning on foreseeable outcomes—involves far less legal luck than the thin skull doctrine which provides for liability for unforeseeable outcomes.

Moreover, adopting something like Herman's approach suggests that in cases of legal luck—unlike cases of plain luck—legal status turns on luck in facts that do not impact one's moral record, raising normative concerns in cases wherein legal status ought to somehow track moral record. Which might explain the possible moral drawback inherent to legal luck, thereby vindicating "legal luck" as a category worthy of special moral reflection.

Notes

1 In adopting a control-based account of "luck" I follow the literature on both "moral luck" and "legal luck."
2 The term is Zimmerman's (1987).

References

Alexander, L. (1994) "Crime and Culpability," *Journal of Contemporary Legal Issues* 5, 1–30.
Calabresi, G. (1970) *The Cost of Accidents*, New Haven, CT: Yale University Press.
Davis, M. (1986) "Why Attempts Deserve Less Punishment than Completed Crimes," *Law and Philosophy* 5, 1–32.
Duff, R.A. (1990) "Auctions, Lotteries, and the Punishment of Attempts," *Law and Philosophy* 9, 1–37.
———. (2001) *Punishment, Communication, and Community*, Oxford: Oxford University Press.
Eisikovits, N. (2005) "Moral Luck and the Criminal Law," in M. Campbell, M. O'Rourke, & D. Shier (eds.) *Law and Social Justice*, Cambridge, MA: MIT Press.
Enoch, D. (2008) "Luck Between Morality, Law, and Justice," *Theoretical Inquiries in Law* 9(23), 23–59.
Feinberg, J. (1962) "Responsibility in Law and Morals," *The Philosophical Review* 71(3), 340–351.
Goldberg, J.C.P., & Zipursky, B.C. (2007) "Tort Law and Moral Luck," *Cornell Law Review* 92, 1123–1176.
Hart, H.L.A. (1968) *Punishment and Responsibility*, Oxford: Oxford University Press.
Hartman, R. (2017) *In Defense of Moral Luck: Why Luck Often Affects Praiseworthiness and Blameworthiness*, New York & London: Routledge.
Herman, B. (1995) "Feinberg on Luck and Failed Attempts," *Arizona Law Review* 37, 143–149.
Holmes, O.W. (1881) *The Common Law*.
Honore, T. (1988) "Responsibility and Luck," *The Law Quarterly Review* 104, 530–553.
Kadish, S.H. (1994) "Forward: the Criminal Law and the Luck of the Draw," *The Journal of Criminal Law and Criminology* 84(4), 679–702.
Katz, L. (2000) "Why the Successful Assassin Is More Wicked than the Unsuccessful One," *California Law Review* 88, 791–812.
Keating, G. (2006) "Strict Liability and the Mitigation of Moral Luck," *Journal of Ethics and Social Philosophy* 2(1), 1–33.
Kenny, A. (1988) "Aristotle on Moral Luck," in J. Dancy, J.M. Moravcsik, & C.C.W. Taylor (eds.) *Human Agency: Language, Duty, and Value*, Stanford, CA: Stanford University Press.
Kessler, K.D. (1994) "Role of Luck in Criminal Law," University of Pennsylvania Law Review 142, 2183–2237.
Landes, W.M., & Posner, R.A. (1987) *The Economic Structure of Tort Law*, Cambridge, MA: Harvard University Press.
Lewis, D. (1989) "The Punishment that Leaves Something to Chance," *Philosophy and Public Affairs* 18, 227–242.
Moore, M. (1997) *Placing Blame*, Oxford: Oxford University Press.
Nagel, T. (1993) "Moral Luck," in D. Statman (ed.) *Moral Luck*, State University of New York Press, pp. 57–72.
Nelkin, D.K. (2013) "Moral Luck," in *The Stanford Encyclopedia of Philosophy* (Winter 2013 Edition), Edward N. Zalta (ed.) https://plato.stanford.edu/archives/win2013/entries/moral-luck/
Otsuka, M. (2009) "Moral Luck: Optional, Not Brute, Philosophical Perspectives," *Ethics* 23, 373–388.
Posner, R.A. (1972) "A Theory of Negligence," *The Journal of Legal Studies* 1(1), 29–96.
Ripstein, A. (2008) "Closing the Gap," *Theoretical Inquiries in Law* 9(1), 61–95.
———. (2016) *Private Wrongs*, Cambridge, MA: Harvard University Press.
Rogers, W.V.H. (2010) *Winfield and Jolowicz on Tort*, London: Thomas Reuters.
Schroeder, C.H. (1997) "Causation, Compensation, and Moral Responsibility," in D. Owen (ed.) *The Philosophical Foundations of Tort Law*, Oxford: Oxford University Press, pp. 347–361.
Shavel, S. (1990) "Deterrence and the Punishment of Attempts," *Journal of Legal Studies* 19, 435–466.
Statman, D. (1993) "Introduction," in D. Statman (ed.) *Moral Luck*, New York: State University of New York Press, pp. 1–34.
———. (2014) "Moral Luck and the Problem of the Innocent Attacker," *Ratio* 28, 97–111.
Walker, M.U. (1993) "Moral Luck and the Virtues of Impure Agency," in D. Statman (ed.) *Moral Luck*, New York: State University of New York Press, pp. 235–250.

Legal Luck

Waldron, J. (1995) "Moments of Carelessness and Massive Loss," in D. Owen (ed.) *Philosophical Foundations of Tort Law*, Oxford: Clarendon Press, pp. 387–408.
——. (2008) "Lucky in Your Judge," *Theoretical Inquires in Law* 9, 185–216.
Williams, B. (1993) "Moral Luck," in D. Statman (ed.) *Moral Luck*, New York: State University of New York Press, pp. 35–56.
Zimmerman, M. (1987) "Luck and Moral Responsibility," *Ethics* 97, 374–386.
Zipursky, B.C. (2008) "Two Dimensions of Responsibility in Crime, Tort, and Moral Luck," *Theoretical Inquiries in* Law 9(1), 98–137.

Case Law

Hall v Brooklands Auto Racing Club [1933] 1 KB 205.

37

FEMINIST APPROACHES TO MORAL LUCK

Carolyn McLeod and Jody Tomchishen

To a large extent, what we do and the circumstances we find ourselves in are beyond our control.[1] Yet this fact presents a problem for the common view that we can be held responsible only for what we have direct control over. If we have control over very little, if anything at all, then to what extent can we be held responsible? A typical response by feminist philosophers is to accept the absence of control—or in other words, the presence of luck—but to insist that responsibility remains often enough. According to this view, where there is luck, there can also be responsibility (what we call, "luck with responsibility" below). At the same time, feminists accept, of course, that where there is luck, there might not be responsibility (see "luck without responsibility" below). In general, like other philosophers, feminists have a complicated understanding of the relationship between luck and responsibility. In this chapter, we aim to describe how their understandings flow out of their feminist commitments and also what avenues there are for future research on luck and responsibility in feminist philosophy. Avenues that concern luck *without* responsibility are our central concern.

Luck With Responsibility

In saying that luck and responsibility can go hand in hand, feminists are embracing the phenomenon of moral luck. They are accepting, in other words, that "factors decisive for the moral standing of an agent are factors subject to luck" (Walker 1991: 14). In order to make sense of this view, they defend theories of *agency*, *responsibility*, and *virtue* that take seriously the extent to which luck enters into our actions or character. They pay special attention, moreover, to what Lisa Tessman calls "systemic luck" (and what Claudia Card calls the "unnatural lottery")—namely, luck that arises from social systems, particularly those of oppression and privilege (Tessman 2005: 13; Card 1996).[2] According to many feminists, the moral standing of agents can vary depending on their *systemic* luck, along with other types of luck.[3]

Given their prominence within feminist discussions about moral luck, we will explore in some detail the themes of agency, responsibility, and virtue.

Agency

According to some feminists, most notably Margaret Urban Walker (1991), there can be luck with responsibility (and *vice versa*) because of the nature of our moral agency. Walker rejects the common view that we can be morally assessed only for what is due to us, to our agency, as opposed to what is due to luck. Such a view rests on a conception of agency that is problematic, according to Walker. It presumes, in contrasting our agency with luck, that the former is immune to luck, which could be true only if we existed outside of "the world of space, time and causality" (1991: 17). Instead, we are, of course, embedded in this world, "variably conditioned by and conditioning parts of [it]" (p. 22). Thus, we are, to use Walker's language, "impure" rather than "pure" agents. Because we are still agents, however, we can be responsible for ourselves and others. We can therefore be subject to luck and moral assessment simultaneously.

But why embrace the notion of impure agency from a feminist perspective? Walker gives reasons in favor of this idea that are not especially feminist (1991). For example, she points to how it coheres with intuitions we tend to have about moral responsibility, such as the intuition that we can be responsible for easing others' suffering even when we did not cause it. But there are also distinctly feminist reasons to accept the impurity of our agency and deny the purity of it. We want to make these reasons explicit, and in so doing, will add to the feminist literature on moral luck.

First, the feminist claim that moral as well as epistemic agents are "situated"—that is, within sociopolitical structures of gender, race, class, and the like—makes sense only if our agency is impure. Feminists tend to critique mainstream ethics and epistemology for ignoring how our social positioning shapes our moral and epistemic agency, including what we can be responsible for or burdened with (e.g., Card 1996; Tessman 2005, 2014); what knowledge, including moral knowledge, we can possess (e.g., Harding 1992; Code 1981); what moral or other emotions we are likely to have (e.g., Bartky 1990: ch. 6; Little 1995), etc. None of this would be true, however, if our agency were pure. More generally, if, as moral agents, we were immune to luck, then we would also be immune to oppression or privilege and to the effects, both negative and positive, that they can have on our moral and epistemic agency. But this thought simply does not cohere with most feminist ethics and epistemology.

Second, many feminists describe our agency as social or relational, which is also possible only if our agency is impure. Claudia Card puts the point this way in her work on moral luck: "Significant relationships affect who we become. They affect our basic values, our sense of who we are, our commitments, even our abilities to live up to those commitments" (1996: 30; see also, e.g., Mackenzie & Stoljar 2000). These relationships can be oppressive or, alternatively, empowering of people who are oppressed in society. By highlighting how they influence people's values, identities, and the like, feminists are able to explain how psychologically oppressed some people are (Bartky 1990: ch. 2), and how resistant others are to their oppression. The view that agency is social clearly supports the notion that agency is situated. Both ideas rely, in turn, on our agency being impure—on our being subject to the luck, good or bad, that comes along with being shaped by certain relationships and certain social structures.[4]

Third, feminists should accept that agents are impure rather than pure, because a world of pure agents is not one that most feminists would welcome. Walker hints at this view when she explains why such a world is not one that anyone would welcome. As she writes,

> [P]ure agents may not be depended upon, much less morally required, to assume a share of the ongoing and massive human work of caring, healing, restoring, and cleaning-up on which each separate life and the collective one depend. That the very young and old, the weak, the sick, and the otherwise helpless—i.e., all of us at some times—depend on the sense of moral responsibility of others unlucky enough to be stuck with the circumstance of their need will not be the pure agents' problem.
>
> *Walker 1991: 25*

It will not be their problem because they are only responsible for what they have done; but usually they will have done nothing to make it the case that others need caring, healing, or restoring. This fact explains why everyone would, or at least should, deny that moral agency is pure. But what does it reveal about why feminists, *qua* feminists, should do so? The answer surely lies in the fact that to combat gender inequality in the performance of care work, we need to disabuse many men of the "commonsense idea" that they are responsible only for what they have control over. We need, in other words, to insist that their agency, along with women's agency, is impure. We should do so, in short, not just for the practical reason of trying to ensure that people get the care they need, but also for the political reason of promoting equality between men and women.

Last and relatedly, feminists should reject the notion of pure agency because it is, arguably, a patriarchal construction. The idea that we can only be responsible, legitimately, for what we have done has allowed many men to get out of the hard emotional and physical work of caring for others, and to assume that women do this work simply because they desire to do it, not because they know that as human beings or beings in special relationships with others, they are genuinely responsible for meeting others' needs.

In summary, one way that feminists have argued in favor of moral luck (of it being real[5]) is by homing in on the concept of agency and arguing that agency is impure. The main philosopher who has taken this tack is Walker. And although she is not explicit about this fact, there are distinctly *feminist* reasons to support her strategy, reasons that concern the feminist projects of highlighting the social and political dimensions of moral and epistemic agency, of redistributing care work, and of promoting gender equality. The details here point to how luck, including the systemic variety, can influence both our moral agency and our moral standing.

Responsibility

Another approach in the feminist literature to understanding how there can be luck with responsibility is to go into depth about the nature of responsibility and to detach responsibility—some forms of it at least—from control. Claudia Card adopts this strategy in *The Unnatural Lottery* (1996); there, to use her words, she explores "moral responsibility without the illusion of transcending luck" (p. 30). Card contrasts her account of responsibility with that found in Bernard Williams (1981) and Thomas Nagel's (1979) classic work on moral luck. Moreover, she suggests that her account coheres better with the moral experience of people who have little social power compared to people who are privileged. Let us explain, starting with Card's take on what we will call the Williams/Nagel view of responsibility.

The Williams/Nagel view is focused mainly on holding people responsible for what they have done: that is, deciding whether they are the proper objects of praise or blame. Responsibility here is *attributed* to others. In addition, it looks *back* to their past behavior. And it looks *down*, according to Card, since deciding who is deserving of punishment or reward has historically been a prerogative "of the powerful exercised for social control" (1996: 23).

Card proposes instead that "we look *forward* and *up*, toward the future and from the standpoints of those" who are socially marginalized (1996: 23; my emphasis). "From this perspective, we are likely to think more of *taking responsibility* than of attributing it," she argues (p. 23; my emphasis). "The point of taking responsibility is often to construct or to improve situations and relationships rather than to control, contain, or dominate" (p. 23). Taking responsibility, particularly in the context of personal or informal relationships, has historically been the prerogative of women (Card 1990). They have had to take responsibility for the care of children and the care or support of husbands, extended family, and often family friends. They have had to manage their households and organize celebrations (e.g., birthday parties), holidays, visits from plumbers, and the like.[6] Responsibilities of these kinds are forward-looking. And women have often felt that they had to take them on, because otherwise the work would not get done.

Although Card refers quite a bit to responsibility in relationships, she is primarily interested in the idea of taking responsibility for oneself—for who one is and who one becomes—having faced bad luck that is both systemic and that enters into one's character (the latter being what Nagel calls "constitutive luck" (1979: 28)). (On systemic, constitutive luck, see also Tessman 2005: ch. 1; 2014: ch. 7.) Card describes how systemic luck can cause moral damage to the moral characters of people who experience privilege and/or oppression. For example, a common mark of privilege is arrogance, and of oppression, ingratiating behavior toward one's oppressors (Card 1996: 200). Having to take responsibility for the bad elements of one's character that have resulted from privilege or oppression is a matter of luck, as is one's ability to meet this responsibility. Card writes that "luck is involved both in the motivation to take responsibility and in our ability to carry through" (1996: 27). Overall, her account of responsibility helps to explain how social positioning can influence moral luck, especially the constitutive variety.

Card acknowledges that "[i]nstead of taking responsibility freely, we sometimes find ourselves with" responsibilities (1996: 29). Thus, despite focusing on taking responsibility, which is to some degree voluntary, she accepts that responsibilities are often involuntary. They can exist, as many feminists argue (e.g., Kittay 1999; Baier 1994; Held 1993), even when we did not or would not consent to being in the kind of relationship we now find ourselves in (e.g., one where the other party is highly dependent on us) or when we did not control the circumstances that brought these responsibilities about (e.g., the other party's need). The reason why is that certain features of relationships— for example, the vulnerability of one party to the other or the needs of one party that the other is best placed to fulfill—can themselves generate responsibilities (Goodin 1985; Tessman 2014). In short, responsibilities can arise out of relationships (or again, out of certain aspects of them) rather than through any kind of voluntary undertaking.[7] Walker has this idea in mind when she writes that "*responsibilities outrun control*" (1991: 19; her emphasis), and when she discusses why a world of pure agents is not one that any of us would welcome.

To conclude this discussion of responsibility, some feminist philosophers, most notably Card, have dealt with the challenge that moral luck poses by adding "depth to our understanding of responsibility" (1996: 21). The depth comes, moreover, by viewing responsibility from the perspectives of people who are socially marginalized, not only from the perspectives of those who are privileged. The account of responsibility that then emerges is one that both insists on and explains how our responsibilities outrun our control.[8]

Virtue

Feminists have also pointed to virtue to support the phenomenon of moral luck. Lisa Tessman reminds us that virtue theorists, including Aristotle and Rosalind Hursthouse (2001), accept that luck provides occasions for virtue (Tessman 2005: 27, 28). For example, Tessman quotes Aristotle as saying that "the man who is truly good and wise, we think, bears all of the chances of life becomingly" (*NE* 1101a1–5; Tessman 2005: 27). Feminists writing on moral luck tend to agree with the sentiment that virtue can require us to respond in particular ways to luck, good or bad. Yet they also highlight particular virtues that have this effect—what Walker calls "virtues of impure agency" (1991: 20),[9] and what Tessman describes simply as the "virtues of the agent who has moral responsibility for things beyond her control" (2005: 28). Included among these traits are integrity, grace, and lucidity (Walker 1991: 19), although the virtue that feminists give the most attention in this context is integrity. In this section, we will explain why feminists, as feminists, have defined integrity as a virtue of impure agency, and in so doing, illustrate their claim that virtue ties luck and responsibility together.

The idea that integrity is a response to the "vicissitudes" of luck might seem strange (Walker 1991: 20), particularly for readers who are familiar with the philosophical literature on integrity, where there is little mention of luck. But consider popular accounts from this literature that define integrity in terms of consistency or coherence (i.e., among one's desires or commitments) or of having a certain identity and living up to it (see Calhoun 1995). And notice that either achievement—consistency or being true to oneself—depends substantially on luck. That is the case from a feminist perspective at least, according to which people experience oppression and privilege. Relevant here is the fact that oppressed people are subject disproportionately to double binds, where by their own lights, they are damned if they do and damned if they don't (Card 1996: 42; see also Frye 1983). Having an integrated self or being true to commitments that define one's identity ("identity-conferring commitments"; McFall 1987) is often very difficult, and is sometimes impossible, in such circumstances. Being free of these burdens, by contrast, is itself a matter of luck, that is, of privilege. These insights about luck and integrity, popularly understood, come from Card (1996: ch. 2).

Integrity is a virtue of impure agency also according to feminists who have developed new understandings of integrity, ones according to which integrity has social value, not merely the personal value that comes with inner unity or meeting identity-conferring commitments. Walker defends this sort of account in the literature on moral luck (see also Payson (2017) and also Calhoun (1995)). Walker writes that "integrity is the capacity for *reliably* maintaining a coherent moral posture [or identity], and … this capacity is only proven under challenge" (Walker 1991: 21, note 6; our emphasis). For Walker, integrity is as much about reliability or dependability as it is about coherence and identity. People with integrity can be relied on not to "shrug off" serious harms they were unlucky enough to cause, for example (as in the case of a negligent driver who happens to hit a child; Walker (1991: 18)). They have the will to take responsibility in such contexts,[10] and presumably the kinds of commitments that require them to do so.[11] If such claims about integrity are true, then integrity must be both a virtue of impure agency and a social virtue. It is the former because the challenges that provide occasions for people to act with integrity arise, in part at least, because of luck. And it is the latter—a virtue that puts us in the "proper relation to others" (Calhoun 1995: 252)—because it makes us reliable to others.

Feminists such as Walker and Card do not believe that to have integrity, we need to be *so* reliable or *so* consistent that we never change our values. It is important that integrity allows for value change, because bad systemic luck that enters into our characters gives us oppressive values. Thus, Card says that to "develop and maintain integrity, we need to discover, assess, and sometimes make changes in our values" (1996: 33). And in her later work, Walker describes integrity in terms not of mere reliability, but of "*reliable accountability*" (1996: 64; her emphasis). This latter view demands consistency over time not in our values, but in the accounts "we are prepared to give" of them and the actions that flow from them (Walker 1996: 72). In this way, integrity allows for personal transformation, even of a radical sort, which is important for feminists (see also Davion 1991; Payson 2017). Integrity is also designed on this view with systemic luck in mind, which can saddle us with values that, on reflection, we do not endorse.

Thus, feminists argue that integrity is a virtue of impure agency, and that virtues of this type show how luck and responsibility go hand in hand. These traits make us responsible for things that are simply a matter of luck; and feminist insights about oppression, privilege, and systemic luck allow us to see why we should count integrity among them. Intuitions of this sort also direct us toward accounts of agency and responsibility that help us to make sense of moral luck. In summary, then, from a feminist perspective, luck can bring with it responsibility because of the nature of moral agency, responsibility, and virtue.

Luck Without Responsibility

The above discussion reveals that, from a feminist perspective, we can have responsibilities—for helping others in need or healing moral damage to our selves caused by oppression, for example—in the face of luck. But feminists also recognize that there are limits on our ability to be responsible for what is our own good or bad luck, and that is true with respect to both systemic luck and what some feminists call "natural" or just "nonsystemic" luck (Tessman 2014: 243; Tessman 2005: 30; Payson 2017: 351). The debate here centers on whether systemic luck can generate *impossible moral demands*, which occur when we have responsibilities yet cannot fulfill them (particularly forward-looking responsibilities; there is luck without responsibility of this kind[12]). Less discussed is the issue of whether systemic luck can produce *illegitimate moral demands*, specifically in cases where oppressive norms make us feel responsible for things we are not responsible for and for what may be just a matter of natural luck. In what follows, we discuss situations where, from a feminist perspective, luck and responsibility can come apart: more specifically, situations involving impossible or illegitimate moral demands. We also suggest where, in the feminist literature on these topics, there are gaps that future feminist work on moral luck should fill in.

Impossible Moral Demands

Feminists writing on moral luck tend to focus on the burdens that bad systemic luck place on people who are oppressed—those of trying, for example, to overcome moral damage to the self or of navigating through the double binds that are characteristic of oppression. These burdens can be insurmountable; for instance, it can be—and arguably normally is—impossible to rid oneself of psychological oppression. Some feminists debate whether, in such circumstances, the burdens are also moral in nature, in which case the agents in question would be morally responsible for doing what they simply cannot do, and moral failure would be inevitable on their part.[13] The main parties to this debate are Tessman (2014) and Eva Kittay (2016), with the former holding the view that these sorts of demands—impossible moral ones—can arise out of bad systemic luck, and the latter disagreeing with her and with the more general claim Tessman makes that "ought" does not always imply "can."[14]

The question of whether impossible moral demands could ever occur as a result of bad systemic luck really depends on whether "ought implies can." Yet this issue (i.e., of whether "ought" truly does imply "can") is not distinctly feminist,[15] and so we will not rehearse the arguments feminists have given on either side of it. Instead, we will discuss what they have written about the kinds of moral responses people should give when they run up against limits to their own moral agency, ultimately because of bad systemic luck. These are situations in which the agents themselves or others expect them to take responsibility in a forward-looking sense, but they are unable to do so. They are situations of impossible moral demand or at least of the experience of such a demand.

Feminists have named among the appropriate responses to the circumstances just described integrity, anger, and regret.[16] Jessica Payson's (2017) work on integrity is relevant here, for example. She claims that in unjust social systems, the demands of integrity are impossible to fulfill (and thus, accepts the notion of an impossible moral demand). In her view, integrity requires that one not promote serious harm, which one does by participating in oppression, which itself is inevitable, according to Payson. Nevertheless, one can display some integrity—at what she calls a "meta-level"—by acknowledging the extent of one's participation and by objecting to it (2017: 357).

The responses of anger and regret appear in Tessman's work. She suggests that when confronted with what is often, in her view, an impossible demand—that of overcoming bad systemic constitutive luck—"a mixture of anger and agent-regret" is called for (where for her, both anger and regret are virtues; 2005: 30). To explain, she writes:

> While situations of nonsystemic bad luck may just call for special virtues having to do with bearing or enduring the bad luck commendably as well as taking responsibility for its results, in the case of systemic bad luck—since the source of the bad luck can be identified and potentially altered through social or political action—the special virtues that are called for will also be those that help one to protest or even eliminate the systemic source of bad luck.
>
> *2005: 30; see also Payson 2017: 351*

In other words, in circumstances where one cannot fully repair the damage caused by systemic bad luck, one can still resist the sources of this luck and one's moral response to it should reflect this fact. Thus, rather than bear the luck "becomingly," as Aristotle recommended (*NE* 1101a1–5), which presumably involves having more positive emotions than regret or anger, one should feel—and perhaps depending on how bad the luck is, be *seething* with—these negative emotions.

In response to Tessman, we question whether anger and regret are the only, or the main, "virtues" that one ought to display in such circumstances. What about *grace*? Recall that Walker includes grace among the virtues of impure agency that she lists. Is it appropriate for people who are oppressed to display grace, if only occasionally, in response to impossible or difficult moral demands that they experience as oppressed people? Walker defines grace as "acceptance, non-aggrandized daily 'living with' unsupported by fantasies of overcoming or restitution" (1991: 21). Moreover, she, as well as Tessman, suggests that grace (or what Tessman simply calls "acceptance"; 2005: 31) *might* be appropriate when our attempts at healing the damage caused by oppression come up short. Yet nowhere in the feminist literature, that we know of, is there a moral theory of grace. Such a theory might show that, on occasion, one could respond appropriately to the weighty moral burdens of oppression without "fantasies [where they are indeed fantasies] of overcoming" or without negative emotions such as anger and regret, which can be all-consuming. Instead, one could exhibit grace. In that case, the "special virtues" that nonsystemic and systemic luck call for would not be so different that the latter never requires us to endure "the bad luck commendably" (assuming that involves accepting the limits to our powers of "overcoming"; Tessman 2005: 30).

Thus, feminists recognize that in the face of bad systemic luck, we will not always be able to live up to responsibilities that we actually have or that we or others believe we have. We will not be able to take responsibility, particularly in a forward-looking sense. Feminists disagree about whether moral failure is inevitable in such cases, which it would be only if the relevant responsibilities are real. More work is needed surely to settle this disagreement (i.e., over whether ought implies can), although we doubt that the work involved will be particularly feminist. What *is* a uniquely feminist project, however—one that should be taken up—is to develop a moral theory of grace specifically for situations of bad systemic luck.

Illegitimate Moral Demands

Feminists who reject the idea of impossible moral demands will say that expectations of rising above one's bad systemic luck can be illegitimate. More generally, being made to feel responsible when one cannot be responsible is illegitimate. For these feminists, the impossible moral demands that Tessman (2014) refers to are simply illegitimate demands. That there is this sort of reaction to Tessman in the feminist literature shows that there is some awareness there about how systemic luck can impose illegitimate moral demands. But there is little discussion by feminists about this problem in general, including instances where oppressive norms make us feel responsible for what is a matter of pure natural luck. We will illustrate these cases briefly, which involve moral demands that are *clearly* illegitimate. We will also discuss cases where luck is ascribed to someone ("you are so lucky!") in a way that is oppressive and produces an illegitimate moral demand. This second type of case does not appear at all in the feminist literature on moral luck, which is a significant gap, in our view.

One of us has written with Julie Ponesse (McLeod & Ponesse 2008) about a particular kind of case where people—women, specifically—experience an illegitimate moral demand because of bad natural luck combined with bad systemic luck. The relevant demand is that women blame themselves for infertility, so that their bad luck of being infertile (i.e., at a time when they actually wish to be pregnant) is bad moral luck of a certain sort.[17] McLeod and Ponesse argue that these feelings of blame stem, in part at least, from pronatalist norms that make it women's social role to bear and rear children. They exist, in other words, because of women's bad systemic luck in sexist societies. Women's self-blame for infertility is just an instance of a larger phenomenon, we assume, of people who are oppressed being encouraged to take responsibility (in the credit sense or otherwise; see note 6) for what is not their fault. The extent to which these people experience bad moral luck of this sort—where, again, the relevant moral demand is obviously illegitimate—should be a topic of greater concern to feminists.

Feminist Approaches to Moral Luck

Another topic that should garner attention in future feminist work on moral luck is the fact that ascriptions of luck, or of being lucky, can themselves be a matter of moral luck—or more specifically, systemic luck that issues in an illegitimate moral demand. We have in mind cases where people who are members of oppressed groups are told they are so lucky to have X—such as a spot at a prestigious university or the parents who were chosen for them in an adoption—even though others in a similar position would not be called lucky, or called that as often as they are. As well, the luck they are ascribed is moral because it comes with the suggestion that they should be grateful, perhaps abundantly so, for having X. One of us (again, McLeod) has children who experience this sort of thing, children who are transracial, intercountry adoptees. The comments that they (or McLeod) get about how lucky they are usually come right after people learn where they are adopted from. Granted her moral perception in these moments could be completely off, McLeod often feels that these statements are laden with racism and classism. (In that case, they are similar to comments directed at a poor student of color who is told he is so lucky to have got into Harvard.) What is more, they carry with them expectations of gratitude, which we believe are illegitimate.[18] Hence, they are ascriptions not just of luck, but of moral luck. They also involve systemic luck, that is, if they are indeed motivated, if only unconsciously, by oppressive attitudes such as racism.

Our focus in this section has been on cases that feminists have largely ignored where systemic luck is moral and places illegitimate moral demands on oppressed people. In such circumstances, there is luck without any real responsibility, although oppressive norms dictate that there should be some responsibility (e.g., in the form of taking blame). We imagine future feminist work on these kinds of cases being interdisciplinary. For example, a feminist philosopher who has expertise in the literature on moral luck could pair up with a psychologist or sociologist on a project about the kinds of luck ascriptions we discussed in the previous paragraph (about the "lucky" student or adoptee). The psychologist or sociologist could analyze whether indeed, or how often, statements like these occur, and the philosopher could focus on the moral and political implications of them.

Conclusion

Our goals in this chapter have been to reveal what rich discussion there is in feminist philosophy about moral luck, but also the need for further discussion, particularly about the virtue of grace and about illegitimate moral demands in circumstances of bad systemic luck. We have focused on the relationship between luck and (moral) responsibility in feminist philosophy, which is complex as we noted at the beginning. In brief, feminists tend to believe that there can be luck with responsibility, especially the kind of responsibility that involves looking forward in an effort to take care of who or what needs to be taken care of. But they also recognize that there can be luck without responsibility. Their work centers on luck that is systemic, which people experience because they inhabit systems of oppression and privilege. Even bad systemic luck can carry with it responsibility, according to many feminists, which helps to explain both how morally burdened oppressed people can be and how morally wrong their oppression is.

Notes

1 In this chapter, we follow other feminists in interpreting luck in terms of a lack of control (see, e.g., Card 1996: 22).
2 Mainstream philosophical discussions about moral luck generally ignore this type of luck; they describe moral luck as nonsystemic and individualized.
3 Lisa Tessman denies that this is true for Eva Kittay in *Love's Labor* (1999). See Tessman (2014: 242) and Kittay's response (2016).
4 Walker writes that it "is characteristic of those who view moral luck as philosophically problematic or paradoxical to claim it is so in light of 'our' or 'the ordinary' concept of agency" (1991: 23). She questions who the "we" is by putting "our" and "the ordinary" in quotation marks. The "we" is clearly not most feminist philosophers, as our discussion about agency reveals.

433

5 That is, real as opposed to illusory or paradoxical (Walker 1991). Some philosophers say that moral luck is illusory—that "the ordinary" view of moral agency is correct: we are not responsible for what we do not have control over (see, e.g., Zimmerman 2002)—while others, including Thomas Nagel (1979), suggest that moral luck is simply paradoxical.

6 As this discussion suggests, taking responsibility can come in different forms. Card explains that it can involve managing what needs to be managed (the "administrative or managerial sense of responsibility"), making oneself accountable for something (the "accountability sense"), committing oneself to provide care or support (the "care-taking sense"), and also owning up to what one has done (the "credit sense"; 1996: 28). Card emphasizes that only the last of these is backward-looking, which reveals that responsibility takes many more forms than Williams and Nagel recognize.

7 This idea is an element of care ethics (Tessman 2014: ch. 7), although some feminists who endorse it describe themselves as having instead an ethics of responsibility (e.g., Walker 1998; Whitbeck 1983). Regardless, they tend to contrast this view about responsibility or obligation with a contractualist one. (On contractualism, see Ashford & Mulgan 2018.)

8 To be clear, it is not the case for feminists that *all* responsibilities necessarily outrun control—that the fact that we lack control in certain circumstances means that we lack all control. Card (1996) has this view, for example, which is common among compatibilists such as Daniel Dennett (2003, 1984), and John Fischer and Mark Ravizza (1998). Card writes: "Even the embeddedness of my computer software in a world that outruns its controls does not imply that the software does not really control anything or that we are always arbitrary to pick out the software rather than environmental conditions as relevantly responsible" (1996: 27). We are similar to the software in this regard (and we believe Walker would agree; 1991). To use Walker's language, the fact that we are impure agents embedded in the causal structure of the universe does not mean we do not exhibit *any* kind of control.

9 Walker uses the existence of these virtues to defend her account of agency as impure (1991).

10 They will take responsibility not necessarily in the backward-looking sense of accepting blame, but at the very least in a forward-looking sense, perhaps of providing care or support. See note 6.

11 Walker suggests that there might be "minimal standards of correctness or adequacy" for the moral posture of a person with integrity (1991: 21, note 6). It seems clear that her account relies, however, on there actually being the minimal standard of accepting moral challenges that are either orchestrated by others or caused by mere chance (or both).

12 In such circumstances, we could act responsibly in the backward-looking sense of accepting some blame for not doing what we are responsible for doing; but we could not act responsibly in any of the forward-looking senses that Card describes (1996). See note 6.

13 On moral failure of this sort, see Tessman (2014) and Calhoun (1999).

14 A central goal of Tessman's book *Moral Failure* is to argue that some moral requirements violate the principle of "ought implies can" (2014: 1). Kittay explicitly rejects this view in a review of Tessman's book, where she insists that this principle "brings desperately needed sanity" to situations of injustice (Kittay 2016).

15 Related issues that are also not uniquely feminist are whether moral dilemmas can ever be irresolvable (see Hursthouse 2001) or whether there can be "*inexhaustible* source[s] of moral requirements," as Tessman says there are when the needs of people are so great, they can never be fully satisfied (2014: 251).

16 One could add here shame, which is a response that Calhoun discusses (1999: 95; cited in Biss 2016: 564).

17 That is, a sort of moral luck that refers to the praise or blame that a person receives versus the praise or blame that the person deserves. This point of clarification comes from Robert Hartman.

18 Any claim that adopted children should be grateful is illegitimate in our view. Even with adoptions that are good ones (the family is well-functioning; there was no injustice involved in the process of adoption), the children simply get what they deserve, morally speaking. In that case, there is no occasion for gratitude.

References

Aristotle. (1984) *The Complete Works of Aristotle: The Revised Oxford Translation*, Jonathan Barnes (ed.), Princeton, NJ: Princeton University Press.

Ashford, E., & Mulgan, T. (2018) "Contractualism," in *The Stanford Encyclopedia of Philosophy* (Summer 2018 Edition), Edward N. Zalta (ed.) https://plato.stanford.edu/archives/sum2018/entries/contractualism/.

Baier, A. (1994) *Moral Prejudices*, Cambridge, MA: Harvard University Press.

Bartky, S.L. (1990) *Femininity and Domination: Studies in the Phenomenology of Oppression*, New York: Routledge.

Biss, M. (2016) "Radical Moral Imagination and Moral Luck," *Metaphilosophy* 47(4–5), 558–570.

Calhoun, C. (1995) "Standing for Something," *Journal of Philosophy* 92(5), 235–260.

———. (1999) "Moral Failure," in C. Card (ed.) *On Feminist Ethics and Politics*, Lawrence: University Press of Kansas, pp. 81–99.

Card, C. (1990) "Gender and Moral Luck," in O. Flanagan & A.O. Rorty (eds.) *Identity, Character, and Morality*, Cambridge: MIT Press, pp. 199–218.

——. (1996) *The Unnatural Lottery: Character and Moral Luck*, Philadelphia: Temple University Press.

Code, L. (1981) "Is the Sex of the Knower Epistemologically Significant?" *Metaphilosophy* 12, 267–276.

Davion, V. (1991) "Integrity and Radical Change," in C. Card (ed.) *Feminist Ethics*, Lawrence: University of Kansas Press, pp. 180–194.

Dennett, D.C. (1984) *Elbow Room*, Cambridge, MA: MIT Press.

——. (2003) *Freedom Evolves*, New York: Viking Press.

Fischer, J.M., & Ravizza, M. (1998) *Responsibility and Control*, Cambridge: Cambridge University Press.

Frye, M. (1983) "Oppression," in *The Politics of Reality*, Trumansburg: Crossing Press, pp. 1–16.

Goodin, R.E. (1985) *Protecting the Vulnerable*, Chicago, IL: University of Chicago Press.

Harding, S. (1992) "Rethinking Standpoint Epistemology: What Is Strong Objectivity?" *The Centennial Review* 36(3), 437–470.

Held, V. (1993) *Feminist Morality*, Chicago, IL: University of Chicago Press.

Hursthouse, R. (2001) *On Virtue Ethics*, 2nd edition, Oxford: Oxford University Press.

Kittay, E.F. (1999) *Love's Labor*, New York: Routledge.

——. (2016) "Two Dogmas of Moral Theory? Comments on Lisa Tessman's Moral Failure," *Feminist Philosophical Quarterly* 2(1), 3.

Little, M.O. (1995) "Seeing and Caring: The Role of Affect in Feminist Moral Epistemology," *Hypatia* 10(3), 117–137.

Mackenzie, C., & Stoljar, N. (2000) "Introduction: Autonomy Reconfigured," in *Relational Autonomy: Feminist Perspectives on Autonomy, Agency, and the Social Self*, Oxford: Oxford University Press, pp. 3–34.

McFall, L. (1987) "Integrity," *Ethics* 98(1), 5–20.

McLeod, C., & Ponesse, J. (2008) "Infertility and Moral Luck," *International Journal of Feminist Approaches to Bioethics* 1(1), 126–144.

Nagel, T. (1979) "Moral Luck," in *Mortal Questions*, Cambridge: Cambridge University Press, pp. 24–38.

Payson, J. (2017) "The 'Meta' Level of Integrity: Integrity in the Context of Structural Injustice," *Hypatia* 32(2), 347–362.

Tessman, L. (2005) *Burdened Virtues: Virtue Ethics for Liberatory Struggles*, New York: Oxford University Press.

——. (2014) *Moral Failure: On the Impossible Demands of Morality*, New York: Oxford University Press.

Walker, M.U. (1991) "Moral Luck and the Virtues of Impure Agency," *Metaphilosophy* 22(1–2), 14–27.

——. (1996) "Picking Up Pieces: Lives, Stories, and Integrity," in D. Meyers (ed.) *Feminists Rethink the Self*, Boulder, CO: Westview Press, pp. 62–84.

——. (1998) *Moral Understandings: A Feminist Study in Ethics*, New York: Routledge.

Whitbeck, C. (1983) "The Moral Implications of Regarding Women as People: New Perspectives on Pregnancy and Personhood," in W. Bondeson et al. (eds.) *Abortion and the Status of the Fetus*, Dordrecht: Reidel, pp. 247–272.

Williams, B. (1981) "Moral Luck," in *Moral Luck*, Cambridge: Cambridge University Press, pp. 20–39.

Zimmerman, M. (2002) "Taking Luck Seriously," *The Journal of Philosophy* 99(11), 553–576.

38

THE NEW PROBLEM OF RELIGIOUS LUCK

Guy Axtell

Introduction

To speak of religious luck certainly sounds odd to the ear. But then, so does "My faith holds value in God's eye, while yours does not."This chapter will argue that these two concerns—with the concept of religious luck and with asymmetric or sharply differential ascriptions of religious value—are inextricably connected.[1] There is a strong tendency among faith traditions to invoke asymmetric explanations of the religious value or salvific status of the home religion vis-à-vis all others. Philosophy of luck will be presented in this chapter as aiding our understanding of what is going on when persons or theologies ascribe various kinds of religiously relevant traits to insiders and outsiders of a faith tradition in sharply asymmetric fashion.

For qualification, this thesis about "what is going on" is not necessarily reductionistic, or indicative of an error theory. Moral, theological, social scientific, and epistemological perspectives must all hold place in philosophy of luck. Also, theists and naturalists often share recognition of common factors—for instance evolutionary, psychological, and sociological factors—that arouse religious faith tendencies, while disagreeing about whether any combination of naturalistically understood proximate and distal factors are their *sufficient* explanation. For theologians the efficacy of factors of nature and nurture in the development of a religious worldview are, in turn, explainable teleologically in terms of divine will, ultimate plan, and gifts to the faithful. So my thesis more carefully stated is that philosophers, theologians, and the numerous parties contributing to or drawing from the cognitive science of religion (CSR) will mutually benefit from a focus on concerns that arise with asymmetric attributions of religious value.They will benefit in particular from a focus on what we will describe as the *New Problem* of religious luck, which is concerned with the logic and illogic of such attributions in connection with a broader study of *inductive risk*, or the epistemic risk of "getting it wrong" in an inductive context.

Although there has been little written to date directly utilizing the concept of religious luck, described in other terms many of the problems we will canvass have a long history. The first section introduces the existing literature that explicitly utilizes the concept; it also provides initial examples of the wide variety of perspectives from which the family of religious luck-related problems can been addressed. The second section sets out a taxonomy of types of religious luck, beginning with types that inter-connect primarily with the literature on *moral* luck, and ending with types that inter-connect primarily with the literature on *epistemic* luck. These sections also provide examples of how theological positions can differ markedly in the extent to which they "lean on luck," or in other words, aggravate or exacerbate luck-related worries of one specific type or another. But this is all largely preliminary to the argument of the third section developing what I call the New Problem. This is a challenge to the reasonableness, not of faith-based religious commitment generally, but of the response to religious multiplicity characteristic of religious exclusivism: that all salvific efficacy is contained in the teachings of the home religion, or that "my faith holds value in God's eye, while yours does not."

The Multi-sided Interest in Problems of Religious Luck

The study of problems of religious luck, I hope to convince the reader, are a needed focus today, in that this study promotes useful dialogue among theologians, philosophers, and researchers in the cognitive science of religions. I describe them as a *family* of problems because of their inter-connectedness. A first indication of this is how they are found addressed in the literature in three overlapping ways: intra-religiously, inter-religiously, and counter-religiously. Let us start with an example of each of these three ways of addressing problems of religious luck, letting these examples introduce issues we can later develop in more depth.

One of the first attempts to connect philosophical discussions of luck to concerns within philosophy of religion and theology was a 1994 paper by Linda Zagzebski, "Religious Luck." Like many others, Zagzebski finds it troubling that people might be the proper objects of moral evaluation, including praise and blame, and reward and punishment, because of something that is partly due to luck, and to that degree outside of their control. Unlike some who deny the phenomenon of moral luck, Zagzebski believes that these problems do exist and, writing as a Christian philosopher, "that they exist for Christian moral practice and Christian moral theories as well." The author's focus is explicitly intra-religious in that her topic "is a problem internal to the concepts of moral responsibility, reward, and punishment as understood by the Christian." Her central thesis is that Christianity has at least two core traditional teachings, those of "eternal heaven and hell" and of "grace" that potentially "magnify the problem of luck to infinity" (Zagzebski 1994: 397–398, 402). Thus, Zagzebski finds it useful to engage philosophy of luck from the direction of moral theory by drawing upon previous work on the impact of moral luck by Joel Feinberg and Thomas Nagel.

Taking discussion in a comparative direction, Jewish philosopher Charlotte Katzoff (2000), in "Religious Luck and Religious Virtue," compares the role of luck in two accounts of divine election, that of Paul and of Rabbi Judah Loeb. Katzoff agrees that God conferring religious value/status on persons without necessary reference to efforts or deeds is "perplexing." But she argues that Paul's account more than Rabbi Judah's suffers from concerns Zagzebski raises about the concept of grace. To say that the greatest religious virtues are infused by grace meant to Paul that faith, by its very nature, is not under the control of its possessor. Emphasizing that God's plans are paramount and might be indifferent to human will and exertion, Paul presents the virtues as "divine gifts, fortuitous, accidental, as it were." Katzoff points out how this appears to impede the attribution of religious value to the individual on the basis of those virtues. But she argues that this worry is lessened on an account like Rabbi Judah's where the virtues adhere essentially to the character of the individual.

What we called a contra-religious or skeptical focus includes certain problems of luck discussed not just within theological circles, but as challenges to the coherence of divine attributes or to the reasonableness of beliefs of a certain kind. Some of these challenges involve primarily moral concerns, while others, including the New Problem, lead us into connections with epistemic luck. Counter-religious can mean here that a writer raises *de facto* or *de jure* objections. A *de facto* challenge raises reasons for thinking a particular religious teaching must be false; a *de jure* challenge raises reasons for thinking that a certain range of beliefs or attitudes are morally and/or epistemologically irresponsible and rationally unacceptable. With a focus on epistemic luck, John Stuart Mill writes,

[T]he world, to each individual, means the part of it with which he comes in contact; his party, his sect, his church, his class of society ... [I]t never troubles him that mere accident has decided which of these numerous worlds is the object of his reliance, and that the same causes which make him a Churchman in London, would have made him a Buddhist or a Confucian in Pekin[g] .... Nor is his faith in this collective authority at all shaken by his being aware that other ages, countries, sects, churches, classes, and parties have thought, and even now think, the exact reverse.

Mill 1913: 10–11

There is an implicit luck-related *de jure* argument in this passage highlighting the strong contingency of certain kinds of belief on people's found epistemic location—their family or culture, or their time in history. It might suggest some kind of debunking, or it might suggest only the need for epistemic humility. It is enough that we initially take Mill as raising a religious *epistemic* luck-related concern with a vaguely counter-religious intent. There is not enough clarity to this passage to say just what its conclusion is intended to be, or whether he believes that the contingency he draws attention to should be thought any *more* challenging to the well-foundedness of religious beliefs than to others he mentions, such as those associated with party (political orientation) and class. Later we will look closer at other and more carefully formulated demographic contingency arguments, and try to distil their proper scope. But to anticipate just a little, we can say that especially strong epistemic luck-related worries arise for theologies which claim that God saves only those who adhere to one particular religious identity, or who assent to one particular religious creed among the many. Thus Robert Hartman (2014) refers to doxastic requirements on salvation as raising "the soteriological problem of geographic luck." If purported saving knowledge is not uniformly distributed then, as a condition of salvation, one must be environmentally or evidentially lucky; otherwise that religious identity will not plausibly even be what William James referred to as a "live option" for them.[2] This suggests to me that we should best interpret arguments like Mill's, which we will call *epistemic location arguments*, as challenging certain uncritical or dogmatic *ways* that we might hold our beliefs, and certain related responses to diversity or disagreement, rather than as intending to undercut the justification for *whole domains* of belief on account of their being more deeply conditioned than others by one's epistemic location.

To summarize, the study of problems of religious luck is common-ground for theologians and philosophers of religion, though individual thinkers might well approach them in substantially different ways. They might be debated as problems of theological adequacy either intra-religiously or inter-religiously. They might also be posed as challenges to particular teachings, to particular conceptions of faith, or to the coherence of divine attributes. Our next step will be to set in place a functional taxonomy of different types of religious luck, so that we can set the New Problem against this background. The taxonomy provided in the next section could turn out to be far from complete, but it substantially reflects the extant literature on moral and epistemic luck. This task will also provide opportunity to briefly elaborate on certain specific problems that each type of religious luck is associated with.

Types of Religious Luck: A Working Taxonomy

Earlier writers have referred to "religious" (Zagzebski 1994), "salvific" (Davison 1999) and "soteriological" luck (Anderson 2011). This section aims at a more detailed taxonomy, since (much as in discussion of moral and epistemic luck) it might be expected that distinct types raise distinct concerns, and that in articulating and debating risk and related problems, central problems of theory are illuminated. Although in order to focus on taxonomy we will have to bypass detailed treatment of what Hartman (2014) calls theological problems of moral luck, we should note that there has been lively recent debate over soteriology especially among Christian thinkers. A soteriology includes an explanation of suffering, including the suffering of the damned and what moral justification there could be for a divine plan that includes selective salvation and hell. Some of the debate has been between conservatives about binary, eternal, retributive hell (Craig 1989) and escapist or other alternative accounts of divine judgment (Jones 2007; Buckareff & Plug 2009). Religious luck has in some way figured into broader intra-Christian debate involving conceptions of providence, divine foreknowledge and free will from Catholic, Open theist, Skeptical theist, Reformed, and Molinist perspectives. The first types of luck to be described connect mainly with moral luck but we will work toward epistemic types of religious luck that have received relatively less direct attention.

Constitutive religious luck is the term we can use to describe types of (good/bad) religious luck that people enjoy or suffer from when they are ascribed as having or lacking religious value for reasons of inborn traits or inherited social standings. Moral theorists recognize a type of (good/bad) luck that affects persons by manner of what inborn morally relevant capacities they have or lack (biological inheritances), or by what advantageous or disadvantageous social groupings they are born into (cultural inheritances). When this involves being ascribed religiously relevant inclinations, capacities, temperament, or inherited religious identity, we can term it constitutive *religious* luck. To the degree that having or lacking these traits is outside of people's control, but matters to them, it is good/bad luck from a methodologically neutral CSR perspective, regardless of how deterministic the theological explanation might be that ascribes these traits to people. Indeed, the more deterministic or even fatalistic is the given explanation on the theological side, the more will the good/bad constitutive endowment appear beyond human control from a neutral or CSR perspective. For a philosophy of religious luck these are not always mutually negating explanations, but are better seen as co-existing "flip-side" religiously committed and religiously neutral perspectives on the same subject matter: particular instances of religious trait-ascription.

Problems of religious luck are not restricted to any one family of religions; indeed their salience across religions and in comparative studies greatly increases the utility of these problems as a focus of study. In karmic religions (good/bad) karma is claimed to accrue to an individual as a result of past actions through previous incarnations. Its forward-looking sense provides a more just world than is experienced over the course of one lifetime, and is connected with the long-term religious goal of universal (as contrasted with selective) liberation/enlightenment. But the more so as the concept or "law" of karma is appealed to in its backward-looking sense to explain and justify what an individual experiences as their found social conditions, such karmic explanations are examples of *constitutive* religious luck-attributions.

Although the caste system in India is on a path to being de-institutionalized today through a widespread "cast out caste" movement, the privilege or servility that comes from high/low birth are rationalized by the Law of Karma in traditional Hindu thought; so are the lack of social mobility and economic opportunities experienced by *shudras*, and especially by those born into classification as "spiritually polluted" *untouchables*. Deep concern with the potentially post-hoc and surreptitious nature of appeals to people's accrued karma to explain social inequities or to justify caste duties is reflected in the Buddhist critique of Hinduism. Both groups understand karma as offering a kind of soteriology, but Buddhists reject caste and repudiate its justification in terms of a law of karma.

In Abrahamic religions, predetermination teachings are one natural focus for appeals to constitutive luck. One may distinguish God's judgment of the dead from God's "reprobating" before creation. But a theodicy of reprobation seems morally troubling: When God is reprobating there are not as yet any vicious or virtuous people in existence, and so it is perplexing to make sense of the immoral character or personal responsibility of the reprobate—those intended for damnation. Predetermination makes it perplexing to understand how anyone can be deserving of damnation on account of their having a fixed or settled character that rejects God. For in a predetermined world, people arguably must get their fixed character when placed among the elect or the damned, rather than being saved or damned *because* of their fixed character. In such a religiously determinist world, it is always God or gods who do the "fixing." So in general the more a religious worldview devolves toward fatalism, the less that human will *can* matter, and the more each person is like an actor on a stage playing out a pre-set script for the pleasure of the supernatural beings who wrote it.

Another teaching re-describable in terms of constitutive religious luck ascriptions are asymmetric ascriptions to people of either a functional or dysfunctional *sensus divinitatis*. This is a purported sixth sense appealed to especially in Calvinist thought that theologically explains the felt certitude and reliable aetiology of theistic belief among believers, and the otherwise perplexing *lack* of belief among non-theists and dissenters. Paralleling asymmetric attribution of a properly working *sensus divinitatis* is attribution of "work of the Holy Spirit" in some individuals but not others, purportedly infusing specifically Christian beliefs into them. The main point here is that claims concerning *infused* beliefs at either the general theistic or religion-specific level carry the sense of being irresistible and hence outside of one's will or control. Due to their passivity and attendant externalist religious epistemology, they have the logical character of *constitutive* trait-ascriptions.

Resultant religious luck we can define as the (good/bad) luck of ending up on one side or another of divine judgment under conditions of "close moral gaps." How can God be fair in regard to judgments meted out if there must be close gaps between many people's on-balance moral character? This *problem of close gaps* raises at least three distinct moral objections about proportionality in soteriologies of divine judgment. These three are: (a) objections to the morality of divine *punishment*; (b) objections to theologies that teach of *binary* heaven/hell; and (c) objections to theologies that teach of *eternal* hell. It would be all the more lucky for you to benefit from a close-gaps comparison with me, or me with you, when the differences in our respective post-mortem existence are describable as reward for one of us and punishment for the other; and/or when the judgment settles a condition that each of us will necessarily remain in *eternally*.

Criterial religious luck overlaps with resultant religious luck. Criterial luck we can define as enjoying benefits or suffering harms through being judged, rewarded, or punished on a basis (1) which is not principled in such a way that it will be consistently employed across like cases (**CRL₁**); or (2) which the persons judged do not have a clear conception of (**CRL₂**); or (3) which the persons judged might not even be aware that they are subjected to (**CRL₃**). When this regards benefits or harms from the purported judgment of souls by a god or gods, it is criterial *religious* luck. Zagzebski acknowledges this criterial concern when she writes,

> Christian moral theory replaces the concept of moral wrongdoing by the concept of sin, an offense against God, and the concept of an abstract state of moral worth which may or may not be determinable is replaced by the concept of one's moral state as judged by God. And presumably that *should* be determinable.
>
> *Zagzebski 1994: 402*[3]

A conception of God's sovereignty that made it *whimsical* in the sense of normatively unconstrained "power," and apologetic strategies that cut off effort to produce a morally adequate soteriology by saying in an ad hoc way that what we cannot know about God's plan we must simply accept, raise especially strong worries about the leaning of criterial religious luck.

Evidential religious luck we can define as any type of (good/bad) luck that plays a significant role in religious explanations for how persons differ in respect to being situated to discover purported religious truths. It is evidentially lucky if one is situated so as to have experiences or have available sources of evidence that others do not, and religious evidential luck if the experiences or evidence are of such a nature as to contribute to their store of religious beliefs or to their value in God's eyes.

Some theologians and philosophers might hold that being advantageously situated to receive theistic evidence is uniformly a question of evidential luck, which when it leads to an acquired true belief is "benign" luck. This means that while I might be lucky to have a certain belief, there is no problem with my rationality, or (on assumption that the belief is true), on my having propositional knowledge. But the facts of religious disagreement and of epistemic risk strongly suggest that we cannot make such a blanket assumption, or confer on ourselves such easy knowledge. We have to look far more carefully at agents' belief-forming cognitive strategies, and at their broader epistemic situation in order to assess whether the kind of epistemic luck operating in particular real or imagined cases is benign, or instead *malign*, i.e., undercutting of positive epistemic status.

Describing the types of epistemic luck epistemologists consider malign—particularly two types of *veritic* epistemic luck—while at the same time shifting to a more sophisticated modal account of luck, will help us unpack these important issues. Duncan Pritchard holds that externalist (including mixed) epistemologies try to preclude cases of coming to have a true belief through a process dependent on veritic luck from counting as instances of knowing. Epistemologists might seek to do this by way of an ability condition on knowledge, a modal safety condition, etc. (see Pritchard 2015, 2005). Debate is ongoing as to how many and what type of conditions are needed to preclude veritic luck, but it is generally conceded to split into two distinct types: *intervening* luck and *environmental* luck, which both need to be accounted for in an adequate analysis of knowing.

Intervening veritic religious luck is the religious analog for the kind of definitely malign luck that Gettier cases are closely associated with in contemporary epistemology. I believe at least some defences of religious exclusivism can be described, by close attention to their formal logical structure, as plying or "leaning" on asymmetric attributions of this intervening kind of epistemic luck. A prime example is Paul J. Griffiths' (2001) influential articulation and defence of religious exclusivism. He uses Karl Barth's theology as a paradigm example of how to articulate the grounds for a Christian exclusivism. Although of course he is not thinking in these terms, his Barthian argument, I argue, formally parallels the way to construct a Gettier case. A person's initial personal or prima facie justification for a target belief is, in an instance of bad epistemic luck, defeated (whether the defeater is recognized or not). But this defeated status is then "reversed" by a second instance of epistemic luck, this time *good* epistemic luck, such that what the person comes to have is a true belief after all. According to Griffiths' reading of Barth,

1. Religion is part of culture, and every theist is roughly equally subjectively justified on historical, philosophical, and phenomenological grounds in accepting the divine authority of their home religion's scriptures, sacred narratives, prophets, etc.
2. But God views all religions that have ever existed as "nothing more than idolatry, something to be judged and rejected."
3. Yet in a turn of events more fortuitous for some than for others, God *intervenes*: The Christian religion is "chosen by God as the locus of revelation …. God transforms an idol into a means of salvation, but without God's free choice to do so, it would remain an idol" (Griffiths 2001: 152–153).[4]

This exclusivist argument could formally run the same way whether it is the Christian or simply the "home" religion posited as uniquely favored of God. While *ex hypothesi* the agent's epistemic justification in believing the Christian or any other purported testimonial tradition is defeated through the first, bad luck event of how God initially views their value, the subsequent intervention by God coming betwixt the agent and the world results in the Christian (but none other) having a *true* belief about the divine authority of their scriptures. Intervening luck as described in Gettier cases is of just this kind. This strongly suggests that any apologist's re-description of the case as one merely of benign evidential luck is epistemologically flawed. In both the Christian exclusivist and the standard Gettier case we witness a clear disconnect between the agent's intellectual *efforts* and the *success* of her belief. The agent's coming to hold a true belief or system of beliefs is something the cognitive abilities of the agent in the end had little to do with. It is not explained as merit or cognitive achievement on her part, but instead as *felix culpa*—truth attained (only) through a "fortunate fault"!

I suggest describing Barth's interesting faith-based assertion in (3) as *meta-fideism*. Whatever description it is given, the Barthian view is a clear example of asymmetric religious-status attributions that raise worries about "leaning on" luck. Still more troubling is that the specific *type* of epistemic luck Barth's explanatory narrative invokes is widely regarded by philosophers and lay audiences alike as *malign* epistemic luck in the sense of being *knowledge-precluding*. Griffiths articulates this Barthian apologetic for religious exclusivism without noting any such logical or epistemic concerns. That their theologies should so mirror a Gettier case is, I submit, not really so surprising, since this arguably just exemplifies one of *many* ways that strongly fideistic models of faith are drawn to aggravate problems of luck in the course of rationalizing in-group/out-group religious value asymmetries.

Environmental veritic religious luck will be our religious analog of the type of malign epistemic luck that operates in Fake Barn cases. Environmental luck is characterized by getting something right through a process of belief-formation that in the agent's epistemic situation is an unsafe process. Summarizing the epistemological lessons he draws from the much-discussed Barney in Fake Barn County case, Pritchard writes,

> Cases like that of "Barney" illustrate that there is a type of knowledge-undermining epistemic luck, what we might call environmental epistemic luck—which is distinct from the sort of epistemic luck in play in standard Gettier-style cases .... [I]n cases of environmental epistemic luck like that involving Barney, luck of this intervening sort is absent—Barney really does get to see the barn and forms a true belief on this basis—although the epistemically inhospitable nature of the environment ensures that his belief is nevertheless only true as a matter of luck such that he lacks knowledge.
>
> *Pritchard 2010: 47*[5]

A majority of philosophers think that the agent does not know in the barn case, despite the belief arising from the usually reliable faculty of sight. But it seems easy to construct *testimonial transmission* cases that are strongly analogous to fake barn cases. All Barney does, after all, is see the one barn within eyesight, and say, "That's a real barn." So we have merely to swap out "the one real barn" for the exclusivist notion of "the one true theology," and "perceived by eyesight from a distance" for "believed on the basis of the purported special revelation dominant at one's epistemic location." Now, to the extent it is agreed that one would more often get false than true beliefs by this process of belief-acquisition, we again have a luckily true belief, a (by hypothesis) true religious belief but one generated on an unsafe basis. If this is correct, it is not difficult to construct *religious* environmental luck cases, cases analogous to the original barn case where Barney is lucky and gets it right, though he easily could have looked at any number of different barns and got it wrong.

To review, simple evidential luck does not violate the safety principle; evidential luck is simply being lucky *to acquire* a true belief, through being epistemically well-situated to have supporting evidence for it, without ramifying circumstances being present. The ramifying conditions include those that transform innocent evidential luck into environmental luck, with violation of the safety principle being (at least partly) what distinguishes them. For environmental luck is the luck that one's belief *is true*, given a set of modal or other epistemic circumstances that are *inhospitable* to the reliability of the utilized mode of belief-uptake.

Despite the clarity of the distinction between them, when we come to cases, real or constructed, the correct description of the type of luck that is salient is sometimes debatable. This shows a pressing need to more closely study how theologians and philosophers should parse in a principled (i.e., non-ad hoc) way between contexts of benign evidential and malign veritic luck. These consequences for the epistemology of disagreement from how contexts of benign and malign epistemic luck are parsed, has not been examined, as far as I know, either in secular or religious epistemology. The New Problem is constructed to illuminate these issues and provide a context for future discussion, by re-casting safety concerns in terms of the degree of *inductive risk* entailed by people's epistemic context and the belief-forming cognitive process on which they rely.

The New Problem: Inductive Risk as a Challenge to Well-Founded Testimonial Belief

As we earlier saw with our example of J.S. Mill, contingency arguments allege a kind of accidentality to most people's religious identity and attendant beliefs. The proximate causes of one's religious identity and the formation of attendant beliefs are, for most people, a matter of their epistemic location, which in turn appears an accident of birth. Michel de Montaigne gave his own version of a contingency argument when he wrote,

> [W]e receive our religion in our own way and by our own hands, and no differently from the way other religions are received. We happen to find ourselves in the country where it has been practiced; or we value its antiquity or the people who have supported it; or we fear the threats it attaches to wrongdoers, or we follow its promises ... By the same means another country, other witnesses, similar promises and threats, could in the same way imprint in us a contrary belief.
>
> *Montaigne 2003: 6*

Arguments like Montaigne's and Mill's have strengths and weaknesses that are rarely carefully noted. They can be wildly over-ambitious if (mis)interpreted to have the implication of reducing to social causes the contents of all beliefs that are even tinged by cultural contingency (Muscat 2015).

Although religious beliefs are usually the ones singled out, epistemic location arguably has a conditioning or shaping effect over *all* of what, in the epistemology of disagreement, are termed our "controversial views" (see Carter 2017), which include also our moral, political, and philosophical views. While we are not here able to venture into an epistemology of disagreement for controversial views (see Axtell 2019), "contingency anxiety" as Mogensen (2016) and Ballantyne (2013) correctly point out, properly attaches to a far broader group than just religious beliefs. The epistemic worries that contingency arguments raise do not necessarily fall evenly across the four controversial domains, however, and I will argue that the study of asymmetric religious epistemic luck ascriptions helps illuminate the limits of reasonable religious disagreement.

Since we need to think carefully about epistemic location if we are to explicate the force of the epistemology-related religious luck problems, the New Problem tries to present a qualified and refocused set of concerns. It carefully delimits the scope of its *de jure* challenge. In general terms, a *de jure* challenge implicates dereliction of epistemic duty, intellectual viciousness, or some other sense of epistemic unacceptability to some target class of religious belief, narrow or broad (Plantinga 1995). By engaging facts of religious multiplicity and understanding a safety condition in terms of the degrees of inductive risk entailed by a mode of belief-uptake, we can state the specific challenge of the New Problem as a challenge to the reasonableness of religious exclusivist (a) conceptions of faith and (b) responses to religious multiplicity.

Let us clarify some technical terms before going further. *Inductive risk is the study of the chance or possibility of getting it wrong in an inductive context.*[6] *Counter*-inductive thinking entails the highest degrees of inductive risk. *Counter-induction is defined in dictionaries as a strategy that whether self-consciously or not reverses the normal logic of induction.* One example would be ignoring the normativity of a strong pattern of how things are within our past and present experience, while making a prediction about the future. For instance I predict something will happen that is quite counter-point to what the evidence and inductive reasoning would suggest. Another example, closer to our concern, is a strategy of taking a mode of belief-uptake that we ourselves assert or are committed to holding is unsafe/unreliable for the production of true beliefs in *other people*, as a truth-conducive mode of belief-uptake in *our own case*. For our purposes counter-inductive thinking primarily describes a commonplace logical failing: a failing to see reason to apply to one's self (or to one's own epistemic situation) a judgment that one readily and even eagerly applies to others (and their epistemic situations); or a failure to supply sufficient and non-circular epistemic grounds for one's self-exemption from an inductive norm.

We are now in position to lay the New Problem out formally. It will consist of three theses, and a fourth which follows from the first three. The first two theses are about *formal* symmetry, symmetry in the belief-forming cognitive process. The first thesis is:

Familial-Cultural Displacement Symmetry
(DS) For the great majority of religious adherents, had s/he been raised in a family or culture with a different predominant religious identification than that in which s/he was actually raised, but with the same natural capacities and intellectual temperament, s/he very likely would come to identify herself with that religion, with roughly the same degree of personal conviction.

Next we move from this counter-factual claim to a more empirical thesis about a belief-forming cognitive process type that is widespread in the formation of religious beliefs even of widely divergent content. The process type should be wide, but our purpose is again not to challenge as unsafe the aetiology of all religious beliefs, but the aetiology of beliefs associated with a fideistic uptake of a testimonial tradition. Max Baker-Hytch (2014) points out that what a modal reliability (or safety-based) version of the contingency argument should do to serve its purpose is *not* to pick out a process type whose specification involves particular religious texts or particular testimonial chains. Rather,

> selecting a wider process type, whose specification includes no such particulars … achieve[s] the desired result: locating a process type a significant proportion of whose outputs are mutually inconsistent, thus whose overall truth-ratio cannot, even given the truth of one or other consistent subset of the process's outputs, be high enough to satisfy a process type reliability condition.
>
> *Baker-Hytch 2014: 190*[7]

In line with this useful point, our second symmetry thesis is:

Aetiological Symmetry
(AS) The epistemologically relevant level of generality at which to characterize the belief-forming cognitive process by which persons in a great majority of cases, and across epistemic locations, acquire their religion, denomination, or sect-specific beliefs is a level of *testimonial authority-assumption*.

Testimonial authority-assumption is our proposed "wider process type, whose specification includes no such particulars." We can all recognize that accepting the unique authority of a purported revelation is a common way to acquire a religious identity, and often in testimonial traditions such acceptance by the individual is tantamount to what they are taught from an early age that faith consists in. So now we follow up these two (difficult to deny) claims about symmetrical processes of testimony uptake with a thesis about exclusivist *asymmetric* ascriptions of truth and falsity to the beliefs acquired through this mode of belief-uptake. Exclusivist asymmetries (EA) makes a qualified contingency argument *specific to religious exclusivists*:

Exclusivist Asymmetries
(EA) Religious believers of exclusivist orientation in the actual world whose original mode of belief-acquisition is aptly described by (DS) and (AS) would likely, if raised in a different epistemic location with a different but still exclusivist dominant testimonial

tradition, (a) adopt as uniquely true and salvific beliefs that in the actual world they hold to be erroneous; and (b) ascribe falsity and error to beliefs that they hold in the actual world.

Finally, counter-inductive thinking (CIT) draws out the key implication that prior concession to all three of (DS), (AS), and (EA) logically commits one to:

Counter-inductive Thinking
(CIT) Religious believers in the actual world whose mode of belief-acquisition and maintenance is aptly described by (DS), (AS), and (EA) ascribe to a mode of belief-acquisition and maintenance that should by their own lights be acknowledged as *unsafe*, and dependent upon *counter-inductive* thinking.

The intention of this argument is to demonstrate how the mind-set of religious exclusivism is enabled only through counter-inductive thinking. The exclusivist ascribes falsehood to the theological systems of religious aliens, but truth to their own, through what any non-committed party would judge to be a common mode of belief-uptake: testimonial authority-assumption. (CIT) shows this to be an unmotivated self-exemption from the normal logic of induction, where if a form of belief-uptake is judged unreliable for others to use it is probably unreliable for ourselves. Religious exclusivists are among those who are most likely to deny that religious aliens are peer, to dismiss the epistemic significance of religious disagreement, and to maintain themselves as fully rational in what Griffiths refers to as "non-accommodationist" attitudes toward religious aliens. But (CIT) strongly implies that peerhood is not easy to dismiss; it indeed suggests that dismissing it proceeds the same way—by a self-serving self-exemption from inductive norms (i.e., by counter-inductive thinking). Denial of the epistemic significance of religious disagreement is shown vain if the fact of persistent disagreement directly affects the assessment of whether the luck concerns in people's epistemic situations are concerns about evidential or about environmental luck.

In order to deny acknowledging (CIT), exclusivists must deny one or more of (DS), (AS), or (EA), but this is not easy to do. The primary challenge that follows from being logically constrained to accept (CIT) is that the grounding or well-foundedness of the exclusivist's belief will then be shown impacted by malign environmental luck not just in the counter-factual but also in *the actual world*. Your beliefs in both the counter-factual *and* the actual world are acquired on an unsafe basis, under conditions of very high inductive risk, which in turn should be recognized as a strong *de jure* challenge to their epistemic standing. How can one respect the morality and rationality of a mode of belief-uptake that generates sharply *asymmetric* moral, epistemic, and theological trait-ascriptions directed by *some* of its users against *others* of its users? The *de jure* challenge stemming from the New Problem of religious luck is that the mode of belief-uptake characterizable as testimonial authority-assumption is, from an externalist viewpoint, *unsafe*, and from a responsibilist viewpoint, *intellectual viciousness*.

The question just asked leads me to a briefer but perhaps clearer description of the New Problem in terms of a dilemma for religious exclusivists: The **Exceptionalist Dilemma.** The exclusivist, it holds, is caught between embracing two responses to the New Problem, neither of which proves philosophically adequate. The first horn says that the exclusivist cannot without great cost just concede that the formal mode of belief-uptake for adherents of the home religion is of the same general type as that of religious others. For one who grabs the first horn and makes a "same process response" will still want to maintain that the faith-based believing of adherents of the home religion results in *true* belief. But given that they themselves hold that this general process type results in untruth and error in a vast majority of cases, they certainly cannot say that the process is *safe*, as epistemologists use that term. The cost of grabbing this first horn is being saddled with recognition that one's mode of belief-uptake is unsafe, which in turn renders counter-inductive their claim that it produces true belief *in their own case*. If the religious insider's beliefs, like that of all the religious aliens who

445

got theology wrong, are grounded on counter-inductive thinking, then it follows that the religious insider's beliefs are, if true, only *luckily* true from the epistemic point of view. The safety or reliability of a belief-forming process is a condition on knowing and related epistemic standings, and we should conclude that we lack personal doxastic responsibility if we believe on the basis of a mode of belief-uptake that we allow is unsafe. Grabbing the first horn then comes back on the initial asymmetrical positing of truth: The truth status the exclusivist confers on their own specific theological system is now counter-inductive to the falsity they claim for all other theological systems.

It is likely a more appealing option for exclusivists to make a "unique process response," thus denying the charge of counter-inductive thinking that comes with affirming that their beliefs are generated by the same general process as are those of adherents of other testimonial traditions. But the second horn of our dilemma is that all attempts to justify the uniqueness of the mode of belief-uptake ascribed to adherents of the home religion will either be empty or will implicitly rely on self-favoring ascriptions of good religious luck.

To effectively grab the second horn, the uniqueness asserted must genuinely be of *process type*, not just of content. One cannot just appeal to content by saying the process type is a "one off," for instance, by claiming that the experiential or testimonial input to it is self-authenticating, or that the process *must* be reliable because it outputs the content of the one true creed. By strength of analogical inference, the seriousness of the charge of engaging in counter-inductive self-exemption is not avoided by such form/content-conflating responses, but actually re-enforced. To avoid vicious circularity, a response that grabs the second horn of our dilemma needs to argue for uniqueness of process type in an adequately formal sense. The challenge I put forth is that no such unique process response can be given to the Exceptionalist Dilemma that is not empty and cannot be shown to lean once again on a self-serving religious luck ascription.

There are different responses that might be tried out, and numerous counter-analogies or disanalogies that might be raised to try to dislodge our challenge. So rather than claiming that the New Problem or the Exceptionalist Dilemma are debunking of religious belief in some grand (crude) sense, I have emphasized that they are a useful focus for a new discussion between philosophers of luck, theologians, and proponents of CSR. But if *neither* "same process" nor "unique process" responses to the dilemma prove satisfactory, then the adherents of our different religious faith traditions should concede that the *de jure* objection reveals the intellectual poverty of exclusivist conceptions of faith and responses to religious multiplicity.

An Objection and Response

We have space for one objection and reply. Consider this objection: The claim crucial to the New Problem, that home religion testimonial uptake is unsafe, unfairly totalizes over religions. It is easy for the exclusivist, whether on epistemologically internalist or externalist assumptions, to deny this. More particularly it is easy to deny (AS), the Aetiological Symmetry thesis, which seems to say that *testimonial authority-assumption* is all one needs to know about the causal aetiology of belief to determine both its ubiquity across religions, and its epistemic viciousness. For the same reasons it is easy to grab the second horn of the Exceptionalist Dilemma, and maintain that the uniqueness of my religion's testimonial tradition qualifies its transmission as a "different process" from that used by adherents of other faith traditions. The safety of testimonial chains needs to be assessed singly, not in the totalizing way posited by the dilemma. Looked at that way, it can be safe even as I, as an exclusivist, hold that testimonial authority-assumption indeed results in false belief for adherents of alien religions.

In response, let me first remind the objector of the requirements of grabbing the second horn:

> To effectively grab the second horn the uniqueness asserted must genuinely be of *process type*, not just of content. One cannot just appeal to content by saying the process type is a "one off," for instance, by claiming that the experiential or testimonial input to it is

self-authenticating, or that the process *must* be reliable because it outputs the content of the one true creed.

As this passage hints, religious exclusivism has champions who defend it through an internalist apologetic, and others who use an externalist apologetic. If the conditions I place on a "different process" response are correct, the question is whether either apologetic strategy can escape circularity well enough to establish the debate-independence of its supporting reasons.

Starting with internalism, the appeal to unique phenomenology, as de Ridder (2014) points out, is an appeal to internal evidences such as what it feels like to read the Bible and feel its inspiration, or to participate in a ritual or other communal practice. These factors are vitally important to one's religious identity. Indeed, that every religion comes with unique concepts and experiences is an important aspect of my permissivist ethics of belief. Religious narratives place readers where they can feel what it is like to have certain sorts of experience, but they appear not to situate them well for making truth claims, let alone exclusivist ones, on their basis. The question at hand is not whether the inner evidences count as personal or subjective justification—they do—but whether they are adequately independent of the exclusivists' disagreement with non-believers and believers in different faith traditions for their reasoning to have force outside the home religion's circle. And the simple answer to that is negative. It is not easy to infer epistemological differences from phenomenological ones.

Appeals to a first-personal perspective and phenomenology seem ill-equipped to break the default symmetry among people as epistemic peers on a certain matter. They can be used to deny peerhood, but only, I think, in a rhetorical way, by the insulating moves of saying the evidence-sharing condition on peerhood is never met across traditions, and that religious disagreements therefore are not peer disagreements. Adherents of alien religious traditions can easily mirror a self-guaranteeing claim that, "I feel it so strongly, it can't be false." The next move, again shared by all, is to "logically" infer the falsity of any view contrary to one's own orthodoxy. The claim of the self-guaranteeing authority of the home scripture or experience is something religious studies scholars associate with strongly fideistic models of faith, but these claims have never settled any actual disagreement. Arguably, all that radical fideism does is to generate an "enemy in the mirror." Let us use the resources of a philosophy of risk and luck to erase, as I have tried to do, the phenomena of self-constructed enemies in the mirror; doing so, it seems to me, is genuine religiosity—at least, it requires no anti-realism about religious language.

Those who appeal instead to externalist epistemology in order to defend an attitude of religious exclusivism, such as Alvin Plantinga, may also often appeal to unique phenomenology. But they would have us accept that we can deny aetiological and peer symmetries by starting from the other end, from the truth of their religious worldview and from the religious knowledge they purport to have. Unfortunately, jumping ship on the epistemic level and the requirement of independent reasons, by telling a metaphysical/theological story about the *causes* of one's experience that set it apart as especially veritic, has never resolved religious disagreement either.

Despite the twists in Plantinga's account of a divine design plan, I hold the basic belief apologetic to be no less fideistic and circular in reasoning than a phenomenal conservative apologetic strategy. Both make religious knowledge very easy, but falter over why views contrary to their own do not also count as properly basic, warranted, and safe. All one can say ultimately is that beliefs running contrary to the Christian's are not true, and that these other epistemic statuses are dependent on truth. On Plantinga's externalist apologetic strategy, a reliable aetiology (safety or warrant) is assured for general theistic and also for Christian teachings infused irresistibly by the work of the Holy Spirit. But ask him about the possibility on which the Holy Spirit and God do not exist and we find Plantinga forced to concede that neither his religion-specific nor his theistic beliefs would in that case be *warranted*, either. Their warrant depends upon supposition of their truth: no truth, no warrant. This explains why the potential mirroring of contrary views that also assert properly basic beliefs in the Great Pumpkin, for instance, became such a serious problem for Plantinga.

One might think (AS) paints religious belief-acquisition with a broad brushstroke, and that when you look in finer detail, the similarity and formal symmetry of the grounds of belief are very different. It is true that (AS) is framed broadly, but this is a reasonable level of generality at which to describe a good deal of belief-uptake, and the location-switching thought experiment works to confirm that something very like this is the causal aetiology of most people's religious beliefs.

This is of course a claim only about observable proximate causes. That the perspective on causal aetiology in (AS) attends only to proximate causes is a methodological limitation, but it does not beg the question by presupposing that all religions are epistemically on a par. The reader should not confuse methodological neutrality and a defeasible default presumption of peerhood when faced with disagreement, with question-begging. I am not committed to the metaphysical claim that no religious perspective or experience is especially veritic. Similarly, there is nothing in (AS)'s iden-tification of a common proximate cause (home religion testimonial authority-assumption) in the acquisition of religious belief that is blind to the claims that some persons use a safer method than others, and that whatever tradition they acquire their belief from, some persons worker harder than others to improve their epistemic positions. The New Problem encourages attempts to make good on symmetry-breaking reasons, just in order to understand them more clearly and analyze their formal structure. Default symmetry, a weaker notion than parity or peerhood, is a defeasible posit, but one that allows us to focus directly upon particular attempts to *break* symmetry, and on the inductive risk explicitly or implicitly accepted in these attempts.

Contrary to the objection, our methodology thus presupposes qualitative or epistemic differences, and *invites* looking for "finer detail." It looks for this especially in symmetry-breaking reasoning, and in the various models of faith that lead adherents to their response to religious multiplicity. But "finer detail" should not be reduced to an opportunity to substitute a sacred narrative in place of a call for epistemic situation-improving reasons; if the closer look indicates that the purportedly unique pro-cess mirrors known group biases and inductive fallacies, then this is not establishing its uniqueness, but rather works to corroborate the description that (AS) makes of that process. So this goes case-by-case, but if the reasons offered in attempts to grab the second horn are reasonably independent of the disagreement then then symmetry-breaking could be on inductively strong grounds. On the other hand, if these reasons turn out to be circular or to lean explicitly or tacitly on asymmetric attribu-tion of religious luck, then this is weak inductive grounds upon which to claim epistemic superiority. Group psychology and inductive fallacies would then seem to explain it better.

Conclusion

The concept of religious luck grants us significant insights into the moral, theological, and epistemo-logical adequacy of different models of religious faith and the responses to religious multiplicity that they motivate. There is reason to think the denial of epistemic symmetry, and the assertion of sharply asymmetric value in God's eyes between adherents of the home religion and all others, can always be shown on close examination to appeal to one or another kind of religious luck. The study of symmetry-breaking attributions, especially through a philosophy of risk or luck, provides theologians, ethicists, epistemologists, and CSR new insights into the causes of religious disagreement and the limits of reasonable religious disagreement.

The presence of pervasive disagreement and epistemic risk make one's epistemic context *inductive*, since these are contexts in which one cannot hope to properly assess their own reliability apart from considering how reliable others would likely be using their same method, and how reliable they themselves would likely be still using that method but under a range of slightly modally varied circumstances. So our argument in this chapter shows that a philosophy of luck must necessarily be concerned with inductive risk, and that the degree of inductive risk in an epistemic strategy is a formal and sometimes readily assessable issue. Our study further suggests that the high degree of inductive risk in contexts in which testimony-based claims to religious knowledge are typically made is a fully sufficient criterion for determining it to be a context of malign environmental, rather than benign evidential luck.

Finally, degrees of incurred inductive risk might not only be a sound criterion for taking the aetiology of a belief to be affected by malign epistemic luck; they might also prove a useful means of measuring where a particular theology falls on the scale between religious rationalism and religious fideism (Bishop 2007). Over-strong rationalism and over-strong fideism both function to undermine reasonable religious disagreement. Religious rationalists hold that there is no more risk involved in theistic belief than in other more everyday beliefs, while religious fideists hold that faith is necessary because a person whose assent to theistic beliefs is matched only to the degree of rational confidence in their evidence has only an unstable faith. So our approach suggests that these same concerns with inductive risk and safety principle violation also supply a way to distinguish moderate and strong (sometimes called radical or counter-evidential) fideism on the basis of recognizable formal markers—something that might be quite useful in religious studies and CSR.

Notes

1 For a book-length development, see Axtell 2019.
2 Axtell 2017 examines William James' account of moral and doxastic risk, focusing especially on J.S. Mill's influence on James' temperament thesis and understanding of religious and philosophical "overbeliefs." Mill's influence on James includes his liberal ideal of a market-place of ideas where people live out and express divergent "experiments in living." In overlapping papers I develop a neo-Jamesian (pragmatic pluralist) account of doxastic responsibility for religious faith ventures, and for "controversial views" (Axtell forthcoming) more generally.
3 If randomness in the world and lack of certainty in a human judgment have different sources, then at least some religious luck lies on the aleatory side of the aleatory/epistemic distinction. If God does not reveal his criteria to humans, or if theists themselves express skepticism about knowing, then it is, arguably, more akin to genuine randomness (aleatory uncertainty) from the creaturely perspective, than to lack of certainty due to *contingent* factors of presently insufficient evidence.
4 Barth (2010) himself writes, "No religion *is* true … A religion can only *become* true ….The true religion, like the justified human being, is a creature of *grace*."
5 For his recent turn from anti-luck to anti-risk epistemology, see Pritchard (2016).
6 Note that my account does not depend on testimonial knowledge being inductive or inferential; it is neutral with respect to debates between reductionists and anti-reductionists. In the primary sense it is simply the presence of potential *defeaters to justification* (such as the presence of fake barns) that transforms a person's context into an inductive one, (so that characterizing Barney as having a justified *visual* belief misses the need for the agent to know of and to weigh the impact of such potential defeaters in their environment). But if (as I think) testimonial uptake indeed *is* inferential, then this further substantiates logical connections between belief-acquisition through home religion testimonial authority-assumption and high inductive risk.
7 This author and I are both drawing from externalist epistemology and the literature on the *generality problem*.

References

Anderson, M.B. (2011) "Molinism, Open Theism, and Soteriological Luck," *Religious Studies* 47(3), 371–381.
Axtell, G. (2017) "James on Pragmatism and Religion," in J. Goodson (ed.) *William James, Moral Philosophy, and the Ethical Life: The Cries of the Wounded*, Lanham, MD: Lexington Books, pp. 317–336.
———. (forthcoming) "Well-Founded Belief and the Contingencies of Epistemic Location," in J.A. Carter & P. Bondy (eds.) *Well-Founded Belief: New Essays on the Epistemic Basing Relation*, Oxford: Oxford University Press.
———. (2019) *Problems of Religious Luck: Assessing the Limits of Reasonable Religious Disagreement*, Lanham, MD: Lexington Books/Rowman & Littlefield.
Baker-Hytch, M. (2014) "Religious Diversity and Epistemic Luck," *International Journal for Philosophy of Religion* 76(2), 171–191.
Ballantyne, N. (2013) "The Problem of Historical Variability," in D. Machuca (ed.) *Disagreement and Skepticism*, New York: Routledge Press, pp. 239–259.
Barth, K. (2010) *Church Dogmatics, Volume 1*, Peabody, MA: Hendrickson Publishers.
Bishop, J. (2007) *Believing by Faith: An Essay in the Epistemology and Ethics of Religious Belief*, Oxford: Oxford University Press.

Buckareff, A., & Plug, A. (2009) "Escapism, Religious Luck, and Divine Reasons for Action," *Religious Studies* 45(2), 63–72.

Carter, J.A (2017) "On Behalf of Controversial View Agnosticism," *European Journal of Philosophy*, 1–13, https://doi.org/10.1111/ejop.12333.

Craig, W.L. (1989) "'No Other Name': A Middle Knowledge Perspective on the Exclusivity of Salvation through Christ," *Faith and Philosophy* 6, 172–188.

Davison, S. (1999) "Salvific Luck," *International Journal for Philosophy of Religion* 45, 129–137.

de Ridder, J. (2014) "Why Only Externalists Can Be Steadfast," *Erkenntnis* 79(1), 185–199.

Griffiths, P.J. (2001) *Problems of Religious Diversity*, London: Wiley-Blackwell.

Hartman, R.J. (2014) "How to Apply Molinism to the Theological Problem of Moral Luck," *Faith and Philosophy* 31, 68–90.

Jones, R. (2007) "Escapism and Luck," *Religious Studies* 43, 206–216.

Katzoff, C. (2000) "Religious Luck and Religious Virtue," *Religious Studies* 40(1), 97–111.

Mill, J.S. (1913) *On Liberty*, London: Longmans, Green, and Co.

Mogensen, A.L. (2016) "Contingency Anxiety and the Epistemology of Disagreement," *Pacific Philosophical Quarterly* 97(4), 590–611.

Montaigne, M. de (2003) *Apology for Raimond Sebond*, Indianapolis: Hackett Publishing.

Muscat, R. (2015) "The Contingency of Belief: Present Beliefs Stem from Past Happenstance," *Free Inquiry* (Oct./Nov.), 40–42.

Plantinga, A. (1995) "Pluralism: A Defense of Religious Exclusivism," in T.D. Senor (ed.) *The Rationality of Belief and the Plurality of Faith*, Ithaca, NY: Cornell University Press, pp. 191–215.

Pritchard, D. (2005) *Epistemic Luck*, Oxford: Oxford University Press.

——. (2010) *Knowledge and Understanding*, in D. Pritchard, A. Millar, & A. Haddock (eds.) *Three Investigations*, Oxford: Oxford University Press, pp. 5–90.

——. (2015) "The Modal Account of Luck," in D. Pritchard & L.J. Whittington (eds.) *The Philosophy of Luck*, London: Wiley Blackwell, pp. 143–168.

——. (2016) "Epistemic Risk," *The Journal of Philosophy* 113(11), 550–571.

Zagzebski, L. (1994) "Religious Luck," *Faith and Philosophy* 11(3), 397–413.

39

THEOLOGY AND LUCK

Jordan Wessling

In 361 CE, in the city of Caesarea, Christians destroyed the only remaining temple dedicated to the goddess of luck, Tyche. While some Caesareans feared that misfortune would soon befall the city, the great Christian theologian Gregory of Nazianzus (329–390 CE) celebrated the temple's destruction. In his mind, the event amounted to a declaration that humans are free from the tyranny of random chance or luck, which has no place in a world run by God (Pelikan 1993: 160–161). Gregory's attitude toward luck represents the mind of many ancient theologians. Most eschew all talk of "luck," "fortune," and like terms as referring to the way things genuinely are in God's creation (see, e.g., Pelikan 1993: ch. 10), even if some allow for insignificant chance events (see Miller 2016; Silva 2016).

It is understandable why theologians would be suspicious of the idea that the world contains luck. Luck is often thought to be essentially connected to some arbitrary and impersonal force that governs creaturely affairs, or to events that no one intends to occur, which are precluded by divine providence (cf. Oates 1995). Nevertheless, there is a sensible understanding of "luck" that is a concomitant of certain ways in which contemporary theologians render teachings that are central to the Christian faith. I here survey literature related to three of these areas—namely, creation, redemption, and petitionary prayer—and I discuss some approaches that theologians might take to be apparent manifestations of luck. Though I examine these matters from a specifically Christian perspective, much of what is discussed applies to other theistic faiths as well.

The Nature of Luck

For the purposes of this essay, I stipulate that "luck" refers to those good and bad things that happen to an individual that are *significant* (e.g., Ballantyne 2012; Coffman 2007) and yet *not under the control* of that individual (e.g., Broncano-Berrocal 2015; Nagel 1979; Riggs 2009). The level of control that one has over the good and bad things that happen to oneself may vary, as can the level of significance of the good and bad things at issue. Since the degree of control and significance can vary in these ways, so too can the degree of luck. These details aside, most agree that winning the lottery, being born in a peaceable country, and having an excellent genetic makeup are examples of good luck. Bad luck might include getting struck by lightning, being arrested for a murder one did not commit, and losing much of one's money due to an unforeseeable crash in the market.

Described in this manner, few Christian theologians would deny the existence of luck. To replace Judas's apostolic office, for example, lots were cast by the other disciples (Acts 1:24–26). Perhaps God guided the outcome, but Matthias, who was selected by the lot, presumably did little-to-nothing to secure the result. Thus, the selection of Matthias was, for Matthias and those impacted by his ministry, a matter of luck—good luck if the selection was good for Matthias and those he oversaw. More substantially, the books of Job and Ecclesiastes can be read as sensitive treatments of some of the ways in which uncontrollable events lead to tremendous goods and devastating losses (see Brown 2011: 96; Miller 2010: 169; Hecht 2016). These events, no doubt, can be described as instances of good and bad luck. Finally, the doctrine of salvation by grace seems to entail a certain amount of luck, since, on this understanding, the opportunity and occurrence of one's salvation are not entirely controlled (Zagzebski 1994: 403–404). The degree of luck might be increased the more the theologian stresses that salvation is exclusively the act of God (cf. Katzoff 2004), but it is doubtful that even theologians that place a premium on the human ability to appropriate saving grace will go so far as to say that humans are entirely responsible for their salvation. Hence, when luck is characterized as I have done here, most will agree that luck cannot be erased from Christian thought. Since luck is here to stay, the challenge is to provide a fruitful theological account of some of the ways in which luck emerges in a world governed by God.

Creation and Luck

Contemporary scientific data suggests a picture of the world that contains quantum indeterminism, and where chance events seem to play a role within the process of biological evolution. One way of interpreting this data is to maintain that the indeterminacy at the quantum level is not just apparent but genuine (i.e., an objective feature of nature operating according to certain probabilistic laws), and that this indeterminism reverberates "upwards" into biological structures, allowing genetic mutations to arise without any *deterministic* cause. On this way of thinking, the eventual character of creation cannot be predicted by an exhaustive knowledge of its initial states. If we could rewind the history of our universe and play it again, it is highly likely that the cosmos would manifest a different shape and that very different kinds of creatures would emerge, if any complex creatures at all (see, Bartholomew 2008; cf. Gould 1989 and Morris 2003).

As one might imagine, there are different theological responses to this chancy and indeterministic understanding of the natural world. Some suggest that this view of the cosmos provides evidence against the existence of God (e.g., Monod 1972; Smith 1993), whereas others argue that God's existence and nature falsifies this description of the cosmos (Sproul 1994; cf. Plantinga 2011: 11–13). A third group, consisting of theologians, sees things rather differently. For them, a creation that unfolds via stochastic processes allows creation to embody a valuable degree of independence, or autonomy, so as to "make itself" (for a survey, see Johnson 2014: ch. 6). On this autonomous creation view, God does not determine the precise shape of creation, nor what exactly comes to exist within it, even if he has the eventual goal of producing some sentient and rational beings. Rather, God sets up a system that can unfold in various ways, and while God interacts with this creation in important respects, God more or less lets creation unravel as the stochastic processes happen to steer things.

The cosmological interplay of law and chance, given the autonomous creation view, acts as something of a lottery system that generates several kinds of luck. Consider two basic kinds. There is the luck of coming to exist by largely undirected processes, and there is the luck of being harmed by these processes, as suffering and death routinely result from the chance-laced evolutionary mechanisms. Insofar as coming to exist is thought to be good for the relevant organisms, the luck here is good luck. Insofar as suffering and death are bad for the relevant organisms, bad luck emerges.

Coming to exist, on any plausible schema, is lucky—it is not the sort of significant event that can be controlled by the individual who comes to exist. From a traditional theistic perspective, the occurrence of this luck is ultimately to be credited to God, the secondary causes notwithstanding. This remains the case on the autonomous view of creation, only here creation is granted a more significant capacity to generate this kind of good luck. This is because, on the autonomous creation model, God does not control completely who comes to exist and who does not. Instead, the indeterministic processes of creation factor into who or what comes to exist. Beyond that, these processes contribute to the *kinds* of creatures that are granted the good luck to exist. For, given an autonomous creation, there is nothing about the initial conditions, or even divine providence, that ensures that the cosmos will have the contours that it does, or which sentient creatures (if any) will populate it. But then the question must be asked, why would God create a system wherein who or what exists is the product of a kind of random, even if good, luck? One might think that matters of such importance should not be subject to *this* kind of luck.

Then there is the bad luck. On the autonomous conception of creation, stochastic processes give rise to natural catastrophes and genetic mutations that lead to suffering, death, and even extinction. Depending upon the degree of autonomy that is believed to have been given to creation, it might even be claimed that the entire system of predation was never specifically intended by God (even if it was foreseen), which is in turn responsible for countless instances of bad luck. It would not be unreasonable to think that the cost of such bad luck is higher than the value of making creation largely "free" (see Tracy 2007: 162–163).

So, on the autonomous creation view, creation is subject to peculiar kinds of indeterministic or chance-laden good and bad luck. It must be admitted that the autonomous creation model presents us with a rather bizarre perspective on the way in which God chooses to run his world. The challenge for the defender of an autonomous creation, then, is to explain why God might set up a system that is laced with such luck.[1]

The well-known theologian, John Haught, proposes one way of addressing the value of an autonomous creation. He reasons that a fully formed and fully deterministic universe would not be truly other than God, but instead "an emanation or appendage of deity." But a "world that is not clearly distinct from God could not be the recipient of divine love" (Haught 2003: 168; cf. 78). Moreover, the value of God creating a world that can be a recipient of his love is what justifies, at least in part, the good and bad luck discussed (2003: 80).

The philosopher Michael Murray objects to Haught's proposal. To Murray's mind, it is far from clear that a clean line between God and creation requires an autonomous, evolutionary process. After all, a human artist can create a painting that is sufficiently distinct from herself despite the fact that the painting is not at all self-actualizing. Hence, being partially self-actualizing is not required for independence. Furthermore, it is reasonable to think that God created the initial singularity of the cosmos, in an instant, yet this hardly seems to entail that the singularity is an "appendage of deity." Thus, Murray asks Haught, "Why must we think that if an agent directly actualizes a state of affairs then that state of affairs is not distinct from the agent?" (Murray 2011: 173).

John Polkinghorne proposes another way of treating the luck of an autonomous creation, in particular, the bad luck of suffering and death. He applies "a variation of the free-will defence … to the whole created world" (Polkinghorne 1989: 66), and he urges us to realize that "[a] world allowed to make itself through the evolutionary exploration of its potentiality is a better world than one produced ready-made by divine fiat" (Polkinghorne 1998: 94; cf. Miller 2007: 289). The basic idea of his defense is that the value of an autonomous creation offsets the affiliated bad luck in a manner that is analogous to the way in which humans endowed with the ability to form their moral characters through a history of free choices offsets the potential for moral evil.

One might worry, however, that Polkinghorne's emphasis is unrealistically anthropomorphic (Collins 2011: 247). Are we to think that atoms literally *choose* to move where they do? Or if they "choose" in some analogous sense, what is that sense exactly, and why should we value it? As a result, one might wonder whether Polkinghorne's "free-process defense" is strong enough to account for the bad luck in question.[2]

Another proposal is that a universe that unfolds by way of a delicate synergy between law and chance somehow heightens the beauty of creation. Favored metaphors for God's involvement with a largely autonomous cosmos include the following: a grand composer who "beginning with an arrangement of notes in an apparently simple tune, elaborates and expands it into a fugue" (Peacocke 1984: 72); a "theatrical improviser of unsurpassed ingenuity in live performance, who amplifies and embroiders each theme as it presents itself" (Johnson 2014: 77); or a choreographer who dances, and even plays, with creation in a manner that does not interfere with the universe's given rhythm (Peacocke 1979: 108–111; cf. Moltmann 1973: ch. 3). Clearly, aesthetic sensibilities animate the way in which many scientifically engaged theologians think about an autonomous creation (cf. Haught 2010: 276). Nevertheless, these theologians often leave unspecified what makes an autonomous creation beautiful and what relation that beauty might play in explaining why God permits the kinds of good and bad luck of concern.

Joshua Rasmussen and Jordan Wessling (2015) attempt to fill this lacuna, though they do not explicitly affirm that God has, in fact, established an autonomous creation. They suggest that *one* valuable feature of a work of art is its ability to arouse certain emotions in the perceiver,[3] and they propose various ways in which an autonomous creation might be aesthetically valuable for this reason. Rasmussen and Wessling even go so far as to suggest the possibility that an autonomous creation produces in God certain pleasures affiliated with curiosity, anticipation, and surprise (given specific conceptions of divine knowledge). Their proposal has the interesting implication that the potential for *divine* good luck partly accounts for why God might have instilled an autonomous creation. This is because, on their proposal, one reason God creates an autonomous creation is so that he might experience the noted aesthetic pleasures. Whether or not God gets these pleasures, or the degree to which he does, is largely a matter of luck, however, given that these pleasures depend upon processes that are not completely controlled and produce unpredictable results. Rasmussen and Wessling also consider, within an additional article, ways in which the value of this divine luck (though they do not call it that) *partially* offsets the potential for bad luck that is inherent in an autonomous creation (Rasmussen & Wessling 2017). In response, one could question the possibility of this divine good luck, as well as its ability to shed light on why God created a cosmos filled with suffering and death.

Criticisms of the autonomous creation view will vary. Some will find the proposal incompatible with biblical and traditional accounts of divine providence, and thus unworthy of serious consideration. Others will contend that the alleged significance of an autonomous creation is exaggerated because the omniscient God knows, prior to his decision to create, which events would emerge from specific indeterministic sequences; consequently, God has the resources to get more or less all the details that he wants, even if the world develops via indeterministic means (e.g., Ratzsch 1998). Apart from such considerations, however, whether or not an autonomous creation model continues to be taken seriously as a theological option largely will depend upon how one assesses the value, or disvalue, of the good and bad luck affiliated with this mode of creation. Hence, more work on this topic remains to be done by both those who affirm and reject an autonomous creation account.

Soteriological Luck

Contemporary philosophical theologians notice the apparent presence of what is variously termed "religious luck" (Buckareff & Plug 2009; Jones 2007; Zagzebski 1994), "salvific luck" (Davison 1999), and "soteriological luck" (Anderson 2011; Hartman 2014). The differences aside, these three labels refer to the extent to which a person's fit candidacy for either eternal salvation or eternal condemnation is beyond that person's control. Those who raise the issue of soteriological luck as a problem are not principally concerned with the notion that God saves in a gracious manner that implies that salvation is at least partially lucky. Instead, the focus is often (though not always) upon a person's apparently lucky advantages or disadvantages regarding salvation in relation to other persons, or even oneself in counterfactual situations (see, especially, Jones 2007: 206; Anderson 2011; Hartman 2014). This is deemed a theological problem insofar as God's justice is thought to preclude treating people according to luck-based inequality, and insofar as a God of love would seek to remove all luck-based barriers to communion with himself (see, e.g., Davison 1999: 129; Walls 2002: 67, 74–75, 84–89; Buckareff & Plug 2005; Mizrahi 2014). By contrast, those who hold strong predestinarian views about God's saving grace and eternal reprobation are bound to see soteriological luck as less of a problem.

A concrete example might sharpen our focus on the topic at hand. Although theologians disagree about what precisely makes someone a fit candidate for eternal salvation, suppose, for purposes of illustration, that a necessary condition is being disposed to trust God daily, even if done with varying success. With this before us, consider two individuals, Jane and Jill. Jane was raised by Christian parents who exemplified Christ's love for her, who taught her right from wrong, took her to church, and so on. As a result, Jane sees the world as filled with meaning and value, and surrounded by God's love. Jill, however, was not so fortunate. She was raised by neglectful, drug-addicted parents, who taught her that there is no God, nor objective right and wrong. As far back as her memory will take her, Jill has believed that the world is indifferent and cruel, and that she must grab whatever pleasures for herself that she can, since there is no one looking out for her. Apart from these circumstantial differences, Jane is naturally a more sensitive, kind, and trusting person than is Jill. Ostensibly, then, Jane has been given a better shot than Jill at reaching an eternal reward. If so, we have an important kind of luck that brings with it eternal consequences.[4]

For those who judge that the reality of soteriological luck would be a problem, there are two general response-types that have been proposed. One type is to grant that soteriological luck exists, but argue that it is outside of God's control in a manner that exonerates him (relevant here is Rissler (2006)). Another option is to propose ways in which soteriological luck would be eliminated, or else substantially reduced. We shall consider a number of proposals that fall within the latter option, many of which were originally explored by Linda Zagzebski in her groundbreaking article, "Religious Luck" (1994).

To begin with, several philosophical theologians suggest that Molinism mitigates the problem of soteriological luck (Anderson 2011; Craig 1989; Davison 1999: 132–133; Hartman 2014; Zagzebski 1994: 407–408). Roughly, Molinism is the idea that, prior to God's choice to create, God knows what any free creature would do within any circumstance she might be placed, and God uses that knowledge to govern creaturely affairs. To date, the most thorough and sophisticated application of Molinism to the problem of soteriological luck comes from Robert Hartman (2014). Hartman examines several Molinist ways of alleviating the problem of soteriological luck by either eliminating soteriological luck altogether *or* ensuring that the luck is overall good luck. In addition, Hartman addresses the topic of *moral* luck, which occurs when an agent is a fit candidate for moral appraisal even when a significant portion of that for which the agent is morally assessed is beyond the agent's control. Soteriological and moral luck are related, Hartman contends, in that whether or not one appropriates God's saving grace can be judged a matter of moral luck, as can one's good or bad works that factor into the *quality* of one's afterlife (namely, rewards or punishments).

Hartman discusses five Molinist-based proposals in detail. An idea that is common to four out of the five proposals is that God actualizes a world wherein (i) each human's moral worth (i.e., being praiseworthy and blameworthy) is better than is typical across other possible worlds that God can actualize, and (ii) God guarantees that each human freely accepts God's salvific grace in the actual world if she freely accepts it in any possible world that God can actualize (cf. Craig 1989; VanArragon 2001). So, no one is damned in the actual world that would have been saved otherwise in another possible world that God could have actualize, and the quality of each person's afterlife is higher than is typical across feasible worlds. If there is luck here, it is mostly good. Consequently, God's goodness is not impugned.

In the end, Hartman hesitates to affirm, for philosophical and theological reasons, any of the five Molinist proposals he expounds. Nevertheless, he offers Molinists various options for consideration. Perhaps one of these options can be built upon to provide a more satisfying solution to the problem(s) of soteriological luck.

But, of course, Molinist treatments of soteriological luck can be only as plausible as the doctrine that God knows, prior to the decision to create, what free creatures would choose in any circumstance in which they are placed. That doctrine is fairly controversial, however (for an overview of the relevant issues, see Perszyk (2011)). This makes the examination of other, non-Molinist proposals considerably important.

One way of eliminating soteriological luck that does not depend upon Molinism is to maintain that God does not allow luck to factor into his judgments concerning who should and should not receive salvation. Instead, God's moral and spiritual evaluation of the human is curtailed to the proportion of control that each individual has, over the course of her life, over her actions and her opportunities to respond to God's grace, even if the grace is not recognized as such. God, so to speak, grades on a curve. (Relevant here are discussions of *inclusivism*; see D'Costa (2009: ch. 1).)

Zagzebski objects to this proposed solution. Relying on an argument first developed by Joel Feinberg for the conclusion that, in principle, there is no precise determinable degree of moral responsibility given the way in which luck permeates character and actions, Zagzebski contends that not even an omniscient being could specify a determinable degree of luck-free soteriological responsibility (1994: 408). Hence, God cannot accurately grade on a curve, even if this is something that he would like to do.

But why think that there is no precise degree of control of the relevant kind? Zagzebski acknowledges that Feinberg's argument, upon which she relies, has not been given "the care necessary to demonstrate such a dramatic conclusion" (1994: 408). Moreover, though it might be difficult/ impossible for humans always to discern a precise degree of moral and spiritual control, this hardly establishes that there is no such control. Perhaps, then, greater care should be paid to this issue before it is dismissed (cf. Davison 1999: 134).

Zagzebski finds a different kind of response (which she does not affirm) to the problem of soteriological luck in the writings of George Schlesinger. The suggestion here is that the more difficult it is for a person to be saved, the greater she is rewarded for responding to that grace. By contrast, the easier it is for a person to be saved, the less she is rewarded for appropriating God's grace. "So some people gamble for higher stakes with a lower chance of success, while others gamble for lower stakes with a higher chance of success" (Zagzebski 1994: 409).

The problem with this suggestion is that individuals do not get to choose how they gamble with their lives. But this seems to be an unfair form of soteriological luck that is not obviously compatible with God's goodness (cf. Zagzebski 1994: 409).

Another kind of view is that God gives some persons special aid in order to compensate for what would otherwise amount to bad soteriological luck (cf. Zagzebski 1994: 410; Jones 2007). In other words, those who need more help than others to receive a sufficient opportunity for salvation are given this help by God. Zagzebski finds this view compatible with how a loving parent would treat his children, yet she doubts that it is in line with our experience. While "it *might* be the case that corrupted criminals" really do have more than enough opportunity to receive God's salvation, "it certainly does not *seem* this way" (1994: 10). However, this opens the door to the retort that we are not in a position to make such judgments (Davison 1999: 135).

So far, each of these discussed responses to the problem of soteriological luck operates on the assumption that, possibly, some will be eternally damned—minimally, the idea is not repudiated. However, the teaching that some will be eternally damned has been rejected by certain leading Christian theologians, both in our own day and historically (for an overview, see MacDonald (2011a) and Ramelli (2013)). But if everyone is saved, it looks as if the problem of soteriological luck vanishes (for discussions, see Anderson 2011: 378; Jones 2007: 208, 214; Zagzebski 1994: 410–411).

Opting for universal salvation as a way of solving the problem of soteriological luck faces three objections. First, as we learned from Hartman, even if everyone is saved, the quality of rewards in heaven can still be a matter of luck. Hence, a significant kind of soteriological luck perhaps remains

(2014: 73–74). Second, universalism by itself does not exclude the possibility that some are given the opportunity to experience salvation sooner than others, or by way of a less torturous process. Yet it is reasonable to hold that such disparities exist and constitute bad soteriological luck (Jones 2007: 210–212; cf. Buckareff and Plug 2009: 66). Finally, many traditionally minded theologians believe that the affirmation of universalism has been off-limits ever since the condemnation of Origen's doctrine of *apocatastasis* within the fifth ecumenical council (for a discussion, see MacDonald (2011b)). So, even if it were granted that universalism solves the problem of soteriological luck, many theologians would maintain that the solution cannot be affirmed.

There is, however, a closely related solution to the problem of soteriological luck that does not require universalism per se, but a cousin of the doctrine. Andrei Buckareff and Allen Plug defend what they label "escapism," the teaching that God allows the damned an unlimited number of chances to "escape" from hell, be reconciled with God, and enjoy everlasting communion with him (2005; cf. Wessling 2017). In an additional article they then apply escapism to the problem of soteriological luck. They argue that

> if a person chooses to remain in hell, and continually affirms this choice for eternity, then, at some point, that continued affirmation would in no way be due to luck [...] but due to that person's refusal to develop the appropriate character.
>
> *Buckareff & Plug 2009: 65; cf. Jones 2007*

Escapism is not an entirely novel theological position. On the contrary, the basic idea can be found in the writings of some of the early church fathers.[5] Still, it is a teaching that will leave some Christians uncomfortable. There are biblical issues with which to contend (see MacDonald 2008: 150–158), and certain ecclesial traditions explicitly deny any postmortem opportunity to change one's eschatological destination (e.g., Roman Catholicism).[6] I leave further evaluation of such matters to the reader (relevant here are Matheson (2014) and Buckareff and Plug (2015)).

We have canvassed various ways in which one might seek to solve, or at least alleviate, the problem of soteriological luck. For the most part, the various proposals have operated independent from one another. However, as Scott Davison submits, "A more promising solution to the problem of salvific luck could be fashioned by incorporating items from several solutions into one" (1999: 136). While some have attempted to do exactly what Davison suggests (Hartman 2014; Jones 2007), the resulting solutions depend upon controversial doctrines. Thus, there is certainly much more work to be done on providing a fuller response to the problem of soteriological luck.

Before concluding this section, it is worth pointing out that it is not only humans who might be affected by soteriological luck. Even God might be subject to a similar kind of luck, namely, a luck that concerns the results of God's saving efforts. To see this, first suppose, as many contend, that, logically prior to God's decision to create, there is no truth-value concerning how merely would-be creatures would freely (in a sense that is incompatible with determinism) behave (see Rhoda 2008; Zimmerman 2012).[7] Further suppose that God decides to create rational agents who possess freedom over whether or not they appropriate the benefits of saving grace. Finally, suppose that, for any of these rational agents, God cannot ensure that these creatures will freely choose to be saved (*pace* Reitan 2004). If these suppositions are true, God does not know, at least prior to his decision to create, who will freely respond to his salvific grace, nor does he know the number or percentage that will be saved (Grössl & Vicens 2014). But if this is so, it might be said that God becomes the subject of good luck if most or all of the population appropriates his saving grace. Conversely, God might be deemed the subject of bad luck if most, or worse all, reject his grace. On such views, it is sometimes claimed, God takes "risks" in creating free creatures (e.g., Sanders 2007), and these risks can result in good or bad luck for God (cf. Leftow 2005).

Of course, the higher the divine degree of control over who is and is not saved, the lower the degree of the noted kind of divine luck. To eliminate this divine luck completely, though, perhaps one will need to say that God exhaustively controls the eternal fate of every rational creature. But stressing God's control over such matters comes with certain ostensible costs. On the one hand, if God exhaustively controls each person's salvation, and God genuinely wants to save all, then universalism becomes irresistible. But, as already mentioned, some theologians find this doctrine off-limits. An alternative is to take the Augustinian/Calvinistic line that God does not genuinely desire the salvation of all, but simply dispenses salvation as he sees fit. Some theologians welcome this paradigm, whereas others are repulsed. The upshot is that the doctrine that God is subject to luck concerning whom he can save is very much a live issue.

Luck and Petitionary Prayer

Christian theologians agree that prayer may sometimes take the form of a petition, or a request for God to bring about some state of affairs. They disagree, however, about whether or not God answers petitionary prayers—where, roughly, God answers a petition if the request plays an essential role in explaining why God performed the requested action (for a discussion, see Davison 2017a: ch. 2). Reasons for skepticism about God being in the business of answering such prayers vary (Davison 2017b), but one primary issue concerns God's goodness. When it comes to important matters—e.g., matters of life and death, heaven and hell—the claim is that a perfectly good God will do what is best (or sufficiently good) for each person, whether or not God is asked (e.g., Basinger 1983). But if this is the case, how can God be said to respond to petitionary prayers in the sense described? A common response is to claim that, sometimes, it is better for God to bring about something because it is requested than it would be for God to bring about that thing independent of any such request (e.g., Murray and Meyers 1994; Howard-Snyder & Howard-Snyder 2010; Reibsamen forthcoming; Stump 1979).

Consider a scenario where Jim's atheist friend Sally has fallen ill and is given only a few weeks to live. On one of Jim's visits to the hospital, he, entirely of his own initiative, takes Sally's hand, kneels next to her bedside and begins to pray aloud for the miraculous healing of Sally. Much to the surprise of both Jim and Sally, Sally recovers shortly thereafter. The doctors do not know what to make of Sally's speedy recovery, and, as a result, Sally comes to trust in God freely and profoundly. Let us suppose that, for reasons unbeknown to us, it would have been best for God to let Sally die, absent Jim's petition. God only chose to heal Sally because he knew that answering Jim's petition would lead Sally freely to turn to him in faith, and God deems this to be a tremendous good.[8] In such a scenario, it could be said that Jim's prayer provides God with a "scale-tripping" reason for healing Sally—i.e., the prayer factors into giving God adequate reason for bringing about that which is requested, a reason that would have been absent otherwise.

Suppose, for the purposes of illustration, that God answers petitions for important matters only when the petition is intimately tied to a scale-tipping reason for answering it. If luck refers to significant events happening to individuals that are outside of their control, then, provided that petitioners do not enjoy the requisite control over whether their prayers act as scale-tipping reasons for God to answer them, God's answering of relevantly significant petitions is a matter of luck for petitioners. But that is hardly surprising. Who would have thought that humans could control God's answers to their prayers? But there are three additional related kinds of luck that are perhaps more weighty (for discussions of two more kinds of related luck, see Davison 2017a: ch. 5 and 142–146).

First, whether or not God has scale-tipping reasons for answering prayers might often be outside his control, and so whether or not God has adequate reason to answer a petition might often be a matter of luck *for him*. This is the case, at any rate, if we assume that (a) many of the goods connected to God's scale-tipping reasons for answering prayers are inextricably tied to how humans freely choose to respond to God's answers to prayer, and (b) God cannot control how humans freely behave (i.e., if human beings have a kind of indeterminist freedom).

An instance of divine luck of this kind can be found in the Sally scenario. Independent of Jim's prayer, God's total reasons favor letting Sally die. It is only Jim's petition plus Sally's foreknown free response that provides God with a scale-tipping reason for healing Sally. So, it might sometimes be that God has insufficient reason to do something that he finds intrinsically worthwhile (because his total reasons favor not doing it), unless someone asks God to bring about that thing *and* the good of God answering that prayer is affiliated with some free creaturely response that factors into giving God the relevant scale-tipping reason. Said differently, God's ability to bless his children by answering their prayers as an expression of what is best is often a matter of luck, for God.

Certainly, many contend that what God can accomplish with free creatures is often beyond God's complete control, and in that sense a matter of luck (e.g., Fringer & Lane 2015). But there seems to be something especially strange about the idea that for certain kinds of good states of affairs that God has the power to bring about directly (e.g., healing someone), God's ability to secure such good states himself, as an expression of the best, can be a matter of luck. Issues of divine freedom immediately arise (see, Davison 2017a: ch. 3), and further work could be done on this type of divine luck.

Second, there is the luck of being the beneficiary of someone else's petition. Notice, on the Sally and Jim scenario, Sally is healed (in part) because Jim requested it. If Jim had not prayed, Sally would not have been healed. But since Sally had no control over Jim's prayer (suppose that Sally would never have thought to ask for such a thing), her being healed is a matter of luck for her. If God regularly answers petitionary prayers, presumably the beneficiaries of such prayers are often lucky in similar ways.

Some have found this implication untoward. Here is H.D. Lewis on the matter (1959: 255):

> Ought not God to benefit men according to their needs or merits and not in terms of the rather haphazard and arbitrary condition of being the subject of prayer? Should momentous things, like recovery from sickness, depend on someone's asking God?

When it comes to important goods in your life, Lewis thinks, these should not depend upon whether someone else asks God to give them to you. Better, instead, for God simply to grant these goods to you, or make you merit them in some way, and not make them such "haphazard and arbitrary" matters of luck.

Is this kind of luck prohibitively odd? Many profound goods in a person's life are dependent upon the unmerited and "arbitrary" kindness of others, which can be described rightly as luck. Thus, it is not clear that the luck that Lewis highlights is problematic. Moreover, some contend that part of the reason God has set up a system wherein petitionary prayers for others are effective is precisely because it extends the reach of one's responsibility for others beyond its natural boundaries (Swinburne 1998: 115; Choi 2016: 41–42; Howard-Snyder & Howard-Snyder 2010: 51–54). On this way of thinking, I can now positively influence faraway victims of natural disasters that I am unable to help through any other means besides prayer. But if this is so, then, it could be argued, the luck of being the beneficiary of prayer is not radically different from being the beneficiary of other ways of lending a helping hand (cf. Taliaferro 2007: 621).

However, Davison (2017a: 126–129) claims that the idea that petitionary prayer allows one to extend one's responsibility beyond natural borders generates a third kind of luck. Since it is God who chooses whether to grant that which is prayed for, there is the luck of whether or not one's attempts to broaden the reach of one's responsibility succeed. On the assumption that one is morally appraisable for the *results* of one's attempts to broaden one's responsibility through prayer, a kind of moral luck arguably follows: An individual is morally appraisable for certain significant results of her prayer that are beyond the individual's control. Davison acknowledges that one could respond by claiming that God will only morally appraise persons for what they pray, not that which he chooses to bring about in response to these prayers. Yet Davison contends that this response sucks the life out of the extended-responsibility motivation for believing that God answers petitions. This is because it then "seems that extending human responsibility for things through petitionary prayer would not make a difference to God; God would care only about the underlying attitudes and intentions, not the actual responsibility" (2017a: 128).

Much could be said in response to Davison's criticism of the extend-responsibility defense of petitionary prayer (see, e.g., Choi 2016: 54–59). But however one prefers to respond, we see from the foregoing that *if* God answers petitionary prayers, luck is connected to this practice in a variety of ways. Perhaps, then, it is not too much to suggest that an evaluation of the role of petitionary luck should factor prominently within future debates about whether God answers petitions.

Conclusion

Throughout this essay various ways in which creatures, and even God, might be affected by luck have been discussed. It is worth pausing to ask what value there might be in reflecting upon such luck. Is the value merely theoretical, or is there some more immediate spiritual benefit as well?

Begin with the luck that affects creatures. Reflecting on the means by which creatures, especially humans, are affected by luck highlights ways in which the control they have over their lives is quite limited. I submit that reflection upon these luck-based limitations can help stave off pride and abet a sense of dependency on God (cf. Hartman 2017: 14–15; Pollard 1958: 87–88). It is largely God, after all, who chooses which kinds of luck impact his creatures. He sets the rules; creatures are subject to them.

At the same time, if God undergoes luck, much or all of it ultimately stems from his free choice to create. He has then chosen to condescend into a kind of give-and-take relationship with creatures that makes him the subject of significant and uncontrolled good and bad events within his life. God would only do such a thing, it seems, if he greatly cares about, even respects, creatures—at least this appears to be the case for many of the kinds of divine luck surveyed. Given this, it is reasonable to think that reflecting upon the ways in which God's concern for creatures generates luck for himself can also be spiritually rewarding. So, for both theoretical and spiritual reasons, the theology of luck remains an issue worthy of further exploration.[9]

Notes

1 The following authors rarely use the word "luck" in their writings about an autonomous creation. Nevertheless, the concept is certainly there.
2 Polkinghorne responds to this kind of objection as follows: "humanity is so intimately connected with the physical world that gave it birth, that it might be thought that only a universe to which the free-process defence applied could give rise to beings subject to the free will defence" (1998: 4). Very briefly, the problem with this response is that it fundamentally changes the nature of the free-process defense, from the good of a self-creating cosmos to the good of a cosmos that prepares the way for free creatures.
3 After a brief historical survey of philosophical conceptions of beauty, Crispin Sartwell claims that "in almost all treatments of beauty, even the most apparently object or objectively-oriented, there is a moment in which the subjective qualities of the experience of beauty are emphasized: rhapsodically, perhaps, or in terms of pleasure" (Sartwell 2014).
4 Zagzebski argues that soteriological luck is worse than the standard problem of moral luck (1994: 402–404). For a response, see Davison (1999: 130–132).
5 See Maspero (2009: 55–64), and Ramelli (2013: *passim*).
6 See, e.g., the *Catechism of the Catholic Church*: 393, 1021. For Roman Catholic resources for mitigating soteriological luck in a manner that is similar to escapism (see D'Costa 2009: ch. 7; cf. Timpe 2015).
7 God may even be the subject of a kind of soteriological luck if Molinism is true (see Hartman 2014: 85).
8 Alternatively, for our open theist friends, we may suppose that God knows that Sally's trusting in him in response to her being healed is *likely* at this time given her current spiritual and existential state.

Theology and Luck

9 Research for this chapter was supported by the John Templeton Foundation-funded Analytic Theology for Theological Formation project, which is led by Oliver Crisp at Fuller Theological Seminary. Many thanks to Oliver, Fuller Theological Seminary, and the John Templeton Foundation for making this chapter possible. I also owe a debt of gratitude to James Arcadi, Jesse Gentile, Robert Hartman, J.T. Turner, and Chris Woznicki for helpful comments on earlier versions of this essay. Finally, an extra special thanks goes to David Cannon for comments on this chapter as well as help with its preparation.

References

Anderson, M.B. (2011) "Molinism, Open Theism, and Soteriological Luck," *Religious Studies* 47(3), 371–81.

Ballantyne, N. (2012) "Luck and Interests," *Synthese* 185(3), 319–334.

Bartholomew, D. (2008) *God, Chance and Purpose: Can God Have it Both Ways?* Cambridge: Cambridge University Press.

Basinger, D. (1983) "Why Petition an Omnipotent, Omniscient, Wholly Good God?" *Religious Studies* 19(1), 25–42.

Broncano-Berrocal, F. (2015) "Luck as Risk and the Lack of Control Account of Luck," *Metaphilosophy* 46(1), 1–25.

Brown, W.P. (2011) *Ecclesiastes*, Louisville, KY: Westminster John Knox Press.

Buckareff, A.A., & Plug, A. (2005) "Escaping Hell: Divine Motivation and the Problem of Hell," *Religious Studies* 41(1), 39–54.

———. (2009) "Escapism, Religious Luck, and Divine Reasons for Action," *Religious Studies* 45(1), 63–72.

———. (2015) "Escaping Hell but Not Heaven," *International Journal of Philosophy of Religion* 77(3), 247–253.

Catechism of the Catholic Church. (2000) 2nd ed. Washington, DC: Libreria Editrice Vaticana.

Choi, I. (2016) "Is Petitionary Prayer Superfluous?" in Jonathan Kvanvig (ed.) *Oxford Studies in Philosophy of Religion*, vol. 7, Oxford: Oxford University Press, pp. 32–62.

Coffman, E.J. (2007) "Thinking about Luck," *Synthese* 158(3), 385–398.

Collins, R. (2011) "Divine Action and Evolution," in T.P. Flint & M.C. Rea (eds.) *The Oxford Handbook of Philosophical Theology*, New York: Oxford University Press, pp. 241–261.

Craig, W.L. (1989) "'No Other Name': A Middle Knowledge Perspective on the Exclusivity of Salvation through Christ," *Faith and Philosophy* 6(2), 172–188.

Davison, S. (1999) "Salvific Luck," *International Journal for Philosophy of Religion* 45(2), 129–137.

———. (2017a) *Petitionary Prayer: A Philosophical Investigation*, New York: Oxford University Press.

———. (2017b) "Petitionary Prayer," in *The Stanford Encyclopedia of Philosophy* (Summer 2017 Edition), Edward N. Zalta (ed.) https://plato.stanford.edu/archves/sum2017/entries/petitionary-prayer/.

D'Costa, G. (2009) *Christianity and World Religions: Disputed Questions in the Theology of Religions*, Malden, MA: Wiley-Blackwell.

Fringer, R.A., & Lane, J.K. (2015) *Theology of Luck: Fate, Chaos, and Faith.* Kansas City, MO: Beacon Hill.

Gould, S.J. (1989) *Wonderful Life: The Burgess Shale and the Nature of History*, New York: W.W. Norton & Company.

Grössl, J., & Vicens, L. (2014) "Closing the Door on Limited-Risk Open Theism," *Faith and Philosophy* 31(4), 475–485.

Hartman, R.J. (2014) "How to Apply Molinism to the Theological Problem of Moral Luck," *Faith and Philosophy* 31(1), 68–90.

———. (2017) *In Defense of Moral Luck: Why Luck Often Affects Praiseworthiness and Blameworthiness*, New York: Routledge.

Haught, J. (2003) *Deeper than Darwin: The Prospect for Religion in the Age of Evolution*, Boulder, CO: Westview Press.

———. (2010) "Science, God and Cosmic Purpose," in P. Harrison (ed.) *The Cambridge Companion to Science and Religion*, New York, NY: Cambridge University Press, pp. 260–277.

Hecht, J.M. (2016) "Ancient Hebraic Voices of Chance and Choice over Fate and Justice," in K.H. Gibberson (ed.) *Abraham's Dice: Chance and Providence in the Monotheistic Traditions*, New York: Oxford University Press, pp. 14–35.

Howard-Snyder, D., & Howard-Snyder, F. (2010) "The Puzzle of Petitionary Prayer," *European Journal for Philosophy of Religion* 2(2), 43–68.

Johnson, E.A. (2014) *Ask the Beasts: Darwin and the God of Love*, London: Bloomsbury Academic.

Jones, R.E. (2007) "Escapism and Luck," *Religious Studies* 43(2), 206–216.

Katzoff, C. (2004) "Religious Luck and Religious Virtue," *Religious Studies* 40(1), 97–111.

Leftow, B. (2005) "No Best World: Moral Luck," *Religious Studies* 41(2), 165–181.

Lewis, H.D. (1959) *Our Experience of God*, London: Allen & Unwin.

MacDonald, G. (2008) *The Evangelical Universalist: The Biblical Hope that God's Love Will Save Us All*, London: SPCK.

——— (2011a) *"All Shall Be Well": Explorations in Universal Salvation and Christian Theology from Origen to Moltmann*, Cambridge: James Clark & Co.

——. (2011b) "Introduction: Between Heresy and Dogma," in G. McDonald (ed.) *"All Shall Be Well": Explorations in Universal Salvation and Christian Theology from Origen to Moltmann*, Cambridge: James Clark & Co., pp. 1–28.

Maspero, G. (2009) "Apocatastasis," in L.F. Mateo-Seco & G. Maspero (eds.), S. Cherney (trans.) *The Brill Dictionary of Gregory of Nyssa*, Leiden: Brill, pp. 55–64.

Matheson, B. (2014) "Escaping Heaven," *International Journal for Philosophy of Religion* 75(3),197–206.

Miller, D.B. (2010) *Ecclesiastes*, Scottdale, PN: Herald Press.

Miller, K.R. (2007) *Finding Darwin's God: A Scientist's Search for Common Ground between God and Evolution*, New York: Harper.

Miller, R.W. (2016) "Chance and Providence in Early Christianity," in K.H. Gibberson (ed.) *Abraham's Dice: Chance and Providence in the Monotheistic Traditions*, New York: Oxford University Press, pp. 129–157.

Mizrahi, M. (2014) "The Problem of Natural Inequality: A New Problem of Evil," *Philosophia* 42(1), 127–136.

Moltmann, J. (1973) *Theology and Joy*, London: SCM.

Monod, J. (1972) *Chance and Necessity*, New York: Vintage Books.

Morris, S.C. (2003) *Life's Solution: Inevitable Humans in a Lonely Universe*, Cambridge: Cambridge University Press.

Murray, M.J. (2011) *Nature Red in Tooth and Claw: Theism and the Problem of Animal Suffering*, New York: Oxford University Press.

Murray, M., & Meyers, K. (1994) "Ask and It Will Be Given to You," *Religious Studies* 30(3), 311–330.

Nagel, T. (1979) *Mortal Questions*, New York: Cambridge University Press.

Oates, W.E. (1995) *Luck: A Secular Faith*, Louisville, KY: Westminster John Knox Press.

Peacocke, A. (1979) *Creation and the World of Science*, Oxford: Oxford University Press.

——. (1984) *Intimations of Reality*, Greencastle, IN: DePauw University Press.

Pelikan, J. (1993) *Christianity and Classical Culture: The Metamorphosis of Natural Theology in the Christian Encounter with Hellenism*, New Haven, CT: Yale University Press.

Perszyk, K. (ed.) (2011) *Molinism: The Contemporary Debate*, Oxford: Oxford University Press.

Plantinga, A. (2011) *Where the Conflict Really Lies: Science, Religion, and Naturalism*, New York: Oxford University Press.

Polkinghorne, J.C. (1989) *Science and Providence: God's Interaction with the World*, West Conshohocken, PA: Templeton Press.

——. (1998) *Science and Theology: An Introduction*, Minneapolis: Fortress Press.

Pollard, W.G. (1958) *Chance and Providence: God's Action in a World Governed by Scientific Law*, New York: Charles Scribner's Sons.

Pritchard, D. (2005) *Epistemic Luck*, Oxford: Oxford University Press.

Ramelli, I. (2013) *The Christian Doctrine of Apokatastasis: A Critical Assessment from the New Testament to Eriugena*, Boston, MA: Brill.

Rasmussen, J., & Wessling, J. (2015) "Reasons for Randomness: A Solution to the Axiological Problem for Theists," *Theology and Science* 13(3), 288–304.

——. (2017) "A Randomness-Based Theodicy for Evolutionary Evils," *Zygon* 52(4), 984–1004.

Ratzsch, D. (1998) "Design, Chance & Theistic Evolution," in W.A. Dembski (ed.) *Mere Creation: Science, Faith & Intelligent Design*, Downers Grove, IL: InterVarsity Press, pp. 289–312.

Reibsamen, J. (forthcoming) "Divine Goodness and the Efficacy of Petitionary Prayer," *Religious Studies.*

Reitan, E. (2004) "Human Freedom and the Impossibility of Damnation," in R.A. Parry & C.H. Partridge (eds.) *Universal Salvation? The Current Debate*, Grand Rapids, MI: Eerdmans Publishing Co. pp. 125–142.

Rhoda, A.R. (2008) "Generic Open Theism and Some Varieties Thereof," *Religious Studies* 44(2), 225–234.

Riggs, W. (2009) "Luck, Knowledge, and Control," in A. Haddock, A. Millar, & D. Pritchard (eds.) *Epistemic Value*, Oxford: Oxford University Press, pp. 204–221.

Rissler, J.D. (2006) "Open Theism: Does God Risk or Hope?" *Religious Studies* 42(1), 63–74.

Sanders, J. (2007) *The God Who Risks: A Theology of Divine Providence*, 2nd ed., Downers Grove, IL: InterVarsity.

Sartwell, C. (2014) "Beauty," in *The Stanford Encyclopedia of Philosophy* (Spring 2014 Edition), Edward N. Zalta (ed.) http://plato.stanford.edu/archives/spr2014/entries/beauty/.

Silva, I. (2016) "Thomas Aquinas on Natural Contingency and Providence," in K.H. Gibberson (ed.) *Abraham's Dice: Chance and Providence in the Monotheistic Traditions*, New York: Oxford University Press, pp. 158–174.

Smith, Q. (1993) "Infinity and the Past," in W.L. Craig & Q. Smith, *Theism, Atheism, and Big Bang Cosmology*, New York: Oxford University Press, pp. 77–91.

Sproul, R.C. (1994) *Not a Chance: The Myth of Chance in Modern Science*, Grand Rapids, MI: Baker Books.

Stump, E. (1979) "Petitionary Prayer," *American Philosophical Quarterly* 16(2), 81–91.

Swinburne, R. (1998) *Providence and the Problem of Evil*, Oxford: Oxford University Press.

Taliaferro, C. (2007) "Prayer," in C. Meister & P. Copan (eds.) *The Routledge Companion to Philosophy of Religion*, London: Routledge, pp. 617–625.

Timpe, K. (2015) "An Argument for Limbo," *Journal of Ethics* 19(3–4), 277–292.

Tracy, T.F. (2007) "The Lawfulness of Nature and the Problem of Evil," in N. Murphy, R.J. Russell, & W.R. Stoeger, S.J. (eds.) *Physics and Cosmology: Scientific Perspectives on the Problem of Natural Evil*, vol. 1, Vatican Observatory: Vatican City State, pp. 153–178.

VanArragon, R. (2001) "Transworld Damnation and Craig's Contentious Suggestion," *Faith and Philosophy* 18(2), 241–260.

Walls, J.L. (2002) *Heaven: The Logic of Eternal Joy*, New York: Oxford University Press.

Wessling, J. (2017) "How Does a Loving God Punish? On the Unification of God's Love and Punitive Wrath," *International Journal of Systematic Theology* 19(4), 421–443.

Zagzebski, L. (1994) "Religious Luck," *Faith and Philosophy* 11(3), 397–413.

Zimmerman, D. (2012) "The Providential Usefulness of 'Simple Foreknowledge'," in K.J. Clark & M. Rea (eds.) *Reason, Metaphysics, and Mind: New Essays on the Philosophy of Alvin Plantinga*, New York, NY: Oxford University Press, pp. 174–202.

INDEX

Abelard, P. 49–50
ability *see* virtue epistemology
ability-relative safety 312, 315
accident 96, 152
achievement *see* performance normativity; virtue epistemology
action theory 46–7
adaptation 361–2
Aetiological Symmetry (AS) 444, 446, 448
Aëtius 36
agency *see* control; subjectivity
agent causation 239, 244 *see also* indeterminism
agent regret 108, 431–2
Aitken, M. 352
Alexander of Aphrodisias 36–7
Alexander, L. 224
analysandum 149–51
Anderson, E. 80
anger 431–2
anti-luck epistemology 115, 118, 308–10, 401–3; ethical activity 293; experimental philosophy 405–11; extended mind 320–6; Gettier cases 284–7, 290; internalist 289–92; performance normativity 185–8; safety theory 99–101, 287–9, 312–15, 318–26; sensitivity condition 98–9, 285–7, 311–14; virtue epistemology 98, 187–8, 290, 315–16, 403
Aquinas, T. 45–6; action theory 46–7; circumstantial luck 53–5; consequences 50–2; constitutive luck 52–3; *Disputed Questions on Evil* 47–8; frustrated sinners 47–50; resultant luck 50–2; *Summa Theologiae* 48–50
area under the receiver operator curve (AUC) 277–82
aretaic luck 221
Aristotle 13–15, 22, 315, 429; constitutive luck 17–20, 31–2; developmental luck 19–21; happiness 25–32; *Physics* and the *Nicomachean Ethics* 15–16; resultant luck 21–2
asymmetry view 231–3

Athanassoulis, N. 13–22, 151
Austin, J.L. 409
autonomous creation 452–4
axiological luck 220
Axtell, G. 436–49
Ayer, A.J. 94

background knowledge 367–8
Bacon, F. 393
Ballantyne, N. 118, 131, 160–9, 342
Barth, K. 441–2
basis-relative safety 312
Batson, C. 209
belief *see* epistemic luck; epistemology; Gettier cases
Bernard, C. 397
binarism 183, 186
binary gambles 142–3
biological contingency 398
Bion of Borysthenes 35
Black, T. 284–93
blame 109, 222–3, 229–30
Blancha, D. 165
BonJour, L. 127
Bradford, G. 187
broaden and build effect 381–3
Broadie, S. 25–32
Broncano-Berrocal, F. 171–81
Brouwer, R. 34–42
Buckareff, A. 457
Buckwalter, W. 408
Burge, T. 291
Burns, W. 353
Byrd, S. 64–5

Calhoun, C. 430
capacity epistemic luck 96, 263
Card, C. 151, 428–30
Carter, J.A. 318–26
categorization tasks 276–7

Index

causal luck 66–7, 211

causal reasoning 366–7

causation 36–7, 212, 217–18 *see also* determinism; indeterminism; legal causation

Chalmers, D. 320–1

chance *see* probability; probability account of luck

Chisholm, R. 94

choice 16, 21, 244–6 *see also* determinism; indeterminism

Christianity 437, 451–2, 460; creation 452–4; petitionary prayer 458–60; soteriological luck 454–8 *see also* religious luck

Chrysippus of Soli 37

Church, I. 186–7, 261–70

Cicero 39

circumstantial luck 53–5, 62–3, 110, 197–8, 209–10, 229–31

Clark, A. 320–1

Clark, L. 352

close sensitivity 314

closeness heuristic 349

closure principle 99, 286

Coffman, E.J. 95, 131, 150, 154, 157, 164–5, 342

cognitive bias 335, 341; framing 335–9; optimism 339–40, 342–3; serial position effect 337–9 *see also* illusion of control

cognitive emotions 357

cognitive externalism 321–3

cognitive fixedness thesis 319–23, 325–6

cognitive internalism 320

cognitive limits 398–9

Cohen, G.A. 80

Cohen, J. 385

coincidence 156, 177–8

Colaço, D. 406, 408

colonialism 393

compatibilism 243–4, 248–9, 256; Levy's objection 250–4, 256; Pérez de Calleja's objection 254–6

completeness criterion 28

Conee, E. 308

consequences *see* resultant luck

constitutive luck 16–21, 31–2, 111, 155, 210, 251–3; Aquinas 52–3; Kant 59–62; legal 415–16, 422–3; religious 439–40

Construal Level Theory 348

constructivism 161; objectivism 163–4; subjectivism 162–3, 168

content epistemic luck 96, 262–3

contingency 392–3, 399; biological and cognitive limits 398; cultural side effects 398; environmental 397; and history 393–5; pscyhological 396–7; simple 397–8; sources of 395–6; timing 397

contrastive nature of luck 346–8

control 45–6, 54, 96–7, 120–2, 153–4, 156–7, 199, 209, 217–18, 243; aretaic luck 221; axiological luck 220; complete/partial 218, 222; deontic luck 219–20; direct/indirect 218; environmental mastery 384–5; feminism 426–8; guidance 218; hypological luck 221–5; intentional/unintentional 218; legal luck 414–23; tracking and effective 180–1 *see also* illusion of control; lack of control account of luck

coping 361

Counter-inductive Thinking (CIT) 445

counterfactual view 229–31

counterfactuals 346–9, 380–1

Craig, E. 313

creation 452–4

credit theory of knowledge 128

criminal attempts 414

criminal law 421

criterial religious luck 440

Csikszentmihaly, M. 379

cultural variation 407

Cynics 34–6

Cyr, T. 252

Damasio, A. 357

Dancy, J. 95

danger 350–1

Darke, P.R. 352

Darley, J. 209

Davison, S. 457, 459–60

Day, L. 334

de Ridder, J. 447

defeasibility 292

Delfabbro, P.H. 370

Della Porta, M.D. 385

Dennett, D. 370

deontic luck 219–20

derivative responsibility 208

determinism 37–8, 154–5, 248–50, 256, 439–40, 452–3; indeterminism 239–40, 242–6, 249, 254–5, 452–3 *see also* causal luck; causality; compatibilism

developmental luck *see* constitutive luck

diachronic knowledge 300

Diamond, J. 393

Dillon, R.L. 353

Diogenes Laertius 35–6

direct virtue epistemology (DVE) 187–9

discrimination 307–8, 312

dispositional optimism *see* optimism

doxastic epistemic luck 96, 263

Dretske, F. 98

Dual Process Theory 357–8

Duff, A. 421

duty 60–2

early Stoics 34–8

egalitarianism *see* luck egalitarianism; relational egalitarianism

Ejova, A. 365–74

Ekstrom, L.W. 239–46

eliminativism 167–9

emotions 357, 360–2, 431–2; positive 381–3; and risk 357–9; and uncertainty 359–60

endowment 251–3

Enoch, D. 418, 422–3

Index

environmental luck 186, 264, 273–4, 282, 323–4; area under the receiver operator curve (AUC) 281–2; generalized environmental luck 274–6, 281–2; problem of 274–5; religious 442; scientific progress 397

environmental mastery 384–5

Enzle, M.E. 352, 371

Epictetus 41

Epicurus 37

epistemic individualism 308–9

epistemic luck 95–7, 127–8, 198–9, 262–5; extended 323–6; religious 437–8 *see also* environmental luck; intervening luck; veritic luck

epistemic virtue *see* virtue epistemology

epistemology 37–8, 40–2, 94–5, 126–7; cognitive fixedness thesis 319–23, 325–6; modally inspired 98–102, 115–22; performance normativity 184–90 *see also* anti-luck epistemology; Gettier cases; luck/ knowledge incompatibility thesis; skeptical argument

Epstude, K. 348

equality *see* luck egalitarianism

error theory 233–6

escapism 457

ethical activity 293

ethics *see* moral luck

eudaimonia 25–32, 38

event causation 239–40, 242–6 *see also* indeterminism

evidence *see* experimental philosophy

evidential luck/evidential epistemic luck 96, 185–6, 263, 302–3, 319; religious 440–2

exceptionalist dilemma 445–6

Exclusivist Asymmetries (EA) 444–5

executive decision 217–18

expectation 138–43

expected outcomes view (EOV) 184, 187–90

experimental method 393–4

experimental philosophy 401, 404–5; anti-luck epistemology 405–11; limits and recommendations 410–11; negative program 405–9; positive 409–10

explanation 398–9

exploitation 132–3

extended epistemic luck 323–6

extended mind theory (EMT) 320–4, 326

externalism 126–8, 310–15, 320–3 *see also* safety condition; sensitivity condition; virtue epistemology

fallibilism 266–70, 291–2

Familial-Cultural Displacement Symmetry (DS) 444

Feinberg, J. 216, 455

Feit, N. 268–70

Feldman, R. 308

feminism 426, 433; agency 426–8; illegitimate moral demands 432–4; impossible moral demands 431–2; responsibility 428–9; virtue 429–32

Flanders, C. 74

Fodor, J. 396

Forman-Barzilai, F. 76

fortune 156–8

framing 335–9

Fredrickson, B. 381–3

free will *see* compatibilism; determinism; indeterminism

Freedman, J.L. 352

freedom 67

Friedman, O. 406

gamblers 137, 333–4, 340–1, 352–3 *see also* illusion of control

Garrett, A. 71, 74

Gauguin thought experiment 21, 106–8

generalized environmental luck 274–6, 281–2

Gettier cases 94–5, 128, 155, 183, 185–90, 261–2, 270; anti-luck epistemology 284–7, 290; experimental philosophy 401–11; Howard-Snyder et al.'s objection to 268–70; luck/knowledge incompatibility thesis 297–8, 300–1; religious luck 441–2; types of luck 262–5; warrant 265–8

Gettier, E. 94–5, 98–9, 101–2, 126, 296–7

Gettier Problem 95, 188, 261–70, 402

God *see* Christianity; religious luck

Goldberg, J. 420

Goldman, A. 98, 402, 407

good fortune 17–18

good will 60

grace 55, 432, 437, 452

gradability 172, 179, 211–12

gratitude 379–81

Greco, J. 101, 151, 234–5, 240, 305–16, 411

Griffith, M. 239

Griffiths, P.J. 441–2

Griffiths, T.L. 367

guess *see* epistemic luck

guidance control 218

habituation 19–20

Hahn, U. 369, 373

Haji, I. 220, 251

Hales, S. 148, 198–200, 333–43, 353

Hankins, K. 74

Hanley, R.P. 71

happiness 25–32, 57–9, 361–2

harm *see* resultant luck

Harper, W. 96, 152

Hartman, R. 129, 133, 206, 227–36, 253–4, 423, 438, 455

Haught, J. 453

Hause, J. 45–55

Hawthorne, J. 101

Helmer, E. 35

Henry, J. 396

Herdova, M. 209

Herman, B. 423–4

Herstein, O.J. 414–24

Hetherington, S. 295–303, 401

high-chance-close-world principle (HCCW) 101

highest good 26–7

Hinduism 439

historical contingency *see* contingency

Holmes, O.W. 416

Holtzman, G. 408
Honore, T. 419–20
Horvath, J. 407
Howard-Snyder, D. 268–70
Howard-Snyder, F. 268–70
Hume, D. 71–2
Hursthouse, R. 429
Hutcheson, F. 71–2
hypological luck 221–5

idiosyncrasy 396–7
ignorance 37
illegitimate moral demands 432–4
illusion of control 365, 372–4, 384; background
    knowledge 367–8; definition 366–7; modal
    account of luck 370–2; theory of randomness 369;
    theory of supernatural entities 369–70, 372–3
impartiality principle 85–6
impossible moral demands 431–2
incompatibilism *see* indeterminism
indeterminism 239–40, 242–6, 249, 254–5, 452–3;
    determinism 37–8, 154–5, 248–50, 256, 439–40,
    452–3
inductive risk 443–8
infallibilism 266–70
inheritance tax 83
integrity 429–31
intellectual virtue 290
intention 16, 47–50, 72–3 *see also* choice
interest linkage 164, 342
internalism 126–8, 308–10; cognitive 320; skeptical
    argument 308
internalist anti-luck epistemology 289–92
intervening luck 186, 264–5, 267, 274–5, 323–4;
    religious 441–2
invisible hand 71–2

James, W. 438
Jarvis, B. 273–82, 324–5
Jenkins, H.M. 367
Jensen, T.K. 380
Johnson, J.A. 333–43, 353
Judaism 437
justification 106–8, 126–8, 289–90 *see also* Gettier
    cases

Kahan, D.M. 357
Kahneman, D. 335–6, 357
Kampa, S. 160–9
Kant, I. 57, 67–8, 106, 219, 309–10; causal luck 66–7;
    circumstantial luck 62–3; constitutive luck 59–62;
    Critique of Practical Reason 62–3; *Groundwork for
    the Metaphysics of Morals* 57–62; happiness 57–9;
    imputation 64–6; merit 65–6; resultant luck 63–6
Katzoff, C. 437
Kearns, S. 209
Kenny, A. 21
Keren, G.B. 351
Keyes, C.L.M. 384
Kierkegaard, S. 292–3

Kim, M. 407
Kittay, E. 431
knowledge *see* epistemic luck; epistemology
Kripke, S. 155
Kuhn, T. 394, 396

lack of control account of luck (LCAL) 125, 129–30,
    137, 151–2, 216–17, 228, 240–1, 341; exploitation
    132–3; moral luck 129, 199–203; and risk 174,
    179–81; significance condition 130–1
Lackey, J. 118–19, 149, 156–7
Langer, E. 365–6
Lasonen-Aarnio, M. 101
Latus, A. 96, 105–12, 132, 154, 228
legal causation 415–16
legal luck 414–17, 421–4; agency 419–20; justification
    420–1; and moral luck 417–18; and plain luck
    422–3; *pro tanto* 418–20
Levy, N. 148, 154–6, 210, 242, 250–6, 370
Lewis, D. 421
Lewis, H.D. 459
Li, H. 352
libertarianism *see* indeterminism
Lockhart, J. 200–2
Lockhart, T. 200–2
Lucas, R.E. 362
luck binarism 183, 186
luck egalitarianism 80–4; impartiality principle
    85–6; merit principle 86–8; sufficiency
    principle 86
luck/knowledge compatibility thesis 302–3
luck/knowledge incompatibility thesis 295–7;
    an objection and reply 301–2; critical evaluation
    298–9; epistemological significance 297–8;
    examples 300–1
Lyubomirsky, S. 385

McCabe, H. 82
McDowell, J. 290–2
Machery, E. 401–11
McKinnon, R. 183–90
McLeod, C. 426–33
magic luck 352–4
Maltby, J. 334
Mandeville, B. 71, 74
Marcus Aurelius 41
Markovits, D. 80–1
Maslow, A. 379
Mele, A. 251, 255
memory capacity 369
merit principle 86–8
method of cases 404–6
Milburn, J. 401–11
Mill, J.S. 80–1, 437–8, 443; impartiality principle
    85–6; inheritance tax 83; luck egalitarianism
    81–4; merit principle 86–8; primogeniture 82–3;
    relational egalitarianism 89–90; subsistence aid
    83–4; sufficiency principle 86; women's rights
    84–5
Miracchi, L. 187–9

Index

mixed account of luck 148–9, 151–3, 158; control condition 153–4; critiques and responses 155–8; modal condition 154–5; significance condition 153

modal account of luck 97–101, 115–22, 152–3, 285, 311–15, 318, 341, 403; competing accounts 118–22; core modal account of luck 116–17; illusion of control 370–2; and risk 173–4, 177–8; significance condition 97, 117–18, 120–1

Molinism 455–6

Möller, N. 358

Montaigne, M. 443

Montmort, P.R. 333–4

Moore, A. 151

Moore, M. 231, 423

moral agency see control

moral evaluation 109, 234–5

moral justification see justification

moral luck 15–16, 105–6, 206–7, 216–19, 227–9, 417; Aquinas 45–55; aretaic luck 221; axiological luck 220; causal luck 66–7, 211; circumstantial luck 53–5, 62–3, 110, 197–8, 209–10, 229–31; definitional critiques 195–202; deontic luck 219–20; error theory 233–6; feminism 426–33; graded moral responsibility 211–12; hypological luck 221–5; lack of control account of luck (LCAL) 129, 199–203; and legal luck 417–18 see also constitutive luck; Nagel, T.; resultant luck; Williams, B.

moral obligation 219–20; illegitimate 432–3; impossible 431–2

moral responsibility see responsibility

Moran, K. 57–68

Morillo, C. 96, 152

multi-outcome situations 143–5

Murray, M. 453

Nagel, T. 155, 407, 415, 428; epistemic luck 309–10; history of luck 15, 17, 46, 59–60, 62–4, 66–7, 105, 108–12; moral luck 196–200, 202–3, 206–7, 221–3, 240 see also moral luck

natural causes see constitutive luck

natural goods 26–32

natural virtues 18, 52–3 see also virtue

Navarro, D.J. 370

negative experimental philosophy 405–9

negligence 73–4, 414

New Problem (religious luck) 443–8

Nichols, S. 407

non-moral goods 27–32

non-relational sense of luck 172

norms see performative normativity

Nozick, R. 98, 285–7, 361

Nussbaum, M.C. 20, 309, 362

objectivism 154, 161–2, 168; constructivist 163–4; realist 165–8

obligation see moral obligation

odds-luck 137, 143

ontology 36–7, 40–2

optimism 339–40, 342–3, 361, 383–4

"ought" implies "can" (OIC) 219–20

Panaetius 39

parallelism argument 232–3

parity principle 320–1

Pasteur, L. 396

Payson, J. 431

Peels, R. 148–58

Pereboom, D. 244

Pérez de Calleja, M. 254–6

performance normativity 183–5; achievement and skill 187–90; anti-luck 185–7

Persaeus 38

personal luck 352

Perszyk, K. 456

pessimism 339–40, 342–3, 361

petitionary prayer 458–60

piacular 74

plain luck 422–3

Plantinga, A. 98, 447

Plato 38, 94, 295–6, 300, 302–3, 309–10

Plug, A. 457

Plutarch 36–7

Polkinghorne, J. 453

Polybius 40

Ponesse, J. 432

Posidonius 39–40

positive emotions 381–3

positive experimental philosophy 409–10

positive psychology 379, 385; environmental mastery 384–5; gratitude 379–81; optimism 383–4; positive emotions 381–3

pragmatism 118

prayer 458–60

predetermination 439–40

present luck 251–6

Priestley, J. 395–6

primogeniture 82–3

Pritchard, D. 402–4, 410–11, 441–2; epistemic luck 262–5, 285, 287–9, 302, 318; history of luck 95–7, 99–100; moral luck 195–8; nature of luck 115–22, 148, 152, 162–3, 167–9, 174–5, 185–6; psychology of luck 334, 360, 370 see also modal account of luck

private property 88

probability account of luck 96, 100–1, 116, 136–8, 145–6, 277, 333–4, 341, 349; binary gambles 142–3; expectation 138–43; multi-outcome situations 143–5; and risk 173, 176–8; subjectivity 138–40 see also modal account of luck; risk

problem-solving 370, 372–3; background knowledge 367–8; theory of randomness 369; theory of supernatural entities 369–70, 372–3

Proclus 38

progress see scientific progress

property (luck as) 149–50

proportional luck 140

psychological contingency 396–7

punishment 64–5, 421

purposefulness 14

Rabinowitz, D. 94–102
racism 433
random luck 351
randomness 369
Rasmussen, J. 454
rational justification *see* justification
rational perceptual capacities 290–1
realism 161; objectivism 165–8; subjectivism 164–5
reasons-responsiveness 209–10
receiver operating characteristic curve *see* area under the receiver operator curve (AUC)
reductive analysis project 262, 265–7, 270
reference groups 155–6
relational egalitarianism 80–1, 89–90
relational sense of luck 172–3, 427
religious luck 436–9, 448–9, 454–8; constitutive 439–40; criterial 440; environmental 442; evidential 440–1; intervening 441–2; New Problem 443–8; prayer 458–60; resultant 440
Rescher, N. 96, 115, 118–20, 136–46, 160–1, 164–5, 347
responsibility 45–6, 54, 73–6, 108–9, 148, 209–10, 219, 359–61, 428–9; derivative 208; graded 211–12; hypological luck 221–5; luck with 426–30; luck without 430–3; other agents 212–14 *see also* control; lack of control account of luck; moral luck
resultant luck 17, 21–2, 108, 110, 200–2, 207–9, 223, 231–3; Aquinas 50–2; Kant 63–6; legal 415–19, 422–3; religious 440
retroindication problem 325–6
Riggs, W. 120–2, 125–34
Ripstein, A. 420
risk 171–4, 240–1, 349–51, 353, 356; difference to luck 174–6; and emotions 357–9; inductive 443–8; lack of control account of luck 174, 179–81; low levels of 174–5; modal account of luck 173–4, 177–8; negative valence 175–6; probability account of luck 173, 176–8 *see also* probability account of luck
Roese, N.J. 348
Roeser, S. 356–62
Rogers, C. 379
Roman Stoics 39–41
Rotter, J.B. 384
Russell, B. 94–5, 98
Ryff, C.D. 384

safety theory 99–101, 287–9, 312–15, 318–26, 442–4
salvific luck *see* religious luck
Sartorio, C. 206–14
Schechter, J. 275, 282
Scheffler, S. 80
Schlesinger, G. 456
Schliesser, E. 74
Schlosser, M. 245
Schwarz, N. 353
scientific progress 391–2, 399; biological contingency 398–9; contingencies of timing 397; environmental contingency 397; historical contingency 393–5; psychological contingency 396–7; simple

contingencies 397–8; sources of contingency 395–6; unintended consequences 398
Seligman, M. 379
Sellars, W. 290–1
Seneca 39–41
sensitivity condition 98–9, 285–7, 311–14
serial position effect 337–9
Servius 37
Seyedsayamdost, H. 407
significance condition 97, 117–18, 120–1, 130–1, 153, 160–2, 240–1, 341–3; constructivist objectivism 163–4; constructivist subjectivism 162–3, 168; eliminativism 167–9; realist objectivism 165–8; realist subjectivism 164–5; risk 175–6, 179–80
Simons, D. 382
Simplicius 36
situationism 209, 223
skeptical argument 305–8; internalism 308; safety condition 312–15; sensitivity condition 311–14
skill 183–4, 187–90 *see also* performance normativity
Slovic, P. 357–8
Smith, A. (1776) 70–3; invisible hand 71–2, 76–7; the irregularity 73–5; justice 76–7; methodology 70–1; proportion 75–6; responsibility 73–6; *Theory of Moral Sentiments* 70–7; unintended consequences 71–3, 76–7
Smith, A. (2013) 230
Smith, C. 70–7
Smith, M. 334, 360, 370, 377–85
social morality 89–90, 420
social network 381–3
socialism 82–4
Socrates 295–6, 300, 302–3
Solon's dictum 28–30
Sosa, E. 99, 183–5, 187, 287, 312, 315
soteriological luck *see* religious luck
Sphaerus of Borysthenes 36
spontaneity 13–14
Starmans, C. 406
states of affairs 149–51
Statman, D. 195–203, 240–1
Steindl-Rast, D. 381
Stich, S. 407–8
Stobaeus 35–6
Stoics 34, 41–2, 333; early 34–8; Roman 39–41
strokes of luck 150–1
subjectivism 161, 168; constructivist 162–3, 168; realist 164–5
subjectivity 121, 138–40, 309–10
subsistence aid 83–4
sufficiency principle 86
supernatural entities 369–70, 372–3
supervenience principle 233, 308
synchronic knowledge 300
systemic luck 426, 429–33

Teigen, K. 334, 345–53, 379–80
teleology 14, 18
Teles of Megara 35
Tenenbaum, J.B. 367

Index

Tessman, L. 426, 429, 431–2
Themistius 38
theology *see* Christianity; religious luck
thought-action tendencies 382
timing 397
Tinsley, C.H. 353
Tomchishen, J. 426–33
tort law 414, 416, 419–21
Trout, J.D. 391–9
truth *see* epistemology
Turner, P.N. 80–90
Turri, J. 406, 409–11
Tversky, A. 335–6

uncertainty 356, 359–60
Unger, P. 96
unintended consequences 50–2, 71–3, 398 *see also* resultant luck
universal theory of randomness 369
universal theory of supernatural entities 369–70, 372–3
utilitarianism *see* Mill, J.S.

value *see* axiological luck
van Dijk, E. 352
van Inwagen, P. 245, 248
Veenhoven, R. 362
veritic luck 185–6, 263–4, 285, 297, 302, 323–4, 441–2 *see also* environmental luck; intervening luck
virtue 19–21, 26–7, 30–1; aretaic luck 221; divine grace 55; feminism 429–32; and happiness 59; natural virtues 52–3
virtue epistemology 98, 187–8, 290, 315–16, 403
virtuous disposition 38, 221

Vogel, J. 101
volition *see* intention
vulnerability 20

Wagenaar, W.A. 351
Walker, M.U. 426–8, 430
Ward, W.C. 367
warrant 265–70, 290–2
Warren, P.A. 369, 373
Weinberg, J. 407
Wessling, J. 451–60
White, L. 397
Whittington, L.J. 165, 342
Wiegmann, A. 407
Williams, B. 15–16, 21, 105–8, 111–12, 216, 227, 419, 428 *see also* moral luck
Williamson, T. 94, 99–100
wisdom 26–7
Wiseman, R. 334, 378–9, 381, 385
Wohl, M.J.A. 352, 371
women's rights 84–5
Worth, P. 377–85
Wu, Y. 352

Xu, A.J. 353

yield-luck 137–44
Yuan, Y. 407

Zagzebski, L. 185, 265, 267, 315, 437, 440, 455–6
Zeno 34–6, 38, 41–2
Zimmerman, M. 151, 216–25, 229
Zipursky, B. 420
Zwick, R. 353